10633828

THE
STRATEGY PROCESS
COLLEGIATE EDITION

Henry Mintzberg
McGill University

James Brian Quinn
Dartmouth College

John Voyer
University of Southern Maine

Prentice Hall, Englewood Cliffs, New Jersey 07632

Library of Congress Cataloging-in-Publication Data

MINTZBERG, HENRY.

The strategy process/HENRY MINTZBERG, JAMES BRIAN QUINN, JOHN VOYER.—Collegiate ed.
p. cm.
Quinn's name appears first on the earlier ed.
Includes bibliographical references and indexes.
ISBN 0-13-556557-X
1. Strategic planning—Case studies.   I. Quinn, James Brian, [date].   II. Voyer, John.   III. Title.

HD30.28.Q53   1995
658.4'012—dc20   94-19998

Acquisitions editor: *Natalie Anderson*
Associate editor: *Lisamarie Brassini*
Project manager: *Edie Riker*
Interior design: *Rosemarie Paccione*
Cover Design: *Rosemarie Paccione*
Production coordinator: *Herb Klein*
Editorial assistant: *Diane Peirano*

 © 1995 by Prentice-Hall, Inc.
A Simon & Schuster Company
Englewood Cliffs, New Jersey 07632

All rights reserved. No part of this book may be
reproduced, in any form or by any means,
without permission in writing from the publisher.

Printed in the United States of America

10 9 8 7 6 5 4 3 2

ISBN   0-13-556557-X

Prentice-Hall International (UK) Limited, *London*
Prentice-Hall of Australia Pty. Limited, *Sydney*
Prentice-Hall Canada Inc., *Toronto*
Prentice-Hall Hispanoamericana, S.A., *Mexico*
Prentice-Hall of India Private Limited, *New Delhi*
Prentice-Hall of Japan, Inc., *Tokyo*
Simon & Schuster Asia Pte. Ltd., *Singapore*
Editora Prentice-Hall do Brasil, Ltda., *Rio de Janeiro*

CONTENTS

To Carly and Andrew

John Voyer

SECTION IV   CASES

ACKNOWLEDGMENTS

We have been involved in the teaching and practice of strategy formation since the 1960s. What originally brought this book together was our firm belief that this field badly needed a new kind of text. We wanted one that looked at process issues as well as analysis; one that was built around critical strategy concepts and contexts instead of the overworked dichotomy of formulation and implementation; and one that accomplished these aims with writing that was intelligent, eclectic, and lively. We sought to combine theory and practice, and description and prescription, in new ways that offered insights none could achieve alone. All of these goals remain exactly the same in this collegiate edition, except that here we set out to fine tune a basic formula that we feel worked well in the other ones. Our own work on the other editions took far longer and was more difficult than we could have imagined, and the same holds true for this edition. We hope that good students of management will think it worthwhile.

In this edition, Professor Voyer had primary responsibility for the chapter introductions, with support from Professor Mintzberg. Professor Quinn wrote the majority of the cases. Professor Mintzberg's readings are prominently featured. He was also mostly responsible for the selection of the other readings, with help from Professor Voyer.

In any work of this scope, there are far too many people involved to thank each one individually. We would, however, like to acknowledge the special assistance given us by those who went especially out of their way to be helpful.

John Voyer took the lead in adapting the general editions of this book to the collegiate market, and, in particular, wrote the chapter introductions. He would particularly like to thank, at the University of Southern Maine, Dean Robert Patton, who was most supportive. His willingness to grant release time was absolutely crucial to the successful completion of this book. Also at Southern Maine, graduate students James Grinnell and Pamela Diehl provided crucial research and editing support for the case and bibliography portions of the book. At Prentice Hall, Natalie Anderson, Lisamarie Brassini, and Diane Peirano were extraordinarily helpful and encouraging, and we thank them.

One last word; this book is not "finished." Our text, like the subject of so much of its content, is an ongoing process, not a static statement, as we believe the reader will find reflected in this edition. So much of this book is so different from conventional strategy textbooks that there are bound to be all kinds of opportunities for improvement. We would like to ask you to help us in this regard. We shall revise the text to improve it to keep up with this exciting field. Please write to any of us with your suggestions on how to improve the readings, the cases, and the organization of the book at large and its presentation. Strategy making, we believe, is a learning process; we are also engaged in a learning process. And for that we need your feedback. Thank you and enjoy what follows.

Henry Mintzberg
James Brian Quinn
John Voyer

INTRODUCTION

In our first edition, we set out to produce a different kind of textbook in the field of business policy or, as it is now more popularly called, strategic management. We tried to provide the reader with a richness of theory, a richness of practice, and a strong basis for linkage between the two. We rejected the strictly case study approach, which leaves theory out altogether, or soft-pedals it, and thereby denies the accumulated benefits of many years of careful research and thought about management processes. We also rejected an alternate approach that forces on readers a highly rationalistic model of how the strategy process *should* function. We collaborated on this book because we believe that in this complex world of organizations a range of concepts is needed to cut through and illuminate particular aspects of that complexity. There is no "one best way" to create strategy, nor is there "one best form" of organization. Quite different forms work well in particular contexts. We believe that exploring a fuller variety systematically will create a deeper and more useful appreciation of the strategy process. In this collegiate edition, we remain loyal to these beliefs and objectives.

This text, unlike most others, is therefore eclectic. Presenting published articles and portions of other books in their original form, rather than filtered through our minds and pens, is one way to reinforce this variety. Each author has his or her own ideas and his or her own best way of expressing them (ourselves included!). Summarized by us, these readings would lose a good deal of their richness.

We do not apologize for contradictions among the ideas of leading thinkers. The world is full of contradictions. The real danger lies in using pat solutions to a nuanced reality, not in opening perspectives up to different interpretations. The effective strategist is one who can live with contradictions, learn to appreciate their causes and effects, and reconcile them sufficiently for effective action. The readings have, nonetheless, been ordered by chapter to suggest some ways in which that reconciliation can be considered. Our own chapter introductions are also intended to assist in this task and to help place the readings themselves in perspective.

ON THEORY

A word on theory is in order. We do not consider theory a dirty word, nor do we apologize for making it a major component of this book. To some people, to be theoretical is to be detached, impractical. But a bright social scientist once said that "there is nothing so practical as a good theory." And every successful doctor, engineer, and physicist would have to agree: they would be unable to practice their modern work without theories. Theories are useful because they shortcut the need to store masses of data. It is easier to remember a simple framework about some phenomenon than it is to consider every detail you ever observed. In a sense, theories are a bit like cataloging systems in libraries; the world would be impossibly confusing without them. They enable you to store and conveniently access your own experiences as well as those of others.

One can, however, suffer not just from an absence of theories, but also from being dominated by them without realizing it. To paraphrase the words of John Maynard Keynes, most "practical men" are the slaves of some defunct theorist. Whether we realize it or not, our behavior is guided by the systems of ideas that we have internalized over the years. Much can be learned by bringing these out in the open, examining them more carefully, and comparing them with alternative ways to view the world—including ones based on systematic study (that is, research). One of our prime intentions in this book is to expose the limitations of conventional theories and to offer alternate explanations that can be superior guides to understanding and taking action in specific contexts.

Prescriptive versus Descriptive Theory

Unlike many textbooks in this field, this one tries to explain the world as it is, rather than as someone thinks it is *supposed* to be. Although there has sometimes been a tendency to disdain such *descriptive* theories, *prescriptive* (or normative) ones have often been the problem, rather than the solution, in the field of management. There is no one best way in management; no prescription works for all organizations. Even when a prescription seems effective in some context, it requires a sophisticated understanding of exactly what that context is and how it functions. In other words, one cannot decide reliably what should be done in a system as complicated as a contemporary organization without a genuine understanding of how that organization really works. In engineering, no student ever questions having to learn physics, in medicine, having to learn anatomy. Imagine an engineering student's hand shooting up in a physics class; "Listen, prof, it's fine to tell us how the atom does work. But what we really want to know is how the atom *should* work." Why should a managment student's similar demand in the realm of strategy or structure be considered any more appropriate? How can people manage complex systems they do not understand?

Nevertheless, we have not ignored prescriptive theory when it appears useful. A number of prescriptive techniques (industry analysis, value chain analysis, portfolio analysis, etc.) are discussed. But these are associated both with other readings and with cases that will help you understand the context and limitations of their usefulness. Both cases and readings offer opportunities to pursue the full complexity of strategic situations. You will find a wide range of issues and perspectives addressed. One of our main goals is to integrate a variety of views, rather than allow strategy to be fragmented into just "human issues" and "economics issues." The text and cases provide a basis for treating the full complexity of strategic management.

ON SOURCES

How were all the readings selected and edited? One popular textbook boasted a few years back that all its readings were published since 1980 (except one dated 1979!). We make no such claim; indeed we would like to make quite a different boast; many of our readings have been around quite a while, long enough to mature, like fine wine. Our criterion for inclusion was not the newness of the article so much as the quality of its insight—that is, its ability to explain some aspect of the strategy process better than any other article. Time does not age the really good articles. Quite the opposite—it distinguishes their quality (but sometimes it brings us back to the old habits of masculine gender; we apologize to our readers for this). We are, of course, not biased toward old articles—just toward good ones. Hence, the materials in this book range from classics of the 1960s to some published just before our final selection was made (as well as a few hitherto unpublished pieces). You will find articles from the most serious academic journals, the best practitioner magazines, books, and some very obscure sources. The best can sometimes be found in strange places!

We have opted to include many shorter readings rather than fewer longer ones, and we have tried to present as wide a variety of good ideas as possible while maintaining clarity. To do so we often had to cut within readings. We have, in fact, put a great deal of effort into the cutting in order to extract the key messages of each reading in as brief, concise, and clear a manner as possible. Unfortunately, our cutting sometimes forced us to eliminate interesting examples and side issues. (In the readings, as well as some of the case materials from published sources, dots . . . signify portions that have been deleted from the original, while square brackets [ ] signify our own insertions of minor clarifications into the original text.) We apologize to you, the reader, as well as to the authors, for having done this, but hope that the overall result has rendered these changes worthwhile.

We have also included a number of our own works. Perhaps we are biased, having less objective standards by which to judge what we have written. But we have messages to convey, too, and our own writings do examine the basic themes that we feel are important in policy and strategy courses today.

ON CASES

A major danger of studying the strategy process—probably the most enticing subject in the management curriculum, and at the pinnacle of organizational processes—is that students and professors can become detached from the basics of the enterprise. The "Don't bore me with the operating details; I'm here to tackle the really big issues" syndrome has been the death of many business policy or strategy courses (not to mention managerial practices!). The big issues *are* rooted in little details. We have tried to recognize this in both the readings and the cases. Effective strategy processes always come down to specifics. The cases and the industry reference notes provide a rich soil for investigating strategic realities. Their complexities always extend well below the surface. Each layer peeled back can reveal new insights and rewards.

As useful as they are, however, cases are not really the ideal way to understand strategy: involving oneself in the hubbub of life in a real organization is. We harbor no illusions that reading 20 pages on an organization will make you an expert. But cases remain the most convenient way to introduce practice into the classroom, to tap a wide variety of experiences, and to involve students actively in analysis and decision making. Our cases consciously contain both their prescriptive and descriptive aspects. On the one hand, they provide the data and background for making a major decision. Students can appraise the situation in its full context, suggest what future directions would be best for the organization in question, and discuss how their solutions can realistically be implemented. On the other hand, each case is also an opportunity to understand the dynamics of an organization—the historical context of the problems it faces, the influence of its culture, its probable reactions to varying solutions, and so on. Unlike many cases which focus on only the analytical aspects of a decision, ours constantly force you to consider the messy realities of arriving at decisions in organizations and obtaining a desired response to any decision. In these respects, case study involves a good deal of descriptive *and* prescriptive analysis.

Adopters of this book have access to a wide selection of cases through our custom publishing service. Everything we've said about the cases applies to the custom cases as well.

Linking Cases and Readings

The cases in this book are not intended to emphasize any particular theories, any more than the theoretical materials are included because they explain particular cases. Each case presents a slice of some specific reality, each reading a conceptual interpretation of some phenomenon. The readings are placed in particular groupings because they approach some common aspects or issues in theory.

Analyze each case for its own sake. Cases are intrinsically richer than readings. Each contains a wide variety of issues—many awfully messy—in no particular order. The readings, in contrast, are usually neat and tidy, professing one or a few basic conceptual ideas, and providing some specific vocabulary. When the two connect—sometimes through direct effort, more often indirectly as conceptual ideas are recalled in the situation of a particular case—some powerful learning can take place in the form of clarification or, we hope, revelation.

Try to see how particular theories can help you to understand some of the issues in the cases and provide useful frameworks for drawing conclusions. Perhaps the great military theorist, Von Clausewitz, said it best over a century ago:

> All that theory can do is give the artist or soldier points of reference and standards of evaluation . . . with the ultimate purpose not of telling him how to act but of developing his judgment. (1976:15)

We have designed the book so that the textual materials develop as the chapters unfold. Concepts introduced in earlier chapters become integrated in the later ones. And early cases tend to build knowledge for those appearing later. Problems and their organizational context move from the simple to the more complex. Space limitations and the structured nature of theories require some compartmentalization. But don't take that compartmentalization too literally. In pre-paring each case, use whatever concepts you find helpful both from chapters of this book and from your personal knowledge. The cases themselves deal with real people in real companies. The reality they present is enormously complicated; their dynamics extend to today's newspaper, and *Who's Who,* or any other reference you can imagine. Use any sound source of information that helps you to deal with them. Part of the fun of policy or strategy courses is understanding how major decisions happened to be made and what were their subsequent consequences—local, national, even international.

These are all living cases. In the strictest sense they have no beginning or end.

They have been written in as lively a style as possible; we do not believe business school cases need be dull! Each case deals with a major transition point in the history of an enterprise. Each can be used in a variety of ways to emphasize a particular set of concepts at a particular time in the course. Many lend themselves to sophisticated financial, industry, portfolio, and competitive analyses as well as disconcerning organizational, behavioral, and managerial practice inquiries. And many contain entrepreneurial and technological dimensions rarely found in strategy cases. Trying to figure out what is going on should be challenging as well as fun!

Case Discussion

Management cases provide a concrete information base for students to analyze and share as they discuss management issues. Without this focus, discussions of theory can become quite confusing. You may have in mind an image of an organization or situation that is very different from that of other discussants. As a result, what appears to be a difference in theory will—after much argument—often turn out to be simply a difference in perception of the realities surrounding these examples.

In this text we try to provide three levels of learning: *first,* a chance to share the generalized insights of leading theoreticians (in the readings); *second,* an opportunity to test the applicability and limits of these theories in specific (case) situations; *third,* the capacity to develop one's own special amalgam of insights based upon empirical observations and inductive reasoning (from case analyses). All are useful approaches; some students and professors will find one mix more productive for their special level of experience or mind set. Another will prefer a quite different mix. Hence, we include a wide selection of cases and readings.

The cases are not intended as *examples* of either weak or exceptionally good management practices. Nor, as we noted, do they provide *examples* of the concepts in a particular reading. They are discussion vehicles for probing the benefits and limits of various approaches. And they are analytical vehicles for applying and testing concepts and tools developed in your education and experience. Almost every case has its marketing, operations, accounting, financial, human relations, planning and control, external environmental, ethical, political, and quantitative dimensions. Each dimension should be addressed in preparations and classroom discussions, although some aspects will inevitably emerge as more important in one situation than another.

In each case you should look for several sets of issues. First, you should understand what went on in that situation. Why did it happen this way? What are the strong or weak features of what happened? What could have been changed to advantage? How? Why? Second, there are always issues of what should be done next. What are the key issues to be resolved? What are the major alternatives available? What outcomes could the organization expect from each? Which alternative should it select? Why? Third, there will almost always be "hard" quantitative data and "soft" qualitative impressions about each situation. Both deserve attention. Because the cases deal with real companies, and real people, in real situations, their data bases can be *extended* as far as students and professors wish. They only have to consult their libraries and daily newspapers.

But remember, no realistic strategy situation is *just* an organization behavior problem or *just* a financial or economic analytical one. Both sets of information should be considered, and an *integrated* solution developed. Our cases are consciously constructed for this. Given their complexity we have tried to keep the cases as short as possible. And we have tried to capture some of the flavor of the real organization. Moreover, we have sought to mix product and services cases, technological and "nontech" cases, entrepreneurial, small company, and large enterprise situations. In this cross section, we have tried to capture some of the most important and exciting issues, concepts, and products of our times. We believe management is fun, and important. The cases try to convey this.

There is no "correct" answer to any case. There may be several "good" answers and many poor ones. The purpose of a strategy course should be to help you understand the nature of these "better" answers, what to look for, how to analyze alternatives, and how to see through the complexities of reaching solutions and implanting them in real organizations. A strategy course can only improve your probability of success, not ensure it. The total number of variables in a real strategy situation is typically beyond the control of any one person or group. Hence another caveat: don't rely on what a company actually did as a guide to effective action. The company may have succeeded or failed not because of its specific decisions, but because of luck, an outstanding personality, the bizarre action of an opponent, international actions over which it had no control, and so on. One of the products of a successful strategy course should be a little humility.

Case Study Guides

We have posed a few questions at the end of some cases as discussion guides. Students have generally found these helpful in organizing their thinking about each case. If you answer these questions well, you can probably deal with anything that comes up in class. But each professor may conduct his or her class in a quite different fashion. The questions should help you see relevant issues, but they should not limit your thinking. From time to time there are intermediate "decision points" in a case. Work on the material up to that point just as you would a short case. The case materials immediately following these decision points consciously leave out much detail on what might have happened so that you can arrive at your own specific solutions. Later you can see them in the context of a longer time horizon, much like a mystery story unfolding in phases. Analyze the specific situations, consider alternatives, and arrive at specific conclusions—understanding that later events might have looked a bit different if your solution had been implemented. Like any good mystery story, a case provides many clues, never all, but, surprisingly, sometimes more than executives might have had time to absorb in the real situation.

Believing that no "canned approach" is viable for all strategic situations, we have selected cases that cut across a variety of issues and theoretical constructs. Almost any of these cases is so complex that it can be positioned at a number of different spots in a good strategy course. We leave the final case selection to the style and wisdom of the professor and his or her students.

THIS BOOK'S STRUCTURE

Not Formulation, Then Implementation

The first edition of this text offered a chapter format that was new to the policy or strategy field. Unlike most others, it had no specific chapter or section devoted to "implementation" per se. The assumption in other texts is that strategy is formulated and then implemented, with organizational structures, control systems, and the like following obediently behind strategy. In this text, as in reality, formulation and implementation are intertwined as complex interactive processes in which politics, values, organizational culture, and management styles determine or constrain particular strategic decisions. And strategy, structure, and systems mix together in complicated ways to influence outcomes. While strategy formulation and implementation may be separated in some situations—perhaps in crises, in some totally new ventures, as well as in organizations facing predictable futures—these events are rare. We certainly do not believe in building a whole book (let alone a whole field) around this conceptual distinction.

But Concepts, Then Contexts

The readings are divided roughly into two different parts. The first deals with *concepts,* the second with *contexts*. We introduce strategy and structure as well as power, culture, and several other concepts early in the text as equal partners in the complex web of ideas that make up what we call "the strategy process." In the second half of the text we weave these concepts together in a number of distinct situations, which we call *contexts*.

Our theme diagram illustrates this. Concepts, shown on top, are divided into two groups—strategy and organization—to represent the first two sections of the book. Contexts draw all these concepts together, in a variety of situations—covered in the third section—which we consider the key ones in the field of strategy today (though hardly the only ones). The outline of the text, chapter by chapter, proceeds as follows:

Section I: Strategy

The first section is called *"Strategy"*; it comprises five chapters (two introductory in nature and three on the processes by which strategy making takes place). Chapter 1 intro-

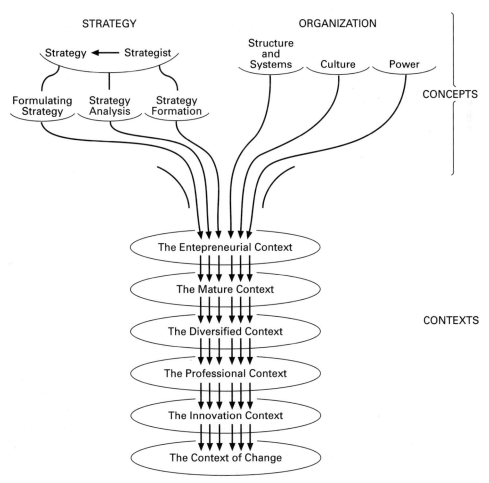

STRATEGY PROCESS THEME DIAGRAM

duces *the strategy concept* and probes the meaning of this important word to broaden your view of it. Here the pattern is set of challenging you to question conventional views, especially when these act to narrow perspectives. The themes introduced in this chapter carry throughout the book and are worth care in understanding.

Chapter 2 introduces a very important character in this book, *the strategist* as general manager. This person may not be the only one who makes strategy in an organization, but he or she is clearly a key player. In examining the work of the general manager and the character of his or her job, we shall perhaps upset a number of widely accepted notions. We do this to help you understand the very real complexities and difficulties of making strategy and managing in contemporary organizations.

Chapters 3, 4, and 5 take up a theme that is treated extensively in the text—to the point of being reflected in its title: the development of an understanding of the *processes* by which strategies are made. Chapter 3 looks at *formulating strategy,* specifically at some widely accepted prescriptive models for how organizations should go about developing their strategies. Chapter 4 extends these ideas to more formal ways of doing *strategy analysis* and considering what, if any, "generic" forms a strategy can take. While readings in later chapters will challenge some of these precepts, what will not be questioned is the importance of having to understand them. They are fundamental to appreciating the strategy process today.

Chapter 5 switches from a prescriptive to a descriptive approach. Concerned with understanding *strategy formation,* it considers how strategies actually *do* form in organizations (not necessarily by being formulated) and *why* different processes may be effective in specific circumstances. This text takes an unconventional stand by viewing planning and other formal approaches as not the only—and often indeed not even the most desirable—ways to make strategy. You will find our emphasis on the descriptive process—as an equal partner with the more traditional concerns for technical and analytical issues—to be one of the unifying themes of this book.

Section II: Foundations of Strategy Formation

In Section I, the readings introduced strategy, the strategist, and various ways in which strategy might be formulated and does in fact form. In Section II we introduce other concepts that constitute part of the strategy process.

In Chapter 6, we consider *structure and systems,* where particular attention is paid to the various forms that structure can take as well as the mechanisms that comprise it. In Chapter 7, we consider *culture,* especially how strong systems of beliefs, called "ideologies," impact on organizations and their strategies and so influence their effectiveness. In Chapter 8, *power* is the focus. We consider two aspects of power: first, the distribution of power among the various actors within the organization and its links to political activity; second, the organization as a political entity in its own right and its power to pursue its own ends, whether or not responsibly, in the face of opposing forces in society. Both aspects will be seen to influence significantly the processes by which strategies are formulated or by which they form.

Section III: Strategy Processes in Context

Section III is called *Strategy Process in Context.* We consider how all of the elements introduced so far—strategy, the processes by which it is formulated and gets formed, the strategist, structure, systems, culture and power—combine to suit particular contexts, six in all.

Chapter 9 deals with the *entrepreneurial context,* where a rather simple organization comes under the close control of a strong leader, often a person with vision.

Chapter 10 examines the *mature context,* one common to many large business and government organizations involved in the mass production or distribution of goods or services.

Chapter 11 develops the contexts of professionalism and innovation, both involving organizations of high expertise. In the professional context, the experts work relatively independently in rather stable conditions, while in the innovation context, they combine in project teams under more dynamic conditions. What these two contexts have in common, however, is that they act in ways that upset many of the widely accepted notions about how organizations should be structured and make strategy.

Chapter 12 examines corporate-level strategy. It introduces the *diversified context,* and deals with organizations that have either vertically integrated or diversified their product or service lines and usually divisionalized their structures to deal with the greater varieties of environments they face. Chapter 13 deals with a special case of corporate-level strategy, the *global context.* It examines organizations that have decided to compete around the world.

In considering each of these widely different contexts, we seek to discuss (where appropriate material is available) the situations in which each is most likely to be found, the structures most suited to it, the kinds of strategies that tend to be pursued, the processes by which these strategies tend to be formed and might be formulated, and the social issues associated with the context.

Chapter 14 is devoted not so much to a specific context as to *managing change* between contexts, or within a context (which we can, of course, characterize as the context of change). The major concerns are how organizations can cope with crises, turnarounds, revitalizations, and new stages in their own lifecycles or those of their key products.

The readings end in Chapter 15 on a provocative note, designed to encourage *thinking strategically,* about strategy itself and the whole process of management.

Well, there you have it. We have worked hard on this book, in both the earlier and this edition, to get it right. We have tried to think things through from the basics, with a resulting text that in style, format, and content is unusual for the field of policy or strategy. Our product may not be perfect, but we believe it is good—indeed better than any other text available. Now it's your turn to find out if you agree. Have fun doing so!

THE STRATEGY CONCEPT

▼

What is strategy? This seems like a straightforward question for a text dealing with the concept of strategy, but unfortunately, the answer is not so clear. The word *strategy* has been used in many different ways and contexts through the years. The most common use has been military, where the idea of strategy has been prominent for centuries. The word has been used more recently in a business context. Another well-known use of the word *strategy* has been in sports and games, particularly chess. In this chapter, we examine what strategy means.

MILITARY ROOTS

The English word *strategy* comes from the Greek *strategos*, meaning "a general." That word in turn comes from roots meaning "army" and "lead." The Greek verb *stratego* means to "plan the destruction of one's enemies through effective use of resources."[1] Strategy as a concept in military and political contexts has been well-known for hundreds of years. For modern-day businesspeople with competitive tendencies, these roots for the concept of strategy have obvious appeal. Although business strategists do not necessarily "plan the destruction" of their competitors, most are trying to outsell or otherwise outperform their rivals.

An early use of the strategy concept in a business context occurred during Greek antiquity, when Socrates comforted the Greek militarist Nichomachides. The Athenians had just held an election for general. Nichomachides was upset because Antisthenes, a businessman, had defeated him. Socrates, comparing the activities of a businessman to those of a general, pointed out to Nichomachides that in each job successful practitioners have to plan and mobilize resources to meet objectives.[2] Jeffrey Bracker pointed out that this viewpoint seemed to have disappeared with the fall of the

Greek city-states and it did not appear to have risen again until after the Industrial Revolution.[3]

![gray bar separator]

MODERN VIEWS

The first modern scholars to associate the concept of strategy to business were Von Neumann and Morgenstern in their work on game theory. They defined business strategy as a series of actions by a firm that are selected according to the particular situation.[4] It is easy to see how this definition grew out of game theory. In his classic 1954 book, *The Practice of Management,* Peter Drucker asserted that strategy requires managers to analyze the present situation and to change it if need be. Part of his definition was the idea that managers should find out what their firm's resources are and what they should be.[5]

Many scholars agree that the first modern definition of business strategy was in Alfred Chandler's 1962 work, *Strategy and Structure.* In that book he painstakingly analyzed the early twentieth-century activities of four giants of American industry— DuPont, Standard Oil of New Jersey, General Motors, and Sears, Roebuck. Based on that study, Chandler defined *strategy* as the determinant of the basic long-term goals of an enterprise, and the adoption of courses of action and the allocation of resources necessary for carrying out these goals.[6]

Seven years later, Chandler's Harvard colleague Kenneth Andrews offered a similar definition. This one influenced a generation of students at the Harvard Business School and around the world: "Strategy is the pattern of objectives, purposes, or goals and the major policies and plans for achieving these goals, stated in such a way to define what business the company is in or is to be in and the kind of company it is or is to be."[7] According to this definition, the strategist must design a set of objectives and plans that reveals the firm's business area and its approach to that business.

In between Chandler and Andrews, in 1965, Igor Ansoff had offered a more analytic yet action-oriented definition. He viewed strategy as the "common thread" among a firm's activities and product/markets.[8] Strategy becomes a rule for making decisions; the common thread would have four components—product/market scope (the products the firm offered and the markets in which the firm operated); growth vector (the changes the firm planned to make in its product/market scope); competitive advantage (those particular properties of individual product/markets that gave the firm a strong position relative to its competitors); and synergy (a measure of how well the different parts of the firm could work together to achieve more than they could have by each working alone).[9]

![gray bar separator]

THE "STANDARD" MODEL OF STRATEGY

Together, the Andrews and Ansoff definitions formed two closely related ways of thinking about strategy that would dominate textbooks and research work for a generation. Chaffee says that this approach has two versions. The first she calls the *linear model*; she chose this term because this approach focuses on objective-setting and planning, and the word *linear* has the right methodical, directed, and sequential connotations. She calls the second version the *adaptive model*; this approach is concerned with finding the best match between the firm's environment and its resources.[10] Mintzberg refers to Andrews' approach as the "Design School," and to Ansoff's as the "Planning School."[11] (We will discuss these two models of Mintzberg's in more detail in Chapter Seven.) With one notable exception, the definitions of *strategy* that have been stated since then are variations on the Andrews and Ansoff definitions.[12]

All these definitions have four common elements. The first is the idea of an **environment**, a set of conditions external to the firm, to which it must respond. Some of these conditions are negative (threats), and some are positive (opportunities). Second, the firm must establish major goals or objectives. The highest-level objective is typically called the **mission**, a statement of the firm's reason for existence.[13] Third, the firm's management must perform a **situational analysis**, to determine its posture in the environment and its level of resources. This is often called a *SWOT analysis* (which stands for *Strengths, Weaknesses, Opportunities,* and *Threats*). Lastly, the firm **plans how to use its resources** to achieve its goals and get the best "fit" possible with its environment.[14]

We will examine this approach to strategy in detail in Chapter Three. For now, it is important to point out two of its major assumptions. The first is that analysis must always come before action. The goal-setting, situational analysis, and planning must *always* occur before any actions by the firm. This is usually referred to as **strategy formulation**.[15] Whatever learning takes place comes from the efforts of planners, upper level managers or other analysts. It does not come from trial and error on the part of, or feedback from, middle-level managers or workers. The second assumption is that action, often called **strategy implementation**,[16] is done by people other than the analysts, upper level managers or planners. These "others" typically hope to carry out their formulations with as little surprise as possible.[17]

A DIFFERENT VIEW OF STRATEGY

Henry Mintzberg has developed a very different approach to the strategy concept. It is an historical method of defining strategy. In his view, the firm's objectives, plans, and resource base at a given moment are no more important than what the firm has actually done and is actually doing.[18] He defines *strategy* as *"a pattern in a stream of actions over time."*[19]

The standard model emphasizes analysis; Mintzberg's approach stresses *action*. According to this view, a firm can have a strategy even without doing any planning. It can also have a strategy even if no one in the firm takes the time to develop formal objectives, let alone a mission statement. All that is required is a *pattern* in a stream of organizational actions. A pattern implies a coherence to the firm's actions; the coherence may or may not be the result of formal planning or goal-setting. In the definitions discussed above, strategy *was* formal planning and goal-setting.

Mintzberg builds his view on this contrast between analysis and action. One way of viewing strategy is as something that is based in **strategic intentions**. This emphasis on prior reflection typifies the standard strategy approach. Another way of viewing strategy is as a convergent series of actions taken by the firm, a **realized strategy**. This typifies Mintzberg's action-oriented approach. If a firm can formulate intentions and move to their realization, we have an example of what Mintzberg calls **deliberate strategy**. If the firm is taking consistent actions that were not part of its formal intentions, we have an example of **emergent strategy**. The strategy takes shape, "happens," despite a lack of formally stated intentions. It may be that, later on, the firm will formally adopt these emergent strategies, but at the time that they arise, they are not conscious or deliberate. (There is a third possibility—that the firm will not be able to implement its strategic intentions. Mintzberg calls this **unrealized strategy**.) Mintzberg gives more details on his definition, as well as some other approaches, in his reading "Five P's for Strategy," discussed below. Let us first examine James Brian Quinn's ideas about the concept of strategy.

STRATEGIES FOR CHANGE

In his reading "Strategies for Change," James Brian Quinn examines the strategy concept from a traditional perspective, even drawing on a classic military confrontation, Philip and Alexander's actions at Chaeronea (338 B.C.), to illustrate his points. He starts by distinguishing between strategic formulation and programmatic planning. The latter is short-range. It simply aims resources at the accomplishment of the limited objectives that flow from a broader strategic plan. Quinn's point is that one cannot even have an intelligent operating or tactical plan without first having a broader strategy. A "true strategy," as Quinn puts it, goes well beyond mere coordinative plans and programs. It is a whole new set of concepts, aimed at ensuring the effectiveness of the organization. These new concepts are based on organizational strengths and weaknesses, changes in the environment, and the moves of intelligent competitors. This kind of analysis is much more far-reaching than that of any programmatic plan. It is apparent that Quinn's definition of strategy fits what earlier was called the "standard model" of strategy.

Despite this traditional-sounding discussion, Quinn argues that analysts should study patterns rather than formal strategic documents. He points out that one would often be hard-pressed to find complete formal statements of corporate strategy that are actually followed. Secondly, objective observers may be able to deduce the existence of a strategy, even if it is not apparent to the executives making critical decisions. Lastly, Quinn implies that formal strategic documents may not reflect what the firm is actually doing. As he puts it, "One . . . must look at the actual emerging pattern of the enterprise's operant goals, policies, and major programs to see what its true strategy is." We see here a kinship to Mintzberg's approach.

Quinn nevertheless argues that there is good analogy from military strategy to business strategy. Just as military organizations have multiple echelons of grand, theater, area, battle, infantry, and artillery strategies, so should other complex organizations have a number of hierarchically related and mutually supporting strategies. Along these lines, Quinn asserts that effective formal strategies have three essential elements: (1) goals, (2) policies, and (3) programs. Secondly, effective strategies, like effective military plans, develop around a few key concepts and thrusts, which give them cohesion, balance, and focus. A third point is that strategy deals not only with the unpredictable but also with the unknowable. A general rarely can predict the outcome of a military campaign, even less what will happen during a battle. Similarly, in organizations it is impossible to know everything that is going to happen. As Quinn puts it, "No analyst could predict the precise ways in which all impinging forces could interact with each other, be distorted by nature or human emotions, or be modified by the imaginations and purposeful counteractions of intelligent opponents." Under these assumptions, effective strategy will be the creation of a strong and flexible organization that is able to respond intelligently *regardless* of what happens.

Quinn concludes his reading with an interesting list of criteria for effective strategies: (1) clear, decisive objectives, (2) maintainence of the initiative, (3) concentration (pinpoint aiming of superior power in a decisive way), (4) flexibility, (5) coordinated and committed leadership, (6) surprise, and (7) security (protecting resources, having a good intelligence system). It is easy to see the military roots of these criteria, but their usefulness is also apparent. One of the most interesting is "concentration." Too often, strategists squander their organization's resources by scattering them. It is almost always better to concentrate the firm's strengths on things at which it excels. We will see this again in a later chapter, in Michael Porter's **focus strategy**.[20]

FIVE Ps FOR STRATEGY

In this reading, Henry Mintzberg offers five distinctive views on the nature of strategy. Mintzberg thinks that strategy is usually defined in one way but used implicitly in different ways. Most people define strategy as a *plan*—a consciously intended course of action. Plans are made in advance of the actions to which they apply, and they are developed consciously and purposefully. This fits the standard model of strategy very well. Strategy can also be a *ploy*—a "maneuver" intended to outwit an opponent or a competitor.

But defining strategy as a plan is not sufficient. Mintzberg thinks we need a definition that encompasses the resulting behavior. As mentioned above, he argues that strategy may be a *pattern* in a stream of actions. By this definition, strategy is consistency in behavior, whether or not intended. For some firms, strategies would be less likely to exist in the absence of intention. A good example might be utilities. To a great extent, the absence of intention would be unlikely for most bureaucratic organizations and multidivisional firms because these kinds of organizations are large, and standardization is an integral part of their functioning. These factors make the formulation of intentions prior to action more feasible, and sometimes even necessary.

Other types of organizations, notably innovative ones, often plunge right into action, without the prior development of formalized intentions. Any kind of firm that faces an uncertain and dynamic environment is a good candidate for forming strategies out of a pattern of action with minimal intentions. In larger, complex organizations, subunits exist that often act without explicit sets of intentions from upper management. Patterns emerge from their activities; these subunit strategies may later be adopted by the overall organization. Hence, even in large organizations it is possible for strategies to form in the relative absence of intention.

Even though few people would define strategy this way, i.e., as a pattern, many seem at one time or another to so use it. From this way of thinking about strategy, Mintzberg derives his notions of deliberate and emergent strategy mentioned above. Purely deliberate or purely emergent strategies are probably rare. Most strategies probably sit on a continuum between the two. In this reading, Mintzberg gives some details on eight types of strategy that flow from his pattern definition: (1) planned, (2) entrepreneurial, (3) ideological, (4) umbrella, (5) process, (6) disconnected, (7) consensus, and (8) imposed.

Mintzberg's fourth definition is that strategy is a *position*; that is, a means of locating an organization in an "environment." This is compatible with the standard, analytical view mentioned earlier. In a departure from this, Mintzberg offers a fifth definition that looks inside the organization, indeed inside the heads of the collective strategists. Strategy is a *perspective*, its content consisting not just of a chosen position but also of an ingrained way of perceiving the world.

NOTES TO CHAPTER ONE

1. Bracker, Jeffrey, "The Historical Development of the Strategic Management Concept." *Academy of Management Review* 5 (1980): 219–24. Much of the following discussion is based on this article.

2. Xenophon, *The Anabasis or Expedition of Cyrus and the Memorabilia of Socrates*, trans. J. S. Watson. New York: Harper and Row, 1869.

3. Bracker, "Historical Development," p. 219.

4. Von Neumann, J., and O. Morgenstern, *Theory of Games and Economic Behavior,* 2nd ed. Princeton: Princeton University Press, 1947, pp 79–84.

5. Drucker, Peter, *The Practice of Management.* New York: Harper & Brothers, 1954.

6. Chandler, Alfred, *Strategy and Structure: Chapters in the History of American Industrial Enterprise.* Cambridge, Mass: M.I.T. Press, 1962, p. 13.

7. Learned, E., R. C. Christensen, K. Andrews, and W. D. Guth, *Business Policy: Test and Cases.* Homewood, Ill.: Richard D. Irwin, 1969, p. 15.

8. Ansoff, H. Igor, *Corporate Strategy: An Analytic Approach to Business Policy for Growth and Expansion.* New York: McGraw-Hill, 1965, pp. 118–21.

9. Hofer, C., and D. Schendel, *Strategy Formulation: Analytical Concepts.* St. Paul: West Publishing, 1978, p. 17.

10. Chaffee, Ellen Earle, "Three Models of Strategy." *Academy of Management Review* 10 (1985): 89–98.

11. Mintzberg, Henry, "Strategy Formation: Schools of Thought." In *Perspectives on Strategic Management,* James W. Frederickson, ed. New York: Harper Business, 1990, pp. 105–235.

12. Bracker, "Historical Development," pp. 220–21, gives a detailed analysis of most of these definitions.

13. Pearce, J. A., and F. David, "Corporate Mission Statements: The Bottom Line." *Academy of Management Executive* 1 (1987): 109–16.

14. Bracker, "Historical Development," p. 221; Chaffee, "Three Models of Strategy," p. 90.

15. Hofer, C., and D. Schendel, *Strategy Formulation: Analytical Concepts.* St. Paul: West Publishing, 1978.

16. Galbraith, J., and R. Kazanjian, *Strategy Implementation.* St. Paul: West Publishing, 1986.

17. Mintzberg, H. and J. Waters, "Of Strategies, Deliberate and Emergent." *Strategic Management Journal* 6 (1985): 257–72.

18. Mintzberg, H., "Patterns in Strategy Formation." *Management Science* 24 (1978): 934–48.

19. Mintzberg and Waters, "Of Strategies, Deliberate and Emergent," p. 257.

20. Porter, M. E., *Competitive Strategy.* New York: Free Press, 1980.

STRATEGIES FOR CHANGE*

By James Brian Quinn

SOME USEFUL DEFINITIONS

Because the words *strategy, objectives, goals, policy,* and *programs* . . . have different meanings to individual readers or to various organizational cultures, I [try] to use certain definitions consistently . . . For clarity—not pedantry—these are set forth as follows:

A **strategy** is the *pattern* or *plan* that *integrates* an organization's *major* goals, policies, and action sequences into a *cohesive* whole. A well-formulated strategy helps to *marshal* and *allocate* an organization's resources into a *unique and viable posture* based on its relative *internal competencies* and *shortcomings,* anticipated *changes in the environment,* and contingent moves by *intelligent opponents.*

Goals (or **objectives**) state *what* is to be achieved and *when* results are to be accomplished, but they do not state *how* the results are to be achieved. All organizations have multiple goals existing in a complex hierarchy (Simon, 1964): from value objectives, which express the broad value premises toward which the company is to strive; through overall organizational objectives, which establish the intended *nature* of the enterprise and the *directions* in which it should move; to a series of less permanent goals that define targets for each organizational unit, its subunits, and finally all major program activities within each subunit. Major goals—those that affect the entity's overall direction and viability—are called *strategic goals.*

Policies are rules or guidelines that express the *limits* within which action should occur. These rules often take the form of contingent decisions for resolving conflicts among specific objectives. For example: "Don't exceed three months' inventory in any item without corporate approval." Like the objectives they support, policies exist in a hierarchy throughout the organization. Major policies—those that guide the entity's overall direction and posture or determine its viability—are called *strategic policies.*

Programs specify the *step-by-step sequence of actions* necessary to achieve major objectives. They express *how* objectives will be achieved within the limits set by policy. They ensure that resources are committed to achieve goals, and they provide the dynamic track against which progress can be measured. Those major programs that determine the entity's overall thrust and viability are called *strategic programs.*

Strategic decisions are those that determine the overall direction of an enterprise and its ultimate viability in light of the predictable, the unpredictable, and the unknowable changes that may occur in its most important surrounding environments. They intimately shape the true goals of the enterprise. They help delineate the broad limits within which the enterprise operates. They dictate both the resources the enterprise will have accessible for its tasks and the principal patterns in which these resources will be allocated. And they determine the effectiveness of the enterprise—whether its major thrusts are in the right directions given its resource potentials—rather than whether individual tasks are performed efficiently. Management for efficiency, along with the myriad decisions necessary to maintain the daily life and services of the enterprise, is the domain of operations.

Guidelines

---

* Excerpted from James Brian Quinn, *Strategies for Change: Logical Incrementalism* (copyright © Richard D. Irwin, Inc., 1980), Chaps. 1 and 5; reprinted by permission of the publisher.

Strategies versus Tactics

Strategies normally exist at many different levels in any large organization. For example, in government there are world trade, national economic, treasury department, military spending, investment, fiscal, monetary supply, banking, regional development, and local reemployment strategies—all related to each other somewhat hierarchically yet each having imperatives of its own. Similarly, businesses have numerous strategies from corporate levels to department levels within divisions. Yet if strategies exist at all these levels, how do strategies and tactics differ? Often the primary difference lies in the scale of action or the perspective of the leader. What appears to be a "tactic" to the chief executive officer (or general) may be a "strategy" to the marketing head (or lieutenant) if it determines the ultimate success and viability of his or her organization. In a more precise sense, tactics can occur at either level. They are the short-duration, adaptive, action-interaction realignments that opposing forces use to accomplish limited goals after their initial contact. Strategy defines a continuing basis for ordering these adaptations toward more broadly conceived purposes.

A genuine strategy is always needed when the potential actions or responses of intelligent opponents can seriously affect the endeavor's desired outcome—regardless of that endeavor's organizational level in the total enterprise. This condition almost always pertains to the important actions taken at the top level of competitive organizations. However, game theorists quickly point out that some important top-level actions—for example, sending a peacetime fleet across the Atlantic—merely require elaborate coordinative plans and programs (Von Neumann and Morgenstern, 1944; Shubik, 1975; McDonald, 1950). A whole new set of concepts, a true strategy, is needed if some people or nations decide to oppose the fleet's purposes. And it is these concepts that in large part distinguish strategic formulation from simpler programmatic planning.

Strategies may be looked at as either a priori statements to guide action or a posteriori results of actual decision behavior. In most complex organizations . . . one would be hard pressed to find a complete a priori statement of a total strategy that actually is followed. Yet often the existence of a strategy (or strategy change) may be clear to an objective observer, although it is not yet apparent to the executives making critical decisions. One, therefore, must look at the actual emerging *pattern* of the enterprise's operant goals, policies, and major programs to see what its true strategy is (Mintzberg, 1972). Whether it is consciously set forth in advance or is simply a widely held understanding resulting from a stream of decisions, this pattern becomes the real strategy of the enterprise. And it is changes in this pattern—regardless of what any formal strategic documents may say—that either analysts or strategic decision makers must address if they wish to comprehend or alter the concern's strategic posture. . . .

THE CLASSICAL APPROACH TO STRATEGY

Military-diplomatic strategies have existed since prehistoric times. In fact, one function of the earliest historians and poets was to collect the accumulated lore of these successful and unsuccessful life-and-death strategies and convert them into wisdom and guidance for the future. As societies grew larger and conflicts more complex, generals, statesmen, and captains studied, codified, and tested essential strategic concepts until a coherent body of principles seemed to emerge. In various forms these were ultimately distilled into the maxims of Sun Tzu (1963), Machiavelli (1950), Napoleon (1940), Von Clausewitz (1976), Foch (1970), Lenin (1927), Hart (1954), Montgomery (1958), or Mao Tse-Tung (1967). Yet with a few exceptions—largely introduced by modern technology—the most basic principles of strategy were in place and recorded long before the

Christian era. More modern institutions primarily adapted and modified these to their own special environments.

Although one could choose any number of classical military-diplomatic strategies as examples, Philip and Alexander's actions at Chaeronea (in 338 B.C.) contain many currently relevant concepts (Varner and Alger, 1978; Green, 1970). . . .

A CLASSICAL STRATEGY

A Grand Strategy

Philip and his young son, Alexander, had very *clear goals.* They sought to rid Macedonia of influence by the Greek city-states and to *establish dominance* over what was then essentially northern Greece. They also wanted Athens to *join a coalition* with them against Persia on their eastern flank. *Assessing their resources,* they *decided to avoid* the overwhelming superiority of the Athenian fleet and *chose to forego* attack on the powerful walled cities of Athens and Thebes where their superbly trained phalanxes and cavalry would not *have distinct advantages.*

Philip and Alexander *used an indirect approach* when an invitation by the Amphictyonic Council brought their army south to punish Amphissa. In a *planned sequence of actions and deceptive maneuvers,* they cut away from a direct line of march to Amphissa, *bypassed the enemy,* and *fortified a key base,* Elatea. They then took steps to *weaken their opponents politically and morally* by pressing restoration of the Phoenician communities earlier dispersed by the Thebans and by having Philip declared a champion of the Delphic gods. Then *using misleading messages* to make the enemy believe they had moved north to Thrace and also *using developed intelligence sources,* the Macedonians in a *surprise attack* annihilated the Greeks' positions near Amphissa. This *lured their opponents away from their defensive positions* in the nearby mountain passes to *consolidate their forces* near the town of Chaeronea.

There, *assessing the relative strengths* of their opponents, the Macedonians first *attempted to negotiate* to achieve their goals. When this was unsuccessful they had a *well-developed contingency plan* on how to *attack and overwhelm* the Greeks. Prior to this time, of course, the Macedonians had *organized* their troops into the famed phalanxes, and had *developed the full logistics* needed for their field support including a longer spear, which helped the Macedonian phalanxes penetrate the solid shield wall of the heavily massed Greek formations. *Using the natural advantages* of their grassy terrain, the Macedonians had developed cavalry support for their phalanxes' movements far beyond the Greek capability. Finally, using a *relative advantage*—the *command structure* their hierarchical *social system* allowed—against the more democratic Greeks, the Macedonian nobles had *trained their personnel* into one of the most *disciplined and highly motivated forces* in the world.

The Battle Strategy

Supporting this was the battle strategy at Chaeronea, which emerged as follows. Philip and Alexander first *analyzed their specific strengths and weaknesses and their opponents' current alignments and probable moves.* The Macedonian strength lay in their new spear technology, the *mobility* of their superbly disciplined phalanxes, and the powerful cavalry units led by Alexander. Their weaknesses were that they were badly outnumbered and faced—in the Athenians and the Theban Band—some of the finest foot troops in the world. However, their opponents had two weak points. One was the Greek left flank with lightly armed local troops placed near the Chaeronean Acropolis and next to some more heavily armed—but hastily assembled—hoplites bridging to the strong center held by the Athenians. The famed Theban Band anchored the Greek right wing near a swamp on the Cephissus River. [See Figure 1.]

Philip and Alexander *organized their leadership to command key positions;* Philip took over the right wing and Alexander the cavalry. They *aligned their forces* into a *unique posture* which *used their strengths* and *offset their weaknesses.* They decided on those spots at which they would *concentrate their forces,* what *positions to concede,* and what *key points* they *must take and hold.* Starting with their units angled back from the Greek lines (see map), they developed a *focused major thrust* against the Greek left wing and *attacked their opponents' weakness*—the troops near Chaeronea—with the most disciplined of the Macedonian units, the guards' brigade. After building up pressure and stretching the Greek line to its left, the guards' brigade abruptly began a *planned withdrawal.* This *feint* caused the Greek left to break ranks and rush forward, believing the Macedonians to be in full re-

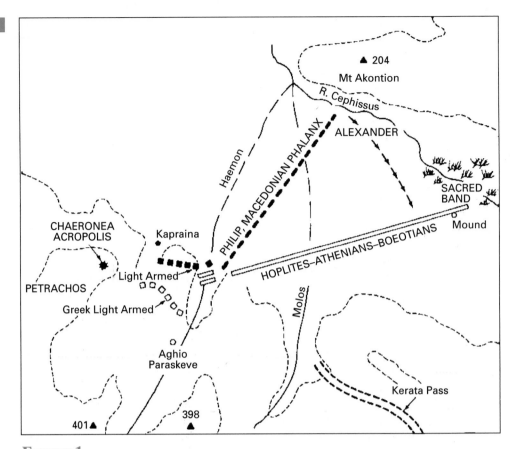

FIGURE 1

The Battle of Chaeronea

Source: Modified with permission from P. Green, Alexander the Great, *Praeger Publishers, New York, 1970.*

treat. This *stretched the opponents' resources* as the Greek center moved left to *maintain contact* with its flank and to attack the "fleeing" Macedonians.

Then *with predetermined timing,* Alexander's cavalry *attacked the exposure* of the stretched line at the same moment Philip's phalanxes *re-formed as planned* on the high ground at the edge of the Heamon River. Alexander *broke through* and *formed a bridge-head* behind the Greeks. He *refocused his forces against a segment* of the opponents' line; his cavalry *surrounded and destroyed* the Theban Band as the *overwhelming power* of the phalanxes poured through the gap he had created. From its *secured position,* the Macedonian left flank then turned and *attacked the flank* of the Athenians. With the help of Philip's *planned counterattack,* the Macedonians *expanded their dominance and over-whelmed the critical target,* i.e., the Greek center. . . .

Modern Analogies

Similar concepts have continued to dominate the modern era of formal strategic thought. As this period begins, Scharnhorst still points to the need to *analyze social forces and structures* as a basis for *understanding effective command styles* and *motivational stimuli* (Von Clausewitz, 1976:8). Frederick the Great proved this point in the field. Presumably based on such analyses, he adopted *training, discipline,* and *fast maneuvers* as the central concepts for a tightly disciplined German culture that had to be constantly ready to fight on two fronts (Phillips, 1940). Von Bülow (1806) continued to emphasize the dominant strategic roles of *geographical positioning* and *logistical support systems* in strategy. Both Jomini (1971) and Von Bülow (1806) stressed the concepts of *concentration, points of domination,* and *rapidity of movement* as central strategic themes and even tried to develop them into mathematically precise principles for their time.

Still later Von Clausewitz expounded on the paramountcy of *clear major objectives* in war and on developing war strategies as a component of the nation's *broader goals* with *time horizons* extending beyond the war itself. Within this context he postulated that an effective strategy should be focused around a relatively *few central principles,* which can *create, guide,* and *maintain dominance* despite the enormous frictions that occur as one tries to position or maneuver large forces in war. Among these he included many of the concepts operant in Macedonian times: *spirit or morale, surprise, cunning, concentration in space, dominance of selected positions, use of strategic reserves, unification over time, tension and release,* and so on. He showed how these broad principles applied to a number of specific attack, defense, flanking, and retreat situations; but he always stressed the intangible of *leadership.* His basic positioning and organizational principles were to be mixed with boldness, perseverance, and genius. He constantly emphasized—as did Napoleon—the need for *planned flexibility* once the battle was joined.

Later strategic analysts adapted these classic themes for larger-scale conflicts. Von Schlieffen linked together the huge numerical and production *strengths* of Germany and the vast *maneuvering capabilities* of Flanders fields to pull the nation's might together conceptually behind a *unique alignment of forces* ("a giant hayrake"), which would *outflank* his French opponents, *attack weaknesses* (their supply lines and rear), capture and *hold key political centers* of France, and *dominate or destroy* its weakened army in the field (Tuchman, 1962). On the other side, Foch and Grandmaison saw *morale* ("élan"), *nerve* ("cran"), and continuous *concentrated attack* ("attaque à outrance") as *matching the values* of a volatile, recently defeated, and vengeful French nation, which had decided (for both moral and *coalition* reasons) to *set important limits* on its own actions in World War I—that is, not to attack first or through Belgium.

As these two strategies lost shape and became the head-on slaughter of trench warfare, Hart (1954) revitalized the *indirect approach,* and this became a central theme of British strategic thinking between the wars. Later in the United States, Matloff and Snell (1953) began to stress planning for *large-scale coalitions* as the giant forces of World War II developed. The Enigma group *moved secretly to develop the intelligence network* that was so crucial in the war's outcome (Stevenson, 1976). But once engaged in war, George Marshall still saw the only hope for Allied victory in *concentrating overwhelming forces* against one enemy (Germany) first, then after *conceding early losses* in the Pacific, *refocusing Allied forces* in a gigantic *sequential coordinated movement* against Japan. In the eastern theater, MacArthur first *fell back, consolidated a base* for operations, *built up his logistics, avoided his opponent's strengths, bypassed* Japan's established defensive positions, and in a *gigantic flanking maneuver* was ready to invade Japan after *softening its political and psychological will* through saturation bombing (James, 1970).

All these modern thinkers and practitioners utilized classical principles of strategy dating back to the Greek era, but perhaps the most startling analogies of World War II lay in Patton's and Rommel's battle strategies, which were almost carbon copies of the Macedonians' concepts of planned concentration, rapid breakthrough, encirclement, and attack on the enemy's rear (Essame, 1974; Farago, 1964; Irving, 1977; Young, 1974).

Similar concepts still pervade well-conceived strategies—whether they are government, diplomatic, military, sports, or business strategies. What could be more direct than the parallel between Chaeronea and a well-developed business strategy that first probes and withdraws to determine opponents' strengths, forces opponents to stretch their commitments, then concentrates resources, attacks a clear exposure, overwhelms a selected market segment, builds a bridgehead in that market, and then regroups and expands from that base to dominate a wider field? Many companies have followed just such strategies with great success. . . .

DIMENSIONS OF STRATEGY

Analysis of military-diplomatic strategies and similar analogies in other fields provides some essential insights into the basic dimensions, nature, and design of formal strategies.

First, effective formal strategies contain three essential elements: (1) the most important *goals* (or objectives) to be achieved, (2) the most significant *policies* guiding or limiting action, and (3) the major *action sequences* (or programs) that are to accomplish the defined goals within the limits set. Since strategy determines the overall direction and action focus of the organization, its formulation cannot be regarded as the mere generation and alignment of programs to meet predetermined goals. Goal development is an integral part of strategy formulation. . . .

Second, effective strategies develop around a *few key concepts and thrusts,* which give them cohesion, balance, and focus. Some thrusts are temporary; others are carried through to the end of the strategy. Some cost more per unit gain than others. Yet resources must be *allocated in patterns* that provide sufficient resources for each thrust to succeed regardless of its relative cost/gain ratio. And organizational units must be coordinated and actions controlled to support the intended thrust pattern or else the total strategy will fail. . . .

Third, strategy deals not just with the unpredictable but also with the *unknowable.* For major enterprise strategies, no analyst could predict the precise ways in which all impinging forces could interact with each other, be distorted by nature or human emotions, or be modified by the imaginations and purposeful counteractions of intelligent opponents (Braybrooke and Lindblom, 1963). Many have noted how large-scale systems can respond quite counterintuitively (Forrester, 1971) to apparently rational actions or how a seemingly bizarre series of events can conspire to prevent or assist success (White, 1978; Lindblom, 1959). . . .

Consequently, the essence of strategy—whether military, diplomatic, business, sports, (or) political . . .—is to *build a posture* that is so strong (and potentially flexible) in selective ways that the organization can achieve its goals despite the unforeseeable ways external forces may actually interact when the time comes.

Fourth, just as military organizations have multiple echelons of grand, theater, area, battle, infantry, and artillery strategies, so should other complex organizations have a number of hierarchically related and mutually supporting strategies (Vancil and Lorange, 1975; Vancil, 1976). Each such strategy must be more or less complete in itself, congruent with the level of decentralization intended. Yet each must be shaped as a cohesive element of higher-level strategies. Although, for reasons cited, achieving total cohesion among all of a major organization's strategies would be a superhuman task for any chief executive officer, it is important that there be a systematic means for testing each component strategy and seeing that it fulfills the major tenets of a well-formed strategy.

The criteria derived from military-diplomatic strategies provide an excellent framework for this, yet too often one sees purported formal strategies at all organizational levels that are not strategies at all. Because they ignore or violate even the most basic strategic principles, they are little more than aggregates of philosophies or agglomerations of programs. They lack the cohesiveness, flexibility, thrust, sense of positioning against intelligent opposition, and other criteria that historical analysis suggests effective strategies must contain. Whether formally or incrementally derived, strategies should be at least intellectually tested against the proper criteria.

Criteria for Effective Strategy

In devising a strategy to deal with the unknowable, what factors should one consider? Although each strategic situation is unique, are there some common criteria that tend to define a good strategy? The fact that a strategy worked in retrospect is not a sufficient criterion for judging any strategy. Was Grant really a greater strategist than Lee? Was Foch's strategy better than Von Schlieffen's? Was Xerxes's strategy superior to that of Leonidas? Was it the Russians' strategy that allowed them to roll over the Czechoslovaks in 1968? Clearly other factors than strategy—including luck, overwhelming resources, superb or stupid implementation, and enemy errors—help determine ultimate results. Besides, at the time one formulates a strategy, one cannot use the criterion of ultimate success because the outcome is still in doubt. Yet one clearly needs some guidelines to define an effective strategic structure.

A few studies have suggested some initial criteria for evaluating a strategy (Tilles, 1963; Christensen et al., 1978). These include its clarity, motivational impact, internal consistency, compatibility with the environment, appropriateness in light of resources, degree of risk, match to the personal values of key figures, time horizon, and workability. . . . In addition, historical examples—from both business and military-diplomatic settings—suggest that effective strategies should at a minimum encompass certain other critical factors and structural elements. . . .

- *Clear, decisive objectives:* Are all efforts directed toward clearly understood, decisive, and attainable overall goals? Specific goals of subordinate units may change in the heat of campaigns or competition, but the overriding goals of the strategy for all units must remain clear enough to provide continuity and cohesion for tactical choices during the time horizon of the strategy. All goals need not be written down or numerically precise, but they must be understood and be decisive—that is, if they are achieved they should ensure the continued viability and vitality of the entity vis-à-vis its opponents.

- *Maintaining the initiative:* Does the strategy preserve freedom of action and enhance commitment? Does it set the pace and determine the course of events rather than reacting to them? A prolonged reactive posture breeds unrest, lowers morale, and surrenders the advantage of timing and intangibles to opponents. Ultimately such a posture increases costs, decreases the number of options available, and lowers the probability of achieving sufficient success to ensure independence and continuity.

- *Concentration:* Does the strategy concentrate superior power at the place and time likely to be decisive? Has the strategy defined precisely what will make the enterprise superior in power—that is, "best" in critical dimensions—in relation to its opponents. A distinctive competency yields greater success with fewer resources and is the essential basis for higher gains (or profits) than competitors. . . .

- *Flexibility:* Has the strategy purposely built in resource buffers and dimensions for flexibility and maneuver? Reserved capabilities, planned maneuverability, and repositioning allow one to use minimum resources while keeping opponents at a relative disadvantage. As corollaries of concentration and concession, they permit the strategist to reuse the same forces to overwhelm selected positions at different times. They also force less flexible opponents to use more resources to hold predetermined positions, while simultaneously requiring minimum fixed commitment of one's own resources for defensive purposes.

- *Coordinated and committed leadership:* Does the strategy provide responsible, committed leadership for each of its major goals? . . . [Leaders] must be so chosen and motivated that their own interests and values match the needs of their roles. Successful strategies require commitment, not just acceptance.

- *Surprise:* Has the strategy made use of speed, secrecy, and intelligence to attack exposed or unprepared opponents at unexpected times? With surprise and correct timing, success can be achieved out of all proportion to the energy exerted and can decisively change strategic positions. . . .

- *Security:* Does the strategy secure resource bases and all vital operating points for the enterprise? Does it develop an effective intelligence system sufficient to prevent surprises by opponents? Does it develop the full logistics to support each of its major thrusts? Does it use coalitions effectively to extend the resource base and zones of friendly acceptance for the enterprise? . . .

These are critical elements of strategy, whether in business, government, or warfare.

READING FIVE PS FOR STRATEGY*

By Henry Mintzberg

Human nature insists on a definition for every concept. But the word strategy has long been used implicitly in different ways even if it has traditionally been defined in only one. Explicit recognition of multiple definitions can help people to maneuver through this difficult field. Accordingly, five definitions of strategy are presented here—as plan, ploy, pattern, position, and perspective—and some of their interrelationships are then considered.

STRATEGY AS PLAN

To almost anyone you care to ask, **strategy is a plan**—some sort of *consciously intended* course of action, a guideline (or set of guidelines) to deal with a situation. A kid has a "strategy" to get over a fence, a corporation has one to capture a market. By this definition, strategies have two essential characteristics: they are made in advance of the actions to which they apply, and they are developed consciously and purposefully. A host of definitions in a variety of fields reinforce this view. For example:

- in the military: Strategy is concerned with "draft[ing] the plan of war . . . shap[ing] the individual campaigns and within these, decid[ing] on the individual engagements" (Von Clausewitz, 1976:177).
- in Game Theory: Strategy is "a complete plan: a plan which specifies what choices [the player] will make in every possible situation" (von Neumann and Morgenstern, 1944:79).
- in management: "Strategy is a unified, comprehensive, and integrated plan . . . designed to ensure that the basic objectives of the enterprise are achieved" (Glueck, 1980:9).

As plans, strategies may be general or they can be specific. There is one use of the word in the specific sense that should be identified here. As plan, **a strategy can be a ploy**, too, really just a specific "maneuver" intended to outwit an opponent or competitor. The kid may use the fence as a ploy to draw a bully into his yard, where his Doberman pinscher awaits intruders. Likewise, a corporation may threaten to expand plant capacity to discourage a competitor from building a new plant. Here the real strategy (as plan, that is, the real intention) is the threat, not the expansion itself, and as such is a ploy.

In fact, there is a growing literature in the field of strategic management, as well as on the general process of bargaining, that views strategy in this way and so focuses attention on its most dynamic and competitive aspects. For example, in his popular book, *Competitive Strategy,* Porter (1980) devotes one chapter to "Market Signals" (including

---

* Originally published in the *California Management Review* (Fall 1987), © 1987 by the Regents of the University of California. Reprinted with deletions by permission of the *California Management Review.*

discussion of the effects of announcing moves, the use of "the fighting brand," and the use of threats of private antitrust suits) and another to "Competitive Moves" (including actions to preempt competitive response). And Schelling (1980) devotes much of his famous book, *The Strategy of Conflict,* to the topic of ploys to outwit rivals in a competitive or bargaining situation.

STRATEGY AS PATTERN

But if strategies can be intended (whether as general plans or specific ploys), surely they can also be realized. In other words, defining strategy as a plan is not sufficient; we also need a definition that encompasses the resulting behavior. Thus a third definition is proposed: **strategy is a pattern**—specifically, a pattern in a stream of actions (Mintzberg and Waters, 1985). By this definition, when Picasso painted blue for a time, that was a strategy, just as was the behavior of the Ford Motor Company when Henry Ford offered his Model T only in black. In other words, by this definition, strategy is *consistency* in behavior, *whether or not* intended.

This may sound like a strange definition for a word that has been so bound up with free will ("strategos" in Greek, the art of the army general[1]). But the fact of the matter is that while hardly anyone defines strategy in this way, many people seem at one time or another to so use it. Consider this quotation from a business executive: "Gradually the successful approaches merge into a pattern of action that becomes our strategy. We certainly don't have an overall strategy on this" (quoted in Quinn, 1980:35). This comment is inconsistent only if we restrict ourselves to one definition of strategy: what this man seems to be saying is that his firm has strategy as pattern, but not as plan. Or consider this comment in *Business Week* on a joint venture between General Motors and Toyota:

> The tentative Toyota deal may be most significant because it is another example of how GM's strategy boils down to doing a little bit of everything until the market decides where it is going. (*Business Week,* October 31, 1983)

A journalist has inferred a pattern in the behavior of a corporation and labeled it strategy.

The point is that every time a journalist imputes a strategy to a corporation or to a government, and every time a manager does the same thing to a competitor or even to the senior management of his own firm, they are implicitly defining strategy as pattern in action—that is, inferring consistency in behavior and labeling it strategy. They may, of course, go further and impute intention to that consistency—that is, assume there is a plan behind the pattern. But that is an assumption, which may prove false.

Thus, the definitions of strategy as plan and pattern can be quite independent of each other: plans may go unrealized, while patterns may appear without preconception. To paraphrase Hume, strategies may result from human actions but not human designs (see Majone, 1976–77). If we label the first definition *intended* strategy and the second *realized* strategy, as shown in Figure 1, then we can distinguish *deliberate* strategies, where intentions that existed previously were realized, from *emergent* strategies, where patterns developed in the absence of intentions, or despite them (which went *unrealized*).

For a strategy to be truly deliberate—that is, for a pattern to have been intended *exactly* as realized—would seem to be a tall order. Precise intentions would have had to

---

[1] Evered (1983) discusses the Greek origins of the word and traces its entry into contemporary Western vocabulary through the military.

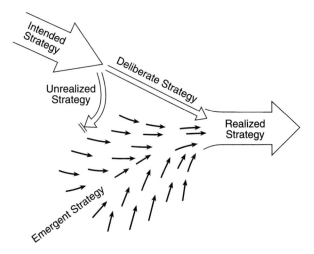

FIGURE 1
Deliberate and Emergent Strategies

be stated in advance by the leadership of the organization; these would have had to be accepted as is by everyone else, and then realized with no interference by market, technological, or political forces and so on. Likewise, a truly emergent strategy is again a tall order, requiring consistency in action without any hint of intention. (No consistency means *no* strategy, or at least unrealized strategy.) Yet some strategies do come close enough to either form, while others—probably most—sit on the continuum that exists between the two, reflecting deliberate as well as emergent aspects. Table 1 lists various kinds of strategies along this continuum.

Strategies about What?

Labeling strategies as plans or patterns still begs one basic question: *strategies about what?* Many writers respond by discussing the deployment of resources, but the question remains: which resources and for what purposes? An army may plan to reduce the number of nails in its shoes, or a corporation may realize a pattern of marketing only products painted black, but these hardly meet the lofty label "strategy." Or do they?

As the word has been handed down from the military, "strategy" refers to the important things, "tactics" to the details (more formally, "tactics teaches the use of armed forces in the engagement, strategy the use of engagements for the object of the war," von Clausewitz, 1976:128). Nails in shoes, colors of cars; these are certainly details. The problem is that in retrospect details can sometimes prove "strategic." Even in the military: "For want of a Nail, the Shoe was lost; for want of a Shoe the Horse was lost . . . ," and so on through the rider and general to the battle, "all for want of Care about a Horseshoe Nail" (Franklin, 1977:280). Indeed one of the reasons Henry Ford lost his war with General Motors was that he refused to paint his cars anything but black.

Rumelt (1979) notes that "one person's strategies are another's tactics—that what is strategic depends on where you sit." It also depends on *when* you sit; what seems tactical today may prove strategic tomorrow. The point is that labels should not be used to imply that some issues are *inevitably* more important than others. There are times when it pays to manage the details and let the strategies emerge for themselves. Thus there is good reason to refer to issues as more or less "strategic," in other words, more or less "important" in some context, whether as intended before acting or as realized after it. Accordingly, the answer to the question, strategy about what, is: potentially about anything. About products and processes, customers and citizens, social responsibilities and self interests, control and color.

Two aspects of the content of strategies must, however, be singled out because they are of particular importance.

TABLE 1 **Various Kinds of Strategies, from Rather Deliberate to Mostly Emergent***

Planned Strategy: Precise intentions are formulated and articulated by a central leadership, and backed up by formal controls to ensure their surprise-free implementation in an environment that is benign, controllable, or predictable (to ensure no distortion of intentions); these strategies are highly deliberate.

Entrepreneurial Strategy: Intentions exist as the personal, unarticulated vision of a single leader, and so are adaptable to new opportunities; the organization is under the personal control of the leader and located in a protected niche in its environment; these strategies are relatively deliberate but can emerge too.

Ideological Strategy: Intentions exist as the collective vision of all the members of the organization, controlled through strong shared norms; the organization is often proactive vis-à-vis its environment; these strategies are rather deliberate.

Umbrella Strategy: A leadership in partial control of organizational actions defines strategic targets or boundaries within which others must act (for example, that all new products be high priced and at the technological cutting edge, although what these actual products are to be is left to emerge); as a result, strategies are partly deliberate (the boundaries) and partly emergent (the patterns within them); this strategy can also be called deliberately emergent, in that the leadership purposefully allows others the flexibility to maneuver and form patterns within the boundaries.

Process Strategy: The leadership controls the process aspects of strategy (who gets hired and so gets a chance to influence strategy, what structures they work within, etc.), leaving the actual content of strategy to others; strategies are again partly deliberate (concerning process) and partly emergent (concerning content), and deliberately emergent.

Disconnected Strategy: Members or subunits loosely coupled to the rest of the organization produce patterns in the streams of their own actions in the absence of, or in direct contradiction to the central or common intentions of the organization at large; the strategies can be deliberate for those who make them.

Consensus Strategy: Through mutual adjustment, various members converge on patterns that pervade the organization in the absence of central or common intentions; these strategies are rather emergent in nature.

Imposed Strategy: The external environment dictates patterns in actions, either through direct imposition (say, by an outside owner or by a strong customer) or through implicitly preempting or bounding organizational choice (as in a large airline that must fly jumbo jets to remain viable); these strategies are organizationally emergent, although they may be internalized and made deliberate.

* Adapted from Mintzberg and Waters (1985:270).

STRATEGY AS POSITION

The fourth definition is that **strategy is a position**—specifically, a means of locating an organization in what organization theorists like to call an "environment." By this definition, strategy becomes the mediating force—or "match," according to Hofer and Schendel (1978:4)—between organization and environment, that is, between the internal and the external context. In ecological terms, strategy becomes a "niche"; in economic terms, a place that generates "rent" (that is "returns to [being] in a 'unique' place" (Bowman, 1974:47)); in management terms, formally, a product-market "domain" (Thompson, 1967), the place in the environment where resources are concentrated.

Note that this definition of strategy can be compatible with either (or all) of the preceding ones; a position can be preselected and aspired to through a plan (or ploy) and/or it can be reached, perhaps even found, through a pattern of behavior.

In military and game theory views of strategy, it is generally used in the context of what is called a "two-person game," better known in business as head-on competition (where ploys are especially common). The definition of strategy as position, however, implicitly allows us to open up the concept, to so-called n-person games (that is, many players), and beyond. In other words, while position can always be defined with respect to a single competitor (literally so in the military, where position becomes the site of battle), it can also be considered in the context of a number of competitors or simply with respect to markets or an environment at large. But strategy as position can extend beyond competition too, economic and otherwise. Indeed, what is the meaning of the word "niche" but a position that is occupied to *avoid* competition. Thus, we can move from the definition employed by General Ulysses Grant in the 1860s, "Strategy [is] the deployment of one's resources in a manner which is most likely to defeat the enemy," to that of Professor Richard Rumelt in the 1980s, "Strategy is creating situations for economic rents and finding ways to sustain them,"[2] that is, any viable position, whether or not directly competitive.

Astley and Fombrun (1983), in fact, take the next logical step by introducing the notion of "collective" strategy, that is, strategy pursued to promote cooperation between organizations, even would-be competitors (equivalent in biology to animals herding together for protection). Such strategies can range "from informal arrangements and discussions to formal devices such as interlocking directorates, joint ventures, and mergers" (p. 577). In fact, considered from a slightly different angle, these can sometimes be described as *political* strategies, that is strategies to subvert the legitimate forces of competition.

STRATEGY AS PERSPECTIVE

While the fourth definition of strategy looks out, seeking to locate the organization in the external environment, and down to concrete positions, the fifth looks inside the organization, indeed inside the heads of the collective strategist, but up to a broader view. Here, **strategy is a perspective**, its content consisting not just of a chosen position, but of an ingrained way of perceiving the world. There are organizations that favor marketing and build a whole ideology around that (an IBM); Hewlett-Packard has developed the "H-P way," based on its engineering culture, while McDonald's has become famous for its emphasis on "quality, service, cleanliness, and value."

Strategy in this respect is to the organization what personality is to the individual. Indeed, one of the earliest and most influential writers on strategy (at least as his ideas have been reflected in more popular writings) was Philip Selznick (1957:47), who wrote about the "character" of an organization—distinct and integrated "commitments to ways of acting and responding" that are built right into it. A variety of concepts from other fields also capture this notion; anthropologists refer to the "culture" of a society and sociologists to its "ideology"; military theorists write of the "grand strategy" of armies; while management theorists have used terms such as the "theory of the business" and its "driving force" (Drucker, 1974; Tregoe and Zimmerman, 1980); and Germans perhaps capture it best with their word "Weltanschauung," literally "worldview," meaning collective intuition about how the world works.

This fifth definition suggests above all that strategy is a *concept*. This has one im-

---

[2] Expressed at the Strategic Management Society Conference, Montreal, October 1982.

portant implication, namely, that all strategies are abstractions which exist only in the minds of interested parties. It is important to remember that no one has ever seen a strategy or touched one; every strategy is an invention, a figment of someone's imagination, whether conceived of as intentions to regulate behavior before it takes place or inferred as patterns to describe behavior that has already occurred.

What is of key importance about this fifth definition, however, is that the perspective is *shared.* As implied in the words Weltanschauung, culture, and ideology (with respect to a society), but not the word personality, strategy is a perspective shared by the members of an organization, through their intentions and/or by their actions. In effect, when we are talking of strategy in this context, we are entering the realm of the *collective mind*—individuals united by common thinking and/or behavior. A major issue in the study of strategy formation becomes, therefore, how to read that collective mind—to understand how intentions diffuse through the system called organization to become shared and how actions come to be exercised on a collective yet consistent basis.

INTERRELATING THE Ps

As suggested above, strategy as both position and perspective can be compatible with strategy as plan and/or pattern. But, in fact, the relationships between these different definitions can be more involved than that. For example, while some consider perspective to *be* a plan (Lapierre, 1980, writes of strategies as "dreams in search of reality"), others describe it as *giving rise* to plans (for example, as positions and/or patterns in some kind of implicit hierarchy). But the concept of emergent strategy is that a pattern can emerge and be recognized so that it gives rise to a formal plan, perhaps within an overall perspective.

We may ask how perspective arises in the first place. Probably through earlier experiences: the organization tried various things in its formative years and gradually consolidated a perspective around what worked. In other words, organizations would appear to develop "character" much as people develop personality—by interacting with the world as they find it through the use of their innate skills and natural propensities. Thus pattern can give rise to perspective too. And so can position. Witness Perrow's (1970:161) discussion of the "wool men" and "silk men" of the textile trade, people who developed an almost religious dedication to the fibers they produced.

No matter how they appear, however, there is reason to believe that while plans and positions may be dispensable, perspectives are immutable (Brunsson, 1982). In other words, once they are established, perspectives become difficult to change. Indeed, a perspective may become so deeply ingrained in the behavior of an organization that the associated beliefs can become subconscious in the minds of its members. When that happens, perspective can come to look more like pattern than like plan—in other words, it can be found more in the consistency of behaviors than in the articulation of intentions.

Of course, if perspective is immutable, then change in plan and position within perspective is easy compared to change outside perspective. In this regard, it is interesting to take up the case of Egg McMuffin. Was this product when new—the American breakfast in a bun—a strategic change for the McDonald's fast-food chain? Posed in MBA classes, this earth-shattering (or at least stomach-shattering) question inevitably evokes heated debate. Proponents (usually people sympathetic to fast food) argue that of course it was: it brought McDonald's into a new market, the breakfast one, extending the use of existing facilities. Opponents retort that this is nonsense; nothing changed but a few ingredients: this was the same old pap in a new package. Both sides are, of course, right—and wrong. It simply depends on how you define strategy. Position changed;

perspective remained the same. Indeed—and this is the point—the position could be changed easily because it was compatible with the existing perspective. Egg McMuffin is pure McDonald's, not only in product and package, but also in production and propagation. But imagine a change of position at McDonald's that would require a change of perspective—say, to introduce candlelight dining with personal service (your McDuckling à l'Orange cooked to order) to capture the late evening market. We needn't say more, except perhaps to label this the "Egg McMuffin syndrome."

THE NEED FOR ECLECTICISM IN DEFINITION

While various relationships exist among the different definitions, no one relationship, nor any single definition for that matter, takes precedence over the others. In some ways, these definitions compete (in that they can substitute for each other), but in perhaps more important ways, they complement. Not all plans become patterns nor are all patterns that develop planned; some ploys are less than positions, while other strategies are more than positions yet less than perspectives. Each definition adds important elements to our understanding of strategy, indeed encourages us to address fundamental questions about organizations in general.

As plan, strategy deals with how leaders try to establish direction for organizations, to set them on predetermined courses of action. Strategy as plan also raises the fundamental issue of cognition—how intentions are conceived in the human brain in the first place, indeed, what intentions really mean. The road to hell in this field can be paved with those who take all stated intentions at face value. In studying strategy as plan, we must somehow get into the mind of the strategist, to find out what is really intended.

As ploy, strategy takes us into the realm of direct competition, where threats and feints and various other maneuvers are employed to gain advantage. This places the process of strategy formation in its most dynamic setting, with moves provoking countermoves and so on. Yet ironically, strategy itself is a concept rooted not in change but in stability—in set plans and established patterns. How then to reconcile the dynamic notions of strategy as ploy with the static ones of strategy as pattern and other forms of plan?

As pattern, strategy focuses on action, reminding us that the concept is an empty one if it does not take behavior into account. Strategy as pattern also introduces the notion of convergence, the achievement of consistency in an organization's behavior. How does this consistency form, where does it come from? Realized strategy, when considered alongside intended strategy, encourages us to consider the notion that strategies can emerge as well as be deliberately imposed.

As position, strategy encourages us to look at organizations in their competitive environments—how they find their positions and protect them in order to meet competition, avoid it, or subvert it. This enables us to think of organizations in ecological terms, as organisms in niches that struggle for survival in a world of hostility and uncertainty as well as symbiosis.

And finally as perspective, strategy raises intriguing questions about intention and behavior in a collective context. If we define organization as collective action in the pursuit of common mission (a fancy way of saying that a group of people under a common label—whether a General Motors or a Luigi's Body Shop—somehow find the means to cooperate in the production of specific goods and services), then strategy as perspective raises the issue of how intentions diffuse through a group of people to become shared as norms and values, and how patterns of behavior become deeply ingrained in the group.

Thus, strategy is not just a notion of how to deal with an enemy or a set of competitors or a market, as it is treated in so much of the literature and in its popular usage. It also draws us into some of the most fundamental issues about organizations as instruments for collective perception and action.

To conclude, a good deal of the confusion in this field stems from contradictory and ill-defined uses of the term strategy. By explicating and using various definitions, we may be able to avoid some of this confusion, and thereby enrich our ability to understand and manage the processes by which strategies form.

C H A P T E R   2

. . . .

THE STRATEGIST

What is a strategist? And what is his or her role in the strategy-making process? Over the years, there have been varying opinions on these questions. The dominant view until recently has been of the strategist as completely rational, and this approach is probably still the prevailing one in the literature. In this chapter we will examine a variety of thoughts on the subject and will offer a different view from the dominant one.

FIVE MODELS OF THE STRATEGIST

Bourgeois and Brodwin[1] created a typology of approaches to strategic implementation. They call them "models." These models are useful for pointing out some different ways of thinking about strategists.

The Strategist as Rational Actor

Their first model is the **commander model**, where the CEO is a rational actor, much like the firm in classic microeconomics. He or she has considerable power, and has access to almost complete information. The commander uses power and information to do exhaustive rational analyses before taking any action. Then, his or her objectives guide strategic actions in the organization. This model captures the essence of the mainstream description of the strategist.

The commander model stresses formulation over implementation, analysis over action. It implies that the strategist has comprehensive and correct information about the firm's internal strengths and weaknesses and about its external environment. There are problems if the firm is in a fast-moving environment, if there are organizational disincentives built into the plan, and if planners cannot be totally objective. Lastly, because this model divides the firm up into thinkers and doers, people who formulate (the commander and her/his planning staff) and people who implement (everybody else), it can breed demotivation (always working on someone else's plan) and non-innovation (withholding alternatives that stand little chance of acceptance). Another problem is that there is considerable evidence, from observed behavior in firms[2], that many strategic ideas come from lower-level participants who identify and champion opportunities. Nevertheless, the commander model is very popular.

The Strategist as Architect

The second model, the **change model**, starts where the commander model leaves off—with implementation. In this model, strategic recommendations have been received in some way (perhaps from a commander-like planner), and now the strategist must get the organization to carry them out. The CEO's role is that of architect—designing structures and systems to secure execution of the strategy, pushing the organization toward goal achievement. This model recommends that the strategist use management and behavioral science tools to implement strategy. These include: **structure and staffing;**[3] **planning systems;**[4] **information systems;**[5] **incentive compensation schemes;**[6] and **organization development,** including survey feedback,[7] team-building,[8] intergroup activities,[9] and whole-system interventions.[10]

A major improvement of this model is that the strategist considers implementation directly, not merely passing on the strategic intent to subordinates, but remaining actively involved throughout the implementation process. But the model does nothing to address other shortcomings: the strategist still needs timely and accurate information, must still be very powerful, still needs a strategy with no built-in disincentives, and still faces the motivational and innovating problems associated with dividing the strategy-making task into a "thinking" part and a "doing" part. Like the cultural model, it takes a long time to implement systems.

The Strategist as Coordinator

In the **collaborative model**, the strategist is concerned with how to get the top management team to help develop and commit to a good set of goals and strategies.[11] The CEO uses group dynamics and brainstorming techniques to get the top management team to develop ideas for the firm's strategy. He or she acts as coordinator, trying to elicit good ideas from the team. There are many variations on the kinds of activities the team could do, including: planning exercises;[12] taking the "devil's advocacy" approach, where a plan developed either by the team or by experts is formally criticized by designated devil's advocates;[13] and leading dialectical inquiry, when two plans are developed—a thesis and an antithesis, in other words, a plan and a counterplan—and the advocates of the two plans engage in a formal debate, arriving at a synthesis.[14]

This model allows for the possibility that the "strategist" could be more than one person. Involving several minds reduces the information accuracy and cognitive processing limits of the commander model. Securing commitment to the strategy overcomes the motivational problems of both the previous models. These benefits are most apparent in turbulent and complex environments.

The Strategist as Coach

The **cultural model** asks the question, "How can I get my whole organization committed to our goals and strategies?"[15] The CEO is like a coach, exhorting people in the firm to believe in the firm's mission, but allowing them to create the details of their compliance with it. In other words, the CEO tries to create a culture—a collection of values, beliefs, and ways of thinking that is shared by organizational members.[16] In applying this model, the strategist would use the full array of cultural tools available, which we will discuss in Chapter Seven.

The cultural model begins to bridge the gap between thinkers and doers. The strategist sets the general tone, even spends much time and energy articulating a vision. Lower-level participants are the ones who create the details of their strategy's conformity to the vision. Inculcating a culture takes a very long time, which can hurt, but once it is established, there is a double payoff—execution is swift and politics are reduced. However, there are many potential problems with a strong culture that could cause the firm to lose touch with their environment. The consistency fostered by a strong culture can make organizational members too inward-looking. They can suffer from xenophobia (the dislike of those not part of the culture). Their members can resist deviance, an ingredient often needed for true innovation. This can also breed homogeneity in the organization, as deviants leave for other firms, and can retard attempts to change in positive ways.[17]

The Strategist as Orchestrator and Judge

Bourgeois and Brodwin's final model of implementation is what they call the **crescive model,** where the CEO encourages managers to develop, champion, and implement sound strategies. The word "crescive" comes from the Latin word *crescere,* to grow. In this model, strategy grows from within the firm, typically from the bottom up. Instead of being a designer, the CEO sets assumptions or boundaries for organizational action, and then appraises the value of suggested strategies. The most important parts of the job are defining organizational purposes broadly enough to allow for innovation and selecting judiciously from the suggested projects.

The crescive model seems to fit many aspects of organizational reality quite well. In highly diversified companies, or in companies that are in highly dynamic industries, CEOs cannot know everything, and what information they get may be outdated. An executive's power, although it is substantial, is more limited than most people think. Power is offset by key subordinates in several ways—they can leave, they may control important information, and they may have control over important customer relationships.[18] Executives have limited time to spend on planning and strategizing.[19] All these things show that CEOs need to rely heavily on subordinates when formulating strategy. The executive needs timely information about conditions in each industry in which the firm operates. Executives also need subordinates to formulate or review business strategies, and to endorse operating goals. Despite the prevalent ideology of the commander model, it is uncommon for strategies to be formulated by single individuals. Strategy formulation is typically a group process, and group processes are riddled with potential problems. These mostly involve avoidance of uncertainty, a tendency to smooth over differences prematurely, and groupthink—a condition that occurs when people who work together accept each other's biases and lose their ability to think critically.[20] The CEO can alleviate this partly by shaping premises—by directing the attention of subordinates to distinctive content areas, by endorsing a specific planning methodology, and by altering organization structure.[21] It is to these kinds of actions that the crescive model points.

STRATEGISTS AND MODELS OF STRATEGY MAKING

Mintzberg identified three conceptual models[22] of strategy making—entrepreneurial, planning, and adaptive. In the entrepreneurial mode, power is centralized in the hands of the chief executive, whose behavior is dominated by the active search for opportunities, by the pursuit of the goal of growth above all, and by the taking of dramatic leaps forward in the face of uncertainty. The planning mode is characterized by an emphasis on analysis (especially assessing the costs and benefits of competing proposals), a major role for staff personnel, and an attempt to formally integrate global strategies that are designed to achieve efficiency and growth. In the adaptive mode, power is divided among many constituencies in the firm, goals are indeterminate, the firm reacts to existing problems rather than searching for new opportunities, and decisions are disjointed and incremental. The role of the strategist in each of these modes is very different.

In a study tracking strategy in an entrepreneurial firm, Mintzberg and Waters[23] found that strategists in that mode practiced "controlled boldness"; that is, not plunging in until they had tested the waters. At first glance, the entrepreneurial mode seems like a variation on the command model discussed earlier. But Mintzberg and Waters found that for entrepreneurs the strategy is not a plan on paper but a vision in the mind; this vision is based on intimate, detailed knowledge of the business. Mintzberg and Waters sum up the strategist's role in the entrepreneurial mode this way:

> Leadership in . . . the entrepreneurial mode is very much tied up with the creation of vision, essentially with concept attainment. . . . The focus is on the leader, the organization is malleable and responsive to the leader's initiatives, and the environment for the most part remains benign, the result of the leader's selecting . . . the correct niche for his or her organization.[24]

Of the three modes, this is the one where the strategist is most easily identified. "There is one leader, and that person invents or conceives strategy."[25] We will examine the entrepreneurial mode in greater detail in Chapter Nine.

In the planning mode, leadership is dominated by the organization's bureaucratic apparatus. The strategist in this mode is akin to the architect of the change model discussed above. He or she designs planning structures and systems that are supposed to scan the external and internal environments and then formulate appropriate strategies. In another study, Mintzberg[26] found that planning mode firms tended to adopt "mainline strategies"—standard, accepted ones in the industry. He found that planning seems to be the mode for operationalizing strategy, not for creating it. Mintzberg and Waters sum up the role of the strategist in the planning mode by saying

> If the strategist of the [entrepreneurial mode] is a concept attainer, then that of the [planning mode] is . . . a pigeonholer who slots generic strategies into well-defined conditions and then hangs onto them for dear life.[27]

In a summary paper on this work, Mintzberg and Waters argue, ironically, that it is simultaneously easy and difficult to pick out a strategist in the planning mode. In one sense, there is no strategist, except the entrepreneur who may have developed the firm's original strategy at some point in the past. As for the current members of the planning mode organization, "Those who call themselves strategists . . . tend to be planners of sorts, protecting, extrapolating, and marginally modifying—in effect, programming or implementing—the strategies the organization already pursues."[28] We will examine the planning mode in greater detail in Chapter Ten.

Organizations in the adaptive mode are close to the crescive model. In a study of a film company, Mintzberg and McHugh found that these firms tend not to have dominant individual strategists.[29] They rely instead on mutual adjustment among all their members; this mutual adjustment is designed to help the organization discern what the firm's customers want. In other words, these firms adapt to what they think their environments want. Mintzberg and Waters describe the strategist in adaptive firms this way:

> . . . The strategist of the [adaptive mode] is a *pattern recognizer*, seeking to detect emerging patterns (inside and outside the [strategic] umbrella). That way the appropriate ones can be encouraged through more conscious attention and concentration of resources (narrowing the umbrella or moving it over), while others deemed inappropriate can be discouraged.[30]

Identifying a specific strategist can be very difficult in the complex situations inhabited by firms in the adaptive mode. Since strategies come about through the mutual adjustment of large numbers of people, it is reasonable to say "every person is a strategist."[31]

THE TRANSFORMATIVE STRATEGIST

Warren Bennis, a noted scholar of leadership, found that successful CEOs display five competencies.[32] The first is **vision**: the capacity to create and express a compelling vision of a desired state of affairs—to impart clarity to this vision and induce commitment to it. Related to this, Bennis found that effective executives have **communication** and **alignment** skills; they can express their vision to gain the support of their multiple constituencies. Effective CEOs also have **persistence, consistency,** and **focus**—the capacity to maintain the organization's direction, especially when the going gets tough. Bennis discovered that effective leaders have the capacity to create environments that can tap and harness the energies and abilities necessary to cause the desired results, a capacity he called **empowerment**. Lastly, there is the skill Bennis called **organizational learning**—finding ways for the organization to oversee its own performance, relate results to established objectives, create and use up-to-date information on which to review past actions and base future ones, and decide how and if the organizational structure and key personnel must be restructured or reassigned when faced with new conditions.

Bennis called this kind of leadership **transformative**, since it has the capacity to create progressive change in an organization. The five skills clearly relate to the strategic role of an executive, especially the role mentioned in the crescive model. The executive must create the general premises (vision) but also must communicate them persistently. Executives must also empower lower-level participants so that they will create strategy and realize the strategic vision. It is also an executive's responsibility to help the organization's members act as judges of how well the organization is doing.

THE STRATEGIST IN HIGH-PERFORMING SYSTEMS

Peter Vaill has done some interesting work on high-performing systems and the characteristics of the people who manage them. He defines high-performing systems as "organizations or groups that meet one or more of the following criteria":[33]

1. They are performing excellently against a known external standard.
2. They are performing excellently against what is assumed to be their potential level of performance.
3. They are performing excellently in relation to where they were at some earlier point in time.
4. They are judged by informed observers to be doing substantially better qualitatively than other comparable systems.
5. They are doing whatever they do with significantly fewer resources than it is assumed are needed to do what they do.
6. They are perceived as exemplars of the way to do whatever they do, and thus they become a source of ideas and inspiration for others.
7. They are perceived to fulfill at a high level the ideals for the culture within which they exist—that is, they have "nobility."
8. They are the only organizations that can do what they do at all, although it might seem that what they do is not that difficult or mysterious a thing.

Having identified some high-performing systems (HPSs), Vaill found that they had the following characteristics:[34]

1. HPSs are clear on their broad purposes and on nearer-term objectives for fulfilling these purposes.
2. Commitment to these purposes is never perfunctory. Motivation is always high and unique to the HPS's members. The members express their energy and commitment by getting into a "groove" of some kind.
3. Teamwork in HPSs is focused on the task. The distinction between task functions and maintenance functions dissolves.
4. Leadership in HPSs is strong and clear, not ambivalent. The source of initiative is never in doubt, although it may not always be the same person. Leadership style varies from HPS to HPS but is always consistent, reliable, and predictable within a given HPS.
5. HPSs are fertile sources of inventions and new methods within the scope of the task they have defined and within the form they have chosen. They tend to avoid going outside that domain.
6. HPSs are clearly bounded from their environments, and a considerable amount of energy, particularly by leaders, is usually devoted to maintaining these boundaries. There is a strong consciousness that "we are different."
7. HPSs are often seen as "a problem" by entities in their environment—even those entities that have a great deal of power over them. HPSs avoid external control. They produce what they want by their standards, not what someone else wants.
8. Above all, HPSs are systems that have "jelled," even though the phenomenon is very difficult to talk about.

Leadership Implications from High-Performing Systems

Vaill points out that clarity of purpose may be the most important thing that distinguishes high-performing systems from ordinary systems. But this clarity is dependent on some degree of stability in environmental demands, members' own expectations and needs, the technologies they are operating, and the structures through which they are bound together.[35] As we saw earlier in this chapter, stability is increasingly rare in modern organizations. How do high-performing systems manage to create clarity of purpose in the face of environmental turbulence?

Vaill says that the leaders do it through **purposing,** which he defines as "that continuous stream of actions by an organization's formal leadership that has the effect of inducing clarity, consensus, and commitment regarding the organization's basic purpose."[36] The words *purpose* and *propose* come from the same Latin root, *proponere.* Vaill argues that the members of high-performing systems create streams of proposals that they ultimately translate into purposes. The leaders are the ones responsible for this process, which is very similar to Bourgeois and Brodwin's crescive model.

In his research, Vaill did not find any *personal* characteristics of leaders that were common across all high-performing systems. He *did* find patterns of behavior that "appear 100 percent of the time in the actions of leaders of high-performing systems."[37] They are:

1. Leaders of high-performing systems put in extraordinary amounts of *time*.
2. Leaders of high-performing systems have very strong *feelings* about the attainment of the system's purposes
3. Leaders of high-performing systems *focus* on key issues and variables.[38]

TIME. Leaders of high-performing systems work very hard. Their conscious thinking is dominated by the system's issues and events. For them, the immediacy of the system does not respect the clock or space—they work long hours, and they think about work no matter where they are. Vaill makes the interesting observation that it is very important that these leaders put in large amounts of both microtime and macrotime. Microtime is the hour-to-hour, day-to-day kind of investment, which is what most people think of when discussing how much a person works. Macrotime is the amount of time a person stays in a position. "Leaders of high-performing systems tend to stay in their jobs for many years; they do not simply 'pass through.' "[39]

FEELING. Vaill quotes a colleague as saying, "An executive ought to want something."[40] Leaders of high-performing systems care deeply about the system, including its purposes, its structure and conduct, its history, its future security, and its people. For these people, sustained vigorous purposing is a natural expression of feeling, of their deep values and beliefs.

Feeling is typically the foundation on which the leader's large commitment of microtime is built. Since the leader cares, it seems perfectly natural to spend so much time on the job. Macrotime plays a different role—it helps develop feeling and can affect its expression. It often takes a long time for a leader to appreciate fully why a system is special, why he or she should care about it. The investment of macrotime helps develop this appreciation. One downside of feeling is that it can blind the leader to what the system needs as the environment changes.

FOCUS. What is it that the boss ought to be working on? Vaill found no list of variables that are important in any organization. But in high-performing systems "there is always some short list of priorities that leaders have clearly in mind."[41] Leaders are also good at communicating this focus to the members of the high-performing system.

This latter skill is very important, since at any given moment there will be many demands for action. Effective strategists will cut through this noise and focus on the few things that are truly important. Strategic management is primarily the study of focus. Vaill points out that effective strategists do as Peters and Waterman discovered—they use "simultaneous loose–tight controls,"[42] tight over the important things, loose over everything else.

Time, Feeling, and Focus: How They Fit Together

Vail concludes his development of the time-feeling-focus model by saying that all three must be present for a high-performing system to have effective leadership. For example, strategic planning (a way to determine focus) is an "empty technical exercise" without time and feeling. Time with no feeling or focus leads to compulsive behavior. Time and feeling with no focus denotes a strategist who needs to step back and understand the system better. Time and focus without feeling is the detached, rational, "professional" manager so typical of the analytical approaches to management and strategy. Feeling without time or focus leads to either idealism or cynicism; either of these can have a place, especially idealism, but Vaill says that these are not found in the leaders of high-performing systems. Feeling and focus without time leads to the staff person who "punches out" at five o'clock, or the consultant who drifts in and out of the organization. A similar mode is focus without time or feeling. Vaill says that, sadly, in modern society it is possible to become a leader of an organization without time, feeling, and focus. This clearly will not lead to high performance.

The readings in this chapter take a closer look at some themes discussed above. In his reading "Good Managers Don't Make Policy Decisions," H. Edward Wrapp takes an entertaining look at what Bourgeois and Brodwin would call the crescive model. But first, let us examine Henry Mintzberg's look at the true nature of managerial work.

THE MANAGER'S JOB: FOLKLORE OR FACT?

Almost all introductory textbooks on management rely on the familiar four-part classification of the manager's job as planning, organizing, coordinating, and controlling, originally developed by Henri Fayol.[43] Mintzberg is not interested in perpetuating Fayol's conceptual scheme. He wants to examine what managers actually do and to develop a descriptive classification. The resulting framework is what this reading is all about. It identifies ten roles of the manager, clustered into three types. **Interpersonal roles** including *figurehead, leader,* and *liaison.* **Informational roles** include *monitor, disseminator,* and *spokesman* Lastly, the **decisional roles** are *entrepreneur, disturbance handler, resource allocator,* and *negotiator.* The reading discusses these in detail.

Mintzberg says that managers aren't reflective, systematic planners. He recognizes that managers must often act systematically. But it is equally true that often they cannot and should not. As mentioned above, the key may lie in what Peters and Waterman asserted in *In Search of Excellence*[44]—like the organizations they manage, managers must be simultaneously loose and tight. The typical view of the manager's job holds that managers should delegate and try to do as little as possible themselves. Mintzberg's empirical model proves that there are some things managers simply can't delegate. They must process certain information, they must link to the outside, they must allocate resources, and so on.

Mintzberg clearly believes that managers are often better off favoring oral communication than written communication, especially computer printouts. Oral media are clearly richer than written media. Research has shown that upper-level managers need large quantities of rich data. Top managers may not benefit from the lean information provided by an MIS. On the other hand, some lower-level managers could use aggregated data more effectively.

Mintzberg argues that for the most part it is difficult to characterize managerial work as professional. The term *professional* can usually be properly applied only to work which is complex yet formalizable through training. Managerial work is complex, but it is not formalizable in that way. Yes, we do teach financial skills that help in the allocation of resources, but research has shown that innate political skills are just as important in determining "who gets what." The parts of management education that come closest to the professional deal with the application of quantitative skills to the solution of structured problems. But those kinds of problems make up only a fraction of the problems faced by managers. Most of the tasks that need to be done—leading, figurehead duties, communicating, disturbance handling, entrepreneurship, negotiating, resource allocating—are not very structured tasks. Being a manager is not like being a doctor or a lawyer or a public accountant, where one can turn to the recognized references in physiology or constitutional law or financial accounting standards.

One role that deserves special mention is the entrepreneur. Mintzberg's description of the entrepreneur has two characteristics concerning the projects he or she develops. The first is that the development projects "emerge as a series of small decisions and actions sequenced over time." The second is that managers sponsor many (possibly up to fifty) projects, at various stages of development, at any one time. The implications of this, which will be explored in greater depth in the reading by Wrapp in this chapter and Quinn's Chapter Eleven reading, "Managing Innovation: Controlled Chaos," are that effective managers may not be looking for "home runs." Strategies for the organization will develop over time as the product of many small, seemingly unrelated efforts by its members. The manager is in the unique position of being able to appreciate all of these streams of action and to integrate them. Another implication is related to innovation. Research on innovation has highlighted its "probabilistic" nature; that is, it takes many attempts to get a few winners. Mintzberg's description of the entrepreneur role jives with this: effective managers will juggle many projects at once, in the hopes that some of them will succeed. All of this is reminiscent of the crescive model discussed earlier.

GOOD MANAGERS DON'T MAKE POLICY DECISIONS

Also reminiscent of the crescive model is Wrapp's reading. The author says that it is a mistake for top managers to avoid involvement with operating problems. In the mainstream view top managers should be concerned with the "big picture" and should never be involved with the operating details. Wrapp says that top managers—like anybody else—need concrete experiences from which to build their mental models. Finding the right balance of big picture thinking and involvement in operating detail will help this process. This idea is similar to Peters and Waterman's mention in *In Search of Excellence* that excellent firms are characterized by "hands on" management.

Wrapp claims that effective managers should limit themselves to three or four major objectives during any single period of sustained activity. Otherwise they may dissipate their energy. Another reason is that the rest of the organization will have an easier time focusing on what is needed to achieve the objectives. This is reminiscent of Vaill's notion of focus. Bear in mind that Wrapp is not advocating that organizations and managers *do* only three or four things. They have to do *many* things, but these things should be directed toward the achievement of a limited number of objectives.

Wrapp urges effective managers to find "corridors of comparative indifference." This is an interesting and useful idea. He argues that for any given proposal, it is possible, for an executive who is sensitive to the power structure, to plot the sentiments of the various "interest groups" in the organization. Some parts of the proposal will be repugnant to certain groups, other parts will be objectionable to other groups. But some aspects (however narrow) of the proposal will be neutral for all the groups. Compared to the parts they do not like, the interest groups will be indifferent to these neutral elements. These are "corridors" in the mental plot drawn by the executive, corridors of comparative indifference. If you think of the "territory" bounded by the proposal as a mine field, riddled with objections, the corridor of indifference is a lane where the interest groups have forgotten to bury mines. The executive can walk through this part of the mine field in comparative safety. Executives can use these corridors to craft a program that moves the organization toward its objectives. This is again reminiscent of the crescive model and of Vaill's purposing idea.

Wrapp claims that it is good for managers to have only "hazy" notions of their objectives, timetables, and available means. This assertion reflects the reality that exists in most firms. Most effective executives have a good *general* idea of what they want the firm to accomplish but would rather not be too specific about it—too many things can change. It is best to be generally clear about general desires and a little less specific, until the time is right, about detailed objectives. Also, the executive does not know when that time will be right, so a detailed timetable may simply not be possible. Lastly, it takes time for the executive to assess all the key individuals and groups in the organization. Better to wait until the corridors of comparative indifference become clearly delineated; otherwise, good ideas may be blocked or stalled. Wrapp outlines the similar reasons why it is wise for a manager to avoid public commitment to a specific set of objectives. This stands in interesting contrast to some of the ideas that will be presented in the next chapter.

The author argues that "objectives get communicated only over time by a consistency or pattern in operating decisions," a statement very much like Mintzberg's idea of emergent strategy. As Wrapp puts it, "such decisions are more meaningful than words." It is one thing to say that you are going to do something, it is quite another to do it. What the firm *does* communicates a great deal to its members. Actual decisions and actions suggest those things to which the organization is truly committed. Members are usually skilled at interpreting the meaning of these actions and decisions. So, over time, they become aware of what the firm's true objectives are.

Wrapp contends that well-defined policies are not typical of well-managed companies and offers some interesting reasons about why his assertion might be true. First, detailed policies often give rise to time-consuming arbitration of disputes which distract the company from moving forward. Second, detailed statements of policy are often a sign of atrophy. Lastly, the policies of well-managed companies "are those which evolve over time from an indescribable mix of operating decisions. From any single operating decision might have come a very minor dimension of the policy as the organization understands it; from a series of decisions comes a pattern of guidelines for various levels of the organization." Again, this is very close to the crescive and emergent models we have examined here.

Wrapp says that a top manager is "skilled as an analyst, but even more talented as a conceptualizer." Most management literature emphasizes the analytical. The problem is that management is not primarily an analytical activity. It is mostly the *piecing together of parts* into a coherent whole, what Wrapp calls conceptualizing. Wrapp argues that the most important management skill is "spotting opportunities and relationships in the stream of operating problems and decisions." This fits with the notion that strategic management is a synthesis-oriented activity, the putting together of pieces into a whole. It is also consistent with the idea that a primary responsibility of top management is to guide the organizational and political process in a subtle, incremental way, not by the handing down of full-blown (and probably overly specific) plans from above, as in the commander model.

NOTES TO CHAPTER TWO

1. Much of the following few sections is based on Bourgeois, L. J., and D. A. Brodwin, "Strategic Implementation: Five Approaches to an Elusive Phenomenon." *Strategic Management Journal* 5 (1984): 241–64.

2. Bower, J., *Managing the Resource Allocation Process.* Boston: Harvard Graduate School of Business Administration, 1970; Burgelman, R., "A Model of the Interaction of Strategic Behavior, Corporate Context, and the Concept of Strategy." *Academy of Management Review* 8 (1983): 61–70.

3. Galbraith, J. R., and R. K. Kazanjian, *Strategy Implementation: Structure, Systems and Process.* St. Paul: West Publishing, 1986.

4. Lorange, P., *Corporate Planning.* Englewood Cliffs, N.J.: Prentice Hall, 1980.

5. Wightman, D. W. L., "Competitive Advantage through Information Technology." *Journal of General Management* 12 (1987): 36–45; Bissett, M. J., "Competitive Advantage—Through Controlling the Middle Ground." Southcourt Conference: Improving Business Based IT Strategy (1986); Stamen, J. P. "Decision Support Systems Help Planners Hit Their Targets." *Journal of Business Strategy* (March–April 1990), pp. 30–33.

6. Galbraith and Kazanjian; *Strategy Implementation,* St. Paul: West Publishing, 1986; Lawler, E. E., "The Design of Effective Reward Systems." In *Handbook of Organizational Behavior,* ed. J. W. Lorsch. Englewood Cliffs, N.J.: Prentice Hall, 1987, pp. 386–422.

7. Nadler, D. A., *Feedback and Organizational Development: Using Data-Based Methods.* Reading, Mass.: Addison-Wesley, 1977.

8. Dyer, W. G., *Team Building: Issue and Alternatives.* Reading, Mass.: Addison-Wesley, 1977.

9. Blake, R. R., and J. S. Mouton. *The Managerial Grid III.* Houston: Gulf, 1985.

10. Weisbord, M., *Productive Workplaces.* San Francisco: Jossey-Bass, 1987; Senge, P., *The Fifth Discipline.* New York: Doubleday Currency, 1990.

11. Bourgeois and Brodwin, "Strategic Implementation," p. 248.

12. Below, P. J., G. L. Morrisey, and B. L. Acomb, *The Executive Guide to Strategic Planning.* San Francisco: Jossey-Bass, 1987.

13. Cosier, R. A., and J. C. Aplin, "A Critical View of Dialectic Inquiry in Strategic Planning." *Strategic Management Journal* 1 (1980): 343–56.

14. Mason, R. O., "A Dialectic Approach to Strategic Planning." *Management Science* 13 (1969): 403–14.

15. Bourgeois and Brodwin, "Strategic Implementation," p. 250.

16. Duncan, W. J., "Organizational Culture: Getting a 'Fix' on an Elusive Concept." *Academy of Management Executive* 3 (1989): 229–36; Smircich, L., "Concepts of Culture and Organizational Analysis." *Administrative Science Quarterly* 28 (1983): 339–58; Sathe, V., "Implications of Corporate Culture: A Manager's Guide to Action." *Organizational Dynamics* (Autumn 1983), pp. 5–23.

17. Ouchi, W., *Theory Z: How American Business Can Meet the Japanese Challenge.* Reading, Mass.: Addison-Wesley, 1981.

18. Ibid.

19. Mintzberg, H., *The Nature of Managerial Work.* New York: Harper & Row, 1973.

20. Janis, I., *Victims of Groupthink.* Boston: Houghton-Mifflin, 1972.

21. Bourgeois and Brodwin, "Strategic Implementation," p. 259.

22. Mintzberg, H., "Strategy-Making in Three Modes." *California Management Review* (Winter 1973), pp. 44–53.

23. Mintzberg, H., and J. Waters, "Tracking Strategy in an Entrepreneurial Firm." *Academy of Management Journal* 25 (1981): 465–99.

24. Mintzberg, H., and J. Waters. "The Mind of the Strategist(s)." In *The Executive Mind,* eds. S. Srivastva and associates. San Francisco: Jossey-Bass, 1983, pp. 58–83. Emphasis in original.

25. Ibid., p. 82.

26. Mintzberg, H., "Patterns in Strategy Formation." *Management Science* 24 (1978): 934–48.

27. Mintzberg and Waters, "The Mind of the Strategist(s)," p. 75.

28. Ibid., p. 82.

29. Mintzberg, H., and A. McHugh, "Strategy Formation in an Adhocracy." *Administrative Science Quarterly* 30 (1985): 160–97.

30. Mintzberg and Waters, "The Mind of the Strategist(s)," p. 81.

31. Ibid., p. 82.

32. This section is based largely on Bennis, W., "The Artform of Leadership." In *The Executive Mind,* eds. S. Srivastva and associates, pp. 15–24.

33. Vaill, P., "The Purposing of High-Performing Systems." *Organizational Dynamics* (Autumn 1982), pp. 23–39. These criteria are listed on p. 25.

34. Ibid., pp. 26–27.

35. Ibid., pp. 28–29.

36. Ibid., p. 29.

37. Ibid., p. 31.

38. Ibid., p. 31.

39. Ibid., p. 33.

40. Ibid., p. 32.

41. Ibid., p. 33.

42. Peters, T., and R. Waterman, *In Search of Excellence.* New York: Harper & Row, 1982.

43. Fayol, H., *General and Industrial Management.* London: Pitman, 1949.

44. Peters and Waterman, *In Search of Excellence.*

By Henry Mintzberg

If you ask managers what they do, they will most likely tell you that they plan, organize, coordinate, and control. Then watch what they do. Don't be surprised if you can't relate what you see to these four words.

When they are called and told that one of their factories has just burned down, and they advise the caller to see whether temporary arrangements can be made to supply customers through a foreign subsidiary, are they planning, organizing, coordinating, or controlling? How about when they present a gold watch to a retiring employee? Or when they attend a conference to meet people in the trade? Or on returning from that conference, when they tell one of their employees about an interesting product idea they picked up there?

The fact is that these four words, which have dominated management vocabulary since the French industrialist Henri Fayol first introduced them in 1916, tell us little about what managers actually do. At best, they indicate some vague objectives managers have when they work.

My intention in this article is simple: to break the reader away from Fayol's words and introduce him or her to a more supportable, and what I believe to be a more useful, description of managerial work. This description derives from my review and synthesis of the available research on how various managers have spent their time.

In some studies, managers were observed intensively ("shadowed" is the term some of them used); in a number of others, they kept detailed diaries of their activities; in a few studies, their records were analyzed. All kinds of managers were studied—foremen, factory supervisors, staff managers, field sales managers, hospital administrators, presidents of companies and nations, and even street gang leaders. These "managers" worked in the United States, Canada, Sweden, and Great Britain.

A synthesis of these findings paints an interesting picture, one as different from Fayol's classical view as a cubist abstract is from a Renaissance painting. In a sense, this picture will be obvious to anyone who has ever spent a day in a manager's office, either in front of the desk or behind it. Yet, at the same time, this picture may turn out to be revolutionary, in that it throws into doubt so much of the folklore that we have accepted about the manager's work.

I first discuss some of this folklore and contrast it with some of the findings of systematic research—the hard facts about how managers spend their time. Then I synthesize those research findings in a description of ten roles that seem to describe the essential content of all managers' jobs. In a concluding section, I discuss a number of implications of this synthesis for those trying to achieve more effective management.

SOME FOLKLORE AND FACTS ABOUT MANAGERIAL WORK

There are four myths about the manager's job that do not bear up under careful scrutiny of the facts.

FOLKLORE: *The manager is a reflective, systematic planner.* The evidence on this issue is overwhelming, but not a shred of it supports this statement.

* Originally published in the *Harvard Business Review* (July–August 1975) and winner of the McKinsey prize for the best article in the *Review* in 1975. Copyright © 1975 by the President and Fellows of Harvard College; all rights reserved. Reprinted with deletions by permission of the *Harvard Business Review.*

FACT: *Study after study has shown that managers work at an unrelenting pace, that their activities are characterized by brevity, variety, and discontinuity, and that they are strongly oriented to action and dislike reflective activities.* Consider this evidence:

> Half the activities engaged in by the five [American] chief executives [that I studied in my own research (Mintzberg, 1973a)] lasted less than nine minutes, and only 10% exceeded one hour. A study of 56 U.S. foremen found that they averaged 583 activities per eight-hour shift, an average of 1 every 48 seconds (Guest, 1956:478). The work pace for both chief executives and foremen was unrelenting. The chief executives met a steady stream of callers and mail from the moment they arrived in the morning until they left in the evening. Coffee breaks and lunches were inevitably work related, and ever-present subordinates seemed to usurp any free moment.

> A diary study of 160 British middle and top managers found that they worked for a half hour or more without interruption only about once every two days (Stewart, 1967).

> Of the verbal contacts of the chief executives in my study, 93% were arranged on an ad hoc basis. Only 1% of the executives' time was spent in open-ended observational tours. Only 1 out of 368 verbal contacts was unrelated to a specific issue and could be called general planning. Another researcher finds that "in *not one single case* did a manager report the obtaining of important external information from a general conversation or other undirected personal communication" (Aguilar, 1967:102).

> No study has found important patterns in the way managers schedule their time. They seem to jump from issue to issue, continually responding to the needs of the moment.

Is this the planner that the classical view describes? Hardly. How, then, can we explain this behavior? The manager is simply responding to the pressures of the job. I found that my chief executives terminated many of their own activities, often leaving meetings before the end and interrupted their desk work to call in subordinates. One president not only placed his desk so that he could look down a long hallway but also left his door open when he was alone—an invitation for subordinates to come in and interrupt him.

Clearly, these managers wanted to encourage the flow of current information. But more significantly, they seemed to be conditioned by their own work loads. They appreciated the opportunity cost of their own time, and they were continually aware of their ever-present obligations—mail to be answered, callers to attend to, and so on. It seems that no matter what he or she is doing, the manager is plagued by the possibilities of what he or she might do and must do.

When the manager must plan, he or she seems to do so implicitly in the context of daily actions, not in some abstract process reserved for two weeks in the organization's mountain retreat. The plans of the chief executives I studied seemed to exist only in their heads—as flexible, but often specific, intentions. The traditional literature notwithstanding, the job of managing does not breed reflective planners; the manager is a real-time responder to stimuli, an individual who is conditioned by his or her job to prefer live to delayed action.

FOLKLORE: *The effective manager has no regular duties to perform.* Managers are constantly being told to spend more time planning and delegating, and less time seeing customers and engaging in negotiations. These are not, after all, the true tasks of the manager. To use the popular analogy, the good manager, like the good conductor, carefully orchestrates everything in advance, then sits back to enjoy the fruits of his or her labor, responding occasionally to an unforeseeable exception. . . .

FACT: *In addition to handling exceptions, managerial work involves performing a number of regular duties, including ritual and ceremony, negotiations, and processing of soft information that links the organization with its environment.* Consider some evidence from the research studies:

- A study of the work of the presidents of small companies found that they engaged in routine activities because their companies could not afford staff specialists and were so thin on operating personnel that a single absence often required the president to substitute (Choran in Mintzberg, 1973a).
- One study of field sales managers and another of chief executives suggest that it is a natural part of both jobs to see important customers, assuming the managers wish to keep those customers (Davis, 1957; Copeman, 1963).
- Someone, only half in jest, once described the manager as that person who sees visitors so that everyone else can get his or her work done. In my study, I found that certain ceremonial duties—meeting visiting dignitaries, giving out gold watches, presiding at Christmas dinners—were an intrinsic part of the chief executive's job.
- Studies of managers' information flow suggest that managers play a key role in securing "soft" external information (much of it available only to them because of their status) and in passing it along to their subordinates.

FOLKLORE: *The senior manager needs aggregated information, which a formal management information system best provides.* In keeping with the classical view of the manager as that individual perched on the apex of a regulated, hierarchical system, the literature's manager was to receive all important information from a giant, comprehensive MIS.

But this never proved true at all. A look at how managers actually process information makes the reason quite clear. Managers have five media at their command—documents, telephone calls, scheduled and unscheduled meetings, and observational tours.

FACT: *Managers strongly favor the verbal media—namely, telephone calls and meetings.* The evidence comes from every single study of managerial work: Consider the following:

- In two British studies, managers spent an average of 66% and 80% of their time in verbal (oral) communication (Stewart, 1967; Burns, 1954). In my study of five American chief executives, the figure was 78%.
- These five chief executives treated mail processing as a burden to be dispensed with. One came in Saturday morning to process 142 pieces of mail in just over three hours, to "get rid of all the stuff." This same manager looked at the first piece of "hard" mail he had received all week, a standard cost report, and put it aside with the comment, "I never look at this."
- These same five chief executives responded immediately to 2 of the 40 routine reports they received during the five weeks of my study and to four items in the 104 periodicals. They skimmed most of these periodicals in seconds, almost ritualistically. In all, these chief executives of good-sized organizations initiated on their own—that is, not in response to something else—a grand total of 25 pieces of mail during the 25 days I observed them.

An analysis of the mail the executives received reveals an interesting picture—only 13% was of specific and immediate use. So now we have another piece in the puzzle: not much of the mail provides live, current information—the action of a competitor, the mood of a government legislator, or the rating of last night's television show. Yet this is the information that drove the managers, interrupting their meetings and rescheduling their workdays.

Consider another interesting finding. Managers seem to cherish "soft" information, especially gossip, hearsay, and speculation. Why? The reason is its timeliness; today's gossip may be tomorrow's fact. The manager who is not accessible for the telephone call informing him or her that the firm's biggest customer was seen golfing with its main competitor may read about a dramatic drop in sales in the next quarterly report. But then it's too late.

Consider the words of Richard Neustadt, who studied the information-collecting habits of Presidents Roosevelt, Truman, and Eisenhower:

> It is not information of a general sort that helps a President see personal stakes; not summaries, not surveys, not the *bland amalgams.* Rather . . . it is the odds and ends of *tangible detail* that pieced together in his mind illuminate the underside of issues put before him. To help himself he must reach out as widely as he can for every scrap of fact, opinion, gossip, bearing on his interests and relationships as President. He must become his own director of his own central intelligence (1960:153–154; italics added).

The manager's emphasis on the verbal media raises two important points:

First, verbal information is stored in the brains of people. Only when people write this information down can it be stored in the files of the organization—whether in metal cabinets or on magnetic tape—and managers apparently do not write down much of what they hear. Thus the strategic data bank of the organization is not in the memory of its computers but in the minds of its managers.

Second, the managers' extensive use of verbal media helps to explain why they are reluctant to delegate tasks. When we note that most of the managers' important information comes in verbal form and is stored in their heads, we can well appreciate their reluctance. It is not as if they can hand a dossier over to someone; they must take the time to "dump memory"—to tell that someone all they know about the subject. But this could take so long that the managers may find it easier to do the task themselves. Thus the managers are damned by their own information systems to a "dilemma of delegation"—to do too much themselves or to delegate to their subordinates with inadequate briefing.

FOLKLORE: *Management is, or at least is quickly becoming, a science and a profession.* By almost any definitions of *science* and *profession,* this statement is false. Brief observation of any manager will quickly lay to rest the notion that managers practice a science. A science involves the enaction of systematic, analytically determined procedures or programs. If we do not even know what procedures managers use, how can we prescribe them by scientific analysis? And how can we call management a profession if we cannot specify what managers are to learn?

FACT: *The managers' programs—to schedule time, process information, make decisions, and so on—remain locked deep inside their brains.* Thus, to describe these programs, we rely on words like *judgment* and *intuition,* seldom stopping to realize that they are merely labels for our ignorance.

I was struck during my study by the fact that the executives I was observing—all very competent by any standard—are fundamentally indistinguishable from their counterparts of a hundred years ago (or a thousand years ago, for that matter). The information they need differs, but they seek it in the same way—by word of mouth. Their decisions concern modern technology, but the procedures they use to make them are the same as the procedures of the nineteenth-century manager. In fact, the manager is in a kind of loop, with increasingly heavy work pressures but no aid forthcoming from management science.

Considering the facts about managerial work, we can see that the manager's job is enormously complicated and difficult. The manager is overburdened with obligations; yet he or she cannot easily delegate tasks. As a result, he or she is driven to overwork and is forced to do many tasks superficially. Brevity, fragmentation, and verbal communication characterize the work. Yet these are the very characteristics of managerial work that have impeded scientific attempts to improve it. As a result, the management scientists have concentrated their efforts on the specialized functions of the organization, where they could more easily analyze the procedures and quantify the relevant information. Thus the first step in providing managers with some help is to find out what their job really is.

BACK TO A BASIC DESCRIPTION OF MANAGERIAL WORK

Now let us try to put some of the pieces of this puzzle together. Earlier, I defined the manager as that person in charge of an organization or one of its subunits. Besides chief executive officers, this definition would include vice presidents, bishops, foremen, hockey coaches, and prime ministers. Can all of these people have anything in common? Indeed they can. For an important starting point, all are vested with formal authority over an organizational unit. From formal authority comes status, which leads to various interpersonal relations, and from these comes access to information. Information, in turn, enables the manager to make decisions and strategies for his or her unit.

The manager's job can be described in terms of various "roles," or organized sets of behaviors identified with a position. My description, shown in Figure 1, comprises ten roles.

Interpersonal Roles

Three of the manager's roles arise directly from formal authority and involve basic interpersonal relationships.

1. First is the *figurehead* role. By virtue of his or her position as head of an organizational unit, every manager must perform some duties of a ceremonial nature. The president greets the touring dignitaries, the foreman attends the wedding of a lathe operator, and the sales manager takes an important customer to lunch.

The chief executives of my study spend 12% of their contact time on ceremonial duties; 17% of their incoming mail dealt with acknowledgments and requests related to their status. For example, a letter to a company president requested free merchandise for a crippled schoolchild; diplomas were put on the desk of the school superintendent for his signature.

Duties that involve interpersonal roles may sometimes be routine, involving little serious communication and no important decision making. Nevertheless, they are important to the smooth functioning of an organization and cannot be ignored by the manager.

2. Because he or she is in charge of an organizational unit, the manager is responsible for the work of the people of that unit. His or her actions in this regard constitute the *leader* role. Some of these actions involve leadership directly—for example, in most organizations the manager is normally responsible for hiring and training his or her own staff.

In addition, there is the indirect exercise of the leader role. Every manager must motivate and encourage his or her employees, somehow reconciling their individual needs with the goals of the organization. In virtually every contact the manager has with these employees, subordinates seeking leadership clues probe his or her actions: "Does he approve?" "How would she like the report to turn out?" "Is he more interested in market share than high profits?"

The influence of managers is most clearly seen in the leader role. Formal authority vests them with great potential power; leadership determines in large part how much of it they will realize.

3. The literature of management has always recognized the leader role, particularly those aspects of it related to motivation. In comparison, until recently it has hardly

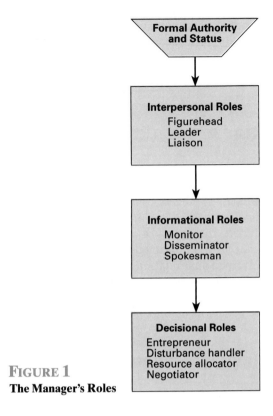

FIGURE 1
The Manager's Roles

mentioned the *liaison* role, in which the manager makes contacts outside his or her vertical chain of command. This is remarkable in light of the finding of virtually every study of managerial work that managers spend as much time with peers and other people outside their units as they do with their own subordinates—and, surprisingly, very little time with their own superiors (generally on the order of 45%, 45%, and 10% respectively).

The contacts the five CEOs made were with an incredibly wide range of people: subordinates; clients, business associates, and suppliers; and peers—managers of similar organizations, government and trade organization officials, fellow directors on outside boards, and independents with no relevant organizational affiliations. The chief executives' time with and mail from these groups is shown in Figure 2.

As we shall see shortly, the manager cultivates such contacts largely to find information. In effect, the liaison role is devoted to building up the manager's own external information system—informal, private, verbal, but, nevertheless, effective.

Informational Roles

By virtue of their interpersonal contacts, both with subordinates and with their network of contacts, managers emerge as the nerve centers of their organizational units. They may not know everything, but they typically know more than any other member of their unit.

Studies have shown this relationship to hold for all managers, from street gang leaders to U.S. presidents. In *The Human Group,* George C. Homans (1950) explains how, because they were at the center of the information flow in their own gangs and were also in close touch with other gang leaders, street gang leaders were better informed than any of their followers. And Richard Neustadt describes the following account from his study of Franklin D. Roosevelt:

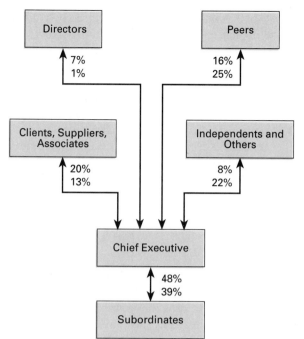

FIGURE 2
The Chief Executives' Contacts

The essence of Roosevelt's technique for information-gathering was competition. "He would call you in," one of his aides once told me, "and he'd ask you to get the story on some complicated business, and you'd come back after a couple of days of hard labor and present the juicy morsel you'd uncovered under a stone somewhere, and *then* you'd find out he knew all about it, along with something else you *didn't* know. Where he got this information from he wouldn't mention, usually, but after he had done this to you once or twice you got damn careful about *your* information." (1960:157).

We can see where Roosevelt "got this information" when we consider the relationship between the interpersonal and informational roles. As leaders, managers have formal and easy access to every member of their units. Hence, as noted earlier, they tend to know more about their own unit than anyone else does. In addition, their liaison contacts expose the managers to external information to which their subordinates often lack access. Many of these contacts are with other managers of equal status, who are themselves nerve centers in their own organization. In this way, managers develop powerful data bases of information.

The processing of information is a key part of the manager's job. In my study, the chief executives spent 40% of their contact time on activities devoted exclusively to the transmission of information; 70% of their incoming mail was purely informational (as opposed to requests for action). The manager does not leave meetings or hang up the telephone in order to get back to work. In large part, communication *is* his or her work. Three roles describe these informational aspects of managerial work.

4. As *monitor,* the manager perpetually scans the environment for information, interrogates his or her liaison contacts and subordinates, and receives unsolicited information, much of it as a result of the network of personal contacts he or she has developed. Remember that a good part of the information the manager collects in the monitor role arrives in verbal form, often as gossip, hearsay, and speculation. By virtue of his or her contacts, the manager has a natural advantage in collecting this soft information.

5. Managers must share and distribute much of this information. Information gleaned from outside personal contacts may be needed within the unit. In their *dis-*

seminator roles, managers pass some of their privileged information directly to their subordinates, who would otherwise have no access to it. When their subordinates lack easy contact with one another, managers will sometimes pass information from one to another.

6. In their *spokesperson* roles, managers send some of their information to people outside their units—a president makes a speech to lobby for an organization cause, or a foreman suggests a product modification to a supplier. In addition, as part of their roles as spokesperson, every manager must inform and satisfy the influential people who control his or her organizational unit. Chief executives especially may spend great amounts of time with hosts of influencers. Directors and shareholders must be advised about financial performance; consumer groups must be assured that the organization is fulfilling its social responsibilities, and so on.

Decisional Roles

Information is not, of course, an end in itself; it is the basic input to decision making. One thing is clear in the study of managerial work: managers play the major role in their unit's decision-making system. As its formal authority, only they can commit the unit to important new courses of action; and as its nerve center, only they have full and current information to make the set of decisions that determine the unit's strategy. Four roles describe the manager as decision maker.

7. As *entrepreneur,* the manager seeks to improve the unit, to adapt it to changing conditions in the environment. In the monitor role, the president is constantly on the lookout for new ideas. When a good one appears, he or she initiates a development project that he or she may supervise himself or delegate to an employee (perhaps with the stipulation that he or she must approve the final proposal).

There are two interesting features about these development projects at the chief executive level. First, these projects do not involve single decisions or even unified clusters of decisions. Rather, they emerge as a series of small decisions and actions sequenced over time. Apparently, chief executives prolong each project so that they can fit it bit by bit into their busy, disjointed schedules and so that they can gradually come to comprehend the issue, if it is a complex one.

Second, the chief executives I studied supervised as many as 50 of these projects at the same time. Some projects entailed new products or processes; others involved public relations campaigns, improvement of the cash position, reorganization of a weak department, resolution of a morale problem in a foreign division, integration of computer operations, various acquisitions at different stages of development, and so on.

The chief executive appears to maintain a kind of inventory of the development projects that he or she supervises—projects that are at various stages of development, some active and some in limbo. Like a juggler, he or she keeps a number of projects in the air; periodically, one comes down, is given a new burst of energy, and is sent back into orbit. At various intervals, he or she puts new projects on-stream and discards old ones.

8. While the entrepreneur role describes the manager as the voluntary initiator of change, the *disturbance handler* role depicts the manager involuntarily responding to pressures. Here change is beyond the manager's control. A strike looms, a major customer has gone bankrupt, or a supplier reneges on his contract.

It has been fashionable, I noted earlier, to compare the manager to an orchestra conductor, just as Peter F. Drucker wrote in *The Practice of Management:*

> The manager has the task of creating a true whole that is larger than the sum of its parts, a productive entity that turns out more than the sum of the resources put into it. One analogy

vidual instrumental parts that are so much noise by themselves become the living whole of music. But the conductor has the composer's score; he is only interpreter. The manager is both composer and conductor. (1954:341–342)

Now consider the words of Leonard R. Sayles, who has carried out systematic research on the manager's job:

> [The manager] is like a symphony orchestra conductor, endeavouring to maintain a melodious performance in which the contributions of the various instruments are coordinated and sequenced, patterned and paced, while the orchestra members are having various personal difficulties, stage hands are moving music stands, alternating excessive heat and cold are creating audience and instrument problems, and the sponsor of the concert is insisting on irrational changes in the program. (1964:162)

In effect, every manager must spend a good part of his or her time responding to high-pressure disturbances. No organization can be so well run, so standardized, that it has considered every contingency in advance. Disturbances arise not only because poor managers ignore situations until they reach crisis proportions but also because good managers cannot possibly anticipate all the consequences of the actions they take.

9. The third decisional role is that of *resource allocator*. To the manager falls the responsibility of deciding who will get what in his or her organizational unit. Perhaps the most important resource the manager allocates is his or her own time. Access to the manager constitutes exposure to the unit's nerve center and decision-maker. The manager is also charged with designing the unit's structure, that pattern of formal relationships that determines how work is to be divided and coordinated.

Also, in his or her role as resource allocator, the manager authorizes the important decisions of the unit before they are implemented. By retaining this power, the manager can ensure that decisions are interrelated; all must pass through a single brain. To fragment this power is to encourage discontinuous decision making and a disjointed strategy.

10. The final decisional role is that of *negotiator*. Studies of managerial work at all levels indicate that managers spend considerable time in negotiations: the president of the football team is called in to work out a contract with the holdout superstar; the corporation president leads her company's contingent to negotiate a new stock issue; the foreman argues a grievance problem to its conclusion with the shop steward. As Leonard Sayles puts it, negotiations are a "way of life" for the sophisticated manager.

These negotiations are duties of the manager's job; perhaps routine, they are not to be shirked. They are an integral part of the job, for only the manager has the authority to commit organizational resources in "real time," and only he or she has the nerve center information that important negotiations require.

The Integrated Job

It should be clear by now that the ten roles I have been describing are not easily separable. In the terminology of the psychologist, they form a gestalt, an integrated whole. No role can be pulled out of the framework and the job be left intact. For example, a manager without liaison contacts lacks external information. As a result, he or she can neither disseminate the information employees need nor make decisions that adequately reflect external conditions. (In fact, this is a problem for the new person in a managerial position, since he or she cannot make effective decisions until he or she has built up his network of contacts.)

To say that the ten roles form a gestalt is not to say that all managers give equal attention to each role. In fact, I found in my review of the various research studies that

. . . sales managers seem to spend relatively more of their time in the interpersonal roles, presumably a reflection of the extrovert nature of the marketing activity;

. . . production managers give relatively more attention to the decisional roles, presumably a reflection of their concern with efficient work flow;

. . . staff managers spend the most time in the informational roles, since they are experts who manage departments that advise other parts of the organization.

Nevertheless, in all cases the interpersonal, informational, and decisional roles remain inseparable.

CONCLUSION

No job is more vital to our society than that of the manager. It is the manager who determines whether our social institutions serve us well or whether they squander our talents and resources. It is time to strip away the folklore about managerial work, and time to study it realistically so that we can begin the difficult task of making significant improvements in its performance.

READING GOOD MANAGERS DON'T MAKE POLICY DECISIONS*

By H. Edward Wrapp

The upper reaches of management are a land of mystery and intrigue. Very few people have ever been there, and the present inhabitants frequently send back messages that are incoherent both to other levels of management and to the world in general. This may account for the myths, illusions, and caricatures that permeate the literature of management—for example, such widely held notions as these:

- Life gets less complicated as a manager reaches the top of the pyramid.
- The manager at the top level knows everything that's going on in the organization, can command whatever resources he may need, and therefore can be more decisive.
- The general manager's day is taken up with making broad policy decisions and formulating precise objectives.
- The top executive's primary activity is conceptualizing long-range plans.
- In a large company, the top executive may be seen meditating about the role of his organization in society.

I suggest that none of these versions alone, or in combination, is an accurate portrayal of what a general manager does. Perhaps students of the management process have been overly eager to develop a theory and a discipline. As one executive I know puts it, "I guess I do some of the things described in the books and articles, but the descriptions are lifeless, and my job isn't."

What common characteristics, then, do successful executives exhibit *in reality?* I shall identify five skills or talents which, in my experience, seem especially significant. . . .

* Originally published in the *Harvard Business Review* (September–October 1967) and winner of the McKinsey prize for the best article in the *Review* in 1967. Copyright © 1967 by the President and Fellows of Harvard College; all rights reserved. Reprinted with deletions by permission of the *Harvard Business Review.*

KEEPING WELL INFORMED

First, each of my heroes has a special talent for keeping himself informed about a wide range of operating decisions being made at different levels in the company. As he moves up the ladder, he develops a network of information sources in many different departments. He cultivates these sources and keeps them open no matter how high he climbs in the organization. When the need arises, he bypasses the lines on the organization chart to seek more than one version of a situation.

In some instances, especially when they suspect he would not be in total agreement with their decision, his subordinates will elect to inform him in advance, before they announce a decision. In these circumstances, he is in a position to defer the decision, or redirect it, or even block further action. However, he does not insist on this procedure. Ordinarily he leaves it up to the members of his organization to decide at what stage they inform him.

Top-level managers are frequently criticized by writers, consultants, and lower levels of management for continuing to enmesh themselves in operating problems, after promotion to the top, rather than withdrawing to the "big picture." Without any doubt, some managers do get lost in a welter of detail and insist on making too many decisions. Superficially, the good manager may seem to make the same mistake—but his purposes are different. He knows that only by keeping well informed about the decisions being made can he avoid the sterility so often found in those who isolate themselves from operations. If he follows the advice to free himself from operations, he may soon find himself subsisting on a diet of abstractions, leaving the choice of what he eats in the hands of his subordinates. As Kenneth Boulding puts it, "The very purpose of a hierarchy is to prevent information from reaching higher layers. It operates as an information filter, and there are little wastebaskets all along the way" (in *Business Week,* February 18, 1967:202). . . .

FOCUSING TIME AND ENERGY

The second skill of the good manager is that he knows how to save his energy and hours for those few particular issues, decisions, or problems to which he should give his personal attention. He knows the fine and subtle distinction between keeping fully informed about operating decisions and allowing the organization to force him into participating in these decisions or, even worse, making them. Recognizing that he can bring his special talents to bear on only a limited number of matters, he chooses those issues which he believes will have the greatest long-term impact on the company, and on which his special abilities can be most productive. Under ordinary circumstances he will limit himself to three or four major objectives during any single period of sustained activity.

What about the situations he elects *not* to become involved in as a decision maker? He makes sure (using the skill first mentioned) that the organization keeps him informed about them at various stages; he does not want to be accused of indifference to such issues. He trains his subordinates not to bring the matters to him for a decision. The communication to him from below is essentially one of: "Here is our sizeup, and here's what we propose to do." Reserving his hearty encouragement for those projects which hold superior promise of a contribution to total corporate strategy, he simply acknowledges receipt of information on other matters. When he sees a problem where the organization needs his help, he finds a way to transmit his know-how short of giving orders—usually by asking perceptive questions.

To what extent do successful top executives push their ideas and proposals through the organization? The rather common notion that the "prime mover" continually creates and forces through new programs, like a powerful majority leader in a liberal Congress, is in my opinion very misleading.

The successful manager is sensitive to the power structure in the organization. In considering any major current proposal, he can plot the position of the various individuals and units in the organization of a scale ranging from complete, outspoken support down to determined, sometimes bitter, and oftentimes well-cloaked opposition. In the middle of the scale is an area of comparative indifference. Usually, several aspects of a proposal will fall into this area, and *here is where he knows he can operate.* He assesses the depth and nature of the blocs in the organization. His perception permits him to move through what I call *corridors* of comparative indifference. He seldom challenges when a corridor is blocked, preferring to pause until it has opened up.

Related to this particular skill is his ability to recognize the need for a few trial-balloon launchers in the organization. He knows that the organization will tolerate only a certain number of proposals which emanate from the apex of the pyramid. No matter how sorely he may be tempted to stimulate the organization with a flow of his own ideas, he knows he must work through idea men in different parts of the organization. As he studies the reactions of key individuals and groups to the trial balloons these men send up, he is able to make a better assessment of how to limit the emasculation of the various proposals. For seldom does he find a proposal which is supported by all quarters of the organization. The emergence of strong support in certain quarters is almost sure to evoke strong opposition in others.

Value of Sense of Timing

Circumstances like these mean that a good sense of timing is a priceless asset for a top executive. . . . As a good manager stands at a point in time, he can identify a set of goals he is interested in, albeit the outline of them may be pretty hazy. His timetable, which is also pretty hazy, suggests that some must be accomplished sooner than others, and that some may be safely postponed for several months or years. He has a still hazier notion of how he can reach these goals. He assesses key individuals and groups. He knows that each has its own set of goals, some of which he understands rather thoroughly and others about which he can only speculate. He knows also that these individuals and groups represent blocks to certain programs or projects, and that these points of opposition must be taken into account. As the day-to-day operating decisions are made, and as proposals are responded to both by individuals and by groups, he perceives more clearly where the corridors of comparative indifference are. He takes action accordingly.

THE ART OF IMPRECISION

The fourth skill of the successful manager is knowing how to satisfy the organization that it has a sense of direction *without ever actually getting himself committed publicly to a specific set of objectives.* This is not to say that he does not have objectives—personal and corporate, long-term and short-term. They are significant guides to his thinking, and he modifies them continually as he better understands the resources he is working with, the competition, and the changing market demands. But as the organization clamors for statements of objectives, these are samples of what they get back from him:

> "Our company aims to be number one in its industry."
> "Our objective is growth with profit."
> "We seek the maximum return on investment."
> "Management's goal is to meet its responsibilities to stockholders, employees, and the public."

In my opinion, statements such as these provide almost no guidance to the various levels of management. Yet they are quite readily accepted as objectives by large numbers of intelligent people.

Maintaining Viability

Why does the good manager shy away from precise statements of his objectives for the organization? The main reason is that he finds it impossible to set down specific objectives which will be relevant for any reasonable period into the future. Conditions in business change continually and rapidly, and corporate strategy must be revised to take the changes into account. The more explicit the statement of strategy, the more difficult it becomes to persuade the organization to turn to different goals when needs and conditions shift.

The public and the stockholders, to be sure, must perceive the organization as having a well-defined set of objectives and clear sense of direction. But in reality the good top manager is seldom so certain of the direction which should be taken. Better than anyone else, he senses the many, many threats to his company—threats which lie in the economy, in the actions of competitors, and, not least, within his own organization.

He also knows that it is impossible to state objectives clearly enough so that everyone in the organization understands what they mean. Objectives get communicated only over time by a consistency or pattern in operating decisions. Such decisions are more meaningful than words. In instances where precise objectives are spelled out, the organization tends to interpret them so they fit its own needs.

Subordinates who keep pressing for more precise objectives are in truth working against their own best interests. Each time the objectives are stated more specifically, a subordinate's range of possibilities for operating are reduced. The narrower field means less room to roam and to accommodate the flow of ideas coming up from his part of the organization.

Avoiding Policy Straitjackets

The successful manager's reluctance to be precise extends into the area of policy decisions. He seldom makes a forthright statement of policy. He may be aware that in some companies there are executives who spend more time in arbitrating disputes caused by stated policies than in moving the company forward. The management textbooks contend that well-defined policies are the sine qua non of a well-managed company. My research does not bear out this contention. For example,

> The president of one company with which I am familiar deliberately leaves the assignments of his top officers vague and refuses to define policies for them. He passes out new assignments with seemingly no pattern in mind and consciously sets up competitive ventures among his subordinates. His methods, though they would never be sanctioned by a classical organization planner, are deliberate—and, incidentally, quite effective.

Since able managers do not make policy decisions, does this mean that well-managed companies operate without policies? Certainly not. But the policies are those which evolve over time from an indescribable mix of operating decisions. From any single operating decision might have come a very minor dimension of the policy as the organization understands it; from a series of decisions comes a pattern of guidelines for various levels of the organization.

The skillful manager resists the urge to write a company creed or to compile a policy manual. Preoccupation with detailed statements of corporate objectives and departmental goals and with comprehensive organization charts and job descriptions—this is often the first symptom of an organization which is in the early stages of atrophy.

The "management by objectives" school, so widely heralded in recent years, suggests that detailed objectives be spelled out at all levels in the corporation. This method is feasible at lower levels of management, but it becomes unworkable at the upper levels. The top manager must think out objectives in detail, but ordinarily some of the objectives must be withheld, or at least communicated to the organization in modest doses. A conditioning process which may stretch over months or years is necessary in order to prepare the organization for radical departures from what it is currently striving to attain.

Suppose, for example, that a president is convinced his company must phase out of the principal business it has been in for 35 years. Although making this change of course is one of his objectives, he may well feel that he cannot disclose the idea even to his vice presidents, whose total know-how is in the present business. A blunt announcement that the company is changing horses would be too great a shock for most of them to bear. And so he begins moving toward this goal but without a full disclosure to his management group.

A detailed spelling out of objectives may only complicate the task of reaching them. Specific, detailed statements give the opposition an opportunity to organize its defenses.

MUDDLING WITH A PURPOSE

The fifth, and most important, skill I shall describe bears little relation to the doctrine that management is (or should be) a comprehensive, systematic, logical, well-programmed science. Of all the heresies set forth here, this should strike doctrinaires as the rankest of all!

The successful manager, in my observation, recognizes the futility of trying to push total packages or programs through the organization. He is willing to take less than total acceptance in order to achieve modest progress toward his goals. Avoiding debates on principles, he tries to piece together particles that may appear to be incidentals into a program that moves at least part of the way toward his objectives. His attitude is based on optimism and persistence. Over and over he says to himself, "There must be some parts of this proposal on which we can capitalize."

Whenever he identifies relationships among the different proposals before him, he knows that they present opportunities for combination and restructuring. It follows that he is a man of wide-ranging interests and curiosity. The more things he knows about, the more opportunities he will have to discover parts which are related. This process does not require great intellectual brilliance or unusual creativity. The wider ranging his interests, the more likely that he will be able to tie together several unrelated proposals. He is skilled as an analyst, but even more talented as a conceptualizer.

If the manager has built or inherited a solid organization, it will be difficult for him to come up with an idea which no one in the company has ever thought of before. His most significant contribution may be that he can see relationships which no one else has seen. . . .

Contrasting Pictures

It is interesting to note, in the writings of several students of management, the emergence of the concept that, rather than making decisions, the leader's principal task is maintaining operating conditions which permit the various decision-making systems to function effectively. The supporters of this theory, it seems to me, overlook the subtle turns of direction which the leader can provide. He cannot add purpose and structure to the balanced judgments of subordinates if he simply rubberstamps their decisions. He must weigh the issues and reach his own decision. . . .

Many of the articles about successful executives picture them as great thinkers who sit at their desks drafting master blueprints for their companies. The successful top executives I have seen at work do not operate this way. Rather than produce a full-grown decision tree, they start with a twig, help it grow, and ease themselves out on the limbs only after they have tested to see how much weight the limbs can stand.

In my picture, the general manager sits in the midst of a continuous stream of operating problems. His organization presents him with a flow of proposals to deal with the problems. Some of these proposals are contained in voluminous, well-documented, formal reports; some are as fleeting as the walk-in visit from a subordinate whose latest inspiration came during the morning's coffee break. Knowing how meaningless it is to say, "This is a finance problem," or, "That is a communications problem," the manager feels no compulsion to classify his problems. He is, in fact, undismayed by a problem that defies classification. As the late Gary Steiner, in one of his speeches, put it, "He has a high tolerance for ambiguity."

In considering each proposal, the general manager tests it against at least three criteria:

1. Will the total proposal—or, more often, will some part of the proposal—move the organization toward the objectives which he has in mind?

2. How will the whole or parts of the proposal be received by the various groups and subgroups in the organization? Where will the strongest opposition come from, which group will furnish the strongest support, and which group will be neutral or indifferent?

3. How does the proposal relate to programs already in process or currently proposed? Can some parts of the proposal under consideration be added on to a program already under way, or can they be combined with all or parts of other proposals in a package which can be steered through the organization? . . .

CONCLUSION

To recapitulate, the general manager possesses five important skills. He knows how to

1. *Keep open many pipelines of information.* No one will quarrel with the desirability of an early warning system which provides varied viewpoints on an issue. However, very few managers know how to practice this skill, and the books on management add precious little to our understanding of the techniques which make it practicable.

2. *Concentrate on a limited number of significant issues.* No matter how skillful the manager is in focusing his energies and talents, he is inevitably caught up in a number of inconsequen-

tial duties. Active leadership of an organization demands a high level of personal involvement, and personal involvement brings with it many time-consuming activities which have an infinitesimal impact on corporate strategy. Hence this second skill, while perhaps the most logical of the five, is by no means the easiest to apply.

3. *Identify the corridors of comparative indifference.* Are there inferences here that the good manager has no ideas of his own, that he stands by until his organization proposes solutions, that he never uses his authority to force a proposal through the organization? Such inferences are not intended. The message is that a good organization will tolerate only so much direction from the top; the good manager therefore is adept at sensing how hard he can push.

4. *Give the organization a sense of direction with open-ended objectives.* In assessing this skill, keep in mind that I am talking about top levels of management. At lower levels, the manager should be encouraged to write down his objectives, if for no other reason than to ascertain if they are consistent with corporate strategy.

5. *Spot opportunities and relationships in the stream of operating problems and decisions.* Lest it be concluded from the description of this skill that the good manager is more an improviser than a planner, let me emphasize that he is a planner and encourages planning by his subordinates. Interestingly, though, professional planners may be irritated by a good general manager. Most of them complain about his lack of vision. They devise a master plan, but the president (or other operating executive) seems to ignore it, or to give it minimum acknowledgment by borrowing bits and pieces for implementation. They seem to feel that the power of a good master plan will be obvious to everyone, and its implementation automatic. But the general manager knows that even if the plan is sound and imaginative, the job has only begun. The long, painful task of implementation will depend on his skill, not that of the planner. . . .

STRATEGY DESIGN AND PLANNING

▼

In this chapter and the next, we examine three prescriptive models of strategy. These models are prescriptive because their adherents recommend them as methods people *should* use to develop strategy. We examine the first two—strategy design and strategy planning—in this chapter. As these are probably the oldest models of strategy making, they tend to form the bulk of most textbooks on strategy. (Strategy analysis, the third prescriptive approach, is the subject of Chapter Four.) As we shall see, these prescriptive approaches have many strengths but also some weaknesses. One positive contribution of these models is that they distinguish between the business and corporate levels of strategy.

LEVELS OF STRATEGY

Business Level

This level of strategy deals with individual businesses operating in one industry. Specifically, it deals with the question, "What must we do as managers to compete successfully in this industry?"[1] At this level, strategists must discover what factors are critical to a firm's success, and then must try to get the firm to perform well on those factors. In some industries, such as pharmaceuticals, research and development is critical. In others, like many consumer products, advertising may be centrally important. The greater part of this book deals with business-level strategy. It will not be until Chapter Twelve that we will examine corporate-level strategy.

Corporate Level

At this level, the managers of firms must address the question, "In which businesses should we compete?"[2] For firms that are in only one business, the business and corporate levels are the same. The vast majority of business firms operate in only one competitive environment. The distinction between levels is valid only for firms in, or considering entering, multiple businesses.

Answering the corporate-level question can take many forms. As mentioned above, most firms answer it by being **single-business** firms. Others, particularly large Fortune 500–type firms, answer it by **diversification**—being in multiple businesses. Even this is less clear-cut than it sounds, since firms may diversify in at least three ways: constrained, where new businesses are entered based on existing skills held by the firm; linked, where the new businesses are more loosely connected to previously existing skills; and unrelated, where the new businesses are entirely unrelated to the existing ones.[3]

Another way for a firm to be in more than one business is through **vertical integration**. To understand this idea, picture a chain of activities that begins with extraction of raw materials (e.g., mining iron ore, growing and harvesting corn), continues through various stages of processing, and ends with retail selling to consumers. Moving from the middle of this imaginary chain toward its beginning is called **backward integration**. For example, a food processing firm might decide to operate its own corn farms. Moving from the middle toward retailing is called **forward integration**. In our illustration, this would be the case if the food processing firm decided to open corn-dog shops in shopping malls. Of course, a firm could do both. Vertical integration involves operating in different businesses, not just different aspects of the same business. In our example, for instance, corn farming is a very different business from food processing, which in turn is very different from corn-dog retailing.

A final component of corporate-level strategy is the decision about whether to operate in one country (commonly called a domestic strategy) or in various parts of the world. Firms electing to do the latter have several options—**exporting, licensing, multidomestic operation,** and **global operation**. We will examine these elements of corporate-level strategy in detail later in this book.

Focus on Business-Level Strategy

For now, we will focus on business-level strategy. There are good reasons for this. First, most firms are single-business enterprises, making this the more relevant approach. Second, most businesses start small; it is only after a business firm has succeeded and grown that issues of geographical expansion, vertical integration, and diversification become important.[4] This stage will not even be reached if firms are unsuccessful at the business level. Lastly, even in a diversified firm, the ultimate success of corporate strategy rests with the success of the firm's business units.[5]

STRATEGY DESIGN: STRATEGY FORMATION AS A CONCEPTUAL PROCESS

The idea that strategy can be designed is perhaps the oldest one in the strategic management literature.[6] The basic idea here is that one person can distill a large amount of information into a streamlined conceptual strategic design.[7] Andrews's reading in this chapter is one of the best examples of the thinking of the design approach. Andrews succinctly says that strategy design is

the intellectual process of ascertaining what a company *might do* in terms of environmental opportunity, of deciding what it *can do* in terms of ability and power, and of bringing these two considerations together in optimal equilibrium. . . . [What] the executives of a company *want to do* must also be brought into the strategic decision . . . [as must] . . . what a company *should do*.[8]

This intellectual design process is followed by the "primarily administrative" process of implementation.[9]

In other words, according to the design model, the strategist does the familiar **SWOT analysis** (standing for *strengths, weaknesses, opportunities,* and *threats*). He or she must assess the firm's external environment for opportunities and threats ("might do"), by identifying the **key success factors** of the industry. Then he or she must examine the internal strengths and weaknesses of the organization ("can do"), which gives the strategist a feel for the firm's **distinctive competences**. These are defined as things the firm does particularly well that are difficult for other firms to copy. In his or her intellectual design process, the strategist must also factor in the firm's **social responsibilities** ("should do") and the **values** of its management ("want to do").

Premises of Strategic Design[10]

Seven premises underlie the idea that strategy can be designed. The first is that strategy formation should be a controlled, conscious process of thought. Thus, strategic design is not action-oriented; it is oriented toward thinking and reflection.

A second premise is that responsibility for the control and deliberateness must rest with the chief executive officer; that person is *the* strategist. This is very similar to the commander model discussed in Chapter Two. Related to this is the third premise, that the model of strategy formation must be kept simple and informal; elaboration will kill it. Simplicity is important so that the strategist will not lose sight of its goal.

The fourth premise is that strategies should be unique, with the best ones resulting from a process of creative design. Strategic design thinking proposes that each situation contains unique strengths, weaknesses, threats, opportunities, values, and social responsibilities. Accordingly, although each design *process* will be similar, the resulting strategic design will be unique.

The fifth premise is the logical conclusion of the first four—strategies emerge from this design process full-blown. Design is not an incremental undertaking. Instead, the designer takes the information about the "specifications"—the strengths, the weaknesses, the opportunities, and the threats, and the values and responsibilities inherent in the situation—and creates a strategy to fit it. Then it is ready to be implemented, which brings us to the sixth premise—strategies should be made explicit and, if possible, articulated, which means they have to be kept simple. That is, the strategy should be clearly understood by the designers, and should be clearly defined to everyone else in the organization, since they will be the implementors of it. This premise of articulation leads to the idea that the strategy should be simple, easily understood by all affected parties—employees, directors, regulators, community residents, and so forth.

The final premise is that only after these unique, full-blown, explicit, and simple strategies are fully formulated can they be implemented. In this approach, thinking is separated from action, formulation from implementation. The activities are sharply different, and the people who do them are sharply different. Top management designs; everyone else carries out the design. To underline how the design approach distinctly separates formulation from implementation, Mintzberg makes the following observation: "It is of interest that the word used is 'implement,' not 'achieve,' the assumption being that given proper implementation, achievement is a foregone conclusion."[11] In other words, design is more important than implementation, so implementation should not be a major hurdle if the strategy has been properly designed.

Strengths and Weaknesses of the Design Approach

There are times when it *is* appropriate for an organization centrally to assess its internal strengths and weaknesses, fitting them to the opportunities and threats in the environment with a fully developed, ready-to-implement strategy. A firm that has created an emergent pattern, for example, might want to apply this as a way to understand the pattern it has created in its stream of action. The design approach has contributed several ideas that have helped to inform strategic thinking. These include the SWOT analysis technique, the idea of fitting the firm's strengths and weaknesses to the environment's opportunities and threats, and the notion of distinctive competence.

In many instances, using the design approach would be unwarranted and perhaps even inappropriate. This would be particularly true in situations where a firm needs to develop its strategies through a learning process. The SWOT analysis, for example, could become a process dominated by a few individuals in a closed room, similar to a classroom case-study discussion. It may not be possible for the individuals in such a small group to know enough for an accurate assessment of strengths, weaknesses, opportunities, and threats. Such knowledge might be obtainable only through learning over time.

The design approach's dichotomy between formulation and implementation also impedes learning. It *is* possible to learn through a purely reflective process like strategy formulation, but it is a mistake to assume that nothing can be learned from action. As Mintzberg points out, the failures of deliberate strategy are often blamed on poor implementation, but the fault may lie not with formulation or implementation so much as with the *separation* of the two, a separation that impedes the natural way people learn.[12]

The design approach says that a firm will modify its structure to fit the strategy.[13] But a firm must also take its existing structure into account as it develops a strategy. Indeed, that probably would be, or should be, part of its assessment of strengths and weaknesses. Lastly, the design approach's prescription for explicitness of strategy may create problems of rigidity. The more clearly a strategy is articulated, the more difficult it is to change.

Mintzberg summarizes the critique of the strategy design approach this way:

> If [the design approach] denies that strategy formation is a long, subtle, and difficult process based on deep understanding, if it encourages managers to detach thinking from acting, remaining in their offices waiting for pithy reports instead of getting outside where the real information for strategy making usually has to be dug out, then it may have done a major disservice to organizations and to society.[14]

STRATEGY PLANNING: STRATEGY FORMATION AS A FORMAL PROCESS

Strategic planning as an approach to strategy is roughly as old as the design approach; its most influential early book, Ansoff's *Corporate Strategy,* was published in 1965.[15] Planning dominated the field through the 1970s, but its influence has declined. One reason is that strategic planning has suffered some highly visible failures.[16] Indeed, thinking in this area has been stagnant almost from the beginning. Mintzberg puts it this way:

> [The] problem was that quantitatively the "strategic planning" literature developed extensively but qualitatively it developed hardly at all. One basic set of ideas, almost trivial in concept and rooted in the design school model, was repeated in this literature in endless variety.[17]

Premises of the Planning Approach

The assumptions upon which the planning approach rests are almost identical to those of the design approach, with two important differences. First, the simple and informal model of the design school is abandoned in favor of an intricate array of procedures, each containing checklists and techniques that must be followed in a formally prescribed order. Ansoff's summary diagram, for example, contains fifty-seven boxes of procedures and subprocedures.[18]

The second difference is the importance of specialized planners in this approach. Although they are supposed to be staff advisers only, much of the recommended practice makes them the major actors in the process. For instance, one planning guide suggested that top managers be informed only at key points, as few as four times a year at one steel company.[19]

Because strategic planning is a very formal analytic process, it emphasizes decomposition, that is, dividing things up into small pieces. The result is that much attention is paid to operational techniques like scheduling, programming, and budgeting, which in turn leads to an accent on a "numbers" approach to strategy. Because of planning's formal decomposition approach, the strategies developed tend to be segmented—into corporate and business levels; and into hierarchies of objectives, programs, action plans, and performance controls.

Mintzberg summarizes the underlying assumptions of the planning approach in this way:

1. Strategy formation should be a controlled, conscious, and formal process, decomposed into distinct steps, each delineated by checklists and supported by techniques.

2. Responsibility for the overall process rests with the chief executive in principle; responsibility for its execution rests with the staff planners in practice.

3. Strategies emerge from the process full-blown, to be explicated so that they can then be implemented through detailed attention to objectives, budgets, programs, and operating plans of various kinds.[20]

Strengths and Weaknesses of the Planning Approach

Besides the well-documented failures of planning mentioned earlier, scholarly investigations of strategic planning in corporations have been unable to prove that it pays. The general result of the studies has been inconclusive.[21] In government, the equivalent to corporate strategic planning was PPBS (Planning, Programming and Budgeting System). Noted public administration scholar Aaron Wildavsky has asserted that "PPBS has failed everywhere at all times."[22] All of this leads Mintzberg to ask some blunt questions, notably "whether the phrase 'strategic planning' is, like progressive conservative or civil engineer, an oxymoron. In other words, can strategy be planned? Can it . . . be made in a formal process?"[23]

Responses to the failures of planning vary widely. Some say that planning should continue despite its failures because of the benefits of going through the planning process.[24] Others suggest the adoption of increasingly more complex and sophisticated approaches.[25] The most popular response has been to blame "pitfalls" that obstruct good planning. Notably the lack of commitment by top management and organizational climates uncongenial to planning practice.[26] Rarely does anyone in the field suggest that the approach may be flawed. But do managers continue to resist? And might a good climate for planning be a bad climate for some organizations in some situations?

Managers may resist planning for two reasons. First, many middle- and lower-level managers resent having plans (and planning processes) imposed on them from above. They feel it preempts their flexibility and their need to function in a more mature way. Second, even top managers may be bypassed in some planning systems, as mentioned above. Their intuition is often derided.[27] Overall, the calculation of planning seems to displace the commitment of managing.

Strategic planning is often touted as an approach suited to dealing with change and turbulent environments. But organizations usually plan to set direction, not to encourage change. Planning, by forcing choice, is designed to be inflexible. Steiner notes, for example, that "plans . . . limit choice . . . [and] reduce initiative in the range of alternatives beyond the plans."[28] This is sometimes a good thing, but not when an organization needs flexibility. There is evidence that the decomposing nature of planning and its use of existing categories make planning a conservative, not a creative, process. Mintzberg puts it this way:

> It can be argued . . . that not just plans but the planning process itself encourages incremental change at the expense of quantum change, generic thinking at the expense of creative thinking, and a short-term orientation at the expense of a long-term perspective. . . . Thus planning tends to preserve the existing categories while serious strategic change generally requires that such categories be reconstituted.[29]

Lastly, if planning fails because of a poor internal climate in an organization, an overly objective and overly formal process may have played a role in creating that climate. Planners who are too dogmatic, or too concerned with their own influence, should not be surprised when their efforts are resisted, either implicitly, through lack of commitment, or explicitly, through organizational politics.

Looking more deeply into the problems, Mintzberg points to four fallacies of strategic planning. The first is the fallacy of *predetermination,* the idea that planners can formally predict the future. Methods to forecast discontinuities remain woefully inadequate. So what really tends to happen is that planners extrapolate from known trends, a method that favors stability (or slow, steady growth) over change. The second fallacy is that of *detachment*—separating strategic management from operating management. Doing this deprives the strategic manager of the rich information that is necessary for developing a good understanding of the business.[30] Third is the fallacy of *formalization.* There is no evidence that breaking a process down into formal steps, each bolstered by "hard" information and rigorous procedures, will result in the formulation of a fresh strategy. In fact, this method is designed to program existing strategies, not to create new ones. That is what so-called strategic planning has been all about. These add up to the "grand fallacy": that analysis can provide synthesis. Analysis means breaking things down; synthesis means putting things together. Management is a synthetic activity, but planning is an analytic activity. It cannot create strategies.[31]

Nonetheless, planners can make at least these positive contributions. They can be *analysts,* particularly of data that managers tend to ignore. They can be *catalysts,* encouraging managers to think strategically; this is what many strategic planning consultants do. Planners can also be *programmers,* as mentioned above, using planning as a tool for operationalizing strategies developed by other means.

A MODEL FOR STRATEGIC PLANNING

This section contains an outline and supporting material for a straightforward model which is a combination of original material and guidelines from a planning book, *The Executive Guide to Strategic Planning.*[32] This book is a good example of the formal, checklist-oriented process described above. Some elements of the model are covered in the next chapter on business-level strategy analysis, so it might be best to read that material in Chapter Four along with this.

The Basic Plan Format

Here is the basic outline that a plan based on this approach would follow:

I. Mission Statement
    A. Business definition
    B. Long-term objectives
II. Scan of External Environment
    A. Industry environment (Porter's Five Forces Model discussed in Chapter Four)
    B. Macroenvironment (political, economic, sociocultural, and technological factors)
    C. Assessment of opportunities and threats
III. Scan of Internal Environment
    A. Value chain analysis (discussed in Chapter Four)
    B. Financial analysis
    C. Assessment of strengths and weaknesses
IV. Business Strategy Statement
V. Integrated Programs

The remainder of this section "fleshes out" the outline above. Most of the procedures described below are based on *The Executive Guide to Strategic Planning.*

Mission Statement

An organization's *mission statement* describes the nature and concept of the organization's future business. It establishes what the organization plans to do, and for whom, along with the major philosophical premises under which it will operate. Its principal application is as an internal guide for major decision makers within the organization so plans that are developed can be tested for compatibility with the total organization's mission. The mission statement should be a visible document that can enable people within the organization to focus his or her efforts. Externally, the mission statement provides clear communication to such groups as customers, suppliers, the financial community, the board of directors, and stockholders.

Here is a checklist taken from *The Executive Guide to Strategic Planning*[33] that may help in clarifying an organization's mission:

1. What business should we be in?
2. Why do we exist (what is our basic purpose)? (NOTE: may not simply be "to make a profit")
3. What is unique or distinctive about our organization? Some possibilities are:

proprietary products/services	key individuals/groups
concentration (or diversity) of products/services	method of sale
geographic concentration (or dispersion)	method of distribution
types of markets/customers	types of support services
unique capabilities/processes	warranties
	legislative mandate
	franchise operation

4. Who are our principal customers, clients, or users?
5. What are our principal products/services, present and future?
6. What are our principal market segments, present and future?

7. What are our principal outlets/distribution channels, present and future?

8. What is different about our business from what it was between three and five years ago?

9. What is likely to be different about our business three to five years in the future?

10. What are our principal economic concerns, and how are they measured?

11. What philosophical issues are important to our organization's future? Some possibilities are:

organizational image	productivity
leadership in industry/profession/community	management approach
environmental impact	
innovation/risk-taking	
quality	

12. What special considerations do we have regarding the following stakeholders (as applicable)?

owners/stockholders/investors/constituents	customers/clients/users
board of directors	suppliers
parent organization	general public
legislative bodies	
employees	

(**Stakeholders** are any groups or individuals who have an interest in the organization's future who may need special consideration.)

EXAMPLES. Here are some examples of mission statements, taken from private, not-for-profit, and governmental organizations. These examples are from *The Executive Guide to Strategic Planning.*[34]

XXXX is in business to supply technically innovative hardware and software I/O solutions to the OEM computer market that provide a long-term benefit to our customers and a long-term return to our investors.

In support of this, we are committed to

- being recognized by our customers for being responsive and oriented to their needs
- being recognized for being a technically superior and innovative supplier of high-quality products
- being recognized by our employees and the business community for excellence and integrity in managing the company's business
- providing an environment for achieving personal excellence and growth for all our employees

* * *

The primary mission of the XXXX Group is to assist our clients in achieving cost-effective results from their employee benefit planning through the marketing, implementation, and administration of creative, individually designed plans.

* * *

The mission of the XXXX County is economically and efficiently to provide and manage delivery systems for diverse programs and services to meet basic human needs. In support of this, we are committed to

- serving as an agent for the federal and state governments to fulfill mandated programs
- providing optional community services as determined by the county board
- providing programs and services in the most cost-effective manner
- encouraging citizen awareness, participation, and involvement in county government
- utilizing community resources as a vehicle for good government

* * *

XXXX supplies products that provide environmentally safe solutions to customer problems associated with the reliable transfer or control of fluids.

* * *

The mission of the Planning Process Group is to provide transferable planning process technology (Integrated Planning Process) that focuses on organizational results for the CEO and key decision makers.

In support of this, we are committed to

- a network with an established CEO/decision maker base
- proprietary materials customized to network requirements
- a visible reputation for consistently achieving planning results
- accelerated financial and professional growth

Long-Term Objectives

Long-term objectives describe what the organization wants to have or become at some point in the future, usually within three to five years. Although these objectives must be measurable to some extent, they will not be as precise as the objectives found in annual operational (sometimes called "tactical") plans. Because long-term objectives are strategic, they focus more on a position to be attained than on specific accomplishments.

Strategic objectives can be established for all areas that a firm thinks is important. Here is a list of areas that are usually mentioned as important.[35]

1. Marketing, including:
   Products offered
   Services offered
   Market needs
   Customer needs
   Method of sale
   Method of distribution
   New markets
2. Profitability (however it is measured)
3. Physical and financial resources, usually meaning:
   Plant (production capacity)
   Equipment
   Assets in general
4. Productivity (i.e., efficiency)
5. Worker performance, attitude, and development
6. Management development
7. Innovation, including:
   Product innovation (new products)
   Process innovation (new production technology)
   Administrative innovation (e.g., reorganizations)
8. Social responsibility
9. Stockholder responsibility
10. Size/growth/diversification

Other areas that would be appropriate for the development of objectives can be added. This list is intended only as a suggestion to get you started.

The authors of *The Executive Guide to Strategic Planning* suggest four criteria against which all objectives should be checked.[36] You will notice immediately the similarity to the Quinn criteria for effective strategy (from Chapter One) and Rumelt's four evaluative tests (from a reading later in this chapter):

1. Is the objective measurable or verifiable? Will you and others affected be able to recognize it when it happens?

2. Is it achievable or feasible?
3. Is it flexible or adaptable?
4. Is it consistent with the rest of the plan?

Here are some examples of long-term objectives, taken from *The Executive Guide to Strategic Planning:*[37]

> To become the dominant supplier of [designated] services to [designated] market segments by [year].
>
> To have at least 20 percent of revenue in [year] from markets not currently being served.
>
> To have a minimum of 20 percent of sales from new products [or services] by [year].
>
> To have a separate research capability in [technology] by [year].
>
> To have a management by objectives process involving all employees in the organization by [year].
>
> To become recognized as one of the top three companies in the industry in terms of service by [year].
>
> To become a multinational corporation with a minimum of 30 percent of net revenue coming from foreign sources by [year].
>
> To have all mature product lines producing a minimum net profit of [percentage] of sales by [year].

Beyond being verifiable, feasible, flexible, and consistent, well-expressed objectives, like the ones in the examples above, have four other characteristics:[38]

1. Each starts with the word *to* followed by an action or accomplishment verb.
2. Each specifies a single measurable result to be accomplished.
3. Each specifies a time span for completion.
4. Each specifies only the *what* and *when*, and avoids venturing into the *why* and *how*.

Scan of External Environment

Most planning experts agree that it is important to do the external analysis *before* the internal analysis. This is primarily so that the people doing the planning examine the external environment objectively. Looking at what is outside the firm *after* looking at what is inside can result in people's having blinders or biases. There could be a tendency to interpret environmental events only through the filter of what people believe is true about the firm.

The analysis of *industry environment,* which could be the first step in the external analysis, is spelled out in great detail in Porter's article on competitive strategy, often called the Five Forces Model, in Chapter Four of this text. Analysis of the *macroenvironment,* as discussed in this chapter, particularly Andrews's reading, should also be done. This includes political, economic, social, and technological (PEST) factors and trends. Lastly, the *assessment of opportunities and threats* summarizes the outside challenges facing the organization.

Scan of Internal Environment and Financial Analysis

Porter's *value chain* framework (described briefly in Mintzberg's Chapter Four reading) can be used to help identify organizational strengths and weaknesses. This model is typically presented as it would be used in a manufacturing company, and has to be adjusted for a service company.

The *financial analysis* includes both past financial performance and future financial requirements for support of the strategic plan, including both capital and operating needs and the alternatives available for the securing of appropriate funding. This analysis typically consists of a full ratio analysis of existing financial statements, or the generation of pro forma financial statements for new firms. Ratio analysis usually encompasses the examination of leverage ratios, liquidity ratios, activity ratios, profitability ratios, and cash flow.

LEVERAGE RATIOS. These ratios measure the extent to which a firm relies on borrowed funds rather than shareholder's equity or internal cash flow to finance operations. These are measures of how these latter sources of funds are *leveraged* by borrowing. The three most commonly used leverage ratios are:
- **Debt-to-assets Ratio.** This most direct measure of leverage is defined as follows:

$$\text{Debt-to-assets} = \frac{\text{Total debt}}{\text{Total assets}}$$

Total debt is the sum of a company's current and long-term liabilities, and total assets are the sum of fixed and current assets.
- **Long-term Debt-to-equity Ratio.** This measures the balance between debt and equity in the long-term capital structure of a firm. It is defined as:

$$\text{Debt-to-equity} = \frac{\text{Long-term debt}}{\text{Total stockholder's equity}}$$

- **Times-covered Ratio.** This measures the degree to which a company's annual interest payments are covered by its gross profit. This ratio's definition is:

$$\text{Times-covered} = \frac{\text{Profits before interest and taxes}}{\text{Total interest charges}}$$

LIQUIDITY RATIOS. Liquidity is a measure of a firm's ability to meet unexpected financial needs, such as, for example, a strike or a prolonged price war. An asset is "liquid" if it can quickly be converted into cash. Inventories and accounts receivable are the most liquid and plant and equipment the least liquid of assets. Two common liquidity ratios are:
- **Current Ratio.** This ratio measures how well the claims of short-term creditors are covered by a company's most liquid assets. In general, this ratio should be at least 1. It is defined as follows:

$$\text{Current ratio} = \frac{\text{Current assets}}{\text{Current liabilities}}$$

- **Quick Ratio.** This ratio assesses a company's ability to pay short-term creditors without having to rely on selling its inventories. Its definition is:

$$\text{Quick ratio} = \frac{\text{Current assets} - \text{inventories}}{\text{Current liabilities}}$$

ACTIVITY RATIOS. These ratios measure a firm's utilization of its short-term and long-term assets. They are a measure of a firm's efficiency. The three most commonly used activity ratios follow.
- **Inventory Turnover.** This measures how many times per year a firm "moves" its inventory, the most important short-term asset. A higher number indicates higher, and therefore better and more efficient, movement. If this ratio is too low compared to sim-

ilar firms, it could mean one of two things. If inventory levels are comparable, then sales need to be boosted. On the other hand, if sales are comparable, then inventory levels are too high. Inventory turnover is defined as follows:

$$\text{Inventory turnover} = \frac{\text{Total sales}}{\text{Average inventory}}$$

- **Fixed Asset Turnover.** This ratio measures how efficiently a firm uses plant and equipment, its long-term assets. The interpretation of this ratio is similar to that of inventory turnover. A ratio that is out of line with the industry could mean either excess plant and equipment or anemic sales. This ratio is defined as:

$$\text{Fixed asset turnover} = \frac{\text{Total sales}}{\text{Fixed assets}}$$

- **Total Asset Turnover.** This ratio measures the efficiency of a firm's utilization of all its assets—fixed as well as short term. It is defined as:

$$\text{Total asset turnover} = \frac{\text{Total sales}}{\text{Total assets}}$$

PROFITABILITY RATIOS. These ratios measure effectiveness; that is, how successfully the firm is creating wealth for its owners, the shareholders. The four most commonly used profitability ratios follow.

- **Gross Profit Margin.** This is an indicator of how much profit a firm generates from its basic physical resources, such as inventory, *before* subtracting the operating expenses (like salaries, maintenance, utilities, etc.) of its value-creating activities. Comparing this ratio to those of similar firms indicates whether pricing is competitive. The ratio's definition is:

$$\text{Gross profit margin} = \frac{\text{Sales revenue} - \text{Cost of goods sold}}{\text{Sales revenue}}$$

- **Net Profit Margin.** This ratio is similar to the previous one, except that it accounts for *all* value-creating expenses. Net profit margin is defined as:

$$\text{Net profit margin} = \frac{\text{Sales revenue} - \text{All expenses}}{\text{Sales revenue}}$$

- **Return on Total Assets.** This ratio, often called *return on investment,* or **ROI,** measures how much profit is generated by the assets the firm has acquired through its equity investments and debts. The standard definition is:

$$\text{Return on total assets} = \frac{\text{Profit after taxes}}{\text{Total assets}}$$

Another definition, for those who wish to account for debt financing of assets, is:

$$\text{Return on total assets} = \frac{\text{Profit after taxes} + \text{Interest}}{\text{Total assets}}$$

- **Return on Stockholder's Equity.** This is often called *return on net worth* or simply *return on equity* or **ROE.** It measures the rate of return to stockholders of just their investments, which may have been leveraged by debt. It is defined this way:

$$\text{Return on equity} = \frac{\text{Profit after taxes and interest}}{\text{Total stockholder's equity}}$$

DUPONT FINANCIAL ANALYSIS. Several ratios mentioned above may be combined to yield an interesting and informative way of analyzing a firm's finances. This is called the Dupont ROI method. Here is how it is defined:

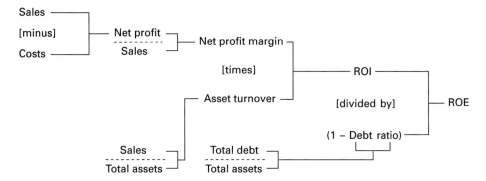

This framework provides a structured way to approach financial analysis. For example, if the net profit margin is too low compared to other firms, the analyst can look to anomalies in either sales or costs. If return on investment is too low, the analyst may investigate whether the difference stems from a low net profit or poor asset turnover. If return on equity is too low, the Dupont method may help reveal whether the problem is poor return on assets or not enough leverage; that is, a debt ratio that is too low compared to the industry.

The final step of internal analysis is the *assessment of strengths and weaknesses,* the firm's summary statement, based on value chain and financial analysis, of internal challenges and capabilities. In each of the areas covered in this section, there will tend to be a lack of information, particularly if the model is used for a case study or a simulation. The problem will be worse in some areas, better in others.

Strategy Statement

Coming up with a strategy statement for a plan is, according to *The Executive Guide to Strategic Planning,* a five-step process:

1. Define and determine the strategic areas that affect the direction of the organization.
2. Establish these in priority order.
3. Determine the organization's Driving Force.®
4. Identify changes that must take place if a new direction is indicated.
5. Formulate a strategy statement that establishes the clear direction of the organization.

Strategic areas represent major factors that decisively affect and influence the direction of the organization. The *Driving Force*® is that strategic area (one of the eight listed below, or another) which is the *primary determiner* of the scope of future products/services and markets. Planning experts believe that although all strategic areas are important, *one and only one* should be the Driving Force.® The ultimate question is, when the final decision about a product or market is made, which strategic area proves to be the most decisive? That one is the Driving Force.® Here are the eight Driving Forces® as developed by Kepner-Tregoe, adapted (with permission) from *Vision in Action* by Tregoe, Zimmerman, Smith and Tobia.[39] You may want to add to or modify this list.

1. Products Offered: "A [products-offered] organization has carefully described the common characteristics of its products and will develop or acquire new products that fit those characteristics. It continually seeks a broader range of customer groups and geographic areas through which to exploit its products."

2. Markets Served: "An organization with this direction has strong and well-defined relationships with its customer groups. This organization is driven by the recognition that its highest exploitable competitive edge is the strength of its relationship with the markets or customer groups it serves. Such an organization is constantly searching for new needs to fill within the base of this customer strength."

3. Return/Profit: "With [this Driving Force], an organization's ability to meet strategically preset return and profit measures is the primary 'hook' determining what businesses this organization will acquire or keep. . . . Typically, organizations with the Return/Profit Driving Force will acquire businesses rather than develop new products or customers."

4. Technology: "An organization pursuing [this Driving Force] builds its strategic vision around a body of knowledge, or a set of technological capabilities. It has the people and the physical resources to develop this basic technology and to apply it in innovative ways in order to satisfy existing, emerging, or completely new fields."

5. Low-Cost Production Capability: "An organization pursuing [this driving force] has a set of production capabilities able to produce products or services at the lowest cost relative to competitive offerings. This type of organization will maintain and increase its cost advantage over its competitors through advanced process technology and cost-conscious management of its production."

6. Operations Capability: This Driving Force means "having a set of capabilities—physical, human, and technical—which, used in a variety of combinations, produces a wide range of products or services."

7. Method of Distribution/Sale: "An organization pursuing [this Driving Force] has a set or system of distribution and sales capabilities and the physical and human resources necessary to fully exploit them in order to provide a variety of products or services with a particular competitive advantage. These distribution and sales capabilities may be unique in their quality, quantity, or position compared with those of competitors."

8. Natural Resources: "An organization pursuing [this Driving Force] owns or controls a significant natural resource (or more than one). It possesses the capability to process that natural resource in usable forms. The organization's competitive advantage rests in the quality, quantity, location, or form of the natural resources themselves."

A *strategy statement* is developed by answering five fundamental questions:

1. What should be our future Driving Force®?
2. How does this differ from our current Driving Force®?
3. What changes will be needed to meet the requirements of our future Driving Force®?
4. How is this compatible with our mission?
5. How is this compatible with the conclusions from our strategic analysis?

Here is an example of an actual strategy statement, taken from *The Executive Guide to Strategic Planning*[40]:

> We intend to move from a services-offered to a customer-needs strategy. The primary reasons are to offset the effect of new competition brought about by deregulation and to meet the financial commitments established in the company's mission. For this to happen, the following changes need to take place:
>
> • more product diversification related to customer needs
> • strong internal focus on employee attitudes, training, and broadening of capabilities to meet the customer-needs posture
> • more accurate analysis of profitability, by customer grouping
> • organizational change to reflect customer-needs posture
> • company image enhancement as a customer-needs-driven organization
> • improved definition of customer service requirements.

Integrated Programs

Integrated programs are the *action steps* of strategic planning. They become integrated because of their cross-functional nature. The purpose of integrated programs is to ensure that the plan will be implemented. They need to be spelled out in enough detail to allow the CEO or planning team to track progress or measure results. Implementation revolves around making the translation from objectives into specific actions and results. *The Executive Guide to Strategic Planning* recommends seven steps for identifying and documenting integrated programs:

1. Identify the results needed to accomplish each long-term objective.
2. Select the five to ten most critical results required to achieve the long-term objective.
3. Reach agreement (as to feasibility, completeness, etc.) on each integrated program.
4. For each integrated program, reach agreement on and document what is needed concerning **results, timetable, resources, accountability,** and **feedback mechanism**. The best way to do this is to create a table for *each* long-term objective, with five columns that correspond to the five elements.
5. Invite review by and comment from the levels of management that will be implementing these programs.
6. Complete final documentation of the integrated programs (that is, write up the plan and the programs).
7. Implement and evaluate (quarterly) the programs.

The authors point out that neither the integrated programs nor the rest of the strategic plan should be cast in concrete.

THE CONCEPT OF CORPORATE STRATEGY

As mentioned earlier, Andrews's reading, "The Concept of Corporate Strategy," is perhaps the classic statement of the design approach to strategy. Since the planning approach is rooted in the design approach, it is relevant for planners as well. Andrews begins with a definition of strategy and a list of what should be contained in a strategy statement. These statements are similar to the material on planning in the previous section. Note, too, that his definition could relate to each of Mintzberg's five *P*'s of strategy from Chapter One.

Andrews goes on to make his well-known statement about the nature of strategy formulation: what the firm might, can, should, and wants to do. He then discusses the environment facing a firm and considers the sources of organizational competence. He concedes that the insight needed to identify strengths does not come naturally, a point Rumelt also makes in the next reading. Andrews offers the interesting opinion that managerial competence is more important than technical competence, which in turn is more important than financial resources. This reflects the high opinion the design approach holds of senior managers. Andrews concludes with the idea, discussed earlier in this chapter, that strategy will be unique for each firm.

THE EVALUATION OF BUSINESS STRATEGY

Rumelt's reading "The Evaluation of Business Strategy" spans the design and planning approaches of this chapter and the positioning approach of the next chapter. It is devoted to the appraisal of a strategy, either an existing or a contemplated one. Rumelt begins with a discussion of how this task is based on knowing the situation and having good insight, two things he suggests are difficult to obtain. He mentions that strategy evaluation requires not problem solving, but problem *structuring,* a skill rarely taught. To help with the task, Rumelt proposes four tests.

The first test, unique to Rumelt's views, is *consistency.* It is designed to make sure the firm's objectives are mutually compatible. The second test is *consonance,* which measures how well the strategy is adapted to general environmental conditions. Then comes the *feasibility* test, intended to appraise a firm's capability to carry out (or continue) a strategy. In this part of the reading, Rumelt echoes Andrews's notion that qualitative factors tend to be more serious limitations on strategy than are quantitative factors, such as money. The consonance and feasibility tests fit squarely into the design and planning approaches; together, they make up the SWOT analysis common to these means of strategy formation.

Rumelt's fourth test is the *advantage* test, designed to assess whether the firm has created and maintained a competitive edge in its industry. This test fits best with the positioning school of thought we shall examine in Chapter Four. For example, Rumelt claims that advantages come from three sources—resources, skills, and position—and that the latter advantage can be based on either size or uniqueness. Size and uniqueness are the sources of two of the generic positioning strategies discussed in the positioning approach to strategy formation in Chapter Four.

NOTES TO CHAPTER THREE

1. Hofer, C. W., and D. Schendel, *Strategy Formulation: Analytical Concepts.* St. Paul: West Publishing, 1978.
2. Ibid.
3. Rumelt, R., *Strategy, Structure and Economic Performance.* Boston: Harvard Business School, 1974.
4. Chandler, A. D., *Strategy and Structure: Chapters in the History of the Industrial Enterprise.* Cambridge, Mass.: M.I.T. Press, 1962.
5. Porter, M. E., "From Competitive Advantage to Corporate Strategy." *Harvard Business Review* (May–June 1987): 43–59.
6. Newman, W. H., *Administrative Action: The Techniques of Organization and Management.* Englewood Cliffs, N.J.: Prentice Hall, 1951.
7. Mintzberg, H., "Strategy Formation: Schools of Thought." In *Perspectives on Strategic Management,* ed. James W. Frederickson. New York: Harper Business, 1990, p. 111.
8. Andrews, K. R., *The Concept of Corporate Strategy.* Homewood, Ill.: Richard D. Irwin, 1980.
9. Ibid.
10. This section is based on Mintzberg, H., "Strategy Formation;" and Mintzberg, H., "The Design School: Reconsidering the Basic Premises of Strategic Management." *Strategic Management Journal* 11 (1990): 171–95.
11. Mintzberg, "The Design School," p. 179.
12. Mintzberg, "Strategy Formation," p. 115.
13. Chandler, *Strategy and Structure.*
14. Mintzberg, "Strategy Formation," p. 116.
15. Ansoff, H. I., *Corporate Strategy.* New York: McGraw-Hill, 1965.
16. "The New Breed of Strategic Planner," *Business Week* (September 17, 1984): 62–66, 68; and Hayes, R. H., "Strategic Planning: Forward in Reverse?" *Harvard Business Review* (November–December 1985): 111–19.
17. Mintzberg, "Strategy Formation," p. 117.
18. Ansoff, *Corporate Strategy.*
19. Pennington, M. W., "Why Has Planning Failed?" *Long Range Planning* 5 no. 1 (1972): 2–9.
20. Mintzberg, "Strategy Formation," p. 119.

21. Bresser, R. K., and R. C. Bishop, "Dysfunctional Effects of Formal Planning: Two Theoretical Explanations." *Academy of Management Review* 8 (1983): 588–99; and Shrader, C. B., L. Taylor, and D. R. Dalton, "Strategic Planning and Organizational Performance: A Critical Appraisal." *Journal of Management* 10 (1984): 149–71.

22. Wildavsky, A., *The Politics of the Budgeting Process,* 2nd ed. Boston: Little, Brown, 1974, p. 205.

23. Mintzberg, "Strategy Formation," p. 120.

24. Steiner, G. A., *Strategic Planning: What Every Manager Must Know.* New York: Free Press, 1979.

25. Ansoff, H. I., "Managing Strategic Surprise by Response to Weak Signals," *California Management Review* 18, no. 2, (1975): 21–33; Ansoff, H. I., *Strategic Management.* New York: Macmillan, 1979; and Ansoff, H. I., *Implanting Strategic Management.* Englewood Cliffs, N.J.: Prentice Hall, 1984.

26. Steiner, *Strategic Planning;* Ringbakk, K. A., "Why Planning Fails." *European Business* 29 (Spring 1971): 15–241.

27. See, for example, Steiner, *Strategic Planning.*

28. Ibid., p. 46.

29. Mintzberg, "Strategy Formation," pp. 121–22.

30. Lengel, R. H., and R. L. Daft, "The Selection of Communication Media as an Executive Skill." *Academy of Management Executive* 2 (August 1988): 225–32.

31. Mintzberg's Chapter Five reading, "Crafting Strategy," explains this in greater detail.

32. Below, P. J., G. L. Morrisey, and B. L. Acomb, *The Executive Guide to Strategic Planning.* San Francisco: Jossey-Bass, 1987.

33. Ibid., pp. 29–34.

34. Ibid., pp. 35–37.

35. Ibid., pp. 58–60.

36. Ibid., pp. 71–73.

37. Ibid., p. 72.

38. Below, P. J., G. L. Morrisey, and B. L. Acomb, *The Executive Guide to Operational Planning.* San Francisco: Jossey-Bass, 1987.

39. Tregoe, B. B., J. W. Zimmerman, R. A. Smith, and P. M Tobia. *Vision in Action.* New York: Fireside Books, 1989. The material in this section is adapted from pp. 45–49 (for numbers 1 through 3) and 209–214 (for numbers 4 through 8).

40. Below, Morrisey, and Acomb. *The Executive Guide to Strategic Planning,* pp. 66–67.

By Kenneth R. Andrews

THE STRATEGY CONCEPT

What Strategy Is

Corporate strategy is the pattern of decisions in a company that determines and reveals its objectives, purposes, or goals, produces the principal policies and plans for achieving those goals, and defines the range of business the company is to pursue, the kind of economic and human organization it is or intends to be, and the nature of the economic and noneconomic contribution it intends to make to its shareholders, employees, customers, and communities. . . .

The strategic decision contributing to this pattern is one that is effective over long periods of time, affects the company in many different ways, and focuses and commits a significant portion of its resources to the expected outcomes. The pattern resulting from a series of such decisions will probably define the central character and image of a company, the individuality it has for its members and various publics, and the position it will occupy in its industry and markets. It will permit the specification of particular objectives to be attained through a timed sequence investment and implementation decisions and will govern directly the deployment or redeployment of resources to make these decisions effective.

Some aspects of such a pattern of decision may be in an established corporation unchanging over long periods of time, like a commitment to quality, or high technology, or certain raw materials, or good labor relations. Other aspects of a strategy must change as or before the world changes, such as product line, manufacturing process, or merchandising and styling practices. The basic determinants of company character, if purposefully institutionalized, are likely to persist through and shape the nature of substantial changes in product-market choices and allocation of resources. . . .

It is important, however, not to take the idea apart in another way, that is, to separate goals from the policies designed to achieve those goals. The essence of the definition of strategy I have just recorded is *pattern*. The interdependence of purposes, policies, and organized action is crucial to the particularity of an individual strategy and its opportunity to identify competitive advantage. It is the unity, coherence, and internal consistency of a company's strategic decisions that position the company in its environment and give the firm its identity, its power to mobilize its strengths, and its likelihood of success in the marketplace. It is the interrelationship of a set of goals and policies that crystallizes from the formless reality of a company's environment a set of problems an organization can seize upon and solve.

What you are doing, in short, is never meaningful unless you can say or imply what you are doing it for: the quality of administrative action and the motivation lending it power cannot be appraised without knowing its relationship to purpose. Breaking up the system of corporate goals and the character-determining major policies for attainment leads to narrow and mechanical conceptions of strategic management and endless logic chopping. . . .

---

* Excerpted from Kenneth R. Andrews, *The Concept of Corporate Strategy,* rev. ed. (copyright © by Richard D. Irwin, Inc., 1980), Chaps. 2 and 3; reprinted by permission of the publisher.

Summary Statements of Strategy

Before we proceed to clarification of this concept by application, we should specify the terms in which strategy is usually expressed. A summary statement of strategy will characterize the product line and services offered or planned by the company, the markets and market segments for which products and services are now or will be designed, and the channels through which these markets will be reached. The means by which the operation is to be financed will be specified, as will the profit objectives and the emphasis to be placed on the safety of capital versus level of return. Major policy in central functions such as marketing, manufacturing, procurement, research and development, labor relations, and personnel, will be stated where they distinguish the company from others, and usually the intended size, form, and climate of the organization will be included.

Each company, if it were to construct a summary strategy from what it understands itself to be aiming at, would have a different statement with different categories of decision emphasized to indicate what it wanted to be or do. . . .

Formulation of Strategy

Corporate strategy is an organization process, in many ways inseparable from the structure, behavior, and culture of the company in which it takes place. Nevertheless, we may abstract from the process two important aspects, interrelated in real life but separable for the purposes of analysis. The first of these we may call *formulation,* the second *implementation.* Deciding what strategy should be may be approached as a rational undertaking, even if in life emotional attachments . . . may complicate choice among future alternatives. . . .

The principal subactivities of strategy formulation as a logical activity include identifying opportunities and threats in the company's environment and attaching some estimate or risk to the discernible alternatives. Before a choice can be made, the company's strengths and weaknesses should be appraised together with the resources on hand and available. Its actual or potential capacity to take advantage of perceived market needs or to cope with attendant risks should be estimated as objectively as possible. The strategic alternative which results from matching opportunity and corporate capability at an acceptable level of risk is what we may call an *economic strategy.*

The process described thus far assumes that strategists are analytically objective in estimating the relative capacity of their company and the opportunity they see or anticipate in developing markets. The extent to which they wish to undertake low or high risk presumably depends on their profit objectives. The higher they set the latter, the more willing they must be to assume a correspondingly high risk that the market opportunity they see will not develop or that the corporate competence required to excel competition will not be forthcoming.

So far we have described the intellectual processes of ascertaining what a company *might do* in terms of environmental opportunity, of deciding what it *can do* in terms of ability and power, and of bringing these two considerations together in optimal equilibrium. The determination of strategy also requires consideration of what alternatives are preferred by the chief executive and perhaps by his or her immediate associates as well, quite apart from economic considerations. Personal values, aspirations, and ideals do, and in our judgment quite properly should, influence the final choice of purposes. Thus what the executives of a company *want to do* must be brought into the strategic decision.

Finally strategic choice has an ethical aspect—a fact much more dramatically illustrated in some industries than in others. Just as alternatives may be ordered in terms of the degree of risk that they entail, so may they be examined against the standards of responsiveness to the expectations of society that the strategist elects. Some alternatives may seem to the executive considering them more attractive than others when the pub-

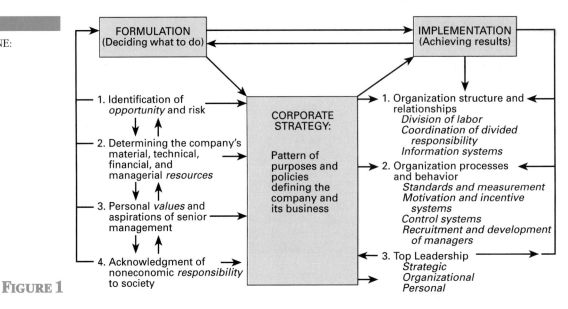

FIGURE 1

lic good or service to society is considered. What a company *should do* thus appears as a fourth element of the strategic decision. . . .

The Implementation of Strategy

Since effective implementation can make a sound strategic decision ineffective or a debatable choice successful, it is as important to examine the processes of implementation as to weigh the advantages of available strategic alternatives. The implementation of strategy is comprised of a series of subactivities which are primarily administrative. If purpose is determined, then the resources of a company can be mobilized to accomplish it. An organizational structure appropriate for the efficient performance of the required tasks must be made effective by information systems and relationships permitting coordination of subdivided activities. The organizational processes of performance measurement, compensation, management development—all of them enmeshed in systems of incentives and controls—must be directed toward the kind of behavior required by organizational purpose. The role of personal leadership is important and sometimes decisive in the accomplishment of strategy. Although we know that organization structure and processes of compensation, incentives, control, and management development influence and constrain the formulation of strategy, we should look first at the logical proposition that structure should follow strategy in order to cope later with the organizational reality that strategy also follows structure. When we have examined both tendencies, we will understand and to some extent be prepared to deal with the interdependence of the formulation and implementation of corporate purpose. Figure 1 may be useful in understanding the analysis of strategy as a pattern of interrelated decisions. . . .

RELATING OPPORTUNITIES TO RESOURCES

Determination of a suitable strategy for a company begins in identifying the opportunities and risks in its environment. This [discussion] is concerned with the identification of a range of strategic alternatives, the narrowing of this range by recognizing the constraints imposed by corporate capability, and the determination of one or more economic strategies at acceptable levels of risk. . . .

The Nature of the Company's Environment

The environment of an organization in business, like that of any other organic entity, is the pattern of all the external conditions and influences that affect its life and development. The environmental influences relevant to strategic decision operate in a company's industry, the total business community, its city, its country, and the world. They are technological, economic, physical, social, and political in kind. The corporate strategist is usually at least intuitively aware of these features of the current environment. But in all these categories change is taking place at varying rates—fastest in technology, less rapidly in politics. Change in the environment of business necessitates continuous monitoring of a company's definition of its business, lest it falter, blur, or become obsolete. Since by definition the formulation of strategy is performed with the future in mind, executives who take part in the strategic planning process must be aware of those aspects of their company's environment especially susceptible to the kind of change that will affect their company's future.

TECHNOLOGY. From the point of view of the corporate strategist, technological developments are not only the fastest unfolding but the most far-reaching in extending or contracting opportunity for an established company. They include the discoveries of science, the impact of related product development, the less dramatic machinery and process improvements, and the progress of automation and data processing. . . .

ECOLOGY. It used to be possible to take for granted the physical characteristics of the environment and find them favorable to industrial development. Plant sites were chosen using criteria like availability of process and cooling water, accessibility to various forms of transportation, and stability of soil conditions. With the increase in sensitivity to the impact on the physical environment of all industrial activity, it becomes essential, often to comply with law, to consider how planned expansion and even continued operation under changing standards will affect and be perceived to affect the air, water, traffic density, and quality of life generally of any area which a company would like to enter. . . .

ECONOMICS. Because business is more accustomed to monitoring economic trends than those in other spheres, it is less likely to be taken by surprise by such massive developments as the internationalization of competition, the return of China and Russia to trade with the West, the slower than projected development of the Third World countries, the Americanization of demand and culture in the developing countries and the resulting backlash of nationalism, the increased importance of the large multinational corporations and the consequences of host-country hostility, the recurrence of recession, and the persistence of inflation in all phases of the business cycle. The consequences of world economic trends need to be monitored in much greater detail for any one industry or company.

INDUSTRY. Although the industry environment is the one most company strategists believe they know most about, the opportunities and risks that reside there are often blurred by familiarity and the uncritical acceptance of the established relative position of competitors. . . .

SOCIETY. Social development of which strategists keep aware include such influential forces as the quest for equality for minority groups, the demand of women for opportunity and recognition, the changing patterns of work and leisure, the effects of urbanization upon the individual, family, and neighborhood, the rise of crime, the decline of conventional morality, and the changing composition of world population.

POLITICS. The political forces important to the business firm are similarly extensive and complex—the changing relations between communist and noncommunist countries

(East and West) and between prosperous and poor countries (North and South), the relation between private enterprise and government, between workers and management, the impact of national planning on corporate planning, and the rise of what George Lodge (1975) calls the communitarian ideology. . . .

Although it is not possible to know or spell out here the significance of such technical, economic, social, and political trends, and possibilities for the strategist of a given business or company, some simple things are clear. Changing values will lead to different expectations of the role business should perform. Business will be expected to perform its mission not only with economy in the use of energy but with sensitivity to the ecological environment. Organizations in all walks of life will be called upon to be more explicit about their goals and to meet the needs and aspirations (for example, for education) of their membership.

In any case, change threatens all established strategies. We know that a thriving company—itself a living system—is bound up in a variety of interrelationships with larger systems comprising its technological, economic, ecological, social, and political environment. If environmental developments are destroying and creating business opportunities, advance notice of specific instances relevant to a single company is essential to intelligent planning. Risk and opportunity in the last quarter of the twentieth century require of executives a keen interest in what is going on outside their companies. More than that, a practical means of tracking developments promising good or ill, and profit or loss, needs to be devised. . . .

For the firm that has not determined what its strategy dictates it needs to know or has not embarked upon the systematic surveillance of environmental change, a few simple questions kept constantly in mind will highlight changing opportunity and risk. In examining your own company or one you are interested in, these questions should lead to an estimate of opportunity and danger in the present and predicted company setting.

1. What are the essential economic, technical, and physical characteristics of the industry in which the company participates? . . .
2. What trends suggesting future change in economic and technical characteristics are apparent? . . .
3. What is the nature of competition both within the industry and across industries? . . .
4. What are the requirements for success in competition in the company's industry? . . .
5. Given the technical, economic, social, and political developments that most directly apply, what is the range of strategy available to any company in this industry? . . .

Identifying Corporate Competence and Resources

The first step in validating a tentative choice among several opportunities is to determine whether the organization has the capacity to prosecute it successfully. The capability of an organization is its demonstrated and potential ability to accomplish, against the opposition of circumstance or competition, whatever it sets out to do. Every organization has actual and potential strengths and weaknesses. Since it is prudent in formulating strategy to extend or maximize the one and contain or minimize the other, it is important to try to determine what they are and to distinguish one from the other.

It is just as possible, though much more difficult, for a company to know its own strengths and limitations as it is to maintain a workable surveillance of its changing environment. Subjectivity, lack of confidence, and unwillingness to face reality may make it hard for organizations as well as for individuals to know themselves. But just as it is essential, though difficult, that a maturing person achieve reasonable self-awareness, so an organization can identify approximately its central strength and critical vulnerability. . . .

To make an effective contribution to strategic planning, the key attributes to be appraised should be identified and consistent criteria established for judging them. If attention is directed to strategies, policy commitments, and past practices in the context of discrepancy between organization goals and attainment, an outcome useful to an individual manager's strategic planning is possible. The assessment of strengths and weaknesses associated with the attainment of specific objectives becomes in Stevenson's (1976) words a "key link in a feedback loop" which allows managers to learn from the success or failures of the policies they institute.

Although [a] study by Stevenson did not find or establish a systematic way of developing or using such knowledge, members of organizations develop judgments about what the company can do particularly well—its core of competence. If consensus can be reached about this capability, no matter how subjectively arrived at, its application to identified opportunity can be estimated.

SOURCES OF CAPABILITIES. The powers of a company constituting a resource for growth and diversification accrue primarily from experience in making and marketing a product line or providing a service. They inhere as well in (1) the developing strengths and weaknesses of the individuals comprising the organization, (2) the degree to which individual capability is effectively applied to the common task, and (3) the quality of coordination of individual and group effort.

The experience gained through successful execution of a strategy centered upon one goal may unexpectedly develop capabilities which could be applied to different ends. Whether they should be so applied is another question. For example, a manufacturer of salt can strengthen his competitive position by offering his customers salt-dispensing equipment. If, in the course of making engineering improvements in this equipment, a new solenoid principle is perfected that has application to many industrial switching problems, should this patentable and marketable innovation be exploited? The answer would turn not only on whether economic analysis of the opportunity shows this to be a durable and profitable possibility, but also on whether the organization can muster the financial, manufacturing, and marketing strength to exploit the discovery and live with its success. The former question is likely to have a more positive answer than the latter. In this connection, it seems important to remember that individual and unsupported flashes of strength are not as dependable as the gradually accumulated product and market-related fruits of experience.

Even where competence to exploit an opportunity is nurtured by experience in related fields, the level of that competence may be too low for any great reliance to be placed upon it. Thus a chain of children's clothing stores might well acquire the administrative, merchandising, buying, and selling skills that would permit it to add departments in women's wear. Similarly, a sales force effective in distributing typewriters might gain proficiency in selling office machinery and supplies. But even here it would be well to ask what *distinctive* ability these companies could bring to the retailing of soft goods or office equipment to attract customers away from a plethora of competitors.

IDENTIFYING STRENGTHS. The distinctive competence of an organization is more than what it can do; it is what it can do particularly well. To identify the less obvious or by-product strengths of an organization that may well be transferable to some more profitable new opportunity, one might well begin by examining the organization's current product line and by defining the functions it serves in its markets. Almost any important consumer product has functions which are related to others into which a qualified company might move. The typewriter, for example, is more than the simple machine for mechanizing handwriting that it once appeared to be when looked at only from the point of view of its designer and manufacturer. Closely analyzed from the point of view of the potential user, the typewriter is found to contribute to a broad range of information processing functions. Any one of these might have suggested an area to be exploited by a typewriter manufacturer. Tacitly defining a typewriter as a replacement for a fountain pen as a writing instrument rather than as an input-output device for word processing is the explanation provided by hindsight for the failure of the old-line typewriter companies to develop before IBM did the electric typewriter and the computer-related input-output devices it made possible. The definition of product which would lead to identification of transferable skills must be expressed in terms of the market needs it may fill rather than the engineering specifications to which it conforms.

Besides looking at the uses or functions to which present products contribute, the would-be diversifier might profitably identify the skills that underlie whatever success has been achieved. The qualifications of an organization efficient at performing its long-accustomed tasks come to be taken for granted and considered humdrum, like the steady provision of first-class service. The insight required to identify the essential strength justifying new ventures does not come naturally. Its cultivation can probably be helped by recognition of the need for analysis. In any case, we should look beyond the company's capacity to invent new products. Product leadership is not possible for a majority of companies, so it is fortunate that patentable new products are not the only major highway to new opportunities. Other avenues include new marketing services, new methods of distribution, new values in quality-price combinations, and creative merchandising. The effort to find or to create a competence that is truly distinctive may hold the real key to a company's success or even to its future development. For example, the ability of a cement manufacturer to run a truck fleet more effectively than its competitors may constitute one of its principal competitive strengths in selling an undifferentiated product.

MATCHING OPPORTUNITY AND COMPETENCE. The way to narrow the range of alternatives, made extensive by imaginative identification of new possibilities, is to match opportunity to competence, once each has been accurately identified and its future significance estimated. It is this combination which establishes a company's economic mission and its position in its environment. The combination is designed to minimize organizational weakness and to maximize strength. In every case, risk attends it. And when opportunity seems to outrun present distinctive competence, the willingness to gamble that the latter can be built up to the required level is almost indispensable to a strategy that challenges the organization and the people in it. Figure 2 diagrams the matching of opportunity and resources that results in an economic strategy.

Before we leave the creative act of putting together a company's unique internal capability and opportunity evolving in the external world, we should note that—aside from distinctive competence—the principal resources found in any company are money and people—technical and managerial people. At an advanced stage of economic development, money seems less a problem than technical competence, and the latter less critical than managerial ability. Do not assume that managerial capacity can rise to any occasion. The diversification of American industry is marked by hundreds of instances in which a company strong in one endeavor lacked the ability to manage an enterprise requiring different skills. The right to make handsome profits over a long period must be earned. Opportunism without competence is a path to fairyland.

Besides equating an appraisal of market opportunity and organizational capability, the decision to make and market a particular product or service should be accompanied by an identification of the nature of the business and the kind of company its management desires. Such a guiding concept is a product of many considerations, including the managers' personal values. . . .

UNIQUENESS OF STRATEGY. In each company, the way in which distinctive competence, organizational resources, and organizational values are combined is or should be unique. Differences among companies are as numerous as differences among individu-

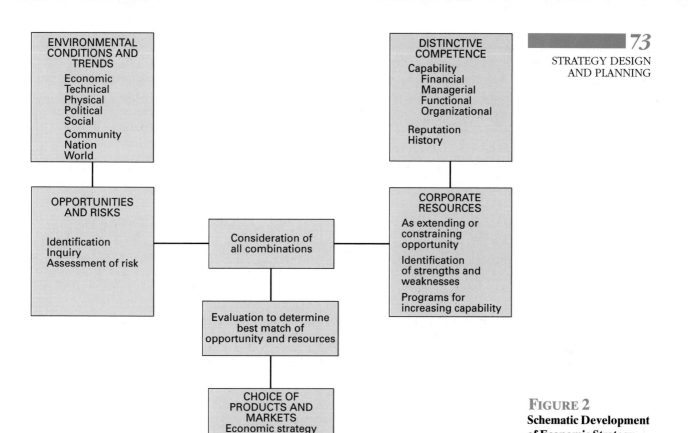

FIGURE 2
**Schematic Development
of Economic Strategy**

als. The combinations of opportunity to which distinctive competences, resources, and values may be applied are equally extensive. Generalizing about how to make an effective match is less rewarding than working at it. The effort is a highly stimulating and challenging exercise. The outcome will be unique for each company and each situation.

THE EVALUATION OF BUSINESS STRATEGY*

READING

By Richard Rumelt

Strategy can neither be formulated nor adjusted to changing circumstances without a process of strategy evaluation. Whether performed by an individual or as part of an organizational review procedure, strategy evaluation forms an essential step in the process of guiding an enterprise.

For many executives strategy evaluation is simply an appraisal of how well a business performs. Has it grown? Is the profit rate normal or better? If the answers to these questions are affirmative, it is argued that the firm's strategy must be sound. Despite its unassailable simplicity, this line of reasoning misses the whole point of strategy—that the critical factors determining the quality of current results are often not directly observable or simply measured, and that by the time strategic opportunities or threats do directly affect operating results, it may well be too late for an effective response. Thus, strategy evaluation is an attempt to look beyond the obvious facts regarding the short-term health of a business and appraise instead those more fundamental factors and trends that govern success in the chosen field of endeavor.

* Originally published in William F. Glueck, *Business Policy and Strategic Management,* 3rd ed. (McGraw-Hill, 1980); reprinted with deletions by permission of the publisher.

THE CHALLENGE OF EVALUATION

However it is accomplished, the products of a business strategy evaluation are answers to these three questions:

1. Are the objectives of the business appropriate?
2. Are the major policies and plans appropriate?
3. Do the results obtained to date confirm or refute critical assumptions on which the strategy rests?

Devising adequate answers to these questions is neither simple nor straightforward. It requires a reasonable store of situation-based knowledge and more than the usual degree of insight. In particular, the major issues which make evaluation difficult and with which the analyst must come to grips are these:

- Each business strategy is unique. For example, one paper manufacturer might rely on its vast timber holdings to weather almost any storm while another might place primary reliance in modern machinery and an extensive distribution system. Neither strategy is "wrong" nor "right" in any absolute sense; both may be right or wrong for the firms in question. Strategy evaluation must, then, rest on a type of situational logic that does not focus on "one best way" but which can be tailored to each problem as it is faced.
- Strategy is centrally concerned with the selection of goals and objectives. Many people, including seasoned executives, find it much easier to set or try to achieve goals than to evaluate them. In part this is a consequence of training in problem structuring. It also arises out of a tendency to confuse *values,* which are fundamental expressions of human personality, with objectives, which are *devices* for lending coherence to action.
- Formal systems of strategic review, while appealing in principle, can create explosive conflict situations. Not only are there serious questions as to who is qualified to give an objective evaluation, the whole idea of strategy evaluation implies management by "much more than results" and runs counter to much of currently popular management philosophy.

THE PRINCIPLES OF STRATEGY EVALUATION

... For our purposes a strategy is a set of objectives, policies, and plans that, taken together, define the scope of the enterprise and its approach to survival and success. Alternatively, we could say that the particular policies, plans, and objectives of a business express its strategy for coping with a complex competitive environment.

One of the fundamental tenets of science is that a theory can never be proven to be absolutely true. A theory can, however, be declared absolutely false if it fails to stand up to testing. Similarly, it is impossible to demonstrate conclusively that a particular business strategy is optimal or even to guarantee that it will work. One can, nevertheless, test it for critical flaws. Of the many tests which could be justifiably applied to a business strategy, most will fit within one of these broad criteria:

- *Consistency:* The strategy must not present mutually inconsistent goals and policies.
- *Consonance:* The strategy must represent an adaptive response to the external environment and to the critical changes occurring within it.
- *Advantage:* The strategy must provide for the creation and/or maintenance of a competitive advantage in the selected area of activity.
- *Feasibility:* The strategy must neither overtax available resources nor create unsolvable subproblems.

A strategy that fails to meet one or more of these criteria is strongly suspect. It fails to perform at least one of the key functions that are necessary for the survival of the business. Experience within a particular industry or other setting will permit the analyst to sharpen these criteria and add others that are appropriate to the situation at hand.

Consistency

Gross inconsistency within a strategy seems unlikely until it is realized that many strategies have not been explicitly formulated but have evolved over time in an ad hoc fashion. Even strategies that are the result of formal procedures may easily contain compromise arrangements between opposing power groups.

Inconsistency in strategy is not simply a flaw in logic. A key function of strategy is to provide coherence to organizational action. A clear and explicit concept of strategy can foster a climate of tacit coordination that is more efficient than most administrative mechanisms. Many high-technology firms, for example, face a basic strategic choice between offering high-cost products with high custom-engineering content and lower-cost products that are more standardized and sold at higher volume. If senior management does not enunciate a clear consistent sense of where the corporation stands on these issues, there will be continuing conflict between sales, design, engineering, and manufacturing people. A clear consistent strategy, by contrast, allows a sales engineer to negotiate a contract with a minimum of coordination—the trade-offs are an explicit part of the firm's posture.

Organizational conflict and interdepartmental bickering are often symptoms of a managerial disorder but may also indicate problems of strategic inconsistency. Here are some indicators that can help sort out these two different problems:

- If problems in coordination and planning continue despite changes in personnel and tend to be issue rather than people based, they are probably due to inconsistencies in strategy.
- If success for one organizational department means, or is interpreted to mean, failure for another department, the basic objective structure is inconsistent.
- If, despite attempts to delegate authority, operating problems continue to be brought to the top for the resolution of *policy* issues, the basic strategy is probably inconsistent.

A final type of consistency that must be sought in strategy is between organizational objectives and the values of the management group. Inconsistency in this area is more of a problem in strategy formulation than in the evaluation of a strategy that has already been implemented. It can still arise, however, if the future direction of the business requires changes that conflict with managerial values. The most frequent source of such conflict is growth. As a business expands beyond the scale that allows an easy informal method of operation, many executives experience a sharp sense of loss. While growth can of course be curtailed, it often will require special attention to a firm's competitive position if survival without growth is desired. The same basic issues arise when other types of personal or social values come into conflict with existing or apparently necessary policies: the resolution of the conflict will normally require an adjustment in the competitive strategy.

Consonance

The way in which a business relates to its environment has two aspects: the business must both match and be adapted to its environment and it must at the same time compete with other firms that are also trying to adapt. This dual character of the relationship between the firm and its environment has its analog in two different aspects of strategic choice and two different methods of strategy evaluation.

TABLE 1 **Generic versus Competitive Strategy**

	GENERIC	COMPETITIVE
Measure of success	Sales growth	Market share
Return to the firm	Value added	Return on investment
Function	Provision of value to the customer	Maintaining or obtaining a defensible position
Basic strategic tasks	Adapting to change and innovation	Creating barriers and deterring rivals
Method of expressing strategy	Product/market terms, functional terms	Policies leading to defensible position
Basic approach to analysis	Study of group of businesses over time	Comparison across rivals at a given time

The first aspect of fit deals with the basic mission or scope of the business and the second with its special competitive position or "edge." Analysis of the first is normally done by looking at changing economic and social conditions over *time.* Analysis of the second, by contrast, typically focuses on the differences across firms at a given time. We call the first the "generic" aspect of strategy and the second "competitive" strategy. Table 1 summarizes the differences between these concepts.

The notion of consonance, or matching, therefore, invites a focus on generic strategy. The role of the evaluator in this case is to examine the basic pattern of economic relationships that characterize the business and determine whether or not sufficient value is being created to sustain the strategy. Most macroanalysis of changing economic conditions is oriented toward the formulation or evaluation of generic strategies. For example, a planning department forecasts that within 10 years home appliances will no longer use mechanical timers or logic. Instead, microprocessors will do the job more reliably and less expensively. The basic message here for the makers of mechanical timers is that their generic strategies are becoming obsolete, especially if they specialize in major home appliances. Note that the threat in this case is not to a particular firm, competitive position, or individual approach to the marketplace but to the basic generic mission.

One major difficulty in evaluating consonance is that most of the critical threats to a business are those which come from without, threatening an entire group of firms. Management, however, is often so engrossed in competitive thinking that such threats are only recognized after the damage has reached considerable proportions. . . .

The key to evaluating consonance is an understanding of why the business, as it currently stands, exists at all and how it assumed its current pattern. Once the analyst obtains a good grasp of the basic economic foundation that supports and defines the business, it is possible to study the consequences of key trends and changes. Without such an understanding, there is no good way of deciding what kinds of changes are most crucial and the analyst can be quickly overwhelmed with data.

Advantage

It is no exaggeration to say that competitive strategy is the art of creating or exploiting those advantages that are most telling, enduring, and most difficult to duplicate.

Competitive strategy, in contrast with generic strategy, focuses on the differences among firms rather than their common missions. The problem it addresses is not so much "how can this function be performed" but "how can *we* perform it either better than, or at least instead of our rivals?" The chain supermarket, for example, represents a successful generic strategy. As a way of doing business, of organizing economic transactions, it has replaced almost all the smaller owner-managed food shops of an earlier era. Yet a potential or actual participant in the retail food business must go beyond this generic strategy and find a way of competing in this business. As another illustration, American Motors' early success in compact cars was generic—other firms soon copied the basic product concept. Once this happened, AMC had to try to either forge a strong competitive strategy in this area or seek a different type of competitive arena.

Competitive advantages can normally be traced to one of three roots:

- Superior resources
- Superior skills
- Superior position

The nature of the advantages produced by the first two are obvious. They represent the ability of a business to do more and/or do it better than its rivals. The critical analytical issue here is the question of which skills and resources represent advantages in which competitive arenas. The skills that make for success in the aerospace electronics industry, for instance, do not seem to have much to do with those needed in consumer electronics. Similarly, what makes for success in the early phases of an industry life cycle may be quite different than what ensures top performance in the later phases.

The idea that certain arrangements of one's resources can enhance their combined effectiveness, and perhaps even put rival forces in a state of disarray, is at the heart of the traditional notion of strategy. This kind of "positional" advantage is familiar to military theorists, chess players, and diplomats. Position plays a crucial role in business strategy as well. . . .

Positional advantage can be gained by foresight, superior skill and/or resources, or just plain luck. Once gained, a good position is defensible. This means that it (1) returns enough value to warrant its continued maintenance and (2) would be so costly to capture that rivals are deterred from full-scale attacks on the core of the business. Position, it must be noted, tends to be self-sustaining as long as the basic environmental factors that underlie it remain stable. Thus, entrenched firms can be almost impossible to unseat, even if their raw skill levels are only average. And when a shifting environment allows position to be gained by a new entrant or innovator, the results can be spectacular.

The types of positional advantage that are most well known are those associated with size or scale. As the scale of operations increases, most firms are able to reduce both the marginal and the total cost of each additional unit produced. Marginal costs fall due to the effects of learning and more efficient processes, and total costs per unit fall even faster as fixed overheads are spread over a larger volume of activity. The larger firm can simply take these gains in terms of increased profitability or it can invest some of the extra returns in position-maintaining activities. By engaging in more research and development, being first to go abroad, having the largest advertising budget, and absorbing the costs involved with acting as an industry spokesman, the dominant business is rechanneling the gains obtained from its advantages into activities designed to maintain those advantages. This kind of positive feedback is the source of the power of position-based advantages—the policies that act to enhance position do not require unusual skills; they simply work most effectively for those who are already in the position in the first place.

While it is not true that larger businesses always have the advantages, it is true that larger businesses will tend to operate in markets and use procedures that turn their size to advantage. Large national consumer-products firms, for example, will normally have an advantage over smaller regional firms in the efficient use of mass advertising, especially network TV. The larger firm will, then, tend to deal in those products where the marginal effect of advertising is most potent, while the smaller firms will seek product-market positions that exploit other types of advantage.

Not all positional advantages are associated with size, although some type of uniqueness is a virtual prerequisite. The principal characteristic of good position is that it permits the firm to obtain advantage from policies that would not similarly benefit rivals without the position. For example, Volkswagen in 1966 had a strong, well-defined position as the preeminent maker of inexpensive, well-engineered, functional automobiles. This position allowed it to follow a policy of not changing its body styling. The policy both enhanced VW's position and reduced costs. Rivals could not similarly benefit from such a policy unless they could also duplicate the other aspects of VW's position. At the other end of the spectrum, Rolls-Royce employed a policy of deliberately limiting its output, a policy which enhanced its unique position and which could do so only because of that position in the first place. Mintzberg (1973b) calls strongly defensible positions and the associated policies "gestalt strategies," recognizing that they are difficult to either analyze or attack in a piecemeal fashion.

Another type of positional advantage derives from successful trade names. These brands, especially when advertised, place retailers in the position of having to stock them which, in turn, reinforces the position and raises the barrier to entry still further. Such famous names as Sara Lee, Johnson & Johnson, and Kraft greatly reduce, for their holders, both the problems of gaining wide distribution for new products and obtaining trial use of new products by the buying public.

Other position-based advantages follow from such factors as:

- The ownership of special raw material sources or long-term supply contracts
- Being geographically located near key customers in a business involving significant fixed investment and high transport costs
- Being a leader in a service field that permits or requires the building of a unique experience base while serving clients
- Being a full-line producer in a market with heavy trade-up phenomena
- Having a wide reputation for providing a needed product or service trait reliably and dependably

In each case, the position permits competitive policies to be adopted that can serve to reinforce the position. *Whenever* this type of positive-feedback phenomena is encountered, the particular policy mix that creates it will be found to be a defensible business position. The key factors that sparked industrial success stories such as IBM and Eastman Kodak were the *early* and rapid domination of strong positions opened up by new technologies.

Feasibility

The final broad test of strategy is its feasibility. Can the strategy be attempted within the physical, human, and financial resources available? The financial resources of a business are the easiest to quantify and are normally the first limitation against which strategy is tested. It is sometimes forgotten, however, that innovative approaches to financing expansion can both stretch the ultimate limitations and provide a competitive advantage, even if it is only temporary. Devices such as captive finance subsidiaries, sale-leaseback arrangements, and tying plant mortgages to long-term contracts have all been used effectively to help win key positions in suddenly expanding industries.

The less quantifiable but actually more rigid limitation on strategic choice is that imposed by the individual and organizational capabilities that are available.

In assessing the organization's ability to carry out a strategy, it is helpful to ask three separate questions.

1. Has the organization demonstrated that it possesses the problem-solving abilities and/or special competences required by the strategy? A strategy, as such, does not and cannot specify in detail each action that must be carried out. Its purpose is to provide structure to

the general issue of the business' goals and approaches to coping with its environment. It is up to the members and departments of the organization to carry out the tasks defined by strategy. A strategy that requires tasks to be accomplished which fall outside the realm of available or easily obtainable skill and knowledge cannot be accepted. It is either infeasible or incomplete.

2. Has the organization demonstrated the degree of coordinative and integrative skill necessary to carry out the strategy? The key tasks required of a strategy not only require specialized skill, but often make considerable demands on the organization's ability to integrate disparate activities. . . .

3. Does the strategy challenge and motivate key personnel and is it acceptable to those who must lend their support? The purpose of strategy is to effectively deploy the unique and distinctive resources of an enterprise. If key managers are unmoved by a strategy, not excited by its goals or methods, or strongly support an alternative, it fails in a major way. . . .

CONCLUSIONS

. . . In most medium- to large-size firms, strategy evaluation is not a purely intellectual task. The issues involved are too important and too closely associated with the distribution of power and authority for either strategy formulation or evaluation to take place in an ivory tower environment. In fact, most firms rarely engage in explicit formal strategy evaluation. Rather, the evaluation of current strategy is a continuing process and one that is difficult to separate from the normal planning, reporting, control, and reward systems of the firm. From this point of view, strategy evaluation is not so much an intellectual task as it is an organizational process.

As process, strategy evaluation is the outcome of activities and events which are strongly shaped by the firm's control and reward systems, its information and planning systems, its structure, and its history and particular culture. Thus, its performance is, in practice, tied more directly to the quality of the firm's strategic management than to any particular analytical scheme. In particular, organizing major units around the primary strategic tasks and making the extra effort required to incorporate measures of strategic success in the control system may play vital roles in facilitating strategy evaluation within the firm.

Ultimately, a firm's ability to maintain its competitive position in a world of rivalry and change may be best served by managers who can maintain a dual view of strategy and strategy evaluation—they must be willing and able to perceive the strategy within the welter of daily activity *and* to build and maintain structures and systems that make strategic factors the object of current activity.

BUSINESS LEVEL STRATEGY ANALYSIS

▼

STRATEGY AS AN ANALYTICAL PROCESS

This chapter deals with the third of the prescriptive models of strategy, the positioning approach. This approach accepts most of the premises of the design and planning approaches, adding to them new content of chiefly economic nature. The approach is called "positioning" because it focuses on how firms in a given context *differ in product-market positions when compared* to one another along any of several dimensions. The search for dimensions of difference has led the positioning approach to concentrate on the actual **content** of a firm's strategy. The result is the identification of **generic strategies;** that is, general types of strategies to be applied in a variety of situations.

In one sense, this is the oldest approach to strategy. Going back as far as 400 B.C. (Sun Tzu[1]), it was also popular in the nineteenth century,[2] as thinkers on military strategy have been concerned with selecting optimal strategies for particular military contexts. In another sense, however, the positioning approach is by far the newest of the three prescriptive approaches. In the 1960s and the 1970s, more positioning-type work was published, based on the work of the Boston Consulting Group (BCG), with its well-known growth-share matrix (with dogs, stars, question marks, and cash cows), and the PIMS (Profit Impact of Market Strategies) project, which gathered enormous amounts of data from many business units to glean strategic prescriptions. The prescriptions resulting from BCG and PIMS were interrelated and tended to be quite directive. For example, market share was considered inherently advantageous, and no matter the context, rapid accumulation of production experience was thought to be beneficial on its face.

The positioning approach solidified its claim as an approach to strategy with the 1980 publication of Michael Porter's book *Competitive Strategy*[3] and his 1985 book *Competitive Advantage.*[4] Moving well beyond the directives of the design and planning approaches, these works spawned a surge of work in the positioning approach, propagating systematic study that put rigor into strategic prescription. Most of the discussion that follows deals with this third wave of the positioning approach. This chapter includes two readings: one by Porter to illustrate the approach to external analysis that he developed in his first book, and one by Mintzberg that discusses generic strategies, including Porter's approach to internal analysis.

81

BUSINESS-LEVEL
STRATEGY ANALYSIS

PREMISES OF STRATEGY AS POSITION

To some extent, the positioning approach built on the bases of the design and planning approaches. Strategy formation is still viewed as a formalized, deliberate thought process that produces fully elaborated strategies, which should be precisely stated before being formally carried out. One difference, however, is that the process focuses much more heavily on calculation, ". . . on the choice of tangible strategic positions rather than the development of integrated strategic perspectives (as in the design school) or of coordinated sets of plans (as in the planning school)."[5]

An additional difference with the other prescriptive models is that the context within which these "tangible positions" are staked out is specified—in an economic and competitive marketplace. Like the design approach, this approach assumes that strategy follows structure, but here the relevant structure is that of the *industry*. This is a legacy of the approach's roots in industrial organization economics; we will discuss industry analysis in detail below.

Like the planning and design approaches, the positioning approach makes the chief executive the center of strategy making in principle, but in actuality it elevates the planner to an even higher role. That person becomes a valued analyst, a technician making sense of large amounts of information and coming up with optimal strategies. However, this approach abandons the notion of "unique" strategy. Here, strategies are **generic**—they fall into a few categories that describe the proper strategic schemes a firm might pursue. The choice of a particular generic strategy typically leads to specific functional strategies. Firms following similar generic strategies tend to have similar functional strategies; these firms cluster into **strategic groups** within an industry.[6]

A summary of the positioning approach follows: Analysts use quantitative data about market structure to calculate the optimal positional strategies, that in turn dictate the organizational structures, systems, and plans that result in a particular performance.

EXTERNAL STRATEGIC ANALYSIS: HOW COMPETITIVE FORCES SHAPE STRATEGY

In our discussion of the design and planning approaches in Chapter Three, we saw how firms were urged to assess their environments. One type of assessment, suggested by Andrews, was macroenvironmental—assessing the environment for "PESTs," the political, economic, sociocultural, and technological factors facing a firm. Rumelt's consonance test, also in Chapter Three, echoed Andrews's suggestions for macroenvironmental analysis. Andrews also urged strategists to assess their industry environment. However, it was Andrews's colleague Michael Porter, the positioning approach's most well-known thinker of recent times, who developed a model for analyzing a firm's industry environment. It goes by various names, including the **Competitive Strategy Model** and the **Five Forces Model**.[7] Porter's reading in this chapter, "How Competitive Forces Shape Strategy," explains the model in detail. This section will briefly summarize the model, which is probably the best one yet developed for addressing Rumelt's advantage test.

True to his training as an economist, Porter's basic point is that the essence of strategy formulation is coping with *competition.* Competition in an industry is rooted in its underlying economics, and this focus enables greater understanding of Rumelt's advantage idea. One shortcoming, though, is that the focus on competition does not address Rumelt's feasibility, consistency and, most of all, consonance tests. But Porter makes a major contribution by broadening our understanding of competition, pointing out that competitive forces go well beyond the familiar established firms in the industry. In addition to these **industry rivals,** Porter tells us that competitive forces include **potential entrants, suppliers, buyers,** and **substitute products.** If these competitive forces are strong in an industry, it means poor long-run profitability prospects; a collection of weaker forces provides a greater opportunity for superior performance. The strategist must, according to Porter, find a position in the industry where the company can best defend itself against these forces or can influence them in its favor. In the reading, Porter describes in detail how the power of each of the five forces intensifies or declines.

STRATEGIC ANALYSIS: GENERIC STRATEGIES FOR LOCATING AND DISTINGUISHING THE CORE BUSINESS

Earlier, we discussed how one feature of the positioning approach that sets it apart has been its emphasis on selecting from among a set of generic strategies. The Mintzberg reading in this chapter examines some generic strategies for locating and distinguishing a core business. These are the ones most relevant to business-level strategy analysis. (A reading in a later chapter will examine generic strategies for elaborating, extending, and reconceiving the core business; these are more appropriate for corporate-level analysis.)

Mintzberg discusses four bases for functional strategies—input, throughput, output, and support—which relate to the position approach's best-known model for internal analysis, Michael Porter's **value chain.** The value chain is based on the idea that firms must create value in the products they produce and the services they provide. The value of a product or service is measured by the amount a buyer is willing to pay for it, in other words, a price.[8] Porter calls the network firm's activities a value chain because the firm wants to transform low-cost inputs into outputs (products or services) whose price exceeds the firm's costs. This excess of price over costs is called **margin.**

Value Chain Analysis

Porter divides the four bases of organizational functioning into two types of activities, primary and support. **Primary activities** are the input, throughput, and output functions mentioned above. Porter identifies them specifically as *inbound logistics, operations, outbound logistics, marketing and sales,* and *service.* These activities are primary because they add value directly, through better product quality, for example, or lower production cost, or even after-sales service that induces buyers to pay a premium price. **Support activities** include *procurement, technology development, human resource management,* and *firm infrastructure.* Unlike the primary activities, support activities do not add value directly. Instead, they enhance the ability of the primary activities to add value. We will examine all these activities below.

The important point of the value chain with respect to gaining competitive advantage is that it provides a framework for identifying or developing a **distinctive competency.** That is, a strategist should strive to obtain a competitive advantage by making his or her firm distinctive in one or more of these activities, preferably a primary one. Distinctive means that it is so outstanding in some way that it becomes difficult for other firms to replicate. Typically, distinctive competencies for a given activity are based on

gaining advantage through one of two approaches. The first and most straightforward is *low cost,* where the firm transforms inputs inexpensively, so that even if the price (value) is low, margin is still created. The second approach is *differentiation,* which is the creation of such meaningful product or service differences that buyers are willing to pay a premium price. It is possible for activities simultaneously to be low cost and differentiated; that is the thrust of much of the recent literature on Total Quality Management.[9] Let us briefly examine the primary and secondary value-creating activities.

Primary Activities

INBOUND AND OUTBOUND LOGISTICS. Inbound logistics are the raw-material input part of a firm's value-adding system. Logistics are relevant mostly for manufacturing firms, not service firms. Once a little-emphasized part of manufacturing activities, logistics have become very important. One aspect of logistics is *inventory management,* which has undergone significant change since the widespread adoption of Just-in-Time (JIT) inventory control systems. Inbound JIT systems are set up so that raw materials, instead of being stockpiled (with attendant high holding costs), arrive just as they are needed by the production process. Outbound JIT systems are set up to provide the same process to a firm's buyers. JIT systems typically yield advantages through cost savings, despite the intense management and coordination needed for them to work properly. The need to coordinate inbound and outbound logistics so closely in JIT systems has recently led some thinkers to suggest that both inbound and outbound logistics be combined into an activity called **materials management,**[10] which integrates procurement, production planning, and distribution.

OPERATIONS. These are the central part of the value chain, the point where inputs are transformed into outputs. For a manufacturing firm, included here are the factories, machines, and ways of organizing production. For a service firm, included are the actual provision of the services.

Expert opinion about manufacturing operations is undergoing a profound shift. For most of this century, mass production was the popular approach to manufacturing. Recently, experts and practitioners have developed entirely different ways of organizing people and machines for manufacturing. One example is **computer-integrated manufacturing,** or **CIM**, which is sometimes referred to as the factory of the future, smart factories, and flexible manufacturing systems. Whatever it is called, the idea of CIM is to link oft-separated manufacturing elements, such as robots, machine tools, product design, and engineering analysis, using one coordinating computer system.[11] Another, much less high-technology approach to organizing manufacturing is called **lean production.** This involves teams of highly trained employees who communicate well, use small inventories, and continuously strive to improve production processes. The result can often be remarkable cost savings and quality improvements.[12]

Service technology is quite different from manufacturing technology. For one thing, production and consumption of the service are simultaneous, in contrast to manufacturing's stockpiling of finished goods for later sale. Outputs of service organizations tend to be customized, particularly for operations such as education, health care, and legal advice. These examples point to another aspect of service technology—the participation of the customer. Service outputs tend to be intangible; even the diploma from a school is just a symbol of the "real" service. Lastly, service technologies are labor intensive.[13] The implications for a service firm wishing to add value are to emphasize employee skill development, with an emphasis both on techniques and interpersonal skills. For example, customer service representatives at a bank not only need to understand the proper procedures for opening accounts, getting information for customers, closing loans, and so forth (which are technical skills) but also must be pleasant and courteous to customers (interpersonal skills).

MARKETING, SALES AND SERVICE. Marketing is often conceived in terms of the **marketing mix,** or the "Four *P*'s" of marketing: product, price, promotion, and placement (also called distribution). Sales is the direct interface between a firm and its buyers, and so is part of marketing. We discuss service here because it can become a major portion of the marketing mix, under either product or placement.

Marketers essentially have two choices to make about managing their marketing mix. One is to decide how much to **differentiate;** that is, to what extent should they act to distinguish their products or services from others'. Possible options for differentiation are *price, image, support, quality,* and *design.* Marketers must also decide the **scope** of their product/service offerings. This is often called **segmentation** because it involves deciding how many customer groups, or segments, to address. The choices can be *unsegmentation* ("one size fits all possible customers"), *segmentation* (virtually limitless possibilities as to type of customer), *niche* (focus on a single segment), and *customizing* (each customer is a unique segment). Mintzberg discusses all these differentiation and scope strategies in detail in his reading at the end of this chapter.

Support Activities

PROCUREMENT. An increasingly important aspect of procurement is controlling the *quality* of inputs. This tends to require forming long-term relationships with single sources of supply, in effect making suppliers part of the firm's activities.[14] The advantages created by this method could be cost savings, differentiation, or both. Of course, good old-fashioned purchasing can add value if the purchasing agents are able to obtain raw materials at low cost, which is helped by a firm being in a concentrated industry buying from a fragmented one.

TECHNOLOGY DEVELOPMENT. This is also called **research and development,** or **R&D.** It can take at least three forms. The first, and perhaps the most familiar, is *product innovation,* the creation of entirely new products. This could also be considered a primary activity in some firms. The second is *product development,* which is the extension and improvement of the features or quality of existing products. This is also close to the marketing function. Lastly, there is *process innovation,* designed to improve a firm's technology so that costs may be lowered and quality improved. This could also be considered part of operations.[15] The very difficulty of separating the three forms of R&D from primary activities illustrates how support activities are supposed to work. Each of these has the potential to directly enhance the performance of a particular primary activity.

HUMAN RESOURCE MANAGEMENT. By definition, organizations are made up of people. Any primary activity on the value chain would be done poorly were a firm to hire incompetent people to do it. Conversely, good people enhance the performance of any primary activity. For that reason alone, good human resources management (HRM) is essential to a firm. But HRM is more than just recruitment; it includes, among many other things, training, development, compensation, and motivation. A firm that seeks competitive advantage from a particular primary activity must recruit, select, train, develop, compensate, and motivate a work force in a way that is consistent with the competitive advantage it seeks. For example, a company that wants to out-market its competitors would need HRM practices that create a first-rate marketing and sales staff. Likewise, a service firm would have to hire good service personnel, then train and compensate them for the kind of customer service it wants.

FIRM INFRASTRUCTURE. This is the corporate setting within which primary and support activities take place. It includes the quality of the management and the quality of established functions, such as planning, finance, accounting, information systems and legal counsel.

Generic Strategies

Porter identifies four generic strategies, discussed briefly by Mintzberg. Firms may seek to gain advantage from low cost or else differentiate, for example on the basis of image, support, quality, and design. And they may choose either a broad or narrow scope. **Cost leadership** is what Porter calls a strategy of broad scope coupled with the seeking of advantage through low cost. Broad scope and differentiation by image or support, etc., is what Porter calls simply **differentiation.** If a firm chooses a narrow scope, Porter identifies two kinds of focus strategies. Narrow scope and low cost result in **cost focus,** while differentiation coupled with narrow scope he calls **differentiation focus.**

STRENGTHS AND WEAKNESSES OF THE POSITIONING APPROACH

The positioning approach suffers from some of the same problems as the design and planning approaches. For example, there remains the problem of separating thinking and action. Formulation, which is done through formal analysis, happens first, then the implementation of the generic strategies takes place "down below." This unduly emphasizes the deliberate aspect of strategy making at the expense of strategic learning. The positioning approach is, like the other prescriptive approaches, undermined by the fallacies mentioned in Chapter Three—of predetermination (discontinuities difficult to predict), detachment (hard data insufficient to inform strategists), and formalization (analysis that cannot produce synthesis).

This approach has some shortcomings as well. One is its narrow focus on quantitative economic data. This can lead to an overemphasis on cost leadership strategies, as opposed to differentiation strategies, since cost data are easier to obtain. One example is the BCG matrix, which placed great emphasis on reducing costs through the experience curve.[16] Because of the bias toward the economic, the political aspects are largely ignored too. This is ironic, since market power can be obtained through means other than economic.[17]

The context of the positioning approach is similarly narrow. Most of its tools (and research) are biased toward large, mainline firms in mature industries. That is where the data are. The BCG approach thus emphasizes the benefits of large scale and high market share, both of which are typically available only to large firms. And Porter discusses strategies to consolidate fragmented industries,[18] but spends little time discussing ways to fragment consolidated industries (a favorite tactic of small firms).[19]

Lastly, strategy itself tends to be narrow in this approach. Instead of being distinctively derived from an appreciation of the circumstances, it tends to be a pat position selected from a list of possible generic options. Yet "some of the most famous battles of business and war have been won not by doing things correctly but by breaking the rules, by *creating* the categories."[20] Two examples are McDonald's in fast food and Polaroid in instant photography.

Mintzberg summarizes the weaknesses of the positioning approach by saying that it ". . . focuses its attention on strategies that have already become generic, on industries that are already established, on groups that have already been formed, and on competitors that have already positioned themselves" and creates ". . . the belief that there is a best generic strategy for a given set of conditions, whereas strategic success may have more to do with commitment than with calculation."[21]

On the other hand, strategy formation is disorderly and ever-changing, but strategic analysis is tidy and unchanging. One of its strengths, therefore, would be as support to the process of strategy formation—conducting studies to feed into strategy making. Even so, this would work best in contexts where conditions are simple and stable enough to provide opportunities for meaningful data analysis. Managers should nevertheless be careful not to let strategy analysis drive out the qualitative factors that arise from experience and familiarity with customers, products, and other aspects of the industry.[22]

NOTES TO CHAPTER FOUR

1. Sun Tzu, *The Art of War;* trans S. G. Griffith. London: Oxford University Press, 1971.

2. Clausewitz, C. von, *On War.* Harmondsworth, Middlesex: Penguin, 1968; Liddell-Hart, B. H., *Strategy,* 2nd ed. New York: Praeger, 1967.

3. Porter, M. E., *Competitive Strategy.* New York: Free Press, 1980.

4. Porter, M. *Competitive Advantage.* New York: Free Press, 1985.

5. Mintzberg, H., "Strategy Formation: Schools of Thought." In *Perspectives on Strategic Management,* ed. James W. Frederickson. New York: Harper Business, 1990, pp. 105–235; this quotation appears on p. 126.

6. A good example of this kind of study is Hatten, K. J., and D. E. Schendel., "Heterogeneity within an Industry: Firm Conduct in the U.S Brewing Industry, 1952–1971." *Journal of Industrial Economics* 26 (1977): 97–113.

7. Porter, *Competitive Strategy.*

8. Porter, *Competitive Advantage.*

9. For a very readable examination of the literature and thinking about Total Quality Management, see Dobyns, L., and C. Crawford-Mason, *Quality or Else.* Boston: Houghton-Mifflin, 1991.

10. Miller, J. G, and P. Gilmour, "Materials Managers: Who Needs Them?" *Harvard Business Review* (July–August 1979): 57.

11. Meredith, J. R., "The Strategic Advantages of the Factory of the Future." *California Management Review* 29 (Spring 1987): 27–41; Jones, A., and T. Webb, "Introducing Computer Integrated Manufacturing." *Journal of General Management* 12 (Summer 1987): 60–74.

12. Womack, J. P., D. T Jones, and D. Roos, *The Machine That Changed the World.* New York: Rawson Associates, 1990.

13. Bowen, D. E., C. Siehl, and B. Schneider, "A Framework for Analyzing Customer Service Orientations in Manufacturing." *Academy of Management Review* 14 (1989): 75–95.

14. See, for example, Crosby, P. B., *Quality Is Free: The Art of Making Quality Certain.* New York: McGraw-Hill, 1979; and Deming, W. E., *Out of the Crisis,* 2nd ed. Cambridge, Mass.: M.I.T. Center for Advanced Engineering Study, 1986.

15. Scarpello, V., W. R. Boulton, and C. W. Hofer, "Reintegrating R&D into Business Strategy." *Journal of Business Strategy* 6 (Spring 1986): 49–56.

16. Mintzberg, "Strategy Formation," p. 131.

17. Porter, *Competitive Strategy,* p. 86.

18. Porter, *Competitive Strategy.*

19. Cooper, A. C., G. E. Willard, and C. Y. Woo, "Strategies of High-Performing New and Small Firms: A Reexamination of the Niche Concept." *Journal of Business Venturing* (1986).

20. Mintzberg, "Strategy Formation," p. 135.

21. Mintzberg, "Strategy Formation," pp. 135–136.

22. Mintzberg, H., "Crafting Strategy." *Harvard Business Review* (July–August 1987); pp. 66–75.

HOW COMPETITIVE FORCES SHAPE STRATEGY*

By Michael E. Porter

The essence of strategy formulation is coping with competition. Yet it is easy to view competition too narrowly and too pessimistically. While one sometimes hears executives complaining to the contrary, intense competition in an industry is neither coincidence nor bad luck.

Moreover, in the fight for market share, competition is not manifested only in the other players. Rather, competition in an industry is rooted in its underlying economics, and competitive forces exist that go well beyond the established combatants in a particular industry. Customers, suppliers, potential entrants, and substitute products are all competitors that may be more or less prominent or active depending on the industry.

The state of competition in an industry depends on five basic forces, which are diagrammed in Figure 1. The collective strength of these forces determines the ultimate

FIGURE 1
Elements of Industry Structure

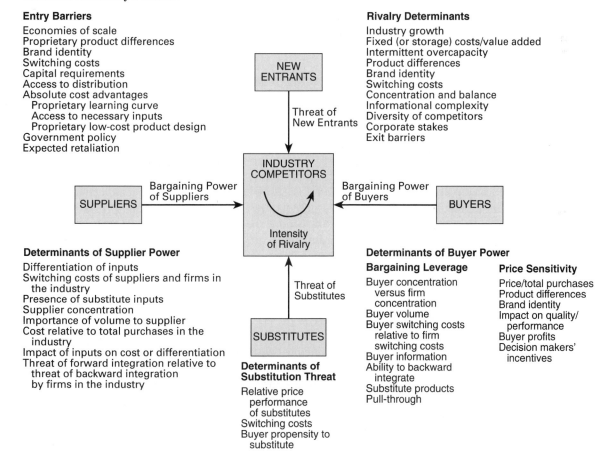

Entry Barriers

Economies of scale
Proprietary product differences
Brand identity
Switching costs
Capital requirements
Access to distribution
Absolute cost advantages
  Proprietary learning curve
  Access to necessary inputs
  Proprietary low-cost product design
Government policy
Expected retaliation

Rivalry Determinants

Industry growth
Fixed (or storage) costs/value added
Intermittent overcapacity
Product differences
Brand identity
Switching costs
Concentration and balance
Informational complexity
Diversity of competitors
Corporate stakes
Exit barriers

NEW ENTRANTS

Threat of New Entrants

INDUSTRY COMPETITORS

Bargaining Power of Suppliers

SUPPLIERS

Intensity of Rivalry

Bargaining Power of Buyers

BUYERS

Threat of Substitutes

SUBSTITUTES

Determinants of Supplier Power

Differentiation of inputs
Switching costs of suppliers and firms in the industry
Presence of substitute inputs
Supplier concentration
Importance of volume to supplier
Cost relative to total purchases in the industry
Impact of inputs on cost or differentiation
Threat of forward integration relative to threat of backward integration by firms in the industry

Determinants of Substitution Threat

Relative price performance of substitutes
Switching costs
Buyer propensity to substitute

Determinants of Buyer Power

Bargaining Leverage

Buyer concentration versus firm concentration
Buyer volume
Buyer switching costs relative to firm switching costs
Buyer information
Ability to backward integrate
Substitute products
Pull-through

Price Sensitivity

Price/total purchases
Product differences
Brand identity
Impact on quality/performance
Buyer profits
Decision makers' incentives

Used with permission of the The Free Press, a Division of Macmillan, Inc., from *Competitive Strategy: Techniques for Analyzing Industries and Competitors* by Michael E. Porter. Copyright © 1980 by The Free Press. [used in place of article's Figure 1 as it contains more detail]

---

* Originally published in the *Harvard Business Review* (March–April, 1979) and winner of the McKinsey prize for the best article in the *Review* in 1979. Copyright © 1979 by the President and Fellows of Harvard College; all rights reserved. Reprinted with deletions by permission of the *Harvard Business Review*.

profit potential of an industry. It ranges from *intense* in industries like tires, metal cans, and steel, where no company earns spectacular returns on investment, to *mild* in industries like oil field services and equipment, soft drinks, and toiletries, where there is room for quite high returns.

In the economists' "perfectly competitive" industry, jockeying for position is unbridled and entry to the industry very easy. This kind of industry structure, of course, offers the worst prospect for long-run profitability. The weaker the forces collectively, however, the greater the opportunity for superior performance.

Whatever their collective strength, the corporate strategist's goal is to find a position in the industry where his or her company can best defend itself against these forces or can influence them in its favor. The collective strength of the forces may be painfully apparent to all the antagonists; but to cope with them, the strategist must delve below the surface and analyze the sources of each. For example, what makes the industry vulnerable to entry? What determines the bargaining power of suppliers?

Knowledge of these underlying sources of competitive pressure provides the groundwork for a strategic agenda of action. They highlight the critical strengths and weaknesses of the company, animate the positioning of the company in its industry, clarify the areas where strategic changes may yield the greatest payoff, and highlight the places where industry trends promise to hold the greatest significance as either opportunities or threats. Understanding these sources also proves to be of help in considering areas for diversification.

CONTENDING FORCES

The strongest competitive force or forces determine the profitability of an industry and so are of greatest importance in strategy formulation. For example, even a company with a strong position in an industry unthreatened by potential entrants will earn low returns if it faces a superior or lower-cost substitute product—as the leading manufacturers of vacuum tubes and coffee percolators have learned to their sorrow. In such a situation, coping with the substitute product becomes the number one strategic priority.

Different forces take on prominence, of course, in shaping competition in each industry. In the oceangoing tanker industry the key force is probably the buyers (the major oil companies), while in tires it is powerful OEM buyers coupled with tough competitors. In the steel industry the key forces are foreign competitors and substitute materials.

Every industry has an underlying structure, or a set of fundamental economic and technical characteristics, that gives rise to these competitive forces. The strategist, wanting to position his company to cope best with its industry environment or to influence that environment in the company's favor, must learn what makes the environment tick.

This view of competition pertains equally to industries dealing in services and to those selling products. To avoid monotony in this article, I refer to both products and services as "products." The same general principles apply to all types of business.

A few characteristics are critical to the strength of each competitive force. I shall discuss them in this section.

Threat of Entry

New entrants to an industry bring new capacity, the desire to gain market share, and often substantial resources. Companies diversifying through acquisition into the industry from other markets often leverage their resources to cause a shakeup, as Philip Morris did with Miller beer.

The seriousness of the threat of entry depends on the barriers present and on the reaction from existing competitors that the entrant can expect. If barriers to entry are high and a newcomer can expect sharp retaliation from the entrenched competitors, obviously he will not pose a serious threat of entering.

There are six major sources of barriers to entry:

1. *Economies of scale*—These economies deter entry by forcing the aspirant either to come in on a large scale or to accept a cost disadvantage. Scale economies in production, research, marketing, and service are probably the key barriers to entry in the mainframe computer industry, as Xerox and GE sadly discovered. Economies of scale can also act as hurdles in distribution, utilization of the sales force, financing, and nearly any other part of a business.

2. *Product differentiation*—Brand identification creates a barrier by forcing entrants to spend heavily to overcome customer loyalty. Advertising, customer service, being first in the industry, and product differences are among the factors fostering brand identification. It is perhaps the most important entry barrier in soft drinks, over-the-counter drugs, cosmetics, investment banking, and public accounting. To create high fences around their businesses, brewers couple brand identification with economies of scale in production, distribution, and marketing.

3. *Capital requirements*—The need to invest large financial resources in order to compete creates a barrier to entry, particularly if the capital is required for unrecoverable expenditures in up-front advertising or R&D. Capital is necessary not only for fixed facilities but also for customer credit, inventories, and absorbing start-up losses. While major corporations have the financial resources to invade almost any industry, the huge capital requirements in certain fields, such as computer manufacturing and mineral extraction, limit the pool of likely entrants.

4. *Cost disadvantages independent of size*—Entrenched companies may have cost advantages not available to potential rivals, no matter what their size and attainable economies of scale. These advantages can stem from the effects of the learning curve (and of its first cousin, the experience curve), proprietary technology, access to the best raw materials sources, assets purchased at preinflation prices, government subsidies, or favorable locations. Sometimes cost advantages are legally enforceable, as they are through patents.

5. *Access to distribution channels*—The new boy on the block must, of course, secure distribution of his product or service. A new food product, for example, must displace others from the supermarket shelf via price breaks, promotions, intense selling efforts, or some other means. The more limited the wholesale or retail channels are and the more that existing competitors have these tied up, obviously the tougher that entry into the industry will be. Sometimes this barrier is so high that, to surmount it, a new contestant must create its own distribution channels, as Timex did in the watch industry in the 1950s.

6. *Government policy*—The government can limit or even foreclose entry to industries with such controls as license requirements and limits on access to raw materials. Regulated industries like trucking, liquor retailing, and freight forwarding are noticeable examples; more subtle government restrictions operate in fields like ski-area development and coal mining. The government also can play a major indirect role by affecting entry barriers through controls such as air and water pollution standards and safety regulations.

The potential rival's expectations about the reaction of existing competitors also will influence its decision on whether to enter. The company is likely to have second thoughts if incumbents have previously lashed out at new entrants or if:

- The incumbents possess substantial resources to fight back, including excess cash and unused borrowing power, productive capacity, or clout with distribution channels and customers.
- The incumbents seem likely to cut prices because of a desire to keep market shares or because of industrywide excess capacity.
- Industry growth is slow, affecting its ability to absorb the new arrival and probably causing the financial performance of all the parties involved to decline.

CHANGING CONDITIONS. From a strategic standpoint there are two important additional points to note about the threat of entry.

First, it changes, of course, as these conditions change. The expiration of

Polaroid's basic patents on instant photography, for instance, greatly reduced its absolute cost entry barrier built by proprietary technology. It is not surprising that Kodak plunged into the market. Product differentiation in printing has all but disappeared. Conversely, in the auto industry economies of scale increased enormously with post–World War II automation and vertical integration—virtually stopping successful new entry.

Second, strategic decisions involving a large segment of an industry can have a major impact on the conditions determining the threat of entry. For example, the actions of many U.S. wine producers in the 1960s to step up product introductions, raise advertising levels, and expand distribution nationally surely strengthened the entry roadblocks by raising economies of scale and making access to distribution channels more difficult. Similarly, decisions by members of the recreational vehicle industry to vertically integrate in order to lower costs have greatly increased the economies of scale and raised the capital cost barriers.

Powerful Suppliers and Buyers

Suppliers can exert bargaining power on participants in an industry by raising prices or reducing the quality of purchased goods and services. Powerful suppliers can thereby squeeze profitability out of an industry unable to recover cost increases in its own prices. By raising their prices, soft drink concentrate producers have contributed to the erosion of profitability of bottling companies because the bottlers, facing intense competition from powdered mixes, fruit drinks, and other beverages, have limited freedom to raise *their* prices accordingly. Customers likewise can force down prices, demand higher quality or more service, and play competitors off against each other—all at the expense of industry profits.

The power of each important supplier or buyer group depends on a number of characteristics of its market situation and on the relative importance of its sales or purchases to the industry compared with its overall business.

A *supplier* group is powerful if:

- It is dominated by a few companies and is more concentrated than the industry it sells to.
- Its product is unique or at least differentiated, or if it has built up switching costs. Switching costs are fixed costs buyers face in changing suppliers. These arise because, among other things, a buyer's product specifications tie it to particular suppliers, it has invested heavily in specialized ancillary equipment or in learning how to operate a supplier's equipment (as in computer software), or its production lines are connected to the supplier's manufacturing facilities (as in some manufacture of beverage containers).
- It is not obliged to contend with other products for sale to the industry. For instance, the competition between the steel companies and the aluminum companies to sell to the can industry checks the power of each supplier.
- It poses a credible threat of integrating forward into the industry's business. This provides a check against the industry's ability to improve the terms on which it purchases.
- The industry is not an important customer of the supplier group. If the industry *is* an important customer, suppliers' fortunes will be closely tied to the industry, and they will want to protect the industry through reasonable pricing and assistance in activities like R&D and lobbying.

A *buyer* group is powerful if:

- It is concentrated or purchases in large volumes. Large-volume buyers are particularly potent forces if heavy fixed costs characterize the industry—as they do in metal containers, corn refining, and bulk chemicals, for example—which raise the stakes to keep capacity filled.

- The products it purchases from the industry are standard or undifferentiated. The buyers, sure that they can always find alternative suppliers, may play one company against another, as they do in aluminum extrusion.
- The products it purchases from the industry form a component of its product and represent a significant fraction of its cost. The buyers are likely to shop for a favorable price and purchase selectively. Where the product sold by the industry in question is a small fraction of buyers' costs, buyers are usually much less price sensitive.
- It earns low profits, which create great incentive to lower its purchasing costs. Highly profitable buyers, however, are generally less price sensitive (that is, of course, if the item does not represent a large fraction of their costs).
- The industry's product is unimportant to the quality of the buyers' products or services. Where the quality of the buyers' products is very much affected by the industry's product, buyers are generally less price sensitive. Industries in which this situation obtains include oil field equipment, where a malfunction can lead to large losses, and enclosures for electronic medical and test instruments, where the quality of the enclosure can influence the user's impression about the quality of the equipment inside.
- The industry's product does not save the buyer money. Where the industry's product or service can pay for itself many times over, the buyer is rarely price sensitive; rather, he is interested in quality. This is true in services like investment banking and public accounting, where errors in judgment can be costly and embarrassing, and in businesses like the logging of oil wells, where an accurate survey can save thousands of dollars in drilling costs.
- The buyers pose a credible threat of integrating backward to make the industry's product. The Big Three auto producers and major buyers of cars have often used the threat of self-manufacture as a bargaining lever. But sometimes an industry engenders a threat to buyers that its members may integrate forward.

Most of these sources of buyer power can be attributed to consumers as a group as well as to industrial and commercial buyers; only a modification of the frame of reference is necessary. Consumers tend to be more price sensitive if they are purchasing products that are undifferentiated, expensive relative to their incomes, and of a sort where quality is not particularly important.

The buying power of retailers is determined by the same rules, with one important addition. Retailers can gain significant bargaining power over manufacturers when they can influence consumers' purchasing decisions, as they do in audio components, jewelry, appliances, sporting goods, and other goods.

STRATEGIC ACTION. A company's choice of suppliers to buy from or buyer groups to sell to should be viewed as a crucial strategic decision. A company can improve its strategic posture by finding suppliers or buyers who possess the least power to influence it adversely.

Most common is the situation of a company being able to choose whom it will sell to—in other words, buyer selection. Rarely do all the buyer groups a company sells to enjoy equal power. Even if a company sells to a single industry, segments usually exist within that industry that exercise less power (and that are therefore less price sensitive) than others. For example, the replacement market for most products is less price sensitive than the overall market.

As a rule, a company can sell to powerful buyers and still come away with above-average profitability only if it is a low-cost producer in its industry or if its product enjoys some unusual, if not unique, features. In supplying large customers with electric motors, Emerson Electric earns high returns because its low-cost position permits the company to meet or undercut competitors' prices.

If the company lacks a low-cost position or a unique product, selling to everyone is self-defeating because the more sales it achieves, the more vulnerable it becomes. The company may have to muster the courage to turn away business and sell only to less potent customers.

Buyer selection has been a key to the success of National Can and Crown Cork & Seal. They focus on the segments of the can industry where they can create product differentiation, minimize the threat of backward integration, and otherwise mitigate the awesome power of their customers. Of course, some industries do not enjoy the luxury of selecting "good" buyers.

As the factors creating supplier and buyer power change with time or as a result of a company's strategic decisions, naturally the power of these groups rises or declines. In the ready-to-wear clothing industry, as the buyers (department stores and clothing stores) have become more concentrated and control has passed to large chains, the industry has come under increasing pressure and suffered falling margins. The industry has been unable to differentiate its product or engender switching costs that lock in its buyers enough to neutralize these trends.

Substitute Products

By placing a ceiling on prices it can charge, substitute products or services limit the potential of an industry. Unless it can upgrade the quality of the product or differentiate it somehow (as via marketing), the industry will suffer in earnings and possibly in growth.

Manifestly, the more attractive the price-performance trade-off offered by substitute products, the firmer the lid placed on the industry's profit potential. Sugar producers confronted with the large-scale commercialization of high-fructose corn syrup, a sugar substitute, are learning this lesson today.

Substitutes not only limit profits in normal times; they also reduce the bonanza an industry can reap in boom times. In 1978 the producers of fiberglass insulation enjoyed unprecedented demand as a result of high energy costs and severe winter weather. But the industry's ability to raise prices was tempered by the plethora of insulation substitutes, including cellulose, rock wool, and styrofoam. These substitutes are bound to become an even stronger force once the current round of plant additions by fiberglass insulation producers has boosted capacity enough to meet demand (and then some).

Substitute products that deserve the most attention strategically are those that (1) are subject to trends improving their price-performance trade-off with the industry's product, or (2) are produced by industries earning high profits. Substitutes often come rapidly into play if some development increases competition in their industries and causes price reduction or performance improvement.

Jockeying for Position

Rivalry among existing competitors takes the familiar form of jockeying for position—using tactics like price competition, product introduction, and advertising slugfests. Intense rivalry is related to the presence of a number of factors:

- Competitors are numerous or are roughly equal in size and power. In many U.S. industries in recent years foreign contenders, of course, have become part of the competitive picture.
- Industry growth is slow, precipitating fights for market share that involve expansion-minded members.
- The product or service lacks differentiation or switching costs, which lock in buyers and protect one combatant from raids on its customers by another.
- Fixed costs are high or the product is perishable, creating strong temptation to cut prices. Many basic materials businesses, like paper and aluminum, suffer from this problem when demand slackens.
- Capacity is normally augmented in large increments. Such additions, as in the chlorine and vinyl chloride businesses, disrupt the industry's supply–demand balance and often lead to periods of overcapacity and price cutting.
- Exit barriers are high. Exit barriers, like very specialized assets or management's loyalty to a particular business, keep companies competing even though they may be earning low or

even negative returns on investment. Excess capacity remains functioning, and the profitability of the healthy competitors suffers as the sick ones hang on. If the entire industry suffers from overcapacity, it may seek government help—particularly if foreign competition is present.

- The rivals are diverse in strategies, origins, and "personalities." They have different ideas about how to compete and continually run head on into each other in the process. . . .

While a company must live with many of these factors—because they are built into industry economics—it may have some latitude for improving matters through strategic shifts. For example, it may try to raise buyers' switching costs or increase product differentiation. A focus on selling efforts in the fastest-growing segments of the industry or on market areas with the lowest fixed costs can reduce the impact of industry rivalry. If it is feasible, a company can try to avoid confrontation with competitors having high exit barriers and can thus sidestep involvement in bitter price cutting.

FORMULATION OF STRATEGY

Once the corporate strategist has assessed the forces affecting competition in his industry and their underlying causes, he can identify his company's strengths and weaknesses. The crucial strengths and weaknesses from a strategic standpoint are the company's posture vis-à-vis the underlying causes of each force. Where does it stand against substitutes? Against the sources of entry barriers?

Then the strategist can devise a plan of action that may include (1) positioning the company so that its capabilities provide the best defense against the competitive force; and/or (2) influencing the balance of the forces through strategic moves, thereby improving the company's position; and/or (3) anticipating shifts in the factors underlying the forces and responding to them, with the hope of exploiting change by choosing a strategy appropriate for the new competitive balance before opponents recognize it. I shall consider each strategic approach in turn.

Positioning the Company

The first approach takes the structure of the industry as given and matches the company's strengths and weaknesses to it. Strategy can be viewed as building defenses against the competitive forces or as finding positions in the industry where the forces are weakest.

Knowledge of the company's capabilities and of the causes of the competitive forces will highlight the areas where the company should confront competition and where to avoid it. If the company is a low-cost producer, it may choose to confront powerful buyers while it takes care to sell them only products not vulnerable to competition from substitutes. . . .

Influencing the Balance

When dealing with the forces that drive industry competition, a company can devise a strategy that takes the offensive. This posture is designed to do more than merely cope with the forces themselves; it is meant to alter their causes.

Innovations in marketing can raise brand identification or otherwise differentiate the product. Capital investments in large-scale facilities or vertical integration affect entry barriers. The balance of forces is partly a result of external factors and partly in the company's control.

Exploiting Industry Change

Industry evolution is important strategically because evolution, of course, brings with it changes in the sources of competition I have identified. In the familiar product life-cycle pattern, for example, growth rates change, product differentiation is said to decline as the business becomes more mature, and the companies tend to integrate vertically.

These trends are not so important in themselves; what is critical is whether they affect the sources of competition. . . .

Obviously, the trends carrying the highest priority from a strategic standpoint are those that affect the most important sources of competition in the industry and those that elevate new causes to the forefront. . . .

The framework for analyzing competition that I have described can also be used to predict the eventual profitability of an industry. In long-range planning the task is to examine each competitive force, forecast the magnitude of each underlying cause, and then construct a composite picture of the likely profit potential of the industry. . . .

The key to growth—even survival—is to stake out a position that is less vulnerable to attack from head-to-head opponents, whether established or new, and less vulnerable to erosion from the direction of buyers, suppliers, and substitute goods. Establishing such a position can take many forms—solidifying relationships with favorable customers, differentiating the product either substantively or psychologically through marketing, integrating forward or backward, establishing technological leadership.

READING

GENERIC STRATEGIES FOR LOCATING, DISTINGUISHING, AND ELABORATING THE CORE BUSINESS*

By Henry Mintzberg

Almost every serious author concerned with "content" issues in strategic management, not to mention strategy consulting "boutique," has his, her, or its own list of strategies commonly pursued by different organizations. The problem is that these lists almost always either focus narrowly on special types of strategies or else aggregate arbitrarily across all varieties of them with no real order.

In 1965, Igor Ansoff proposed a matrix of four strategies that became quite well known—market penetration, product development, market development, and diversification (1965:109). But this was hardly comprehensive. Fifteen years later, Michael Porter (1980) introduced what became the best known list of "generic strategies": cost leadership, differentiation, and focus. But the Porter list was also incomplete: while Ansoff focused on *extensions* of business strategy, Porter focused on *identifying* business strategy in the first place. Families of strategies may be divided into five broad groupings. These are strategies for:

1. *locating* the core business
2. *distinguishing* the core business
3. *elaborating* the core business
4. *extending* the core business
5. *reconceiving* the core business

This reading examines the first three of these, locating, distinguishing and elaborating the core business, since they are more relevant for business-level strategy. A compan-

---

* Abbreviated version prepared for this book of Henry Mintzberg, "Generic Strategies: Toward a Comprehensive Framework," in *Advances in Strategic Management,* Vol. 5 (Greenwich, CT: JAI Press, 1988), pp. 1–67.

ion reading in Chapter Twelve discusses the two more relevant for corporate-level strategy—extending and reconceiving the core business. These five groupings of strategies are presented as a logical hierarchy, although it should be emphasized that strategies do not necessarily develop that way in organizations.

LOCATING THE CORE BUSINESS

A business can be thought to exist at a junction in a network of industries that take raw materials and through selling to and buying from each other produce various finished products (or services). Figure 1, for example, shows a hypothetical canoe business in such a network. Core location strategies can be described with respect to the stage of the business in the network and the particular industry in question.

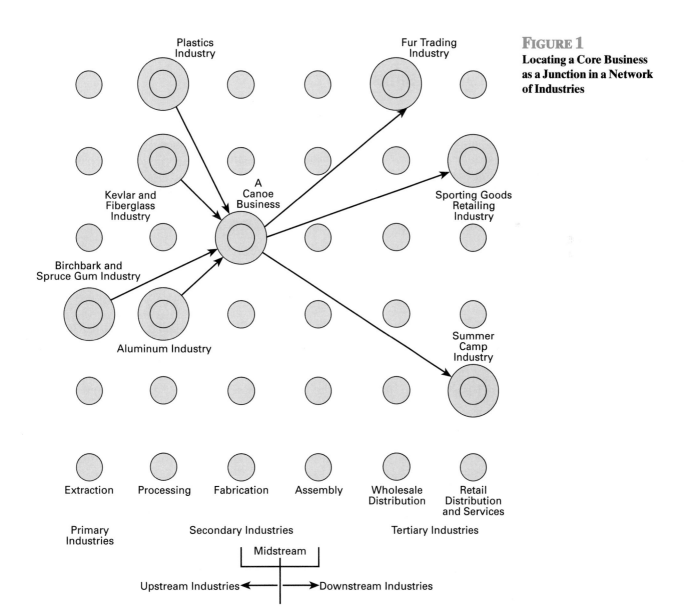

FIGURE 1
Locating a Core Business as a Junction in a Network of Industries

Strategies of Stage of Operations

Traditionally, industries have been categorized as being in the primary (raw materials extraction and conversion), secondary (manufacturing), or tertiary (delivery or other service) stage of operations. More recently, however, stage in the "stream" has been the favored form of description:

UPSTREAM BUSINESS STRATEGY. Upstream businesses function close to the raw material. As shown in the little figure, the flow of product tends to be divergent, from a basic material (wood, aluminum) to a variety of uses for it. Upstream business tends to be technology and capital intensive rather than people intensive, and more inclined to search for advantage through low costs than through high margins and to favor sales push over market pull (Galbraith, 1983:65–66).

MIDSTREAM BUSINESS STRATEGY. Here the organization sits at the neck of an hourglass, drawing a variety of inputs into a single production process out of which flows the product to a variety of users, much as the canoe business is shown in Figure 1.

DOWNSTREAM BUSINESS STRATEGY. Here a wide variety of inputs converge into a narrow funnel, as in the many products sold by a department store.

Strategies of Industry

Many factors are involved in the identification of an industry, so many that it would be difficult to develop a concise set of generic labels. Moreover, change continually renders the boundaries between "industries" arbitrary. Diverse products get bundled together so that two industries become one while traditionally bundled products get separated so that one industry becomes two. Economists in government and elsewhere spend a great deal of time trying to pin these things down, via SIC codes and the like. In effect, they try to fix what strategists try to change: competitive advantage often comes from reconceiving the definition of an industry.

DISTINGUISHING THE CORE BUSINESS

Having located the circle that identifies the core business, the next step is to open it up — to distinguish the characteristics that enable an organization to achieve competitive advantage and so to survive in its own context.

The Functional Areas

This second level of strategy can encompass a whole host of strategies in the various functional areas. As shown in Figure 2, they may include input "sourcing" strategies, throughput "processing" strategies, and output "delivery" strategies, all reinforced by a set of "supporting" strategies.

It has been popular of late to describe organizations in this way, especially since Michael Porter built his 1985 book around the "generic value chain," shown in Figure 3. Porter presents it as "a systematic way of examining all the activities a firm performs and how they interact . . . for analyzing the sources of competitive advantage" (1985:33). Such a chain, and how it performs individual activities, reflects a firm's "history, its strategy, its approach to implementing its strategy, and the underlying economies of the activities themselves" (p. 36). According to Porter, "the goal of any generic strategy" is to "create value for buyers" at a profit. Accordingly,

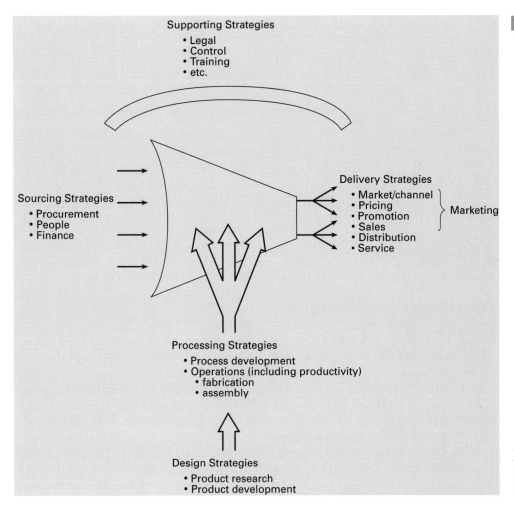

FIGURE 2
Functional Areas,
in Systems Terms

The value chain displays total value, and consists of *value activities* and *margin.* Value activities are the physically and technologically distinct activities a firm performs. These are the building blocks by which a firm creates a product valuable to its buyers. Margin is the difference between total value and the collective cost of performing the value activities. . . .

Value activities can be divided into two broad types, *primary* activities and *support* activities. Primary activities, listed along the bottom of Figure 3 are the activities involved in the physical creation of the product and its sale and transfer to the buyer as well as after-sale assistance. In any firm, primary activities can be divided into the five generic categories shown in Figure 3. Support activities support the primary activities and each other by providing purchased inputs, technology, human resources, and various firmwide functions (p. 38).[1]

---

[1] Our figure differs from Porter's in certain ways. Because he places his major emphasis on the flow of physical materials (for example, referring to "inbound logistics" as encompassing "materials handling, warehousing, inventory control, vehicle scheduling, and returns to suppliers"), he shows procurement and human resource management as support activities, whereas by taking more of a general system orientation, our Figure 2 shows them as inputs, among the sourcing strategies. Likewise, he considers technology development as support whereas Figure 2 considers it as part of processing. (Among the reasons Porter gives for doing this is that such development can pertain to "outbound logistics" or delivery as well as processing. While true, it also seems true that far more technology development pertains to operations than to delivery, especially in the manufacturing firms that are the focus of Porter's attention. Likewise, Porter describes procurement as pertaining to any of the primary activities, or other support activities for that matter. But in our terms that does not make it any less an aspect of sourcing on the inbound side.) In fact, Porter's description would relegate engineering and product design (not to mention human resources and purchasing) to staff rather than line activities, a place that would certainly be disputed in many manufacturing firms (with product design, for example, being mentioned only peripherally in his text (p. 42) alongside other "technology development" activities such as media research and servicing procedures).

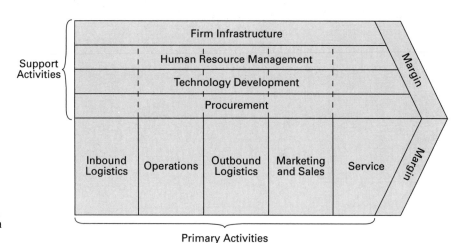

FIGURE 3
The Generic Value Chain
From Porter (1985:37).

Porter's Generic Strategies

Porter's framework of "generic strategies" has also become quite widely used. In our terms, these constitute strategies to distinguish the core business. Porter believes there are but two "basic types of competitive advantage a firm can possess: low cost or differentiation" (1985:11). These combine with the "scope" of a firm's operations (the range of market segments targeted) to produce "three *generic strategies* for achieving above-average performance in an industry: cost leadership, differentiation, and focus" (namely, narrow scope), shown in Figure 4.

To Porter, firms that wish to gain competitive advantage must "make a choice" among these: "being 'all things to all people' is a recipe for strategic mediocrity and below-average performance" (p. 12). Or in words that have become more controversial, "a firm that engages in each generic strategy but fails to achieve any of them is 'stuck in the middle' " (p. 16).

The strategies we describe in this section take their lead from Porter, but depart in some respects. We shall distinguish scope and differentiation, as Porter did in his 1980 book (focus being introduced as narrow scope in his later book), but we shall include cost leadership as a form of differentiation (namely with regard to low price). If, as Porter argues, the intention of generic strategies is to seize and sustain competitive advantage, then it is not taking the leadership on cutting costs that matters so much as using that cost leadership to underprice competitors and so to attract buyers.[2]

Thus two types of strategies for distinguishing a core business are presented here. First is a set of increasingly extensive strategies of *differentiation*. These identify what is fundamentally distinct about a business in the marketplace, in effect as perceived by its customers. Second is a set of decreasingly extensive strategies of *scope*. These identify what markets the business is after, as perceived by itself.

---

[2] In other words, it is the differentiation of price that naturally drives the functional strategy of reducing costs just as it is the differentiation of product that naturally drives the functional strategies of enhancing quality or creating innovation. (To be consistent with the label of "cost leadership," Porter would have had to call his differentiation strategy "product leadership.") A company could, of course, cut costs while holding prices equivalent to competitors. But often that means less service, lower quality, fewer features, etc., and so the customers would have to be attracted by lower prices. [See Mintzberg (1988:14–17) for a fuller discussion of this point.]

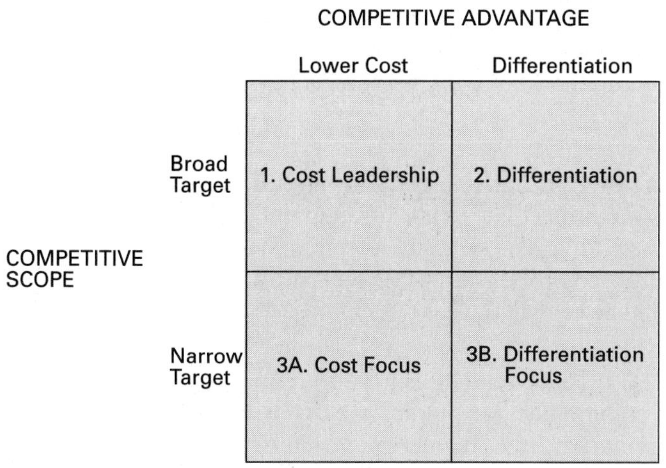

COMPETITIVE ADVANTAGE

	Lower Cost	Differentiation
Broad Target	1. Cost Leadership	2. Differentiation
Narrow Target	3A. Cost Focus	3B. Differentiation Focus

COMPETITIVE SCOPE

FIGURE 4
Porter's Generic Strategies
From Porter (1985:12)

Strategies of Differentiation

As is generally agreed in the literature of strategic management, an organization distinguishes itself in a competitive marketplace by differentiating its offerings in some way—by acting to distinguish its products and services from those of its competitors. An organization can differentiate its offerings in six basic ways:

PRICE DIFFERENTIATION STRATEGY. The most basic way to differentiate a product (or service) is simply to charge a lower price for it. All things being equal, or not too unequal, some people at least will always beat a path to the door of the cheaper product. Price differentiation may be used with a product undifferentiated in any other way—in effect, a standard design, perhaps a commodity. The producer simply absorbs the lost margin, or makes it up through a higher volume of sales. But other times, backing up price differentiation is a strategy of design intended to create a product that is intrinsically cheaper.

IMAGE DIFFERENTIATION STRATEGY. Marketing is sometimes used to feign differentiation where it does not otherwise exist—an image is created for the product. This can also include cosmetic differences to a product that do not enhance its performance in any serious way, for example, putting fins on an automobile or a fancier package around yogurt. (Of course, if it is the image that is for sale, in other words if the product is intrinsically cosmetic, as, say, in "designer" jeans, then cosmetic differences would have to be described as design differentiation.)

SUPPORT DIFFERENTIATION STRATEGY. More substantial, yet still having no effect on the product itself, is to differentiate on the basis of something that goes alongside the product, some basis of support. This may have to do with selling the product (such as special credit or 24-hour delivery), servicing the product (such as exceptional after-sales service), or providing a related product or service alongside the basic one (paddling lessons with the canoe you buy). In an article entitled "Marketing Success Through Differentiation—of Anything," Theodore Levitt has argued the interesting point that "there is no such thing as a commodity" (1980:83). His basic point is that no matter how difficult it may be to achieve differentiation by design, there is always a basis to achieve another substantial form of differentiation, especially by support.

QUALITY DIFFERENTIATION STRATEGY. Quality differentiation has to do with features of the product that make it better—not fundamentally different, just better. The product performs with (1) greater initial reliability, (2) greater long-term durability, and/or (3) superior performance.

DESIGN DIFFERENTIATION STRATEGY. Last but certainly not least is differentiation on the basis of design—offering something that is truly different, that breaks away from the "dominant design" if there is one, to provide unique features. While everyone else was making cameras whose pictures could be seen next week, Edwin Land went off and made one whose pictures could be seen in the next minute.

UNDIFFERENTIATION STRATEGY. To have no basis for differentiation is a strategy too, indeed by all observation a common one, and in fact one that may be pursued deliberately. Given enough room in a market, and a management without the skill or the will to differentiate what it sells, there can be place for copycats.

Scope Strategies

The second dimension to distinguish the core business is by the *scope* of the products and services offered, in effect the extent of the markets in which they are sold. Scope is essentially a demand-driven concept, taking its lead from the market—what exists out there. Differentiation, in contrast, is a supply-driven concept, rooted in the nature of the product itself—what is offered to the market (Smith, 1956). Differentiation, by concentrating on the product offered, adopts the perspective of the customer, existing only when that person perceives some characteristic of the product that adds value. And scope, by focusing on the market served, adopts the perspective of the producer, existing only in the collective mind of the organization—in terms of how it diffuses and disaggregates its markets (in other words, what marketing people call segmentation). Scope strategies include the following:

UNSEGMENTATION STRATEGY. "One size fits all": the Ford Model T, table salt. In fact, it is difficult to think of any product today that is not segmented in some way. What the unsegmented strategy really means then is that the organization tries to capture a wide chunk of the market with a basic configuration of the product.

SEGMENTATION STRATEGIES. The possibilities for segmentation are limitless, as are the possible degrees. We can, however, distinguish a range of this, from a simple segmentation strategy (three basic sizes of paper clips) to a hyperfine segmentation strategy (as in designer lighting). Also, some organizations seek to be *comprehensive,* to serve all segments (department store, large cigarette manufacturers), others to be *selective,* targeting carefully only certain segments (e.g., "clean" mutual funds).

NICHE STRATEGY. Niche strategies focus on a single segment. Just as the panda bear has found its biological niche in the consumption of bamboo shoots, so too is there the canoe company that has found its market niche in the fabrication of racing canoes, or the many firms which are distinguished only by the fact that they provide their highly standardized offerings in a unique place, a geographical niche—the corner grocery story, the regional cement producer, the national Red Cross office. All tend to follow "industry" recipes to the letter, providing them to their particular community. All strategies are in some sense niche, characterized as much by what they exclude as by what they include. No organization can be all things to all people. The all-encompassing strategy is no strategy at all.

CUSTOMIZING STRATEGIES. Customization is the limiting case of segmentation: disaggregation of the market to the point where each customer constitutes a unique segment. *Pure* customization, in which the product is developed from scratch for each customer, is found in the architecturally designed house and the special purpose machine. It infiltrates the entire value chain: the product is not only delivered in a personalized way, not only assembled and even fabricated to order, but is also designed for the individual customer in the first place. Less ambitious but probably more common is *tailored* customization: a basic design is modified, usually in the fabrication stage, to the customer's needs or specifications (certain housing, protheses modified to fit the bone joints of each customer, and so on). *Standardized* customization means that final products are assembled to individual requests for standard components—as in automobiles in which the customer is allowed to choose color, engine, and various accessories. Advances in computer-aided design and manufacturing (CAD, CAM) will doubtlessly cause a proliferation of standardized customization, as well as tailored customization.

ELABORATING THE CORE BUSINESS

An organization can elaborate a business in a number of ways. It can develop its product offerings within that business, it can develop its market via new segments, new channels, or new geographical areas, or it can simply push the same products more vigorously through the same markets. Back in 1965, Igor Ansoff showed these strategies (as well as one to be discussed in the next section) as presented in Figure 5.

PENETRATION STRATEGIES. Penetration strategies work from a base of existing products and existing markets, seeking to penetrate the market by increasing the organization's share of it. This may be done by straight *expansion* or by the *takeover* of existing competitors. Trying to expand sales with no fundamental change in product or market (buying market share through more promotion, etc.) is at one and the same time the most obvious thing to do and perhaps the most difficult to succeed at, because, at least in a relatively stable market, it means extracting market share from other firms, which logically leads to increased competition. Takeover, where possible, obviously avoids this, but perhaps at a high cost. The harvesting strategy, popularized in the 1970s by the Boston Consulting Group, in some ways represents the opposite of the penetration strategies. The way to deal with "cash cows"—businesses with high market shares but low growth potential—was to harvest them, cease investment and exploit whatever potential remained. The mixing of the metaphors may have been an indication of the dubiousness of the strategy, since to harvest a cow is, of course, to kill it.

	Existing Product	New Product
Existing Market	Penetration Strategies	Product Development Strategies
New Market	Market Development Strategies	Diversification Strategies

FIGURE 5

Ways to Elaborate a Given Business

From Ansoff (1965:109), with minor modifications; see also Johnson and Jones (1957:52).

MARKET DEVELOPMENT STRATEGIES. A predominant strategy here is *market elaboration,* which means promoting existing products in new markets—in effect broadening the scope of the business by finding new market segments, perhaps served by new channels. Product substitution is a particular case of market elaboration, where uses for a product are promoted that enable it to substitute for other products. *Market consolidation* is the inverse of market elaboration, namely reducing the number of segments. But this is not just a strategy of failure. Given the common tendency to proliferate market segments, it makes sense for the healthy organization to rationalize them periodically, to purge the excesses.

GEOGRAPHIC EXPANSION STRATEGIES. An important form of market development can be geographic expansion—carrying the existing product offering to new geographical areas, anywhere from the next block to across the world. When this also involves a strategy of geographic rationalization—locating different business functions in different places—it is sometimes referred to as a "global strategy." The IKEA furniture company, for example, designs in Scandinavia, sources in Eastern Europe among other places, and markets in Western Europe and North America.

PRODUCT DEVELOPMENT STRATEGIES. Here we can distinguish a simple *product extension* strategy from a more extensive *product line proliferation* strategy, and their counterparts, *product line rationalization.* Offering new or modified products in the same basic business is another obvious way to elaborate a core business—from cornflakes to bran flakes and rice crispies, eventually offering every permutation and combination of the edible grains. This may amount to differentiation by design, if the products are new and distinctive, or else to no more than increased scope through segmentation, if standardized products are added to the line. Product line proliferation means aiming at comprehensive product segmentation—the complete coverage of a given business. Rationalization means culling products and thinning the line to get rid of overlaps or unprofitable excesses. Again we might expect cycles of product extension and rationalization, at least in businesses (such as cosmetics and textiles) predisposed to proliferation in their product lines.

CHAPTER 5
· ·

STRATEGY FORMATION

As we discussed in Chapter One, most people think of strategy as something that is formulated and then implemented. That is, people tend to believe that organizational members rationally think out their actions before they carry them out. Chapters Three and Four emphasized this view. Those chapters dealt with **prescriptive** ways of thinking (schools of thought) about strategy, or how strategy should be formed.

There are other ways of thinking about strategy. In Chapter One, we introduced the idea that strategy is something that could form as well as be formulated. In this chapter, we begin to examine **descriptive** schools of thought about the strategy process.[1] These schools of thought address the question, "How does strategy actually form in organizations?" As it turns out, accurate description improves prescription: Knowing about how organizations actually form strategies helps managers do a better job of managing strategy.

THE DESCRIPTIVE SCHOOLS

This section briefly discusses the more important descriptive schools of strategy formation—cultural, political, entrepreneurial, environmental, and configurational—that later chapters cover in more detail. We then treat the learning school at length in the balance of this chapter.

THE CULTURAL SCHOOL. We examine this school in Chapter Seven. The cultural school[2] suggests that strategy formation is a process of collective behavior, rooted in the beliefs shared by the members of the organization. The entrepreneurial school (discussed below) is based on individual vision; the cultural school is based on **collective vision**. Organizations that exemplify the cultural school of strategy formation tend not to use design, planning, or analysis. They tend to create patterns in streams of action over time (i.e., strategies) that are based on **norms** and **values** held by their members. A good

103

example would be Sony Corporation, whose strategy is based on strong norms of innovation and service to humanity through the artful combination of mechanics and electronics.

THE POLITICAL SCHOOL. Chapter Eight looks at this approach, which views strategy formation as a power process. Authority is the basis of the design and planning schools, while knowledge is the basis of the positioning or learning schools. Here, however, power becomes the basis of strategy formation, manifested either internally (micro politics)[3] in political conflict, or externally (macro politics)[4] where the whole organization exerts its influence politically.

THE ENTREPRENEURIAL SCHOOL. Chapter Nine examines this way of thinking about strategy formation. In one way, the entrepreneurial school[5] is similar to the design school in that a powerful CEO is the architect of strategy. The difference is that the entrepreneurial school glorifies the entrepreneur *acting alone.* His or her **individual vision** is the root of strategy formation. In contrast to the design school, this vision may never be explicit or articulated, probably not even consciously considered by the entrepreneur. But it guides his or her actions, which in turn govern the actions of the firm's members.

THE ENVIRONMENTAL SCHOOL. The basic idea of this approach is that environmental forces dictate strategy to organizations.[6] Strategy formation therefore becomes a process of adaptation. Strategists, whose role is curtailed, are reduced to finding viable niches to which their firms may adapt. We cover this process to some extent in Chapter Eleven.

THE CONFIGURATIONAL SCHOOL. In a sense, the whole of Part III of this book deals with the configurational school. This approach advocates the idea that we can best describe behaviors of organizations in terms of *distinct, integrated, clusters of characteristics* called **configurations.**[7] Here, strategy formation is an episodic process. For a discernable period, there is a match between a type of organization, a type of environment, and a type of strategy process. For example, a bureaucratic organization, in a simple, stable environment, tends to use elaborate planning techniques to maintain its strategies over long periods of time. One interesting finding from research guided by this school of thought is that changes to new configurations tend to happen rapidly, in **quantum leaps.** Episodes are relatively long, but the changes from one episode to the next are rather short.

THE LEARNING SCHOOL

This school of thought sees strategy formation as an **emergent** process.[8] According to the learning school, strategies evolve, as strategists, sometimes individually but more often collectively, come to know a context and their organization's ability to deal with it. After many tries, using various approaches, the organization converges on a pattern of behavior that works.

One premise of this school is that two things may prevent the organization from deliberately controlling the strategy process. The first is a dynamic and complex environment, where strategies conceived deliberately run the risk of becoming obsolete (or worse) before the organization can implement them. Better to let things emerge, and then make the necessary adjustments. The second obstacle is a knowledge base diffused throughout the organization, not concentrated at the top. In this situation, top managers may not be privy to the information needed to conceive a deliberate strategy. Better to

· ·

let the strategy emerge through the actions of the people who know about the latest advances in technology, or the most recent trends in consumer taste, etc.

No Dichotomy between Formulation and Implementation

One interesting result of this process is that it becomes difficult to distinguish formulation from implementation.[9] In the prescriptive schools, formulation has to end, more or less, before the organization can implement; in other words, action follows thinking. But in the learning school, acting and thinking are intertwined. The organization tries something. It doesn't fully work, so it tries something different. That works better, but various members of the organization see possibilities for improvement. So the organization makes more changes, and the process continues to cycle between action and thinking. Who can say that something clearly identifiable as "formulation" took place before something equally obvious called "implementation"?

A second premise of the learning school is that strategy need not emanate exclusively from an elite strategist, such as a CEO who designs the organization's strategy.[10] Of course the CEO is capable of learning too, but proponents of the learning school argue that learning can occur anywhere in the organization. Strategy may thus be influenced or formed by many different actors. This is particularly true for innovative or professional organizations: the key learning tends to occur at low levels of the organization's hierarchy where the scientists or professional practitioners will be the first to get the critical feedback.

Strategic learning is like any trial-and-error learning—people act, then must make sense of their actions, alter them as seems appropriate, and try again. Actions may be taken by anybody who can learn and has the means to perform the actions and learn from them. This means that strategies can take root in many different kinds of places in the organization. Once the actions are taken, the strategies may be left on their own to flounder or develop, or they may be championed by higher-level managers. These champions may also integrate them into existing strategies. Successful strategies will proliferate, perhaps spontaneously. Or else the process may be conscious, as managers recognize emergent patterns and formally make them deliberate.

This points to a leadership role different from the image presented by the prescriptive schools. Instead of preconceiving deliberate strategies, strategic managers must manage the process of strategic learning. This means paying particular attention to the people involved in the process and to the structures used to foster learning. Strategic management therefore involves artfully weaving together the subtle relationships between thought, action, and learning. These are the themes of Henry Mintzberg's reading, "Crafting Strategy."

CRAFTING STRATEGY

Mintzberg compares strategists to potters. Managers are craftsmen and strategy is their clay. Like potters displaying a retrospective of their work, they sit between a past (of corporate capabilities) and a future (of market opportunities). Like potters, managers should bring an equally intimate knowledge of the materials at hand. As Mintzberg describes it, crafting has many desirable aspects—involvement, intimacy with the materials, long experience, and commitment. Other words he associates with craft are "dedication, experience, involvement with the material, the personal touch, mastery of detail, [and] a sense of harmony and integration."

The prescriptive models assert that to have a coherent strategy, everything must be thought through in advance. Mintzberg asserts that there are other ways to proceed.

People may act and get ideas, good ideas, from their actions. In other words, they learn. This happens for potters and other craftsmen, why shouldn't it also happen for strategists? It is true that good analysis is needed in large organizations, but Mintzberg alludes to problems that arise when this attitude is taken too far. People need to be able to act, then think about their actions. They also need to be allowed to think, then act on their thoughts. Just thinking or just acting is not enough—there must be an intelligent blending of thought and action.[11] Mintzberg points out that *deliberate* strategy, by definition, means going from intention to realization with *little or no deviation.* In other words, a deliberate strategy fulfills a plan, no matter what new information is gained along the way. A purely deliberate strategy would thus preclude learning.

On the other hand, a purely emergent strategy would be very volatile, always in danger of veering off into chaos. Mintzberg points to one of the many paradoxes of strategy—strategy tends to mean stability. That is the meaning of plan as well as pattern in action. Yet if we want strategy to be a learning process, how can we expect it to be stable? After all, learning is not useful unless we change because of what we learned. But just having a strategy creates a situation that goes beyond stability—it creates **resistance to change.** Of course it is during those periods of stability that firms tend to have their greatest successes. You do well by exploiting a strategy, not by searching for it.

The Configurational School points out that the typical strategy cycle is a long stable period, punctuated by a brief quantum leap, followed by another long stable period, and so forth. Why do organizations wait so long, until they are out of synch with their environments, before they make key changes? The main reason seems to be that frequent change is too expensive, monetarily and in human terms. Firms seem to find it more lucrative to live with a slightly out-of-alignment strategy for a while to hold back change until it is absolutely necessary. Smaller, more creative firms, however, seem to have shorter periods of stability and more frequent changes. There seems to be such a movement even in large firms, which is the basis of the "thriving on chaos" idea.[12]

Mintzberg ends with several prescriptions, designed to help strategic managers apply the lessons of the learning school. The first is "managing stability": even though many people think of strategic management as change-oriented, the research shows that firms have their highest levels of performance during stable periods. Successful strategic managers must learn how to exploit this. But they must also learn how to "detect discontinuities" especially through experience. This goes along with the idea that strategic managers have to "know the business," in terms of the details *and* the big picture. Mintzberg also argues that managers need to "manage patterns" and learn how to "reconcile change and continuity," so that strategic change can take place before it's too late and the established patterns have become dysfunctional.

THE HONDA EFFECT

The ideas of the learning school are well illustrated in Richard Pascale's reading, "The Honda Effect," which tells the story of Honda's meteoric rise to dominance in the U.S. motorcycle market. The classic explanation for Honda's success related to planning and positioning. The actual story shows that the roots of success were flexibility and a *willingness to learn.*

The Honda effect highlights the differences between the planning approach and the learning approach. One encourages analysis (reflection), while the other encourages *action.* The Honda story also illustrates the notion that many ideas for successful strategies come from sources other than top management. Pascale calls this the "little brain" theory of strategy. Its opposite, the "big brain" theory, is reminiscent of the design or planning schools. Pascale goes on to say that success in forming strategy is a matter of being persistent (in the sense of always trying to improve), but also making sure to adapt and change as the organization learns what works and what doesn't.

Pascale ends by defining strategy as "all the things necessary for the successful functioning of organization as an adaptive mechanism." This will strike some as messy; it's not a "clean," crisp definition. But that is the point. Strategy is not the precise statement of intentions but the realization of whatever it takes to make things work. This kind of activity is probably going to be messy (even if ultimately successful). It's one thing to know that strategy may form in a learning-oriented kind of way. That does not necessarily help in managing the process. This is the theme of the last reading in this chapter.

STRATEGY FORMATION

LOGICAL INCREMENTALISM: MANAGING STRATEGY FORMATION

Quinn and Voyer discuss logical incrementalism. The first part of the article articulates its advantages, while the second part provides details on its use.

Logical incrementalism neutralizes the negative effects of both the formal planning approach and the power-based approach. There are many corporate decisions that affect strategy but are "soft," that is, not appropriate for quantitative analysis. Changes in overall organizational structure have implications that are not quantifiable. External (especially governmental) relations are riddled with many problematic and unpredictable areas not amenable to quantitative analysis. Questions of acquisition, divestiture, or divisional control often include social, organizational, and political factors. Even more problematic are value and expectation changes, and their effects on worker and professional relationships. And technological changes can not be predicted with the kind of precision necessary for quantitative modeling or forecasting.

The way a firm resolves these kinds of issues can have major effects on its future. No organization can possibly foresee the timing, severity, or even the nature of all precipitating events. Also, there might not be the time, the resources, or the information to do a full formal analysis. Yet decisions made under pressure can be difficult to reverse later. The most logical response may thus be to proceed in small steps that can be assessed, reviewed, and changed, until decision makers have a better idea of what is happening. Quinn and Voyer discuss two examples—diversification and major reorganization.

They emphasize that formal planning can make a contribution but only as an aid to the incremental process. There are two reasons why planning practices might act as a spur for incrementalism. First, most planning is "bottom up," and the people at the bottom have an interest in the existing products and processes. Consequently, managers need to proceed incrementally to overcome some of these vested interests. Second, most plans are meant to be "living" or "ever green," intended as frameworks only. They can be changed as the organization learns; the plans will still be good for providing guidance and consistency to the incremental decisions. Thus, formal plans used as frameworks can be a good support mechanism for incremental logic and can encourage it. They point out, though, that efforts to do "total posture planning" typically fail. Actual strategies *evolve.*

Quinn and Voyer claim that strategy deals with the unknowable, not the uncertain. Uncertainty means that several future events are possible, but that the decision maker cannot assign probabilities to their occurrence. The authors' point is that it is not even realistic to expect decision makers to think of possible future events, let alone probable ones. It is simply not possible to know what the future will bring, at least not in the kind of long period which characterizes strategic decision making. The implication is that managers should strive to make their organizations as flexible, responsive, and adaptive as possible. That way, no matter what happens, there is the chance for an appropriate response. Part of this capability involves using logical incrementalism—proceeding in small steps, going from the broad to the specific, and waiting for as long as possible before committing.

The authors emphasize that logical incrementalism is not "muddling." It is conscious, purposeful, active, *good* management. If a strategist were to proceed incrementally, but without knowing what he or she was doing, without tying everything to an overarching sense of direction, without being aware of the political and social structures that exist in the organization, without trying to build awareness and commitment to what he or she was trying to accomplish—*that* would be muddling. But the *logical* incrementalist proceeds in small steps *because* he or she is aware of these issues. Accordingly, logical incrementalism is conscious, purposeful, productive, *good* management.

Quinn and Voyer list several management processes that characterize logical incremental management. Managers must be ahead of the formal information system. They must strive to build organizational awareness. They must make people in the organization believe that new ideas are credible and legitimate. Since things will not always work out as hoped, managers must be ready to accept tactical shifts and partial solutions. The prescriptive models prescribe that strategy be developed by top management, as an integrated whole, using analytical techniques, *before* any action takes place. Implementation is by lower-level participants. Here, instead, top management encourages others to undertake many small, low-risk projects. These are unlikely to attract opposition, the way a large-scale proposal might. Progress is made, but it is partial, tentative, and experimental. As events unfurl, the solutions to several initially unrelated problems tend to flow together into a new synthesis.

Logical incrementalism is a highly political way of managing. Managers must try to broaden political support for new strategic thrusts. They must also be willing to overcome any serious opposition. They should launch trial balloons and be willing to wait systematically for conditions to improve. Planned delays allow the organization to talk through threatening issues, work out implications of new solutions, and gain an improved information base. Sometimes, strategic ideas that are initially resisted can gain acceptance and commitment simply by the passage of time. Many top executives, planners, and change agents consciously arrange such "gestation periods."

Managers who use logical incrementalism can create pockets of commitment in the organization, by doing things such as sponsoring small projects that could result in a big change. They should consciously build flexibility into the organization. But they must be willing to halt the process by crystallizing the focus of the organization, and by formalizing its commitment to the new direction. Once the organization is moving in its new direction, managers must act to make sure that they do not become too rigid. But these activities do not necessarily come in a linear sequence. The organization must be flexible, responsive, and adaptable. Lastly, the authors point out that incremental does not mean piecemeal. Effective strategic managers keep the organization focused by concentrating on only a few key thrusts, and by managing coalitions rigorously.

Notes to Chapter Five

1. This chapter borrows heavily from Mintzberg, H., "Strategy Formation: Schools of Thought." In *Perspectives on Strategic Management,* ed. James W. Frederickson. New York: Harper Business, 1990, pp. 105–235.

2. This school was pioneered by Rhenman and Normann. See Normann, R., "Organizational Innovativeness: Product Variation and Reorientation." *Administrative Science Quarterly* 16 (1971): 203–15; Normann, R., *Management for Growth.* Chichester: John Wiley, 1977; and Rhenman, E., *Organization Theory for Long-Range Planning.* London: John Wiley, 1973.

3. The most influential source for this school's micro view is Allison, G. T., *Essence of Decision: Explaining the Cuban Missile Crisis.* Boston: Little, Brown, 1971.

4. Some influential sources for the macro approach in this school are: Perrow, C., *Organizational Analysis: A Sociological View.* Belmont, Calif.: Wadsworth, 1970; and Pfeffer, J., and G. R. Salancik, *The External Control of Organizations: A Resource Dependence Perspective.* New York: Harper & Row, 1978.

5. Schumpeter, J. A., *Theory of Economic Development.* Cambridge, Mass.: Harvard University Press, 1934; see also Cole, A. H., *Business Enterprise in Its Social Setting.* Cambridge, Mass.: Harvard University Press, 1959.

6. Aldrich, H. E., and J. Pfeffer, "Environments of Organizations." In *Annual Review of Sociology,* vol. 2., ed. A. Inkeles. Palo Alto, Calif.: Annual Reviews, 1976; Aldrich, H. E., *Organizations and Environments.* Englewood Cliffs, N.J.: Prentice Hall, 1979; and Hannan, M. T., and J. Freeman, "The Population Ecology of Organizations." *American Journal of Sociology* 82 (1977): 929–64.

7. Miller, D., and P. Friesen, *Organizations: A Quantum View.* Englewood Cliffs, N.J.: Prentice Hall, 1984; Miller, D., and H. Mintzberg, "The Case for Configuration." In *Beyond Method,* ed. G. Morgan. Beverly Hills, Calif.: Sage, 1983, pp. 57–73.

8. Mintzberg, H., and J. Waters, "Of Strategies, Deliberate and Emergent." *Strategic Management Journal* 6 (1985): 257–72; and Quinn, J. B., *Strategies for Change: Logical Incrementalism.* Homewood, Ill.: Richard D. Irwin, 1980.

9. Mintzberg, "Strategy Formation," p. 154.

10. Ibid.

11. Weick, K. "Managerial Thought in the Context of Action." In Suresh Srivastva, ed., *The Executive Mind.* San Francisco: Jossey-Bass, 1983, pp. 221–242.

12. Peters, T. *Thriving on Chaos.* New York: Harper & Row, 1987.

CRAFTING STRATEGY*

READING

By Henry Mintzberg

Imagine someone planning strategy. What likely springs to mind is an image of orderly thinking: a senior manager, or a group of them, sitting in an office formulating courses of action that everyone else will implement on schedule. The keynote is reason—rational control, the systematic analysis of competitors and markets, of company strengths and weaknesses, the combination of these analyses producing clear, explicit, full-blown strategies.

Now imagine someone *crafting* strategy. A wholly different image likely results, as different from planning as craft is from mechanization. Craft evokes traditional skill, dedication, perfection through the mastery of detail. What springs to mind is not so much thinking and reason as involvement, a feeling of intimacy and harmony with the materials at hand, developed through long experience and commitment. Formulation and implementation merge into a fluid process of learning through which creative strategies evolve.

My thesis is simple: the crafting image better captures the process by which effective strategies come to be. The planning image, long popular in the literature, distorts these processes and thereby misguides organizations that embrace it unreservedly.

In developing this thesis, I shall draw on the experiences of a single craftsman, a potter, and compare them with the results of a research project that tracked the strategies of a number of corporations across several decades. Because the two contexts are so obviously different, my metaphor, like my assertion, may seem farfetched at first. Yet if we think of a craftsman as an organization of one, we can see that he or she must also re-

*Originally published in the *Harvard Business Review* (July–August 1987) and winner of McKinsey prize for second best article in the *Review* 1987. Copyright © 1987 by the President and Fellows of Harvard College; all rights reserved. Reprinted with deletions by permission of the *Harvard Business Review.*

solve one of the great challenges the corporate strategist faces: knowing the organization's capabilities well enough to think deeply enough about its strategic direction. By considering strategy making from the perspective of one person, free of all the paraphernalia of what has been called the strategy industry, we can learn something about the formation of strategy in the corporation. For much as our potter has to manage her craft, so too managers have to craft their strategy.

At work, the potter sits before a lump of clay on the wheel. Her mind is on the clay, but she is also aware of sitting between her past experiences and her future prospects. She knows exactly what has and has not worked for her in the past. She has an intimate knowledge of her work, her capabilities, and her markets. As a craftsman, she senses rather than analyzes these things; her knowledge is "tacit." All these things are working in her mind as her hands are working the clay. The product that emerges on the wheel is likely to be in the tradition of her past work, but she may break away and embark on a new direction. Even so, the past is no less present, projecting itself into the future.

In my metaphor, managers are craftsmen and strategy is their clay. Like the potter, they sit between the past of corporate capabilities and a future of market opportunities. And if they are truly craftsmen, they bring to their work an equally intimate knowledge of the materials at hand. That is the essence of crafting strategy.

STRATEGIES ARE BOTH PLANS FOR THE FUTURE AND PATTERNS FROM THE PAST

Ask almost anyone what strategy is, and they will define it as a plan of some sort, an explicit guide to future behavior. Then ask them what strategy a competitor or a government or even they themselves have actually pursued. Chances are they will describe consistency in *past* behavior—a pattern in action over time. Strategy, it turns out, is one of those words that people define in one way and often use in another, without realizing the difference.

The reason for this is simple. Strategy's formal definition and its Greek military origins notwithstanding, we need the word as much to explain past actions as to describe intended behavior. After all, if strategies can be planned and intended, they can also be pursued and realized (or not realized, as the case may be). And pattern in action, or what we call realized strategy, explains that pursuit. Moreover, just as a plan need not produce a pattern (some strategies that are intended are simply not realized), so too a pattern need not result from a plan. An organization can have a pattern (or realized strategy) without knowing it, let alone making it explicit.

Patterns, like beauty, are in the mind of the beholder, of course. But finding them in organizations is not very difficult. But what about intended strategies, those formal plans and pronouncements we think of when we use the term *strategy?* Ironically, here we run into all kinds of problems. Even with a single craftsman, how can we know what her intended strategies really were? If we could go back, would we find expressions of intention? And if we could, would we be able to trust them? We often fool ourselves, as well as others, by denying our subconscious motives. And remember that intentions are cheap, at least when compared with realizations.

Reading the Organization's Mind

If you believe all this has more to do with the Freudian recesses of a craftsman's mind than with the practical realities of producing automobiles, then think again. For who knows what the intended strategies of an organization really mean, let alone what they are? Can we simply assume in this collective context that the company's intended strategies are represented by its formal plans or by other statements emanating from the executive suite? Might these be just vain hopes or rationalizations or ploys to fool the competition? And even if expressed intentions do exist, to what extent do various people in the organization share them? How do we read the collective mind? Who is the strategist anyway?

The traditional view of strategic management resolves these problems quite simply, by what organizational theorists call attribution. You see it all the time in the business press. When General Motors acts, it's because its CEO has made a strategy. Given realization, there must have been intention, and that is automatically attributed to the chief.

In a short magazine article, this assumption is understandable. Journalists don't have a lot of time to uncover the origins of strategy, and GM is a large, complicated organization. But just consider all the complexity and confusion that gets tucked under this assumption—all the meetings and debates, the many people, the dead ends, the folding and unfolding of ideas. Now imagine trying to build a formal strategy-making system around that assumption. Is it any wonder that formal strategic planning is often such a resounding failure?

To unravel some of the confusion—and move away from the artificial complexity we have piled around the strategy-making process—we need to get back to some basic concepts. The most basic of all is the intimate connection between thought and action. That is the key to craft, and so also to the crafting of strategy.

STRATEGIES NEED NOT BE DELIBERATE—THEY CAN ALSO EMERGE, MORE OR LESS

Virtually everything that has been written about strategy making depicts it as a deliberate process. First we think, then we act. We formulate, then we implement. The progression seems so perfectly sensible. Why would anybody want to proceed differently?

Our potter is in the studio, rolling the clay to make a waferlike sculpture. The clay sticks to the rolling pin, and a round form appears. Why not make a cylindrical vase? One idea leads to another, until a new pattern forms. Action has driven thinking: a strategy has emerged.

Out in the field, a salesman visits a customer. The product isn't quite right, and together they work out some modifications. The salesman returns to his company and puts the changes through; after two or three more rounds, they finally get it right. A new product emerges, which eventually opens up a new market. The company has changed strategic course.

In fact, most salespeople are less fortunate than this one or than our craftsman. In an organization of one, the implementor is the formulator, so innovations can be incorporated into strategy quickly and easily. In a large organization, the innovator may be ten levels removed from the leader who is supposed to dictate strategy and may also have to sell the idea to dozens of peers doing the same job.

Some salespeople, of course, can proceed on their own, modifying products to suit their customers and convincing skunkworks in the factory to produce them. In effect, they pursue their own strategies. Maybe no one else notices or cares. Sometimes, however, their innovations do get noticed, perhaps years later, when the company's prevalent strategies have broken down and its leaders are groping for something new. Then the salesperson's strategy may be allowed to pervade the system, to become organizational.

Is this story farfetched? Certainly not. We've all heard stories like it. But since we tend to see only what we believe, if we believe that strategies have to be planned, we're unlikely to see the real meaning such stories hold.

Consider how the National Film Board of Canada (NFB) came to adopt a feature-film strategy. The NFB is a federal government agency, famous for its creativity and expert in the production of short documentaries. Some years back, it funded a filmmaker on a project that unexpectedly ran long. To distribute his film, the NFB turned to theaters and so inadvertently gained experience in marketing feature-length films. Other filmmakers caught onto the idea, and eventually the NFB found itself pursuing a feature-film strategy—a pattern of producing such films.

My point is simple, deceptively simple: strategies can *form* as well as be *formulated.* A realized strategy can emerge in response to an evolving situation, or it can be brought about deliberately, through a process of formulation followed by implementation. But when these planned intentions do not produce the desired actions, organizations are left with unrealized strategies.

Today we hear a great deal about unrealized strategies, almost always in concert with the claim that implementation has failed. Management has been lax, controls have been loose, people haven't been committed. Excuses abound. At times, indeed, they may be valid. But often these explanations prove too easy. So some people look beyond implementation to formulation. The strategists haven't been smart enough.

While it is certainly true that many intended strategies are ill conceived, I believe that the problem often lies one step beyond, in the distinction we make between formulation and implementation, the common assumption that thought must be independent of and precede action. Sure, people could be smarter—but not only by conceiving more clever strategies. Sometimes they can be smarter by allowing their strategies to develop gradually, through the organization's actions and experiences. Smart strategists appreciate that they cannot always be smart enough to think through everything in advance.

Hands and Minds

No craftsman thinks some days and works others. The craftsman's mind is going constantly, in tandem with her hands. Yet large organizations try to separate the work of minds and hands. In so doing, they often sever the vital feedback link between the two. The salesperson who finds a customer with an unmet need may possess the most strategic bit of information in the entire organization. But that information is useless if he or she cannot create a strategy in response to it or else convey the information to someone who can—because the channels are blocked or because the formulators have simply finished formulating. The notion that strategy is something that should happen way up there, far removed from the details of running an organization on a daily basis, is one of the great fallacies of conventional strategic management. And it explains a good many of the most dramatic failures in business and public policy today.

Strategies like the NFB's that appear without clear intentions—or in spite of them—can be called emergent. Actions simply converge into patterns. They may become deliberate, of course, if the pattern is recognized and then legitimated by senior management. But that's after the fact.

All this may sound rather strange, I know. Strategies that emerge? Managers who acknowledge strategies already formed? Over the years, we have met with a good deal of resistance from people upset by what they perceive to be our passive definition of a word so bound up with proactive behavior and free will. After all, strategy means control—the ancient Greeks used it to describe the art of the army general.

Strategic Learning

But we have persisted in this usage for one reason: learning. Purely deliberate strategy precludes learning once the strategy is formulated; emergent strategy fosters it. People take actions one by one and respond to them, so that patterns eventually form.

Our craftsman tries to make a freestanding sculptural form. It doesn't work, so she rounds it a bit here, flattens it a bit there. The result looks better, but still isn't quite right. She makes another and another and another. Eventually, after days or months or years, she finally has what she wants. She is off on a new strategy.

In practice, of course, all strategy making walks on two feet, one deliberate, the other emergent. For just as purely deliberate strategy making precludes learning, so purely emergent strategy making precludes control. Pushed to the limit, neither approach makes much sense. Learning must be coupled with control. That is why we use the word *strategy* for both emergent and deliberate behavior.

Likewise, there is no such thing as a purely deliberate strategy or a purely emergent one. No organization—not even the ones commanded by those ancient Greek generals—knows enough to work everything out in advance, to ignore learning en route. And no one—not even a solitary potter—can be flexible enough to leave everything to happenstance, to give up all control. Craft requires control just as it requires responsiveness to the material at hand. Thus deliberate and emergent strategy form the end points of a continuum along which the strategies that are crafted in the real world may be found. Some strategies may approach either end, but many more fall at intermediate points.

EFFECTIVE STRATEGIES DEVELOP IN ALL KINDS OF STRANGE WAYS

Effective strategies can show up in the strangest places and develop through the most unexpected means. There is no one best way to make strategy.

The form for a ceramic cat collapses on the wheel, and our potter sees a bull taking shape. Clay sticks to a rolling pin, and a line of cylinders results. Wafers come into being because of a shortage of clay and limited kiln space while visiting a studio in France. Thus errors become opportunities, and limitations stimulate creativity. The natural propensity to experiment, even boredom, likewise stimulates strategic change.

Organizations that craft their strategies have similar experiences. Recall the National Film Board with its inadvertently long film. Or consider its experiences with experimental films, which made special use of animation and sound. For 20 years, the NFB produced a bare but steady trickle of such films. In fact, every film but one in that trickle was produced by a single person, Norman McLaren, the NFB's most celebrated filmmaker. McLaren pursued a *personal strategy* of experimentation, deliberate for him perhaps (though who can know whether he had the whole stream in mind or simply planned one film at a time?) but not for the organization. Then 20 years later, others followed his lead and the trickle widened, his personal strategy becoming more broadly organizational.

While the NFB may seem like an extreme case, it highlights behavior that can be found, albeit in muted form, in all organizations. Those who doubt this might read Richard Pascale's account of how Honda stumbled into its enormous success in the American motorcycle market [the following article in this book].

Grass-Roots Strategy Making

These strategies all reflect, in whole or part, what we like to call a grass-roots approach to strategic management. Strategies grow like weeds in a garden. They take root in all kinds of places, wherever people have the capacity to learn (because they are in touch with the situation) and the resources to support that capacity. These strategies become organizational when they become collective, that is, when they proliferate to guide the behavior of the organization at large.

Of course, this view is overstated. But it is no less extreme than the conventional view of strategic management, which might be labeled the hothouse approach. Neither is right. Reality falls between the two. Some of the most effective strategies we uncovered in our research combined deliberation and control with flexibility and organizational learning.

Consider first what we call the *umbrella strategy*. Here senior management sets out broad guidelines (say, to produce only high-margin products at the cutting edge of technology or to favor products using bonding technology) and leaves the specifics (such as what these products will be) to others lower down in the organization. This strategy is not only deliberate (in its guidelines) and emergent (in its specifics), but it is also deliberately emergent, in that the process is consciously managed to allow strategies to emerge en route. IBM used the umbrella strategy in the early 1960s with the impending 360 series, when its senior management approved a set of broad criteria for the design of a family of computers later developed in detail throughout the organization. [See the IBM case in this section.]

Deliberately emergent, too, is what we call the *process strategy*. Here management controls the process of strategy formation—concerning itself with the design of the structure, its staffing, procedures, and so on—while leaving the actual content to others.

Both process and umbrella strategies seem to be especially prevalent in businesses that require great expertise and creativity—a 3M, a Hewlett-Packard, a National Film Board. Such organizations can be effective only if their implementors are allowed to be formulators, because it is people way down in the hierarchy who are in touch with the situation at hand and have the requisite technical expertise. In a sense, these are organizations peopled with craftsmen, all of whom must be strategists.

STRATEGIC REORIENTATIONS HAPPEN IN BRIEF, QUANTUM LEAPS

The conventional view of strategic management, especially in the planning literature, claims that change must be continuous: the organization should be adapting all the time. Yet this view proves to be ironic because the very concept of strategy is rooted in stability, not change. As this same literature makes clear, organizations pursue strategies to set direction, to lay out courses of action, and to elicit cooperation from their members around common, established guidelines. By any definition, strategy imposes stability on an organization. No stability means no strategy (no course to the future, no pattern from the past). Indeed, the very fact of having a strategy, and especially of making it explicit (as the conventional literature implores managers to do), creates resistance to strategic change!

What the conventional view fails to come to grips with, then, is how and when to promote change. A fundamental dilemma of strategy making is the need to reconcile the forces for stability and for change—to focus efforts and gain operating efficiencies on the one hand, yet adapt and maintain currency with a changing external environment on the other.

Quantum Leaps

Our own research and that of colleagues suggest that organizations resolve these opposing forces by attending first to one and then to the other. Clear periods of stability and change can usually be distinguished in any organization: while it is true that particular strategies may always be changing marginally, it seems equally true that major shifts in strategic orientation occur only rarely.

In our study of Steinberg, Inc., a large Quebec supermarket chain headquartered in Montreal, we found only two important reorientations in the 60 years from its founding to the mid-1970s: a shift to self-service in 1933 and the introduction of shopping centers and public financing in 1953. At Volkswagenwerk, we saw only one between the late 1940s and the 1970s, the tumultuous shift from the traditional Beetle to the Audi-type design. And at Air Canada, we found none over the airline's first four decades, following its initial positioning.

Our colleagues at McGill, Danny Miller and Peter Friesen (1984), found this pattern of change so common in their studies of large numbers of companies (especially the high-performance ones) that they built a theory around it, which they labeled the quantum theory of strategic change. Their basic point is that organizations adopt two distinctly different modes of behavior at different times.

Most of the time they pursue a given strategic orientation. Change may seem continuous, but it occurs in the context of that orientation (perfecting a given retailing formula, for example) and usually amounts to doing more of the same, perhaps better as well. Most organizations favor these periods of stability because they achieve success not by changing strategies but by exploiting the ones they have. They, like craftsmen, seek continuous improvement by using their distinctive competencies on established courses.

While this goes on, however, the world continues to change, sometimes slowly, occasionally in dramatic shifts. Thus gradually or suddenly, the organization's strategic orientation moves out of sync with its environment. Then what Miller and Friesen call a strategic revolution must take place. That long period of evolutionary change is suddenly punctuated by a brief bout of revolutionary turmoil in which the organization quickly alters many of its established patterns. In effect, it tries to leap to a new stability quickly to reestablish an integrated posture among a new set of strategies, structures, and culture.

But what about all those emergent strategies, growing like weeds around the organization? What the quantum theory suggests is that the really novel ones are generally held in check in some corner of the organization until a strategic revolution becomes necessary. Then, as an alternative to having to develop new strategies from scratch or having to import generic strategies from competitors, the organization can turn to its own emerging patterns to find its new orientation. As the old, established strategy disintegrates, the seeds of the new one begin to spread.

This quantum theory of change seems to apply particularly well to large established, mass-production companies, like a Volkswagenwerk. Because they are especially reliant on standardized procedures, their resistance to strategic reorientation tends to be especially fierce. So we find long periods of stability broken by short disruptive periods of revolutionary change. Strategic reorientations really are cultural revolutions.

In more creative organizations we see a somewhat different pattern of change and stability, one that is more balanced. Companies in the business of producing novel outputs apparently need to run off in all directions from time to time to sustain their creativity. Yet they also need to settle down after such periods to find some order in the resulting chaos—convergence following divergence.

Whether through quantum revolutions or cycles of convergence and divergence, however, organizations seem to need to separate in time the basic forces for change and stability, reconciling them by attending to each in turn. Many strategic failures can be attributed either to mixing the two or to an obsession with one of these forces at the expense of the other.

The problems are evident in the work of many craftsmen. On the one hand, there are those who seize on the perfection of a single theme and never change. Eventually the creativity disappears from their work and the world passes them by—much as it did Volkswagenwerk until the company was shocked into its strategic revolution. And then there are those who are always changing, who flit from one idea to another and never settle down. Because no theme or strategy ever emerges in their work, they cannot exploit or even develop any distinctive competence. And because their work lacks definition, identity crises are likely to develop, with neither the craftsmen nor their clientele knowing what to make of it. Miller and Friesen (1978: 921) found this behavior in conventional business too; they label it "the impulsive firm running blind." How often have we seen it in companies that go on acquisition sprees?

TO MANAGE STRATEGY, THEN, IS TO CRAFT THOUGHT AND ACTION, CONTROL AND LEARNING, STABILITY AND CHANGE

The popular view sees the strategist as a planner or as a visionary, someone sitting on a pedestal dictating brilliant strategies for everyone else to implement. While recognizing the importance of thinking ahead and especially of the need for creative vision in this pedantic world, I wish to propose an additional view of the strategist—as a pattern recognizer, a learner if you will—who manages a process in which strategies (and visions) can emerge as well as be deliberately conceived. I also wish to redefine that strategist, to extend that someone into the collective entity made up of the many actors whose interplay speaks an organization's mind. This strategist *finds* strategies no less than creates them, often in patterns that form inadvertently in its own behavior.

What, then, does it mean to craft strategy? Let us return to the words associated with craft: dedication, experience, involvement with the material, the personal touch, mastery of detail, a sense of harmony and integration. Managers who craft strategy do not spend much time in executive suites reading MIS reports or industry analyses. They are involved, responsive to their materials, learning about their organizations and industries through personal touch. They are also sensitive to experience, recognizing that while individual vision may be important, other factors must help determine strategy as well.

MANAGE STABILITY. Managing strategy is mostly managing stability, not change. Indeed, most of the time senior managers should not be formulating strategy at all; they should be getting on with making their organizations as effective as possible in pursuing the strategies they already have. Like distinguished craftsmen, organizations become distinguished because they master the details.

To manage strategy, then, at least in the first instance, is not so much to promote change as to know *when* to do so. Advocates of strategic planning often urge managers to plan for perpetual instability in the environment (for example, by rolling over five-year plans annually). But this obsession with change is dysfunctional. Organizations that reassess their strategies continuously are like individuals who reassess their jobs or their marriages continuously—in both cases, they will drive themselves crazy or else reduce themselves to inaction. The formal planning process repeats itself so often and so mechanically that it desensitizes the organization to real change, programs it more and more deeply into set patterns, and thereby encourages it to make only minor adaptations.

So-called strategic planning must be recognized for what it is: a means, not to create strategy, but to program a strategy already created—to work out its implications formally. It is essentially analytic in nature, based on decomposition, while strategy creation is essentially a process of synthesis. That is why trying to create strategies through formal planning most often leads to extrapolating existing ones or copying those of competitors.

This is not to say that planners have no role to play in strategy formation. In addition to programming strategies created by other means, they can feed ad hoc analyses into the strategy-making process at the front end to be sure that the hard data are taken into consideration. They can also stimulate others to think strategically. And of course people called planners can be strategists too, so long as they are creative thinkers who are in touch with what is relevant. But that has nothing to do with the technology of formal planning.

DETECT DISCONTINUITY. Environments do not change on any regular or orderly basis. And they seldom undergo continuous dramatic change, claims about our "age of discontinuity" and environmental "turbulence" notwithstanding. (Go tell people who lived through the Great Depression or survivors of the siege of Leningrad during World War II that ours are turbulent times.) Much of the time, change is minor and even temporary and requires no strategic response. Once in a while there is a truly significant discontinuity or, even less often, a gestalt shift in the environment, where everything important seems to change at once. But these events, while critical, are also easy to recognize.

The real challenge in crafting strategy lies in detecting the subtle discontinuities that may undermine a business in the future. And for that, there is no technique, no program, just a sharp mind in touch with the situation. Such discontinuities are unexpected and irregular, essentially unprecedented. They can be dealt with only by minds that are attuned to existing patterns yet able to perceive important breaks in them. Unfortunately, this form of strategic thinking tends to atrophy during the long periods of stability that most organizations experience. So the trick is to manage within a given strategic orientation most of the time yet be able to pick out the occasional discontinuity that really matters. The ability to make that kind of switch in thinking is the essence of strategic management. And it has more to do with vision and involvement than it does with analytic technique.

KNOW THE BUSINESS. Note the kind of knowledge involved in strategic thinking: not intellectual knowledge, not analytical reports or abstracted facts and figures (though these can certainly help), but personal knowledge, intimate understanding, equivalent to the craftsman's feel for the clay. Facts are available to anyone; this kind of knowledge is not. Wisdom is the word that captures it best. But wisdom is a word that has been lost in the bureaucracies we have built for ourselves, systems designed to distance leaders from operating details. Show me managers who think they can rely on formal planning to create their strategies, and I'll show you managers who lack intimate knowledge of their businesses or the creativity to do something with it.

Craftsmen have to train themselves to see, to pick up things other people miss. The same holds true for managers of strategy. It is those with a kind of peripheral vision who are best able to detect and take advantage of events as they unfold.

MANAGE PATTERNS. Whether in an executive suite in Manhattan or a pottery studio in Montreal, a key to managing strategy is the ability to detect emerging patterns and help them take shape. The job of the manager is not just to preconceive specific strategies but also to recognize their emergence elsewhere in the organization and intervene when appropriate.

Like weeds that appear unexpectedly in a garden, some emergent strategies may need to be uprooted immediately. But management cannot be too quick to cut off the unexpected, for tomorrow's vision may grow out of today's aberration. (Europeans, after all, enjoy salads made from the leaves of the dandelion, America's most notorious weed.) Thus some patterns are worth watching until their effects have more clearly manifested themselves. Then those that prove useful can be made deliberate and be incorporated into the formal strategy, even if that means shifting the strategic umbrella to cover them.

To manage in this context, then, is to create the climate within which a wide variety of strategies can grow. In more complex organizations, this may mean building flexible structures, hiring creative people, defining broad umbrella strategies, and watching for the patterns that emerge.

RECONCILE CHANGE AND CONTINUITY. Finally, managers considering radical departures need to keep the quantum theory of change in mind. As Ecclesiastes reminds us, there is a time to sow and a time to reap. Some new patterns must be held in check until the organization is ready for a strategic revolution, or at least a period of divergence. Managers who are obsessed with either change or stability are bound eventually to harm their organizations. As pattern recognizer, the manager has to be able to sense when to exploit an established crop of strategies and when to encourage new strains to displace the old.

While strategy is a word that is usually associated with the future, its link to the past is no less central. As Kierkegaard once observed, life is lived forward but understood backward. Managers may have to live strategy in the future, but they must understand it through the past.

Like potters at the wheel, organizations must make sense of the past if they hope to manage the future. Only by coming to understand the patterns that form in their own behavior do they get to know their capabilities and their potential. Thus crafting strategy, like managing craft, requires a natural synthesis of the future, present, and past.

READING | THE HONDA EFFECT*

By Richard T. Pascale

At face value, "strategy" is an innocent noun. Webster defines it as the large-scale planning and direction of operations. In the business context, it pertains to a process by which a firm searches and analyzes its environment and resources in order to (1) select opportunities defined in terms of markets to be served and products to serve them and (2) make discrete decisions to invest resources in order to achieve identified objectives. (Bower, 1970: 7–8).

But for a vast and influential population of executives, planners, academics, and consultants, strategy is more than a conventional English noun. It embodies an implicit model of how organizations should be guided and consequently, proconfigures our way of thinking. Strategy formulation (1) is generally assumed to be driven by senior management whom we expect to set strategic direction, (2) has been extensively influenced by empirical models and concepts, and (3) is often associated with a laborious strategic planning process that, in some companies, has produced more paper than insight.

A $500-million-a-year "strategy" industry has emerged in the United States and Europe comprised of management consultants, strategic planning staffs, and business school academics. It caters to the unique emphasis that American and European companies place upon this particular aspect of managing and directing corporations.

Words often derive meaning from their cultural context. *Strategy* is one such word and nowhere is the contrast of meanings more pronounced than between Japan and the United States. The Japanese view the emphasis we place on "strategy" as we might regard their enthusiasm for Kabuki or sumo wrestling. They note our interest not with an

---

* Excerpted from an article originally entitled "Perspectives on Strategy: The Real Story Behind Honda's Success," *California Management Review XXVI*, no. 3, pp. 47–72. Copyright © 1984 by the Regents of the University of California. Reprinted by permission of the Regents.

intent of acquiring similar ones but for insight into our peculiarities. The Japanese are somewhat distrustful of a single "strategy" for in their view any idea that focuses attention does so at the expense of peripheral vision. They strongly believe that *peripheral vision* is essential to discerning changes in the customer, the technology or competition, and is the key to corporate survival over the long haul. They regard any prospensity to be driven by a single-minded strategy as a weakness.

The Japanese have particular discomfort with strategic concepts. While they do not reject ideas such as the experience curve or portfolio theory outright they regard them as a stimulus to perception. They have often ferreted out the "formula" of their concept-driven American competitors and exploited their inflexibility. In musical instruments, for example (a mature industry facing stagnation as birthrates in the United States and Japan declined), Yamaha might have classified its products as "cash cows" and gone on to better things (as its chief U.S. competitor, Baldwin United, had done). Instead, beginning with a negligible share of the U.S. market, Yamaha plowed ahead and destroyed Baldwin's seemingly unchallengeable dominance. YKK's success in zippers against Talon (a Textron division) and Honda's outflanking of Harley-Davidson (a former AMF subsidiary) in the motorcycle field provide parallel illustrations. All three cases involved American conglomerates, wedded to the portfolio concept, that had classified pianos, zippers, and motorcycles as mature businesses to be harvested rather than nourished and defended. Of course, those who developed portfolio theory and other strategic concepts protest that they were never intended to be mindlessly applied in setting strategic direction. But most would also agree that there is a widespread tendency in American corporations to misapply concepts and to otherwise become strategically myopic—ignoring the marketplace, the customer, and the problems of execution. This tendency toward misapplication, being both pervasive and persistent over several decades, is a phenomenon that the literature has largely ignored [for exceptions, see Hayes and Abernathy, 1980:67; Hayes and Garvin, 1982:71]. There is a need to identify explicitly the factors that influence how we conceptualize strategy—and which foster its misuse.

HONDA: THE STRATEGY MODEL

In 1975, Boston Consulting Group (BCG) presented the British government its final report: *Strategy Alternatives for the British Motorcycle Industry*. This 120-page document identified two key factors leading to the British demise in the world's motorcycle industry:

- Market share loss and profitability declines
- Scale economy disadvantages in technology, distribution, and manufacturing

During the period 1959 to 1973, the British share of the U.S. motorcycle industry had dropped from 49% to 9%. Introducing BCG's recommended strategy (of targeting market segments where sufficient production volumes could be attained to be price competitive) the report states:

> The success of the Japanese manufacturers originated with the growth of their domestic market during the 1950s. As recently as 1960, only 4 percent of Japanese motorcycle production was exported. By this time, however, the Japanese had developed huge production volumes in small motorcycles in their domestic market, and volume-related cost reductions had followed. This resulted in a highly competitive cost position which the Japanese used as a springboard for penetration of world markets with small motorcycles in the early 1960s (BCG, 1975:xiv).

The BCG study was made public by the British government and rapidly dissemi-
nated in the United States. It exemplifies the necessary (and, I argue, insufficient) strategist's perspective of

- examining competition primarily from an intercompany perspective,
- at a high level of abstraction,
- with heavy reliance on microeconomic concepts (such as the experience curve).

Case writers at Harvard Business School, UCLA, and the University of Virginia
quickly condensed the BCG report for classroom use in case discussions. It currently enjoys extensive use in first-term courses in business policy.

Of particular note in the BCG study, and in the subsequent Harvard Business
School rendition, is the historical treatment of Honda.

The mix of competitors in the U.S. motorcycle market underwent a major shift in the
1960s. Motorcycle registrations increased from 575,000 in 1960 to 1,382,000 in 1965. Prior to
1960 the U.S. market was served mainly by Harley-Davidson of U.S.A., BSA, Triumph and
Norton of U.K. and Moto-Guzzi of Italy. Harley was the market leader with total 1959 sales
of $16.6 million. After the second world war, motorcycles in the U.S.A. attracted a very lim-
ited group of people other than police and army personnel who used motorcycles on the
job. While most motorcyclists were no doubt decent people, groups of rowdies who went
around on motorcycles and called themselves by such names as "Hell's Angels," "Satan's
Slaves" gave motorcycling a bad image. Even leather jackets which were worn by motorcyclists as a protective device acquired an unsavory image. A 1953 movie called "The Wild
Ones" starring a 650cc Triumph, a black leather jacket and Marlon Brando gave the rowdy
motorcyclists wide media coverage. The stereotype of the motorcyclist was a leather-jack-
eted, teenage troublemaker.

Honda established an American subsidiary in 1959—American Honda Motor
Company. This was in sharp contrast to other foreign producers who relied on distributors.
Honda's marketing strategy was described in the 1963 annual report as "With its policy of
selling, not primarily to confirmed motorcyclists but rather to members of the general public who had never before given a second thought to a motorcycle. . . ." Honda started its
push in the U.S. market with the smallest, lightweight motorcycles. It had a three-speed
transmisson, an automatic clutch, five horsepower (the American cycle only had two and a
half), an electric starter and step through frame for female riders. And it was easier to handle. The Honda machines sold for under $250 in retail compared with $1,000–$1,500 for the
bigger American or British machines. Even at that early date Honda was probably superior
to other competitors in productivity.

By June 1960 Honda's Research and Development effort was staffed with 700 de-
signers/engineers. This might be contrasted with 100 engineers/draftsmen employed by . . .
(European and American competitors). In 1962 production per man-year was running at
159 units, (a figure not reached by Harley-Davidson until 1974). Honda's net fixed asset investment was $8170 per employee . . . (more than twice its European and American com-
petitors). With 1959 sales of $55 million Honda was already the largest motorcycle producer
in the world.

Honda followed a policy of developing the market region by region. They started on
the West Coast and moved eastward over a period of four–five years. Honda sold 2,500 machines in the U.S. in 1960. In 1961 they lined up 125 distributors and spent $150,000 on re-
gional advertising. Their advertising was directed to the young families, their advertising
theme was "You Meet the Nicest People on a Honda." This was a deliberate attempt to dis-
sociate motorcycles from rowdy, Hell's Angels type people.

Honda's success in creating demand for lightweight motorcycles was phenomenal.
American Honda's sales went from $500,000 in 1960 to $77 million in 1965. By 1966 the
market share data showed the ascendancy of Japanese producers and their success in selling lightweight motorcycles. [Honda had 63% of the market.] . . . Starting from virtually
nothing in 1960, the lightweight motorcycles had clearly established their lead (Purkayastha, 1981: 5, 10, 11, 12).

QUOTING FROM THE BCG REPORT:

The Japanese motorcycle industry, and in particular Honda, the market leader, present a
[consistent] picture. The basic philosophy of the Japanese manufacturers is that high vol-

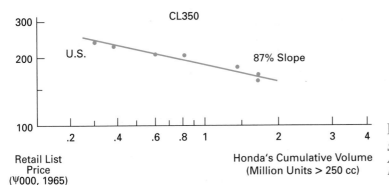

FIGURE 1

Source: BCG (1975) "Strategy Alternatives for the British Motorcycle Industry."

umes per model provide the potential for high productivity as a result of using capital intensive and highly automated techniques. Their marketing strategies are therefore directed towards developing these high model volumes, hence the careful attention that we have observed them giving to growth and market share.

The overall result of this philosophy over time has been that the Japanese have now developed an entrenched and leading position in terms of technology and production methods. . . . The major factors which appear to account for the Japanese superiority in both these areas are . . . (specialized production systems, balancing engineering and market requirements, and the cost efficiency and reliability of suppliers) (BCG, pp. 59, 40).

As evidence of Honda's strategy of taking position as low cost producer and exploiting economies of scale, other sources cite Honda's construction in 1959 of a plant to manufacture 30,000 motorcycles per month well ahead of existing demand at the time. (Up until then Honda's most popular models sold 2,000–3,000 units per month.) (Sakiya, 1982:119)

The overall picture as depicted by the quotes exemplifies the "strategy model." Honda is portrayed as a firm dedicated to being the low price producer, utilizing its dominant market position in Japan to force entry into the U.S. market, expanding that market by redefining a leisure class ("Nicest People") segment, and exploiting its comparative advantage via aggressive pricing and advertising. Richard Rumelt, writing the teaching note for the UCLA adaptation of the case states: "The fundamental contribution of BCG is not the experience curve per se but the ever-present assumption that differences in cost (or efficiency) are the fundamental components of strategy." (Rumelt, 1980:2).

THE ORGANIZATIONAL PROCESS PERSPECTIVE

On September 10, 1982, the six Japanese executives responsible for Honda's entry into the U.S. motorcycle market in 1959 assembled in Honda's Tokyo headquarters. They had gathered at my request to describe in fine grain detail the sequence of events that had led to Honda's ultimate position of dominance in the U.S. market. All were in their sixties; three were retired. The story that unfolded, greatly abbreviated below, highlights miscalculation, serendipity, and organizational learning—counterpoints to the streamlined "strategy" version related earlier. . . .

Any account of Honda's successes must grasp at the outset the unusual character of its founder, Sochiro Honda, and his partner, Takeo Fujisawa. Honda was an inventive genius with a large ego and mercurial temperament, given to bouts of "philandering" (to use his expression) (Sakiya, 1979). . . .

Postwar Japan was in desperate need of transportation. Motorcycle manufacturers proliferated, producing clip-on engines that converted bicycles into makeshift "mopeds." Honda was among these but it was not until he teamed up with Fujisawa in

1949 that the elements of a successful enterprise began to take shape. Fujisawa provided money as well as financial and marketing strengths. In 1950 their first D-type motorcycle was introduced. They were, at that juncture, participating in a fragmented industry along with 247 other manufacturers. Other than its sturdy frame, this introductory product was unnoteworthy and did not enjoy great commercial success. (Sakiya, 1979, 1982).

Honda embodied a rare combination of inventive ability and ultimate self-confidence. His motivation was not primarily commercial. Rather, the company served as a vehicle to give expression to his inventive abilities. A successful company would provide a resource base to pursue, in Fujisawa's words, his "grandiose dream." Fujisawa continues, "There was no end to his pursuit of technology." (Sakiya, 1982).

Fujisawa, in an effort to save the faltering company, pressed Honda to abandon their noisy two-stroke engine and pursue a four-stroke design. The quieter four-stroke engines were appearing on competitive motorcycles, therefore threatening Honda with extinction. Mr. Honda balked. But a year later, Honda stunned Fujisawa with a breakthrough design that doubled the horsepower of competitive four-stroke engines. With this innovation, the firm was off and putting, and by 1951 demand was brisk. There was no organization, however, and the plant was chaotic (Sakiya, 1982). Strong demand, however, required early investment in a simplified mass production process. As a result, *primarily* due to design advantages, and secondarily to production methods, Honda became one of the four or five industry leaders by 1954 with 15 percent market share (data provided by company). . . .

For Fujisawa, the engine innovation meant increased sales and easier access to financing. For Mr. Honda, the higher horsepower engine opened the possibility of pursuing one of his central ambitions in life—to race his motorcycle and win. . . .

Fujisawa, throughout the fifties, sought to turn Honda's attention from his enthusiasm with racing to the more mundane requirements of running an enterprise. By 1956, as the innovations gained from racing had begun to pay off in vastly more efficient engines, Fujisawa pressed Honda to adapt this technology for a commercial motorcycle (Sakiya, 1979, 1982). Fujisawa had a particular segment in mind. Most motorcyclists in Japan were male and the machines were used primarily as an alternative form of transportation to trains and buses. There were, however, a vast number of small commercial establishments in Japan that still delivered goods and ran errands on bicycles. Trains and buses were inconvenient for these activities. The pursestrings of these small enterprises were controlled by the Japanese wife—who resisted buying conventional motorcycles because they were expensive, dangerous, and hard to handle. Fujisawa challenged Honda: Can you use what you've learned from racing to come up with an inexpensive, safe-looking motorcycle that can be driven with one hand (to facilitate carrying packages).

In 1958, the Honda 50cc Supercub was introduced—with an automatic clutch, three-speed transmission, automatic starter, and the safe, friendly look of a bicycle (without the stigma of the outmoded mopeds). Owing almost entirely to its high horsepower but *lightweight 50cc engine* (not to production efficiencies), it was affordable. Overnight, the firm was overwhelmed with orders. Engulfed by demand, they sought financing to build a new plant with a 30,000 unit per month capacity. "It wasn't a speculative investment," recalls one executive. "We had the proprietary technology, we had the market, and the demand was enormous." (The plant was completed in mid-1960.) Prior to its opening, demand was met through makeshift, high cost, company-owned assembly and farmed-out assembly through subcontractors. By the end of 1959, Honda had skyrocketed into first place among Japanese motorcycle manufacturers. Of its total sales that year of 285,000 units, 168,000 were Supercubs.

Fujisawa utilized the Supercub to restructure Honda's channels of distribution. For many years, Honda had rankled under the two-tier distribution system that prevailed in the industry. These problems had been exacerbated by the fact that Honda was a late entry and had been carried as secondary line by distributors whose loyalties lay with their older manufacturers. Further weakening Honda's leverage, all manufacturer sales were on a consignment basis.

Deftly, Fujisawa had characterized the Supercub to Honda's distributors as "something much more like a bicycle than a motorcycle." The traditional channels, to their later regret, agreed. Under amicable terms Fujisawa began selling the Supercub directly to retailers—and primarily through bicycle shops. Since these shops were small and numerous (approximately 12,000 in Japan), sales on consignment were unthinkable. A cash-on-delivery system was installed, giving Honda significantly more leverage over its dealerships than the other motorcycle manufacturers enjoyed.

The stage was now set for exploration of the U.S. market. Mr. Honda's racing conquests in the late 1950s had given substance to his convictions about his abilities. . . .

Two Honda executives—the soon-to-be-named president of American Honda, Kihachiro Kawashima, and his assistant—arrived in the United States in late 1958. Their itinerary: San Francisco, Los Angeles, Dallas, New York, and Columbus. Mr. Kawashima recounts his impressions:

> My first reaction after travelling across the United States was: How could we have been so stupid as to start a war with such a vast and wealthy country! My second reaction was discomfort. I spoke poor English. We dropped in on motorcycle dealers who treated us discourteously and in addition, gave the general impression of being motorcycle enthusiasts who, secondarily, were in business. There were only 3,000 motorcycle dealers in the United States at the time and only 1,000 of them were open five days a week. The remainder were open on nights and weekends. Inventory was poor, manufacturers sold motorcycles to dealers on consignment, the retailers provided consumer financing; after-sales service was poor. It was discouraging.
>
> My other impression was that everyone in the United States drove an automobile—making it doubtful that motorcycles could ever do very well in the market. However, with 450,000 motorcycle registrations in the U.S. and 60,000 motorcycles imported from Europe each year it didn't seem unreasonable to shoot for 10 percent of the import market. I returned to Japan with that report.
>
> In truth, we had no strategy other than the idea of seeing if we could sell something in the United States. It was a new frontier, a new challenge, and it fit the "success against all odds" culture that Mr. Honda had cultivated. I reported my impressions to Fujisawa—including the seat-of-the-pants target of trying, over several years, to attain a 10 percent share of U.S. imports. He didn't probe that target quantitatively. We did not discuss profits or deadlines for breakeven. Fujisawa told me if anyone could succeed, I could and authorized $1 million for the venture.
>
> The next hurdle was to obtain a currency allocation from the Ministry of Finance. They were extraordinarily skeptical. Toyota had launched the Toyopet in the U.S. in 1958 and had failed miserably. "How could Honda succeed?" they asked. Months went by. We put the project on hold. Suddenly, five months after our application, we were given the go-ahead—but at only a fraction of our expected level of commitment. "You can invest $250,000 in the U.S. market," they said, "but only $110,000 in cash." The remainder of our assets had to be in parts and motorcycle inventory.
>
> We moved into frantic activity as the government, hoping we would give up on the idea, continued to hold us to the July 1959 start-up timetable. Our focus, as mentioned earlier, was to compete with the European exports. We knew our products at the time were good but not far superior. Mr. Honda was especially confident of the 250cc and 305cc machines. The shape of the handlebar on these larger machines looked like the eyebrow of Buddha, which he felt was a strong selling point. Thus, after some discussion and with no compelling criteria for selection, we configured our start-up inventory with 25 percent of each of our four products—the 50cc Supercub and the 125cc, 250cc, and 305cc machines. In dollar value terms, of course, the inventory was heavily weighted toward the larger bikes.
>
> The stringent monetary controls of the Japanese government together with the unfriendly reception we had received during our 1958 visit caused us to start small. We chose Los Angeles where there was a large second and third generation Japanese community, a climate suitable for motorcycle use, and a growing population. We were so strapped for cash that the three of us shared a furnished apartment that rented for $80 per month. Two of us slept on the floor. We obtained a warehouse in a run-down section of the city and waited for the ship to arrive. Not daring to spare our funds for equipment, the three of us stacked the motorcycle crates three high—by hand, swept the floors, and built and maintained the parts bin.

We were entirely in the dark the first year. We were not aware the motorcycle business in the United States occurs during a seasonable April-to-August window— and our timing coincided with the closing of the 1959 season. Our hard-learned experiences with distributorships in Japan convinced us to try to go to the retailers direct. We ran ads in the motorcycle trade magazine for dealers. A few responded. By spring of 1960, we had forty dealers and some of our inventory in their stores—mostly larger bikes. A few of the 250cc and 305cc bikes began to sell. Then disaster struck.

By the first week of April 1960, reports were coming in that our machines were leaking oil and encountering clutch failure. This was our lowest moment. Honda's fragile reputation was being destroyed before it could be established. As it turned out, motorcycles in the United States are driven much farther and much faster than in Japan. We dug deeply into our precious cash reserves to air freight our motorcycles to the Honda testing lab in Japan. Through the dark month of April, Pan Am was the only enterprise in the U.S. that was nice to us. Our testing lab worked twenty-four-hour days bench testing the bikes to try to replicate the failure. Within a month, a redesigned head gasket and clutch spring solved the problem. But in the meantime, events had taken a surprising turn.

Throughout our first eight months, following Mr. Honda's and our own instincts, we had not attempted to move the 50cc Supercubs. While they were a smash success in Japan (and manufacturing couldn't keep up with demand there), they seemed wholly unsuitable for the U.S. market where everything was bigger and more luxurious. As a clincher, we had our sights on the import market—and the Europeans, like the American manufacturers, emphasized the larger machines.

We used the Honda 50s ourselves to ride around Los Angeles on errands. They attracted a lot of attention. One day we had a call from a Sears buyer. While persisting in our refusal to sell through an intermediary, we took note of Sears' interest. But we still hesitated to push the 50cc bikes out of fear they might harm our image in a heavily macho market. But when the larger bikes started breaking, we had no choice. We let the 50cc bikes move. And surprisingly, the retailers who wanted to sell them weren't motorcycle dealers, they were sporting goods stores.

The excitement created by the Honda Supercub began to gain momentum. Under restrictions from the Japanese government, we were still on a cash basis. Working with our initial cash and inventory, we sold machines, reinvested in inventory, and sunk the profits into additional inventory and advertising. Our advertising tried to straddle the market. While retailers continued to inform us that our Supercub customers were normal everyday Americans, we hesitated to target toward this segment out of fear of alienating the high margin end of our business—sold through the traditional motorcycle dealers to a more traditional "black leather jacket" customer.

Honda's phenomenal sales and share gains over the ensuing years have been previously reported. History has it that Honda "*redefined*" the U.S. motorcycle industry. In the view of American Honda's start-up team, this was an innovation they backed into— and reluctantly. It was certainly not the strategy they embarked on in 1959. As late as 1963, Honda was still working with its original Los Angeles advertising agency, its ad campaigns straddling all customers so as not to antagonize one market in pursuit of another.

In the spring of 1963, an undergraduate advertising major at UCLA submitted, in fulfillment of a routine course assignment, an ad campaign for Honda. Its theme: You Meet the Nicest People on a Honda. Encouraged by his instructor, the student passed his work on to a friend at Grey Advertising. Grey had been soliciting the Honda account—which with a $5 million a year budget was becoming an attractive potential client. Grey purchased the student's idea—on a tightly kept nondisclosure basis. Grey attempted to sell the idea to Honda.

Interestingly, the Honda management team, which by 1963 had grown to five Japanese executives, was badly split on this advertising decision. The president and treasurer favored another proposal from another agency. The director of sales, however, felt strongly that the Nicest People campaign was the right one—and his commitment eventually held sway. Thus, in 1963, through an inadvertent sequence of events, Honda came to adopt a strategy that directly identified and targeted that large untapped segment of the marketplace that has since become inseparable from the Honda legend.

The Nicest People campaign drove Honda's sales at an even greater rate. By 1964, nearly one out of every two motorcycles sold was a Honda. As a result of the influx of medium income leisure class consumers, banks and other consumer credit companies began to finance motorcycles—shifting away from dealer credit, which had been the traditional purchasing mechanism available. Honda, seizing the opportunity of soaring demand for its products, took a courageous and seemingly risky position. Late in 1964, they announced that thereafter, they would cease to ship on a consignment basis but would require cash on delivery. Honda braced itself for revolt. While nearly every dealer questioned, appealed, or complained, none relinquished his franchise. In one fell swoop, Honda shifted the power relationship from the dealer to the manufacturer. Within three years, this would become the pattern for the industry.

THE "HONDA EFFECT"

The preceding account of Honda's inroads in the U.S. motorcycle industry provides more than a second perspective on reality. It focuses our attention on different issues and raises different questions. What factors permitted two men as unlike one another as Honda and Fujisawa to function effectively as a team? What incentives and understandings permitted the Japanese executives at American Honda to respond to the market as it emerged rather than doggedly pursue the 250cc and 305 cc strategy that Mr. Honda favored? What decision process permitted the relatively junior sales director to overturn the bosses' preferences and choose the Nicest People campaign? What values or commitment drove Honda to take the enormous risk of alienating its dealers in 1964 in shifting from a consignment to cash? In hindsight, these pivotal events all seem ho-hum common sense. But each day, as organizations live out their lives without the benefit of hindsight, few choose so well and so consistently.

The juxtaposed perspectives reveal what I shall call the "Honda Effect." Western consultants, academics, and executives express a preference for oversimplifications of reality and cognitively linear explanations of events. To be sure, they have always acknowledged that the "human factor" must be taken into account. But extensive reading of strategy cases at business schools, consultants' reports, strategic planning documents as well as the coverage of the popular press, reveals a widespread tendency to overlook the process through which organizations experiment, adapt, and learn. We tend to impute coherence and purposive rationality to events when the opposite may be closer to the truth. How an organization deals with miscalculation, mistakes, and serendipitous events *outside its field of vision is often crucial to success over time.* It is this realm that requires better understanding and further research if we are to enhance our ability to guide an organization's destiny. . . .

An earlier section has addressed the shortcomings of the narrowly defined micro-economic strategy model. The Japanese avoid this pitfall by adopting a broader notion of "strategy." In our recent awe of things Japanese, most Americans forget that the original products of the Japanese automotive manufacturers badly missed the mark. Toyota's Toyopet was square, sexless, and mechanically defective. It failed miserably, as did Datsun's first several entries into the U.S. market. More recently, Mazda miscalculated badly with its first rotary engine and nearly went bankrupt. Contrary to myth, the Japanese did not from the onset embark on a strategy to seize the high-quality small-car market. They manufactured what they were accustomed to building in Japan and tried to sell it abroad. Their success, as any Japanese automotive executive will readily agree, did not result from a bold insight by a few big brains at the top. On the contrary, success was achieved by senior managers humble enough not to take their initial strategic positions too seriously. What saved Japan's near-failures was the cumulative impact of "little brains" in the form of salesmen and dealers and production workers, all contributing incrementally to the quality and market position these companies enjoy today. Middle and upper management saw their primary task as guiding and orchestrating this input from below rather than steering the organization from above along a predetermined strategic course.

The Japanese don't use the term "strategy" to describe a crisp business definition or competitive master plan. They think more in terms of "strategic accommodation," or "adaptive persistence," underscoring their belief that corporate direction evolves from an incremental adjustment to unfolding events. Rarely, in their view, does one leader (or a strategic planning group) produce a bold strategy that guides a firm unerringly. Far more frequently, the input is from below. It is this ability of an organization to move information and ideas from the bottom to the top and back again in continuous dialogue that the Japanese value above all things. As this dialogue is pursued, what in hindsight may be "strategy" evolves. In sum, "strategy" is defined as "all the things necessary for the successful functioning of organization as an adaptive mechanism." . . .

READING | LOGICAL INCREMENTALISM: MANAGING STRATEGY FORMATION[*]

*By James Brian Quinn
and John J. Voyer*

THE LOGIC OF LOGICAL INCREMENTALISM

Strategy change processes in well-managed major organizations rarely resemble the rational-analytical systems touted in the literature. Instead, strategic change processes are typically fragmented, evolutionary, and intuitive. Real strategy *evolves* as internal decisions and external events flow together to create a new, widely shared consensus for action.

The Formal Systems Planning Approach

There is a strong literature stating which factors *should* be included in a systematically planned strategy. This systems-planning approach focuses on quantitative factors, and underemphasizes qualitative, organizational, and power factors. Systems planning *can* make a contribution, but it should be just one building block in the continuous stream of events that creates organizational strategy.

The Power-Behavioral Approach

Another body of literature has enhanced our understanding of *multiple goal structures,* the *politics* of strategic decisions, *bargaining* and *negotiation* processes, *satisficing* in decision making, the role of *coalitions,* and the practice of "*muddling*" in public sector management. The shortcomings of this body of literature are that it has typically been far-removed from strategy making, it has ignored the contributions of useful analytical approaches, and it has offered few practical recommendations for the strategist.

---

[*] Based on James Brian Quinn, "Strategic Change: 'Logical Incrementalism.' " *Sloan Management Review,* Fall 1978, pp. 1–21, and James Brian Quinn, "Managing Strategies Incrementally." *Omega: The International Journal of Management Science,* 1982.

Summary Findings from Study of Actual Change Processes

Recognizing the strengths and weaknesses of each of these approaches, the change processes in ten major organizations were documented. Several important findings emerged from these investigations.

- Neither approach above adequately describes strategy processes.
- Effective strategies tend to emerge incrementally and opportunistically, as subsystems of organizational activity (e.g., acquisitions, divestitures, major reorganizations, even formal plans) are blended into a coherent pattern.
- The logic behind this process is so powerful that it may be the best approach to recommend for strategy formation in large companies.
- Because of cognitive and process limits, this approach must be managed and linked together in a way best described as "logical incrementalism."
- Such incrementalism is not "muddling." It is a purposeful, effective, active management technique for improving and integrating *both* the analytical and behavioral aspects of strategy formation.

Critical Strategic Issues

Though "hard data" decisions dominate the literature, there are various "soft" kinds of changes that affect strategy:

- The design of an organization's structure
- The characteristic management style in the firm
- A firm's external (especially governmental) relations
- Acquisitions, divestitures, or divisional control issues
- A firm's international posture and relationships
- An organization's innovative capabilities
- The effects of an organization's growth on the motivation of its personnel
- Value and expectation changes, and their effects on worker and professional relationships in the organization
- Technological changes that affect the organization

Top executives made several important points about these kinds of changes. Few of these issues lend themselves to quantitative modeling or financial analysis. Most firms use different subsystems to handle different types of strategic changes, yet the subsystems were similar across firms. Lastly, no single formal analytical process could handle all strategic variables simultaneously using a planning approach.

PRECIPITATING EVENTS AND INCREMENTAL LOGIC. Executives reported that various events often resulted in interim decisions that shaped the company's future strategy. This was evident in the decisions forced on General Motors by the 1973–74 oil crisis, in the shift in posture pressed upon Exxon by the Prince William Sound oil spill, or in the dramatic opportunities allowed for Haloid Corporation and Pilkington Brothers by the unexpected inventions of xerography and float glass. No organization—no matter how brilliant, rational, or imaginative—could possibly have foreseen the timing, severity, or even the nature of all such precipitating events.

Recognizing this, top executives tried to respond incrementally. They kept early commitments broadly formative, tentative, and subject to later review. Future implications were too hard to understand, so parties wanted to test assumptions and have an opportunity to learn. Also, top executives were sensitive to social and political structures in the organization; they tried to handle things in a way that would make the change process a good one.

THE DIVERSIFICATION SUBSYSTEM. Strategies for diversification provide excellent examples of the value of proceeding incrementally. Incremental processes aid both the formal aspects of diversification (price and strategic fit, for example), and the psychological and political aspects. Most important among the latter are generating a genuine, top-level psychological commitment to diversification, consciously preparing the firm to move opportunistically, building a "comfort factor" for risk taking, and developing a new ethos based on the success of new divisions.

THE MAJOR REORGANIZATION SUBSYSTEM. Large-scale organizational moves may have negative effects on organizational politics and social structure. Logical incrementalism makes it easier to avoid those negative effects. As the organization proceeds incrementally, it can assess the new roles, capabilities, and individual reactions of those involved in the restructuring. It allows new people to be trained and tested, perhaps for extended periods. Logical incrementalism allows organizational actors to modify the idea behind the reorganization as more is learned. It also gives executives the luxury of making final commitments as late as possible. Executives may move opportunistically, step-by-step, selectively moving people as developments warrant (events seldom come together at one convenient time). They may also articulate the broad organizational concept in detail only when the last pieces fit together. Lastly, logical incrementalism works well in large-scale reorganization because it allows for testing, flexibility, and feedback.

Formal Planning in Corporate Strategy

Formal planning techniques do serve some essential functions. They discipline managers to look ahead, and to express goals and resource allocations. Long-term planning encourages longer time horizons, and eases the evaluation of short-term plans. Long-term plans create a psychological backdrop and an information framework about the future against which managers can calibrate short-term or interim decisions. Lastly, "special studies," like the white papers used at Pillsbury to inform the chicken-business divestiture decision, have a large effect at key junctures for specific decisions.

Planning may make incrementalism standard organizational practice, for two reasons. First, most planning is "bottom up," and the people at the bottom have an interest in their existing products and processes. Second, executives want most plans to be "living" or "ever green," intended to be only frameworks, providing guidance and consistency for incremental decisions. To do otherwise would be to deny that further information could have value. Thus, properly used formal planning can be part of incremental logic.

TOTAL POSTURE PLANNING. Occasionally, managements did attempt very broad assessments of their companies' total posture. But these major product thrusts were usually unsuccessful. Actual strategies *evolved,* as each company overextended, consolidated, made errors, and rebalanced various thrusts over time. The executives thought that this was both logical and expected.

Logical Incrementalism

Strategic decisions cannot be aggregated into a single decision matrix, with factors treated simultaneously to achieve an optimum solution. There are cognitive limits, but also "process limits"—timing and sequencing requirements, the needs to create awareness, to build comfort levels, to develop consensus, to select and train people, and so forth.

A STRATEGY EMERGES. Successful executives connect and sequentially arrange a series of strategic processes and decisions over a period of years. They attempt to build a resource base and posture that are strong enough to withstand all but the most devastating events. They constantly reconfigure corporate structure and strategy as new information suggests better—but never perfect—alignments. The process is dynamic, with no definite beginning or end.

Conclusions

Strategy deals with the unknowable, not the uncertain. It involves so many forces, most of which have great strength and the power to combine, that one cannot, in a probabilistic sense, predict events. Therefore, logic dictates that one proceed flexibly and experimentally from broad ideas toward specific commitments. Making the latter concrete as late as possible narrows the bands of uncertainty, and allows the firm to benefit from the best available information. This is the process of "logical incrementalism." It is not "muddling." Logical incrementalism is conscious, purposeful, active, good management. It allows executives to blend analysis, organizational politics, and individual needs into a cohesive new direction.

MANAGING INCREMENTALLY

How can one actively manage the logical incremental process? The study discussed here shows that executives tend to use similar incremental processes as they manage complex strategy shifts.

BEING AHEAD OF THE FORMAL INFORMATION SYSTEM. The earliest signals for strategy change rarely come from formal company systems. Using multiple internal and external sources, managers "sense" the need for change before the formal systems do. T. Vincent Learson at IBM drove the company to develop the 360 series of computers based on his feeling that, despite its current success, IBM was heading toward market confusion. IBM's formal intelligence system did not pick up any market signals until three years after Learson launched the development process.

BUILDING ORGANIZATIONAL AWARENESS. This is essential when key players lack information or psychological stimulation to change. At early stages, management processes are broad, tentative, formative, information-seeking, and purposely avoid irreversible commitments. They also try to avoid provoking potential opponents of an idea.

BUILDING CREDIBILITY/CHANGING SYMBOLS. Symbols may help managers signal to the organization that certain types of changes are coming, even when specific solutions are not yet in hand. Highly visible symbolic actions can communicate effectively to large numbers of people. Grapevines can amplify signals of pending change. Symbolic moves often verify the intention of a new strategy, or give it credibility in its early stages. Without such actions, people may interpret even forceful verbiage as mere rhetoric and delay their commitment to new strategic ideas.

LEGITIMIZING NEW VIEWPOINTS. Planned delays allow the organization to debate and discuss threatening issues, work out implications of new solutions, or gain an improved information base. Sometimes, strategic ideas that are initially resisted can gain acceptance and commitment simply by the passage of time and open discussion of new information. Many top executives, planners and change agents consciously arrange such "gestation periods." For example, William Spoor at Pillsbury allowed more than a year of discussion and information-gathering before the company decided to divest its chicken business.

TACTICAL SHIFTS AND PARTIAL SOLUTIONS. These are typical steps in developing a new strategic posture, especially when early problem resolutions need to be partial, tentative or experimental. Tactical adjustments, or a series of small programs, typically encounter little opposition, while a broad strategic change could encounter much opposition. These approaches allow the continuation of on-going strengths while shifting momentum at the margin. Experimentation can occur with minimized risk, leading to many different ways to succeed.

As events unfurl, the solutions to several problems, which may initially have seemed unrelated, tend to flow together into a new combination. When possible, strategic logic (risk minimization) dictates starting broad initiatives that can be flexibly guided in any of several possible desirable directions.

BROADENING POLITICAL SUPPORT. This is an essential and consciously-active step in major strategy changes. Committees, task forces or retreats tend to be favored mechanisms. By selecting such groups' chairpersons, membership, timing, and agenda the guiding executive can largely influence and predict a desired outcome, yet nudge other executives toward a consensus. Interactive consensus building also improves the quality of decisions, and encourages positive and innovative help when things go wrong.

OVERCOMING OPPOSITION. Unnecessary alienation of managers from an earlier era in the organization's history should be avoided; their talents may be needed. But overcoming opposition is usually necessary. Preferred methods are persuasion, co-optation, neutralization, or moving through zones of indifference (i.e., pushing those portions of a project that are non-controversial to most of the interested parties). To be sure, successful executives honor and even stimulate legitimate differences. Opponents sometimes thoughtfully shape new strategies into more effective directions; sometimes they even change their views. Occasionally, though, strong-minded executives may need to be moved to less-influential positions, or be stimulated to leave.

CONSCIOUSLY STRUCTURED FLEXIBILITY. Flexibility is essential in dealing with the many "unknowables" in the environment. Successful organizations actively create flexibility. This requires active horizon scanning, creating resource buffers, developing and positioning champions, and shortening decision lines. These are the keys to *real* contingency planning, not the usual pre-capsuled (and shelved) programs designed to respond to stimuli that never occur quite as expected.

TRIAL BALLOONS AND SYSTEMATIC WAITING. Strategists may have to wait patiently for the proper option to appear or precipitating event to occur. For example, although he wanted to divest Pillsbury's chicken business, William Spoor waited until his investment bankers found a buyer at a good price. Executives may also consciously launch trial ideas, like Spoor's "Super Box" at Pillsbury, to attract options and concrete proposals. Without making a commitment to any specific solution, the executive mobilizes the organization's creative abilities.

CREATING POCKETS OF COMMITMENT. Executives often need this tactic when they are trying to get organizations to adopt entirely new strategic directions. Small projects, deep within the organization, are used to test options, create skills, or build commitments for several possible options. The executive provides broad goals, proper climate, and flexible resource support, without public commitment. This avoids attention on, and identification with, any project. Yet executives can stimulate the good options, make life harder for the poorer options, or even kill the weakest ones.

CRYSTALLIZING THE FOCUS. At some point, this becomes vital. Early commitments are necessarily vague, but once executives develop information or consensus on desirable ways to proceed, they may use their prestige or power to push or crystallize a particular formulation. This should not be done too early, as it might inadvertently centralize the organization or preempt interesting options. Focusing too early might also provide a common target for otherwise fragmented opposition, or cause the organization to undertake undesirable actions just to carry out a stated commitment. When to crystallize viewpoints and when to maintain open options is a true art of strategic management.

FORMALIZING COMMITMENT. This is the final step in the logical incremental strategy formation process. It usually occurs after general acceptance exists, and when the timing is right. Typically, the decision is announced publicly, programs and budgets are formed, and control and reward systems are aligned to reflect intended strategic emphases.

CONTINUING THE DYNAMICS AND MUTATING THE CONSENSUS. Advocates of the "new" strategy can become as strong a source of inflexible resistance to new ideas as were the advocates of the "old" strategy. Effective strategic managers immediately introduce new ideas and stimuli at the top, to maintain the adaptability of the strategic thrusts they have just solidified. This is a most difficult, but essential, psychological task.

NOT A LINEAR PROCESS. While generation of a strategy generally flows along the sequence presented above, the stages are usually not ordered or discrete. The process is more like fermentation in biochemistry, instead of being like an industrial assembly line. Segments of major strategies are likely to be at different stages of development. They are usually integrated in the minds of top executives, each of whom may nevertheless see things differently. Lastly, the process is so continuous that it may be hard to discern the particular point in time when specific clear-cut decisions are made.

An important point to remember is that the validity of a strategy lies not in its pristine clarity or rigorously maintained structure. Its value lies in its capacity to capture the initiative, to deal with unknowable events, and to redeploy and concentrate resources as new opportunities and thrusts emerge. This allows the organization to use resources most effectively toward selected goals.

Integrating the Strategy

The process described above may be incremental, but it is not piecemeal. Effective executives constantly reassess the total organization, its capacities and its needs as related to the surrounding environment.

CONCENTRATING ON A FEW KEY THRUSTS. Effective strategic managers constantly seek to distill a few (six to ten) "central themes" that draw the firm's actions together. These maintain focus and consistency in the strategy. They make it easier to discuss and monitor intended directions. By contrast, formal models, designed to keep track of divisional progress toward realizing strategy, tend to become bound up in red tape, procedure, and rigid bureaucracy.

COALITION MANAGEMENT. The heart of all controlled strategy development is coalition management. Top managers act at the confluence of pressures from all stakeholders. These stakeholders will form coalitions, so managers must be active in forming their own. People selection and coalition management are the ultimate controls top executives have in guiding and coordinating their companies' strategies.

Conclusions

Many recent attempts to devise strategy using approaches that emphasize formal planning have failed because of poor implementation. This results from the classic trap of thinking about strategy formulation and implementation as separate and sequential processes. Successful managers who operate logically and actively, in an *incremental* mode, build the seeds of understanding, identity and commitment into the very processes that create their strategies. Strategy "formulation" and strategy "implementation" interact in the organization's continuing stream of events.

C H A P T E R   6

STRUCTURE AND SYSTEMS

The last few chapters have sketched out some differences between the prescriptive and descriptive approaches to strategy. In this chapter we will discuss how organizational structure and systems fit into each kind of approach. Briefly, the prescriptive approaches assert that structure and systems are the major part of strategy implementation. After having designed, formally planned, or analyzed which strategy to use, the strategist's responsibility is to use the tools of structure and systems to carry it out. In other words, structure follows strategy.

The descriptive approaches take a different tack. Their assertion, which we will examine in detail in the chapters to come, is that different kinds of structures will lead to different kinds of strategy processes. The kind of process one might find in a small entrepreneurial company is very different from what one would see in a large bureaucracy. Taken to the extreme, the descriptive view says that strategy follows structure.

Of course, as Mintzberg stressed in his Chapter Five reading "Crafting Strategy," strategy walks on two feet—deliberate and emergent. Similarly, we will see in the chapters to come that strategy and structure serve similarly like two feet walking—one always proceeds (and follows!) the other. That is, sometimes structure *does* follow strategy—if the organization can realize its strategy deliberately. Other times, strategy follows structure, as when a loosely coupled innovative organization shows an inclination to form emergent strategies. And sometimes, an organization can change over time from one type of structure to another, creating a different strategy process as it does so.

Though the prescriptive and the descriptive approaches assume contrasting cause-and-effect relationships between strategy and structure, the basic principles of structure and systems are the same for the two approaches. Hence, in this chapter we examine the basics of organizational structure and how they apply to strategy. We also examine organizational control systems and their relationship to strategy.

BASICS OF STRUCTURE AND SYSTEMS

At the end of this chapter, there is an extensive reading by Mintzberg that covers structure and systems in detail. His fundamental point is that managers may choose from among many building blocks at their disposal when they try to design and create organizations. He calls these building blocks "design parameters." We will preview the basics of his analysis here.

There are three important elements in organizational structure and design. The first is the designation of formal reporting relationships, including the number of levels the hierarchy has or should have, and the number of people supervised by managers. The second is grouping—of individuals into departments and of departments into the whole organization. These together are commonly referred to as **structure.** The third element is the design of **systems** to ensure that departments are effective in communicating and coordinating, and in integrating their efforts.[1] For strategists, the second, grouping, and the third, systems, are most important.

Basic Structures

As Mintzberg points out in his reading, there are really only two choices for grouping. *Function* is the first, comprising the means (techniques and activities) that people in the organization employ to do their tasks. Grouping this way results in the pure **functional form,** a familiar structure containing activity-based departments. Mintzberg gives the example of a cultural center that has departments of finance, operations, public relations, box office, and maintenance/garage.

The second way to group units is by *market,* meaning that units focus on particular customers, products, or end services. The result is the pure **divisional form.** Mintzberg's example is the Canadian Post Office, with units grouped first into four regions (Atlantic, Quebec, Ontario, and Western). Each focuses on one geographic market.

It is often necessary to combine functional and market grouping in large organizations. The need for scale may require some units to be grouped by function even while other units in the same organization are grouped by market. This is a **hybrid form,** and an example is a diversified company with a large legal staff and several lines of business. It may be best to group the legal staff into one large unit at headquarters, though the lines of business are grouped into divisions, each serving a different market.

The other basic type of organizational structure is called the **matrix form.** It also combines functional and market grouping, but in a very different way from the hybrid structure. In short, where a hybrid groups functional and market units in different areas of an organization, a matrix *overlaps* functional and product structures. That is, any person working in a matrix works simultaneously for a functional unit and a market unit—for example, an engineer specialized in motor design in an automobile company may also be assigned to a project to design a new high-performance sports car.

Coordinating Mechanisms[2]

Grouping people into units is only one aspect of organization design. Those people and units must communicate with one another, and they must coordinate and integrate their efforts. In short, they must *link* with each other. These linkages must be in two directions: **Vertical linkages** deal with coordination up and down the hierarchy, while **horizontal linkages** promote coordination across units at the same level of the hierarchy.

VERTICAL COORDINATION MECHANISMS. As the need for vertical coordination and control increases in a firm, there are four increasingly powerful mechanisms it can use. The simplest is **hierarchical referral,** which means sending problems from one level up to a higher level of the organization. This is a low-capacity mechanism because it could quickly overwhelm the people at higher levels. It also requires much time to solve problems. If coordination problems are recurrent, the organization can devise **rules and plans** to deal with them. This is much quicker, since rules merely have to be consulted for guidance if the situation is a standardized one. Plans, too, can help coordinate the actions of large numbers of people in an efficient way, merely by having them refer to and follow the plan's guidelines. If managers are still being overwhelmed, the organization can **add positions or levels to the hierarchy.** Thus, if a manager is flooded with problems from, say, fifty subordinates, she can place five people below her in the hierarchy, each with ten people reporting to them; her span of control goes down from fifty to five. Lastly, organizations can increase the efficiency of their coordination by adding **vertical information systems.** Instead of adding referrals, rules, or people, the organization adds to its ability to move information to decision makers.

HORIZONTAL COORDINATION MECHANISMS. Organizations must also break down barriers and ease communication and coordination among units at the same level of the hierarchy. The most direct way to do that is with **paperwork,** the familiar written memoranda and reports. Another way to bridge units is with **direct contact**—face-to-face meetings among people who need to coordinate. These methods have some shortcomings. Although paperwork can be efficient, it is a lean communication mechanism.[3] People who receive memos can easily ignore them or misunderstand them. Direct contact is the opposite—it can be very rich (it is more difficult to ignore someone giving you a face-to-face message), but can become inefficient if many people or units must coordinate.

When two units must coordinate over time but on a limited basis, an organization may use **liaison roles.** This is when someone is given the responsibility of coordinating among departments on matters of ongoing concern to all of them. If several units must coordinate, the liaison people need to meet as a group. If the coordination is for a limited time, members of each unit can meet as a **task force,** a committee that exists for a specified time only. If the several groups have coordination needs that are more-or-less permanent, they may use either a **full-time integrator** or have their liaison people meet as a **team** or **standing committee.** Full-time integrators typically have titles such as product manager, project manager, program manager, or brand manager. A brand manager, for example, would coordinate all the marketing functions relevant to his or her brand—sales, distribution, and advertising. Project teams are permanent groups made up of the liaison people from the relevant departments. Teams are the highest-capacity coordination mechanisms, allowing members of functional units to deal directly with one another on a permanent basis, on issues related to their project.

ORGANIZATIONAL CONTROL SYSTEMS

In Chapter One we saw how strategies fall on a continuum from deliberate to emergent. As we will see in later chapters, managers have control choices to make about each of these strategy processes. At the more deliberate end, the choice is how to control the implementation of the intended strategy. In between, the choice is about how to control the premises of strategy making. At the emergent end, the choices are about how to allow the most adaptive strategies to emerge. Depending on the type of strategy process and the type of organization, managers have three fundamental options for organizational control.

Bureaucratic Control

As Mintzberg points out in his reading in this chapter, managers may choose to control either actions or outputs. Action planning systems specify behavior in advance and expect to get desired outcomes. For example, an insurance company may specify standard procedure for how its claims agents should process the paperwork for a claim. Performance control systems specify desired outcomes and are indifferent to the behaviors used to achieve those results. For example, a manufacturing firm may have a target for the percentage of defects in a production run but leaves it up to the people in the plants how they will achieve that target. Either of these is an example of **bureaucratic control,**[4] using standardization methods, such as rules, policies, and specifications, either to regulate behavior or to assess performance.

Bureaucratic control often takes the form of *management control systems,*[5] a constellation of four techniques: **budgets,** which are used to specify financial resource allocations; **statistical reports,** which managers use to oversee and assess nonfinancial performance; **performance appraisal,** which consists of various techniques (for example, Management by Objectives) for evaluating people or organizational units; and **standard operating procedures,** the familiar rules and regulations specifying correct job performance.

Bureaucratic control is common in machine organizations, a form Mintzberg describes in detail in this chapter's readings. It is likely to be used in situations where an organization wishes to pursue a planned strategy. It is also common in situations where there are no external forces that can help control the organization. Most government agencies would be good examples. But even a manufacturing plant could use it to help it achieve nonfinancial targets, like percentage of defects. A variant of bureaucratic control might be used to influence process too. Instead of applying controls directly on its employees, managers use bureaucratic processes to select or promote people who are sympathetic to the processes the managers prefer to use.

Market Control

A special case of performance control is **market control.** This requires a price mechanism, competition among organizations in the market, and viable exchange relationships between organizations and their customers. If these conditions exist, an organization may be evaluated as to whether the market accepts its outputs. Typical measures would be sales, market share, and profit.

This type of organizational control is both common and appropriate in diversified organizations. For example, a corporation with three divisions, each of which operated in a different business, could establish sales, market share, and profit performance targets for each division, in effect seeking to standardize their performance through financial measures.

Under market control, the central headquarters of the organization worries mostly about the divisions' results and is indifferent to the methods used to achieve them. This means that within each division, managers would be free to use either bureaucratic control, described earlier, or clan control.

Clan Control

Clan control is the use of culture, beliefs, traditions, values and commitment to ensure that people in an organization work together in the desired way and on the desired things. Like market control, clan control can be used only if certain requirements are met. At minimum, there have to be shared values and trust among employees.

THE 7-*S* FRAMEWORK

Underlying everything written earlier in this chapter is the idea that somehow a variety of factors must be pulled together if an organization is to succeed in realizing an effective strategy. Waterman, Peters, and Phillips' reading, "The Seven-*S* Framework," is a closer look at the factors that must be combined and balanced. They point to seven interconnected ones.

The first two, strategy and structure, have been mainstays of strategic thought for decades, as is already clear from previous chapters. The third, systems, as well as structure, has been covered so far in this chapter. Style is the fourth element, and Waterman and his associates seem to equate it with how managers in an organization tend to make decisions. Much of the discussion of Chapter Two in this text is relevant to their discussion.

Skills, the fifth element of the Seven-*S* Framework, has also been touched on in this text. Skills are the things that make up a firm's distinctive competency, a concept we examined in Chapters Three and Four. Waterman, Peters, and Phillips also recognize the importance of people, making staff their sixth element. They argue that having and developing good people is critically important to an organization's effectiveness. The final element of the framework is superordinate goals, which Peters and Waterman retitled "shared values" in their book *In Search of Excellence.*[6] This is the culture of the firm, the thing that makes clan control possible.

The fundamental point that these authors assert is that there is no implicit or explicit hierarchy among these seven elements. All seven must be simultaneously balanced. Much discussion of organizational effectiveness has focused on the relationship between strategy and structure: Should strategy follow structure, or should structure follow strategy? Waterman, Peters, and Phillips argue that this debate is too limited. Managers need to look at these two factors together with systems, style, skills, staff, and shared values. Everything must fit together well for an organization to succeed.

STRUCTURES, FORCES AND FORMS IN EFFECTIVE ORGANIZATIONS

Mintzberg's reading, "Structures, Forces and Forms in Effective Organizations," picks up the theme of fit. He first identifies the many pieces that must ultimately fit together. Chief among these are the parts of the organization: the strategic apex (top management), the middle line (middle management), the operating core (the direct operators), the technostructure (the people who design work processes), the support staff (those who provide indirect support), and the ideology (which many people call culture).

He follows this with a discussion of the six ways to coordinate organizational action. The first, and perhaps the oldest, is mutual adjustment, where the people working a same task communicate directly with one another to get things accomplished. Another classic approach is direct supervision, where a boss tells his or her subordinates what to do. The four other coordinating mechanisms are all ways of standardizing activity. The first is the standardization of work processes, a familiar phenomenon in large bureaucracies. The second is the standardization of output, such as financial performance measures in a diversified firm. The third form of standardization is of skills, which dominates organizations composed of professionals. Lastly is the standardization of norms, to enhance the culture.

Mintzberg also discusses what he calls "design parameters," the many choices for grouping people and units, coordinating these units, and designing the decision-making apparatus of the firm. These were briefly discussed earlier in this chapter.

The middle portion of Mintzberg's reading is about seven classic ways that all these pieces can fit together. Mintzberg calls them configurations—entrepreneurial, machine, professional, diversified, innovative, missionary, and political. Each is a distinctive blend of various parts that cluster together coherently. For example, the machine organization, which many people will recognize as classic bureaucracy, has a powerful strategic apex, a very well-developed technostructure that designates rules for everyone else in the organization, a middle line that is stuck between the powerful strategic apex and a large but weak operating core, and a well-developed support staff that services all the remaining pieces of the organization.

In the latter portion of the reading, Mintzberg writes about the difference between lumping and splitting. Management literature has been filled with material of the "splitter" variety for a long time. But lumping is important, too. For the lumpers, Mintzberg has already proposed a set of forms, the configurations. So for the splitters he offers a set of forces that correspond to the seven pure configurations—direction (entrepreneurial), efficiency (machine), proficiency (professional), concentration (diversified), learning (innovative), cooperation (missionary), and competition (political). Mintzberg argues that both the forms and the forces must be appreciated in order for organizations to be effectively developed.

The lumpers have to realize that in the real world, no organization takes a pure form—all have to split, too, in other words give attention to a variety of the forces. Some, in fact, are hybrids—roughly equal balances of two or more forms—while others exist in transition between different forms—for example, an entrepreneurial organization on its way to becoming a more established machine one.

Ideology helps to manage the balancing of forms and forces in several ways. It is the driving force for cooperation in the organization. It encourages members to look to its vision. Most important is ideology's ability to help members reconcile the many contradictions they will encounter in their organizations. But there are problems. Ideologies are difficult to build and to maintain. And established ideologies can get in the way of effectiveness; they inhibit major change by forcing everyone to work within the same set of beliefs.

Politics is the force for competition, conflict, and confrontation. If it dominates, it may create a politicized organization. But it can also help. If reactionary forces dominate a firm, it may be politics that forces it to change, by challenging the status quo.

All this leads Mintzberg to consider five approaches to organizational effectiveness. The first he calls **convergence,** the idea that there is "one best way" to design and manage an organization. The second is **congruence,** typically called the contingency approach, that "it all depends" on matching organizational design to conditions. The third is the focus of the earlier part of the reading, the **configuration** approach. These three approaches are familiar enough, but the fourth and fifth are somewhat different. The fourth approach to organizational effectiveness is **contradiction,** which requires management of the dynamic tension between the contradictory forces mentioned above. Lastly is **creation,** the invention of completely new approaches to organizing.

NOTES TO CHAPTER SIX

1. Child, J., *Organization.* New York: Harper & Row, 1984.

2. The following discussion is based on Galbraith, J., *Designing Complex Organizations.* Reading, Mass.: Addison-Wesley, 1973; and Galbraith, J., *Organization Design.* Reading, Mass.: Addison-Wesley, 1977.

3. Daft, R. L., and R. H. Lengel, "Information Richness: A New Approach to Managerial Behavior and Organizational Design." In *Research in Organizational Behavior* vol. 6., eds. B. Staw and L. Cummings, Greenwich, Conn.: JAI Press, 1984.

4. Ouichi, W. G., "A Conceptual Framework for the Design of Organizational Control Mechanisms." *Management Science* 25 (1979): 833–48.

5. Daft, R. L., and N. B. Macintosh, "The Nature and Use of Formal Control Systems for Management Control and Strategy Implementation." *Journal of Management* 10 (1984): 43–66.

6. Peters, T. J., and R. H. Waterman. *In Search of Excellence.* New York: Harper & Row, 1982.

THE 7-S FRAMEWORK*

By Robert H. Waterman, Jr., Thomas J. Peters, and Julien R. Phillips

The Belgian surrealist René Magritte painted a series of pipes and titled the series *Ceci n'est pas une pipe:* this is not a pipe. The picture of the thing is not the thing. In the same way, a structure is not an organization. We all know that, but like as not, when we reorganize, what we do is to restructure. Intellectually all managers and consultants know that much more goes on in the process of organizing than the charts, boxes, dotted lines, position descriptions, and matrices can possibly depict. But all too often we behave as though we didn't know it; if we want change we change the structure. . . .

Our assertion is that productive organization change is not simply a matter of structure, although structure is important. It is not so simple as the interaction between strategy and structure, although strategy is critical too. Our claim is that effective organizational change is really the relationship between structure, strategy, systems, style, skills, staff, and something we call superordinate goals. (The alliteration is intentional: it serves as an aid to memory.)

Our central idea is that organization effectiveness, stems from the interaction of several factors—some not especially obvious and some underanalyzed. Our framework for organization change, graphically depicted in Figure 1, suggests several important ideas:

- First is the idea of a multiplicity of factors that influence an organization's ability to change and its proper mode of change. Why pay attention to only one or two, ignoring the others? Beyond structure and strategy, there are at least five other identifiable elements. The divi-

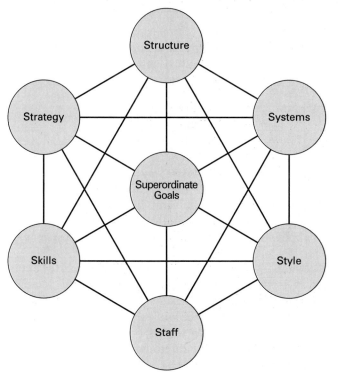

FIGURE 1
A New View of Organization

*Originally published as "Structure is Not Organization" in *Business Horizons* (June 1980); copyright © 1980 by the Foundation for the School of Business at Indiana University; all rights reserved. Reprinted with deletions by permission of the publisher.

sion is to some extent arbitrary, but it has the merit of acknowledging the complexity identified in the research and segmenting it into manageable parts.

- Second, the diagram is intended to convey the notion of the interconnectedness of the variables—the idea is that it's difficult, perhaps impossible, to make significant progress in one area without making progress in the others as well. Notions of organization change that ignore its many aspects or their interconnectedness are dangerous.

- In [an] article on strategy, *Fortune* commented that perhaps as many as 90% of carefully planned strategies don't work. If that is so, our guess would be that the failure is a failure in execution, resulting from inattention to the other S's. Just as a logistics bottleneck can cripple a military strategy, inadequate systems or staff can make paper tigers of the best-laid plans for clobbering competitors.

- Finally, the shape of the diagram is significant. It has no starting point or implied hierarchy. A priori, it isn't obvious which of the seven factors will be the driving force in changing a particular organization at a particular point in time. In some cases, the critical variable might be strategy. In others, it could be systems or structure.

STRUCTURE

To understand this model of organization change better, let us look at each of its elements, beginning—as most organization discussions do—with structure. What will the new organization of the 1980s be like? If decentralization was the trend of the past, what is next? Is it matrix organization? What will "Son of Matrix" look like? Our answer is that those questions miss the point. . . .

The central problem in structuring today . . . is not the one on which most organization designers spend their time—that is, how to divide up tasks. It is one of emphasis and coordination—how to make the whole thing work. The challenge lies not so much in trying to comprehend all the possible dimensions of organization structure as in developing the ability to focus on those dimensions which are currently important to the organization's evolution—and to be ready to refocus as the crucial dimensions shift.

STRATEGY

If structure is not enough, what is? Obviously, there is strategy. It was Alfred Chandler (1962) who first pointed out that structure follows strategy, or more precisely, that a strategy of diversity forces a decentralized structure. Throughout the past decade, the corporate world has given close attention to the interplay between strategy and structure. Certainly, clear ideas about strategy make the job of structural design more rational.

By "strategy" we mean those actions that a company plans in response to or anticipation of changes in its external environment—its customers, its competitors. Strategy is the way a company aims to improve its position vis-à-vis competition—perhaps through low-cost production or delivery, perhaps by providing better value to the customer, perhaps by achieving sales and service dominance. It is, or ought to be, an organization's way of saying: "Here is how we will create unique value."

As the company's chosen route to competitive success, strategy is obviously a central concern in many business situations—especially in highly competitive industries where the game is won or lost on share points. But "structure follows strategy" is by no means the be-all and end-all of organization wisdom. We find too many examples of large, prestigious companies around the world that are replete with strategy and cannot execute any of it. There is little if anything wrong with their structures; the causes of their inability to execute lie in other dimensions of our framework. When we turn to nonprofit and public sector organizations, moreover, we find that the whole meaning of "strategy" is tenuous—but the problem of organizational effectiveness looms as large as ever.

Strategy, then, is clearly a critical variable in organization design—but much more is at work.

SYSTEMS

By systems we mean all the procedures, formal and informal, that make the organization go, day by day and year by year: capital budgeting systems, training systems, cost accounting procedures, budgeting systems. If there is a variable in our model that threatens to dominate the others, it could well be systems. Do you want to understand how an organization really does (or doesn't) get things done? Look at the systems. Do you want to change an organization without disruptive restructuring? Try changing the systems.

A large consumer goods manufacturer was recently trying to come up with an overall corporate strategy. Textbook portfolio theory seemed to apply: find a good way to segment the business, decide which segments in the total business portfolio are most attractive, invest most heavily in those. The only catch: reliable cost data by segment were not to be had. The company's management information system was not adequate to support the segmentation. . . .

[One] intriguing aspect of systems is the way they mirror the state of an organization. Consider a certain company we'll call International Wickets. For years management has talked about the need to become more market oriented. Yet astonishingly little time is spent in their planning meetings on customers, marketing, market share, or other issues having to do with market orientation. One of their key systems, in other words, remains *very* internally oriented. Without a change in this key system, the market orientation goal will remain unattainable no matter how much change takes place in structure and strategy.

To many business managers the word "systems" has a dull, plodding, middle-management sound. Yet it is astonishing how powerfully systems changes can enhance organizational effectiveness—without the disruptive side effects that so often ensue from tinkering with structure.

STYLE

It is remarkable how often writers, in characterizing a corporate management for the business press, fall back on the word "style." . . . The trouble we have with style is not in recognizing its importance, but in doing much about it. Personalities don't change, or so the conventional wisdom goes.

We think it is important to distinguish between the basic personality of a top-management team and the way that team comes across to the organization. Organizations may listen to what managers say, but they believe what managers do. Not words, but patterns of actions are decisive. The power of style, then, is essentially manageable.

One element of a manager's style is how he or she chooses to spend time. As Henry Mintzberg has pointed out managers don't spend their time in the neatly compartmentalized planning, organizing, motivating, and controlling modes of classical management theory. Their days are a mess—or so it seems. There's a seeming infinity of things they might devote attention to. No top executive attends to all of the demands of his time; the median time spent on any one issue is nine minutes.

What can a top manager do in nine minutes? Actually, a good deal. He can signal what's on his mind; he can reinforce a message; he can nudge people's thinking in a desired direction. Skillful management of his inevitably fragmented time is, in fact, an immensely powerful change lever. . . .

Another aspect of style is symbolic behavior. Companies most successful in finding mineral deposits typically have more people on the board who understand exploration or have headed exploration departments. Typically they fund exploration more consistently (that is, their year-to-year spending patterns are less volatile). They define fewer and more consistent exploration targets. Their exploration activities typically report at a higher organizational level. And they typically articulate better reasons for exploring in the first place.

STAFF

Staff (in the sense of people, not line/staff) is often treated in one of two ways. At the hard end of the spectrum, we talk of appraisal systems, pay scales, formal training programs, and the like. At the soft end, we talk about morale, attitude, motivation, and behavior.

Top management is often, and justifiably, turned off by both these approaches. The first seems too trivial for their immediate concern ("Leave it to the personnel department"), the second too intractable ("We don't want a bunch of shrinks running around, stirring up the place with more attitude surveys").

Our predilection is to broaden and redefine the nature of the people issue. What do the top-performing companies do to foster the process of developing managers? How, for example, do they shape the basic values of their management cadre? Our reason for asking the question at all is simply that no serious discussion of organization can afford to ignore it (although many do). Our reason for framing the question around the development of managers is our observation that the superbly performing companies pay extraordinary attention to managing what might be called the socialization process in their companies. This applies especially to the way they introduce young recruits into the mainstream of their organizations and to the way they manage their careers as the recruits develop into tomorrow's managers. . . .

Considering people as a pool of resources to be nurtured, developed, guarded, and allocated is one of the many ways to turn the "staff" dimension of our 7-S framework into something not only amenable to, but worthy of practical control by senior management.

We are often told, "Get the structure 'right' and the people will fit" or "Don't compromise the 'optimum' organization for people considerations." At the other end of the spectrum we are earnestly advised, "The right people can make any organization work." Neither view is correct. People do count, but staff is only one of our seven variables.

SKILLS

We added the notion of skills for a highly practical reason: It enables us to capture a company's crucial attributes as no other concept can do. A strategic description of a company, for example, might typically cover markets to be penetrated or types of products to be sold. But how do most of us characterize companies? Not by their strategies or their structures. We tend to characterize them by what they do best. We talk of IBM's orientation to the marketplace, its prodigious customer service capabilities, or its sheer market power. We talk of Du Pont's research prowess, Procter & Gamble's product management capability, ITT's financial controls, Hewlett-Packard's innovation and quality, and Texas Instruments' project management. These dominating attributes, or capabilities, are what we mean by skills.

Now why is this distinction important? Because we regularly observe that organizations facing big discontinuities in business conditions must do more than shift strategic focus. Frequently they need to add a new capability, that is to say, a new skill. . . . These dominating capability needs, unless explicitly labeled as such, often get lost as the company "attacks a new market" (strategy shift) or "decentralizes to give managers autonomy" (structure shift).

Additionally, we frequently find it helpful to *label* current skills, for the addition of a new skill may come only when the old one is dismantled. Adopting a newly "flexible and adaptive marketing thrust," for example, may be possible only if increases are accepted in certain marketing or distribution costs. Dismantling some of the distracting attributes of an old "manufacturing mentality" (that is, a skill that was perhaps crucial in the past) may be the only way to ensure the success of an important change program. Possibly the most difficult problem in trying to organize effectively is that of weeding out old skills—and their supporting systems, structures, and so on—to ensure that important new skills can take root and grow.

SUPERORDINATE GOALS

The word "superordinate" literally means "of higher order." By superordinate goals, we mean guiding concepts—a set of values and aspirations, often unwritten, that goes beyond the conventional formal statement of corporate objectives.

Superordinate goals are the fundamental ideas around which a business is built. They are its main values. But they are more as well. They are the broad notions of future direction that the top management team wants to infuse throughout the organization. They are the way in which the team wants to express itself, to leave its own mark. Examples would include Theodore Vail's "universal service" objective, which has so dominated AT&T; the strong drive to "customer service" which guides IBM's marketing. . . .

In a sense, superordinate goals are like the basic postulates in a mathematical system. They are the starting points on which the system is logically built, but in themselves are not logically derived. The ultimate test of their value is not their logic but the usefulness of the system that ensues. Everyone seems to know the importance of compelling superordinate goals. The drive for their accomplishment pulls an organization together. They provide stability in what would otherwise be a shifting set of organization dynamics.

Unlike the other six S's, superordinate goals don't seem to be present in all, or even most, organizations. They are, however, evident in most of the superior performers.

To be readily communicated, superordinate goals need to be succinct. Typically, therefore, they are expressed at high levels of abstraction and may mean very little to outsiders who don't know the organization well. But for those inside, they are rich with significance. Within an organization, superordinate goals, if well articulated, make meanings for people. And making meanings is one of the main functions of leadership.

CONCLUSION

We have passed rapidly through the variables in our framework. What should the reader have gained from the exercise?

We started with the premise that solutions to today's thorny organizing problems that invoke only structure—or even strategy and structure—are seldom adequate. The inadequacy stems in part from the inability of the two-variable model to explain why organizations are so slow to adapt to change. The reasons often lie among the other variables: systems that embody outdated assumptions, a management style that is at odds with the stated strategy, the absence of a superordinate goal that binds the organization together in pursuit of a common purpose, the refusal to deal concretely with "people problems" and opportunities.

At its most trivial, when we merely use the framework as a checklist, we find that it leads into new terrain in our efforts to understand how organizations really operate or to design a truly comprehensive change program. At a minimum, it gives us a deeper bag in which to collect our experiences.

More importantly, it suggests the wisdom of taking seriously the variables in organizing that have been considered soft, informal, or beneath the purview of top management interest. We believe that style, systems, skills, superordinate goals can be observed directly, even measured—if only they are taken seriously. We think that these variables can be at least as important as strategy and structure in orchestrating major change; indeed, that they are almost critical for achieving necessary, or desirable change. A shift in systems, a major retraining program for staff, or the generation of top-to-bottom enthusiasm around a new superordinate goal could take years. Changes in strategy and structure, on the surface, may happen more quickly. But the pace of real change is geared to all seven S's.

At its most powerful and complex, the framework forces us to concentrate on interactions and fit. The real energy required to redirect an institution comes when all the variables in the model are aligned. One of our associates looks at our diagram as a set of compasses. "When all seven needles are all pointed the same way," he comments, "you're looking at an *organized* company."

READING | ## STRUCTURES, FORCES AND FORMS IN EFFECTIVE ORGANIZATIONS*

By Henry Mintzberg

The "one best way" approach has dominated our thinking about organizational structure since the turn of the century. There is a right way and a wrong way to design an organization. A variety of failures, however, has made it clear that organizations differ, that, for example, long-range planning systems or organizational development programs are good for some but not others. And so recent management theory has moved away from the "one best way" approach, toward an "it all depends" approach, formally known as "contingency theory." Structure should reflect the organization's situation—

---

*Excerpted originally from *The Structuring of Organizations* (Prentice Hall, 1979), with added sections from *Power in and Around Organizations* (Prentice Hall, 1983). This chapter was rewritten for this edition of the text, based on two other excerpts, "A Typology of Organizational Structure," published as Chapter 3 in Danny Miller and Peter Friesen, *Organizations: A Quantum View* (Prentice Hall, 1984), "Deriving Configurations," Chapter 6 in *Mintzberg on Management: Inside Our Strange World of Organizations* (Free Press, 1989), and the Chapter called "Beyond Configuration: Forces and Forms in Effective Organization" in the same book.

for example, its age, size, type of production system, the extent to which its environment is complex and dynamic.

This reading argues that the "it all depends" approach does not go far enough, that structures are rightfully designed on the basis of a third approach, which might be called the "getting it all together" or, "configuration" approach. Spans of control, types of formalization and decentralization, planning systems, and matrix structures should not be picked and chosen independently, the way a shopper picks vegetables at the market. Rather, these and other elements of organizational design should logically configure into internally consistent groupings.

When the enormous amount of research that has been done on organizational structure is looked at in the light of this conclusion, much of its confusion falls away, and a convergence is evident around several configurations, which are distinct in their structural designs, in the situations in which they are found, and even in the periods of history in which they first developed.

To understand these configurations, we must first understand each of the elements that make them up. Accordingly, the first four sections of this reading discuss the basic parts of organizations, the mechanisms by which organizations coordinate their activities, the parameters they use to design their structures, and their contingency, or situational, factors. The next section introduces the structural configurations, each of which will be discussed at length in Section III of this text. The reading concludes with a discussion of how the forces and forms can be combined, and how they interact in other ways.

SIX BASIC PARTS OF THE ORGANIZATION

At the base of any organization can be found its operators, those people who perform the basic work of producing the products and rendering the services. They form the *operating core.* All but the simplest organizations also require at least one full-time manager who occupies what we shall call the *strategic apex,* where the whole system is overseen. And as the organization grows, more managers are needed—not only managers of operators but also managers of managers. A *middle line* is created, a hierarchy of authority between the operating core and the strategic apex.

As the organization becomes still more complex, it generally requires another group of people, whom we shall call the analysts. They, too, perform administrative duties—to plan and control formally the work of others—but of a different nature, often labeled "staff." These analysts form what we shall call the *technostructure,* outside the hierarchy of line authority. Most organizations also add staff units of a different kind, to provide various internal services, from a cafeteria or mailroom to a legal counsel or public relations office. We call these units and the part of the organization they form the *support staff.*

Finally, every active organization has a sixth part, which we call its *ideology* (by which is meant a strong "culture"). Ideology encompasses the traditions and beliefs of an organization that distinguish it from other organizations and infuse a certain life into the skeleton of its structure.

This gives us six basic parts of an organization. As shown in Figure 1, we have a small strategic apex connected by a flaring middle line to a large, flat operating core at the base. These three parts of the organization are drawn in one uninterrupted sequence to indicate that they are typically connected through a single chain of formal authority. The technostructure and the support staff are shown off to either side to indicate that

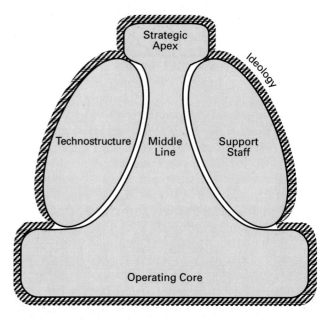

FIGURE 1
The Six Basic Parts of the Organization

they are separate from this main line of authority, influencing the opening core only in-directly. The ideology is shown as a kind of halo that surrounds the entire system.

These people, all of whom work inside the organization to make its decisions and take its actions—full-time employees or, in some cases, committed volunteers—may be thought of as *influencers* who form a kind of *internal coalition*. By this term, we mean a system within which people vie among themselves to determine the distribution of power.

In addition, various outside people also try to exert influence on the organization, seeking to affect the decisions and actions taken inside. These external influencers, who create a field of forces around the organization, can include owners, unions and other employee associations, suppliers, clients, partners, competitors, and all kinds of publics, in the form of governments, special interest groups, and so forth. Together they can all be thought to form an *external coalition*.

Sometimes the external coalition is relatively *passive* (as in the typical behavior of the shareholders of a widely held corporation or the members of a large union). Other times it is *dominated* by one active influencer or some group of them acting in concert (such as an outside owner of a business firm or a community intent on imposing a certain philosophy on its school system). And in still other cases, the external coalition may be *divided,* as different groups seek to impose contradictory pressures on the organization (as in a prison buffeted between two community groups, one favoring custody, the other rehabilitation).

SIX BASIC COORDINATING MECHANISMS

Every organized human activity—from the making of pottery to the placing of a man on the moon—gives rise to two fundamental and opposing requirements: the *division of labor* into various tasks to be performed and the *coordination* of those tasks to accom-plish the activity. The structure of an organization can be defined simply as the total of the ways in which its labor is divided into distinct tasks and then its coordination achieved among those tasks.

1. *Mutual adjustment* achieves coordination of work by the simple process of informal communication. The people who do the work interact with one another to coordinate, much as two canoeists in the rapids adjust to one another actions. Figure 2a shows mutual adjustment in terms of an arrow between two operators. Mutual adjustment is obviously used in the simplest of organizations—it is the most obvious way to coordinate. But, paradoxically, it is also used in the most complex, because it is the only means that can be relied upon under extremely difficult circumstances, such as trying to figure out how to put a man on the moon for the first time.

2. *Direct supervision* in which one person coordinates by giving orders to others, tends to come into play after a certain number of people must work together. Thus, fifteen people in a war canoe cannot coordinate by mutual adjustment; they need a leader who, by virtue of instructions, coordinates their work, much as a football team requires a quarterback to call the plays. Figure 2b shows the leader as a manager with the instructions as arrows to the operators.

Coordination can also be achieved by *standardization*—in effect, automatically, by virtue of standards that predetermine what people do and so ensure that their work is coordinated. We can consider four forms—the standardization of the work processes themselves, of the outputs of the work, of the knowledge and skills that serve as inputs to the work, or of the norms that more generally guide the work.

3. *Standardization of work processes* means the specification—that is, the programming—of the content of the work directly, the procedures to be followed, as in the case of the assembly instructions that come with many children's toys. As shown in Figure 2c, it is typically the job of the analysts to so program the work of different people in order to coordinate it tightly.

4. *Standardization of outputs* means the specification not of what is to be done but of its results. In that way, the interfaces between jobs is predetermined, as when a machinist is told to drill holes in a certain place on a fender so that they will fit the bolts being welded by someone else, or a division manager is told to achieve a sales growth of 10% so that the corporation can meet some overall sales target. Again, such standards generally emanate from the analysts, as shown in Figure 2d.

5. *Standardization of skills,* as well as knowledge, is another, though looser way to achieve coordination. Here, it is the worker rather than the work or the outputs that is standardized. He or she is taught a body of knowledge and a set of skills which are subsequently applied to the work. Such standardization typically takes place outside the organization—for example in a professional school of a university before the worker takes his or her first job—indicated in Figure 2e. In effect, the standards do not come from the analyst; they are

FIGURE 2
The Basic Mechanisms of Coordination

(a) Mutual Adjustment

(b) Direct Supervision

(c) Standardization of Work

(d) Standardization of Outputs

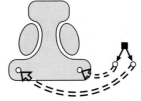

(e) Standardization of Skills

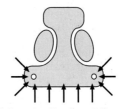

(f) Standardization of Norms

internalized by the operator as inputs to the job he or she takes. Coordination is then achieved by virtue of various operators' having learned what to expect of each other. When an anesthetist and a surgeon meet in the operating room to remove an appendix, they need hardly communicate (that is, use mutual adjustment, let alone direct supervision); each knows exactly what the other will do and can coordinate accordingly.

6. *Standardization of norms* means that the workers share a common set of beliefs and can achieve coordination based on it, as implied in Figure 2f. For example, if every member of a religious order shares a belief in the importance of attracting converts, then all will work together to achieve this aim.

These coordinating mechanisms can be considered the most basic elements of structure, the glue that holds organizations together. They seem to fall into a rough order: As organizational work becomes more complicated, the favored means of coordination seems to shift from mutual adjustment (the simplest mechanism) to direct supervision, then to standardization, preferably of work processes or norms, otherwise of outputs or of skills, finally reverting back to mutual adjustment. But no organization can rely on a single one of those mechanisms; all will typically be found in every reasonably developed organization.

Still, the important point for us here is that many organizations do favor one mechanism over the others, at least at certain stages of their lives. In fact, organizations that favor none seem most prone to becoming politicized, simply because of the conflicts that naturally arise when people have to vie for influence in a relative vacuum of power.

THE ESSENTIAL PARAMETERS OF DESIGN

Strategists who wish to design their organizations for effectiveness have series of parameters at their disposal. Depending on the circumstances, they may adjust these in a variety of ways. The first set of parameters concerns the design of individual positions in the organization.

- **Job specialization** refers to the number of tasks in a given job and the worker's control over these tasks. A job is *horizontally* specialized to the extent that it encompasses a few narrowly defined tasks, *vertically* specialized to the extent that the worker lacks control of the tasks performed. *Unskilled* jobs are typically highly specialized in both dimensions; skilled or *professional* jobs are typically specialized horizontally but not vertically. "Job enrichment" refers to the enlargement of jobs in both the vertical and horizontal dimension.

- **Behavior formalization** refers to the standardization of work processes by the imposition of operating instructions, job descriptions, rules, regulations, and the like. Structures that rely on any form of standardization for coordination may be defined as *bureaucratic,* those that do not as *organic.*

- **Training** refers to the use of formal instructional programs to establish and standardize in people the requisite skills and knowledge to do particular jobs in organizations. Training is a key design parameter in all work we call professional. Training and formalization are basically substitutes for achieving the standardization (in effect, the bureaucratization) of behavior. In one, the standards are learned as skills, in the other they are imposed on the job as rules.

- **Indoctrination** refers to programs and techniques by which the norms of the members of an organization are standardized, so that they become responsive to its ideological needs and can thereby be trusted to make its decisions and take its actions. Indoctrination too is a substitute for formalization, as well as for skill training, in this case the standards being internalized as deeply rooted beliefs.

The second set of design parameters deals with the design of the superstructure, that is, the overall network of subunits reflected in the organizational chart.

- **Unit grouping** refers to the choice of the bases by which positions are grouped together into units, and those units into higher-order units (typically shown on the organization chart). Grouping encourages coordination by putting different jobs under common supervision, by requiring them to share common resources and achieve common measures of performance, and by using proximity to facilitate mutual adjustment among them. The various bases for grouping—by work process, product, client, place, and so on—can be reduced to two fundamental ones—the *function* performed and the *market* served. The former (illustrated in Fig. 3) refers to means, that is to a single link in the chain of processes by which products or services are produced, the latter (in Fig. 4) to ends, that is, the whole chain for specific end products, services, or markets.

Organization designers must consider four criteria when trying to decide on unit grouping. The first is *workflow links,* sometimes called *workflow interdependencies.* If links between

FIGURE 3
Grouping by Function: A Cultural Center

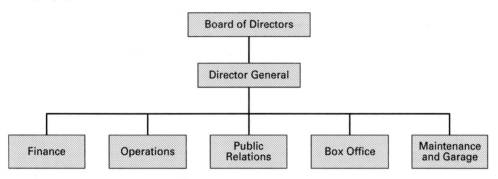

FIGURE 4
Grouping by Market: The Canadian Post Office

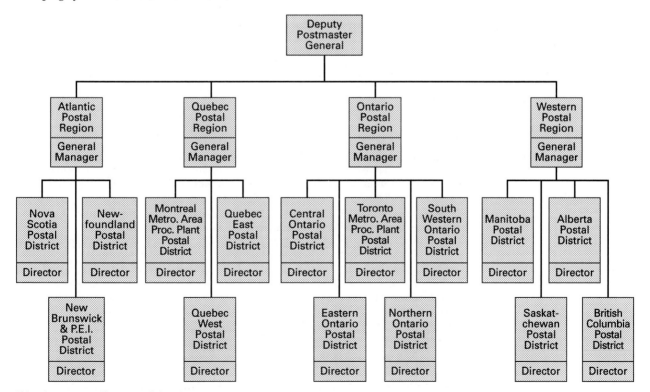

*Headquarter staff groups deleted.

units are tight, or should be, those units should be grouped together to facilitate coordination. An example would be a product where design, production, and marketing need to coordinate closely to meet customer needs. Instead of having a few people in a large design unit coordinate with a few people in a large production unit and a few people in a large marketing department, it may be best to group all the design, production and marketing people for a given product into one product division. The second criterion is *process interdependencies*—tasks that are similar but are in different workflows, like maintenance on machines in different assembly lines. It sometimes makes sense to group these together, so that the people can learn from one another or borrow one another's tools and equipment and so on. Organization designers also need to consider *scale interdependencies,* which are situations when units need to be grouped because it would be inefficient to separate them. For example, all maintenance people in a factory may have to be grouped together because no single department has enough maintenance work for one person. Lastly, there are *social interdependencies,* which are the need to group people together for social reasons. A good example is mining, where mutual support under dangerous working conditions can be a factor in deciding how to group people.

What are the advantages and disadvantages of functional versus market grouping? Functional grouping is best for handling process and scale interdependencies, and it fosters specialization. However, it encourages narrow perspectives and a focus on means instead of ends. Market grouping is better for managing workflow interdependencies, and allows the organization to do a greater variety of tasks and to better meet the needs of markets. But it does these things at some cost. Market grouping is less able to do repetitive and specialized tasks well, and is more wasteful because it does not take advantage of economies of scale and often duplicates resources. The implications for organization designers are clear. Use functional grouping if standardization can contain workflow interdependencies, or if process and scale interdependencies are very important. Use market grouping if workflow interdependencies are high and cannot easily be handled by standardization. Except for very small organizations, it is likely that both forms of grouping will be needed in different parts of the organization.

- **Unit size** refers to the number of positions (or units) contained in a single unit. The equivalent term, *span of control,* is not used here, because sometimes units are kept small despite an absence of close supervisory control. For example, when experts coordinate extensively by mutual adjustment, as in an engineering team in a space agency, they will form into small units. In this case, unit size is small and span of control is low despite a relative absence of direct supervision. In contrast, when work is highly standardized (because of either formalization or training), unit size can be very large, because there is little need for direct supervision. One foreman can supervise dozens of assemblers, because they work according to very tight instructions.

The next set of design parameters pertains to the lateral linkages used to flesh out the superstructure.

- **Planning and control systems** are used to standardize outputs. They may be divided into two types: *action planning* systems, which specify the results of specific actions before they are taken (for example, that holes should be drilled with diameters of 3 centimeters); and *performance control* systems, which specify the desired results of whole ranges of actions after the fact (for example, that sales of a division should grow by 10% in a given year).

- **Liaison devices** refer to a whole series of mechanisms used to encourage mutual adjustment within and between units. Four are of particular importance:

  - *Liaison positions* are jobs created to coordinate the work of two units directly, without having to pass through managerial channels, for example, the purchasing engineer who sits between purchasing and engineering or the sales liaison person who mediates between the sales force and the factory. These positions carry no formal authority per se; rather, those who serve in them must use their powers of persuasion, negotiation, and so on to bring the two sides together.

  - *Task forces and standing committees* are institutionalized forms of meetings which bring members of a number of different units together on a more intensive basis, in the first case to deal with a temporary issue, in the second, in a more permanent and regular way to discuss issues of common interest.

  - *Integrating managers*—essentially liaison personnel with formal authority—provide for stronger coordination. These "managers" are given authority not over the units they

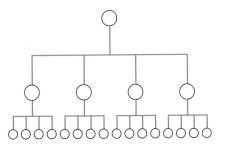

(a) Hierarchical Structure

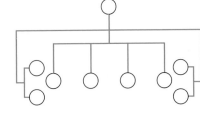

(b) Line and Staff Structure

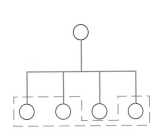

(c) Liaison Overlay Structure
(e.g., Task Force)

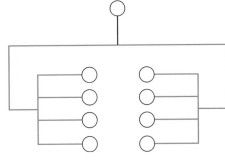

(d) Matrix Structure

FIGURE 5
**Structures to Deal with
Residual Interdependencies**

link, but over something important to those units, for example, their budgets. One example is the brand manager in a consumer goods firm who is responsible for a certain product but who must negotiate its production and marketing with different functional departments.

- *Matrix structure* carries liaison to its natural conclusion. No matter what the bases of grouping at one level in an organization, some interdependencies always remain. Figure 5 suggests various ways to deal with these "residual interdependencies": a different type of grouping can be used at the next level in the hierarchy; staff units can be formed next to line units to advise on the problems; or one of the liaison devices already discussed can be overlaid on the grouping. But in each case, one basis of grouping is favored over the others. The concept of matrix structure is balance between two (or more) bases of grouping, for example functional with market (or for that matter, one kind of market with another—say, regional with product). This is done by the creation of a dual authority structure—two (or more) managers, units, or individuals are made jointly and equally responsible for the same decisions. We can distinguish a *permanent* form of matrix structure, where the units and the people in them remain more or less in place, as shown in the example of a whimsical multinational firm in Figure 6, and a *shifting* form, suited to project work, where the units and the people in them move around frequently. Shifting matrix structures are common in high-technology industries, which group specialists in functional departments for housekeeping purposes (process interdependencies, etc.) but deploy them from various departments in project teams to do the work, as shown for NASA in Figure 7.

Lastly, strategists have at their disposal a set of parameters that may be adjusted to design the decision-making system of the organization.

- **Decentralization** refers to the diffusion of decision-making power. When all the power rests at a single point in an organization, we call its structure centralized; to the extent that the power is dispersed among many individuals, we call it relatively decentralized. *Vertical decentralization* is the delegation of formal power down the hierarchy to line managers. *Horizontal decentralization* is the extent to which formal or informal power is dispersed out of the line hierarchy to nonmanagers (like operators, analysts, and support staffers). Decentralization may also be *selective* or *parallel*. Selective means the dispersal of power over different decisions to different places in the organization. Parallel means the dispersal

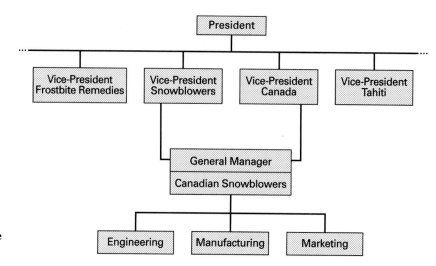

FIGURE 6
**A Permanent Matrix Structure
in an International Firm**

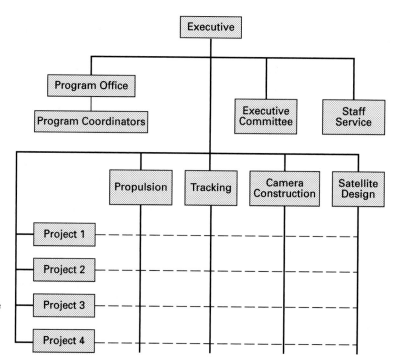

FIGURE 7
**Shifting Matrix Structure in
the NASA Weather Satellite
Program**

*Source: Modified from Delbecq
and Filley (1974:16).*

of power over the same kinds of decisions to the same place (e.g., all division managers have
the same set of decision powers). The result is a continuum with pure centralization at one
extreme, pure decentralization at the other, and various limited forms of decentralization in
the middle.

THE SITUATIONAL FACTORS

A number of "contingency" or "situational" factors influence the choice of these design
parameters. The design parameters may also influence the situation. These factors (age,
size, technical system, environment, and power) are summarized below.

Age

- In older organizations, the jobs are more specified, that is, more formalized.
- Older industries are populated by organizations that are more formalized.

Size

- In larger organizations, the jobs are more specified, i.e., formalized.
- Larger organizations are more specialized and have a greater proportion of administrative personnel.
- Larger organizations have units that are larger, on average.

Technical System

Technical system refers to the instruments used in the operating core to produce the outputs. This is not the same thing as "technology," which refers to the knowledge base of an organization.

- Technical systems that control the work of the operators lead to specified jobs and bureaucratic structure.
- Complex technical systems lead to larger, more professional support staff. That staff tends to get decision-making authority. The use of liaison devices goes up.
- Automating the operating core lets the management structure be more organic, less bureaucratic.

Environment

The environment refers to various characteristics of the organization's outside context, related to markets, political climate, economic conditions, and so on.

- Fast-moving environments are associated with organic structures.
- Complex environments are associated with decentralization.
- Diverse markets lead to market-based divisions.
- Bad times lead to temporary centralization of an organization's structure.
- If the environment has a lot of diversity, the organization is encouraged to adopt market grouping, so long as economies of scale are favorable.

Power

- If an organization is controlled by outside forces, it will become bureaucratic.
- If there is conflict among the outside forces, there will be more politics inside the organization, and vice versa.
- Managers adopt some organization structures because those structures may be fashionable. This will sometimes happen even if that structure is the wrong one for that firm.

THE CONFIGURATIONS

We have now introduced various attributes of organizations—parts, coordinating mechanisms, design parameters, situational factors. How do they all combine?

We proceed here on the assumption that a limited number of configurations can help explain much of what is observed in organizations. We have introduced in our dis-

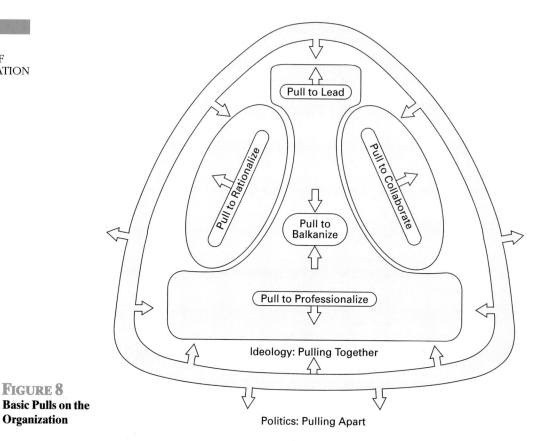

FIGURE 8
Basic Pulls on the Organization

cussion six basic parts of the organization, six basic mechanisms of coordination, as well as six basic types of decentralization. In fact, there seems to be a fundamental correspondence between all of these sixes, which can be explained by a set of pulls exerted on the organization by each of its six parts, as shown in Figure 8. When conditions favor one of these pulls, the associated part of the organization becomes key, the coordinating

CONFIGURATION	PRIME COORDINATING MECHANISM	KEY PART OF ORGANIZATION	TYPE OF DECEN-TRALIZATION
Entrepreneurial organization	Direct supervision	Strategic apex	Vertical and horizontal centralization
Machine organization	Standardization of work processes	Technostructure	Limited horizontal decentralization
Professional organization	Standardization of skills	Operating core	Horizontal decentralization
Diversified organization	Standardization of outputs	Middle line	Limited vertical decentralization
Innovative organization	Mutual adjustment	Support staff	Selected decentralization
Missionary organization	Standardization of norms	Ideology	Decentralization
Political organization	None	None	Varies

mechanism appropriate to itself becomes prime, and the form of decentralization that passes power to itself emerges. The organization is thus drawn to design itself as a particular configuration. We list here and then introduce briefly the six resulting configurations, together with a seventh that tends to appear when no one pull or part dominates.

The Entrepreneurial Organization

The name tells it all. And the figure above shows it all. The structure is simple, not much more than one large unit consisting of one or a few top managers, one of whom dominates by the pull to lead, and a group of operators who do the basic work. Little of the behavior in the organization is formalized and minimal use is made of planning, training, or the liaison devices. The absence of standardization means that the structure is organic and has little need for staff analysts. Likewise there are few middle line managers because so much of the coordination is handled at the top. Even the support staff is minimized, in order to keep the structure lean, the organization flexible.

The organization must be flexible because it operates in a dynamic environment, often by choice since that is the only place where it can outsmart the bureaucracies. But that environment must be simple, as must the production system, or else the chief executive could not for long hold on to the lion's share of the power. The organization is often young, in part because time drives it toward bureaucracy, in part because the vulnerability of its simple structure often causes it to fail. And many of these organizations are often small, since size too drives the structure toward bureaucracy. Not infrequently the chief executive purposely keeps the organization small in order to retain his or her personal control.

The classic case is of course the small entrepreneurial firm, controlled tightly and personally by its owner. Sometimes, however, under the control of a strong leader, the organization can grow large. Likewise, entrepreneurial organizations can be found in other sectors too, like government, where strong leaders personally control particular agencies, often ones they have founded. Sometimes under crisis conditions, large organizations also revert temporarily to the entrepreneurial form to allow forceful leaders to try to save them.

The Machine Organization

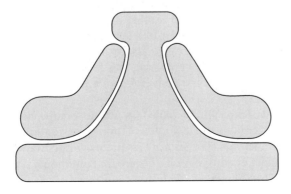

The machine organization is the offspring of the industrial revolution, when jobs became highly specialized and work became highly standardized. As can be seen in the figure above, in contrast to entrepreneurial organizations, the machine one elaborates is administration. First, it requires a large technostructure to design and maintain its systems of standardization, notably those that formalize its behaviors and plan its actions. And by virtue of the organization's dependence on these systems, the technostructure gains a good deal of informal power, resulting in a limited amount of horizontal decentralization, reflecting the pull to rationalize. A large hierarchy of middle-line managers emerges to control the highly specialized work of the operating core. But the middle line hierarchy is usually structured on a functional basis all the way up to the top, where the real power of coordination lies. So the structure tends to be rather centralized in the vertical sense.

To enable the top managers to maintain centralized control, both the environment and the production system of the machine organization must be fairly simple, the latter regulating the work of the operators but not itself automated. In fact, machine organizations fit most naturally with mass production. Indeed it is interesting that this structure is most prevalent in industries that date back to the period from the Industrial Revolution to the early part of this century.

The Professional Organization

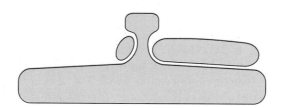

There is another bureaucratic configuration, but because this one relies on the standardization of skills rather than of work processes or outputs for its coordination, it emerges as dramatically different from the machine one. Here the pull to professionalize dominates. In having to rely on trained professionals—people highly specialized, but with considerable control over their work, as in hospitals or universities—to do its operating tasks, the organization surrenders a good deal of its power not only to the professionals themselves but also to the associations and institutions that select and train them in the first place. So the structure emerges as highly decentralized horizontally; power over many decisions, both operating and strategic, flows all the way down the hierarchy, to the professionals of the operating core.

Above the operating core we find a rather unique structure. There is little need for a technostructure, since the main standardization occurs as a result of training that takes place outside the organization. Because the professionals work so independently, the size of operating units can be very large, and few first line managers are needed. The support staff is typically very large too, in order to back up the high-priced professionals.

The professional organization is called for whenever an organization finds itself in an environment that is stable yet complex. Complexity requires decentralization to highly trained individuals, and stability enables them to apply standardized skills and so to work with a good deal of autonomy. To ensure that autonomy, the production system must be neither highly regulating, complex, nor automated.

The Diversified Organization

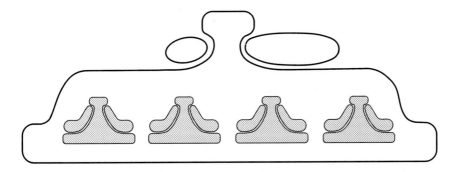

Like the professional organization, the diversified one is not so much an integrated organization as a set of rather independent entities coupled together by a loose administrative structure. But whereas those entities of the professional organization are individuals, in the diversified one they are units in the middle line, generally called "divisions," exerting a dominant pull to Balkanize. This configuration differs from the others in one major respect: it is not a complete structure, but a partial one superimposed on the others. Each division has its own structure.

An organization divisionalizes for one reason above all, because its product lines are diversified. And that tends to happen most often in the largest and most mature organizations, the ones that have run out of opportunities—or have become bored—in their traditional markets. Such diversification encourages the organization to replace functional by market-based units, one for each distinct product line (as shown in the diversified organization figure), and to grant considerable autonomy to each to run its own business. The result is a limited form of decentralization down the chain of command.

How does the central headquarters maintain a semblance of control over the divisions? Some direction supervision is used. But too much of that interferes with the necessary divisional autonomy. So the headquarters relies on performance control systems, in other words, the standardization of outputs. To design these control systems, headquarters creates a small technostructure. This is shown in the figure, across from the small central support staff that headquarters sets up to provide certain services common to the divisions such as legal counsel and public relations. And because headquarters' control constitutes external control, as discussed in the first hypothesis on power, the structure of the divisions tend to be drawn toward the machine form.

The Innovative Organization

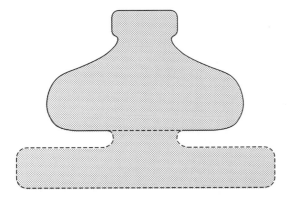

None of the structures so far discussed suits the industries of our age, industries such as aerospace, petrochemicals, think tank consulting, and film making. These organizations need above all to innovate in very complex ways. The bureaucratic structures are too inflexible, and the entrepreneurial one too centralized. These industries require "project structures," ones that can fuse experts drawn from different specialties into smoothly functioning creative teams. That is the role of our fifth configuration, the innovative organization, which we shall also call "adhocracy," dominated by the experts' pull to collaborate.

Adhocracy is an organic structure that relies for coordination on mutual adjustment among its highly trained and highly specialized experts, which it encourages by the extensive use of the liaison devices—integrating managers, standing committees, and above all task forces and matrix structure. Typically the experts are grouped in functional units for housekeeping purposes but deployed in small market based project teams to do their work. To these teams, located all over the structure in accordance with the decisions to be made, is delegated power over different kinds of decisions. So the structure becomes decentralized selectively in the vertical and horizontal dimensions, that is, power is distributed unevenly, all over the structure, according to expertise and need.

All the distinctions of conventional structure disappear in the innovative organization, as can be seen in the figure above. With power based on expertise, the line-staff distinction evaporates. With power distributed throughout the structure, the distinction between the strategic apex and the rest of the structure blurs.

These organizations are found in environments that are both complex and dynamic, because those are the ones that require sophisticated innovation, the type that calls for the cooperative efforts of many different kinds of experts. One type of adhocracy is often associated with a production system that is very complex, sometimes automated, and so requires a highly skilled and influential support staff to design and maintain the technical system of the operating core. (The dashed lines of the figure designate the separation of the operating core from the adhocratic administrative structure.) Here the projects take place in the administration to bring new operating facilities on line (as when a new complex is designed in a petrochemicals firm). Another type of adhocracy produces its projects directly for its clients (as in a think tank consulting firm or manufacturer of engineering prototypes). Here, as a result, the operators also take part in the projects, bringing their expertise to bear on them; hence the operating core blends into the administrative structure (as indicated in the figure above the dashed line). This second type of adhocracy tends to be young on average, because with no standard products or services, many tend to fail while others escape their vulnerability by standardizing some products or services and so converting themselves to a form of bureaucracy.[1]

The Missionary Organization

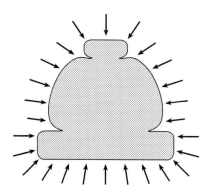

---

[1] We shall clarify in a later reading these two basic types of adhocracies. Toffler employed the term adhocracy in his popular book *Future Shock,* but it can be found in print at least as far back as 1964.

Our sixth configuration forms another rather distinct combination of the elements we have been discussing. When an organization is dominated by its ideology, its members are encouraged to pull together, and so there tends to be a loose division of labor, little job specialization, as well as a reduction of the various forms of differentiation found in the other configurations—of the strategic apex from the rest, of staff from line or administration from operations, between operators, between divisions, and so on.

What holds the missionary together—that is, provides for its coordination—is the standardization of norms, the sharing of values and beliefs among all its members. And the key to ensuring this is their socialization, effected through the design parameter of indoctrination. Once the new member has been indoctrinated into the organization—once he or she identifies strongly with the common beliefs—then he or she can be given considerable freedom to make decisions. Thus the result of effective indoctrination is the most complete form of decentralization. And because other forms of coordination need not be relied upon, the missionary organization formalizes little of its behavior as such and makes minimal use of planning and control systems. As a result, it has little technostructure. Likewise, external professional training is not relied upon, because that would force the organization to surrender a certain control to external agencies.

Hence, the missionary organization ends up as an amorphous mass of members, with little specialization as to job, differentiation as to part, division as to status.

Missionaries tend not to be very young organizations—it takes time for a set of beliefs to become institutionalized as an ideology. Many missionaries do not get a chance to grow very old either (with notable exceptions, such as certain long-standing religious orders). Missionary organizations cannot grow very large per se—they rely on personal contacts among their members—although some tend to spin off other enclaves in the form of relatively independent units sharing the same ideology. Neither the environment nor the technical system of the missionary organization can be very complex, because that would require the use of highly skilled specialists, who would hold a certain power and status over others and thereby serve to differentiate the structure. Thus we would expect to find the simplest technical systems in these organizations, usually hardly any at all, as in religious orders or in the primitive farm cooperatives.

The Political Organization

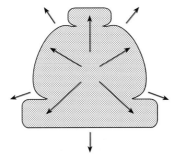

Finally, we come to a form of organization characterized, structurally at least, by what it lacks. When an organization has no dominate part, no dominant mechanism of coordination, and no stable form of centralization or decentralization, it may have difficulty tempering the conflicts within its midst, and a form of organization called the *political* may result. What characterizes its behavior is the pulling apart of its different parts, as shown in the figure above.

Political organizations can take on different forms. Some are temporary, reflecting difficult transitions in strategy or structure that evoke conflict. Others are more permanent, perhaps because the organization must face competing internal forces (say, between necessarily strong marketing and production departments), perhaps because a kind of political rot has set in but the organization is sufficiently entrenched to support it (being, for example, a monopoly or a protected government unit).

Together, all these configurations seem to encompass and integrate a good deal of what we know about organizations. It should be emphasized however, that as presented, each configuration is idealized—a simplification, really a caricature of reality. No real organization is ever exactly like any one of them, although some do come remarkably close, while others seem to reflect combinations of them, sometimes in transition from one to another.

The first five represent what seem to be the most common forms of organizations; thus these will form the basis for the "context" section of this book—labeled entrepreneurial, mature, diversified, innovation, and professional. There, a reading in each chapter will be devoted to each of these configurations, describing its structure, functioning, conditions, strategy-making process, and the issues that surround it. Other readings in these chapters will look at specific strategies in each of these contexts, industry conditions, strategy techniques, and so on.

The other two configurations—the missionary and the political—seem to be less common, represented more by the forces of culture and conflict that exist in all organizations than by distinct forms as such. Hence they will be discussed in the two chapters that immediately follow this one, on "Dealing with Power" and "Dealing with Culture." But because all these configurations themselves must not be taken as hard and fast, indeed because ideology and politics work within different configurations in all kinds of interesting ways, a final section seeks to broaden this view of organizations.

BEYOND CONFIGURATION

"Lumpers" are people who categorize, who synthesize. "Splitters" are people who analyze, who see all the nuances. From the standpoint of organization, both are right and both are wrong. Without categories, it would be impossible to practice management. With only categories, it could not be practiced effectively.

The author was mostly a lumper until a friend asked him if he wanted to play "jigsaw puzzle" or "LEGO" with his concepts. In other words, do all these concepts fit together in set ways and known images (puzzle), or were they to be used creatively to create new images? The remainder of this reading is presented in the spirit of playing "organizational LEGO." It tries to show how we can use splitting as well as lumping to understand what makes organizations effective as well as what causes many of their fundamental problems.

FORMS AND FORCES

The configurations described above are *forms,* and they are laid out at the nodes of a pentagon in Figure 9. Many organizations seem to fit naturally into one of the original five, but some do not fit, to the lumpers' chagrin. To respond to this, five *forces* have been added, each associated with one of the original forms:

- *Direction* in the entrepreneurial form, for some sense of where the organization must go. This is often called "strategic vision." Without direction the various activities of an organization cannot easily work together to achieve common purpose.

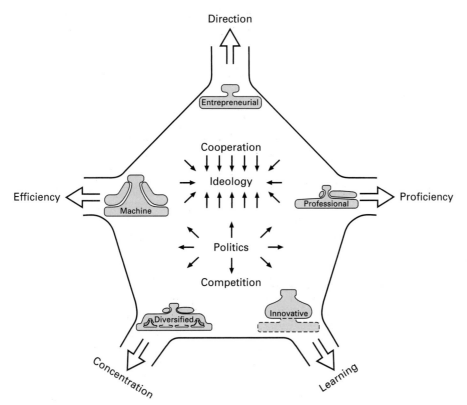

Figure 9
**An Integrating Pentagon of
Forces and Forms**

- *Efficiency* in the machine form. This ensures a viable ratio of benefits gained to costs in-curred. Lack of concern for efficiency would cause all but the most protected organization to fade.
- *Proficiency* in the professional form. Organizations need this to carry out tasks with high levels of knowledge and skill. The difficult work of organizations would otherwise simply not get done.
- *Concentration* in the diversified form. If individual units in an organization fail to concen-trate their efforts on particular markets, it becomes almost impossible to manage a diversi-fied organization.
- *Learning* in the innovative or adhocracy form. Organizations need to be able to learn, to discover new things for their customers and themselves—to adapt and to innovate.

Two other forces exist that are not necessarily associated with a particular form:

- *Cooperation,* represented by ideology. This is the force for pulling together.
- *Competition,* represented by politics. This is the force for pulling apart.

For the lumpers we now have a *portfolio of forms,* and for the splitters we now have a *system of forces.* Both views are critical for the practice of management. One represents the most fundamental forces that act on organizations. All serious organizations experi-ence all seven of them, at one time or another, if not all the time. The other represents the most fundamental forms that organizations can take, which some of them do some of the time. Together, these forces and forms appear to constitute a powerful diagnostic framework by which to understand what goes on in organizations and to prescribe ef-fective change in them.

When one force dominates an organization, it is drawn toward the associated *con-figuration,* but must deal with *contamination.* When no force dominates, the organiza-tion is a balanced *combination* of forces, including periods of *conversion* from one form to another; there is a problem of *cleavage.* Contamination and cleavage require the man-agement of *contradiction,* which is where ideology and politics come in.

Dominant forces drive an organization to one of the pure forms discussed earlier—entrepreneurial, machine, professional, diversified, innovative, missionary or political. These are not "real," but are abstract models designed to capture some reality. Some organizations *do* match the pure forms closely. If the form fits, the organization should wear it. Configuration has benefits. With configuration, an organization achieves a sense of order, or integration. There is internal consistency, synergy among processes, fit with the external context. Configuration also helps outsiders understand an organization. The consistency of configuration keeps workers from being confused, and helps the organization be effective and efficient. For classification, for comprehension, for diagnosis, and for design, configuration seems to be effective. But only so long as everything holds still. Introduce the dynamics of evolutionary change and, sooner or later, configuration becomes ineffective.

Contamination by Configuration

The harmony, consistency, and fit that is configuration's greatest strength is also its greatest weakness. The dominant force can become so strong that it drives out everything else. For example, control in machine organizations may contaminate the innovators in research. Machine organizations recognize this when they put their research and development facilities away from the head office, to avoid the contaminating effects of the central efficiency experts. The opposite case is also well known—the "looseness" in adhocracies may contaminate the accountants. This contamination may be a small price to pay for being coherently organized, until things go out of control.

Configuration Out of Control

When the need arises for change, the dominating force may act to hold the organization in place. The other forces have atrophied, and so the organization goes out of control. For instance, the machine organization in need of a new strategy may have no entrepreneurs and no innovators left to give it its new direction. The dominating force may drive the organization out of control directly, by simply becoming too strong, e.g., an obsession with control in the machine organization. Miller and Kets de Vries (1987) have developed five organizational "neuroses" that correspond roughly to what can happen in extreme cases of contamination in the five forms. Each is an example of a system that may once have been healthy but has run out of control.

- *Dramatic:* the entrepreneur, freed from other forces, may take the organization on an ego trip. This can even occur in large diversified organizations that are dominated by strong CEOs.
- *Compulsive:* happens when there is completeness of control in machine organizations. This is the classic overbearing bureaucracy.
- *Paranoid:* paranoia is often a collective tendency in some professional organizations like universities and hospitals. Professors and doctors are always suspicious that their peers, or worse, the "administration," are planning to undermine their efforts.
- *Depressive:* can be the result of an obsession with the bottom line in diversified organizations. Being a cash cow that is constantly being "milked" is very bad for morale.
- *Schizoid:* the need to innovate, but to get the commercial benefits from innovation, means that adhocracies are in a constant oscillation between divergent and convergent thinking.

In other words, behaviors that were once functional become dysfunctional when pursued to excess.

Containment of Configuration

Truly effective organizations do not exist in pure form. What keeps a configuration effective is not only the dominance of a single force but also the constraining effects of other forces. This is *containment.* To manage configuration effectively is to exploit one form but also to reconcile the different forces. Machine organizations must exploit their efficiency but must still allow for innovation. Innovative forms must exploit their power to create, but must find a way to make it financially lucrative.

COMBINATION

Configuration is nice if you can have it. But some organizations all of the time, and all organizations some of the time, are unable to have it. They must instead balance competing forces. Organizations like this are called *combinations;* instead of being a node in the pentagon, they are somewhere within it. It is probable that roughly half of all organizations are combinations.

Kinds of Combinations

When only two of the five forces meet in rough balance, that is a *hybrid.* A symphony orchestra is an example, being a rough balance of entrepreneurial and professional forms. Some organizations experience *multiple combinations.* Apple Computer may be a combination of adhocracy (a legacy of its founder, Steve Jobs), machine (developed by John Scully to increase efficiency in production and distribution), entrepreneurial (in the person of a dynamic sales manager), and professional (in marketing and training). In some cases the combined forces interact in a steady state. This would probably be the case in a symphony orchestra. In other cases, the interaction is separable in place and/or time, as it is at Apple Computer.

Cleavage in Combinations

If configuration encourages contamination, sometimes combination encourages *cleavage.* Instead of one force dominating, two or more confront each other to the point of paralyzing the organization. A common example from business organizations is the innovative drive of R&D against the machine-like drive of production.

Despite the problems created by having to balance forces, combination of one kind or another is probably necessary in most organizations. Effective organizations usually balance many forces. Configuration merely means a tilt toward one force; combination is more balanced.

CONVERSION

The preceding discussions of configuration and combination implied stability. But few organizations stay in one form or combination; they undergo *conversion* from one configuration or combination to another. Often these result from external changes. For example, an innovative organization decides to settle down to exploit an innovation. Or a suddenly unstable market makes a machine become more innovative. Conversions are often temporary, as in the machine organization that becomes an entrepreneurial organization during a crisis.

Cycles of Conversion

The forces that may destroy the organization may instead drive it to another, perhaps more viable, configuration. For example, the entrepreneurial form is inherently vulnerable, because of its reliance on a single leader. It may work well for the young organization, but with aging and growth a dominant need for direction may be displaced by that for efficiency. Then conversion to the machine form becomes necessary—the power of one leader must be replaced by that of administrators.

The implication is that organizations go through stages as they develop, sequenced into so-called life cycles. The most common life cycle is the one mentioned above. It begins with the entrepreneurial form and moves down along the left edge of the pentagon. Growth leads to the machine form, and even greater growth leads ultimately to the diversified form. Another life cycle, depicted along the right edge of the pentagon, occurs for firms dependent on expertise. They move from the entrepreneurial form to either the professional form (if they can standardize their services) or the innovative form (if their services are more creative). Another common conversion is when an innovative form decides to exploit and perfect the skills it has developed and settles into a professional form, a common conversion in consulting.

Ideology and politics play a role in conversion. Ideology is a more important force in young organizations. That is because cultures can develop more easily in younger firms, especially with charismatic leadership in the entrepreneurial stage. By comparison, it is extremely difficult to build a strong and lasting culture in a mature organization. By contrast, politics typically spreads as the energy of the young firm dissipates and its activities become more diffuse. As the organization becomes more formalized, its culture is blunted, and politics becomes a more important force as an organization ages.

Cleavage in Conversion

Some conversions are easy because they are so overdue. Most are more difficult and conflictual, requiring periods of transition, prolonged and agonizing. As the organization in transition sits between its old and new forms, it becomes a kind of combination. The forces that create the conversion also create the possibility of cleavage. How does the organization deal with the contradictions?

CONTRADICTION

Organizations that have to reconcile contradictory forces, especially in dealing with change, often turn to the cooperative force of ideology or the competitive force of politics. Indeed, these two forces themselves represent a contradiction that must be managed if an organization is not to run out of control.

While it is true that each can dominate an organization, and so draw it toward a missionary or political form, more commonly they act differently, as *catalysts*. Ideology tends to draw behavior inwards toward a common core; politics drives behavior away from any central place. Both can act to promote change or also to prevent it. Either way, they sometimes render an organization more effective, sometimes less.

Cooperation through Ideology

Ideology represents the force for cooperation in an organization, for collegiality and consensus. It encourages members to look inward, to take their lead from the imperatives of the organization's own vision. One important implication is that the infusion of ideology renders any particular configuration more effective. People get fired up to pursue efficiency or proficiency or whatever else drives the organization. When this happens to a machine organization—as in a McDonald's, very responsive to its customers and very sensitive to its employees—we have a "snappy bureaucracy." Bureaucratic machines are not supposed to be snappy, but ideology changes the nature of their quest for efficiency.

Another implication is that ideology helps an organization manage contradiction and so to deal with change. The innovative machine and the tightly controlled innovative organization are inherent contradictions. These organizations handle their contradictions by having strong cultures. Such organizations can more easily reconcile their opposing forces because what matters to their people is the organization itself, not any of its particular parts. This is how Toyota gets efficiency and high quality at the same time.

Limits to Cooperation

Ideologies sound completely wonderful, but they are difficult to build and sustain. And established ideologies can get in the way of organizational effectiveness. They may discourage change by forcing everyone to work within the same set of beliefs. This has implications for strategy. Change *within* strategic perspective, to a new position, is facilitated by a strong ideology. But change *of* perspective—fundamental change—is discouraged by it.

Competition through Politics

Politics represents the force for competition in an organization, for conflict and confrontation. It can infuse any of the configurations or combinations, aggravating contamination and cleavage. In a configuration, the representatives of the dominant force "lord it" over others. This could lead to contamination. In a combination, representatives of the various forces relish opportunities to do battle with each other, potentially leading to cleavage.

One problem facing strategic managers is that politics may be a more "natural" force than ideology. Left to themselves, organizations seem to pull apart rather easily. Keeping them together requires considerable and constant effort.

Benefits of Competition

If pulling together discourages people from addressing fundamental change, then pulling apart may become the only way to ensure that happens. Change requires challenging the status quo. Politics may facilitate this; if there are no entrepreneurial or innovative forces stimulating strategic change, it may be the *only* available force for change.

Both politics and ideology can promote organizational effectiveness as well as undermine it. Ideology can be a force for revitalization, energizing the organization and making its people more responsive. But it can also hinder fundamental change. Likewise, politics often impedes necessary change and wastes valuable resources. But it can also promote important change that may be available in no other way. It can enable those who realize the need for change to challenge those who do not. The last remaining contradiction is the one between ideology and politics themselves.

Combining Cooperation and Competition

Ideology and politics themselves have to be reconciled. Pulling together ideologically infuses life; splitting apart politically challenges the status quo. Only by encouraging both can an organization sustain its viability. Ideology helps secondary forces to contain a dominant one; politics encourages them to challenge it.

The balance between ideology and politics should be a dynamic equilibrium. Most of the time ideology should be pulling things together, contained by healthy internal competition. When fundamental change becomes necessary, politics should help pull the organization apart.

COMPETENCE

What makes an organization effective? The "Peterian" view (named after Tom Peters of *In Search of Excellence* fame) is that organizations should be "hands on, value driven." The "Porterian" view (named after Michael Porter) says that organizations should use competitive analysis. To Porter, effectiveness resides in strategy, while to Peters it is the operations that count. We must find out what really makes an organization truly effective. We need to understand what takes it to a viable strategy in the first place, what makes it excellent there, and how some organizations are able to sustain viability and excellence in the face of change.

Here are five views to guide us in our search for organizational effectiveness:

CONVERGENCE: First is the *convergence* hypothesis. Its motto is that there is "one best way" to design an organization. This is usually associated with the machine form. A good structure is one with a rigid hierarchy of authority, with spans of control no greater than six, with heavy use of strategic planning, MIS, and whatever else happens to be in the current fashion of the rationalizers. In *In Search of Excellence,* by contrast, Peters and Waterman argued that ideology was the key to an organization's success. We cannot dismiss this hypothesis—sometimes there *are* proper things to do in most, perhaps all, organizations. But we must take issue with its general thrust. Society has paid an enormous price for "one best way" thinking over the course of this century, on the part of all its organizations that have been drawn into using what is fashionable rather than functional. We need to look beyond the obvious, beyond the convergence hypothesis.

CONGRUENCE: Beyond convergence is the *contingency* or "it all depends" approach. Introduced into organization theory in the 1960s, it suggests that running an organization is like choosing dinner from a buffet table—a little bit of this, a little bit of that, all selected according to specific needs. Organizational effectiveness thus becomes a question of matching a given set of internal attributes, treated as a kind of portfolio, with various situational factors. The congruence hypothesis has certainly been an improvement, but like a dinner plate stacked with an old assortment of foods, it has not been good enough.

CONFIGURATION: The motto of the *configuration* hypothesis is "getting it all together." Design your organization as you would a jigsaw puzzle, fitting the organizational pieces together to create a coherent, harmonious picture. There is reason to believe that organizations succeed in good part because they are consistent in what they do; they are certainly easier to manage that way. But, as we have seen, configuration has its limits, too.

CONTRADICTION: While the lumpers may like the configuration hypothesis, splitters prefer the *contradiction* hypothesis. Their call is to manage the dynamic tension between contradictory forces. They point to the common occurrence of combinations and conversions, where organizations are forced to manage contradictory forces. This is an important hypothesis—together with that of configuration, which are in their own dynamic tension, it is an important clue to organizational effectiveness. But still it is not sufficient.

CREATION: The truly great organization transcends all of the foregoing while building on it to achieve something more. It respects the *creation* hypothesis. Creativity is its forte, "understand your inner nature" is its motto, LEGO its image. The most interesting organizations live at the edges, far from the logic of conventional organizations, where as Raphael (1976: 5–6) has pointed out in biology (for example, between the sea and the land, or at the forest's edge), the richest, most varied, and most interesting forms of life can be found. These organizations invent novel approaches that solve festering problems and so provide all of us with new ways to deal with our world of organizations.

ORGANIZATIONAL CULTURE AND STRATEGY

▼

In this chapter we examine what is becoming an increasingly popular way for organizations to gain effectiveness—by using strong cultures. We will examine the basics of culture and how it can be used as the basis for strategy formation.

BASICS OF ORGANIZATIONAL CULTURE

Culture is made up of intangible things that are shared by the people in an organization—values, beliefs that guide action, understandings, even ways of thinking.[1] Some organizations have poorly developed cultures or hardly any distinct ones at all. Organizations with weak cultures can be called stylistically barren. In contrast, some firms have very strong cultures, either by coincidence or by design. These could be called stylistically rich.[2] Here, members get a sense of organizational identity and commit to inspiring values and beliefs. Such values help keep an organization stable, and provide new members with tools for understanding events and activities that go on in the organization.[3]

Culture typically exists at two levels. The observable level has the visible artifacts—the way people behave and dress, physical settings, symbols, ceremonies, and stories. We will discuss these later. Below the surface are the deeper values and beliefs that represent the "real" culture.[4] Some common and significant elements of culture are rites and ceremonies, stories, symbols, and language.[5]

RITES AND CEREMONIES. These well-deveoped, prearranged, formal activities are usually staged for the benefit of an audience, and they make up special events in an organization. Organizational managers can use them to reinforce values or highlight the efforts of people who symbolize what the organization holds valuable. There are four kinds of rites. **Rites of passage** are used to help employees move into new social roles. A good example is induction and basic training into the U. S. Army. Another example is the speech the top management at Sony makes to all new employees every year. **Rites of enhancement** are ceremonies that help people develop stronger social identities; they also raise employees' status in the organization. A good example is an organization's annual awards night; people who are rewarded for outstanding effort identify more with the organization, and their status is raised in the eyes of everyone else attending the ceremony. **Rites of renewal** are designed to improve organizational functioning using training or development activities. An example would be a series of faculty development seminars at a college. Even a series of advanced word-processing–skills seminars for clerical staff would be a rite of renewal. An elaborate series of organizational development activities (e.g., team building) is another example. **Rites of integration** are used to bond organizational members closer together, creating good feelings among them, in order to build commitment. Monthly brown-bag lunches among faculty in universities are one example. An office holiday party is another.

STORIES. These are accounts based on factual events from the organization's past; they are usually widely shared among employees and are told to new people to inform them about what is considered exemplary in the organization. Many stories are about **heroes,** people who are models or ideals of what the organization values; these are usually quite reliable types of stories. Then there are **legends,** stories grounded in actual events from an organization's history which may have been embellished with made-up details to drive home the connection to what the organization values. Finally there are **myths,** stories that fit well with the organization's values and beliefs but which are based mostly on fictional events.[6]

SYMBOLS. A symbol is one thing that represents another thing. Since rites and stories represent, in their own way, the deeper values held by an organization's members, they are types of symbols, too. But people typically think of symbols as physical artifacts. For example, at the L. L. Bean mail order firm, love of the outdoors is so important that the retail store has a fully stocked trout pond in a central location, and the corporate letterhead shows a scene of a mountain lake. In some organizations, office size and decor symbolize a person's status. In other organizations, awards can be powerful symbols; for example, top salespeople at Mary Kay Cosmetics are allowed to use pink Cadillacs for a year.

LANGUAGE. Many organizations have special slogans, sayings, and metaphors that often convey special meanings to members of the organization. Hewlett-Packard uses the catch-all phrase "The H-P Way" to capture the feeling of the company's freewheeling sense of creativity and freedom to innovate. L. L. Bean displays sayings by founder Leon Leonwood Bean in all areas of the retail store, offices, warehouses, and manufacturing plants.

SPONTANEOUS AND MANAGED CULTURE

Aspects of culture in organizations generally arise without anyone consciously trying to create them. People in the organization interact over a long period, coming to implicit agreements about what is important (values), about what they need to do (guiding beliefs), about what makes the organization and its industry "tick" (examples of understandings), and about how all the components of their system fit together (ways of thinking or mental maps).[7]

But sometimes, culture is less spontaneous, more managed.[8] The term **ideology** has the connotation of a set of doctrines or beliefs forming the basis of an organizational system[9], although in his readings in this chapter, Mintzberg uses the term to mean strong culture. Organizations that use ideology will tend to frame their organization's system of beliefs as a set of doctrines to which members must adhere, not simply learn about. You may recall that in his reading in Chapter Six on structure and systems, while discussing the parts of the organization, Mintzberg mentioned indoctrination as one of the design parameters. The implication was that if managers want to develop ideologies for organizations, they must be willing to use indoctrination.

CULTURE, IDEOLOGY, AND STRATEGY

An organization can use culture or ideology as the basis of its strategy formation. This idea, which we referred to as the cultural school[10] in Chapter Five, suggests that strategy formation is a process of collective vision, rooted in the beliefs shared by the members of the organization (as opposed to the entrepreneurial school's individual vision, discussed in Chapter Nine).

Organizations that exemplify the cultural school of strategy formation tend not to emphasize planning or analysis. They prefer to create strategies based on **norms** and **values** held by their members. A good example is Sony Corporation, whose strategy is based on strong norms of innovation and service to humanity through the artful combination of mechanics and electronics. Sony uses no elaborate rational planning techniques.

Ideological Strategy and Japanese Management Practices

Creating strategy through an ideological process may seem "soft" compared to the usual rigorous planning processes. But ideological strategy requires a deliberate, integrated effort that may be even more rigorous than planning. Elite Japanese companies such as Sony, Toyota, Honda, Matsushita, Nissan, and Mitsubishi have come to exemplify the kind of integrated effort required. In their article "Management Practices in Japan and Their Impact on Business Strategy,"[11] Vladimir Pucik and Nina Hatvany outline the elements of ideological strategy in the elite Japanese company.

STRATEGIC THRUSTS OF JAPANESE MANAGEMENT PRACTICES. These Japanese organizations focus on human resources. This translates into three strategic thrusts. The first is the organization as an *internal labor market*. The firm tries to assure its workers of lifetime employment and allocates labor according to internal rules, not external demand and supply conditions. This requires much skill training within the firm, but the skills become "company specific," discouraging employee mobility. A second strategic thrust is having an *articulated and unique company philosophy*. This presents a clear picture of the goals, norms, and values of the firm. Individuals get clear direction, are more motivated, yet have some constraints placed on their behavior. The third thrust of Japanese ideological strategy is *intensive socialization*. Ensuring that employees know and understand the company philosophy is one of the primary functions of the company's socialization effort. In Japan, it is also important to develop cohesiveness based on moderate views and a harmonious personality. The process begins with the initial training program, but continues with "resocialization" each time the recruit enters a new position.

MANAGEMENT TECHNIQUES IN JAPAN. These three strategic thrusts are expressed in six management techniques. The first is *open communication*—management is committed to developing a climate of trust in the corporation through sharing information across departmental boundaries. Team spirit and networks of contacts encourage face-to-face communication. Second is *job rotation, slow promotion,* and *internal training*; under conditions of lifetime employment, promotion is unlikely to be rapid. Firms tend to identify "elite" workers informally early on, rewarding them with carefully planned

lateral transfers. There is also a "dual" promotion system: status and position. If a good performer can't be promoted because there are no vacancies, he or she can be promoted in status. The emphasis on job rotation creates an environment in which the employee becomes a generalist, rather than a specialist.

The third management technique that creates the Japanese system of ideological strategy is the *competitive appraisal system.* Competition focuses on how to build networks of people who will be future rivals for promotion. Fourth, elite Japanese companies *emphasize work groups.* Most company policies revolve around groups. Cohesion is aided by delegating responsibility to work groups and by job rotation and group-based performance feedback. The groups themselves solve operational problems. Quality Control (QC) circles are widely used. Fifth is *consultative decision making;* extensive face-to-face communication is often mistaken for participative decision making, but most proposals are made by middle managers at the request of top managers. It is more of a top-down or interactive-consultative process.

Lastly, elite Japanese companies are characterized by *concern for the employee*— informal communication gives managers the chance to express concern about the personal well-being of employees, on which they spend a great deal of time. (Quality of relationships is part of their evaluation.) The company sponsors cultural, athletic, and other recreational activities, which are supposed to be voluntary but in which virtually all members participate. Many companies give benefits like family, commuting, and other job-related allowances. Some also have company housing, dormitories, housing loans, company nurseries, company scholarships, credit extension, savings plans, and insurance.

RESULTING STRENGTHS OF THE JAPANESE MANAGEMENT SYSTEM. These six management techniques are burdensome, intense, and difficult to execute. The result is a system of ideological strategy that provides some distinctive strengths to the elite Japanese firm. The first of these is a *competitive spirit,* where the firm is seen as good and the rest of the world is seen as needing to be defeated. Another result is a *long-term perspective.* Since decision makers are around for a long time, they cannot escape the consequences of their decisions; this minimizes the danger of taking advantage of short-term gains to the detriment of long-term goals. Since the individual's welfare is tied to the company's welfare, this increases the long-term view.

The third effect of the Japanese ideological approach is an *emphasis on market share* which fits the Japanese system well because it provides an objective measurement of competitive standing. Fourth, elite Japanese firms *emphasize internal growth;* Japanese values put a premium on maintaining the organization as an intact, bonded group. Mergers and acquisitions, even divestitures, are rare in Japan, and hostile takeovers, so common in the United States until recently, are almost impossible. As a result, firms must concentrate on efficiently making high-quality products that meet customer needs. Top managers may focus on production, meaning product and process improvement, free from worry about takeovers or defense against takeovers. Also, Japanese firms tend to diversify by building on strengths built up over the long term, a method that research has shown to be the best approach to diversification.[12]

Lastly, Japanese firms are *aggressive innovators.* They do not segregate R&D, production, and marketing from one another but diffuse the innovation process widely throughout the organization. This has recently become the method of choice in the West, called the horizontal linkage model.[13]

It seems apparent that even though this management system does not closely resemble the usually prescribed rational planning approach, it is just as intense in its own way, even more so; the effort required to create and maintain the ideology is enormous. Also, some research has shown that organizational competencies built on people's skills and attitudes are more durable and distinctive than those built on other resources.[14] For these reasons, companies using ideological strategy can be formidable competitors.

CULTURE AND ORGANIZATIONAL EFFECTIVENESS

Denison studied the fit among strategy, culture, and environment[15] that sheds some light on why the elite Japanese firms discussed above are so successful. He found four types of organizational cultures, depending on whether the organization had an internal or an external strategic focus and on whether it faced a stable or a dynamic environment.

Firms with external emphases that faced environments needing change and flexibility tended to have **adaptability cultures.** The norms and values of this type of culture favor interaction with customers and other external stakeholders, in an effort to identify their needs and meet them through the firm's efforts. This type of culture is common in electronics firms, advertising agencies, marketing companies, and fashion companies. It is obviously appropriate for turbulent environments, but things can get frenetic in adaptability cultures.

Companies whose strength and focus are internal, but who face dynamic environments, tend to have **involvement cultures.** These cultures focus on involving all members of the organization in meeting the needs of external constituents. High involvement and participation create commitment and greater feelings of responsibility. This type of culture is possibly the closest to the elite Japanese-company culture described above. Firms that build their distinctive competencies by developing people and getting them to work together can be formidable competitors. This culture type can be very pleasant in which to work, but some employees might find it stifling.

The **mission culture** is similar to Mintzberg's missionary organization, discussed below. The emphasis is on a shared vision of what the organization is about, which tends to be meeting some well-defined yet stable external need. Sony, with its well-articulated desire to provide unique electromechanical products to consumers around the world, is a good example. Many not-for-profit organizations, religious and otherwise, fit into this culture type. Clearly, firms with this culture type could run into difficulty should their environments change. These firms would also tend to select their members carefully, since belief in the mission cannot waver.

When the environment is stable and the focus is internal, the culture is likely to be a **consistency culture.** What is important in such an organization is following established ways of doing things. Due process is critical; methodical approaches are highly valued. Professional organizations, like law firms, accounting firms, and universities, tend to have consistency cultures. As we will see in a later chapter, organizations with these types of cultures can be very pleasant for their employees but can have great difficulty adapting to change, even slow change.

IDEOLOGY AND THE MISSIONARY ORGANIZATION

In his reading "Ideology and the Missionary Organization," Henry Mintzberg shows how ideology develops in an organization. It typically starts with the actions of a charismatic entrepreneur, is elaborated through the kinds of stories described above, and is maintained through four kinds of what Mintzberg calls **identification.** This identification is the degree to which individuals relate to or feel linked to the organization.

Mintzberg describes the **missionary organization** as stylistically rich, where the majority of members identify with the organization's mission. That mission tends to be clear, focused, inspiring, and distinctive. He ends by showing how the missionary form may be an overlay on conventional organizations. This is common in stylistically rich organizations with strong ideologies, such as the elite Japanese firms discussed above.

172

ORGANIZATIONAL CULTURE: "GETTING A FIX" ON AN ELUSIVE CONCEPT

W. Jack Duncan provides a very practical reading for managers about culture. He starts with a description of the surface elements of culture, a discussion that parallels our discussion above. He continues by defining culture and describing a set of techniques, called **triangulation,** which managers can use to try to uncover the subsurface elements of their organization's culture. Using a detailed example from a rehabilitation center, he shows how one must first understand the culture that is in place, and then move to create the kind of culture (or ideology) that can move the organization in the desired direction.

NOTES TO CHAPTER SEVEN

1. Duncan, W. J., "Organizational Culture: Getting a 'Fix' on an Elusive Concept." *Academy of Management Executive* 3 (1989): 229–36; Smircich, L., "Concepts of Culture and Organizational Analysis." *Administrative Science Quarterly* 28 (1983): 339–58; Sathe, V., "Implications of Corporate Culture: A Manager's Guide to Action." *Organizational Dynamics* (Autumn 1983): 5–23.

2. Edwards, J. P., "Strategy Formulation as a Stylistic Process." *International Studies of Management and Organization* (Summer 1977), pp. 13–27.

3. Smircich, "Concepts of Culture and Organizational Analysis"; Peters, T. J., and R. H. Waterman, *In Search of Excellence*. New York: Harper & Row, 1982.

4. Schein, E. H., "Organizational Culture." *American Psychologist* 45 (February 1990): 109–19.

5. Trice, H. M., and J. M. Beyer, "Studying Organizational Cultures through Rites and Ceremonials." *Academy of Management Review* 9 (1984): 653–69; Beyer, J. M., and H. M. Trice, "How an Organization's Rites Reveal Its Culture." *Organizational Dynamics* 15 (Spring 1987): 5–24.

6. Most of the preceding section was based on Trice and Beyer, "Studying Organizational Cultures through Rites and Ceremonials."

7. See Senge, P., *The Fifth Discipline*. New York: Doubleday Currency, 1990, especially Chapter 3, for a discussion of how ways of thinking can trap organizational members.

8. See, for example, Kunda, G., *Engineering Culture*. Philadelphia: Temple University Press, 1992.

9. Based on the definition of *ideology* in *The American Heritage Dictionary of the English Language*, 3rd ed. Boston: Houghton-Mifflin, 1992, p. 896.

10. This school was pioneered by Rhenman and Normann. See Normann, R., "Organizational Innovativeness: Product Variation and Reorientation." *Administrative Science Quarterly* 16 (1971): 203–15; Normann, R., *Management for Growth*. Chichester: John Wiley, 1977; and Rhenman, E., *Organization Theory for Long-Range Planning*. London: John Wiley, 1973.

11. Pucik, V., and N. Hatvany, "Management Practices in Japan and Their Impact on Business Strategy." *Advances in Strategic Management,* vol. 1. Greenwich, Conn.: JAI Press, 1983, pp. 103–31.

12. Rumelt, R., *Strategy, Structure and Economic Performance*. Boston: Harvard Business School, 1974.

13. Daft, R., *Organization Theory and Design,* 4th ed. St. Paul: West Publishing, 1992, pp. 262–63.

14. Barney, J., "Organizational Culture: Can It Be a Source of Competitive Advantage?" *Academy of Management Review* 11 (1986): 656–65.

15. Denison, D., *Corporate Culture and Organizational Effectiveness*. New York: John Wiley, 1990.

IDEOLOGY AND THE MISSIONARY ORGANIZATION

By Henry Mintzberg

We all know that 2 + 2 = 4. But general systems theory, through the concept of synergy, suggests that it can also equal 5, that the parts of a system may produce more working together than they can apart. A flashlight and a battery add up to just so many pieces of hardware; together they form a working system. Likewise an organization is a working system that can entice from its members more than they would produce apart—more effort, more creativity, more output (or, of course, less). This may be "strategic"—deriving from the way components have been combined in the organization. Or it may be motivational: The group is said to develop a "mood," an "atmosphere," to have some kind of "chemistry." In organizations, we talk of a "style," a "culture," a "character." One senses something unique when one walks into the offices of IBM; the chemistry of Hewlett-Packard just doesn't feel the same as that of Texas Instruments, even though the two have operated in some similar businesses.

All these words are used to describe something—intangible yet very real, over and above the concrete components of an organization—that we refer to as its *ideology*. Specifically, an ideology is taken here to mean a rich system of values and beliefs about an organization, shared by its members, that distinguishes it from other organizations. For our purposes, the key feature of such an ideology is its unifying power: It ties the individual to the organization, generating an "esprit de corps," a "sense of mission," in effect, an integration of individual and organizational goals that can produce synergy.

THE DEVELOPMENT OF AN ORGANIZATIONAL IDEOLOGY

The development of an ideology in an organization will be discussed here in three stages. The roots of the ideology are planted when a group of individuals band together around a leader and, through a sense of mission, found a vigorous organization, or invigorate an existing one. The ideology then develops over time through the establishment of traditions. Finally, the existing ideology is reinforced when new members enter the organization and identify with its system of beliefs.

Stage 1: The Rooting of Ideology in a Sense of Mission

Typically, an organization is founded when a single prime mover identifies a mission—some product to be produced, service to be rendered—and collects a group around him or her to accomplish it. Some organizations are, of course, founded by other means, as when a new agency is created by a government or a subsidiary by a corporation. But a prime mover often can still be identified behind the founding of the organization.

The individuals who come together don't do so at random, but coalesce because they share some values associated with the fledgling organization. At the very least they see something in it for themselves. But in some cases, in addition to the mission per se there is a "sense of mission," that is, a feeling that the group has banded together to create something unusual and exciting. This is common in new organizations for a number of reasons.

First, unconstrained by procedure and tradition, new organizations offer wide lat-

Adapted from Henry Mintzberg *Power in and Around Organizations* (copyright © Prentice-Hall, 1983), Chaps. 11 and 21; used by permission of the publisher; based on a summary that appeared in *Mintzberg on Management: Inside Our Strange World of Organizations* (New York: Free Press, 1989).

itude for maneuver. Second, they tend to be small, enabling the members to establish personal relationships. Third, the founding members frequently share a set of strong basic beliefs, sometimes including a sense that they wish to work together. Fourth, the founders of new organizations are often "charismatic" individuals, and so energize the followers and knit them together. Charisma, as Weber (1969:12) used the term, means a sense of "personal devotion" to the leader for the sake of his or her personal qualities rather than formal position. People join and remain with the organization because of dedication to the leader and his or her mission. Thus the roots of strong ideologies tend to be planted in the founding of organizations.

Of course, such ideologies can also develop in existing organizations. But a review of the preceding points suggests why this should be much more difficult to accomplish. Existing organizations *are* constrained by procedures and traditions, many are *already* large and impersonal, and their *existing* beliefs tend to impede the establishment of new ones. Nonetheless, with the introduction of strong charismatic leadership reinforced by a strong new sense of mission, an existing organization can sometimes be invigorated by the creation of a new ideology.

A key to the development of an organizational ideology, in a new or existing organization, is a leadership with a genuine belief in mission and an honest dedication to the people who must carry it out. Mouthing the right words might create the veneer of an organizational ideology, but it is only an authentic feeling on the part of the leadership—which followers somehow sense—that sets the roots of the ideology deep enough to sustain it when other forces, such as impersonal administration (bureaucracy) or politics, challenge it.

Stage 2: The Development of Ideology through Traditions and Sagas

As a new organization establishes itself or an existing one establishes a new set of beliefs, it makes decisions and takes actions that serve as commitments and establish precedents. Behaviors reinforce themselves over time, and actions become infused with value. When those forces are strong, ideology begins to emerge in its own right. That ideology is strengthened by stories—sometimes called "myths"—that develop around important events in the organization's past. Gradually the organization establishes its own unique sense of history. All of this—the precedents, habits, myths, history—form a common base of tradition, which the members of the organization share, thus solidifying the ideology. Gradually, in Selznick's (1957) terms, the organization is converted from an expendable "instrument" for the accomplishment of externally imposed goals into an "institution," a system with a life of its own. It "acquires a self, a distinctive identity."

Thus Clark described the "distinctive college," with reference particularly to Reed, Antioch, and Swarthmore. Such institutions develop, in his words, an "organizational saga," "a collective understanding of a unique accomplishment based on historical exploits," which links the organization's present with its past and "turns a formal place into a beloved institution." (1972:178). The saga captures allegiance, committing people to the institution (Clark 1970:235).

Stage 3: The Reinforcement of Ideology through Identifications

Our description to this point makes it clear that an individual entering an organization does not join a random collection of individuals, but rather a living system with its own culture. He or she may come with a certain set of values and beliefs but there is little doubt that the culture of the organization can weigh heavily on the behavior he or she will exhibit once inside it. This is especially true when the culture is rich—when the organization has an emerging or fully developed ideology. Then the individual's *identification* with and *loyalty* to the organization can be especially strong. Such identification can develop in a number of ways:

- Most simply, identification occurs *naturally* because the new member is attracted to the organization's system of beliefs.
- Identification may also be *selected.* New members are chosen to "fit in" with the existing beliefs, and positions of authority are likewise filled from among the members exhibiting the strongest loyalty to those beliefs.
- Identification may also be *evoked.* When the need for loyalty is especially great, the organization may use informal processes of *socialization* and formal programs of *indoctrination* to reinforce natural or selected commitment to its system of beliefs.
- Finally, and most weakly, identification can be *calculated.* In effect, individuals conform to the beliefs not because they identify naturally with them not because they even necessarily fit in with them, not because they have been socialized or indoctrinated into them, but simply because it pays them to identify with the beliefs. They may enjoy the work or the social group, may like the remuneration, may work to get ahead through promotion and the like. Of course, such identification is fragile. It disappears as soon as an opportunity calculated to be better appears.

Clearly, the higher up this list an organization's member identifications tend to be, the more likely it is to sustain a strong ideology, or even to have such an ideology in the first place. Thus, strong organizational belief systems can be recognized above all by the presence of much natural identification. Attention to selected identification indicates the presence of an ideology, since it reflects an organization's efforts to sustain its ideology, as do efforts at socialization and indoctrination. Some organizations require a good deal of the latter two, because of the need to instill in their new members a complex system of beliefs. When the informal processes of socialization tend to function naturally, perhaps reinforced by more formal programs of indoctrination, then the ideology would seem to be strong. But when an organization is forced to rely almost exclusively on indoctrination, or worse to fall back on forms of calculated identification, then its ideology would appear to be weakening, if not absent to begin with.

THE MISSIONARY ORGANIZATION

While some degree of ideology can be found in virtually every organization, that degree can vary considerably. At one extreme are those organizations, such as religious orders or radical political movements, whose ideologies tend to be strong and whose identifications are primarily natural and selected. Edwards (1977) refers to organizations with strong ideologies as "stylistically rich," Selznick (1957) as "institutions." It is the presence of such an ideology that enables an organization to "have a life of its own," to emerge as "a living social institution" (Selznick 1949:10). At the other extreme are those organizations with relatively weak ideologies, "stylistically barren," in some cases business organizations with strongly utilitarian reward systems. History and tradition have no special value in these organizations. In the absence of natural forms of identification on the part of their members, these organizations sometimes try to rely on the process of indoctrination to integrate individual and organizational goals. But usually they have to fall back on calculated identifications and especially formal controls.

We can refer to "stylistically rich" organizations as *missionaries,* because they are somewhat akin in their beliefs to the religious organizations by that name. Mission counts above all—to preserve it, extend it, or perfect it. That mission is typically (1) clear and focused, so that its members are easily able to identify with it; (2) inspiring, so that the members do, in fact, develop such identifications; and (3) distinctive, so that the organization and its members are deposited into a unique niche where the ideology can flourish. As a result of their attachment to its mission, the members of the organization resist strongly any attempt to change it, to interfere with tradition. The mission and the rest of the ideology must be preserved at all costs.

The missionary organization is a distinct configuration of the attributes of structure, internally highly integrated yet different from other configurations. What hold this organization together—that is, provides for its coordination—is the standardization of its norms, in other words, the sharing of values and beliefs among its members. As was noted, that can happen informally, either through natural selection or else the informal process of socialization. But from the perspective of structural design the key attribute is indoctrination, meaning formalized programs to develop or reinforce identification with the ideology. And once the new member has been selected, socialized, and indoctrinated, he or she is accepted into the system as an equal partner, able to participate in decision making alongside everyone else. Thus, at the limit, the missionary organization can achieve the purest form of decentralization: All who are accepted into the system share its power.

But that does not mean an absence of control. Quite the contrary. No matter how subtle, control tends to be very powerful in this organization. For here, the organization controls not just people's behavior but their very souls. The machine organization buys the "workers' " attention through imposed rules; the missionary organization captures the "members' " hearts through shared values. As Jay noted in his book *Management and Machiavelli* (1970), teaching new Jesuit recruits to "love God and do what you like" is not to do what they like at all but to act in strict conformance with the order's beliefs (1970:70).

Thus, the missionary organization tends to end up as an amorphous mass of members all pulling together within the common ideology, with minimum specialization as to job, differentiation as to part, division as to status. At the limit, managers, staffers, and operators, once selected, socialized, and indoctrinated, all seem rather alike and may, in fact, rotate into each other's positions.

The traditional Israeli kibbutz is a classic example of the missionary organization. In certain seasons, everyone pitches in and picks fruit in the fields by day and then attends the meetings to decide administrative issues by night. Managerial positions exist but are generally filled on a rotating basis so that no one emerges with the status of office for long. Likewise, staff support positions exist, but they too tend to be filled on a rotating basis from the same pool of members, as are the operating positions in the fields. (Kitchen duty is, for example, considered drudgery that everyone must do periodically.) Conversion to industry has, however, threatened that ideology. As suggested, it was relatively easy to sustain the egalitarian ideology when the work was agricultural. Industry, in contrast, generally called for greater levels of technology, specialization, and expertise, with a resulting increase in the need for administrative hierarchy and functional differentiation, all a threat to the missionary orientation. The kibbutzim continue to struggle with this problem.

A number of our points about the traditional kibbutz are summarized in a table developed by Rosner, which contrasts the "principles of kibbutz organization"—classic missionary—with those of "bureaucratic organization," in our terms, the classic machine.

Principles of Bureaucratic Organization	**Principles of Kibbutz Organization**
1. Permanency of office.	Impermanency of office.
2. The office carries with it impersonal, fixed privileges and duties.	The definition of office is flexible—privileges and duties are not formally fixed and often depend on the personality of the official.

3. A hierarchy of functional authorities expressed in the authority of the officials.	A basic assumption of the equal value of all functions without a formal hierarchy of authority.
4. Nomination of officials is based on formal objective qualifications.	Officials are elected, not nominated. Objective qualifications are not decisive, personal qualities are more important in election.
5. The office is a full-time occupation.	The office is usually supplementary to the full-time occupation of the official. (Rosner, 1969)

We can distinguish several forms of the pure missionary organization. Some are *reformers* that set out to change the world directly—anything from overthrowing a government to ensuring that all domestic animals are "decently" clothed. Other missionaries can be called *converters*, their mission being to change the world indirectly, by attracting members and changing them. The difference between the first two types of missionaries is the difference between the Women's Christian Temperance Union and Alcoholics Anonymous. Their ends were similar, but their means differed, seeking to reduce alcoholism in one case by promoting a general ban on liquor sales, in the other by discouraging certain individuals, namely joined members, from drinking. Third are the *cloister* missionaries that seek not to change things so much as to allow their members to pursue a unique style of life. The monasteries that close themselves off from the outside world are good examples, as are groups that go off to found new isolated colonies.

Of course, no organization can completely seal itself off from the world. All missionary organizations, in fact, face the twin opposing pressures of isolation and assimilation. Together these make them vulnerable. On one side is the threat of *isolation*, of growing ever inward in order to protect the unique ideology from the pressures of the ordinary world until the organization eventually dies for lack of renewal. On the other side is the threat of *assimilation*, of reaching out so far to promote the ideology that it eventually gets compromised. When this happens, the organization may survive but the ideology dies, and so the configuration changes (typically to the machine form).

IDEOLOGY AS AN OVERLAY ON CONVENTIONAL ORGANIZATIONS

So far we have discussed what amounts to the extreme form of ideological organization, the missionary. But more organizations have strong ideologies that can afford to structure themselves in this way. The structure may work for an Israeli kibbutz in a remote corner of the Negev desert, but this is hardly a way to run a Hewlett-Packard or a McDonald's, let alone a kibbutz closer to the worldly pressures of Tel Aviv.

What such organizations tend to do is overlay ideological characteristics on a more conventional structure—perhaps machinelike in the case of McDonald's and that second kibbutz, innovative in the case of Hewlett-Packard. The mission may sometimes seem ordinary—serving hamburgers, producing instruments and computers—but it is carried out with a good dose of ideological fervor by employees firmly committed to it.

Best known for this are, of course, certain of the Japanese corporations, Toyota being a prime example. Ouchi and Jaeger (1978:308) contrast in the table reproduced below the typical large American corporation (Type A) with its Japanese counterpart (Type J).

Type A (for American)	Type J (for Japanese)
Short-term employment	Lifetime employment
Individual decision making	Consensual decision making
Individual responsibility	Collective responsibility
Rapid evaluation and promotion	Slow evaluation and promotion
Explicit, formalized control	Implicit, informal control
Specialized career path	Nonspecialized career path
Segmented concern	Holistic concern

Ouchi and Jaeger (1978) in fact make their point best with an example in which a classic Japanese ideological orientation confronts a conventional American bureaucratic one:

> [D]uring one of the author's visits to a Japanese bank in California, both the Japanese president and the American vice-presidents of the bank accused the other of being unable to formulate objectives. The Americans meant that the Japanese president could not or would not give them explicit, quantified targets to attain over the next three or six months, while the Japanese meant that the Americans could not see that once they understood the company's philosophy, they would be able to deduce for themselves the proper objective for any conceivable situation. (p. 309)

In another study, however, Ouchi together with Johnson (1978) discussed a native American corporation that does resemble the Type J firm (labeled "Type Z"; Ouchi (1981) later published a best seller about such organizations). In it, they found greater loyalty, a strong collective orientation, less specialization, and a greater reliance on informal controls. For example, "a new manager will be useless for at least four or five years. It takes that long for most people to decide whether the new person really fits in, whether they can really trust him." That was in sharp contrast to the "auction market" atmosphere of a typical American firm: It "is almost as if you could open the doors each day with 100 executives and engineers who had been randomly selected from the country, and the organization would work just as well as it does now" (1978:302).

The trends in American business over several decades—"professional" management, emphasis on technique and rationalization, "bottom-line" mentality—have worked against the development of organizational ideologies. Certainly the missionary configuration has hardly been fashionable in the West, especially the United States. But ideology may have an important role to play there, given the enormous success many Japanese firms have had in head-on competition with American corporations organized in machine and diversified ways, with barren cultures. At the very least, we might expect more ideological overlays on the conventional forms of organizations in the West. But this, as we hope our discussion has made clear, may be both for better and for worse.

ORGANIZATIONAL CULTURE: "GETTING A FIX" ON AN ELUSIVE CONCEPT

READING

By W. Jack Duncan

The study of organizational culture, some believe, is merely the latest in a long line of management fads. The concept has been trivialized by definitions like "Organizational culture is the glue that holds organizations together, or the lubrication that makes the gears mesh."

Consequently, it is tempting to ignore the whole issue. Even some of the most de-

The Academy of Management EXECUTIVE, 1989, Vol. III, No. 3, pp. 229–236.

voted students of organizational culture confess to disturbing doubts about their ability to make sense out of this vague concept.

Yet a survey of chief executive officers revealed that most believed that organizational cultures are real, and that strong cultures contribute to corporate success. Forty percent said they believed strongly enough to try to "deal with culture in a serious manner."[1]

Let's look closely at the elements that are said to make up a corporate culture. First are the organization's myths, symbols, and labels. Few people doubt that managers traffic in images and more often act as evangelists or psychologists than accountants or engineers.[2] Their job requires that they be skilled interpreters of (1) organizational stories that possess underlying meanings; (2) organizational histories that stir the emotions; and (3) myths—those dramatic narratives of imagined events that contribute to corporate legends, help unify groups, and can build competitive advantages.[3] Moreover, rites and rituals can be useful in helping new staff members adapt to the organization, and parting ceremonies can ease the pain and disorientation of plant closings, layoffs, or the closing of an entire organization.[4]

While all of these cultural realities are elusive, the manager can ill afford to ignore them. If they are meaningful to people, managers must consider them important. If we believe that organizational culture is real, then we must agree that managers and researchers need to find ways to adequately describe and ultimately use the concept and, ultimately, use it to help companies accomplish their organizational goals.[5]

A consultant with McKinsey and Company has stated that to manage successfully, a company must (1) decide what kind of culture is needed in the organization, (2) evaluate the existing culture to determine where gaps exist between the actual and desired cultures, (3) decide how to close these gaps, and (4) repeat the entire process periodically.[6] The process of managing culture, therefore, begins with our ability to describe the kind of culture we want and determine how our existing culture deviates from the desired one.

This article reports on the application of a multi-method technique known as "triangulation" to the study of one organization's culture. The use of obtrusive observation, self-administered questionnaires, and personal interviews made it possible to construct a holistic picture of the organization's culture that helped management manage it better.

WHAT IS ORGANIZATIONAL CULTURE?

A good definition of organizational culture was provided almost four decades ago by Eliott Jacques:

> The customary or traditional ways of thinking and doing things, which are shared to a greater or lesser extent by all members of the organization and which new members must learn and at least partially accept in order to be accepted into the service of the firm.[7]

This definition highlights three important characteristics of organizational culture: It is learned, it is shared, and it is transmitted.[8]

In describing the concept of organizational culture, we must specifically consider three important dimensions along which culture can be analyzed. The first is the objective/subjective dimension. Objective aspects of culture are those that exist outside the minds of organization members. They include physical artifacts like monuments to and pictures of heroes, organizational stories, sagas, myths, ceremonies, and rituals.

Subjective aspects are the organization's viewpoint, mindsets, and assumptions.

They cannot be directly perceived by the senses but are nonetheless real. Examples of subjective aspects include (1) shared assumptions (i.e., where we begin our thinking around here); (2) shared values (i.e., what we believe in around here); (3) shared meanings (i.e., how we interpret things around here); and (4) shared understandings (i.e., how things are done around here).

The second dimension of organizational culture is the *qualitative/quantitative* dimension. Qualitative aspects of culture are interpretations—the way people describe, decode, translate, and otherwise come to terms with the meaning of culture-related phenomena. Quantitative aspects, by contrast, include what people say about (as opposed to the meaning of) a culture.

Finally, the third dimension is the *observer (outsider)/native (insider)* dimension. Observer aspects are the meanings assigned to collected responses or observed behavior by an individual outside the organization. Gaining an outsider's perspective on a culture is important because an observer can sometimes detect features that elude insiders. At the same time, outsiders impose their own perspectives on events, creating the danger that the meaning derived may not represent the meaning that the person being observed intended. Observers of culture attempt to enter the world of the studied so they may understand that world in terms of its own standards.[9]

GETTING A FIX ON CULTURE

Neither conventional employee surveys nor personal interviews nor careful observations alone can tell managers all they need to know to understand and manage their organization's culture. In fact, no single technique can effectively measure all the important aspects of culture.

Learning from the Culture

The research site for this study was a rehabilitation center for handicapped individuals, which was located in a public 400-bed hospital.

The rehabilitation center was established as a "comprehensive, multidisciplinary, short-term residential facility for the rehabilitation of handicapped adults." It operated as an autonomous organization, even though it was governed by the hospital's policies, which, in turn, were based on Civil Service regulations. Since its establishment in 1979, the center had been given priority funding, and it had successfully attracted supplemental research and training funds. As a result, it was better financed than other hospital units. Old-timers in the hospital said the center was enjoying a fiscal honeymoon.

Fifty employees worked in the center, and all but four were highly trained professionals. The typical employee was younger than 40, had an undergraduate degree and was working on a graduate degree, and had more than five but less than ten years' experience working with the handicapped. The center had an equal number of male and female employees, and a simple hierarchical structure—a director, an assistant director, and a supervisor heading up each of four functional units.

The center was selected as the research site because of the director's interest in managing organizational culture and her invitation to conduct the study. The director's interest was stimulated by changing funding priorities and frequent messages from top management that the funding "honeymoon" was over. She had worked hard to build an environment that attracted the best and the brightest, and she knew that the scarcity of resources would necessitate radical adjustments on the part of her staff.

Gathering Facts and Opinions

Data were collected by means of "triangulation," a multimethod approach that derives its name from the navigational technique of using multiple reference points to locate an object's exact location. In the same way, managers can improve their understanding of organizational culture by looking at different kinds of data that have a bearing on it.[10]

Keep in mind that triangulation is not a new methodology for studying culture. Anthropologists, sociologists, and other behavioral scientists have used it for years, although applied management researchers have used it less frequently.

THE CENTER'S CULTURE

The observations conducted at the center provided the following picture of the rehabilitation unit.

• *Six of the eight observers specifically noted that the center was a favored child of the funding agency.* In contrast to other areas of the hospital, the observers indicated, the center was (1) well illuminated and freshly painted, (2) equipped with state-of-the-art technology, (3) supportive of purposeful, goal-oriented employee behavior, and (4) free of artifacts like mottos and pictures of heroes, which were frequently observed in other parts of the hospital.

• *The same six observers made reference to the appearance and behavior of the staff,* stating that they were (1) dressed casually, as opposed to employees in other parts of the hospital, where the color of an individual's uniform clearly denoted his or her status; (2) informal and congenial—employees were on a first-name basis, whereas in other parts of the hospital name tags carried references to earned degrees and certifications, and titles were used; and (3) less preoccupied with symbols of rank and position than others in the hospital were.

• *Five observers mentioned office furnishings,* noting that they were (1) neat, except for supervisors' spaces, which were more cluttered, and (2) inviting—open doors were the rule.

• *Half the observers indicated that employee conversations,* focused on (1) party planning, (2) pleasant topics, (3) concern over retrenchment and rumored budget cuts, (4) the lack of upward mobility and the importance the organization placed on long tenure, (5) educational qualifications and training, and (6) technical jargon. In other parts of the hospital, conversations focused on the organization's limited resources, its overcrowded space, the inconvenience caused by what seemed to be perpetual construction, and retirement.

• *Six observers described staff meetings* as (1) ceremoniously conducted, (2) carefully run according to circulated agendas, and (3) the focal point of culture building, since they included discussions of core values like the importance of clients and interdisciplinary cooperation.

Insider Responses

The more quantitative and objective insider's view of the center's culture was obtained through a self-administered questionnaire. According to T .E. Deal and A. A. Kennedy, "If values are the soul of the culture, then heroes personify those values and epitomize the strength of the organization."[11] The questionnaires indicated that center personnel recognized two heroes: the director, who was listed as a hero by 70% of the respondents, and the assistant director, who was listed by 80%. The director was seen as living proof that it was possible to be a fast tracker in a public system that seemed to value longevity

more than performance, and loyalty more than change. The assistant director suffered from the same handicap as the center's clients. He was viewed as a hero because he was a role model and, more important, a symbol to the employees of the special nature of their jobs.

These types of heroes were essential to the center's staff. First, responses to other questions confirmed that most of them did not believe the hospital's culture supported fast trackers. Sixty percent believed the primary focus of the hospital was on the past and present, while the focus of the center was on the present and the future. In addition, 80% were convinced that the primary concern of everyone in the center was the clients' welfare, and the center's mission was to rehabilitate clients to the extent that they became emotionally adjusted to their handicap and able to function independently in society.

When asked to characterize the center's culture according to familiar categories presented by Deal and Kennedy, employees gave some interesting responses, which are illustrated by the line marked "questionnaire" in Exhibit 1. Forty percent of the respondents said the center had a work hard/play hard culture (i.e., a culture marked by fun and action with high levels of low-risk activities); 30% said the center had a "you bet your organization" culture (i.e., a culture in which people played for high stakes and willingly took risks); 20% said it had a tough guy/macho culture (i.e., a culture with high-risk stakes and quick feedback); and only 10% believed the center's culture was process oriented and bureaucratic. This was interesting because responses to other questions revealed a general concern among members about bureaucratic behavior and the "lack of opportunities for young, fast-moving professionals." Sixty-one percent agreed that following policies and procedures for getting work done in the center were crucial for smooth operation. Only 9% disagreed. Center staff clearly described the larger hospital environment as bureaucratic.

Almost half the respondents attributed the center's success to the staff's commitment to interdisciplinary problem solving, teamwork, and cooperation. Respondents also recognized that the center preserved and reinforced certain management rituals, including staff meetings (called "staffings") during which the core values of team building, interdisciplinary cooperation, and concern for clients were emphasized and reinforced; and parting ceremonies, during which interns who rotated through the hospital's departments were "roasted" by the permanent staff. In the words of respondents, "these ceremonies and rituals bonded staff members to one another and helped build confidence and trust."

What Members Think

The final stage of data collection involved structured personal interviews, which were conducted to obtain qualitative views. (Of course, these views passed through the filter of the interviewer.) While the interviews were structured to ensure that essential information was obtained from each person, the interviewers were instructed to let people talk freely, and to record their diversions as well as direct responses to questions. Some of the more important elaborations indicated the following:

1. *Employees generally felt that they worked for an elite part of the hospital.* This feeling largely stemmed from the high level of funding the center received. Employees were uneasy about the possibility that the fiscal honeymoon would soon be over. Nevertheless, many emphasized that the center was not really part of the larger system. In fact, 40% of those interviewed took pride in describing the center as a "subculture" where personnel were younger, better educated, more professional, and more innovative.

2. *Many interviewees characterized the center's culture as "work hard/play hard," rather than bureaucratic.* This characterization came up more often in personal interviews (50% of the time) than on the self-administered questionnaires (40%). Interes-

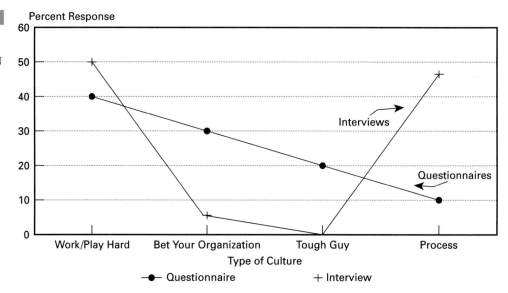

EXHIBIT 1
Alternative Views of the Center's Culture

tingly, 46% of interviewees admitted that the culture was process oriented and bureaucratic, compared with only 10% of the questionnaire respondents. Only 4% said the center had a "you bet your organization" culture, and no one thought of it as tough guy/macho. (See Exhibit 1.)

3. *Interviewees insisted, "There are no heroes around here."* Center personnel devoted considerable energy to convincing interviewers that "everyone is critical to the organization's success. We do not develop nor do we recognize heroes in this organization." Neither the director nor the assistant director were described as heroes during the interviews.

4. *Center personnel more openly discussed ceremonies and rituals during the interviews than they did on the questionnaires.* Three major categories of rituals and ceremonies were identified: rituals of transition, like the parting ceremonies for interns; rituals of socialization, like the new-employee orientation program; and rituals of intimidation and degradation, of which the center was uniformly perceived to be the victim, with those outside the center carrying out these rituals.

5. *While clients were frequently mentioned, more than 50% of those interviewed indicated that the center's real mission was to prove the feasibility of large-scale, interdisciplinary problem solving in the care and treatment of handicapped people.* As devoted as the personnel were to the clients, it was clear that the desire to prove that the multidisciplinary treatment of the handicapped could be successful was the driving force behind the efforts of a majority of the staff.

6. *Interviews were characterized by specialized jargon.* Such jargon, however, was not specific to individuals in certain functional lines as the self-administered questionnaires indicated.

IMPLICATIONS FOR MANAGERS

The findings of this study are important for two reasons: They illustrate that a practical and inexpensive technique can help managers learn more about the culture of an organization, and they offer some implications for effectively managing organizational cultures.

It is important to remember that the purpose of using triangulation was to gain a holistic view of the center's culture rather than to validate the content or the reliability of any single technique. Therefore, we will begin by looking at some of the things one technique told us and adding the insights provided by the other methodologies into a holistic picture.

The difference in results produced by the self-administered questionnaires and personal interviews about the center's heroes is important to consider. The questionnaire evidently provided respondents with an opportunity to make two points to themselves and others. First, people—especially those in rehabilitative settings—need to feel that what they do is special. The assistant director was a constant reminder to center employees that what they did *was* special; thus, he was a hero. Second, center employees had invested a great deal—personally and financially—to educate themselves for their work. Thus, they tried hard to convince themselves that fast tracking was possible, even within a large system that discouraged it. The director's success proved that fast trackers existed in their environment.

During the personal interviews, however, employees denied the importance of heroes in an attempt to convince the interviewer that everyone's contribution was equally important. At the same time, center staff knew the interviewer was aware that promotions were rare. The director was described by the interviewees as an anomaly rather than a hero. Center employees evidently wanted the interviewer to get the message that they all were professional, unconcerned with rank and status, and equally essential to the successful accomplishment of the organization's mission.

Consider also that on the self-administered questionnaire, respondents said the center had a work hard/play hard or "you bet your organization" culture. Only the hospital was thought of as bureaucratic. During the personal interviews, however, employees had to admit that the center was bureaucratic in order to support their belief that the center had no heroes. Thus, they could perpetuate an image of themselves as entrepreneurial professionals trapped in a system that allowed little innovation. They differentiated themselves from the hostile hospital environment by focusing on their cohesiveness, emphasizing the importance of their rituals and culture-building "staffings."

Respondents to the self-administered questionnaire agreed that the center's mission was to rehabilitate clients so they could live useful, productive lives. Observations and the personal interviews found, however, that a more frequently discussed goal was to prove that the comprehensive multidisciplinary approach to which the center and its personnel were dedicated was more feasible, practical, and cost effective. This is not to suggest clients were unimportant to employees; however, the employees' real agenda was to prove that they were devoting themselves to a viable concept.

As a final note, this study again confirmed people's tendency to internalize success and externalize failure. The interviews, observations, and questionnaire responses showed that most employees believed their successes were the result of their own training, the group's commitment to teamwork, and everyone's willingness to go beyond the call of duty; their failures were the result of the larger system, which was threatening to hold back the one resource that had made the center relatively autonomous and innovative: money.

The findings from each of these three data-gathering techniques were different enough for us to infer that no consistent perceptions about factors like heroes and culture stereotypes existed. Thus, insights provided by each data-collection technique should be considered equally important; a holistic picture of the center's culture would have been impossible to obtain had we used a single technique. Considered alone, the observations, self-administered questionnaire, and interviews each would have painted a less-than-complete picture of the center; the different sets of perspectives highlighted conflicts and thus revealed the center's true nature.

More specifically, the picture of the culture provided by the multimethod approach gave the center's director important information she could use to develop an action plan for the future.

A Helpful Subculture

The dominant culture in this study was the hospital's bureaucratic/process culture. Within any dominant culture, three types of subcultures may exist: an *enhancing subculture,* which embraces the dominant culture's values more fervently than the dominant culture does; a *counterculture,* which challenges the values of the dominant culture; and an *orthogonal subculture,* which accepts the values of the dominant culture as well as a nonconfirming set of values that it considers its own. The center's personnel did accept some of the values upon which the hospital's culture was based, but their careful disregard for most of its core values provided the foundations of a counterculture.[12]

The director's immediate task was to recognize, first, that the center would never be an enhancing subculture—its core values were simply too different. In fact, the center's innovativeness, resulting from its rejection of the bureaucratic/process culture, provided many benefits to the hospital. In addition, she needed to realize that as it faced reduced resources and increased accountability, the center would most likely no longer enjoy the autonomy or funding that had enabled it to survive as a counterculture. Finally, she needed to see that for the center and hospital to prosper, she had to take steps to redirect some of the center personnel's actions and attitudes, and bring them more in line with those of the rest of the hospital's staff.

In other words, the director needed to convert the center's subculture into an orthogonal subculture. To do that, she had to:

1. *Plan symbolic acts that would reinforce the mutual dependency of the hospital and the center.* She could begin to do this by redesigning the new-employee orientation program so that it placed more emphasis on hospital values, as opposed to center values.

2. *Strategically place a few of the hospital's artifacts in the center.* The hospital's motto could be displayed, and a section of the hospital's newsletter could feature the center, discussing its role in meeting hospital goals.

3. *Reinforce the importance of the client.* She could plan for celebrations to occur when a group of clients completed their programs, as opposed to when interns rotated.

4. *Monitor the accomplishments of ex-clients.* Organizational publications could feature ex-clients and emphasize the importance of the staff's contribution to the ex-clients' accomplishments.

5. *Emphasize cooperativeness between the center and the hospital.* She could place less emphasis on competing with and outperforming the hospital.

6. *Encourage employees to continue to behave innovatively and entrepreneurially.* Of course, she had to be sure not to create false expectations about the hospital's potential to respond.

7. *Aggressively emphasize the role of the center within the hospital.* Less attention needed to be paid to the center's uniqueness.

8. *Seek symbiosis to help the hospital, center, and all personnel meet their goals.*

A PRACTICAL TOOL

Triangulation is a practical technique and should not be restricted to the arsenals of researchers. Different signals, even when they initially confuse us, eventually can provide us with useful information.

Managers believe in organizational cultures, as do organizational researchers. Before executives can confidently devote resources and time to the management of culture, more accurate and innovative ways of defining and measuring it are needed.

Triangulation may help us better understand the phenomenon of organizational culture. It is not a perfect tool, but the manager who uses it can be more confident in his or her efforts to come to grips with this important and exciting aspect of organization.

NOTES TO CHAPTER SEVEN

1. M. Gardner, "Creating A Corporate Culture for the Eighties," *Business Horizons,* January/February 1985, 59–63. For some of the problems involved in creating a culture, see A. L. Wilkins and N. J. Bristow, "For Successful Organizational Culture, Honor Your Past," *Academy of Management Executive,* August 1987, 221–229.

2. Karl E. Weick, *The Social Psychology of Organizing,* Reading, MA: Addison-Wesley, 1979.

3. For examples of stories, sagas, and myths, see Joanne Martin, M. S. Feldman, M. J. Hatch, and S. B. Sitkin, "The Uniqueness Paradox in Organizational Stories," *Administrative Science Quarterly,* 28, 1983, 438–453; T. E. Deal and A. A. Kennedy, *Corporate Culture,* Reading, MA: Addison-Wesley, 1982; and H. M. Trice and J. M. Beyer, "Studying Organizational Culture Through Rites and Ceremonies," *Academy of Management Review,* 9, 1984, 653–669.

4. S. G. Harris and R. I. Sutton, "Functions of Parting Ceremonies in Dying Organizations," *Academy of Management Journal,* Vol. 29, 1986, 5–30.

5. R. L. Daft, "The Evolution of Organizational Analysis in ASQ, 1959–1979," *Administrative Science Quarterly,* 25, 632–636.

6. Edwin L. Baker, "Managing Organizational Culture," *Management Review,* July 1980, 8–13.

7. Eliott Jacques, *The Changing Culture of a Factory,* London: Tavistock Institute, 1951, p. 251.

8. Paul Bate, "The Impact of Organizational Culture on Approaches to Organizational Problem Solving," *Organizational Studies,* 5(1), 1984, 43–66.

9. K. L. Gregory, "Native-View Paradigms: Multiple Cultures and Culture Conflict in Organizations," *Administrative Science Quarterly,* 28, 1983, 359–376. Also see John Van Maanen, James Dabbs, Jr., and Robert R. Faulkner, *Varieties in Qualitative Research,* Beverly Hills, CA: Sage Publications, 1982.

10. See T. D. Jick, "Mixing Qualitative and Quantitative Methods: Triangulation in Action," *Administrative Science Quarterly,* 24, 1979, 602–611. For a comprehensive examination of this methodology and examples see John Van Maanen, James Dabbs, Jr., and Robert R. Faulkner, *Varieties in Qualitative Research,* Beverly Hills, CA: Sage Publications, 1982; and Joanne Martin, "Breaking Up the Mono-Method Monopolies in Organizational Research," Research Report No. 613, Graduate School of Business, Stanford University, Palo Alto, CA, Revised Version, March 1984.

11. T. E. Deal and A. A. Kennedy, *Corporate Culture,* Reading, MA: Addison-Wesley, 1982.

12. Joanne Martin and Caren Siehl, "Organizational Culture and Countercultures: An Uneasy Symbiosis." *Organizational Dynamics,* Autumn, 1983, 52–64.

POWER AND POLITICS

▼

In the previous two chapters we have examined two important sets of contextual dimensions—structure and systems in Chapter Six, and culture and ideology in Chapter Seven. In this chapter we examine the last of the important contextual elements, power and politics. Once we have examined all three building blocks, we can move on to see how they can be put together to form distinct configurations.

POWER AND POLITICS

Power is commonly defined as the capacity of a person or department to influence other people or departments to work toward outcomes the power holder desires.[1] Note the use of the word *capacity*; power is like a *stock* of something. It is like potential energy, acquired and stored until it is used. **Politics** is the use of power to exert influence over others so that the political actor's objectives, including the obtainment of more power, are achieved.[2] Note that politics, although related to power, is more of a *flow*; it is like kinetic energy, that is, power in motion. In this chapter we will examine how people, departments, and organizations obtain and use power. We will examine the implications of power and politics for organizational strategy and conclude with a brief examination of ethics in strategy formation.

SOURCES OF POWER IN ORGANIZATIONS

Power Sources for Top Management

Whether a firm is using a deliberate or emergent approach, the people with the ultimate responsibility for strategy formation are top management. Accordingly, it is important to understand how people in top management get power. The first and most obvious source of power is top management's **formal position**.[3] Being officially named top management grants a certain amount of legitimacy. This kind of power is a special case called **authority**; it is legally and formally granted by the organization to designated individuals, to be respected as such by other members.

It is common for top managers, in the normal course of affairs, to have control over important **resources**,[4] be they money, equipment, or physical plant. Since granting resource requests is a form of reward, and denying those requests a form of punishment, control over resources can be a potent source of power.

Top management is in an excellent position to have **control of decision premises and information**.[5] Top management sets agendas for meetings and decisions and articulates restrictions on the decisions that can be made by lower-level participants. Control over information allows top management to direct the understanding of those who receive the information. These types of control can enhance the power of top management, who can regulate what decisions get made, and how, and who can frame the problems facing the organization in ways helpful to their own interests.

Lastly, top management has what is called **network centrality**.[6] This means simply being located in the organization's networks of people and information, which enhances its exposure. It can place protégés in crucial positions and use them to keep itself informed about the important things happening throughout the organization.

Power Sources for Organizational Units

We tend to think of top management as having most of the power in modern organizations. But other locations in the organization can amass power as well. In fact, at any given level of the hierarchy, departments and people will differ in how much power they have. **Strategic contingencies**[7] are events and activities at which the organization must do well if it is to succeed. To the extent that people and departments can help the organization meet these contingencies, they will have power. Scholars have identified five sources of power related to strategic contingencies.

Dependency is the first such source of power. A department will have power over other departments if it has something they need, that is, if they are dependent on it.[8] In Chapter Six, for example, we discussed workflow and process interdependencies. If a unit is early in a workflow, units downstream must wait for it, and therefore it has greater power. Or if many other units depend on the process skills provided by a given unit, say an engineering department in a manufacturing company, it will have greater power.

If a department is good at generating **financial resources**,[9] it will have greater power. For example, an academic department that obtains many grants will garner power in a university. The retail store that generates the most sales in a chain will have greater power than those at other locations. **Centrality**[10] refers to a department's importance in the primary activity of the organization. In manufacturing organizations, it is common for production units to have the greatest power. Similarly, in organizations driven by new products, research and development is typically a powerful department.

A department whose function cannot be performed by any other department will have great power; this is called **nonsubstitutability**.[11] An example is computer programming; when computers were first invented, programmers were extremely powerful, since typically no one else in the organization was capable of making these machines function properly. As programmers have become more common, and as computers have become more user-friendly, the power of programmers has diminished.[12]

Organizations often face environments that are dynamic and complex, leading to great uncertainty. A department that excels at **coping with uncertainty** will achieve power in this situation. Some may do it by *obtaining prior information* about the environment, such as a good forecasting group. Other departments may help with the *prevention* of uncertainty, such as a good government lobbying group. And some departments may be good at *absorbing* uncertainty, such as an able research and development department that quickly develops new products in response to competitors' moves.

POLITICS: USING POWER IN ORGANIZATIONS

Upper-Level Politics: Using Power in Top Management

What is interesting about the sources of power for top management is how closely they mirror what Wrapp discussed in his Chapter Two article, "Good Managers Don't Make Policy Decisions." According to him, two of the most important skills of good managers are to keep informed and to play the power game. Yet the good manager does this subtly, with little overt exercise of power. The position source of power merely sets the stage, giving top managers legitimacy. Control over resources could be exercised bluntly but should probably be done with subtlety, keeping in mind the organization's power structure. Control over decision premises can provide the top manager with superb opportunities for unobtrusive control over the organization's activities. These three sources of power—position, resources, decision premises—are things that top management can use to channel the flow of organizational activity in the desired direction. In other words, they are tools for creating strategies. The power source of network centrality supports this enterprise by giving the good manager reliable sources of information without appearing intrusive.

There is almost an analogy to Porter's value chain, only with regard to politics. Position, resources, and control of decision premises are the direct ways in which top management can control the organization's direction. Network centrality gives top management an informational support activity for political action. Each of these four sources of power could also be used to reinforce top management's power. For example, if a top manager is successful in setting direction for the firm, he or she will gain legitimacy in the eyes of the board and fellow employees, solidifying his or her position. Or if he or she uses his or her centrally located information sources well, he or she will perhaps gain greater discretion over resources, thereby gaining power.[13]

Politics throughout the Organization

The power sources of organizational units, discussed above, can be used by them in two ways—to gain more power or to achieve desired outcomes. The implications are clear for how the power sources can be used to garner more power. Departments could get involved in areas of high uncertainty for the organization.[14] Another obvious way to increase power is to create dependencies.[15] Equally obvious, but not necessarily easy to do, is to provide resources.[16] Lastly, a department could invent ways to meet one or more of the organization's strategic contingencies.[17]

If a department wishes to use its accumulated power to achieve outcomes it wants, it should probably start by building coalitions. This involves meeting in informal groups with managers and others from various parts of the organization, attempting to persuade them of the department's point of view.[18] Related to this is the tactic of expanding networks. Just as top managers can be at the center of a network of contacts throughout the organization, so can a department. Departments can expand networks by gradually spinning some of its members off into other units, while keeping in touch with them. Or it can try to co-opt actual or potential dissenters by including them in the department's network.[19]

A department, like top managers, can try to control decision premises. It can try to share information selectively to make itself look as good as possible. It can try to get particular items on the agendas of decision-making groups.[20] Departments can make use of their legitimacy and expertise to get even more power. For example, a financial manager might recommend a financial strategy that could have the side benefit of gaining more power for the finance department. Others in the organization would probably accept this suggestion because of the finance manager's expertise and legitimacy, possibly without even considering the benefits to the finance department.[21]

POWER, ORGANIZATION, AND STRATEGY

Our discussion of power so far has been mostly positive. Top management and departments can accumulate power in various ways. Then in situations where goals differ, they can engage in political tactics that offer an opportunity to use their power to achieve their desired ends. Conceived this way, power and politics are indispensable parts of strategy making. Indeed, Wrapp said as much in his Chapter Two reading.

There is obviously a downside to politics, and Henry Mintzberg, in his article, "Politics and the Political Organization," has written about it. He takes a very different view of politics. You might recall from Chapter Six that he views politics as the force in organizations that drives organizations apart, in contrast to ideology, which pulls them together. Let us examine Mintzberg's views in some detail.[22]

He points out that organizations function with four systems of influence: (1) authority, (2) ideology, (3) expertise, and (4) politics. Mintzberg thinks the first three are legitimate and the last is not. *Authority* is formally authorized power, by definition legitimate. *Ideology* is a set of widely accepted beliefs that legitimizes influence. *Expertise* is influence that is officially certified by professional organizations or educational achievements. Politics, he says, reflects power that is technically illegitimate, since it does not fit into any of the above three categories. He asserts that political power in the organization is not formally authorized, widely accepted, or officially certified. It is therefore often divisive and conflictive, in his view.

The alternative view, discussed in detail earlier in this chapter, is that power (the currency of politics) is often gained in informal ways that could nevertheless be characterized as legitimate. Departments that help the organization meet its strategic contingencies usually have greater power. This greater power may be widely accepted, even though it is informal. Authority, ideology, and expertise are merely special cases of power sources. Each could be used in political activity, well or poorly. The value judgment is likely to be based mostly on the judger's point of view, not some objective criterion.

Political Games in Organizations

Mintzberg thinks that political activity can be described as "game playing," and he identifies thirteen games:

- **Insurgency game:** Lower-level participants resist authority.
- **Counterinsurgency game:** Authority fights back.
- **Sponsorship game:** Lower-level members attach themselves to authority figures to build a power base. This is the other side of the network centrality coin.
- **Alliance-building game:** Peers negotiate implicit contracts of support to build a power base. This is the coalition-building tactic mentioned earlier.
- **Empire-building game:** Managers build power bases with subordinates. This is a variation of top-management network expansion.

- **Budgeting game:** Played overtly, governed by rules, to build power with resources. This is clearly related to the resource power source of top managers.
- **Expertise game:** Nonsanctioned use of expertise to build power base; experts play by flaunting their expertise; non-experts play by trying to have their work viewed as expert.
- **Lording game:** Building power by "lording it" over those without it, i.e., illegitimate use of legitimate power. This has the same self-defeating quality built into it as does the expertise game.
- **Line vs. staff game:** Pits line managers with legitimate power against staff advisers with expertise; played to defeat rivals. This obviously can be destructive if playing the game becomes an end, as opposed to using authority or expertise to achieve worthwhile, but disputed, ends.
- **Rival camps game:** Played when an alliance- or empire-building game evolves into a two-competitor, zero-sum game. This can be acceptable if it is the only way to resolve a dispute over goals in the organization. If it is a game played for its own sake, it dissipates energy that should otherwise be expended on productive activity.
- **Strategic candidates game:** Individuals or groups play to politically promote their favored strategic changes.
- **Whistle-blowing game:** Inside information is used to expose unethical or illegal behavior; typically a brief and simple game. We will discuss ethics further below.
- **Young Turks game:** This is a high-stakes game. "Young Turks" near the center of power seek to effect change (strategic, ideological, expert/technological, or of the leadership).

Mintzberg asserts that politics may be present in an organization, but not dominant, or it may be the dominant system of influence. The latter situation gives rise to the type of configuration Mintzberg calls political.

Forms of Political Organization

Unlike the other configurations discussed in Chapter Six, political organizations are best understood in terms of power, not structure. They have no preferred method of coordination, no key part, no clear type of decentralization. Everything depends on the fluidity of informal power, marshaled to win individual issues. When factions in the organization clash politically, the result is conflict.

Conflict, according to the Mintzberg reading, falls into two dimensions: moderate/enduring vs. intense/brief, and confined vs. pervasive. This leads to four forms of political organization. **Confrontation** is an organization where conflict is confined and intense/brief, for example, a takeover. A **shaky alliance** is a political organization where conflict is confined and moderate/enduring; a good example is often a professional organization operating in the public sector, like a large social services agency. A **politicized organization** has pervasive conflict that is moderate/enduring, as in many a regulatory agency. A **complete political arena** is an organization whose conflict is pervasive and intense/brief. This form is so unstable as to be rarely found for any period of time. The other three endure, the first by moderating conflict, the second by containing conflict, and the third by doing both.

The Functional Role of Politics in Organizations

Mintzberg's view of the types of political organizations highlights what he sees as the dysfunctional influences of politics. Politics can be divisive and costly and can burn up energy. It is often used to sustain outmoded systems of power or introduce unjustified new ones. Political activity of a very intense nature can paralyze an organization.

However, Mintzberg sees the potential functional influences of politics. In general, he believes that politics can correct deficiencies in the legitimate systems of influence. Politics can act in a Darwinian way to ensure that the strongest members of an organization are brought into positions of leadership. It can ensure that all sides of an issue are fully debated, whereas the other systems of influence may promote only one. The system of politics is often required to stimulate necessary change that is blocked by the legitimate systems of influence. Lastly, the system of politics can ease the path for the execution of decisions.

Politics and Strategy

Whether one accepts Mintzberg's dark view of politics or the more neutral view articulated earlier, one must accept the role of politics in forming strategy. A prescriptive analyst should consider a firm's power structure during an internal analysis, and again in choosing the proper way to implement the formulated strategy.

From a descriptive view, in a situation where strategy emerges, undoubtedly one factor shaping the strategy will be the firm's power structure. Whether that is good or bad depends mostly on the perspective of the observer. The point is that for strategy to form, the various power blocs in the firm must mobilize and act. A large part of the logical incrementalism approach is based on explicit management of organizational politics, as we saw in Chapter Five. This was also seen in Wrapp's Chapter Two reading on how effective executives channel organizational action. On these bases, a case could be made that politics is a major part of the strategic learning school. However, Mintzberg points to the chief danger of organizational politics—if it gets out of hand and is played for its own sake, it can be destructive, preventing the creation of a coherent pattern in organizational actions over time. Another problem is that if power becomes entrenched, the organization will certainly realize a pattern in a stream of action over time, that is, a strategy. But it may be a non-adaptive, ineffective strategy.

THE INSTITUTIONAL FUNCTION OF MANAGEMENT: INTERORGANIZATIONAL POWER

Organizations operate in industry and social contexts, and may have power in those contexts. In this section we briefly examine power in an industry. Later, we will discuss how organizations may have power in, and therefore responsibility toward, society.

Economic Sources of Industry Power

Michael Porter's model of competitive strategy, discussed in Chapter Four, showed one way in which firms may gain power in their industries. They may be able to raise barriers to entry, perhaps through economies of scale or brand loyalty, or else can neutralize substitutes by creating unfavorable price-performance tradeoffs for the substitutes. A firm may have power over its suppliers because it is one of few firms using raw materials provided by many vendors. The list of examples could get quite long; Porter's Chapter Four reading goes into detail about the various sources of power for a firm in a competitive environment. Porter's main point is that by becoming a cost leader or by successfully differentiating or focusing, a firm can become powerful enough in an industry that it overcomes the potentially deleterious effects of the different competitive forces.

Political Sources of Industry Power

Another way of looking at the bases of a firm's power in its industry is by using a framework similar to that used earlier to analyze the power of a department in a company. A firm will have power to the extent that it meets strategic contingencies in an industry. For example, it may make buyers or suppliers at least partially dependent on it or be mildly nonsubstitutable because of its differentiation. On the other hand, if it wants to help other members of the industry system (especially suppliers and buyers) cope with uncertainty, it may have to do it using methods less arms-length than what Porter suggests. This is what Jeffrey Pfeffer discusses in his reading in this chapter, "The Institutional Function of Management."

The institutional function of management means managing the organization's relationships with other organizations. All members of an industry face uncertainty and interdependence. Managing the institutional level can help firms deal with these twin problems. Pfeffer suggests doing this through a "political" strategy, namely, the establishment of favorable exchange relationships with other organizations. He examines in detail the strengths and weaknesses of six such strategies: merger, joint ventures, cooptation and interlocking directorates, executive recruitment, regulation, and, lastly, direct political action such as lobbying.

WHO SHOULD CONTROL THE CORPORATION? STRATEGY AND ETHICS

If an organization can manage its relationship with society and other aspects of its institutional environment, it has associated responsibilities to society. That is one major point of Henry Mintzberg's reading, "Who Should Control the Corporation?" Mintzberg uses what he calls a "conceptual horseshoe" to explain the continuum of techniques society can use to control corporate behavior. The continuum is set in the shape of a horseshoe instead of a straight line because its endpoints both call for control of the corporation by distinct outside forces, even if they represent the two ends of the political spectrum.

At the extreme left is "nationalize it," meaning direct government control of the corporation. Mintzberg explains how even in a market economy this approach, generally taboo, occasionally is used. At the extreme right is "restore it," the idea that corporate control legitimately rests only with its legal owners, the stockholders. Mintzberg points out several problems, many of them technical, with having exclusive shareholder control. He also discusses several philosophical issues related to full ownership control, among them the idea that in a democratic society, ownership control is not necessarily more legitimate than worker control, consumer control, or even public control.

In the middle part of his horseshoe are several other approaches that are often used to control corporate behavior. Moving from left-wing to right-wing, the first approach he discusses is "democratize it," meaning the institutionalizing of corporate democracy, either through worker or public or other representation on the board of directors (representative democracy) or direct worker or public involvement in decision making (participatory democracy). Next is a very familiar approach, "regulate it"; Mintzberg explains when this approach is and is not appropriate. The approach that emerges as Mintzberg's favored one in this reading is "pressure it," the idea that all kinds of "stakeholders" should constantly prod the corporation to do the right thing, to "keep it honest." At the midpoint of the horseshoe is "trust it," a position we shall discuss in more detail below.

Next comes "ignore it," a position Mintzberg vigorously urges readers to disregard. This approach calls for no change in corporate behavior. It assumes that social needs are met while pursuing economic goals. The argument is that "it pays to be good." But in instances where the status quo is not socially enlightened, "ignore it" makes a good case for "pressure it," in Mintzberg's view, "forcing it to be good." "Induce it," the next position on the horseshoe, is the converse of "regulate it." When the situation is not appropriate for regulation, the government may choose to create incentives for acceptable behavior instead of punishments for transgressions.

"Trust It": Ethics in Strategic Management

In his discussion of "trust it," Mintzberg explains the argument of those who say we should trust managers: When the corporation has responsible managers, there is no reason for it to be nationalized, democratized, regulated, or pressured: The corporation's leaders can be trusted to attend to social goals. Some have criticized this doctrine as all rhetoric. Others claim that businesspeople lack the qualifications to make these social choices. The most extensive criticism, from both the left and the right, is that managers have no right to make these kinds of choices.

Mintzberg argues that we have to trust managers for two reasons: (1) strategic decisions inevitably involve social as well as economic consequences; and (2) there is always some degree of discretion involved in corporate decision making. Socially, things could be better, but with irresponsible managers they could be an awful lot worse. Mintzberg says that we must socialize our managers to be trustworthy. Society must aspire to higher standards of conduct. "Without responsible and ethical people in important places," he says, "our society is not worth very much."

Ethical Frameworks

The question raised by this approach is, "Are there ethical guidelines available to managers to make them more trustworthy?" The answer is clearly yes. Lawrence Kohlberg[23] found that people move through three stages of moral development. The **preconventional stage** characterizes the moral condition of children. The justification for actions comes from authority and its associated punishment. The perspective at the **conventional stage** is on the group and what it thinks is appropriate; actions are justified on the basis of group norms. Adolescents can be great examples of this; they are confronted by a myriad of norms: family, peer group, legal, and organizational. Most people are at the conventional stage. Some get stuck at the preconventional level of moral development. They will not act ethically on their own; they must be compelled by authority or the punishment. But others are stuck at the conventional level and will act ethically only in the context of their group. Ethical behavior will not extend to other groups or cultures.

People who continue to develop morally reach the **postconventional stage.** The perspective at this level of development is extremely broad. People at this level tend to look universally, beyond their immediate group. Actions are justified by broad moral principles. Kohlberg found that broader perspectives led to better ethical results. There are three ethical approaches available that provide these broader perspectives and help people make better ethical decisions.

The first of these is the **utilitarian approach,** which argues that people should make decisions that result in the greatest good for the greatest number of people. This idea is generally associated with the philosopher Jeremy Bentham.[24] Applying this model is straightforward but complex. One must identify the various alternatives, that is, strategies. The decision maker must then learn the costs and benefits for each stakeholder. This means not only *economic* costs and benefits but also *social* ones. This also means that *all* stakeholders must be considered. From this calculation, the decision maker must select the best alternative.

The second approach is the **human rights approach.** This approach is based on the idea that all people have fundamental rights because they are human beings. Rights are necessary for people to have self-respect, and they support freedom and well-being. These rights are *independent* of whether or not one is a member of social institutions. Indeed, human rights can be the measure of institutions. Institutions that violate human rights are subject to criticism and to the "pressure it" approach discussed above.

The rights approach is usually associated with the philosopher Immanuel Kant.[25] A contemporary expression of Kant's "Categorical Imperative," that respect for persons leads directly to human rights, is:[26]

- Only act if the principle of your action applied universally is not self-defeating. For example, cheating fails this test; one only gains from cheating if no one else cheats. If everyone cheats, they defeat themselves.
- Always act with recognition of every person's right, including yourself, to be treated with respect. Treat people as ends, not means.
- Act as if you were a member of a moral community governed by moral principles of universality and respect for persons. This is the way to put the first two points into action. This approach has clear implications for hierarchical organizations such as the ones we have been discussing in this book.

The result of all this is the existence of two basic kinds of rights: liberty and welfare. Some standard liberty rights are privacy, free speech, free consent, and freedom of conscience. Typical welfare rights include the rights to employment, food, housing, and education. For every right, decision makers have an associated duty—they must not interfere with liberty rights, and they must provide to the extent possible what is needed to assure welfare rights. The task of the ethical decision maker under this approach is to assess how particular decisions and actions will affect the rights of all the people affected by the decisions.

The third approach is the **justice approach**, which has its roots in the writings of Aristotle and Plato.[27] The essence of this approach is to treat people the same, unless they differ in relevant ways; for example, characteristics that are related to the task or need. This approach argues that standards of fairness, equity, and impartiality must be upheld in both the final decision and during the process leading up to the decision. Decisions that conform to those standards will be ethical.

Notes to Chapter Eight

1. See Dahl, R. A., "The Concept of Power." *Behavioral Science* 2 (1957): 201–15; Astley, W. G., and P. S. Sachdeva, "Structural Sources of Intraorganizational Power: A Theoretical Synthesis." *Academy of Management Review* 9 (1984): 104–13; and Salancik, G. R., and J. Pfeffer, "The Bases and Use of Power in Organizational Decision-Making: The Case of the University." *Administrative Science Quarterly* 19 (1974): 453–73.

2. Pfeffer, J., *Power in Organizations.* Marshfield, Mass.: Pitman, 1981.

3. Hardy, C., "The Nature of Unobtrusive Power." *Journal of Management Studies* 22 (1985): 384–99; Pfeffer, *Power in Organizations;* Peabody, R. L., "Perceptions of Organizational Authority." *Administrative Science Quarterly* 6 (1962): 479.

4. Pfeffer, *Power in Organizations.*

5. Bradshaw-Camball, P., and V. Murray, "Multiple Theoretical Perspectives on Politics in Organizations." *Organization Science* 3 (1991); Pettigrew, A., "Information Control as a Power Resource." *Sociology* 6 (1972): 187–204.

6. Astley and Sachdeva, "Structural Sources of Intraorganizational Power."

7. Hickson, D. J., C. R. Himings, C. A. Lee, R. E. Schneck, and J. M. Pennings, "A Strategic Contingencies Theory of Intraorganizational Power." *Administrative Science Quarterly* 16 (1971): 216–29; Salancik, G. R., and J. Pfeffer, "Who Gets Power—and How They Hold On to It." *Organization Dynamics* (Winter 1977): 3–21.

8. Emerson, R. M, "Power-Dependence Relations." *American Sociological Review* 27 (1962): 31–41.

9. Pfeffer, J., and G. Salancik, "Organizational Decision-Making as a Political Process: The Case of a University Budget." *Administrative Science Quarterly* 19 (1974): 135–51.

10. Hickson et al., "A Strategic Contingencies Theory of Intraorganizational Power."

11. Ibid.

12. Pettigrew, A., *The Politics of Organizational Decision-Making.* London: Tavistock, 1973.

13. This self-reinforcing aspect of power is a major theme in Pfeffer, *Power in Organizations.*

14. Hickson et al., "A Strategic Contingencies Theory of Intraorganizational Power."

15. Pfeffer, *Power in Organizations.*

16. Pfeffer and Salancik, "Organizational Decision-Making as a Political Process."

17. Hickson et al., "A Strategic Contingencies Theory of Intraorganizational Power."

18. Merrell, V. D., *Huddling: The Informal Way to Management Success.* New York: AMACOM, 1979.

19. Vredenburgh, D. J., and J. G. Maurer, "A Process Framework of Organizational Politics." *Human Relations* 37 (1984): 47–66.

20. Pfeffer, *Power in Organizations.*

21. Ibid.

22. The bulk of this section is based on Mintzberg, H., "Politics and the Political Organization." In *The Strategy Process,* 2nd ed., ed. H. Mintzberg and J. B Quinn. Englewood Cliffs, N. J.: Prentice Hall, 1991, pp. 371–77.

23. Kohlberg, L., "Moral Stages and Moralization: The Cognitive-Developmental Approach." In *Moral Development and Behavior: Theory, Research, and Social Issues*, ed. T. Likona. New York: Holt, Rinehart & Winston, 1976.

24. Bentham, J., *An Introduction to the Principles of Morals and Legislation.* Oxford: Clarendon Press, 1897. For more modern treatments of utilitarianism, see Hardin, R., *Morality within the Limits of Reason.* Chicago: University of Chicago Press, 1988; and Singer, P., *Practical Ethics.* New York: Cambridge University Press, 1979.

25. Kant, I., *Critique of Practical Reason,* trans. L. W. Beck. Indianapolis: Bobbs-Merrill, 1956; Kant, I., *Groundwork of the Metaphysic of Morals,* trans. H. J. Paton. New York: Harper & Row, 1964.

26. The contemporary expression of the Categorical Imperative is taken from the materials for the Arthur Andersen Conference on Teaching Business Ethics held at Lake Charles, Illinois, in June 1991. Those materials were prepared by Dr. Norman E. Bowie and Dr. Manual Velasquez.

27. Aristotle, *Nichomachean Ethics, Book V* (several editions). A modern treatment of the justice approach is Rawls, J., *A Theory of Justice.* Boston: Harvard University Press, 1971.

THE INSTITUTIONAL FUNCTION OF MANAGEMENT

READING

By Jeffrey Pfeffer

Theory, research, and education in the field of organizational behavior and management have been dominated by a concern for the management of people *within* organizations. The question of how to make workers more productive has stood as the foundation for management theory and practice since the time of Frederick Taylor. Such an emphasis neglects the institutional function of management. While managing people within organizations is critical, managing the organization's relationships with other organizations such as competitors, creditors, suppliers, and governmental agencies is frequently as critical to the firm's success.

Parsons (1960) noted that there were three levels of organizations: (1) the technical level, where the technology of the organization was used to produce some product or service; (2) the administrative level, which coordinated and supervised the technical

Originally published as "Beyond Management and the Worker: The Institutional Function of Management," in the *Academy of Management Review* (April 1976); copyright © *Academy of Management Review.* Reprinted with deletions by the permission of the *Academy of Management Review* and the author.

level; and (3) the institutional level, which was concerned with the organization's legitimacy and with organization-environment relations. Organization and management theory has primarily concentrated on administrative level problems, frequently at very low hierarchical levels in organizations.

Practicing managers and some researchers do recognize the importance of the institutional context in which the firm operates. There is increasing use of institutional advertising, and executives from the oil industry, among others, have been active in projecting their organizations' views in a variety of contexts. Mintzberg (1973a) has identified the liaison role as one of ten roles managers fill. Other authors explicitly have noted the importance of relating the organization to other organizations (Pfeffer and Nowak, n.d., Whyte, 1955). . . .

The purposes of this article are: (a) to present evidence of the importance of the institutional function of management, and (b) to review data consistent with a model of institutional management. This model argues that managers behave as if they were seeking to manage and reduce uncertainty and interdependence arising from the firm's relationships with other organizations. Several strategic responses to interorganizational exchange, including their advantages and disadvantages, are considered.

INSTITUTIONAL PROBLEMS OF ORGANIZATIONS

Organizations are open social systems, engaged in constant and important transactions with other organizations in their environments. Business firms transact with customer and supplier organizations, and with sources of credit; they interact on the federal and local level with regulatory and legal authorities which are concerned with pollution, taxes, antitrust, equal employment, and myriad other issues. Because firms do interact with these other organizations, two consequences follow. First, organizations face uncertainty. If an organization were a closed system so that it could completely control and predict all the variables that affected its operation, the organization could make technically rational, maximizing decisions and anticipate the consequences of its actions. As an open system, transacting with important external organizations, the firm does not have control over many of the important factors that affect its operations. Because organizations are open, they are affected by events outside their boundaries.

Second, organizations are interdependent with other organizations with which they exchange resources, information or personnel, and thus open to influence by them. The extent of this influence is likely to be a function of the importance of the resource obtained, and inversely related to the ease with which the resource can be procured from alternative sources (Jacobs, 1974; Thompson, 1967). Interdependence is problematic and troublesome. Managers do not like to be dependent on factors outside their control. Interdependence is especially troublesome if there are few alternative sources, so the external organization is particularly important to the firm.

Interdependence and uncertainty interact in their effects on organizations. One of the principal functions of the institutional level of the firm is the management of this interdependence and uncertainty.

THE IMPORTANCE OF INSTITUTIONAL MANAGEMENT

Katz and Kahn (1966) noted that organizations may pursue two complementary paths to effectiveness. The first is to be as efficient as possible, and thereby obtain a competitive advantage with respect to other firms. Under this strategy, the firm succeeds because it operates so efficiently that it achieves a competitive advantage in the market. The second strategy, termed "political," involves the establishment of favorable exchange relationships based on considerations that do not relate strictly to price, quality, service, or efficiency. Winning an order because of the firm's product and cost characteristics would be an example of the strategy of efficiency; winning the order because of interlocks in the directorates of the organizations involved, or because of family connections between executives in the two organizations, would illustrate political strategies.

The uses and consequences of political strategies for achieving organizational success have infrequently been empirically examined. Hirsch (1975) has . . . compared the ethical drug and record industries, noting great similarities between them. Both sell their products through gatekeepers or intermediaries—in the case of pharmaceuticals, through doctors who must write the prescriptions, and in the case of records, through disc jockeys who determine air time and, consequently, exposure. Both sell products with relatively short life cycles, and both industries place great emphasis on new products and product innovation. Both depend on the legal environment of patents, copyrights, and trademarks for market protection.

Hirsch noted that the rate of return for the average pharmaceutical firm during the period 1956–1966 was more than double the rate of return for the average firm in the record industry. Finding no evidence that would enable him to attribute the striking differences in profitability to factors associated with internal structural arrangements, Hirsch concluded that at least one factor affecting the relative profitability of the two industries is the ability to manage their institutional environments, and more specifically, the control over distribution, patent and copyright protection, and the prediction of adoption by the independent gatekeepers.

In a review of the history of both industries, Hirsch indicated that in pharmaceuticals, control over entry was achieved by (a) amending the patent laws to permit the patenting of naturally occurring substances, antibiotics and (b) instituting a long and expensive licensing procedure required before drugs could be manufactured and marketed, administered by the Food and Drug Administration (FDA). In contrast, record firms have much less protection under the copyright laws; as a consequence, entry is less controlled, leading to more competition and lower profits. While there are other differences between the industries, including size and expenditures on research and development, Hirsch argued that at least some of the success of drug firms derives from their ability to control entry and their ability to control information channels relating to their product through the use of detail personnel and advertising in the American Medical Association Journals. Retail price maintenance, tariff protection, and licensing to restrict entry are other examples of practices that are part of the organization's institutional environment and may profoundly affect its success.

MANAGING UNCERTAINTY AND INTERDEPENDENCE

The organization, requiring transactions with other organizations and uncertain about their future performance, has available a variety of strategies that can be used to manage uncertainty and interdependence. Firms face two problems in their institutional relationships: (a) managing the uncertainty caused by the unpredictable actions of competitors and (b) managing the uncertainty resulting from noncompetitive interdependence with suppliers, creditors, government agencies, and customers. In both instances, the same set of strategic responses is available: merger, to completely absorb the interdependence and resulting uncertainty; joint ventures; interlocking directorates, to partially absorb interdependence; the movement and selective recruiting of executives and other personnel, to develop interorganizational linkages; regulation, to provide government enforced stability; and other political activity to reduce competition, protect markets, and sources of supply, and otherwise manage the organization's environment.

Because organizations are open systems, each strategy is limited in its effect. While merger or some other interorganizational linkage may manage one source of organizational dependence, it probably at the same time makes the organizations dependent on yet other organizations. For example, while regulation may eliminate effective price competition and restrict entry into the industry (Jordan, 1972; Pfeffer, 1974a; Posner, 1974), the regulated organizations then face the uncertainties involved in dealing with the regulatory agency. Moreover, in reducing uncertainty for itself, the organization must bargain away some of its own discretion (Thompson, 1967). One can view institutional management as an exchange process—the organization assures itself of needed resources, but at the same time, must promise certain predictable behaviors in return. Keeping these qualifications in mind, evidence on use of the various strategies of institutional management is reviewed.

Merger

There are three reasons an organization may seek to merge—first, to reduce competition by absorbing an important competitor organization; second, to manage interdependence with either sources of input or purchasers of output by absorbing them; and third, to diversify operations and thereby lessen dependence on the present organizations with which it exchanges (Pfeffer, 1972b). While merger among competing organizations is presumably proscribed by the antitrust laws, enforcement resources are limited, and major consolidations do take place. . . .

The classic expressed rationale for merger has been to increase the profits or the value of the shares of the firm. In a series of studies beginning as early as 1921, researchers have been unable to demonstrate that merger active firms are more profitable or have higher stock prices following the merger activity. This literature has been summarized by Reid (1968), who asserts that mergers are made for growth, and that growth is sought because of the relationship between firm size and managerial salaries.

Growth, however, does not provide information concerning the desired characteristics of the acquired firm. Under a growth objective, any merger is equivalent to any other of the same size. Pfeffer (1972b) has argued that mergers are undertaken to manage organizational interdependence. Examining the proportion of merger activity occurring within the same two-digit SIC industry category, he found that the highest proportion of within-industry mergers occurred in industries of intermediate concentration. The theoretical argument was that in industries with many competitors, the absorption of a single one did little to reduce competitive uncertainty. At the other extreme, with only a few competitors, merger would more likely be scrutinized by the antitrust authorities and coordination could instead be achieved through more informal arrangements, such as price leadership.

The same study investigated the second reason to merge: to absorb the uncertainty among organizations vertically related to each other, as in a buyer–seller relationship. He found that it was possible to explain 40% of the variation in the distribution of merger activity over industries on the basis of resource interdependence, measured by estimates of the transactions flows between sectors of the economy. On an individual industry basis, in two-thirds of the cases a measure of transactions interdependence accounted for 65% or more of the variation in the pattern of merger activity. The study indicated that it was possible to account for the industry of the likely merger partner firm by considering the extent to which firms in the two industries exchanged resources.

While absorption of suppliers or customers will reduce the firm's uncertainty by bringing critical contingencies within the boundaries of the organization, this strategy has some distinct costs. One danger is that the process of vertical integration creates a larger organization which is increasingly tied to a single industry.

The third reason for merger is diversification. Occasionally, the organization is confronted by interdependence it cannot absorb, either because of resource or legal limitations. Through diversifying its activities, the organization does not reduce the uncertainty, but makes the particular contingency less critical for its success and well-being. Diversification provides the organization with a way of avoiding, rather than absorbing, problematic interdependence.

Merger represents the most complete solution to situations of organizational independence, as it involves the total absorption of either a competitor or a vertically related organization, or the acquisition of an organization operating in another area. Because it does involve total absorption, merger requires more resources and is a more visible and substantial form of interorganizational linkage.

Joint Ventures

Closely related to merger is the joint venture: the creation of a jointly owned, but independent organization by two or more separate parent firms. Merger involves the total pooling of assets by two or more organizations. In a joint venture, some assets of each of several parent organizations are used, and thus only a partial pooling of resources is involved (Bernstein, 1965). For a variety of reasons, joint ventures have been prosecuted less frequently and less successfully than mergers, making joint ventures particularly appropriate as a way of coping with competitive interdependence.

The joint subsidiary can have several effects on competitive interdependence and uncertainty. First, it can reduce the extent of new competition. Instead of both firms entering a market, they can combine some of their assets and create a joint subsidiary to enter the market. Second, since joint subsidiaries are typically staffed, particularly at the higher executive levels, with personnel drawn from the parent firms, the joint subsidiary becomes another location for the management of competing firms to meet. Most importantly, the joint subsidiary must set price and output levels, make new product development and marketing decisions and decisions about its advertising policies. Consequently, the parent organizations are brought into association in a setting in which exactly those aspects of the competitive relationship must be jointly determined.

In a study of joint ventures among the manufacturing and oil and gas companies during the period 1960–1971, Pfeffer and Nowak (1976a, 1976b) found that 56% involved parent firms operating in the same two-digit industry. Further, in 36% of the 166 joint ventures studied, the joint subsidiary operated in the same industry as both parent organizations. As in the case of mergers, the proportion of joint venture activities undertaken with other firms in the same industry was related to the concentration of the firm's industry being intermediate. The relationship between concentration and the proportion of joint ventures undertaken within the same industry accounted for some 25% of the variation in the pattern of joint venture activities.

In addition to considering the use of joint ventures in coping with competitive interdependence, the Pfeffer and Nowak study of joint ventures examined the extent to which the creation of joint subsidiaries was related to patterns of transaction interdependence across industries. While the correlations between the proportion of transactions and the proportion of joint ventures undertaken between industry pairs were lower than in the case of mergers, statistically significant relationships between this form of interorganizational linkage activity and patterns of resource exchange were observed. The difference between mergers and joint ventures appears to be that mergers are used relatively more to cope with buyer–seller interdependence, and joint ventures are more highly related to considerations of coping with competitive uncertainty.

Cooptation and Interlocking Directorates

Cooptation is a venerable strategy for managing interdependence between organizations. Cooptation involves the partial absorption of another organization through the placing of a representative of that organization on the board of the focal organization. Corporations frequently place bankers on their boards; hospitals and universities offer trustee positions to prominent business leaders; and community action agencies develop advisory boards populated with active and strong community political figures. . . .

Interlocks in the boards of directors of competing organizations provide a possible strategy for coping with competitive interdependence and the resulting uncertainty. The underlying argument is that in order to manage interorganizational relationships, information must be exchanged, usually through a joint subsidiary or interlocking directorate. While interlocks among competitors are ostensibly illegal, until very recently there was practically no prosecution of this practice. In a 1965 study, a subcommittee of the House Judiciary Committee found more than 300 cases in which direct competitors had interlocking boards of directors (House of Representatives, 1965). In a study of the extent of interlocking among competing organizations in a sample of 109 manufacturing organizations, Pfeffer and Nowak (n.d.) found that the proportion of directors on the board from direct competitors was higher for firms operating in industries in which concentration was intermediate. This result is consistent with the result found for joint ventures and mergers as well. In all three instances, linkages among competing organizations occurred more frequently when concentration was in an intermediate range.

Analyses of cooptation through the use of boards of directors have not been confined to business firms. Price (1963) argued that the principal function of the boards of the Oregon Fish and Game Commissions was to link the organizations to their environments. Zald (1967) found that the composition of YMCA boards in Chicago matched the demography of their operating areas, and affected the organizations' effectiveness, particularly in raising money. Pfeffer (1973) examined the size, composition, and function of hospital boards of directors, finding that variables of organizational context, such as ownership, source of funds, and location, were important explanatory factors. He also found a relationship between cooptation and organizational effectiveness. In 1972, Pfeffer (1972a) found that regulated firms, firms with a higher proportion of debt in their capital structures, and larger firms tended to have more outside directors. Allen (1974) also found that size of the board and the use of cooptation was predicted by the size of the firm, but did not replicate Pfeffer's earlier finding of a relationship between the organization's capital structure and the proportion of directors from financial institutions. In a study of utility boards, Pfeffer (1974b) noted that the composition of the board tended to correlate with the demographics of the area in which the utility was regulated.

The evidence is consistent with the strategy of organizations using their boards of directors to coopt external organizations and manage problematic interdependence. The role of the board of directors is seen not as the provision of management expertise or control, but more generally as a means of managing problematic aspects of an organization's institutional environment.

Executive Recruitment

Information also is transferred among organizations through the movement of personnel. The difference between movement of executives between organizations and cooptation is that in the latter case, the person linking the two organizations retains membership in both organizations. In the case of personnel movement, dual organizational membership is not maintained. When people change jobs, they take with themselves information about the operations, policies, and values of their previous employers, as well as contacts in the organization. In a study of the movement of faculty among schools of business, Baty et al. (1971) found that similar orientations and curricula developed among schools exchanging personnel. The movement of personnel is one method by which new techniques of management and new marketing and product ideas are diffused through a set of organizations.

Occasionally, the movement of executives between organizations has been viewed as intensifying, rather than reducing, competition. Companies have been distressed by the raiding of trade secrets and managerial expertise by other organizations. While this perspective must be recognized, the exchange of personnel among organizations is a revered method of conflict *reduction* between organizations (Stern, Sternthal, and Craig, 1973). Personnel movement inevitably involves sharing information among a set of organizations.

If executive movement is a form of interfirm linkage designed to manage competitive relationships, the proportion of executives recruited from within the same industry should be highest at intermediate levels of industrial concentration. Examining the three top executive positions in twenty different manufacturing industries, the evidence on executive backgrounds was found to be consistent with this argument (Pfeffer and Leblebici, 1973). The proportion of high level executives with previous jobs in the same industry but in a different company was found to be negatively related to the number of firms in the industry. The larger the number of firms, the less likely that a single link among competitors will substantially reduce uncertainty, but the larger the available supply of external executive talent. The data indicated no support for a supply argument, but supported the premise that interorganizational linkages are used to manage interdependence and uncertainty.

The use of executive movement to manage noncompetitive interorganizational relationships is quite prevalent. The often-cited movement of personnel between the Defense Department and major defense contractors is only one example, because there is extensive movement of personnel between many government departments and industries interested in the agencies decisions. The explanation is frequently proposed that organizations are acquiring these personnel because of their expertise. The expertise explanation is frequently difficult to separate from the alternative that personnel are being exchanged to enhance interorganizational relationships. Regardless of the motivation, exchanging personnel inevitably involves the transfer of information and access to the other organization.

Regulation

Occasionally, institutional relationships are managed through recourse to political intervention. The reduction of competition and its associated uncertainty may be accomplished through regulation. Regulation, however, is a risky strategy for organizations to pursue. While regulation most frequently benefits the regulated industry (Jordan, 1972; Pfeffer, 1974a), the industry and firms have no assurance that regulatory authority will not be used against their interests. Regulation is very hard to repeal. Successful use of regulation requires that the firm and industry face little or no powerful political opposition, and that the political future can be accurately forecast.

The benefits of regulation to those being regulated have been extensively reviewed (Posner, 1974; Stigler, 1971). Regulation frequently has been sought by the regulated industry. . . . Estimates of the effects of regulation on prices in electric utilities, airlines, trucking, and natural gas have indicated that regulation either increases price or has no effect.

The theory behind these outcomes is still unclear. One approach suggests that regulation is created for the public benefit, but after the initial legislative attention, the regulatory process is captured by the firms subject to regulation. Another approach proposes that regulation, like other goods, is acquired subject to supply and demand considerations (Posner, 1974). Political scientists, focusing on the operation of interest groups, argue that regulatory agencies are "captured" by organized and well-financed interests. Government intervention in the market can solve many of the interdependence problems faced by firms. Regulation is most often accompanied by restriction of entry and the fixing of prices, which tend to reduce market uncertainties. Markets may be actually allocated to firms, and with the reduction of risk, regulation may make access to capital easier. Regulation may alter the organization's relationships with suppliers and customers. One theory of why the railroads were interested in the creation of the Interstate Commerce Commission (ICC) in 1887 was that large users were continually demanding and winning discriminatory rate reductions, disturbing the price stability of railroad price fixing cartels. By forbidding price discrimination and enforcing this regulation, the ICC strengthened the railroads' position with respect to large customers (MacAvoy, 1965).

Political Activity

Regulation is only one specific form of organizational activity in governmental processes. Business attempts to affect competition through the operation of the tariff laws date back to the 1700's (Bauer et al., 1968). Epstein (1969) provided one of the more complete summaries of the history of corporate involvement in politics and the inevitability of such action. The government has the power of coercion, possessed legally by no other social institution. Furthermore, legislation and regulation affect most of our economic institutions and markets, either indirectly through taxation, or more directly through purchasing, market protection or market creation. For example, taxes on margarine only recently came to an end. Federal taxes, imposed in 1886 as a protectionist measure for dairy interests, were removed in 1950, but a law outlawing the sale of oleo in its colored form lasted until 1967 in Wisconsin.

As with regulation, political activities carry both benefits and risks. The risk arises because once government intervention in an issue on behalf of a firm or industry is sought, then political intervention becomes legitimated, regardless of whose interests are helped or hurt. The firm that seeks favorable tax legislation runs the risk of creating a setting in which it is equally legitimate to be exposed to very unfavorable legislation. After an issue is opened to government intervention, neither side will find it easy to claim that further government action is illegitimate.

In learning to cope with a particular institutional environment, the firm may be unprepared for new uncertainties caused by the change of fundamental institutional relationships, including the opening of price competition, new entry and the lack of protection from overseas competition.

CONCLUSION

. . . Considering its probable importance to the firm, the institutional function of management has received much less concern than it warrants. It is time that this aspect of management receives the systematic attention long reserved for motivational and productivity problems associated with relationships between management and workers.

WHO SHOULD CONTROL THE CORPORATION?

By Henry Mintzberg

Who should control the corporation? How? And for the pursuit of what goals? Historically, the corporation was controlled by its owners—through direct control of the managers if not through direct management—for the pursuit of economic goals. But as shareholding became dispersed, owner control weakened; and as the corporation grew to very large size, its economic actions came to have increasing social consequences. The giant, widely held corporation came increasingly under the implicit control of its managers, and the concept of social responsibility—the voluntary consideration of public social goals alongside the private economic ones—arose to provide a basis of legitimacy for their actions.

To some, including those closest to the managers themselves, this was accepted as a satisfactory arrangement for the large corporation. "Trust it" to the goodwill of the managers was their credo; these people will be able to achieve an appropriate balance between social and economic goals.

But others viewed this basis of control as fundamentally illegitimate. The corporation was too large, too influential, its actions too pervasive to be left free of the direct and concerted influence of outsiders. At the extreme were those who believed that legitimacy could be achieved only by subjecting managerial authority to formal and direct external control. "Nationalize it," said those at one end of the political spectrum, to put ultimate control in the hands of the government so that it will pursue public social goals. No, said those at the other end, "restore it" to direct shareholder control, so that it will not waiver from the pursuit of private economic goals.

Other people took less extreme positions. "Democratize it" became the rallying cry for some, to open up the governance of the large, widely held corporation to a variety of affected groups—if not the workers, then the customers, or conservation interests, or minorities. "Regulate it" was also a popular position, with its implicit premise that only by sharing their control with government would the corporation's managers attend to certain social goals. Then there were those who accepted direct management control so long as it was tempered by other, less formal types of influence. "Pressure it," said a generation of social activists, to ensure that social goals are taken into consideration. But others argued that because the corporation is an economic instrument, you must "induce it" by providing economic incentives to encourage the resolution of social problems.

Finally, there were those who argued that this whole debate was unnecessary, that a kind of invisible hand ensures that the economic corporation acts in a socially responsible manner. "Ignore it" was their implicit conclusion.

This article is written to clarify what has become a major debate of our era, *the* major debate revolving around the private sector: Who should control the corporation, specifically the large, widely held corporation, how, and for the pursuit of what goals? The answers that are eventually accepted will determine what kind of society we and our children shall live in. . . .

As implied earlier, the various positions of who should control the corporation, and how, can be laid out along a political spectrum, from nationalization at one end to the restoration of shareholder power at the other. From the managerial perspective, however, those two extremes are not so far apart. Both call for direct control of the corporation's managers by specific outsiders, in one case the government to ensure the pur-

Originally published in the *California Management Review* (Fall 1984), pp. 90–115, based on a section of Henry Mintzberg, *Power in and Around Organizations* (Prentice Hall, 1983). Copyright © 1984 by The Regents of the University of California. Reprinted with deletions by permission of The Regents.

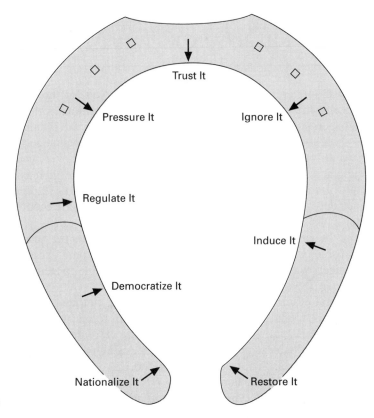

FIGURE 1
The Conceptual Horseshoe

suit of social goals, in the other case the shareholders to ensure the pursuit of economic ones. It is the moderate positions—notably, trusting the corporation to the social responsibility of its managers—that are farthest from the extremes. Hence, we can fold our spectrum around so that it takes the shape of a horseshoe.

Figure 1 shows our "conceptual horseshoe," with "nationalize it" and "restore it" at the two ends. "Trust it" is at the center, because it postulates a natural balance of social and economic goals. "Democratize it," "regulate it," and "pressure it" are shown on the left side of the horseshoe, because all seek to temper economic goals with social ones. "Induce it" and "ignore it," both of which favor the exclusive pursuit of economic goals, are shown on the right side.

This conceptual horseshoe provides a basic framework to help clarify the issues in this important debate. We begin by discussing each of these positions in turn, circling the horseshoe from left to right. Finding that each (with one exception) has a logical context, we conclude—in keeping with our managerial perspective—that they should be thought of as forming a portfolio from which society can draw to deal with the issue of who should control the corporation and how.

"NATIONALIZE IT"

Nationalization of the corporation is a taboo subject in the United States—in general, but not in particular. Whenever a major corporation runs into serious difficulty (i.e., faces bankruptcy with possible loss of many jobs), massive government intervention, often including direct nationalization, inevitably comes up as an option. This option has been exercised: U. S. travelers now ride on Amtrak; Tennessee residents have for years been getting their power from a government utility; indeed, the Post Office was once a private enterprise. Other nations have, of course, been much more ambitious in this regard.

From a managerial and organizational perspective, the question is not whether nationalization is legitimate, but whether it works—at least in particular, limited circumstances. As a response to concerns about the social responsibility of large corporations, the answer seems to be no. The evidence suggests that social difficulties arise more from the size of an organization and its degree of bureaucratization than from its form of ownership (Epstein, 1977; Jenkins, 1976). On the other hand, contrary to popular belief in the United States, nationalization does not necessarily harm economic efficiency. Over the years, Renault has been one of the most successful automobile companies outside Japan; it was nationalized by the French government shortly after World War II. . . . When people believe that government ownership leads to interference, politicization, and inefficiency, that may be exactly what happens. However, when they believe that nationalization *has* to work, then state-owned enterprises may be able to attract the very best talent in the country and thereby work well.

But economic efficiency is no reason to favor nationalization any more than is concern about social responsibility. Nationalization does, however, seem to make sense in at least two particular circumstances. The first is when a mission deemed necessary in a society will not be provided adequately by the private sector. That is presumably why America has its Amtrak [and why Third World nations often create state enterprises]. . . . The second is when the activities of an organization must be so intricately tied to government policy that it is best managed as a direct arm of the state. The Canadian government created Petrocan to act as a "window" and a source of expertise on the sensitive oil industry.

Thus, it is not rhetoric but requirement that should determine the role of this position as a solution to who should control the corporation. "Nationalize it" should certainly not be embraced as a panacea, but neither should it be rejected as totally inapplicable.

"DEMOCRATIZE IT"

A less extreme position—at least in the context of the American debate—is one that calls for formal devices to broaden the governance of the corporation. The proponents of this position either accept the legal fiction of shareholder control and argue that the corporation's power base is too narrow, or else they respond to the emergent reality and question the legitimacy of managerial control. Why, they ask, do stockholders or self-selected managers have any greater right to control the profound decisions of these major institutions than do workers or customers or the neighbors downstream.

This stand is not to be confused with what is known as "participative management." The call to "democratize it" is a legal, rather than ethical one and is based on power, not generosity. Management is not asked to share its power voluntarily; rather, that power is to be reallocated constitutionally. That makes this position a fundamental and important one, *especially* in the United States with its strong tradition of pluralist control of its institutions.

The debate over democratization of the corporation has been confusing in part because many of the proposals have been so vague. We can bring some order to it by considering, in organizational terms, two basic means of democratization and two basic

GROUPS INVOLVED

	Internal Employees	External Interest Groups
Board of Directors	Worker Representative Democracy (European style, e.g., "co-determination" or worker ownership)	Pluralistic Representative Democracy (American style, e.g., "public interest" directors)
Internal Decision-Making Process	Worker Participatory Democracy (e.g., works councils)	Pluralistic Participatory Democracy (e.g., outsiders on new product committees)

FOCUS OF ATTENTION

FIGURE 2

Four Basic Forms of Corporate Democracy

constituencies that can be involved. As shown in Figure 2, they suggest four possible forms of corporate democracy. One means is through the election of representatives to the board of directors, which we call *representative democracy.* The other is through formal but direct involvement in internal decision making processes, which we call *participatory democracy.* Either can focus on the *workers* . . . or else on a host of outside interest groups, the latter giving rise to a *pluralistic* form of democracy. These are basic forms of corporate democracy in theory. With one exception, they have hardly been approached—let alone achieved—in practice. But they suggest where the "democratize it" debate may be headed.

The European debate has focused on worker representative democracy. This has, in some sense, been achieved in Yugoslavia, where the workers of all but the smallest firms elect the members of what is the equivalent of the American board of directors. In Germany, under the so-called *Mitbestimmung* ("codetermination"), the workers and the shareholders each elect half of the directors.

The evidence on this form of corporate democracy has been consistent, and it supports neither its proponents nor its detractors. Workers representation on the board seems to make relatively little difference one way or the other. The worker representatives concern themselves with wage and welfare issues but leave most other questions to management. Worker-controlled firms (not unlike the state-owned ones) appear to be no more socially responsible than private ones. . . .

On the other hand, worker representative democracy may have certain positive benefits. German Chancellor Helmut Schmidt is reported to have said that "the key to [his] country's postwar economic miracle was its sophisticated system of workers' participation" (in Garson, 1977:63). While no one can prove this statement, codetermination certainly does not seem to have done the German economy much harm. By providing an aura of legitimacy to the German corporation and by involving the workers (at least officially) in its governance, codetermination may perhaps have enhanced the spirit of enterprise in Germany (while having little real effect on how decisions are actually made). More significantly, codetermination may have fostered greater understanding and cooperation between the managers and the union members who fill most of the worker seats on the boards. . . .

. . . the embryonic debate over representative democracy in the United States has shown signs of moving in a different direction. Consistent with the tradition of pluralism in America's democratic institutions, there has been increasing pressure to elect outside directors who represent a wide variety of special interest groups—that is, consumers, minorities, environmentalists, and so on. . . .

Critics . . . have pointed out the problems of defining constituencies and finding the means to hold elections. "One-person, one-vote" may be easily applied to electing representatives of the workers, but no such simple rule can be found in the case of the consumer or environmental representatives, let alone ones of the "public interest." Yet it is amazing how quickly things become workable in the United States when Americans decide to put their collective mind to it. Indeed, the one case of public directors that I came across is telling in this regard. According to a Conference Board report, the selection by the Chief Justice of the Supreme Court of New Jersey of 6 of the 24 members of the board of Prudential Insurance as public directors has been found by the company to be "quite workable" (Bacon and Brown, 1975:48). . . . [Note—see the associated box on "The Power of the Board," page 210.]

Despite its problems, representative democracy is crystal clear compared with participatory democracy. What the French call "autogestion" (as opposed to "cogestion," or codetermination) seems to describe a kind of bottom-up, grass-roots democracy in which the workers participate directly in decision making (instead of overseeing management's decisions from the board of directors) and also elect their own managers (who then become more administrators than bosses). Yet such proposals are inevitably vague, and I have heard of no large mass production or mass service firm—not even one owned by workers or a union—that comes close to this. . . .

What has impeded worker participatory democracy? In my opinion, something rather obvious has stood in its way; namely, the structure required by the very organizations in which the attempts have been made to apply it. Worker participatory democracy—and worker representative democracy too, for that matter—has been attempted primarily in organizations containing large numbers of workers who do highly routine, rather unskilled jobs that are typical of most mass production and service— what I have elsewhere called Machine Bureaucracies. The overriding requirement in Machine Bureaucracy is for tight coordination, the kind that can only be achieved by central administrators. For example, the myriad of decisions associated with producing an automobile at Volvo's Kalmar works in Sweden cannot be made by autonomous groups, each doing as it pleases. The whole car must fit together in a particular way at the end of the assembly process. These decisions require a highly sophisticated system of bureaucratic coordination. That is why automobile companies are structured into rigid hierarchies of authority. . . .

Participatory democracy *is* approached in other kinds of organizations . . . the autonomous professional institutions such as universities and hospitals, which have very different needs for central coordination. . . . But the proponents of democracy in organizations are not lobbying for changes in hospitals or universities. It is the giant mass producers they are after, and unless the operating work in these corporations becomes largely skilled and professional in nature, nothing approaching participative democracy can be expected.

In principal, the pluralistic form of participatory democracy means that a variety of groups external to the corporation can somehow control its decision-making processes directly. In practice, of course, this concept is even more elusive than the worker form of participatory democracy. To fully open up the internal decision-making processes of the corporation to outsiders would mean chaos. Yet certain very limited forms of outside participation would seem to be not only feasible but perhaps even desirable. . . . Imagine telephone company executives resolving rate conflicts with consumer groups in quiet offices instead of having to face them in noisy public hearings.

To conclude, corporate democracy—whether representative or participatory in form—may be an elusive and difficult concept, but it cannot be dismissed. It is not just another social issue, like conservation or equal opportunity, but one that strikes at the most fundamental of values. Ours has become a society of organizations. Democracy will have decreasing meaning to most citizens if it cannot be extended beyond political and judicial processes to those institutions that impinge upon them in their daily lives— as workers, as consumers, as neighbors. This is why we shall be hearing a great deal more of "democratize it."

THE POWER OF THE BOARD

Proposals for representative democracy, indeed those for nationalization and the restoration of shareholder control as well, rest on assumptions about the power of the board of directors. It may, therefore, be worth considering at this point the roles that boards of directors play in organizations and the board's resulting powers.

In law, traditionally, the business of a corporation was to be "managed" by its board. But of course, the board does no such thing. Managers manage, although some may happen to sit on the board. What, then, are the roles of the board, particularly of its "outside" directors?

The most tangible role of the board, and clearly provided for in law, is to name, and of course to dismiss as well, the chief executive officer, that person who in turn names the rest of the management. A second role may be to exercise direct control during periods of crisis, for example when the management has failed to provide leadership. And a third is to review the major decisions of the management as well as its overall performance.

These three constitute the board's roles of control, in principal at least because there is no shortage of evidence that boards have difficulty doing even these effectively, especially outside directors. Their job is, after all, part-time, and in a brief meeting once in a while they face a complex organization led by a highly organized management that deals with it every day. The result is that board control tends to reduce to naming and replacing the chief executive, and that person's knowledge of that fact, nothing more. Indeed, even that power is circumscribed, because a management cannot be replaced very often. In a sense, the board is like a bee hovering near a person picking flowers. The person must proceed carefully, so as not to provoke the bee, but can proceed with the task. But if the bee does happen to be provoked, it only gets to sting once. Thus many boards try to know only enough to know when the management is not doing its job properly, so that they can replace it.

But if boards tend to be weaker than expected in exercising *control over* the organization, they also tend perhaps to be stronger than expected in providing *service to* the organization. Here board membership plays at least four other roles. First, it "co-opts" influential outsiders: The organization uses the status of a seat on its board to gain the support of people important to it (as in the case of the big donors who sit on university boards). Second, board membership may be used to establish contacts for the organization (as when retired military officers sit on the boards of weapons manufacturing firms). This may be done to help in such things as the securing of contracts and the raising of funds. Third, seats on the board can be used to enhance an organization's reputation (as when an astronaut or some other type of celebrity is given a seat). And fourth, the board can be used to provide advice for the organization (as in the case of many of the bankers and lawyers who sit on the boards of corporations).

How much do boards serve organizations, and how much do they control them? Some boards do, of course, exercise control, particularly when their members represent a well-defined constituency, such as the substantial owner of a corporation. But, as noted, this tends to be a loose control at best. And other boards hardly do even that, especially when their constituencies are widely dispersed.

To represent everyone is ultimately to represent no one, especially when faced with a highly organized management that knows exactly what it wants. (Or from the elector's point of view, having some distant representative sitting on a board somewhere hardly brings him or her closer to control over the things that

THE POWER OF THE BOARD (continued)

impinge on daily life—the work performed, the products consumed, the rivers polluted.) In corporations, this has been shown to be true of the directors who represent many small shareholders no less than those who represent many workers or many customers, perhaps even those who represent government, since that can be just a confusing array of pressure groups. These boards become, at best, tools of the organization, providing it with the variety of the services discussed above, at worst mere façades of formal authority.

"REGULATE IT"

In theory, regulating the corporation is about as simple as democratizing it is complex. In practice, it is, of course, another matter. To the proponents of "regulate it," the corporation can be made responsive to social needs by having its actions subjected to the controls of a higher authority—typically government, in the form of a regulatory agency or legislation backed up by the courts. Under regulation, constraints are imposed externally on the corporation while its internal governance is left to its managers.

Regulation of business is at least as old as the Code of Hammurabi. In America, it has tended to come in waves. . . .

To some, regulation is a clumsy instrument that should never be relied upon; to others, it is a panacea for the problems of social responsibility. At best, regulation sets minimum and usually crude standards of acceptable behavior; when it works, it does not make any firm socially responsible so much as stop some from being grossly irresponsible. Because it is inflexible, regulation tends to be applied slowly and conservatively, usually lagging public sentiment. Regulation often does not work because of difficulties in enforcement. The problems of the regulatory agencies are legendary—limited resources and information compared with the industries they are supposed to regulate, the cooptation of the regulators by industries, and so on. When applied indiscriminately, regulation either fails dramatically or else succeeds and creates havoc.

Yet there are obvious places for regulation. A prime one is to control tangible "externalities"—costs incurred by corporations that are passed on to the public at large. When, for example, costly pollution or worker health problems can be attributed directly to a corporation, then there seems to be every reason to force it (and its customers) to incur these costs directly, or else to terminate the actions that generate them. Likewise, regulation may have a place where competition encourages the unscrupulous to pull all firms down to a base level of behavior, forcing even the well-intentioned manager to ignore the social consequences of his actions. Indeed, in such cases, the socially responsible behavior is to encourage sensible regulation. "Help us to help others," businessmen should be telling the government. . . .

Most discouraging, however, is Theodore Levitt's revelation some years ago that business has fought every piece of proposed regulatory or social legislation throughout this century, from the Child Labor Acts on up. In Levitt's opinion, much of that legislation has been good for business—dissolving the giant trusts, creating a more honest and effective stock market, and so on. Yet, "the computer is programmed to cry wolf" (Levitt, 1968:83). . . .

In summary, regulation is a clumsy instrument but not a useless one. Were the business community to take a more enlightened view of it, regulation could be applied more appropriately, and we would not need these periodic housecleanings to eliminate the excesses.

"PRESSURE IT"

"Pressure it" is designed to do what "regulate it" fails to do: provoke corporations to act beyond some base level of behavior, usually in an area that regulation misses entirely. Here, activists bring ad hoc campaigns of pressure to bear on one or a group of corporations to keep them responsive to the activists' interpretation of social needs. . . .

"Pressure it" is a distinctively American position. While Europeans debate the theories of nationalization and corporate democracy in their cafés, Americans read about the exploits of Ralph Nader et al. in their morning newspapers. Note that "pressure it," unlike "regulate it," implicitly accepts management's right to make the final decisions. Perhaps this is one reason why it is favored in America.

While less radical than the other positions so far discussed, "pressure it" has nevertheless proved far more effective in eliciting behavior sensitive to social needs . . . [activist groups] have pressured for everything from the dismemberment of diversified corporations to the development of day care centers. Of special note is the class action suit, which has opened up a whole new realm of corporate social issues. But the effective use of the pressure campaign has not been restricted to the traditional activist. President Kennedy used it to roll back U. S. Steel price increases in the early 1960s, and business leaders in Pittsburgh used it in the late 1940s by threatening to take their freight-haulage business elsewhere if the Pennsylvania Railroad did not replace its coal burning locomotives to help clean up their city's air.

"Pressure it" as a means to change corporate behavior is informal, flexible, and focused; hence, it has been highly successful. Yet it is irregular and ad hoc, with different pressure campaigns sometimes making contradictory demands on management. Compared to the positions to its right on the horseshoe, "pressure it," like the other positions to its left, is based on confrontation rather than cooperation.

"TRUST IT"

To a large and vocal contingent, which parades under the banner of "social responsibility," the corporation has no need to act irresponsibly, and therefore there is no reason for it to either be nationalized by the state, democratized by its different constituencies, regulated by the government, or pressured by activists. This contingent believes that the corporation's leaders can be trusted to attend to social goals for their own sake, simply because it is the noble thing to do. (Once this position was known as *noblesse oblige,* literally "nobility obliges.")

We call this position "trust it," or, more exactly, "trust the corporation to the goodwill of its managers," although looking from the outside in, it might just as well be called "socialize it." We place it in the center of our conceptual horseshoe because it alone postulates a natural balance between social and economic goals—a balance which is to be attained in the heads (or perhaps the hearts) of responsible businessmen. And, as a not necessarily incidental consequence, power can be left in the hands of the managers; the corporation can be trusted to those who reconcile social and economic goals.

The attacks on social responsibility, from the right as well as the left, boil down to whether corporate managers should be trusted when they claim to pursue social goals; if so, whether they are capable of pursuing such goals; and finally, whether they have any right to pursue such goals.

The simplest attack is that social responsibility is all rhetoric, no action. E. F. Cheit refs to the "Gospel of Social Responsibility" as "designed to justify the power of managers over an ownerless system" (1964:172). . . .

Others argue that businessmen lack the personal capabilities required to pursue social goals. Levitt claims that the professional manager reaches the top of the hierarchy by dedication to his firm and his industry; as a result, his knowledge of social issues is highly restricted (Levitt, 1968:83). Others argue that an orientation to efficiency renders business leaders inadept at handling complex social problems (which require flexibility and political finesse, and sometimes involve solutions that are uneconomic). . . .

The most far reaching criticism is that businessmen have no right to pursue social goals. "Who authorized them to do that?" asks Braybrooke (1967:224), attacking from the left. What business have they—self-selected or at best appointed by shareholders—to impose *their* interpretation of the public good on society. Let the elected politicians, directly responsible to the population, look after the social goals.

But this attack comes from the right, too. Milton Friedman writes that social responsibility amounts to spending other people's money—if not that of shareholders, then of customers or employees. Drawing on all the pejorative terms of right-wing ideology, Friedman concludes that social responsibility is a "fundamentally subversive doctrine," representing "pure and unadulterated socialism," supported by businessmen who are "unwitting puppets of the intellectual forces that have been undermining the basis of a free society these past decades." To Friedman, "there is one and only one social responsibility of business—to use its resources and engage in activities designed to increase its profits so long as it stays within the rules of the game" (1970). Let businessmen, in other words, stick to their own business, which is business itself.

The empirical evidence on social responsibility is hardly more encouraging. Brenner and Molander, comparing their 1977 survey of *Harvard Business Review* readers with one conducted fifteen years earlier, concluded that the "respondents are somewhat more cynical about the ethical conduct of their peers" than they were previously (1977:59). Close to half the respondents agreed with the statement that "the American business executive tends not to apply the great ethical laws immediately to work. He is preoccupied chiefly with gain" (p. 62). Only 5% listed social responsibility as a factor "influencing ethical standards" whereas 31% and 20% listed different factors related to pressure campaigns and 10% listed regulation. . . .

The modern corporation has been described as a rational, amoral institution —its professional managers "hired guns" who pursue "efficiently" any goals asked of them. The problem is that efficiency really means measurable efficiency, so that the guns load only with goals that can be quantified. Social goals, unlike economic ones, just don't lend themselves to quantification. As a result, the performance control systems—on which modern corporations so heavily depend—tend to drive out social goals in favor of economic ones (Ackerman, 1975). . . .

In the contemporary large corporation, professional amorality turns into economic morality. When the screws of the performance control systems are turned tight . . . economic morality can turn into social immorality. And it happens often: A *Fortune* writer found that "a surprising number of [big companies] have been involved in blatant illegalities" in the 1970s, at least 117 of 1,043 firms studied (Ross, 1980:57). . . .

How, then, is anyone to "trust it"?

The fact is that we have to trust it, for two reasons. First, the strategic decisions of large organizations inevitably involve social as well as economic consequences that are inextricably intertwined. The neat distinction between economic goals in the private sector and social goals in the public sector just doesn't hold up in practice. Every important decision of the large corporation—to introduce a new product line, to close an old plant, whatever—generates all kinds of social consequences. There is no such thing as purely economic decisions in big business. Only a conceptual ostrich, with his head deeply buried in the abstractions of economic theory, could possibly use the distinction between economic and social goals to dismiss social responsibility.

The second reason we have to "trust it" is that there is always some degree of discretion involved in corporate decision making, discretion to thwart social needs or to attend to them. Things could be a lot better in today's corporation, but they could also be an awful lot worse. It is primarily our ethics that keep us where we are. If the performance control systems favored by diversified corporations cut too deeply into our ethical standards, then our choice is clear; to reduce these standards or call into question the whole trend toward diversification.

To dismiss social responsibility is to allow corporate behavior to drop to the lowest level, propped up only by external controls such as regulation and pressure campaigns. Solzhenitsyn, who has experienced the natural conclusion of unrestrained bureaucratization, warns us (in sharp contrast to Friedman) that "a society with no other scale but the legal one is not quite worthy of man. . . . A society which is based on the letter of the law and never reaches any higher is scarcely taking advantage of the high level of human possibilities" (1978:B1).

This is not to suggest that we must trust it completely. We certainly cannot trust it unconditionally by accepting the claim popular in some quarters that only business can solve the social ills of society. Business has no business using its resources without constraint in the social sphere—whether to support political candidates or to dictate implicitly through donations how nonprofit institutions should allocate their efforts. But where business is inherently involved, where its decisions have social consequences, that is where social responsibility has a role to play: where business creates externalities that cannot be measured and attributed to it (in other words, where regulation is ineffective); where regulation would work if only business would cooperate with it; where the corporation can fool its customers, or suppliers, or government through superior knowledge; where useful products can be marketed instead of wasteful or destructive ones. In other words, we have to realize that in many spheres we must trust it, or at least socialize it (and perhaps change it) so that we can trust it. Without responsible and ethical people in important places, our society is not worth very much.

"IGNORE IT"

"Ignore it" differs from the other positions on the horseshoe in that explicitly or implicitly it calls for no change in corporate behavior. It assumes that social needs are met in the course of pursuing economic goals. We include this position in our horseshoe because it is held by many influential people and also because its validity would preempt support for the other positions. We must, therefore, investigate it alongside the others.

It should be noted at the outset that "ignore it" is not the same position as "trust it." In the latter, to be good is the right thing to do; in the present case, "it pays to be good." The distinction is subtle but important, for now it is economics, not ethics, that elicits the desired behavior. One need not strive to be ethical; economic forces will ensure that social needs fall conveniently into place. Here we have moved one notch to the right on our horseshoe, into the realm where the economic goals dominate. . . .

"Ignore it" is sometimes referred to as "enlightened self-interest," although some of its proponents are more enlightened than others. Many a true believer in social responsibility has used the argument that it pays to be good to ward off the attacks from the right that corporations have no business pursuing social goals. Even Milton Friedman must admit that they have every right to do so if it pays them economically. The danger of such arguments, however—and a prime reason "ignore it" differs from "trust it"—is that they tend to support the status quo: Corporations need not change their behavior because it already pays to be good.

Sometimes the case for "ignore it" is made in terms of corporations at large, that the whole business community will benefit from socially responsible behavior. Other times the case is made in terms of the individual corporation, that it will benefit directly from its own socially responsible actions. . . . Others make the case for "ignore it" in "social investment" terms, claiming that socially responsible behavior pays off in a better image for the firm, a more positive relationship with customers, and ultimately a healthier and more stable society in which to do business.

Then, there is what I like to call the "them" argument: "If we're not good, *they* will move in"—"they" being Ralph Nader, the government, whoever. In other words, "Be good or else." The trouble with this argument is that by reducing social responsibility to simply a political tool for sustaining managerial control of the corporation in the face of outside threats, it tends to encourage general pronouncements instead of concrete actions (unless of course, "they" actually deliver with pressure campaigns). . . .

The "ignore it" position rests on some shaky ground. It seems to encourage average behavior at best; and where the average does not seem to be good enough, it encourages the status quo. In fact, ironically, "ignore it" makes a strong case for "pressure it," since the whole argument collapses in the absence of pressure campaigns. Thus while many influential people take this position, we question whether in the realities of corporate behavior it can really stand alone.

"INDUCE IT"

Continuing around to the right, our next position drops all concern with social responsibility per se and argues, simply, "pay it to be good," or, from the corporation's point of view, "be good only where it pays." Here, the corporation does not actively pursue social goals at all, whether as ends in themselves or as means to economic ends. Rather, it undertakes socially desirable programs only when induced economically to do so— usually through government incentives. If society wishes to clean up urban blight, then let its government provide subsidies for corporations that renovate buildings; if pollution is the problem, then let corporations be rewarded for reducing it.

"Induce it" faces "regulate it" on the opposite side of the horseshoe for good reason. While one penalizes the corporation for what it does do, the other rewards it for doing what it might not otherwise do. Hence these two positions can be direct substitutes: Pollution can be alleviated by introducing penalties for the damage done or by offering incentives for the improvements rendered.

Logic would, however, dictate a specific role for each of these positions. Where a corporation is doing society a specific, attributable harm—as in the case of pollution— then paying it to stop hardly seems to make a lot of sense. If society does not wish to outlaw the harmful behavior altogether, then surely it must charge those responsible for it—the corporation and, ultimately, its customers. Offering financial incentives to stop causing harm would be to invite a kind of blackmail—for example, encouraging corporations to pollute so as to get paid to stop. And every citizen would be charged for the harm done by only a few.

On the other hand, where social problems exist which cannot be attributed to specific corporations, yet require the skills of certain corporations for solution, then financial incentives clearly make sense (so long, of course, as solutions can be clearly defined and tied to tangible economic rewards). Here, and not under "trust it," is where the "only business can do it" argument belongs. When it is true that only business can do it (and business has not done it to us in the first place), then business should be encouraged to do it. . . .

Our last position on the horseshoe tends to be highly ideological, the first since "democratize it" to seek a fundamental change in the governance and the goals of the corporation. Like the proponents of "nationalize it," those of this position believe that managerial control is illegitimate and must be replaced by a more valid form of external control. The corporation should be restored to its former status, that is, returned to its "rightful" owners, the shareholders. The only way to ensure the relentless pursuit of economic goals—and that means the maximization of profit, free of the "subversive doctrine" of social responsibility—is to put control directly into the hands of those to whom profit means the most.

A few years ago this may have seemed to be an obsolete position. But thanks to its patron saint Milton Friedman . . . , it has recently come into prominence. Also, other forms of restoring it, including the "small is beautiful" theme, have also become popular in recent years.

Friedman has written,

> In a free-enterprise, private-property system, a corporate executive is an employee of the owners of the business. He has direct responsibility to his employers. That responsibility is to conduct the business in accordance with their desires, which generally will be to make as much money as possible while conforming to the basic rules of the society, both those embodied in law and those embodied in ethical custom. (1970:33)

Interestingly, what seems to drive Friedman is a belief that the shift over the course of this century from owner to manager control, with its concerns about social responsibility, represents an unstoppable skid around our horseshoe. In the opening chapter of his book *Capitalism and Freedom,* Friedman seems to accept only two possibilities—traditional capitalism and socialism as practiced in Eastern Europe. The absence of the former must inevitably lead to the latter:

> The preservation and expansion of freedom are today threatened from two directions. The one threat is obvious and clear. It is the external threat coming from the evil men in the Kremlin who promised to bury us. The other threat is far more subtle. It is the internal threat coming from men of good intentions and good will who wish to reform us. (1962:20)

The problem of who should control the corporation thus reduces to a war between two ideologies—in Friedman's terms, "subversive" socialism and "free" enterprise. In this world of black and white, there can be no middle ground, no moderate position between the black of "nationalize it" and the white of "restore it," none of the gray of "trust it." Either the owners will control the corporation or else the government will. Hence: " 'restore it' or else." Anchor the corporation on the right side of the horseshoe, Friedman seems to be telling us, the only place where "free" enterprise and "freedom" are safe.

All of this, in my view, rests on a series of assumptions—technical, economic, and political—which contain a number of fallacies. First is the fallacy of the technical assumption of shareholder control. Every trend in ownership during this century seems to refute the assumption that small shareholders are either willing or able to control the large, widely held corporation. The one place where free markets clearly still exist is in stock ownership, and that has served to detach ownership from control. When power is widely dispersed—among stockholders no less than workers or customers—those who share it tend to remain passive. It pays no one of them to invest the effort to exercise their power. Hence, even if serious shareholders did control the boards of widely held corporations (and one survey of all the directors of the *Fortune* 500 in 1977 found that only 1.6% of them represented significant shareholder interests, [Smith, 1978]), the question remains open as to whether they would actually try to control the management. (This is obviously not true of closely held corporations, but these—probably a decreasing minority of the *Fortune* 500—are "restored" in any event.)

The economic assumptions of free markets have been discussed at length in the literature. Whether there exists vibrant competition, unlimited entry, open information, consumer sovereignity, and labor mobility is debatable. Less debatable is the conclusion that the larger the corporation, the greater is its ability to interfere with these processes. The issues we are discussing center on the giant corporation. It is not Luigi's Body Shop that Ralph Nader is after, but General Motors, a corporation that employs more than half a million people and earns greater revenues than many national governments.

Those who laid the foundation for conventional economic theory—such as Adam Smith and Alfred Marshall—never dreamed of the massive amounts now spent for advertising campaigns, most of them designed as much for affect as for effect; of the waves of conglomeration that have combined all kinds of diverse businesses into single corporate entities; of chemical complexes that cost more than a billion dollars; and of the intimate relationships that now exist between giant corporations and government, as customer and partner not to mention subsidizer. The concept of arm's length relationships in such conditions is, at best, nostalgic. What happens to consumer sovereignty when Ford knows more about its gas tanks than do its customers? And what does labor mobility mean in the presence of an inflexible pension plan, or commitment to a special skill, or a one-factory town? It is an ironic twist of conventional economic theory that the worker is the one who typically stays put, thus rendering false the assumption of labor mobility, while the shareholder is the mobile one, thus spoiling the case for owner control.

The political assumptions are more ideological in nature, although usually implicit. These assumptions are that the corporation is essentially amoral, society's instrument for producing goods and services, and, more broadly, that a society is "free" and "democratic" so long as its governmental leaders are elected by universal suffrage and do not interfere with the legal activities of businessmen. But many people—a large majority of the general public, if polls are to be believed—seem to subscribe to one or more assumptions that contradict these "free enterprise" assumptions.

One assumption is that the large corporation is a social and political institution as much as an economic instrument. Economic activities, as noted previously, produce all kinds of social consequences. Jobs get created and rivers get polluted, cities get built and workers get injured. These social consequences cannot be factored out of corporate strategic decisions and assigned to government.

Another assumption is that society cannot achieve the necessary balance between social and economic needs so long as the private sector attends only to economic goals. Given the pervasiveness of business in society, the acceptance of Freidman's prescriptions would drive us toward a one-dimensional society—a society that is too utilitarian and too materialistic. Economic morality, as noted earlier, can amount to a social immorality.

Finally, the question is asked: Why the owners? In a democratic society, what justifies owner control of the corporation any more than worker control, or consumer control, or pluralistic control? Ours is not Adam Smith's society of small proprietors and shopkeepers. His butcher, brewer, and baker have become Iowa Beef Packers, Anheuser-Bush, and ITT Continental Baking. What was once a case for individual democracy now becomes a case for oligarchy. . . .

I see Friedman's form of "restore it" as a rather quaint position in a society of giant corporations, managed economies, and dispersed shareholders—a society in which the collective power of corporations is coming under increasing scrutiny and in which the distribution between economic and social goals is being readdressed.

Of course, there are other ways [than Friedman's] to "restore it." "Divest it" could return the corporation to the business or central theme it knows best, restoring the role of allocating funds between different businesses to capital markets instead of central headquarters. Also, boards could be restored to positions of influence by holding directors legally responsible for their actions and by making them more independent of managers (for example, by providing them with personal staffs and by precluding full-time managers from their ranks, especially the position of chairman). We might even wish to extend use of "reduce it" where possible, to decrease the size of those corporations that have grown excessively large on the basis of market or political power rather than economies of scale, and perhaps to eliminate certain forms of vertical integration. In many cases it may prove advantageous, economically as well as socially, to have the corporation trade with its suppliers and customers instead of being allowed to ingest them indiscriminately.[1]

I personally doubt that these proposals could be any more easily realized in today's society than those of Friedman, even though I believe them to be more desirable. "Restore it" is the nostalgic position on our horseshoe, a return to our fantasies of a glorious past. In this society of giant organizations, it flies in the face of powerful economic and political forces.

CONCLUSION: IF THE SHOE FITS . . .

I believe that today's corporation cannot ride on any one position any more than a horse can ride on part of a shoe. In other words, we need to treat the conceptual horseshoe as a portfolio of positions from which we can draw, depending on circumstances. Exclusive reliance on one position will lead to a narrow and dogmatic society, with an excess concentration of power . . . the use of a variety of positions can encourage the pluralism I believe most of us feel is necessary to sustain democracy. If the shoe fits, then let the corporation wear it.

I do not mean to imply that the eight positions do not represent fundamentally different values and, in some cases, ideologies as well. Clearly they do. But I also believe that anyone who makes an honest assessment of the realities of power in and around today's large corporations must conclude that a variety of positions have to be relied upon [even if they themselves might tilt to the left, right or center of our horseshoe]. . . .

I tilt to the left of center, as has no doubt been obvious in my comments to this point. Let me summarize my own prescriptions as follows, and in the process provide some basis for evaluating the relevant roles of each of the eight positions.

FIRST "TRUST IT," OR AT LEAST "SOCIALIZE IT." Despite my suspicions about much of the rhetoric that passes for social responsibility and the discouraging evidence about the behavior of large contemporary organizations (not only corporations), I remain firmly convinced that without honest and responsible people in important places, we are in deep trouble. We need to trust it because, no matter how much we rely on the other positions, managers will always retain a great deal of power. And that power necessarily has social no less than economic consequences. The positions on the right side of our horseshoe ignore these social consequences while some of those on the left fail to recognize the difficulties of influencing these consequences in large, hierarchical organizations. Sitting between these two sets of positions, managers can use their discretion to satisfy or to subvert the wishes of the public. Ultimately, what managers do is determined by their sense of responsibility as individual members of society.

---

[1] A number of these proposals would be worthwhile to pursue in the public and parapublic sectors as well, to divide up overgrown hospitals, school systems, social service agencies, and all kinds of government departments.

Although we must "trust it," we cannot *only* "trust it." As I have argued, there is an appropriate and limited place for social responsibility—essentially to get the corporation's own house in order and to encourage it to act responsibly in its own sphere of operations. Beyond that, social responsibility needs to be tempered by other positions around our horseshoe.

THEN "PRESSURE IT," CEASELESSLY. As we have seen, too many forces interfere with social responsibility. The best antidote to these forces is the ad hoc pressure campaign, designed to pinpoint unethical behavior and raise social consciousness about issues. The existence of the "pressure it" position is what most clearly distinguishes the western from the eastern "democracies." Give me one Ralph Nader to all those banks of government accountants.

In fact, "pressure it" underlies the success of most of the other positions. Pressure campaigns have brought about necessary new regulations and have highlighted the case for corporate democracy. As we have seen, the "ignore it" position collapses without "pressure it". . . .

AFTER THAT, TRY TO "DEMOCRATIZE IT." A somewhat distant third in my portfolio is "democratize it," a position I view as radical only in terms of the current U.S. debate, not in terms of fundamental American values. Democracy matters most where it affects us directly—in the water we drink, the jobs we perform, the products we consume. How can we call our society democratic when many of its most powerful institutions are closed to governance from the outside and are run as hierarchies of authority from within?

As noted earlier, I have no illusions about having found the means to achieve corporate democracy. But I do know that Americans can be very resourceful when they decide to resolve a problem—and this is a problem that badly needs resolving. Somehow, ways must be found to open the corporation up to the formal influence of the constituencies most affected by it—employees, customers, neighbors, and so on—without weakening it as an economic institution. At stake is nothing less than the maintenance of basic freedoms in our society.

THEN, ONLY WHERE SPECIFICALLY APPROPRIATE, "REGULATE IT" AND "INDUCE IT." Facing each other on the horseshoe are two positions that have useful if limited roles to play. Regulation is neither a panacea nor a menace. It belongs where the corporation can abuse the power it has and can be penalized for that abuse—notably where externalities can be identified with specific corporations. Financial inducements belong, not where a corporation has created a problem, but where it has the capability to solve a problem created by someone else.

OCCASIONALLY, SELECTIVELY, "NATIONALIZE IT" AND "RESTORE IT," BUT NOT IN FRIEDMAN'S WAY. The extreme positions should be reserved for extreme problems. If "pressure it" is a scalpel and "regulate it" a cleaver, then "nationalize it" and "restore it" are guillotines.

Both these positions are implicitly proposed as alternatives to "democratize it." One offers public control, the other "shareholder democracy." The trouble is that control by everyone often turns out to be control by no one, while control by the owners—even if attainable—would remove the corporation even further from the influence of those most influenced by it.

Yet, as noted earlier, nationalization sometimes makes sense—when private enterprise cannot provide a necessary mission, at least in a sufficient or appropriate way, and when the activities of a corporation must be intricately tied in to government policy.

As for "restore it," I believe Friedman's particular proposals will aggravate the problems of political control and social responsibility, strengthening oligarchical tendencies in society and further tilting what I see as the current imbalance between social and economic goals. In response to Friedman's choice between "subversive" socialism and "free" enterprise, I say "a pox on both your houses." Let us concentrate our efforts on the intermediate positions around the horseshoe. However, other forms of "restore it" are worth considering—to "divest it" where diversification has interfered with capital markets, competition, and economic efficiency; to "*dis*integrate it" vertically where a trading network is preferable to a managerial hierarchy; to strengthen its board so that directors can assess managers objectively; and to "reduce it" where size represents a power game rather than a means to provide better and more efficient service to the public. I stand with Friedman in wishing to see competitive markets strengthened; it is just that I believe his proposals lead in exactly the opposite direction.

FINALLY, ABOVE ALL, DON'T "IGNORE IT." I leave one position out of my portfolio altogether, because it contradicts the others. The one thing we must not do is ignore the large, widely held corporation. It is too influential a force in our lives. Our challenge is to find ways to distribute the power in and around our large organizations so that they will remain responsive, vital, and effective.

C H A P T E R   9

STRUCTURE AND STRATEGY IN ENTREPRENEURIAL ORGANIZATIONS

As we have discussed earlier in this book, strategies can fall somewhere on a continuum between deliberate (full realization of intentions) and emergent (realization of something that was not intended). As Mintzberg put it in his Chapter One reading, "Five Ps for Strategy," for entrepreneurial strategy "intentions exist as the personal, unarticulated vision of a single leader, and so are adaptable to new opportunities. . . ." This makes entrepreneurial strategy somewhat deliberate, in that the entrepreneur tries to move the organization in directions consistent with his or her unarticulated vision. But individual vision is obviously a flexible thing, so entrepreneurial strategy can be somewhat emergent, too, as the entrepreneur learns about the conditions facing the firm and adjusts to them.

Mintzberg also pointed out that in entrepreneurial firms "the organization is under the personal control of the leader and located in a protected niche in its environment. . . ." As we will see later in this chapter, this means that the organization tends to prefer the direct supervision coordinating mechanism, relying greatly on its leader's industry-specific knowledge. Consequently, entrepreneurial strategy is built on three foundations: individual vision, technical or industry expertise, and the individual leader's personality traits.

INDIVIDUAL VISION

Entrepreneurial leaders start with a vision, a mental image of what they want their business to look like. This vision is rarely articulated by the leader, and often it is not even fully elaborated in his or her mind. He or she just "knows" that something will work. Successful entrepreneurs are usually seen as the heroes of business, for example, H. Ross Perot, Steve Jobs, Ray Kroc, and Henry Ford. Because of this hero worship, we have come to associate the word *"vision"* with something lofty or profound, but those adjectives need not describe the typical entrepreneurial vision. A person could have an idea for a perfectly ordinary restaurant, dry-cleaning store, or auto repair shop. The important thing is that the idea for the business is in the mind of the entrepreneur. Often, a person who is unhappy with his or her job sees an opportunity to create a coherent new venture based on ideas that have been rejected by the budding entrepreneur's current employer; other times the idea is unrelated to current employment.[1]

TECHNICAL OR INDUSTRY EXPERTISE

No matter whether the new venture is based on rejected work ideas or another interest, it is essential for the entrepreneur to be very knowledgeable about the industry and the technology used in that industry. Research on organizational life cycles has shown that the driving force of new businesses is creativity and technical knowledge.[2] The founders must know enough about the business and the industry to create a product and ensure survival in the marketplace. Once the business is a going concern, the entrepreneur must keep current on the state of the industry. This need for industry and technical knowledge belies the notion of the entrepreneur as a bold pioneer. One study found that the best way to characterize entrepreneurs is as hardworking, practical, and greatly familiar with their market and industry.[3] Mintzberg discusses this idea of "controlled boldness" in his reading in this chapter.

THE ENTREPRENEURIAL PERSONALITY[4]

The chief personality trait traditionally attributed to entrepreneurs was greed. However, in the 1950s scholars began to paint a more flattering picture of entrepreneurs. One of the first findings was that the need to achieve is what drives most entrepreneurs. This means that entrepreneurs are motivated to do well and to pick situations where attaining success is likely. People high in achievement motivation like to set their own goals, which tend to be moderately challenging. High achievers also like to set targets for which they can obtain feedback about their success.[5]

Internal locus of control is another characteristic of entrepreneurs. This means that they believe they are in control of their own destinies and that external forces have little influence. Entrepreneurs are convinced that they make the difference between success or failure, so they are motivated to do what needs to be done to set up a new venture. Since this requires much effort, entrepreneurs tend to have **high energy levels.** Also related to internal locus of control is the tendency of entrepreneurs to be **high in self-confidence.** They believe that they can handle anything that exists or could conceivably come up. They also tend to be **aware of passing time;** entrepreneurs are impatient and avoid procrastination.

Lastly, entrepreneurs have **tolerance for ambiguity.** Many people need structure, specific instructions, and complete information. By contrast, tolerance for ambiguity allows a person to be unbothered by uncertainty and disorder. Since there are few situations more uncertain than starting a new business, it seems likely that entrepreneurs would tolerate ambiguity better than other people.

THE ENTREPRENEURIAL ORGANIZATION

The Structure

In his reading in this chapter, "The Entrepreneurial Organization," Henry Mintzberg begins by describing the basic structure of the entrepreneurial organization. It is the simple structure described in Chapter Six—at the extreme, little or no staff, a loose division of labor, and a small managerial hierarchy. It is not formalized and makes minimal use of planning or training. Power focuses on the chief executive, who exercises it personally by relying on direct supervision for coordination.

The external environment is usually simple (understandable by one person) and dynamic (good for flexible structures). These firms are often young and aggressive, searching for the risky markets that scare off the bureaucracies. But Mintzberg also points out that some entrepreneur organizations are not so aggressive or visionary; many settle down to pursue common strategies in small geographic niches. But the focus on one leader can be the Achilles heel of the entrepreneurial organization too. That leader may get bogged down in operating detail; being knowledgeable about operations is good, but being excessively involved sometimes is not. The entrepreneurial organization's coordination mechanism is fragile—it is one person, who could be wiped out by a heart attack. Also, the organization's adaptability would be sharply reduced if the leader resisted change. Lastly, many people find working for an all-powerful boss too restrictive.

Most new organizations, whatever the sector, seem to adopt the entrepreneurial configuration, because they have to rely on personalized leadership to get themselves going. Some older organizations will retain the form as long as their founders are still around. Lastly, Mintzberg points out that the entrepreneurial organization also arises in any other type of organization that faces severe crisis, a point to which we will return in the next chapter.

Strategy Formation in the Entrepreneurial Organization

Mintzberg discusses how entrepreneurial strategy is rooted in vision. He examines one entrepreneurial firm in detail, the Steinberg supermarket chain. It is here that he mentions "controlled boldness." Sam Steinberg exemplified how ideas can be bold, but execution careful. If a business can be understood in one mind, the entrepreneurial approach is powerful, perhaps the best approach. Nothing else combines integrated vision with flexibility quite so effectively. As mentioned in "Crafting Strategy" (in Chapter Five), conceiving a new strategy is an exercise in synthesis; synthesis happens best within a single, knowledgeable mind. Of course, great success ultimately leads to large size, which is difficult to handle using an entrepreneurial approach.

The genius of the entrepreneur is his or her ability to pursue one vision for a long time and then to change that vision at the appropriate time. Mintzberg examines this process of shifting a firm's vision through a detailed look at Canadelle, a Canadian women's undergarment manufacturer. The first step is the realization that things have changed. The second, and by far the most difficult and painful, is to "step into the void"—to shed comfortable old notions and try to figure out what changes need to be made. This realization typically comes in a "eureka"-type flash. Lastly, the firm must relentlessly and single-mindedly work toward the realization of the new vision.

COMPETITIVE STRATEGY IN EMERGING INDUSTRIES

Emerging industries are newly formed or reformed industries that have been created by technological innovations, shifts in cost relationships, or the emergence of new consumer needs or other potentially viable business opportunities.[6] Michael Porter's reading, "Competitive Strategy in Emerging Industries," deals with this type of industry, which is another context in which entrepreneurial organizations abound. The basic situation in emerging industries is that no "rules of the game" yet exist. Everything is uncertain—technology, strategy, information about rival firms, even who the rival firms *are*. Costs may initially be high but then may plummet. Many firms in the industry are spinoffs from larger firms, but others may be embryonic start-ups. There are many first-time buyers, and typically all firms have a short time horizon. Clearly this is the kind of environment where entrepreneurial organizations should flourish.

In the early stages of an industry, the things that make success possible are not necessarily rooted in a firm's ability to obtain massive resources. Instead, success is based more on its ability to shoulder risk, to be innovative with technology, and to be thoughtful and farsighted enough to marshal needed inputs and distribution channels. Porter points out that strategic uncertainty in emerging industries is so high that success may go to the firm that seizes the opportunity to shape the structure and "rules" of the industry. Firms must also take advantage of being "first movers" by trying to secure the loyalty of both early buyers and suppliers, and by taking advantage of the "honeymoon" period that new industries often enjoy with Wall Street. Porter concludes on a sobering note by pointing out that the long-term attractiveness of an industry rests not on its current growth rate, but on its predicted *ultimately* favorable structure. Because discerning this ideal is difficult, it must rest on a thorough analysis of the five forces of competition.

COMPETITIVE STRATEGY IN FRAGMENTED INDUSTRIES

Fragmented industries are ones where no firm has a significant market share and none can strongly influence the industry outcome. They are usually populated by several of what we have been calling entrepreneurial organizations. Michael Porter's reading in this chapter, "Competitive Strategy in Fragmented Industries," describes fragmented industries in some detail. Some factors that lead to fragmentation, according to Porter, are low entry barriers, lack of size advantages, diverse market needs, local regulation, and newness.

Porter then discusses how entrepreneurial organizations should handle these and other situations. Suggested ways of coping with fragmentation are to decentralize operations but keep financial control central, to use "formula" facilities like franchises, to increase value added by emphasizing service or custom fabrication, or various forms of specialization (by product type or segment, by customer type, or by order type), by focusing on a geographic area, by going to a "no frills" approach, and, lastly, by backward integration.

STRATEGIES OF HIGH-PERFORMING NEW AND SMALL FIRMS

"A Reexamination of the Niche Concept"

Cooper, Willard and Woo's reading in this chapter examines a situation where entrepreneurial organizations can outperform the industry's larger firms. The typical advice to entrepreneurial organizations is to service only the "niches" left unserviced by large rivals. These authors urge us to reexamine the niche concept, saying that it is often possible for small firms to compete directly with industry giants. The reading examines the experiences of five small firms that challenged established leaders.

The authors point out that several kinds of changes can create opportunities for all firms in an industry but may especially create openings for small firms. Among these are changes in regulation, technology, and consumer preferences, along with innovations in organization and management. These opportunities may involve adding or subtracting services or features, or adopting lower-cost technology. Successful challengers need a clear concept of what they seek, so that they may develop a competitive advantage. As we saw earlier, entrepreneurial organizations excel at developing this kind of vision. The final ingredients for success, the authors say, are adequate (though not necessarily abundant) financial resources and talented managers who can shape the organization to realize the innovative strategies.

Cooper, Willard, and Woo discuss in detail the many things about large firms that make it more difficult for them to respond to challenges from entrepreneurial organizations. But they give equal time to the things that erode the advantages that challengers may initially develop. They conclude by pointing out that although the strategies discussed in the article may seem like focused, niche strategies, observers should not be misled into thinking that the entrepreneurial firms are going after only segments of no interest to their larger competitors. On the contrary, firms that take advantage of new opportunities may end in direct, and successful, competition with industry leaders.

NOTES TO CHAPTER NINE

1. Kuehl, C. R., and P. A. Lambing, *Small Business: Planning and Management.* Chicago: The Dryden Press, 1990.
2. Quinn, R. E., and K. Cameron, "Organizational Life Cycles and Shifting Criteria of Effectiveness: Some Preliminary Evidence." *Management Science* 29 (1983), 33–51; Greiner, L. E., "Evolution and Revolution as Organizations Grow." *Harvard Business Review* 50 (July–August 1972): 37–46.
3. Case, J., "The Origins of Entrepreneurship." *INC.* (June 1989), 51–63.
4. Much of this section is based on Kuehl and Lambing, *Small Business.*
5. McClelland, D. C., *The Achieving Society.* New York: Van Nostrand, 1961.
6. See Porter, M., "Competitive Strategy in Emerging Industries," later in this chapter.

By Henry Mintzberg

Consider an automobile dealership with a flamboyant owner, a brand-new government department, a corporation or even a nation run by an autocratic leader, or a school system in a state of crisis. In many respects, these are vastly different organizations. But the evidence suggests that they share a number of basic characteristics. They form a configuration we shall call the entrepreneurial organization.

THE BASIC STRUCTURE

The structure of the entrepreneurial organization is often very simple, characterized about all by what it is not: elaborated. As shown in the opening figure, typically it has little or no staff, a loose division of labor, and a small managerial hierarchy. Little of its activity is formalized, and it makes minimal use of planning procedure or training routines. In a sense, it is nonstructure; in my "structuring" book, I called it *simple structure.*

Power tends to focus on the chief executive, who exercises a high personal profile. Formal controls are discouraged as a threat to the chief's flexibility. He or she drives the organization by sheer force of personality or by more direct interventions. Under the leader's watchful eye, politics cannot easily arise. Should outsiders, such as particular customers or suppliers, seek to exert influence, such leaders are as likely as not to take the organizations to a less exposed niche in the marketplace.

Thus, it is not uncommon in small entrepreneurial organizations for everyone to report to the chief. Even in ones not so small, communication flows informally, much of it between the chief executive and others. As one group of McGill MBA students commented in their study of a small manufacturer of pumps: "It is not unusual to see the president of the company engaged in a casual conversation with a machine shop mechanic. [That way he is] informed of a machine breakdown even before the shop superintendent is advised."

Decision making is likewise flexible, with a highly centralized power system allowing for rapid response. The creation of strategy is, of course, the responsibility of the chief executive, the process tending to be highly intuitive, even oriented to the aggressive search for opportunities. It is not surprising, therefore, that the resulting strategy tends to reflect the chief executive's implicit vision of the world, often an extrapolation of his or her own personality.

Handling disturbances and innovating in an entrepreneurial way are perhaps the most important aspects of the chief executive's work. In contrast, the more formal aspects of managerial work—figurehead duties, for example, receive less attention, as

Adapted from *The Structuring of Organizations* (Prentice Hall, 1979, Chap. 17 on "The Simple Structure"), *Power in and around Organizations* (Prentice Hall, 1983, Chap. 20 on "The Autocracy"), and the material on strategy formation from "Visionary Leadership and Strategic Management," *Strategic Management Journal,* (1989, coauthored with Frances Westley); see also, "Tracking Strategy in an Entrepreneurial Firm," *Academy of Management Journal* (1982), and "Researching the Formation of Strategies: The History of a Canadian Lady, 1939–1976," in R. B. Lamb, ed., *Competitive Strategic Management* (Prentice Hall, 1984), the last two coauthored with James A. Waters. A chapter similar to this appeared in *Mintzberg on Management: Inside Our Strange World of Organizations* (Free Press, 1989).

does the need to disseminate information and allocate resources internally, since knowledge and power remain at the top.

CONDITIONS OF THE ENTREPRENEURIAL ORGANIZATION

A centrist entrepreneurial configuration is fostered by an external context that is both simple and dynamic. Simpler environments (say, retailing food as opposed to designing computer systems) enable one person at the top to retain so much influence, while it is a dynamic environment that requires flexible structure, which in turn enables the organization to outmaneuver the bureaucracies. Entrepreneurial leaders are naturally attracted to such conditions.

The classic case of this is, of course, the entrepreneurial firm, where the leader is the owner. Entrepreneurs often found their own firms to escape the procedures and control of the bureaucracies where they previously worked. At the helm of their own enterprises, they continue to loathe the ways of bureaucracy, and the staff analysts that accompany them, and so they keep their organizations lean and flexible. Figure 1 shows the organigram for Steinberg's, a supermarket chain we shall be discussing shortly, during its most classically entrepreneurial years. Notice the identification of people above positions, the simplicity of the structure (the firm's sales by this time were on the order of $27 million), and the focus on the chief executive (not to mention the obvious family connections).

Entrepreneurial firms are often young and aggressive, continually searching for the risky markets that scare off the bigger bureaucracies. But they are also careful to avoid the complex markets, preferring to remain in niches that their leaders can comprehend. Their small size and focused strategies allow their structures to remain simple, so that the leaders can retain tight control and maneuver flexibly. Moreover, business entrepreneurs are often visionary, sometimes charismatic or autocratic as well (sometimes both, in sequence!). Of course, not all "entrepreneurs" are so aggressive or visionary; many settle down to pursue common strategies in small geographic niches. Labeled the *local producers,* these firms can include the corner restaurant, the town bakery, the regional supermarket chain.

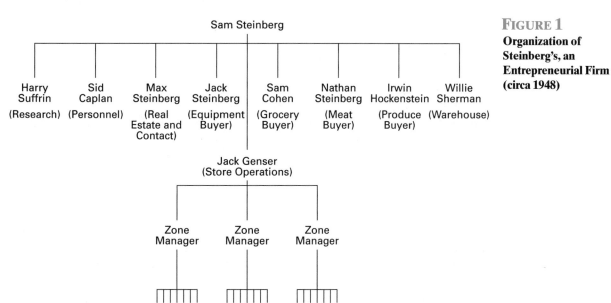

FIGURE 1

Organization of Steinberg's, an Entrepreneurial Firm (circa 1948)

But an organization need not be owned by an entrepreneur, indeed need not even operate in the profit sector, to adopt the configuration we call entrepreneurial. In fact, most new organizations seem to adopt this configuration, whatever their sector, because they generally have to rely on personalized leadership to get themselves going—to establish their basic direction, or *strategic vision,* to hire their first people and set up their initial procedures. Of course, strong leaders are likewise attracted to new organizations, where they can put their own stamp on things. Thus, we can conclude that most organizations in business, government, and not-for-profit areas pass through the entrepreneurial configuration in their formative years, during *start-up.*

Moreover, while new organizations that quickly grow large or that require specialized forms of expertise may make a relatively quick transition to another configuration, many others seem to remain in the entrepreneurial form, more or less, as long as their founding leaders remain in office. This reflects the fact that the structure has often been built around the personal needs and orientation of the leader and has been staffed with people loyal to him or her.

This last comment suggests that the personal power needs of a leader can also, by themselves, give rise to this configuration in an existing organization. When a chief executive hoards power and avoids or destroys the formalization of activity as an infringement on his or her right to rule by fiat, then an autocratic form of the entrepreneurial organization will tend to appear. This can be seen in the cult of personality of the leader, in business (the last days of Henry Ford) no less than in government (the leadership of Stalin in the Soviet Union). Charisma can have a similar effect, though different consequences, when the leader gains personal power not because he or she hoards it but because the followers lavish it on the leader.

The entrepreneurial configuration also tends to arise in any other type of organization that faces severe crisis. Backed up against a wall, with its survival at stake, an organization will typically turn to a strong leader for salvation. The structure thus becomes effectively (if not formally) simple, as the normal powers of existing groups—whether staff analysts, line managers, or professional operators, and so on, with their perhaps more standardized forms of control—are suspended to allow the chief to impose a new integrated vision through his or her personalized control. The leader may cut costs and expenses in an attempt to effect what is known in the strategic management literature as an *operating turnaround,* or else reconceive the basic product and service orientation, to achieve *strategic turnaround.* Of course, once the turnaround is realized, the organization may revert to its traditional operations, and, in the bargain, spew out its entrepreneurial leader, now viewed as an impediment to its smooth functioning.

STRATEGY FORMATION IN THE ENTREPRENEURIAL ORGANIZATION

How does strategy develop in the entrepreneurial organization? And what role does that mysterious concept known as "strategic vision" play? We know something of the entrepreneurial mode of strategy making, but less of strategic vision itself, since it is locked in the head of the individual. But some studies we have done at McGill do shed some light on both these questions. Let us consider strategic vision first.

Visionary Leadership

In a paper she coauthored with me, my McGill colleague Frances Westley contrasted two views of visionary leadership. One she likened to a hypodermic needle, in which the active ingredient (vision) is loaded into a syringe (words) which is injected into the employees to stimulate all kinds of energy. There is surely some truth to this, but Frances prefers another image, that of drama. Drawing from a book on theater by Peter Brook (1968), the legendary director of the Royal Shakespeare Company, she conceives strategic vision, like drama, as becoming magical in that moment when fiction and life blend together. In drama, this moment is the result of endless "rehearsal," the "performance" itself, and the "attendance" of the audience. But Brook prefers the more dynamic equivalent words in French, all of which have English meanings—"repetition," "representation," and "assistance." Frances likewise applies these words to strategic vision.

"Repetition" suggests that success comes from deep knowledge of the subject at hand. Just as Sir Laurence Olivier would repeat his lines again and again until he had trained his tongue muscles to say them effortlessly (Brook, p. 154), so too Lee Iococca "grew up" in the automobile business, going to Chrysler after Ford because cars were "in his blood" (Iococca, 1984:141). The visionary's inspiration stems not from luck, although chance encounters can play a role, but from endless experience in a particular context.

"Representation" means not just to perform but to make the past live again, giving it immediacy, vitality. To the strategist, that is vision articulated, in words and actions. What distinguishes visionary leaders is their profound ability with language, often in symbolic form, as metaphor. It is not just that they "see" things from a new perspective but that they get others to so see them.

Edwin Land, who built a great company around the Polaroid camera he invented, has written of the duty of "the inventor to build a new gestalt for the old one in the framework of society" (1975:50). He himself described photography as helping "to focus some aspect of [your] life"; as you look through the viewfinder, "it's not merely the camera you are focusing: you are focusing yourself . . . when you touch the button, what is inside of you comes out. It's the most basic form of creativity. Part of you is now permanent" (*Time,* 1972:84). Lofty words for 50 tourists filing out of a bus to record some pat scene, but powerful imagery for someone trying to build an organization to promote a novel camera. Steve Jobs, visionary (for a time) in his promotion, if not invention, of the personal computer, placed a grand piano and a BMW in Apple's central foyer, with the claim that "I believe people get great ideas from seeing great products" (in Wise, 1984:146).

"Assistance" means that the audience for drama, whether in the theater or in the organization, empowers the actor no less than the actor empowers the audience. Leaders become visionary because they appeal powerfully to specific constituencies at specific periods of time. That is why leaders once perceived as visionary can fall so dramatically from grace—a Steve Jobs, a Winston Churchill. Or to take a more dramatic example, here is how Albert Speer, arriving skeptical, reacted to the first lecture he heard by his future leader: "Hitler no longer seemed to be speaking to convince; rather, he seemed to feel that he was experiencing what the audience, by now transformed into a single mass, expected of him" (1970:16).

Of course, management is not theater; the leader who becomes a stage actor, playing a part he or she does not live, is destined to fall from grace. It is integrity—a genuine feeling behind what the leader says and does—that makes leadership truly visionary, and that is what makes impossible the transition of such leadership into any formula.

This visionary leadership is style and strategy, coupled together. It is drama, but not playacting. The strategic visionary is born and made, the product of a historical moment. Brook closes his book with the following quotation:

> In everyday life, "if " is a fiction, in the theatre "if " is an experiment.
> In everyday life, "if " is an evasion, in the theatre "if " is the truth.
> When we are persuaded to believe in this truth, then the theatre and life are one.
> This is a high aim. It sounds like hard work.

To play needs much work. But when we experience the work as play, then it is no work any more.
A play is play. (p. 157)

In the entrepreneurial organization, at best, "theater," namely strategic vision, becomes one with "life," namely organization. That way leadership creates drama; it turns work into play.

Let us now consider the entrepreneurial approach to strategy formation in terms of two specific studies we have done, one of a supermarket chain, the other of a manufacturer of women's undergarments.

The Entrepreneurial Approach to Strategy Formation in a Supermarket Chain

Steinberg's is a Canadian retail chain that began with a tiny food store in Montreal in 1917 and grew to sales in the billion-dollar range during the almost 60-year reign of its leader. Most of that growth came from supermarket operations. In many ways, Steinberg's fits the entrepreneurial model rather well. Sam Steinberg, who joined his mother in the first store at the age of 11 and personally made a quick decision to expand it 2 years later, maintained complete formal control of the firm (including every single voting share) to the day of his death in 1978. He also exercised close managerial control over all its major decisions, at least until the firm began to diversify after 1960, primarily into other forms of retailing.

It has been popular to describe the "bold stroke" of the entrepreneur (Cole, 1959). In Steinberg's we saw only two major reorientations of strategy in the sixty years, moves into self-service in the 1930s and into the shopping center business in the 1950s. But the stroke was not bold so much as tested. The story of the move into self-service is indicative. In 1933 one of the company's eight stores "struck it bad," in the chief executive's words, incurring "unacceptable" losses ($125 a week). Sam Steinberg closed the store one Friday evening, converted it to self-service, changed its name from "Steinberg's Service Stores" to "Wholesale Groceteria," slashed its prices by 15–20%, printed handbills, stuffed them into neighborhood mailboxes, and reopened on Monday morning. That's strategic change! But only once these changes proved successful did he convert the other stores. Then, in his words, "We grew like Topsy."

This anecdote tells us something about the bold stroke of the entrepreneur— "controlled boldness" is a better expression. The ideas were bold, the execution careful. Sam Steinberg could have simply closed the one unprofitable store. Instead he used it to create a new vision, but he tested that vision, however ambitiously, before leaping into it. Notice the interplay here of problems and opportunities. Steinberg took what most businessmen would probably have perceived as a *problem* (how to cut the losses in one store) and by treating it as a *crisis* (what is wrong with our *general* operation that produces these losses) turned it into an *opportunity* (we can grow more effectively with a new concept of retailing). That was how he got energy behind actions and kept ahead of his competitors. He "oversolved" his problem and thereby remade his company, a characteristic of some of the most effective forms of entrepreneurship.

But absolutely central to this form of entrepreneurship is intimate, detailed knowledge of the business or of analogous business situations, the "repetition" discussed earlier. The leader as conventional strategic "planner"—the so-called architect of strategy—sits on a pedestal and is fed aggregate data that he or she uses to "formulate" that are "implemented" by others. But the history of Steinberg's belies that image. It suggests that clear, imaginative, integrated strategic vision depends on an involvement with detail, an intimate knowledge of specifics. And by closely controlling "implementation" personally, the leader is able to reformulate en route, to adapt the evolving vision through his or her own process of learning. That is why Steinberg tried his new ideas in one store first. And that is why, in discussing his firm's competitive advantage, he told us: "Nobody knew the grocery business like we did. Everything has to do with your knowledge." He added: "I knew merchandise, I knew cost, I knew selling, I knew customers, I knew everything . . . and I passed on all my knowledge; I kept teaching my people. That's the advantage we had. They couldn't touch us."

Such knowledge can be incredibly effective when concentrated in one individual who is fully in charge (having no need to convince others, not subordinates below, not superiors at some distant headquarters, nor market analysts looking for superficial pronouncements) and who retains a strong, long-term commitment to the organization. So long as the business is simple and focused enough to be comprehended in one brain, the entrepreneurial approach is powerful, indeed unexcelled. Nothing else can provide so clear and complete a vision, yet also allow the flexibility to elaborate and rework that vision when necessary. The conception of a new strategy is an exercise in synthesis, which is typically best carried out in a single, informed brain. That is why the entrepreneurial approach is at the center of the most glorious corporate successes.

But in its strength lies entrepreneurship's weakness. Bear in mind that strategy for the entrepreneurial leader is not a formal, detailed plan on paper. It is a personal vision, a concept of the business, locked in a single brain. It may need to get "represented," in words and metaphors, but that must remain general if the leader is to maintain the richness and flexibility of his or her concept. But success breeds a large organization, public financing, and the need for formal planning. The vision must be articulated to drive others and gain their support, and that threatens the personal nature of the vision. At the limit, as we shall see later in the case of Steinberg's, the leader can get captured by his or her very success.

In Steinberg's, moreover, when success in the traditional business encouraged diversification into new ones (new regions, new forms of retailing, new industries), the organization moved beyond the realm of its leader's personal comprehension, and the entrepreneurial mode of strategy formation lost its viability. Strategy making became more decentralized, more analytic, in some ways more careful, but at the same time less visionary, less integrated, less flexible, and ironically, less deliberate.

Conceiving a New Vision in a Garment Firm

The genius of an entrepreneur like Sam Steinberg was his ability to pursue one vision (self-service and everything that entailed) faithfully for decades and then, based on a weak signal in the environment (the building of the first small shopping center in Montreal), to realize the need to shift that vision. The planning literature makes a big issue of forecasting such discontinuities, but as far as I know there are no formal techniques to do so effectively (claims about "scenario analysis" notwithstanding). The ability to perceive a sudden shift in an established pattern and then to conceive a new vision to deal with it appears to remain largely in the realm of informed intuition, generally the purview of the wise, experienced, and energetic leader. Again, the literature is largely silent on this. But another of our studies, also concerning entrepreneurship, did reveal some aspects of this process.

Canadelle produces women's undergarments, primarily brassieres. It too was a highly successful organization, although not on the same scale as Steinberg's. Things were going well for the company in the late 1960s, under the personal leadership of Larry Nadler, the son of its founder, when suddenly everything changed. A sexual revolution of sorts was accompanying broader social manifestations, with bra burning a symbol of its resistance. For a manufacturer of brassieres the threat was obvious. For many other women the miniskirt had come to dominate the fashion scene, obsoleting the girdle and giving rise to pantyhose. As the executives of Canadelle put it, "the bottom fell out of the girdle business." The whole environment—long so receptive to the company's strategies—seemed to turn on it all at once.

At the time, a French company had entered the Quebec market with a light, sexy, molded garment called "Huit," using the theme, "just like not wearing a bra." Their target market was 15–20-year-olds. Though the product was expensive when it landed in Quebec and did not fit well in Nadler's opinion, it sold well. Nadler flew to France in an attempt to license the product for manufacture in Canada. The French firm refused, but, in Nadler's words, what he learned in "that one hour in their offices made the trip worthwhile." He realized that what women wanted was a more natural look, not no bra but less bra. Another trip shortly afterward, to a sister American firm, convinced him of the importance of market segmentation by age and life-style. That led him to the realization that the firm had two markets, one for the more mature customer, for whom the brassiere was a cosmetic to look and feel more attractive, and another for the younger customer who wanted to look and feel more natural.

Those two events led to a major shift in strategic vision. The CEO described it as sudden, the confluence of different ideas to create a new mental set. In his words, "all of a sudden the idea forms." Canadelle reconfirmed its commitment to the brassiere business, seeking greater market share while its competitors were cutting back. It introduced a new line of more natural brassieres for the younger customers, for which the firm had to work out the molding technology as well as a new approach to promotion.

We can draw on Kurt Lewin's (1951) three-stage model of unfreezing, changing, and refreezing to explain such a gestalt shift in vision. The process of *unfreezing* is essentially one of overcoming the natural defense mechanisms, the established "mental set" of how an industry is supposed to operate, to realize that things have changed fundamentally. The old assumptions no longer hold. Effective managers, especially effective strategic managers, are supposed to scan their environments continually, looking for such changes. But doing so continuously, or worse, trying to use technique to do so, may have exactly the opposite effect. So much attention may be given to strategic monitoring when nothing important is happening that when something really does, it may not even be noticed. The trick, of course, is to pick out the discontinuities that matter, and as noted earlier that seems to have more to do with informed intuition than anything else.

A second step in unfreezing is the willingness to step into the void, so to speak, for the leader to shed his or her conventional notions of how a business is supposed to function. The leader must above all avoid premature closure—seizing on a new thrust before it has become clear what its signals really mean. That takes a special kind of management, one able to live with a good deal of uncertainty and discomfort. "There is a period of confusion," Nadler told us, "you sleep on it . . . start looking for patterns . . . become an information hound, searching for [explanations] everywhere."

Strategic *change* of this magnitude seems to require a shift in mind-set before a new strategy can be conceived. And the thinking is fundamentally conceptual and inductive, probably stimulated (as in this case) by just one or two key insights. Continuous bombardment of facts, opinions, problems, and so on may prepare the mind for the shift, but it is the sudden *insight* that is likely to drive the synthesis—to bring all the disparate elements together in one "eureka"-type flash.

Once the strategist's mind is set, assuming he or she has read the new situation correctly and has not closed prematurely, then the *refreezing* process begins. Here the object is not to read the situation, at least not in a global sense, but in effect to block it out. It is a time to work out the consequences of the new strategic vision.

It has been claimed that obsession is an ingredient in effective organizations (Peters, 1980). Only for the period of refreezing would we agree, when the organization must focus on the pursuit of the new orientation—the new mind-set—with full vigor. A management that was open and divergent in its thinking must now become closed and convergent. But that means that the uncomfortable period of uncertainty has passed, and people can now get down to the exciting task of accomplishing something new. Now the organization knows where it is going; the object of the exercise is to get there using

all the skills at its command, many of them formal and analytic. Of course, not everyone accepts the new vision. For those steeped in old strategies, *this* is the period of discomfort, and they can put up considerable resistance, forcing the leader to make greater use of his or her formal powers and political skills. Thus, refreezing of the leader's mind-set often involves the unfreezing, changing, and refreezing of the organization itself! But when the structure is simple, as it is in the entrepreneurial organization, that problem is relatively minor.

Leadership Taking Precedence in the Entrepreneurial Configuration

To conclude, entrepreneurship is very much tied up with the creation of strategic vision, often with the attainment of a new concept. Strategies can be characterized as largely deliberate, since they reside in the intentions of a single leader. But being largely personal as well, the details of those strategies can emerge as they develop. In fact, the vision can change too. The leader can adapt en route, can learn, which means new visions can emerge too, sometimes, as we have seen, rather quickly.

In the entrepreneurial organization, as shown in Figure 2, the focus of attention is on the leader. The organization is malleable and responsive to that person's initiatives, while the environment remains benign for the most part, the result of the leader's selecting (or "enacting") the correct niche for his or her organization. The environment can, of course, flare up occasionally to challenge the organization, and then the leader must adapt, perhaps seeking out a new and more appropriate niche in which to operate.

SOME ISSUES ASSOCIATED WITH THE ENTREPRENEURIAL ORGANIZATION

We conclude briefly with some broad issues associated with the entrepreneurial organization. In this configuration, decisions concerning both strategy and operations tend to be centralized in the office of the chief executive. This centralization has the important advantage of rooting strategic response in deep knowledge of the operations. It also allows for flexibility and adaptability: Only one person need act. But this same executive can get so enmeshed in operating problems that he or she loses sight of strategy; alternatively, he or she may become so enthusiastic about strategic opportunities that the more routine operations can wither for lack of attention and eventually pull down the whole organization. Both are frequent occurrences in entrepreneurial organizations.

This is also the riskiest of organizations, hinging on the activities of one individual. One heart attack can literally wipe out the organization's prime means of coordination. Even a leader in place can be risky. When change becomes necessary, everything hinges on the chief's response to it. If he or she resists, as is not uncommon where that person developed the existing strategy in the first place, then the organization may have no means to adapt. Then the great strength of the entrepreneurial organization—the vision of its leader plus its capacity to respond quickly—becomes its chief liability.

233

Another great advantage of the entrepreneurial organization is its sense of mission. Many people enjoy working in a small, intimate organization where the leader—often charismatic—knows where he or she is taking it. As a result, the organization tends to grow rapidly, with great enthusiasm. Employees can develop a solid identification with such an organization.

But other people perceive this configuration as highly restrictive. Because one person calls all the shots, they feel not like the participants on an exciting journey, but like cattle being led to market for someone else's benefit. In fact, the broadening of democratic norms into the sphere of organizations has rendered the entrepreneurial organization unfashionable in some quarters of contemporary society. It has been described as paternalistic and sometimes autocratic, and accused of concentrating too much power at the top. Certainly, without countervailing powers in the organization the chief executive can easily abuse his or her authority.

Perhaps the entrepreneurial organization is an anachronism in societies that call themselves democratic. Yet there have always been such organizations, and there always will be. This was probably the only structure known to those who first discovered the benefits of coordinating their activities in some formal way. And it probably reached its heyday in the era of the great American trusts of the late nineteenth century, when powerful entrepreneurs personally controlled huge empires. Since then, at least in Western society, the entrepreneurial organization has been on the decline. Nonetheless, it remains a prevalent and important configuration, and will continue to be so as long as society faces the conditions that require it: the prizing of entrepreneurial initiative and the resultant encouragement of new organizations, the need for small and informal organizations in some spheres and of strong personalized leadership despite larger size in others, and the need periodically to turn around ailing organizations of all types.

READING COMPETITIVE STRATEGY IN EMERGING INDUSTRIES

By Michael E. Porter

Emerging industries are newly formed or reformed industries that have been created by technological innovations, shifts in relative cost relationships, emergence of new consumer needs, or other economic and sociological changes that elevate a new product or service to the level of a potentially viable business opportunity. . . .

The essential characteristic of an emerging industry from the viewpoint of formulating strategy is that there are no rules of the game. The competitive problem in an emerging industry is that all the rules must be established such that the firm can cope with and prosper under them.

THE STRUCTURAL ENVIRONMENT

Although emerging industries can differ a great deal in their structures, there are some common structural factors that seem to characterize many industries in this stage of their development. Most of them relate either to the absence of established bases for competition or other rules of the game or to the initial small size and newness of the industry.

Excerpted from *Competitive Strategy: Techniques for Analyzing Industries and Competitors,* by Michael E. Porter. Copyright © 1980 by The Free Press, a division of Macmillan, Inc. Reprinted by permission of the publisher.

Common Structural Characteristics

TECHNOLOGICAL UNCERTAINTY. There is usually a great deal of uncertainty about the technology in an emerging industry: What product configuration will ultimately prove to be the best? Which production technology will prove to be the most efficient? . . .

STRATEGIC UNCERTAINTY. . . . No "right" strategy has been clearly identified, and different firms are groping with different approaches to product/market positioning, marketing, servicing, and so on, as well as betting on different product configurations or production technologies. . . . Closely related to this problem, firms often have poor information about competitors, characteristics of customers, and industry conditions in the emerging phase. No one knows who all the competitors are, and reliable industry sales and market share data are often simply unavailable, for example.

HIGH INITIAL COSTS BUT STEEP COST REDUCTION. Small production volume and newness usually combine to produce high costs in the emerging industry relative to those the industry can potentially achieve. . . . Ideas come rapidly in terms of improved procedures, plant layout, and so on, and employees achieve major gains in productivity as job familiarity increases. Increasing sales make major additions to the scale and total accumulated volume of output produced by firms. . . .

EMBRYONIC COMPANIES AND SPIN-OFFS. The emerging phase of the industry is usually accompanied by the presence of the greatest proportion of newly formed companies (to be contrasted with newly formed units of established firms) that the industry will ever experience. . . .

FIRST-TIME BUYERS. Buyers of the emerging industry's product or service are inherently first-time buyers. The marketing task is thus one of inducing substitution, or getting the buyer to purchase the new product or service instead of something else. . . .

SHORT TIME HORIZON. In many emerging industries the pressure to develop customers or produce products to meet demand is so great that bottlenecks and problems are dealt with expediently rather than as a result of an analysis of future conditions. At the same time, industry conventions are often born out of pure chance. . . .

SUBSIDY. In many emerging industries, especially those with radical new technology or that address areas of societal concern, there may be subsidization of early entrants. Subsidy may come from a variety of government and nongovernment sources. . . . Subsidies often add a great degree of instability to an industry, which is made dependent on political decisions that can be quickly reversed or modified. . . .

Early Mobility Barriers

In an emerging industry, the configuration of mobility barriers is often predictably different from that which will characterize the industry later in its development. Common early barriers are the following:

- proprietary technology
- access to distribution channels
- access to raw materials and other inputs (skilled labor) of appropriate cost and quality
- cost advantages due to experience, made more significant by the technological and competitive uncertainties
- risk, which raises the effective opportunity cost of capital and thereby effective capital barriers

. . . The nature of the early barriers is a key reason why we observe newly created companies in emerging industries. The typical early barriers stem less from the need to command massive resources than from the ability to bear risk, be creative technologically, and make forward-looking decisions to garner input supplies and distribution channels. . . . There may be some advantages to late entry, however. . . .

Strategic Choices

Formulation of strategy in emerging industries must cope with the uncertainty and risk of this period of an industry's development. The rules of the competitive game are largely undefined, the structure of the industry unsettled and probably changing, and competitors hard to diagnose. Yet all these factors have another side—the emerging phase of an industry's development is probably the period when the strategic degrees of freedom are the greatest and when the leverage from good strategic choices is the highest in determining performance.

SHAPING INDUSTRY STRUCTURE. The overriding strategic issue in emerging industries is the ability of the firm to shape industry structure. Through its choices, the firm can try to set the rules of the game in areas like product policy, marketing approach, and pricing strategy. . . .

EXTERNALITIES IN INDUSTRY DEVELOPMENT. In an emerging industry, a key strategic issue is the balance the firm strikes between industry advocacy and pursuing its own narrow self-interest. Because of potential problems with industry image, credibility, and confusion of buyers . . . in the emerging phase the firm is in part dependent on others in the industry for its own success. The overriding problem for the industry is inducing substitution and attracting first-time buyers, and it is usually in the firm's interest during this phase to help promote standardization, police substandard quality and fly-by-night producers, and present a consistent front to suppliers, customers, government, and the financial community. . . .

It is probably a valid generalization that the balance between industry outlook and firm outlook must shift in the direction of the firm as the industry begins to achieve significant penetration. Sometimes firms who have taken very high profiles as industry spokespersons, much to their and the industry's benefit, fail to recognize that they must shift their orientation. As a result, they can be left behind as the industry matures. . . .

CHANGING ROLE OF SUPPLIERS AND CHANNELS. Strategically, the firm in an emerging industry must be prepared for a possible shift in the orientation of its suppliers and distribution channels as the industry grows in size and proves itself. Suppliers may become increasingly willing (or can be forced) to respond to the industry's special needs in terms of varieties, service, and delivery. Similarly, distribution channels may become more receptive to investing in facilities, advertising, and so forth in partnership with the firms. Early exploitation of these changes in orientation can give the firm strategic leverage.

SHIFTING MOBILITY BARRIERS. As outlined earlier . . . the early mobility barriers may erode quickly in an emerging industry, often to be replaced by very different ones as the industry grows in size and as the technology matures. This factor has a number of implications. The most obvious is that the firm must be prepared to find new ways to defend its position and must not rely solely on things like proprietary technology and a unique product variety on which it has succeeded in the past. Responding to shifting mobility barriers may involve commitments of capital that far exceed those that have been necessary in the early phases.

Another implication is that the nature of entrants into the industry may shift to more established firms attracted to the larger and increasingly proven (less risky) industry, often competing on the basis of the newer forms of mobility barriers, like scale and marketing clout. . . .

Timing Entry

A crucial strategic choice for competing in emerging industries is the appropriate timing of entry. Early entry (or pioneering) involves high risk but may involve otherwise low entry barriers and can offer a large return. Early entry is appropriate when the following general circumstances hold:

- Image and reputation of the firm are important to the buyer, and the firm can develop an enhanced reputation by being a pioneer.
- Early entry can initiate the learning process in a business in which the learning curve is important, experience is difficult to imitate, and it will not be nullified by successive technological generations.
- Customer loyalty will be great, so that benefits will accrue to the firm that sells to the customer first.
- Absolute cost advantages can be gained by early commitment to supplies of raw materials, distribution channels, and so on. . . .

TACTICAL MOVES. The problems limiting development of an emerging industry suggest some tactical moves that may improve the firm's strategic position:

- Early commitments to suppliers of raw materials will yield favorable priorities in times of shortages.
- Financing can be timed to take advantage of a Wall Street love affair with the industry if it happens, even if financing is ahead of actual needs. This step lowers the firm's cost of capital. . . .

The choice of which emerging industry to enter is dependent on the outcome of a predictive exercise such as the one described above. An emerging industry is attractive if its ultimate structure (not its initial structure) is one that is consistent with above-average returns and if the firm can create a defendable position in the industry in the long run. The latter will depend on its resources relative to the mobility barriers that will evolve.

Too often firms enter emerging industries because they are growing rapidly, because incumbents are currently very profitable, or because ultimate industry size promises to be large. These may be contributing reasons, but the decision to enter must ultimately depend on a structural analysis. . . .

COMPETITIVE STRATEGY IN FRAGMENTED INDUSTRIES   READING

By Michael E. Porter

An important structural environment in which many firms compete is the fragmented industry, that is, an industry in which no firm has a significant market share and can strongly influence the industry outcome. Usually fragmented industries are populated by a large number of small- and medium-sized companies, many of them privately held. . . . The essential notion that makes these industries a unique environment in

Excerpted from *Competitive Strategy: Techniques for Analyzing Industries and Competitors,* by Michael E. Porter. Copyright © 1980 by The Free Press, a division of Macmillan, Inc.; reprinted by permission of publisher.

which to compete is the absence of market leaders with the power to shape industry events. . . .

Some fragmented industries, such as computer software and television program syndication, are characterized by products or services that are differentiated, whereas others, such as oil tanker shipping, electronic component distribution, and fabricated aluminum products, involve essentially undifferentiated products. Fragmented industries also vary greatly in their technological sophistication, ranging from high technology businesses like solar heating to garbage collection and liquor retailing. . . .

WHAT MAKES AN INDUSTRY FRAGMENTED?

. . . in many industries there are underlying economic causes [of fragmentation] and the principal ones seem to be as follows:

LOW OVERALL ENTRY BARRIERS. Nearly all fragmented industries have low overall entry barriers. Otherwise they could not be populated by so many small firms. . . .

ABSENCE OF ECONOMIES OF SCALE OR EXPERIENCE CURVE. Most fragmented industries are characterized by the absence of significant scale economies or learning curves in any major aspect of the business. . . .

HIGH TRANSPORTATION COSTS. High transportation costs limit the size of an efficient plant or production location despite the presence of economies of scale. . . .

HIGH INVENTORY COSTS OR ERRATIC SALES FLUCTUATIONS. Although there may be intrinsic economies of scale in the production process, they may be reaped if inventory carrying costs are high and sales fluctuate. . . . Small-scale, less specialized facilities or distribution systems are usually more flexible in absorbing output shifts than large, more specialized ones, even though they may have higher operating costs at a steady operating rate.

NO ADVANTAGES OF SIZE IN DEALING WITH BUYERS OR SUPPLIERS. . . . Buyers, for example, might be so large that even a large firm in the industry would only be marginally better off in bargaining with them than a smaller firm. . . .

DISECONOMIES OF SCALE IN SOME IMPORTANT ASPECT. [Rapid product changes or style changes, need to maintain low overhead, a highly diverse product line, heavy creative content, need for close local control (as in restaurants), personal service or local image or contacts are key.]

DIVERSE MARKET NEEDS. In some industries buyers' tastes are fragmented, with different buyers each desiring special varieties of a product and willing (and able) to pay a premium for it rather than accept a more standardized version. . . .

HIGH PRODUCT DIFFERENTIATION, PARTICULARLY IF BASED ON IMAGE. . . . Performing artists, for example, may prefer dealing with a small booking agency or record label that carries the image they desire to cultivate.

EXIT BARRIERS. If there are exit barriers, marginal firms will tend to stay in the industry and thereby hold back consolidation. . . .

LOCAL REGULATION. Local regulation, by forcing the firm to comply with standards that may be particularistic, or to be attuned to a local political scene, can be a major source of fragmentation in an industry, even where the other conditions do not hold....

GOVERNMENT PROHIBITION OF CONCENTRATION. Legal restrictions prohibit consolidation in industries such as electric power and television and radio stations....

NEWNESS. An industry can be fragmented because it is new and no firm or firms have yet developed the skills and resources to command a significant market share, even though there are no other impediments to consolidation....

COPING WITH FRAGMENTATION

It takes the presence of only one of these characteristics to block the consolidation of an industry....

In many situations, industry fragmentation is ... the result of underlying industry economics that cannot be overcome. Fragmented industries are characterized not only by many competitors but also by a generally weak bargaining position with suppliers and buyers. Marginal profitability can be the result. In such an environment, strategic *positioning* is of particularly crucial significance. The strategic challenge is to cope with fragmentation by becoming one of the most successful firms, although able to garner only a modest market share.

Since every industry is ultimately different, there is no generalized method for competing most effectively in a fragmented industry. However, there are a number of possible strategic alternatives for coping with a fragmented structure that should be considered when examining any particular situation. These are specific approaches to pursuing the low cost, differentiate, or focus generic strategies....

TIGHTLY MANAGED DECENTRALIZATION. Since fragmented industries often are characterized by the need for intense coordination, local management orientation, high personal service, and close control, an important alternative for competition is tightly managed decentralization. Rather than increasing the scale of operations at one or a few locations, this strategy involves deliberately keeping individual operations small and as autonomous as possible. This approach is supported by tight central control and performance-oriented compensation for local managers....

"FORMULA" FACILITIES. Another alternative, related to the previous one, is to view the key strategic variable in the business as the building of efficient, low-cost facilities at multiple locations. This strategy involves designing a standard facility, whether it be a plant or a service establishment, and polishing to a science the process of constructing and putting the facility into operation at minimum cost....

INCREASED VALUE ADDED. Many fragmented industries produce products or services that are commodities or otherwise difficult to differentiate; many distribution businesses, for example, stock similar if not identical product lines to their competitors'. In cases such as these, an effective strategy may be to increase the value added of the business by providing more service with sale, by engaging in some final fabrication of the product (like cutting to size or punching holes), or by doing subassembly or assembly of components before they are sold to the customer.....

SPECIALIZATION BY PRODUCT TYPE OR PRODUCT SEGMENT. When industry fragmentation results from or is accompanied by the presence of numerous items in the product line, an effective strategy for achieving above-average results can be to specialize on a tightly constrained group of products. . . . [This] can allow the firm to achieve some bargaining power with suppliers by developing a significant volume of their products. It may also allow the enhancement of product differentiation with the customer as a result of the specialist's perceived expertise and image in the particular product area. . . .

SPECIALIZATION BY CUSTOMER TYPE. If competition is intense because of a fragmented structure, a firm can potentially benefit by specialization on a particular category of customer in the industry. . . .

SPECIALIZATION BY TYPE OF ORDER. Regardless of the customer, the firm can specialize in a particular type of order to cope with intense competitive pressure in a fragmented industry. One approach is to service only small orders for which the customer wants immediate delivery and is less price sensitive. Or the firm can service only custom orders to take advantage of less price sensitivity or to build switching costs. Once again, the cost of such specialization may be some limitation in volume.

A FOCUSED GEOGRAPHIC AREA. Even though a significant industry-wide share is out of reach or there are no national economies of scale (and perhaps even diseconomies), there may be substantial economies in blanketing a given geographic area by concentrating facilities, marketing attention, and sales activity. This policy can economize on the use of the sales force, allow more efficient advertising, allow a single distribution center, and so on. . . .

BARE BONES/NO FRILLS. Given the intensity of competition and low margins in many fragmented industries, a simple but powerful strategic alternative can be intense attention to maintaining a bare bones/no frills competitive posture—that is, low overhead, low-skilled employees, tight cost control, and attention to detail. This policy places the firm in the best position to compete on price and still make an above-average return.

BACKWARD INTEGRATION. Although the causes of fragmentation can preclude a large share of the market, selective backward integration may lower costs and put pressure on competitors who cannot afford such integration. . .

READING | A REEXAMINATION OF THE NICHE CONCEPT

*By Arnold C. Cooper,
Gary E. Willard, and
Carolyn Y. Woo*

. . . Despite the number and importance of new and small firms, there has been little explicit examination of their strategies. Founders of new firms must find ways to compete in a world which had gotten along without them before. Starting with no reputation and limited financial and human resources, they must seek out opportunities and develop strategies which enable them to compete, sometimes in industries dominated by large, established companies. Since almost any strategy involves competing with someone, they need to consider which established competitors might be challenged and whether sustainable competitive advantages could be achieved.

The extant literature generally advises small firms not to meet larger competitors head on. They should concentrate on specialized products, localize business operations,

Originally published in the *Journal of Business Venturing* (1986) under the title "Strategies of High-Performing New and Small Firms: A Reexamination of the Niche Concept." Copyright © 1986 by Elsevier Science Publishing Company, New York; reprinted with deletions by permission of the authors and publisher.

and provide products which require a high degree of craftsmanship (Hosmer, 1957; Gross, 1967). Small businesses are also seen to benefit from the provision of customer service, product customization, and other factors which are inimical to large-scale production (Cohn and Lindberg, 1972). The above recommendations would often limit the opportunities open to new and small firms to "niches" too small to be of interest to larger firms. . . . We suggest that this concept of the niche, although descriptive of the strategies of many small firms, is unduly limiting; in fact, it does not describe the strategies of some of the most successful new and small companies. Under some conditions, and for some firms, exceptional opportunities exist for competing directly with large established companies. These smaller challengers pursue "niche" strategies in the sense of being focused and directed at serving the needs of a particular group of customers. However, they do not avoid direct competition with market leaders or confine themselves to segments of no interest to them. If we were to apply the test of asking who the young firm takes customers away from, the answer would be clear. It is the largest, the most established, often the most successful firms in the industry that the smaller firm is competing with. . . .

The objective of this article is to reexamine the concept of the niche strategy with particular attention to the new firms challenging industry leaders. In no sense do we argue that such strategies of direct competition are feasible under all conditions or should be undertaken by all new firms. In this article we will discuss what conditions might support the choice of this strategy. . . .

The concepts discussed will be illustrated by reference to five successful challenges which developed strategies of direct competition against much larger established industry leaders. These are

1. MCI, which competed directly with AT&T
2. Amdahl Corporation, which competed directly with IBM
3. Iowa Beef Processors, which competed directly against large meat packers such as Armour and Wilson
4. People Express Airline, which competed directly against larger airlines such as Eastern
5. Nucor, which competed directly against old-line steel companies such as US Steel and Bethlehem

CONDITIONS UNDER WHICH SUCCESSFUL DIRECT COMPETITION MAY BE POSSIBLE

Opportunities to compete directly with large firms vary widely across industries. Of particular importance is whether an industry is changing, the nature of those changes, and whether the managements of the leading firms recognize their implications. In any industry the leading companies have been the most successful in developing strategies to exploit previously existing opportunities. Over time they have mastered existing technologies, fine-tuned their strategies, and developed organizations trained and committed to these ways of competing. If there are no changes, there are few opportunities for challengers.

However, changes in the form of deregulation, new technology, organizational and management innovations, and changing consumer preferences create opportunities for new firms. Thus, deregulation in air transportation and telecommunications enabled People Express Airline and MCI to confront established firms not attuned to competing against new entrants. Nucor took advantage of technology in the form of electric furnaces and continuous casting which permitted it to compete directly against steel mills locked into old technology. . . .

Although change can create opportunities, other industry conditions may make it easier for a small firm to achieve advantages or to keep from being overwhelmed by larger competitors. If there are opportunities for differentiation, for offering a product or service which is somewhat different, then the small firm may be able to achieve an advantage in serving some segment of the market. Frequently, differentiation is perceived to be the process of adding services or product features which some customers value. But, differentiation may also be achieved by subtracting a feature or service included by large firms in their standard offering, but which a segment of the market does not value highly. People Express Airline, for example, eliminated the "meals-in-flight" feature and baggage handling from the standard airline product, reduced the price, and found a ready market from among the major airlines' price-sensitive passengers.

By contrast, if products are nondifferentiated—"commodity-like"—then alternative ways of competing are more limited. Although established firms may already be organized to compete on the basis of price, the new firm can, in certain cases, adopt a different (and inherently lower cost) technology for providing the commodity-like product. Nucor, a successful "mini-mill," adopted the electric furnace technology for making steel directly from scrap-iron, and avoided the heavy capital investments associated with making steel from ore. Low-cost technology similarly enabled Iowa Beef to undercut prices of industry leaders.

The relative importance of economies of scale and/or experience curve effects also bears upon the opportunities for direct competition. If it is possible to compete on a small scale or with little experience and not incur a substantial cost disadvantage, then small firms (with little volume) or new firms (with little experience) may be able to compete directly with success. Nucor and other mini-mills positioned themselves in a segment of the steel industry in which small scale was not a disadvantage. Mini-mills can achieve cost advantage despite annual tonnages of only 250,000 tons per year, a mere "drop in the ladle" in the steel industry.

NATURE OF SUCCESSFUL CHALLENGERS

Even within industries offering opportunities for direct competition, only some new firms may be in a position to adopt such strategies. There must be the right combination of insight, assets, and commitment.

Central to success is a concept, a strategy, which enables the new firm to earn a competitive advantage. Although all of the small firms considered here confronted much larger companies, none competed in exactly the same way as their larger competitors. All were headed by entrepreneurs who innovated and challenged the conventional wisdom within their industries. At first, their strategies were untested and their potential was unclear. However, all saw possibilities not evident to others and all served as champions of the new strategies which their firms developed.

Financial and managerial resources are critical to all firms, but particularly to those following these strategies. The emphasis on innovation, the development of larger markets, and direct confrontation with powerful competitors all require more resources than needed for many small businesses. In addition, these strategies are characterized by experimentation, by feedback from the marketplace, and by adaptation to competitive response. All require time and sufficient capital to stay in the game. Some new firms run out of money (or credibility with investors) before they can perfect and implement their strategy. Thus, Amdahl, after developing its initial product line, but before market introduction, was confronted by a newly introduced IBM product in 1972. It was necessary for Amdahl to go back to its investors for an additional $16 million in order to upgrade its product line before it had realized any revenues.

The early capital of these five firms (after initial public offerings) ranged from $956 thousand to $105 million. Although these amounts were substantially more than the capitalization of most new firms, they were far less than those of their major competitors. For example, the initial capital of People Express Airline was $28 million versus $2 billion for Eastern Airline at that time, and that for MCI was $105 million, compared to $29 billion for AT&T. In no way were these challengers in a position to outspend their major competitors.

Those small competitors suited for strategies of direct confrontation must also be able to capitalize upon their potential for achieving organizational commitment and for shaping organizations attuned to these innovative strategies. A young firm, such as those considered here, does not have a stake in the status quo. Employees' security and influence are not tied to traditional ways of competing. If the young firm is led by management with vision and leadership ability, it may be possible to recruit, train, and motivate a cadre of people dedicated to the new strategy. Thus, the new employees of People Express knew they would be operating out of dingy headquarters in Newark, with "previously owned" aircraft, and a work schedule in which jobs would be rotated. An enthusiastic management, which led by example, was able to achieve a high degree of organizational commitment to the new strategy.

BARRIERS TO RESPONSE

In each of the five examples considered here, these young companies competed directly with established large firms. Despite limited finances, reputation, and organizations, they developed and implemented strategies which captured customers away from large, established competitors. We might have expected direct and massive retaliation. Yet, in many cases, this did not occur.

The literature on barriers that prevent response to competitive challenge offers some insights worth noting. MacMillan and Jones (1984) suggest that response will be difficult in situations in which the challenged firm is organized around a particular activity/output configuration. To the extent that response will divert the challenged firm from "doing what it does best," violate existing product-market boundary charters, or result in cannibalization of existing product offering, the competitive reaction will likely be delayed (Coyne, 1986; Kotter and Schlesinger, 1979; McIntyre, 1982).

If the response requires fundamental changes in the organizational or reporting relationships within the challenged firm, the response lag is likely to be greater (MacMillan, McCaffery, and Van Wijk, 1985). Coyne (1986) suggests that response may be delayed if "capability gaps" exist because of facility locations or regulatory/legal restrictions. MacMillan (1982) and Coyne (1986) refer to inertia barriers which may prevent competitive response.

The literature above suggests several reasons why the challenged firm may be unable to answer the competitive attack promptly. In our study of five local firms, we found some support for these, as well as some additional considerations.

Locked into Existing Product Packages and Prices

STANDARDIZED PRODUCTS. Large firms often develop a common approach to serving broad markets, even though customer preferences may not be uniform. This practice enables firms to simplify the structure of their supporting organizations and to standardize policies with respect to production, customer services, distribution, pricing, and other functional activities. Thus, established airlines had developed strategies of providing full services for all of their customers. Organizations were developed and employees trained to provide ticketing assistance, baggage handling, and meals inflight. Having defined their "product" in this fashion, and having developed the supporting logistic structure, it was difficult for them to "unbundle" these services for those passengers who would rather not pay for them.

PRICING DISTORTIONS. Similar distortions may occur when one product is priced to recover the cost of another product. The unprofitable product may be justified on the basis of social benefits, attempt to gain distribution power, utilization of excess capacity or other reasons. AT&T, for example, had long used the profits from long-distance service to subsidize local telephone rates. As a regulated monopoly, it had been considered "in the public interest" to provide this subsidy, which was estimated to be as high as 35% of long-distance revenues. When MCI was permitted to compete in the long distance market, paying a much lower subsidy to local phone service than AT&T, the latter faced a competitive challenge which was difficult to respond to. This disparity was reported to account for 70% of MCI's ability to undercut AT&T. AT&T [was] bound to this local subsidy until 1988, when it [began to] be phased out. Meanwhile, they must rely on the short-term solution of emphasizing nonprice characteristics in the face of 15–50% price discounts offered by MCI and other new competitors.

CANNIBALIZATION OF EXISTING PRODUCTS. In meeting a confrontation, established firms are constrained by the extent to which their response would affect sales of products which are not directly challenged. Efforts to protect a particular product may lead to loss of sales on other products.

At IBM, the pricing policy reflected a constant price/performance ratio across the entire family of computers. This policy paid off for IBM inasmuch as the lineup of products was developed to derive maximum revenues. While still employed at IBM, Gene Amdahl proposed to IBM a large central processor which would be profitable under two conditions. First, to gain market acceptance, this machine would have to be priced lower than that stipulated by the existing pricing strategy. Second, two additional machines would have to be placed between the IBM 370 family and the largest processor to generate sufficient volume. These steps, however, would upset IBM's overall pricing ratio and threaten the demand for those machines for which the price/performance ratio would become less attractive. Thus, IBM rejected this proposal, and Amdahl subsequently left to found his own firm. He eventually gained success by offering an advanced central processor (the 470 V/6) priced at a level consistent with market demand and not hampered by consideration of whether it would cannibalize smaller machines.

Manufacturing Barriers

The challengers in our examples all demonstrated superior cost advantages. These became feasible through a combination of policies which departed from traditional industry practice. However, the established firms found themselves "locked into" higher cost positions, which reflected historic decisions about wages, work rules, locations, processes, and the skills needed to compete.

WAGE RATES AND WORK RULES. At People Express, the salary structure was substantially lower than that of the established airlines. Initially, its pilots earned $30,000 per year and worked 70 hours per month, compared with industry averages of $60,000 and 45 hours.

Operating by work rules which were much more flexible than those of the industry, People Express promoted efficiency by rotating all its employees through different job assignments. This practice extended to managers, pilots, maintenance personnel, and flight attendants (known as customer service managers at People Express). Hence, People Express "produced" at significantly lower costs than would have been the case had they accepted the high salary structures and rigid job classifications of their larger rivals. Its labor costs were about 20% of revenues, compared with 37% for major airlines as a group. The competing major airlines had wage contracts in place; they also had pilots and managers who would regard the rotation of job assignments as demeaning and unacceptable.

EXISTING FACILITIES AND PROCESSES. IBP's decision to locate its cattle slaughtering facilities in the heart of cattle feeding country, rather than only in the traditional stockyard terminal cities of Kansas City, St. Louis, or Chicago, not only resulted in lower wage rates, but also lower real estate and building costs. Moreover, this strategy drastically reduced the shrinkage normally experienced when livestock were transported long distances from the feedlot to the slaughter site.

And redefining the manner in which slaughter cattle were processed, IBP introduced the moving "disassembly" line. Unskilled or semiskilled laborers were used to perform simple repetitive tasks, replacing the skilled butchers required by the traditional meat packing process. The combination of efficient, one-story plants, redefined process operations and lower wage rates gave IBP a "kill" cost of around $18 per head compared to $30–35 per head for old-line packers.

IBP led the industry in cleaving and trimming carcasses into loins, ribs, and other cuts and boxing the pieces at the plant, which further reduced the transportation costs by removing excess weight. The innovative plastic packaging introduced by IBP virtually eliminated shrinkage due to refrigeration and quadrupled the shelf-life of fresh meat from 7 to 28 days. In fact, IBP claimed it could deliver boxed beef to a supermarket at prices as much as $36 less per head than the retailer could buy and process carcasses himself.

The established meat packers had commitments to existing plants and facilities. They had already trained skilled butchers, and were paying them accordingly. Their entire organizations were oriented toward the traditional way of slaughtering and shipping beef.

JOINT MANUFACTURING. Components shared across product lines can give rise to economies of scale in production, lower design, engineering, and service costs. On the other hand, this practice often promotes standardization and exacts a compromise in product performance.

In IBM's case, the component division recognized that the largest mainframe computers represented only a small market. To attain economies of scale, components for the large processor would also be designed for use in the smaller computers in the company's line. This commonality would lead to lower production costs, particularly across the entire family of products, but also would lead to sacrifices in product performance. When Gene Amdahl proposed the development of a large central processing unit, he could not obtain assurances that the components needed would not be downgraded. Yet without such guarantees, he felt that the desired performance specifications would be compromised. When Amdahl later left IBM and developed his own central processor, utilizing only those components appropriate to its design, IBM was faced with a dilemma. Should it retain emphasis on commonality, leading to lower development, manufacturing, and service costs across a family of products, or should it seek to match the price/performance ratios of the Amdahl computers through using components uniquely suited to large central processors?

Organizational Structure and Culture

ORGANIZATIONAL STRUCTURES. The organizational structures of large companies influence their ability to respond to direct competition by small firms. High degrees of centralization and thick policy manuals make it more difficult to modify policies or respond quickly to the moves of smaller competitors. Layers of organization also are often associated with high overhead rates. AT&T was characterized by strong central staff groups, careful and deliberate study of proposed policy changes—including pricing, and concern about systemwide consistency. The corporation was noted for many strengths, but not for internal entrepreneurship. Thus, MCI's development of a lean, stripped-down organization with innovative pricing and marketing techniques, was difficult for AT&T to match.

ORGANIZATION CULTURES. The organizational cultures of established firms evolve through long periods of hiring, training, and motivating employees to implement particular strategies. Employees become proud of organizational capabilities, such as offering a full product line or excellent service.

The integrated steel companies competed on the basis of offering broad product lines. Many major steel companies had integrated backward to the point of iron and coal mining and forward to the point of steel service centers where structural shapes were prepared for individual customers. The traditional "big steel" claim of "If it's done in steel, we do it" required a large investment in metallurgical skills and facilities which had come to be accepted as a necessary requirement of being in the steel business.

But, at Nucor Steel, Iverson did not need or want a full product line. Hence, he had no requirement for the extensive staff, large-capacity furnaces, rolling equipment, re-heating facilities, and other investments required of an integrated steel producer. In fact, the investment cost of Nucor's "mini-mills" ran only about $150 per ton of annual output, compared to the nearly $1400 per ton of annual output for an integrated mill.

The young firms in this study created cultures which were difficult for the large firms to replicate. In the early days of Amdahl, Gene Amdahl visited customers and closed the sale himself—an approach that was difficult for IBM to match. Nucor created a culture in which every employee was made to feel important. They even listed the name of every employee on the back page of their annual report!

ABILITY TO INNOVATE. Innovation can vary widely across established firms. Often, they are well equipped to deal with incremental innovations leading to gradual improvements in cost or performance. However, dramatic changes in the concept of the products, services, or production systems may encounter significant organizational barriers. Initially, it is not clear whether the new concepts will be successful or how large their market potential might be. The methods of analysis used in large corporations often emphasize "hard data" and systematic analysis more suited to incremental innovation than to major changes in strategy. Moreover, innovative strategies often call into question the long-established success formula of the corporation. Such changes threaten managers whose power bases depend on the existing strategy and who may have spent careers developing skills which would no longer be valued.

By contrast, the entrepreneurs within these new companies were the product champions. Gene Amdahl of Amdahl Corporation and Gitner and Burr of People Express Airline had dreams of what they hoped to bring about through their new companies. They could rely upon their "feel" for the technology and marketplace based upon personal experience. Unencumbered by high administrative overhead and large organizations, they could achieve success at relatively low sales volumes. Thus, their small firms were almost ideal settings for experimentation with innovative strategies.

BARRIERS TO RESPONSE. In examining these barriers to response, we should not underestimate the role of *government regulation* and *union contracts*. Established firms are visible and accumulate, over time, a history of agreements. AT&T certainly was subject to regulatory constraints, such as the requirement to provide low-cost local service. MCI was faced with no such requirement. Major airlines and old-line beef packers were obligated to labor agreements which restricted flexible work assignments and called for much higher hourly wage rates than those faced by competitors such as People Express or Iowa Beef.

FACTORS BEARING ON WHETHER CHALLENGER ADVANTAGES MAY BE ERODED

Young firms engaged in strategies of direct competition may achieve initial success, based upon some of the advantages just considered. The firms illustrated in this study . . . all achieved substantial growth. . . . Their 1984 sales ranged from more than $500 million to over $5 billion.

This is not to suggest that the conditions which give rise to this success, and the effectiveness of strategies which exploited these opportunities will persist permanently [as, for example, in the case of People Express]. Much depends on how the industry evolves and how established competitors respond. Responses may be of a short-term tactical nature, or they may involve basic changes in the large firms' strategies and organization structures.

Small firms must also be aware that, as they grow, they may lose some of the characteristics which contributed to their success. New players, encouraged by the visible success of challengers, may enter and crowd the markets. Managements of challenging firms must assess these developments and how they may threaten their competitive advantage.

The previous literature clearly notes that early success may not endure and that "sustainable competitive advantage" is required for continuing success (Coyne, 1986; Porter, 1985). The ability to sustain advantage may depend, in part, upon how well the new firm deals with the continuing crises of growth (Buchele, 1967; Baumback and Mancuso, 1975). Even as the firm grows to substantial size, management confronts a series of internal challenges, of evolutions and revolutions (Greiner, 1972). Outside the firm, continuing industry development may shift the focus of competition (Porter, 1980). In some cases early success may attract excessive numbers of competitors, which coupled with rapid change and customer instability, can lead to disappointing performance for many participants (Sahlman and Stevenson, 1985).

The five challengers considered here all had to deal with a succession of responses by established competitors, internal changes, and confrontations with new entrants.

Responses by Established Firms

Responses by established firms can be tactical or strategic. Tactical responses do not stem from fundamental changes in the firm's policies. They represent short term responses by established firms to protect critical segments, to test the commitment of challengers, or to buy time to implement new strategies or organizational changes. In certain key markets, established airlines slashed ticket prices by over 50% to meet People Express's low fares in an all-out price war. One United ad directly attacked the upstart with the slogan, "You can fly or you can be shipped." Established airlines also lobbied the CAB to eliminate subsidies relating to the lower penalties People Express faced if luggage was lost or confirmed passengers were bumped.

Strategic actions, on the other hand, involve major adjustments in the large competitors' products, processes, and organizational structures. Two years after Amdahl sold its first 470 V/6, IBM announced a radical new product, Model 3033, which would bring a price/performance improvement of some 140% over its predecessor. . . . Major efforts were also undertaken by leading airlines to pare down operations, evaluate route structures, and negotiate with unions for lower wage rates.

247

When faced with these tactical and strategic countermoves, what might challengers do? They must choose their battlefields carefully, taking into account their more limited resources. . . .

Challenging firms must also be prepared to compete more aggressively as established firms react. As MCI's cost advantage over AT&T began to slide, MCI increased its marketing emphasis and expanded its sales force to contact wavering customers. Moreover, it continued to adopt an aggressive posture, spending heavily to expand capacity, work force, and upgrade microwave transmitters.

Evolution of Small Firms

If challengers are successful in developing markets, they will eventually evolve into larger organizations. As these firms grow, they become more complex and the necessary administrative processes may cause such firms to take on characteristics of larger competitors, slowing response time and dulling the competitive edge they once held. . . .

Challengers must recognize those dimensions of their cultures which were relevant not only to their past success, but would be critical to their future performance as well. Only half-jokingly, McGowan said he would abolish the existing MCI to build a new company "to keep employees on their toes." This statement, albeit made in jest, reflected his acknowledgment of the need to maintain MCI's fighting spirit despite experiences of success. Nucor, to affirm its belief in the importance of its workers, has continued to print the names of employees on its annual reports. Only now the organization has grown so large that even the front cover is used for this purpose. Nucor's workers have always enjoyed generous bonuses based on production levels. The base levels on which such bonuses are calculated have remained unchanged despite significant technology-driven productivity gains.

Entrance of Other Firms

In the beginning, it is usually not clear whether innovative small firms are developing strategies with great potential. However, as their success becomes visible, other competitors, both established corporations and new ventures, may begin to copy their strategies. For example, MCI and AT&T subsequently competed not only with each other, but also with Sprint, Allnet, US Telephone, and SBS. In the meat-packing industry, IBP competed not only against the old-line packers, but also against such firms as MBPXL and Monfort, which were following strategies similar to their own. Suppliers of supercomputers subsequently included not only IBM and Amdahl, but Cray Research and Control Data as well.

The innovative small firm may thus confront a variety of competitors, with different strategies and strengths. Management must anticipate these competitive pressures. This may include being careful not to overextend the firm and developing the financial strength or competitive alliances needed to survive under more difficult conditions. It also means sharpening the distinctive skills which led to their early successes and being careful not to let creeping changes in strategy take the firm away from its core strengths. . . .

CONCLUSIONS

. . . The strategies considered here are niche strategies in the sense that they concentrate on serving the needs of limited groups of customers. They are also "focus strategies" as described by Porter (1980), in the sense of emphasizing lower costs, differentiation, or both, in dealing with a portion of the market. However, contrary to the prevailing thinking in much of the literature, these niche or focus strategies do not limit young firms to markets that are of no interest to leading competitors. Those firms with the right combination of corporate resources and industry opportunity may be able to develop strategies of direct competition which lead to continuing and enviable success.

In no way do we suggest that a direct confrontation strategy is appropriate for all small businesses. The sample considered is small and may not be broadly representative. However, these observations may challenge the dominant perspective and hopefully, invite future entrepreneurs and researchers to think more broadly and aggressively about the distinctive competencies of small and new businesses.

STRUCTURE AND STRATEGY IN MATURE ORGANIZATIONS

▼

As we saw in Chapter Six, older mature industries are populated by organizations that are more formalized. In other words, the typical firm in a mature industry is what Mintzberg calls a machine organization. Explaining strategy formation in machine organizations is challenging because what the strategy textbooks say is *supposed* to happen (prescriptive strategy) in such firms is rarely the way strategies *form* in them (descriptive strategy). In this chapter we examine the strategy formation process in the mature organization from both the prescriptive and descriptive strategy perspectives.

PRESCRIPTIVE STRATEGY FOR MACHINE ORGANIZATIONS

The kind of strategy typically associated with machine organizations is what Mintzberg calls *planned strategy*. In planned strategy, "precise intentions are formulated and articulated by a central leadership, and backed up by formal controls to ensure their surprise-free implementation in an environment that is benign, controllable, or predictable (to ensure no distortion of intentions); these strategies are highly deliberate."[1]

One can see from this definition that to understand fully how strategy is supposed to form in mature organizations, one would only have to reread Chapters Three and Four of this book. Those chapters dealt with the design, planning, and positioning schools. Strategy in the machine organization is supposed to emanate from the top of the hierarchy, where the perspective is broadest and the power most focused. The people at the top formulate an integrated strategy. If they do it alone, it is an example of the strategy-as-design approach; if they follow a formal process, it is the planned strategy approach. Lastly, if they formulate the integrated strategy with the assistance of analysts, which is often the case, it is an example of strategy-as-position. In any event, implementation follows as top management hands the concept, plan, or analysis down the hierarchy to the people who are supposed to execute it.

THE CONTEXT OF THE MACHINE ORGANIZATION

Henry Mintzberg's reading in this chapter, "The Machine Organization," starts with a discussion of the structure of machine organizations. Machine organizations emphasize functional grouping, standardization of work process into simple tasks, a high level of formalization, and obsession with control. The reading then moves to a description of the environmental context within which machine organizations operate. The work of machine organizations is found in *simple, stable* environments. This is because work associated with complex environments is difficult to rationalize into simple tasks, which is the trademark of the machine organization. Similarly, it is difficult to predict, standardize, and make repetitive the work associated with dynamic environments.

As mentioned above, the machine configuration characterizes mature (large and old) organizations. It may also be found in organizations that use regulating technical systems, for example, mass production firms. The environment may be stable because the organization has acted aggressively to stabilize it, using advertising, long-term supply contracts, cartels, vertical integration, and so on. This configuration is found in many types of enterprises: large and sometimes small manufacturing firms, routine service firms, some government agencies, and so on. In this type of environment, a machine organization could thrive, and the prescriptive strategy process described above could work. Things would be stable enough for a design, planning, or analytical approach to be sensible. But what if this environment occurs less frequently than theorists think?

Michael Porter's reading in this chapter, "The Transition to Industry Maturity," gives a very different description of what happens as an industry matures. The differences start with the industry's driving force shifting from growth to market share. Buyers behave differently, since they are now experienced. Competition becomes more oriented toward cost and service. Capacity planning moves from expansion to restraint. Functional areas like manufacturing, marketing, distribution, selling, and research are changing. New products and applications are harder to come by. Competition becomes increasingly international. Profits fall. Dealers and distributors become more powerful because their number decreases. This type of environment seems anything but simple and stable.

POSITIONING STRATEGIES IN MATURE INDUSTRIES

Fortunately, scholars from the positioning school have developed some ideas about the kinds of strategies that mature organizations might follow in an industry with the characteristics Porter mentions. Porter details some of these strategies in his reading. In this section we discuss other methods that firms might use to reduce industry rivalry, both directly and by preventing entry by new firms (which would intensify rivalry).

Market Signaling

One thing that creates a barrier to entry is the potential of retaliation by incumbent firms. Similarly, the jockeying for position of firms already in the industry might moderate in light of what their rivals might do in retaliation. Market signaling is what firms use to let rivals or potential entrants know their intentions. Some of these are product/market moves, potential competitive moves, or responses to the competitive moves of others.[2] A firm might use market signaling to reveal to rivals its intention of responding robustly to market moves such as price cuts or promotional blitzes. Or it might signal to potential entrants that it will cut prices or promote products vigorously in response to their entry attempts. Another use of market signaling is to send signals aimed at pre-empting competitors' moves, such as letting the market know about plans for new product introductions or new production capacity.

Lastly, market signaling may even be used to coordinate indirectly the actions of the firms in an industry. For example, a firm might announce that it is cutting prices to reduce the rate at which buyers substitute the industry's products for products not part of the industry. This signal would be designed to let rivals know that the firm is not trying to start a price war; by implication, rivals would be invited to lower their prices for the same reason. If they followed suit, the balance of intra-industry rivalry would remain unchanged. This use of market signaling is intended to give rivals information so that they can understand the firm's competitive moves and make desired responses.

Price Leadership

Another way to moderate the level of destructive competition in a mature industry is **price leadership**. This is when a firm in the industry takes the responsibility for setting industry prices.[3] When this firm sets prices, other firms adjust their prices. In this way, the firm implicitly formulates price levels for the industry. The firm could be the strongest one, which might set prices low to keep other firms' margins low. Or it could be the weakest firm — since its margins are likely to be the slimmest in the industry, using it as the price leader would result in higher margins for the other, stronger firms.

Because of antitrust laws, firms cannot use price leadership formally. But when an industry's firms successfully achieve price leadership informally, it can greatly moderate price competition and other types of rivalry, and can increase industry profitability. The danger of price leadership is that it may lull the price leader into complacency, opening the door for entrants (or incumbents) with lower costs. The latter could lower their prices, taking market share away from the price leader and its followers.

Competitive Product Differentiation

Firms in mature industries look for ways to compete that do not involve price. If an industry is mature, using pricing to compete hurts all firms by lowering profits. One alternative is **competitive product differentiation**, such as *market penetration,* when a firm expands its market share in segments where it is already doing business.[4] The firm typically does this using advertising and promotion, not pricing. This approach is the way of life in industries such as brewing and detergents, where firms advertise and promote heavily.

If a firm chooses to compete by introducing new or improved products in its existing segments, it is pursuing a strategy of *product development.*[5] This is the strategy behind different "versions" of programs in the software industry; each version has better features than the last, prompting the release of new versions by firms with rival programs. Another approach to competitive product differentiation is *market development,* when a firm tries to offer its existing products to new market segments. An example would be Avon's Skin-So-Soft, which was developed as a bath oil but later became a popular insect repellent. The last and broadest strategy of competitive product differentiation is *product proliferation.*[6] A firm using this approach offers a wide array of products to many market segments. By tailoring products to specific segments, a company makes it more difficult for firms to enter any given segment. This approach also puts pressure on rivals already in the industry, but not in a price-oriented way.

Competitive Pricing

Although firms in mature industries would prefer to compete in ways other than pricing, price wars are virtually inevitable. However, incumbent firms may use various forms of competitive pricing to deter entry by other firms. One method is **limit pricing**, useful when an industry has good profits.[7] In that situation, firms outside the industry might be motivated to enter. Incumbent firms can use market signaling or price leadership to hold prices down to a level that provides acceptable profits but avoids signaling to potential entrants the true profit potential of the industry. This is obviously a difficult strategy to execute, since the firms trying to do it have no way to control the actions of each other or of potential rivals.

Another, more common approach to competitive pricing is to **charge a high price initially and then cut prices aggressively**.[8] This allows a firm to garner high profits in the short-term, and then try to gain market share, while simultaneously deterring entry, over the longer term. This strategy is usually more effective against weak rivals or entrants.

Capacity Control

An important and common problem in mature industries is *excess capacity*. An industry has excess capacity when the combined manufacturing (or service-providing) capacity of all its firms is greater than the industry's buyers' total demand. Excess capacity can occur when new technology is introduced, but the old plant is continued in service. It can also happen when new firms enter the industry and add capacity. Lastly, it can happen if incumbent firms try to take market share away from each other; in anticipation of success, many firms will add capacity simultaneously. Since they all won't succeed (that would happen only in a growth industry, not the mature industry we are discussing here), there will be too much capacity.

In general, there are only two choices available to companies that wish to control capacity in the industry. One is to **preempt rivals or entrants** by signaling their intention to add capacity. If rivals or entrants take these signals seriously, they may be deterred from entering or adding capacity.

The other approach is to **coordinate with other companies**. This works like price leadership, except that market signaling is used to coordinate informally the capacity-building actions, not the pricing actions, of industry incumbents. This approach is less risky than preemption, since it does not necessarily require investment. It has risks all its own, analogous to those faced by price leaders—entrants may invade the industry anyway, disrupting the coordination of its incumbents.

Supply and Distribution

Since mature industries tend to be consolidated, firms operating in them have the potential to be powerful vis-a-vis their suppliers and buyers. Firms in such industries can use this to their advantage. They can structure their relationships with suppliers to gain better margins (typical among U.S. firms) or higher quality (typical for Japanese firms). They can nurture relationships with distributors in a way that enhances their product reputation—for example, by choosing only high-profile outlets or by working with them on promotional campaigns. Or firms can try to increase their margins—for example, by demanding and getting higher prices from distributors. Going through the hard work of managing relationships with suppliers and buyers can help firms control costs and prices, and even their reputation and quality. These are important concerns in mature industries.

OTHER PROBLEMS FACING MACHINE ORGANIZATIONS IN MATURE INDUSTRIES

A natural question at this point is, "How good are machine organizations at carrying out the kinds of responses discussed in the previous section?" After all, the prototypical machine organization with its centrally planned strategy process is supposed to operate in simple, stable environments, but mature environments often change.

As we saw in the Cooper, Willard, and Woo reading in the previous chapter, machine organizations suffer from problems that make it difficult for them to respond to the changes in their industries. First, they tend to be locked into strategies with standardized products, set pricing, and the potential for cannibalization of existing products. Second, they often have manufacturing barriers such as wage rates and work rules, existing facilities and processes to which they are committed, and manufacturing arrangements with subcontractors. Lastly, there may be organizational structure and culture issues, such rigid organizational structures, organizational cultures that intensify resistance to change, a stunted ability to innovate in ways other than incrementally, and barriers to response created by long-term contracts and government regulations.

When one combines these problems with the description Porter gives of the mature industry, the picture that emerges is of rigid bureaucracies having a difficult time keeping up with industry changes. In other words, the environment for which theorists say machine organizations are best suited often shift to a more hostile type. What does this mean for the kind of strategy process that is prescribed for machine organizations? In other words, do machine organizations use strategy design, planning, and analysis? In the next section, we will examine the process that machine organizations seem to use.

STRATEGY FORMATION IN THE MACHINE ORGANIZATION

Mintzberg's reading in this chapter has a section that describes strategy formation in machine organizations in some detail. He also provides extensive examples. Here, we review his major points.

Planning is rarely responsible for formulating strategy. It is more a tool for carrying out strategies that have already been conceived; it is a programming tool. Planning tends to extrapolate industry trends; rarely does it result in a novel strategy. It is too analysis-oriented, while strategy formation, like most other aspects of management, is synthesis-oriented. Planners are most useful when they are used to lead analyses at the beginning of strategy-making and to program the strategies that come out of it.

Perhaps Mintzberg's main point is that the prescriptive model of strategy formulation in machine organizations errs greatly when it separates formulation from implementation. This can work only if the environment stays simple and stable, or at least predictable, enough for some highly placed person in the firm to formulate. But when real changes have to be made, formulation and implementation must be collapsed. The result is that there are two ways by which strategy tends to form in machine organizations. One is where the formulator implements; that is, the CEO concentrates power at the top and behaves entrepreneurially. In other words, the machine organization temporarily adopts the entrepreneurial configuration. The other way strategy forms is for the implementors to formulate. That is, people closest to what is going on with customers and other factors in the industry get the power to develop strategy. This is the strategy formation model in the innovative organization, which we will examine in more detail in the next chapter. Because of all these factors, machine organizations seem to

pursue set strategies for long periods, interrupted by short bursts of change, which can be called "strategic revolutions."

This reading concludes with the thought that machine organizations can be highly effective in their context, but once their situations become more unstable, they falter. When that happens, they need to adopt another configuration's strategy formation process temporarily, either the entrepreneurial process or the innovative process.

THE TRANSITION TO INDUSTRY MATURITY

As mentioned earlier, Michael Porter's reading in this chapter, "The Transition to Industry Maturity," begins with a description of the dynamics of the mature industry. Porter goes on in some detail about some strategic implications of industry maturity. The first of these is that mature firms need to become even more astute about selecting a good generic strategy. They need to learn how to do sophisticated cost analysis, to insulate themselves against the dangers of inevitable price wars. Machine organizations need to excel at process innovation and design for manufacturing. Both these skills help keep costs down and may also provide non-price advantages such as product quality. Firms in mature industries must learn to adjust to changes in the buying habits of their customers. They should strive to buy the cheap assets that typically become available as firms fail. They could find cost curves in market niches that give them advantages, even if their total costs are not in line with industry levels. Lastly, they should be assertive about competing internationally; their costs may be lower in different countries.

NOTES TO CHAPTER TEN

1. See Mintzberg's reading "Five Ps for Strategy" in Chapter One.
2. Porter, M. E., *Competitive Strategy: Techniques for Analyzing Industries and Competitors.* New York: Free Press, 1980, pp. 76–86.
3. Scherer, F. M., *Industrial Market Structure and Economic Performance,* 2nd ed. Boston: Houghton-Mifflin, 1980, Ch. 6.
4. Ansoff, H. I., *Corporate Strategy.* London: Penguin Books, 1984, pp. 97–100.
5. Ansoff, *Corporate Strategy,* pp. 98–99.
6. Brander, J., and J. Eaton, "Product Line Rivalry." *American Economic Review* (June 1984), pp. 323–34.
7. Scherer, *Industrial Market Structure and Economic Performance,* Ch. 8.
8. Milgrom, P., and J. Roberts, "Predation, Reputation, and Entry Deterrence." *Journal of Economic Theory* 27 (1982): 280–312.

THE MACHINE ORGANIZATION

By Henry Mintzberg

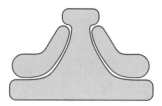

A national post office, a custodial prison, an airline, a giant automobile company, even a small security agency—all these organizations appear to have a number of characteristics in common. Above all, their operating work is routine, the greatest part of it rather simple and repetitive; as a result, their work processes are highly standardized. These characteristics give rise to the machine organizations of our society, structures fine-tuned to run as integrated, regulated, highly bureaucratic machines.

THE BASIC STRUCTURE

A clear configuration of the attributes has appeared consistently in the research: highly specialized, routine operating tasks; very formalized communication throughout the organization; large-size operating units; reliance on the functional basis for grouping tasks; relatively centralized power for decision making; and an elaborate administrative structure with a sharp distinction between line and staff.

The Operating Core and Administration

The obvious starting point is the operating core, with its highly rationalized work flow. This means that the operating tasks are made simple and repetitive, generally requiring a minimum of skill and training, the latter often taking only hours, seldom more than a few weeks, and usually in-house. This in turn results in narrowly defined jobs and an emphasis on the standardization of work processes for coordination, with activities highly formalized. The workers are left with little discretion, as are their supervisors, who can therefore handle very large spans of control.

To achieve such high regulation of the operating work, the organization has need for an elaborate administrative structure—a fully developed middle-line hierarchy and technostructure—but the two clearly distinguished.

The managers of the middle line have three prime tasks. One is to handle the disturbances that arise in the operating core. The work is so standardized that when things fall through the cracks, conflict flares, because the problems cannot be worked out informally. So it falls to managers to resolve them by direct supervision. Indeed, many

Adapted from *The Structure of Organizations* (Prentice Hall, 1979), Chap. 18 on "The Machine Bureaucracy"; also *Power in and around Organizations* (Prentice Hall, 1983), Chaps. 18 and 19 on "The Instrument" and "The Closed System"; the material on strategy formation from "Patterns in Strategy Formation," *Management Science* (1978); Does Planning Impede Strategic Thinking? Tracking the Strategies of Air Canada, from 1937–1976" (coauthored with Pierre Brunet and Jim Waters), in R. B. Lamb and P. Shrivastava, eds., *Advances in Strategic Management,* Volume IV (JAI press, 1986); and "The Mind of the Strategist(s)" (coauthored with Jim Waters), in S. Srivastva, ed., *The Executive Mind* (Jossey-Bass, 1983); the section on the role of planning, plans, and planners is drawn from a book in process on strategic planning. A chapter similar to this appeared in *Mintzberg on Management: Inside Our Strange World of Organizations* (Free Press, 1989).

problems get bumped up successive steps in the hierarchy until they reach a level of common supervision where they can be resolved by authority (as with a dispute in a company between manufacturing and marketing that may have to be resolved by the chief executive). A second task of the middle-line managers is to work with the staff analysts to incorporate their standards down into the operating units. And a third task is to support the vertical flows in the organization—the elaboration of action plans flowing down the hierarchy and the communication of feedback information back up.

The technostructure must also be highly elaborated. In fact this structure was first identified with the rise of technocratic personnel in early-nineteenth-century industries such as textiles and banking. Because the machine organization depends primarily on the standardization of its operating work for coordination, the technostructure—which houses the staff analysts who do the standardizing—emerges as the key part of the structure. To the line managers may be delegated the formal authority for the operating units, but without the standardizers—the cadre of work-study analysts, schedulers, quality control engineers, planners, budgeters, accountants, operations researchers, and many more—these structures simply could not function. Hence, despite their lack of formal authority, considerable informal power rests with these staff analysts, who standardize everyone else's work. Rules and regulations permeate the entire system: The emphasis on standardization extends well beyond the operating core of the machine organization, and with it follows the analysts' influence.

A further reflection of this formalization of behavior are the sharp divisions of labor all over the machine organization. Job specialization in the operating core and the pronounced formal distinction between line and staff have already been mentioned. In addition, the administrative structure is clearly distinguished from the operating core; unlike the entrepreneurial organization, here managers seldom work alongside operators. And they themselves tend to be organized along functional lines, meaning that each runs a unit that performs a single function in the chain that produces the final outputs. Figure 1 shows this, for example, in the organigram of a large steel company, traditionally machinelike in structure.

All this suggests that the machine organization is a structure with an obsession— namely, control. A control mentality pervades it from top to bottom. At the bottom, consider how a Ford Assembly Division general foreman described his work:

> I refer to my watch all the time. I check different items. About every hour I tour my line. About six thirty, I'll tour labor relations to find out who is absent. At seven, I hit the end of the line. I'll check paint, check my scratches and damage. Around ten I'll start talking to all the foremen. I make sure they're all awake. We can't have no holes, no nothing.

And at the top, consider the words of a chief executive:

> When I was president of this big corporation, we lived in a small Ohio town, where the main plant was located. The corporation specified who you could socialize with, and on what level. (His wife interjects: "Who were the wives you could play bridge with."). In a small town they didn't have to keep check on you. Everybody knew. There are certain sets of rules. (Terkel, 1972:186, 406)

The obsession with control reflects two central facts about these organizations. First, attempts are made to eliminate all possible uncertainty, so that the bureaucratic machine can run smoothly, without interruption, the operating core perfectly sealed off from external influence. Second, these are structures ridden with conflict; the control systems are required to contain it. The problem in the machine organization is not to develop an open atmosphere where people can talk the conflicts out, but to enforce a closed, tightly controlled one where the work can get done despite them.

The obsession with control also helps to explain the frequent proliferation of support staff in these organizations. Many of the staff services could be purchased from out-

FIGURE 1
**Organigram of a Large Steel
Company**

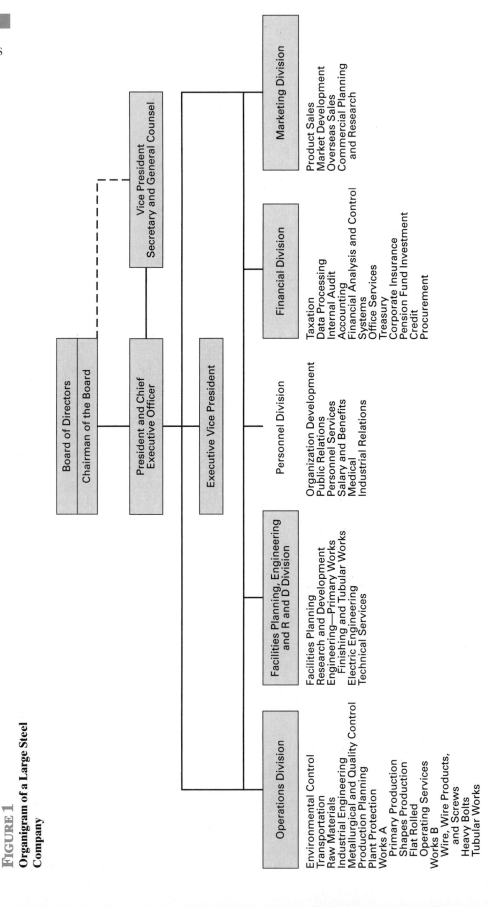

side suppliers. But that would expose the machine organization to the uncertainties of the open market. So it "makes" rather than "buys," that is, it envelops as many of the support services as it can within its own structure in order to control them, everything from the cafeteria in the factory to the law office at headquarters.

The Strategic Apex

The managers at the strategic apex of these organizations are concerned in large part with the fine-tuning of their bureaucratic machines. Theirs is a perpetual search for more efficient ways to produce the given outputs.

But not all is strictly improvement of performance. Just keeping the structure together in the face of its conflicts also consumes a good deal of the energy of top management. As noted, conflict is not resolved in the machine organization; rather it is bottled up so that the work can get done. And as in the case of a bottle, the cork is applied at the top: Ultimately, it is the top managers who must keep the lid on the conflicts through their role of handling disturbances. Moreover, the managers of the strategic apex must intervene frequently in the activities of the middle line to ensure that coordination is achieved there. The top managers are the only generalists in the structure, the only managers with a perspective broad enough to see all the functions.

All this leads us to the conclusion that considerable power in the machine organization rests with the managers of the strategic apex. These are, in other words, rather centralized structures: The formal power clearly rests at the top; hierarchy and chain of authority are paramount concepts. But so also does much of the informal power, since that resides in knowledge, and only at the top of the hierarchy does the formally segmented knowledge of the organization come together.

Thus, our introductory figure shows the machine organization with a fully elaborated administrative and support structure—both parts of the staff component being focused on the operating core—together with large units in the operating core but narrower ones in the middle line to reflect the tall hierarchy of authority.

CONDITIONS OF THE MACHINE ORGANIZATION

Work of a machine bureaucratic nature is found, above all, in environments that are simple and stable. The work associated with complex environments cannot be rationalized into simple tasks, and that associated with dynamic environments cannot be predicted, made repetitive, and so standardized.

In addition, the machine configuration is typically found in mature organizations, large enough to have the volume of operating work needed for repetition and standardization, and old enough to have been able to settle on the standards they wish to use. These are the organizations that have seen it all before and have established standard procedures to deal with it. Likewise, machine organizations tend to be identified with technical systems that regulate the operating work, so that it can easily be programmed. Such technical systems cannot be very sophisticated or automated (for reasons that will be discussed later).

Mass production firms are perhaps the best-known machine organizations. Their operating work flows through an integrated chain, open at one end to accept raw materials, and after that functioning as a sealed system that processes them through sequences of standardized operations. Thus, the environment may be stable because the organization has acted aggressively to stabilize it. Giant firms in such industries as transportation, tobacco, and metals are well known for their attempts to influence the forces of supply and demand by the use of advertising, the development of long-term supply contacts, sometimes the establishment of cartels. They also tend to adopt strategies of "vertical integration," that is, extend their production chains at both ends, becoming both their own suppliers and their own customers. In that way they can bring some of the forces of supply and demand within their own planning processes.

Of course, the machine organization is not restricted to large, or manufacturing, or even private enterprise organizations. Small manufacturers—for example producers of discount furniture or paper products—may sometimes prefer this structure because their operating work is simple and repetitive. Many service firms use it for the same reason, such as banks or insurance companies in their retailing activities. Another condition often found with machine organizations is external control. Many government departments, such as post offices and tax collection agencies, are machine bureaucratic not only because their operating work is routine but also because they must be accountable to the public for their actions. Everything they do—treating clients, hiring employees, and so on—must be seen to be fair, and so they proliferate regulations.

Since control is the forte of the machine bureaucracy, it stands to reason that organizations in the business of control—regulatory agencies, custodial prisons, police forces—are drawn to this configuration, sometimes in spite of contradictory conditions. The same is true for the special need for safety. Organizations that fly airplanes or put out fires must minimize the risks they take. Hence they formalize their procedures extensively to ensure that they are carried out to the letter: A fire crew cannot arrive at a burning house and then turn to the chief for orders or discuss informally who will connect the hose and who will go up the ladder.

MACHINE ORGANIZATIONS AS INSTRUMENTS AND CLOSED SYSTEMS

Control raises another issue about machine organizations. Being so pervasively regulated, they themselves can easily be controlled externally, as the *instruments* of outside influencers. In contrast, however, their obsession with control runs not only up the hierarchy but beyond, to control of their own environments, so that they can become *closed systems* immune to external influence. From the perspective of power, the instrument and the closed system constitute two main types of machine organizations.

In our terms, the instrument form of machine organization is dominated by one external influencer or by a group of them acting in concert. In the "closely held" corporation, the dominant influencer is the outside owner; in some prisons, it is a community concerned with the custody rather than the rehabilitation of prisoners.

Outside influencers render an organization their instrument by appointing the chief executive, charging that person with the pursuit of clear goals (ideally quantifiable, such as return on investment or prisoner escape measures), and then holding the chief responsible for performance. That way outsiders can control an organization without actually having to manage it. And such control, by virtue of the power put in the hands of the chief executive and the numerical nature of the goals, acts to centralize and bureaucratize the internal structure, in other words, to drive it to the machine form.

In contrast to this, Charles Perrow, the colorful and outspoken organizational sociologist, does not quite see the machine organization as anyone's instrument:

> Society is adaptive to organizations, to the large, powerful organizations controlled by a few, often overlapping, leaders. To see these organizations as adaptive to a "turbulent," dynamic, very changing environment is to indulge in fantasy. The environment of most powerful organizations is well controlled by them, quite stable, and made up of other organizations with similar interests, or ones they control. (1972:199)

Perrow is, of course, describing the closed system form of machine organization, the one that uses its bureaucratic procedures to seal itself off from external control and control others instead. It controls not only its own people but its environment as well: perhaps its suppliers, customers, competitors, even government and owners too.

Of course, autonomy can be achieved not only by controlling others (for example, buying up customers and suppliers in so-called vertical integration) but simply by avoiding the control of others. Thus, for example, closed system organizations sometimes form cartels with ostensible competitors or, less blatantly, diversify markets to avoid dependence on particular customers, finance internally to avoid dependence on particular financial groups, and even buy back their own shares to weaken the influence of their own owners. Key to being a closed system is to ensure wide dispersal, and therefore pacification, of all groups of potential external influence.

What goals does the closed system organization pursue? Remember that to sustain centralized bureaucracy the goals should be operational, ideally quantifiable. What operational goals enable an organization to serve itself, as a system closed to external influence? The most obvious answer is growth. Survival may be an indispensable goal and efficiency a necessary one, but beyond those what really matters here is making the system larger. Growth serves the system by providing greater rewards for its insiders—bigger empires for managers to run or fancier private jets to fly, greater programs for analysts to design, even more power for unions to wield by virtue of having more members. (The unions may be external influencers, but the management can keep them passive by allowing them more of the spoils of the closed system.) Thus the classic closed system machine organization, the large, widely held industrial corporation, has long been described as oriented far more to growth than to the maximization of profit per se (Galbraith, 1967).

Of course, the closed system form of machine organization can exist outside the private sector too, for example in the fundraising agency that, relatively free to external control, becomes increasingly charitable to itself (as indicated by the plushness of its managers' offices), the agricultural or retail cooperative that ignores those who collectively own it, even government that becomes more intent on serving itself than the citizens for which it supposedly exists.

The communist state, at least up until very recently, seemed to fit all the characteristics of the closed system bureaucracy. It had no dominant external influencer (at least in the case of the Soviet Union, if not the other East European states, which were its "instruments"). And the population to which it is ostensibly responsible had to respond to its own plethora of rules and regulations. Its election procedures, traditionally offering a choice of one, were similar to those for the directors of the "widely held" Western corporation. The government's own structure was heavily bureaucratic, with a single hierarchy of authority and a very elaborate technostructure, ranging from state planners to KGB agents. (As James Worthy [1959:77] noted, Frederick Taylor's "Scientific Management had its fullest flowering not in America but in Soviet Russia.") All significant resources were the property of the state—the collective system—not the individual. And, as in other closed systems, the administrators tend to take the lion's share of the benefits.

SOME ISSUES ASSOCIATED WITH THE MACHINE ORGANIZATION

No structure has evoked more heated debate than the machine organization. As Michel Crozier, one of its most eminent students, has noted,

On the one hand, most authors consider the bureaucratic organization to be the embodiment of rationality in the modern world, and, as such, to be intrinsically superior to all other possible forms of organizations. On the other hand, many authors—often the same ones—consider it a sort of Leviathan, preparing the enslavement of the human race. (1964:176)

Max Weber, who first wrote about this form of organization, emphasized its rationality; in fact, the word *machine* comes directly from his writings (see Gerth and Mills, 1958). A machine is certainly precise; it is also reliable and easy to control; and it is efficient—at least when restricted to the job it has been designed to do. Those are the reasons many organizations are structured as machine bureaucracies. When an integrated set of simple, repetitive tasks must be performed precisely and consistently by human beings, this is the most efficient structure—indeed, the only conceivable one.

But in these same advantages of machinelike efficiency lie all the disadvantages of this configuration. Machines consist of mechanical parts; organizational structures also include human beings—and that is where the analogy breaks down.

Human Problems in the Operating Core

James Worthy, when he was an executive of Sears, wrote a penetrating and scathing criticism of the machine organization in his book *Big Business and Free Men*. Worthy traced the root of the human problems in these structures to the "scientific management" movement led by Frederick Taylor that swept America early in this century. Worthy acknowledged Taylor's contribution to efficiency, narrowly defined. Worker initiative did not, however, enter into his efficiency equation. Taylor's pleas to remove "all possible brain work" from the shop floor also removed all possible initiative from the people who worked there: the "machine has no will of its own. Its parts have no urge to independent action. Thinking, direction—even purpose—must be provided from outside or above." This had the "consequence of destroying the meaning of work itself," which has been "fantastically wasteful for industry and society," resulting in excessive absenteeism, high worker turnover, sloppy workmanship, costly strikes, and even outright sabotage (1959:67, 79, 70). Of course, there are people who like to work in highly structured situations. But increasing numbers do not, at least not *that* highly structured.

Taylor was fond of saying, "In the past the man has been first; in the future the system must be first" (in Worthy 1959:73). Prophetic words, indeed. Modern man seems to exist for his systems; many of the organizations he created to serve him have come to enslave him. The result is that several of what Victor Thompson (1961) has called "bureaupathologies"—dysfunctional behaviors of these structures—reinforce each other to form a vicious circle in the machine organization. The concentration on means at the expense of ends, the mistreatment of clients, the various manifestations of worker alienation—all lead to the tightening of controls on behavior. The implicit motto of the machine organization seems to be, "When in doubt, control." All problems have to be solved by the turning of the technocratic screws. But since that is what caused the bureaupathologies in the first place, increasing the controls serves only to magnify the problems, leading to the imposition of further controls, and so on.

Coordination Problems in the Administrative Center

Since the operating core of the machine organization is not designed to handle conflict, many of the human problems that arise there spill up and over, into the administrative structure.

It is one of the ironies of the machine configuration that to achieve the control it requires, it must mirror the narrow specialization of its operating core in its administrative structure (for example, differentiating marketing managers from manufacturing managers, much as salesmen are differentiated from factory workers). This, in turn, means problems of communication and coordination. The fact is that the administrative structure of the machine organization is also ill suited to the resolution of problems through mutual adjustment. All the communication barriers in these structures—horizontal, vertical, status, line/staff—impede informal communication among managers and with staff people. "Each unit becomes jealous of its own prerogatives and finds ways to protect itself against the pressure or encroachments of others" (Worthy, 1950:176). Thus narrow functionalism not only impedes coordination; it also encourages the building of private empires, which tends to produce top-heavy organizations that can be more concerned with the political games to be won than with the clients to be served.

Adaptation Problems in the Strategic Apex

But if mutual adjustment does not work in the administrative center—generating more political heat than cooperative light—how does the machine organization resolve its coordination problems? Instinctively, it tries standardization, for example, by tightening job descriptions or proliferating rules. But standardization is not suited to handling the nonroutine problems of the administrative center. Indeed, it only aggravates them, undermining the influence of the line managers and increasing the conflict. So to reconcile these coordination problems, the machine organization is left with only one coordinating mechanism, direct supervision from above. Specifically, nonroutine coordination problems between units are "bumped" up the line hierarchy until they reach a common level of supervision, often at the top of the structure. The result can be excessive centralization of power, which in turn produces a host of other problems. In effect, just as the human problems in the operating core become coordination problems in the administrative center, so too do the coordination problems in the administrative center become adaptation problems at the strategic apex. Let us take a closer look at these by concluding with a discussion of strategic change in the machine configuration.

STRATEGY FORMATION IN THE MACHINE ORGANIZATION

Strategy in the machine organization is supposed to emanate from the top of the hierarchy, where the perspective is broadest and the power most focused. All the relevant information is to be sent up the hierarchy, in aggregated, MIS-type form, there to be formulated into integrated strategy (with the aid of the technostructure). Implementation then follows, with the intended strategies sent down the hierarchy to be turned into successively more elaborated programs and action plans. Notice the clear division of labor assumed between the formulators at the top and the implementors down below, based on the assumption of perfectly deliberate strategy produced through a process of planning.

That is the theory. The practice has been shown to be another matter. Drawing on our strategy research at McGill University, we shall consider first what planning really proved to be in one machinelike organization, how it may in fact have impeded strategic thinking in a second, and how a third really did change its strategy. From there we shall consider the problems of strategic change in machine organizations and their possible resolution.

Planning as Programming in a Supermarket Chain

What really is the role of formal planning? Does it produce original strategies? Let us return to the case of Steinberg's in the later years of its founder, as large size drove this retailing chain toward the machine form, and as is common in that form, toward a planning mode of management at the expense of entrepreneurship.

One event in particular encouraged the start of planning at Steinberg's: the company's entry into capital markets in 1953. Months before it floated its first bond issue (stock, always nonvoting, came later), Sam Steinberg boasted to a newspaper reporter that "not a cent of any money outside the family is invested in the company." And asked about future plans, he replied: "Who knows? We will try to go everywhere there seems to be a need for us." A few months later he announced a $5 million debt issue and with it a $15 million five-year expansion program, one new store every two months for a total of thirty, the doubling of sales, new stores to average double the size of existing ones.

What happened in those ensuing months was Sam Steinberg's realization, after the opening of Montreal's first shopping center, that he needed to enter the shopping center business himself to protect his supermarket chain and that he could not do so with the company's traditional methods of short-term and internal financing. And, of course, no company is allowed to go to capital markets without a plan. You can't just say: "I'm Sam Steinberg and I'm good," though that was really the issue. In a "rational" society, you have to plan (or at least appear to do so).

But what exactly was that planning? One thing for certain: It did not formulate a strategy. Sam Steinberg already had that. What planning did was justify, elaborate, and articulate the strategy that already existed in Sam Steinberg's mind. Planning operationalized his strategic vision, programmed it. It gave order to that vision, imposing form on it to comply with the needs of the organization and its environment. Thus, planning followed the strategy-making process, which had been essentially entrepreneurial.

But its effect on that process was not incidental. By specifying and articulating the vision, planning constrained it and rendered it less flexible. Sam Steinberg retained formal control of the company to the day of his death. But his control over strategy did not remain so absolute. The entrepreneur, by keeping his vision personal, is able to adapt it at will to a changing environment. But by being forced to program it, the leader loses that flexibility. The danger, ultimately, is that the planning mode forces out the entrepreneurial one; procedure replaces vision. As its structure became more machinelike, Steinberg's required planning in the form of strategic programming. But that planning also accelerated the firm's transition toward the machine form of organization.

Is there, then, such a thing as "strategic planning"? I suspect not. To be more explicit, I do not find that major new strategies are formulated through any formal procedure. Organizations that rely on formal planning procedures to formulate strategies seem to extrapolate existing strategies, perhaps with marginal changes in them, or else copy the strategies of other organizations. This came out most clearly in another of our McGill studies.

Planning as an Impediment to Strategic Thinking in an Airline

From about the mid-1950s, Air Canada engaged heavily in planning. Once the airline was established, particularly once it developed its basic route structure, a number of factors drove it strongly to the planning mode. Above all was the need for coordination, both of flight schedules with aircraft, crews, and maintenance, and of the purchase of expensive aircraft with the structure of the route system. (Imagine someone calling out in the hangar: "Hey, Fred, this guy says he has two 747s for us; do you know who ordered them?") Safety was another factor: The intense need for safety in the air breeds a mentality of being very careful about what the organization does on the ground, too. This is the airlines' obsession with control. Other factors included the lead times inherent in key decisions, such as ordering new airplanes or introducing new routes, the sheer cost of the capital equipment, and the size of the organization. You don't run an intricate system like an airline, necessarily very machinelike, without a great deal of formal planning.

But what we found to be the consequence of planning at Air Canada was the absence of a major reorientation of strategy during our study period (up to the mid-1970s). Aircraft certainly changed—they became larger and faster—but the basic route system did not, nor did markets. Air Canada gave only marginal attention, for example, to cargo, charter, and shuttle operations. Formal planning, in our view, impeded strategic thinking.

The problem is that planning, too, proceeds from the machine perspective, much as an assembly line or a conventional machine produces a product. It all depends on the decomposition of analysis: You split the process into a series of steps or component parts, specify each, and then by following the specifications in sequence you get the desired product. There is a fallacy in this, however. Assembly lines and conventional machines produce standardized products, while planning is supposed to produce a novel strategy. It is as if the machine is supposed to design the machine; the planning machine is expected to create the original blueprint— the strategy. To put this another way, planning is analysis oriented to decomposition, while strategy making depends on synthesis oriented to integration. That is why the term "strategic planning" has proved to be an oxymoron.

Roles of Planning, Plans, Planners

If planning does not create strategy, then what purpose does it serve? We have suggested a role above, which has to do with the programming of strategies already created in other ways. This is shown in Figure 2, coming out of a box labeled strategy formation— meant to represent what is to planning a mysterious "black box." But if planning is restricted to programming strategy, plans and planners nonetheless have other roles in play, shown in Figure 2 and discussed alongside that of planning itself.

FIGURE 2
Specific Roles of Planning, Plans, Planners

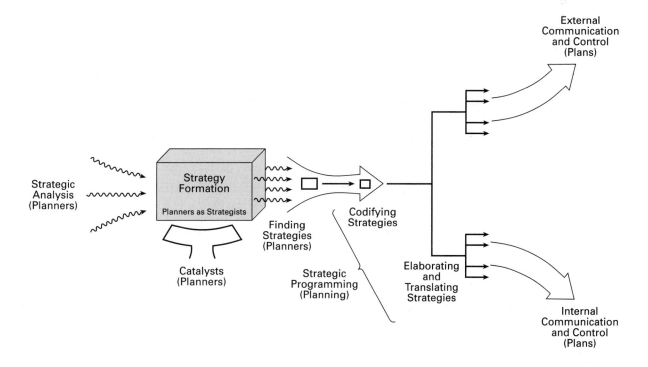

ROLE OF PLANNING. Why do organizations engage in formal planning? The answer seems to be: not to create strategies, but to program the strategies they already have, that is, to elaborate and operationalize the consequences of those strategies formally. We should really say that *effective* organizations so engage in planning, at least when they require the formalized implementation of their strategies. Thus strategy is not the *consequence* of planning but its starting point. Planning helps to translate the intended strategies into realized ones, taking the first step that leads ultimately to implementation.

This *strategic programming,* as it might properly be labeled, can be considered to involve a series of steps, namely the *codification* of given strategy, including its clarification and articulation, the *elaboration* of that strategy into substrategies, ad hoc action programs, and plans of various kinds, and the *translation* of those substrategies, programs, and plans into routine budgets and objectives. In these steps, we see planning as an analytical process that takes over after the synthesis of strategic formation is completed.

Thus formal planning properly belongs in the *implementation* of strategy, not in its formulation. But it should be emphasized that strategic programming makes sense when viable intended strategies are available, in other words when the world is expected to hold still while these strategies unfold, so that formulation can logically precede implementation, and when the organization that does the implementing in fact requires clearly codified and elaborated strategies. In other circumstances, strategic programming can do organizations harm by preempting the flexibility that managers and others may need to respond to changes in the environment, or to their own internal processes of learning.

ROLES OF PLANS. If planning is programming, then plans clearly serve two roles. They are a medium for communication and a device for control. Both roles draw on the analytical character of plans, namely, that they represent strategies in decomposed and articulated form, if not quantified then often at least quantifiable.

Why program strategy? Most obviously for coordination, to ensure that everyone in the organization pulls in the same direction, a direction that may have to be specified as precisely as possible. In Air Canada, to use our earlier example, that means linking the acquisition of new aircraft with the particular routes that are to be flown, and scheduling crews and planes to show up when the flights are to take off, and so on. Plans, as they emerge from strategic programming as programs, schedules, budgets, and so on, can be prime media to communicate not just strategic intention but also the role each individual must play to realize it.

Plans, as communication media, inform people of intended strategy and its consequences. But as control devices they can go further, specifying what role departments and individuals must play in helping to realize strategy and then comparing that with performance in order to feed control information back into the strategy-making process.

Plans can help to effect control in a number of ways. The most obvious is control of the strategy itself. Indeed what has long paraded under the label of "strategy planning" has probably had more to do with "strategic control" than many people may realize. Strategic control has to do with keeping organizations on their strategic tracks: to ensure the realization of intended strategy, its implementation as expected, with resources appropriately allocated. But there is more to strategic control than this. Another aspect includes the assessment of the realization of strategies in the first place, namely, whether the patterns realized corresponded to the intentions specified beforehand. In other words, strategic control must assess behavior as well as performance. Then the more routine and traditional form of control can come in to consider whether the strategies that were in fact realized proved effective.

ROLES OF PLANNERS. Planners, of course, play key roles in planning (namely, strategic programming), and in using the resulting plans for purposes of communication and control. But many of the most important things planners do have little to do with planning or even plans per se. Three roles seem key here.

First, planners can play a role in finding strategies. This may seem curious, but if strategies really do emerge in organizations, then planners can help to identify the patterns that are becoming strategies, so that consideration can be given to formalizing them, that is, making them deliberate. Of course, finding the strategies of competitors—for assessment and possible modified adoption—is also important here.

Second, planners play the roles of analysts, carrying out ad hoc studies to feed into the black box of strategy making. Indeed, one could argue that this is precisely what Michael Porter proposes with his emphasis on industry and competitive analysis. The ad hoc nature of such studies should, however, be emphasized because they feed into a strategy-making process that is itself irregular, proceeding on no schedule and following no standard sequence of steps. Indeed, regularity in the planning process can interfere with strategic thinking, which must be flexible, responsive, and creative.

The third role of the planner is as a catalyst. This refers not to the traditional role long promoted in the literature of selling formal planning as some kind of religion, but to encourage strategic *thinking* throughout the organization. Here the planner encourages *informal* strategy making, trying to get others to think about the future in a creative way. He or she does not enter the block box of strategy making so much as ensure that the box is occupied with active line managers.

A PLANNER FOR EACH SIDE OF THE BRAIN. We have discussed various roles for planning, plans, and planners, summarized around the block box of strategy formation in Figure 2. These roles suggest two different orientations for planners.

On one hand (so to speak), the planner must be a highly analytic, convergent type of thinker, dedicated to bringing order to the organization. Above all, this planner programs intended strategies and sees to it that they are communicated clearly and used for purposes of control. He or she also carries out studies to ensure that the managers concerned with strategy formation take into account the necessary hard data that they may be inclined to miss and that the strategies they formulate are carefully and systematically evaluated before they are implemented.

On the other hand, there is another type of planner, less conventional a creative, divergent thinker, rather intuitive, who seeks to open up the strategy-making process. As a "soft analyst," he or she tends to conduct "quick and dirty" studies, to find strategies in strange places, and to encourage others to think strategically. This planner is inclined toward the intuitive processes identified with the brain's right hemisphere. We might call him or her a *left-handed planner*. Some organizations need to emphasize one type of planner, others the other type. But most complex organizations probably need some of both.

Strategic Change in an Automobile Firm

Given planning itself is not strategic, how does the planning-oriented machine bureaucracy change its strategy when it has to? Volkswagenwerk was an organization that had to. We interpreted its history from 1934 to 1974 as one long cycle of a single strategic perspective. The original "people's car," the famous "Beetle," was conceived by Ferdinand Porsche; the factory to produce it was built just before the war but did not go into civilian automobile production until after. In 1948, a man named Heinrich Nordhoff was given control of the devastated plant and began the rebuilding of it, as well as of the organization and the strategy itself, rounding out Porsche's original conception. The firm's success was dramatic.

By the late 1950s, however, problems began to appear. Demand in Germany was moving away from the Beetle. The typically machine-bureaucratic response was not to rethink the basic strategy—"it's okay" was the reaction—but rather to graft another piece onto it. A new automobile model was added, larger than the Beetle but with a similar no-nonsense approach to motoring, again air-cooled with the engine in the back. Volkswagenwerk added position but did not change perspective.

But that did not solve the basic problem, and by the mid-1960s the company was in crisis. Nordhoff, who had resisted strategic change, died in office and was replaced by a lawyer from outside the business. The company then underwent a frantic search for new models, designing, developing, or acquiring a whole host of them with engines in the front, middle, and rear; air and water cooled; front- and rear-wheel drive. To paraphrase the humorist Stephen Leacock, Volkswagenwerk leaped onto its strategic horse and rode off in all directions. Only when another leader came in, a man steeped in the company and the automobile business, did the firm consolidate itself around a new strategic perspective, based on the stylish front-wheel drive, water-cooled designs of one of its acquired firms, and thereby turn its fortunes around.

What this story suggests, first of all, is the great force of bureaucratic momentum in the machine organization. Even leaving planning aside, the immense effort of producing and marketing a new line of automobiles locks a company into a certain posture. But here the momentum was psychological, too. Nordhoff, who had been the driving force behind the great success of the organization, became a major liability when the environment demanded change. Over the years, he too had been captured by bureaucratic momentum. Moreover, the uniqueness and tight integration of Volkswagenwerk's strategy—we labeled it *gestalt*—impeded strategic change. Change an element of a tightly integrated gestalt and it *dis*integrates. Thus does success eventually breed failure.

Bottleneck at the Top

Why the great difficulty in changing strategy in the machine organization? Here we take up that question and show how changes generally have to be achieved in a different configuration, if at all.

As discussed earlier, unanticipated problems in the machine organization tend to get bumped up the hierarchy. When these are few, which means conditions are relatively stable, things work smoothly enough. But in times of rapid change, just when new strategies are called for, the number of such problems magnifies, resulting in a bottleneck at the top, where senior managers get overloaded. And that tends either to impede strategic change or else to render it ill considered.

A major part of the problem is information. Senior managers face an organization decomposed into parts, like a machine itself. Marketing information comes up one channel, manufacturing information up another, and so on. Somehow it is the senior managers themselves who must integrate all that information. But the very machine bureaucratic premise of separating the administration of work from the doing of it means that the top managers often lack the intimate, detailed knowledge of issues necessary to effect such an integration. In essence, the necessary power is at the top of the structure, but the necessary knowledge is often at the bottom.

Of course, there is a machinelike solution to that problem too—not surprisingly in the form of a system. It is called a management information system, or MIS, and what it does is combine all the necessary information and package it neatly so that top managers can be informed about what is going on—the perfect solution for the overloaded executive. At least in theory.

Unfortunately, a number of real-world problems arise in the MIS. For one thing, in the tall administrative hierarchy of the machine organization, information must pass through many levels before it reaches the top. Losses take place in each one. Good news gets highlighted while bad news gets blocked on the way up. And "soft" information, so necessary for strategy information, cannot easily pass through, while much of the hard MIS-type information arrives only slowly. In a stable environment, the manager may be able to wait; in a rapidly changing one, he or she cannot. The president wants to be told right away that the firm's most important customer was seen playing golf yesterday with a main competitor, not to find out six months later in the form of a drop in a sales report. Gossip, hearsay, speculation—the softest kinds of information—warn the manager of impeding problems; the MIS all too often records for posterity ones that have already been felt. The manager who depends on an MIS in a changing environment generally finds himself or herself out of touch.

The obvious solution for top managers is to bypass the MIS and set up their own informal information systems, networks of contacts that bring them the rich, tangible, instant information they need. But that violates the machine organization's presuppositions of formality and respect for the chain of authority. Also, this takes the managers' time, the lack of which caused the bottleneck in the first place. So a fundamental dilemma faces the top managers of the machine organization a result of its very own design: in times of change, when they most need the time to inform themselves, the system overburdens them with other pressures. They are thus reduced to acting superficially, with inadequate, abstract information.

The Formulation/Implementation Dichotomy

The essential problem lies in one of the chief tenets of the machine organization, that strategy formation must be sharply separated from strategy implementation. One is thought out at the top, the other then acted out lower down. For this to work assume two conditions: first, that the formulator has full and sufficient information, and second, that the world will hold still, or at least change in predictable ways, during the implementation, so that there is no need for *re*formulation.

Now consider why the organization needs a new strategy in the first place. It is because its world has changed in an unpredictable way, indeed may continue to do so. We have just seen how the machine bureaucratic structure tends to violate the first condition—it misinforms the senior manager during such times of change. And when change continues in an unpredictable way (or at least the world unfolds in a way not yet predicted by an ill-informed management), then the second condition is violated too—it hardly makes sense to lock in by implementation a strategy that does not reflect changes in the world around it.

What all this amounts to is a need to collapse the formulation/implementation dichotomy precisely when the strategy of machine bureaucracy must be changed. This can be done in one of two ways.

In one case, the formulator implements. In other words, power is concentrated at the top, not only for creating the strategy but also for implementing it, step by step, in a personalized way. The strategist is put in close personal touch with the situation at hand (more commonly a strategist is appointed who has or can develop that touch) so that he or she can, on one hand, be properly informed and, on the other, control the implementation en route in order to reformulate when necessary. This, of course, describes the entrepreneurial configuration, at least at the strategic apex.

In the other case, the implementers formulate. In other words, power is concentrated lower down, where the necessary information resides. As people who are naturally in touch with the specific situations at hand take individual actions—approach new customers, develop new products, et cetera—patterns form, in other words, strategies emerge. And this describes the innovative configuration, where strategic initiatives often originate in the grass roots of the organization, and then are championed by managers at middle levels who integrate them with one another or with existing strategies in order to gain their acceptance by senior management.

We conclude, therefore, that the machine configuration is ill suited to change its fundamental strategy, that the organization must in effect change configuration temporarily in order to change strategy. Either it reverts to the entrepreneurial form, to allow a single leader to develop vision (or proceed with one developed earlier), or else it overlays an innovative form on its conventional structure (for example, creates an informed network of lateral teams and task forces) so that the necessary strategies can emerge. The former can obviously function faster than the latter; that is why it tends to be used for drastic *turnaround,* while the latter tends to proceed by the slower process of *revitalization.* (Of course, quick turnaround may be necessary because there has been no slow revitalization.) In any event, both are characterized by a capacity to *learn*—that is the essence of the entrepreneurial and innovative configurations, in one case learning centralized for the simpler context, in the other, decentralized for the more complex one. The machine configuration is not so characterized.

This, however, should come as no surprise. After all, machines are specialized instruments, designed for productivity, not for adaptation. In Hunt's (1970) words, machine bureaucracies are performance systems, not problem-solving ones. Efficiency is their forte, not innovation. An organization cannot put blinders on its personnel and then expect peripheral vision. Managers here are rewarded for cutting costs and improving standards, not for taking risks and ignoring procedures. Change makes a mess of the operating systems: change one link in a carefully coupled system, and the whole chain must be reconceived. Why, then, should we be surprised when our bureaucratic machines fail to adapt?

Of course, it is fair to ask why we spend so much time trying to make them adapt. After all, when an ordinary machine becomes redundant, we simply scrap it, happy that it served us for as long and as well as it did. Converting it to another use generally proves more expensive than simply starting over. I suspect the same is often true for bureaucratic machines. But here, of course, the context is social and political. Mechanical parts don't protest, nor do displaced raw materials. Workers, suppliers, and customers do, however, protest the scrapping of organizations, for obvious reasons. But that the cost of this is awfully high in a society of giant machine organizations will be the subject of the final chapter of this book.

Strategic Revolutions in Machine Organizations

Machine organizations do sometimes change, however, at times effectively but more often it would seem at great cost and pain. The lucky ones are able to overlay an innovative structure for periodic revitalization, while many of the other survivors somehow manage to get turned around in entrepreneurial fashion.

Overall, the machine organizations seem to follow what my colleagues Danny Miller and Peter Friesen (1984) call a "quantum theory" of organization change. They pursue their set strategies through long periods of stability (naturally occurring or created by themselves as closed systems), using planning and other procedures to do so efficiently. Periodically these are interrupted by short bursts of change, which Miller and Friesen characterize as "strategic revolutions" (although another colleague, Mihaela Firsirotu [1985], perhaps better labels it "strategic turnaround as cultural revolution").

Organization Taking Precedence in the Machine Organization

To conclude, as shown in Figure 3, it is organization—with its systems and procedures, its planning and its bureaucratic momentum—that takes precedence over leadership and environment in the machine configuration. Environment fits organization, either because the organization has slotted itself into a context that matches its procedures, or else because it has forced the environment to do so. And leadership generally falls into

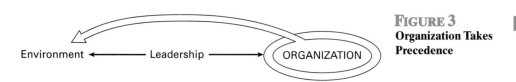

FIGURE 3
Organization Takes
Precedence

271
STRUCTURE AND
STRATEGY IN MATURE
ORGANIZATIONS

place too, supporting the organization, indeed often becoming part of its bureaucratic momentum.

This generally works effectively, though hardly nonproblematically, at least in times of stability. But in times of change, efficiency becomes ineffective and the organization will falter unless it can find a different way to organize for adaptation.

All of this is another way of saying that the machine organization is a configuration, a species, like the others, suited to its own context but ill suited to others. But unlike the others, it is the dominant configuration in our specialized societies. As long as we demand inexpensive and so necessarily standardized goods and services, and as long as people continue to be more efficient than real machines at providing them, and remain willing to do so, then the machine organization will remain with us—and so will all its problems.

THE TRANSITION TO INDUSTRY MATURITY

READING

By Michael E. Porter

As part of their evolutionary process, many industries pass from periods of rapid growth to the more modest growth of what is commonly called industry maturity. . . . industry maturity does not occur at any fixed point in an industry's development, and it can be delayed by innovations or other events that fuel continued growth for industry participants. Moreover, in response to strategic breakthroughs, mature industries may regain their rapid growth and thereby go through more than one transition to maturity. With these important qualifications in mind, however, let us consider the case in which a transition to maturity is occurring. . . . .

INDUSTRY CHANGE DURING TRANSITION

Transition to maturity can often signal a number of important changes in an industry's competitive environment. Some of the probable tendencies for change are as follows:

1. *Slowing growth means more competition for market share.* With companies unable to maintain historical growth rates merely by holding market share, competitive attention turns inward toward attacking the shares of the others. . . . Not only are competitors probably going to be more aggressive, but also the likelihood of misperceptions and "irrational" retaliation is great. Outbreaks of price, service, and promotional warfare are common during transition to maturity.

2. *Firms in the industry increasingly are selling to experienced, repeat buyers.* The product is no longer new but an established legitimate item. Buyers are often increasingly knowledgeable and experienced, having already purchased the product, sometimes repeatedly. The buyers' focus shifts from deciding whether to purchase the product at all to making choices among brands. Approaching these differently oriented buyers requires a fundamental reassessment of strategy.

Excerpted from *Competitive Strategy: Techniques for Analyzing Industries and Competitors,* by Michael E. Porter. Copyright © by The Free Press, a division of Macmillan, Inc.; reprinted by permission of the publisher.

3. *Competition often shifts toward greater emphasis on cost and service.* As a result of slower growth, more knowledgeable buyers, and usually greater technological maturity, competition tends to become more cost and service-oriented. . . .

4. *There is a topping-out problem in adding industry capacity and personnel.* As the industry adjusts to slower growth, the rate of capacity addition in the industry must slow down as well or overcapacity will occur. . . . [But the necessary] shifts in perspective rarely occur in maturing industries, and overshooting of industry capacity relative to demand is common. Overshooting leads to a period of overcapacity, accentuating the tendency during transition toward price warfare. . . .

5. *Manufacturing, marketing, distributing, selling, and research methods are often undergoing change.* These changes are caused by increased competition for market share, technological maturity, and buyer sophistication. . . .

6. *New products and applications are harder to come by.* Whereas the growth phase may have been one of rapid discovery of new products and applications, the ability to continue product change generally becomes increasingly limited, or the costs and risks greatly increase, as the industry matures. This change requires, among other things, a reorientation of attitude toward research and new product development.

7. *International competition increases.* As a consequence of technological maturity, often accompanied by product standardization and increasing emphasis on costs, transition is often marked by the emergence of significant international competition. . . .

8. *Industry profits often fall during the transition period, sometimes temporarily and sometimes permanently.* Slowing growth, more sophisticated buyers, more emphasis on market share, and the uncertainties and difficulties of the required strategic changes usually mean that industry profits fall in the short run from the levels of the pre-transition growth phase. . . . Whether or not profits will rebound depends on the level of mobility barriers and other elements of industry structure. . . .

9. *Dealers' margins fall, but their power increases.* For the same reasons that industry profits are often depressed, dealers' margins may be squeezed, and many dealers may drop out of business—often *before* the effect on manufacturers' profits is noticeable. . . . Such trends tighten competition among industry participants for dealers, who may have been easy to find and hold in the growth phase but not upon maturity. Thus, dealers' power may increase markedly.

SOME STRATEGIC IMPLICATIONS OF TRANSITION

. . . Some characteristic strategic issues often arise in transition. These are presented as issues to examine rather than generalizations that will apply to all industries; like humans, all industries mature a little differently. Many of these approaches can be a basis for the entry of new firms into an industry even though it is mature.

Overall Cost Leadership versus Differentiate versus Focus— The Strategic Dilemma Made Acute by Maturity

Rapid growth tends to mask strategic errors and allow most, if not all, companies in the industry to survive and even to prosper financially. Strategic experimentation is high, and a wide variety of strategies can coexist. Strategic sloppiness is generally exposed by industry maturity, however. Maturity may force companies to confront, often for the first time, the need to choose among the three generic strategies described (in Chapter 4 of this text). It becomes a matter of survival.

Sophisticated Cost Analysis

Cost analysis becomes increasingly important in maturity to (1) rationalize the product mix and (2) price correctly.

RATIONALIZING THE PRODUCT MIX. . . . a quantum improvement in the sophistication of product costing is necessary to allow pruning of unprofitable items from the line and to focus attention on items either that have some distinctive advantage (technology, cost, image, etc.) or whose buyers are "good" buyers. . . .

CORRECT PRICING. Related to product line rationalization is the change in pricing methodology that is often necessary in maturity. Although average-cost pricing, or pricing the line as a whole rather than as individual items, may have been sufficient in the growth era, maturity often requires increased capability to measure costs on individual items and to price accordingly. . . .

We might summarize this and the other points in this section by saying that an enhanced level of "financial consciousness" along a variety of dimensions is often necessary in maturity, whereas in the developmental period of the industry areas such as new products and research may have rightly held center stage. . . .

Process Innovation and Design for Manufacture

The relative importance of process innovations usually increases in maturity, as does the payoff for designing the product and its delivery system to facilitate lower-cost manufacturing and control. . . .

INCREASING SCOPE OF PURCHASES. Increasing purchases of existing customers may be more desirable than seeking new customers. . . . Such a strategy may take the firm out of the industry into related industries. This strategy is often less costly than finding new customers. In a mature industry, winning new customers usually means battling for market share with competitors and is consequently quite expensive. . . .

Buy Cheap Assets

Sometimes assets can be acquired very cheaply as a result of the company distress that is caused by transition to maturity. A strategy of acquiring distressed companies or buying liquidated assets can improve margins and create a low-cost position if the rate of technological change is not too great. . . .

Buyer Selection

As buyers become more knowledgeable and competitive pressures increase in maturity, buyer selection can sometimes be a key to continued profitability. Buyers who may not have exercised their bargaining power in the past, or had less power because of limited product availability, will usually not be bashful about exercising their power in maturity. Identifying "good" buyers and locking them in . . . becomes crucial.

Different Cost Curves

There is often more than one cost curve possible in an industry. The firm that is *not* the overall cost leader in a mature market can sometimes find new cost curves which may actually make it a lower-cost producer for certain types of buyers, product varieties, or order sizes. This step is key to implementing the generic strategy of focus. . . .

Competing Internationally

A firm may escape maturity by competing internationally where the industry is more favorably structured. Sometimes equipment that is obsolete in the home market can be used quite effectively in international markets, greatly lowering the costs of entry there. . . .

STRATEGIC PITFALLS IN TRANSITION

In addition to failure to recognize the strategic implications of transition described above, there is the tendency for firms to fall prey to some characteristic strategic pitfalls:

1. *A company's self-perceptions and its perception of the industry.* Companies develop perceptions or images of themselves and their relative capabilities ("we are the quality leader"; "we provide superior customer service"), which are reflected in the implicit assumptions that form the basis of their strategies. . . . These self-perceptions may be increasingly inaccurate as transition proceeds, buyers' priorities adjust, and competitors respond to new industry conditions. Similarly, firms have assumptions about the industry, competitors, buyers, and suppliers which may be invalidated by transition. Yet altering these assumptions, built up through actual past experience, is sometimes a difficult process.

2. *Caught in the middle.* The problem of being caught in the middle described [earlier] is particularly acute in transition to maturity. Transition often squeezes out the slack that has made this strategy viable in the past.

3. *The cash trap—investments to build share in a mature market.* Cash should be invested in a business only with the expectation of being able to remove it later. In a mature, slow-growing industry, the assumptions required to justify investing new cash in order to build market share are often heroic. Maturity of the industry works against increasing or maintaining margins long enough to recoup cash investments down the road, by making the present value of cash inflows justify the outflows. Thus businesses in maturity can be cash traps, particularly when a firm is not in a strong market position but is attempting to build a large market share in a maturing market. The odds are against it.

A related pitfall is placing heavy attention on revenues in the maturing market instead of on profitability. This strategy may have been desirable in the growth phase, but it usually faces diminishing returns in maturity. . . .

4. *Giving up market share too easily in favor of short-run profits.* In the face of the profit pressures in transition, there seems to be a tendency for some companies to try to maintain the profitability of the recent past—which is done at the expense of market share or by foregoing marketing, R&D, and other needed investments, which in turn hurts future market position. . . . A period of lower profits may be inevitable while industry rationalization occurs, and a cool head is necessary to avoid overreaction.

5. *Resentment and irrational reaction to price competition* (*"we will not compete on price"*). It is often difficult for firms to accept the need for price competition after a period in which it has not been necessary. . . .

6. *Resentment and irrational reaction to changes in industry practices* (*"they are hurting the industry"*). Changes in industry practices, such as marketing techniques, production methods, and the nature of distributor contracts are often an inevitable part of transition. They may be important to the industry's long-run potential, but there is often resistance to them. . . .

7. *Overemphasis on "creative," "new" products rather than improving and aggressively selling existing ones.* Although past success in the early and growth phases of an industry may have been built on research and on new products, the onset of maturity often

means that new products and applications are harder to come by. It is usually appropriate that the focus of innovative activity should change, putting standardization rather than newness and fine tuning at a premium. Yet this development is not satisfying to some companies and is often resisted.

8. *Clinging to "higher quality" as an excuse for not meeting aggressive pricing and marketing moves of competitors.* High quality can be a crucial company strength, but quality differentials have a tendency to erode as an industry matures. . . . Yet it is difficult for many companies to accept the fact that they do not possess the highest-quality product or that their quality is unnecessarily high.

9. *Overhanging excess capacity.* As a result of capacity overshooting demand, or because of capacity increases that inevitably accompany the plant modernization required to compete in the mature industry, some firms may have some excess capacity. Its mere presence creates both subtle and unsubtle pressures to utilize it, and it can be used in ways that will undermine the firm's strategy. . . .

STRUCTURE AND STRATEGY IN PROFESSIONAL AND INNOVATIVE ORGANIZATIONS

▼

In this chapter we examine how strategy forms in two types of organizations—professional organizations and innovative organizations—that are similar in two ways but very different in most other ways. One similarity is in the kind of people who work in them, namely professionally trained experts. The other is in the nature of their work, which is very complex. Despite these seemingly important similarities, what goes on in these two types of organizational forms differs greatly. For example, their typical strategy formation processes are quite different. Most aspects of organizational structure differ between the two, as do the prime coordination mechanisms. Innovation seldom occurs in one, often in the other, and so on. Let us start with an examination of the professional organization and its typical strategy process.

THE PROFESSIONAL ORGANIZATION

Structure

Mintzberg's reading, "The Professional Organization," covers the structural and strategy formation aspects of the professional organization in detail. In this part of the chapter we touch on only the points that merit greater emphasis. Examples of professional organizations are hospitals or other large medical practices, law firms, accounting firms, and universities. The most important part of professional organizations like these are their operating cores, which are populated by highly trained professionals, such as physicians, lawyers, certified public accountants, and professors.

Professionals rely for coordination on the similarity (Mintzberg calls it the standardization) of their skills.[1] This standardization results from their extensive training, be it in medical school, law school, university accounting programs, or doctoral study. This is usually supplemented by on-the-job training and indoctrination. Mintzberg points out that other forms of standardization do not work easily in professional organizations because the work is too complex to be standardized by analysts; outputs of professionals cannot be easily measured; and direct supervision and mutual adjustment impede professional autonomy.

277

STRUCTURE AND
STRATEGY IN
PROFESSIONAL AND
INNOVATIVE
ORGANIZATIONS

The work of the professionals in the professional organization becomes patterned into **pigeonholing**.[2] In effect the professional organization is a set of standard programs—a repertoire of professional skills—applied to known situations, called contingencies. Professionals have two main tasks—to diagnose the contingency and to execute the program. In other words, the professional must put a problem in the right pigeonhole and then select the correct standardized skill program to handle it, much as doctors diagnose their patients or universities put students into set programs. The machine organization, as we saw earlier, is a single-purpose structure. By contrast, the professional organization applies more varied programs, but in a circumscribed way. It is typically found in complex yet stable situations, since unstable ones require more fully open-ended diagnosis, as we shall see with no programming.

Strategy

The prescriptive strategy models are almost totally at odds with what really seems to happen in professional organizations. However, if one considers strategy as a pattern in a stream of action over time, then strategy certainly forms in professional organizations. The real questions in this kind of organization are "Which actions?" and "What processes?"

With regard to the first of these questions, Mintzberg argues that the most important strategy making in any organization deals with the elaboration of the basic mission. In a professional organization, the central mission is the provision of the profession's basic services. In a law firm, this would be legal representation; in a university, it would be education and research, and so on for other kinds of professional organizations. This idea, combined with the earlier discussion of structure and work in professional organizations, points to a critical realization—elaboration of the basic mission is significantly controlled by *individual professionals*. Other aspects of strategy making in professional organizations (e.g., resource inputs, governance) can be partially controlled by professionals as well, along with administrators.

With respect to the process question, Mintzberg's reading describes three ways that strategies may form in professional organizations. The first is when **decisions are made by professional judgment**, as in the elaboration of the basic mission, discussed above. The second is when the leadership makes **decisions by administrative fiat**, which is usually restricted to issues not directly related to professional work. Most support services are like this, for example, the construction of a new parking garage on a university campus. The third way in which strategies form in professional organizations is when **decisions are made by collective choice**, whether collegially, through common interest,[3] or politically through self-interest.

The result of these different processes is "disconnected" strategy, with "members or subunits loosely coupled to the rest of the organization [producing] patterns in the streams of their own actions in the absence of, or in direct contradiction to, the central or common intentions of the organization at large."[4] Several of the ideas expressed in this quotation fit well with the conditions found in professional organizations. "Members or subunits loosely coupled to the rest of the organization" is, as Weick has pointed out,[5] an apt description of how professionals relate to the organizations they populate. For example, each senior partner in a large law or accounting firm may have his or her own set of clients. In a large university, professors in the departments of philosophy and English hardly ever need to coordinate their efforts. The next thought, producing "patterns in the streams of their own actions," is a result of the autonomy of professionals. The law and accounting partners mentioned above may be providing services that are coherent and steady over time, even though they are not connected to

anything else that goes on in the firm. The professors may well develop teaching and research styles that are consistent over time, that is, a strategy. The other thought in the
Mintzberg quotation is that patterns are created "in the absence of . . . central or common intentions of the organization at large." The law or accounting firm may have only
the barest overall intended strategy, that is, to provide legal or accounting services.
Somehow, all the lawyers and accountants acting independently create a firm that provides good professional services to its clients. Similarly, the university may not elaborate
its espoused goal beyond saying that it provides high-quality education.

Most of the strategy processes that Mintzberg discussed in Chapter One are centrally coordinated in some way. Planned strategy is controlled by formal processes.
Entrepreneurial strategy is integrated inside the mind of a visionary individual.
Ideological strategy emanates from a strongly held culture. Umbrella and process
strategies, although "deliberately emergent," are channeled or directed by the articulation of acceptable boundaries or the manipulation of processes, respectively. Even consensus strategy, the hallmark of the innovative organization (which we will discuss
below) uses mutual adjustment to gain general agreement about how to proceed.
Disconnected strategy has no central coordinating force. In a sense, it is "additive"—
add up what all the professionals are doing, and you have the strategy of the organization. The question becomes, can patterns exist in such an organizational environment?
The short answer is, yes.

First, although the process of strategy making may be different from what it is in
other types of organizations, professional organizations are inundated with strategies,
that is, with patterns in streams of action. Second, this occurs despite the disconnected
nature of the professional strategy process, because many forces in professional organizations promote the formation even of common patterns. For example, standardization
of skills encourages patterning based on similarity of skill or trained outlook.
Collegiality promotes consistency of behavior. Even politics can work to resist changes
in existing patterns.[6] Although many people are involved in the strategy-making
process, there are forces that encourage strategic cohesion: the centralized forces of administrative fiat; the broad negotiations of collective action; and the forces of habit, tradition, and ideology, all of which can be strong in professional organizations.

Despite the prevalence of disconnected strategy, strategies in professional organizations are fairly stable. The fragmentation of activity and the influence of the individual professionals and their outside associations are forces that discourage strategic
revolutions. However, smaller, more focused changes happen constantly—new contingencies, new programs, new clients, new pigeonholes. The result is an interesting paradox: The professional organization is stable at the broadest level and constantly
changing at the narrowest one.

We turn now to the other kind of organization that is heavily populated by experts,
but whose strategy process is strikingly different—the innovative organization.

THE INNOVATIVE ORGANIZATION

Structure

The second reading by Mintzberg in this chapter, "The Innovative Organization," describes in detail this organizational configuration and its typical strategy process. Here,
we will cover the most important points about this organizational form capable of sophisticated innovation. Entrepreneurial organizations can innovate but only in simple
ways. The machine organization and the professional organization are performance-,

not innovative-, oriented. For sophisticated innovation we need *adhocracies,* to borrow a term from Bennis and Slater[7] which Mintzberg calls innovative organizations.

279

STRUCTURE AND
STRATEGY IN
PROFESSIONAL AND
INNOVATIVE
ORGANIZATIONS

The innovative organization is a configuration with a distinctive blend of design parameters. It has a highly organic structure, little formalization, and specialized jobs based on expert training (but not as autonomous and independent as the ones in the professional organization). It has functional grouping for "housekeeping," for example, billing clients, but small project teams for the work itself. This latter characteristic is one major distinction with the professional organization, which has few teams for the operating work but many independent professionals.

Mutual adjustment is the key coordinating mechanism in the adhocracy. None of the four kinds of standardization can be relied upon because standardization drives out innovation. Direct supervision, which works well in the entrepreneurial organization, cannot be used because the work is too complex. In other words, people on the project teams need to talk to each other and work together on problems. The experts in this configuration coordinate in ways that allow the combining of their skills and expertise. Lastly, there is considerable decentralization to the teams, in contrast to the individual decentralization of the professional organization. This allows power over decisions to flow to those with the information to make them—the experts.

Mintzberg points out that there are two kinds of adhocracies. In some industries, there is a split between the basic work done by the organization's operating core and the administrative work. The operating work might be routine and, therefore, be best handled by a typical machine organization. But the industry might be dynamic and complex, so that tasks like new product development might better be done with an adhocracy. A good example would be a large biotechnology company. Producing large quantities of pharmaceuticals using biotechnology is very routine, employing large vats in a rigidly controlled process. Biotechnological production is best done by a machine organization. By contrast, the science behind biotechnology is complex and constantly changing. The administration of the research end of the biotechnology industry would therefore better be handled with an adhocracy. He calls this an **administrative adhocracy**.

In other industries and organizations, the adhocracy innovates and solves problems *directly* for its clients. This is called an **operating adhocracy**. Here, administrative and operating work tend to blend into a single effort. Examples of this are design firms, film companies, creative consulting firms, big project organizations (e.g., to put on an Olympic Games), and some (usually smaller) software development firms.

Strategy

As stated above, adhocracies try to create novel solutions. They do this by trying to understand client needs and then meeting those needs by organizing into multidisciplinary, skill-blending teams. A good model for understanding how this is done is the **horizontal linkage model**.[8] It has three components. First, the key departments of Research and Development (R&D), Marketing, and Production each become highly *specialized* within their own discipline. This maximizes the expertise of the members of each department. Second, they must *span organizational boundaries* by linking to the relevant elements of the firm's environment. For R&D this would be the technical developments occurring in their field. For Marketing it would be customer needs. Third, to complete the connections, the technical, production, and marketing people must *horizontally link* by sharing knowledge and ideas. Research people let marketing people know about interesting developments in technology, to see if there might be some potential for commercialization. Marketing people let research people know about customer problems, to see if there are any developments in technology that might solve them. Both have to link with production to test the manufacturing feasibility of product ideas, or to find ways to improve product quality.

The horizontal linkage model applies best to the innovative organization, and it has three key elements—expertise, deep understanding of customer needs, and flexible internal organization to speed response to those needs. These elements give clues about the nature of strategy formation in innovative organizations. Innovative organizations cannot rely on deliberate strategy; their actions must be decided upon individually, according to the needs of the moment. They cannot rely excessively on action planning, because, as we have seen in earlier chapters, those tend to separate thinking from action. That would severely impede the flexibility of the organization to respond creatively to its complex and dynamic environment. How, then, does strategy form in innovative organizations?

The fundamental characteristic of strategy in innovative organizations is that it is *emergent*. But there are three variations on this emergent theme, discussed in the "crafting strategy" reading in Chapter Five. The "purest" is **consensus strategy,** which occurs when "through mutual adjustment, various members converge on patterns that pervade the organization in the absence of central or common intentions."[9] In the horizontal linkage example, the members of the three departments would use their knowledge of customer needs and technology to suggest possible solutions to those needs. There would be disagreements about the effectiveness of those solutions, so the team members would "mutually adjust"; that is, they would argue about how best to combine their expertise for the client's benefit. After a while, they would agree on the proper approach. Consensus strategy in its purest form is likely to be found in small operating adhocracies.

Two other kinds of strategy processes that are likely to exist in larger firms that subdivide into smaller, innovative operating units. These are **umbrella strategy** and **process strategy**. In umbrella strategy, "a leadership in partial control of organizational actions defines strategic targets or boundaries within which others must act. . . ; as a result, strategies are partly deliberate . . . and partly emergent; this strategy can also be called deliberately emergent, in that the leadership purposefully allows others the flexibility to maneuver and form patterns within the boundaries."[10] Process strategy works in a similar way, except that the leadership sets the boundaries less explicitly, using organizational processes, such as hiring, structure, and reward systems, to control how the strategy "deliberately emerges." Another way of thinking about umbrella and process strategy is that consensus strategy is allowed to take place, but in a more "confined" way than in the pure form discussed first.

MANAGING INNOVATION: CONTROLLED CHAOS

Umbrella and process strategies may well be the waves of the future. Larger firms that wish to become more innovative can use them very profitably. First, the firm subdivides itself into many smaller units, each with an adhocracy structure. Second, the firm's corporate level articulates a strategic umbrella, or a set of controls processes, to channel strategic activity in the firm. Third, this allows the small, innovative units' strategies to emerge. Lastly, the units converge on streams of action that seem to make the most sense.

James Brian Quinn, in an article called "Managing Innovation: Controlled Chaos,"[11] discusses how large firms that have been successful with this approach have done it. First, they create the proper **atmosphere and vision**, that is, an umbrella. They manage their company's value system and atmosphere to support innovation. Innovative managements project clear long-term visions for their organizations that go beyond simple economic measures. In an example of process strategy, they attract quality people to the company and give focus to their creative and entrepreneurial drives. They channel growth by concentrating attention on profitable actions.

Second, successful large-scale innovators have an **orientation to the market**, tying

281

STRUCTURE AND
STRATEGY IN
PROFESSIONAL AND
INNOVATIVE
ORGANIZATIONS

their visions to the practical realities of the marketplace. Even at the very top of the company, they have a strong market orientation as well as mechanisms to ensure inter-actions between technical and marketing people at lower levels (that is, they use the horizontal linkage model). Third, these kinds of firms prefer **flat organizations** and small units, trying to restrict the total number of levels and the number of people on project teams. They also try to keep their operating divisions and total technical units small. Fourth, they use **multiple approaches**. No one can be sure which of several approaches will dominate a field, because technologies advance in "accidents." Innovative enter-prises move quickly from paper studies to physical testing, encouraging several proto-types to proceed in parallel.

Fifth, successful large-scale innovators often use **developmental "shoot-outs,"** competitions among prototypes. This practice provides more objective information, de-creases risk, and helps ensure that winning options move ahead with committed teams. The sixth tool of such firms is the **skunkworks**, which are small teams of engineers, tech-nicians, designers, and model makers hidden in pockets for developing new products from idea to commercial prototype with minimal restrictions. These are, in other words, adhocracies. They speed communication and experimentation, and instill a high level of group identity and loyalty.

Lastly, they employ **interactive learning**, a point we made earlier in Chapter Five in discussing the learning school of strategy. What this means is that large innovative companies draw upon multiple outside sources of technology, including their cus-tomers' capabilities. They try to form closer relationships with customers, even with competitors—joint ventures, consortia, and partnerships.

Designing the Large Firm for Innovation

Quinn also discusses how other firms may set up their structures and processes to take advantage of adhocracy's benefits. They can cultivate **an opportunity orientation**; that is, let employees know that if they come up with good ideas, the firms will find the nec-essary capital. Management can also **structure the firm for innovation** by thinking care-fully about how innovation fits with its technology, skills, resources, and organizational commitments. Firms can engage in **complex portfolio planning** —to allocate resources strategically for innovation, management needs to define the broad, long-term actions necessary within and across divisions.

NOTES TO CHAPTER ELEVEN

1. Spencer, F. C, "Deductive Reasoning in the Lifelong Continuing Education of a Cardiovascular Surgeon." *Archives of Surgery* (1976), 1177–83.
2. Weick, K. E., "Educational Organizations as Loosely Coupled Systems." *Administrative Science Quarterly* (1976), 1–19.
3. Taylor, W. H., "The Nature of Policy Making in Universities." *The Canadian Journal of Higher Education* (1983), pp. 17–32.
4. Mintzberg, H., "Five Ps for Strategy" in Chapter One.
5. Weick, "Educational Organizations as Loosely Coupled Systems."
6. Pfeffer, J., *Power in Organizations.* Marshfield, Mass.: Pitman, 1982.
7. Bennis, W. G., and P. Slater, *The Temporary Society.* New York: Harper & Row, 1964.
8. Daft, R. L., *Organization Theory and Design,* 4th ed. St Paul: West Publishing, 1992, pp. 262–63.
9. Mintzberg, H., "Five Ps for Strategy" in Chapter One.
10. Ibid.
11. This section draws heavily from Quinn, J. B., "Managing Innovation: Controlled Chaos." *Harvard Business Review* (May–June 1985).

THE PROFESSIONAL ORGANIZATION

By Henry Mintzberg

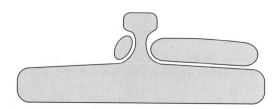

THE BASIC STRUCTURE

An organization can be bureaucratic without being centralized. This happens when its work is complex, requiring that it be carried out and controlled by professionals, yet at the same time remains stable, so that the skills of those professionals can be perfected through standardized operating programs. The structure takes on the form of *professional* bureaucracy, which is common in universities, general hospitals, public accounting firms, social work agencies, and firms doing fairly routine engineering or craft work. All rely on the skills and knowledge of their operating professionals to function; all produce standardized products or services.

The Work of the Professional Operators

Here again we have a tightly knit configuration of the attributes of structure. Most important, the professional organization relies for coordination on the standardization of skills, which is achieved primarily through formal training. It hires duly trained specialists—professionals—for the operating core, then gives them considerable control over their own work.

Control over their work means that professionals work relatively independently of their colleagues but closely with the clients they serve—doctors treating their own patients and accountants who maintain personal contact with the companies whose books they audit. Most of the necessary coordination among the operating professionals is then handled automatically by their set skills and knowledge—in effect, by what they have learned to expect from each other. During an operation as long and as complex as open-heart surgery, "very little needs to be said [between the anesthesiologist and the surgeon] preceding chest opening and during the procedure on the heart itself . . . [most of the operation is] performed in absolute silence" (Gosselin, 1978). The point is perhaps best made in reverse by the cartoon that shows six surgeons standing around a patient on an operating table with one saying, "Who opens?"

Just how standardized the complex work of professionals can be is illustrated in a paper read by Spencer before a meeting of the International Cardiovascular Society. Spencer notes that an important feature of surgical training is "repetitive practice" to evoke "an automatic reflex." So automatic, in fact, that this doctor keeps a series of surgical "cookbooks" in which he lists, even for "complex" operations, the essential steps

Adapted from The Structuring of Organizations (Prentice Hall, 1979), Chap. 19 on "The Professional Bureaucracy"; also Power In and Around Organizations (Prentice Hall, 1983), Chap. 22 on "The Meritocracy"; the material on strategy formation from "Strategy Formation in the University Setting," coauthored with Cynthia Hardy, Ann Langley, and Janet Rose, in J. L. Bess (ed.) College and University Organization (New York University Press, 1984). A chapter similar to this one appeared in Mintzberg on Management: Inside Our Strange World of Organizations (Free Press, 1989).

as chains of thirty to forty symbols on a single sheet, to "be reviewed mentally in sixty to 120 seconds at some time during the day preceding the operation" (1976:1179, 1182).

283

STRUCTURE AND
STRATEGY IN
PROFESSIONAL AND
INNOVATIVE
ORGANIZATIONS

But no matter how standardized the knowledge and skills, their complexity ensures that considerable discretion remains in their application. No two professionals—no two surgeons or engineers or social workers—ever apply them in exactly the same way. Many judgments are required.

Training, reinforced by indoctrination, is a complicated affair in the professional organization. The initial training typically takes place over a period of years in a university or special institution, during which the skills and knowledge of the profession are formally programmed into the students. There typically follows a long period of on-the-job training, such as internship in medicine or articling in accounting, where the formal knowledge is applied and the practice of skills perfected. On-the-job training also completes the process of indoctrination, which began during the formal education. As new knowledge is generated and new skills develop, of course (so it is hoped) the professional upgrades his or her expertise.

All that training is geared to one goal, the internalization of the set procedures, which is what makes the structure technically bureaucratic (structure defined earlier as relying on standardization for coordination). But the professional bureaucracy differs markedly from the machine bureaucracy. Whereas the latter generates its own standards—through its technostructure, enforced by its line managers—many of the standards of the professional bureaucracy originate outside its own structure, in the self-governing associations its professionals belong to with their colleagues from other institutions. These associations set universal standards, which they ensure are taught by the universities and are used by all the organizations practicing the profession. So whereas the machine bureaucracy relies on authority of a hierarchical nature—the power of office—the professional bureaucracy emphasizes authority of a professional nature—the power of expertise.

Other forms of standardization are, in fact, difficult to rely on in the professional organization. The work processes themselves are too complex to be standardized directly by analysts. One need only try to imagine a work-study analyst following a cardiologist on rounds or timing the activities of a teacher in a classroom. Similarly, the outputs of professional work cannot easily be measured and so do not lend themselves to standardization. Imagine a planner trying to define a cure in psychiatry, the amount of learning that takes place in a classroom, or the quality of an accountant's audit. Likewise, direct supervision and mutual adjustment cannot be relied upon for coordination, for both impede professional autonomy.

The Pigeonholing Process

To understand how the professional organization functions at the operating level, it is helpful to think of it as a set of standard programs—in effect, the repertoire of skills the professionals stand ready to use—that are applied to known situations, called contingencies, also standardized. As Weick notes of one case in point, "schools are in the business of building and maintaining categories" (1976:8). The process is sometimes known as *pigeonholing*. In this regard, the professional has two basic tasks: (1) to categorize, or "diagnose," the client's need in terms of one of the contingencies, which indicates which standard program to apply, and (2) to apply, or execute, that program. For example, the management consultant carries a bag of standard acronymic tricks: MBO, MIS, LRP, OD. The client with information needs gets MIS; the one with managerial conflicts, OD. Such pigeonholing, of course, simplifies matters enormously; it is also what enables each professional to work in a relatively autonomous manner.

It is in the pigeonholing process that the fundamental differences among the machine organization, the professional organization, and the innovative organization (to be discussed next) can best be seen. The machine organization is a single-purpose structure. Presented with a stimulus, it executes its one standard sequence of programs, just as we kick when tapped on the knee. No diagnosis is involved. In the professional organization, diagnosis is a fundamental task, but one highly circumscribed. The organization seeks to match a predetermined contingency to a standardized program. Fully open-ended diagnosis—that which seeks a creative solution to a unique problem—requires the innovative form of organization. No standard contingencies or programs can be relied upon there.

The Administrative Structure

Everything we have discussed so far suggests that the operating core is the key part of the professional organization. The only other part that is fully elaborated is the support staff, but that is focused very much on serving the activities of the operating core. Given the high cost of the professionals, it makes sense to back them up with as much support as possible. Thus, universities have printing facilities, faculty clubs, alma mater funds, publishing houses, archives, libraries, computer facilities, and many, many other support units.

The technostructure and middle-line management are not highly elaborated in the professional organization. They can do little to coordinate the professional work. Moreover, with so little need for direct supervision of, or mutual adjustment among, the professionals, the operating units can be very large. For example, the McGill Faculty of Management functions effectively with 50 professors under a single manager, its dean, and the rest of the university's academic hierarchy is likewise thin.

Thus, the diagram at the beginning of this chapter shows the professional organization, in terms of our logo, as a flat structure with a thin middle line, a tiny technostructure, but a fully elaborated support staff. All these characteristics are reflected in the organigram of a university hospital, shown in Figure 1.

Coordination within the administrative structure is another matter, however. Because these configurations are so decentralized, the professionals not only control their own work but they also gain much collective control over the administrative decisions that affect them—decisions, for example, to hire colleagues, to promote them, and to distribute resources. This they do partly by doing some of the administrative work themselves (most university professors, for example, sit on various administrative committees) and partly by ensuring that important administrative posts are staffed by professionals or at least sympathetic people appointed with the professionals' blessing. What emerges, therefore, is a rather democratic administrative structure. But because the administrative work requires mutual adjustment for coordination among the various people involved, task forces and especially standing committees abound at this level, as is in fact suggested in Figure 1.

Because of the power of their professional operators, these organizations are sometimes described as inverse pyramids, with the professional operators on top and the administrators down below to serve them—to ensure that the surgical facilities are kept clean and the classrooms well supplied with chalk. Such a description slights the power of the administrators of professional work, however, although it may be an accurate description of those who manage the support units. For the support staff—often more numerous than the professional staff, but generally less skilled—there is no democracy in the professional organization, only the oligarchy of the professionals. Such support units as housekeeping in the hospital or printing in the university are likely to be managed tightly from the top, in effect as machinelike enclaves within the professional configuration. Thus, what frequently emerges in the professional organization are parallel and separate administrative hierarchies, one democratic and bottom-up for the professionals, a second machinelike and top-down for the support staff.

FIGURE 1

Organization of a University Hospital

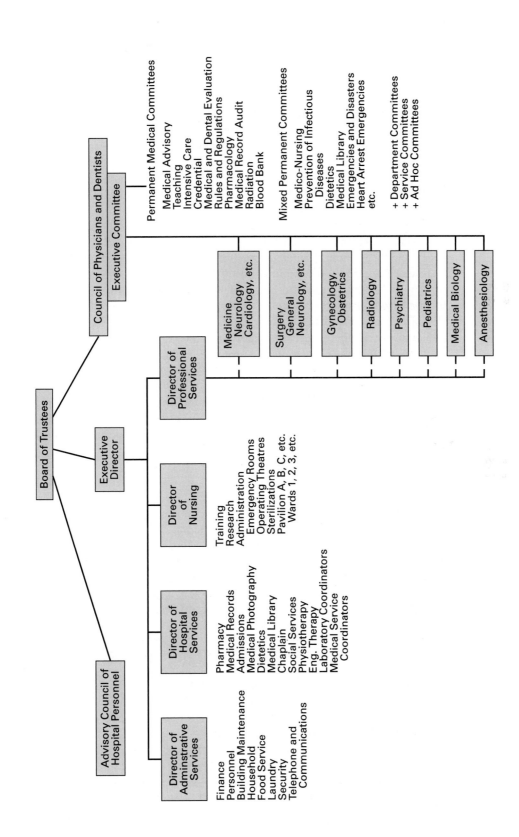

The Roles of the Administrators of Professional Work

Where does all this leave the administrators of the professional hierarchy, the executive directors and chiefs of the hospitals and the presidents and deans of the universities? Are they powerless? Compared with their counterparts in the entrepreneurial and machine organizations, they certainly lack a good deal of power. But that is far from the whole story. The administrator of professional work may not be able to control the professionals directly, but he or she does perform a series of roles that can provide considerable indirect power.

First, this administrator spends much time handling disturbances in the structure. The pigeonholing process is an imperfect one at best, leading to all kinds of jurisdictional disputes between the professionals. Who should perform mastectomies in the hospitals, surgeons who look after cutting or gynecologists who look after women? Seldom, however, can one administrator impose a solution on the professionals involved in a dispute. Rather, various administrators must often sit down together and negotiate a solution on behalf of their constituencies.

Second, the administrators of professional work—especially those at higher levels—serve in key roles at the boundary of the organization, between the professionals inside and the influencers outside: governments, client associations, benefactors, and so on. On the one hand, the administrators are expected to protect the professionals' autonomy, to "buffer" them from external pressures. On the other hand, they are expected to woo those outsiders to support the organization, both morally and financially. And that often leads the outsiders to expect these administrators, in turn, to control the professionals, in machine bureaucratic ways. Thus, the external roles of the manager—maintaining liaison contacts, acting as figurehead and spokesman in a public relations capacity, negotiating with outside agencies—emerge as primary ones in the administration of professional work.

Some view the roles these administrators are called upon to perform as signs of weakness. They see these people as the errand boys of the professionals, or else as pawns caught in various tugs of war—between one professional and another, between support staffer and professional, between outsider and professional. In fact, however, these roles are the very sources of administrators' power. Power is, after all, gained at the locus of uncertainty, and that is exactly where the administrators of professionals sit. The administrator who succeeds in raising extra funds for his or her organization gains a say in how they are distributed; the one who can reconcile conflicts in favor of his or her unit or who can effectively buffer the professionals from external influence becomes a valued, and therefore powerful, member of the organization.

We can conclude that power in these structures does flow to those professionals who care to devote effort to doing administrative instead of professional work, so long as they do it well. But that, it should be stressed, is not laissez-faire power; the professional administrator maintains power only as long as the professionals perceive him or her to be serving their interests effectively.

CONDITIONS OF THE PROFESSIONAL ORGANIZATION

The professional form of organization appears wherever the operating work of an organization is dominated by skilled workers who use procedures that are difficult to learn yet are well defined. This means a situation that is both complex and stable—complex enough to require procedures that can be learned only through extensive training yet stable enough so that their use can become standardized.

Note that an elaborate technical system can work against this configuration. If highly regulating or automated, the professionals' skills might be amenable to rational-

287

STRUCTURE AND
STRATEGY IN
PROFESSIONAL AND
INNOVATIVE
ORGANIZATIONS

ization, in other words, to be divided into simple, highly programmed steps that would destroy the basis for professional autonomy and thereby drive the structure to the machine form. And if highly complicated, the technical system would reduce the professionals' autonomy by forcing them to work in multidisciplinary teams, thereby driving the organization toward the innovative form. Thus the surgeon uses a scalpel, and the accountant a pencil. Both must be sharp, but both are otherwise simple and commonplace instruments. Yet both allow their users to perform independently what can be exceedingly complex functions.

The prime example of the professional configuration is the personal-service organization, at least the one with complex, stable work not reliant on a fancy technical system. Schools and universities, consulting firms, law and accounting offices, and social work agencies all rely on this form of organization, more or less, so long as they concentrate not on innovating in the solution of new problems but on applying standard programs to well-defined ones. The same seems to be true of hospitals, at least to the extent that their technical systems are simple. (In those areas that call for more sophisticated equipment—apparently a growing number, especially in teaching institutions—the hospital is driven toward a hybrid structure, with characteristics of the innovative form. But this tendency is mitigated by the hospital's overriding concern with safety. Only the tried and true can be relied upon, which produces a natural aversion to the looser innovative configuration.)

So far, our examples have come from the service sector. But the professional form can be found in manufacturing too, where the above conditions hold up. Such is the case of the craft enterprise, for example the factory using skilled workers to produce ceramic products. The very term *craftsman* implies a kind of professional who learns traditional skills through long apprentice training and then is allowed to practice them free of direct supervision. Craft enterprises seem typically to have few administrators, who tend to work, in any event, alongside the operating personnel. The same would seem to be true for engineering work oriented not to creative design so much as to modification of existing dominant designs.

STRATEGY FORMATION IN THE PROFESSIONAL ORGANIZATION

It is commonly assumed that strategies are formulated before they are implemented, that planning is the central process of formulation, and that structures must be designed to implement these strategies. At least this is what one reads in the conventional literature of strategic management. In the professional organization, these imperatives stand almost totally at odds with what really happens, leading to the conclusion either that such organizations are confused about how to make strategy, or else that the strategy writers are confused about how professional organizations must function. I subscribe to the latter explanation.

Using the definition of strategy as pattern in action, strategy formation in the professional organization takes on a new meaning. Rather than simply throwing up our hands at its resistance to formal strategic planning, or, at the other extreme, dismissing professional organizations as "organized anarchies" with strategy-making processes as mere "garbage cans" (March and Olsen, 1976) we can focus on how decisions and actions in such organizations order themselves into patterns over time.

Taking strategy as pattern in action, the obvious question becomes, which actions? The key area of strategy making in most organizations concerns the elaboration of the basic mission (the products or services offered to the public); in professional organizations, we shall argue, this is significantly controlled by individual professionals. Other important areas of strategy here include the inputs to the system (notably the choice of professional staff, the determination of clients, and the raising of external funds), the

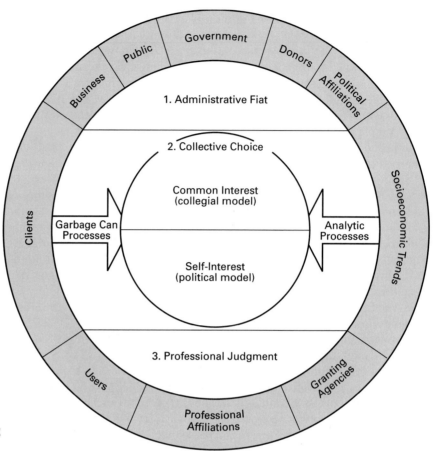

FIGURE 2
Three Levels of Decision Making in the Professional Organization

means to perform the mission (the construction of buildings and facilities, the purchase of research equipment, and so on), the structure and forms of governance (design of the committee system, the hierarchies, and so on), and the various means to support the mission.

Were professional organizations to formulate strategies in the conventional ways, central administrators would develop detailed and integrated plans about these issues. This sometimes happens, but in a very limited number of cases. Many strategic issues come under the direct control of individual professionals, while others can be decided neither by individual professionals nor by central administrators, but instead require the participation of a variety of people in a complex collective process. As illustrated in Figure 2, we examine in turn the decisions controlled by individual professionals, by central administrators, and by the collectivity.

Decisions Made by Professional Judgment

Professional organizations are distinguished by the fact that the determination of the basic mission—the specific services to be offered and to whom—is in good part left to the judgment of professionals as individuals. In the university, for example, each professor has a good deal of control over what is taught and how, as well as what is researched and how. Thus the overall product-market strategy of McGill University must be seen as the composite of the individual teaching and research postures of its 1,200 professors.

That, however, does not quite constitute full autonomy, because there is a subtle but not insignificant constraint on that power. Professionals are left to decide on their own only because years of training have ensured that they will decide in ways generally accepted in their professions. Thus professors choose course contents and adopt teaching methods highly regarded by their colleagues, sometimes even formally sanctioned by their disciplines; they research subjects that will be funded by the granting agencies (which usually come under professional controls); and they publish articles acceptable to the journals referred by their peers. Pushed to the limit, then, individual freedom becomes professional control. It may be explicit freedom from administrators, even from peers in other disciplines, but it is not implicit freedom from colleagues in their own discipline. Thus we use the label "professional judgment" to imply that while judgment may be the mode of choice, it is informed judgment, mightily influenced by professional training and affiliation.

289

STRUCTURE AND
STRATEGY IN
PROFESSIONAL AND
INNOVATIVE
ORGANIZATIONS

Decisions Made by Administrative Fiat

Professional expertise and autonomy, reinforced by the pigeonholing process, sharply circumscribe the capacity of central administrators to manage the professionals in the ways of conventional bureaucracy—through direct supervision and the designation of internal standards (rules, job descriptions, policies). Even the designation of standards of output or performance is discouraged by the intractable problem of operationalizing the goals of professional work.

Certain types of decisions, less related to the professional work per se, do however fall into the realm of what can be called administrative fiat, in other words, become the exclusive prerogative of the administrators. They include some financial decisions, for example, to buy and sell property and embark on fund-raising campaigns. Because many of the support services are organized in a conventional top-down hierarchy, they too tend to fall under the control of the central administration. Support services more critical to professional matters, however, such as libraries or computers in the universities, tend to fall into the realm of collective decision making, where the central administrators join the professionals in the making of choices.

Central administrators may also play a prominent role in determining the procedures by which the collective process functions: what committees exist, who gets nominated to them, and so on. It is the administrators, after all, who have the time to devote to administration. This role can give skillful administrators considerable influence, however indirect, over the decisions made by others. In addition, in times of crisis administrators may acquire more extensive powers, as the professionals become more inclined to defer to leadership to resolve the issues.

Decisions Made by Collective Choice

Many decisions are, however, determined neither by administrators nor by individual professionals. Instead they are handled in interactive processes that combine professionals with administrators from a variety of levels and units. Among the most important of these decisions seem to be ones related to the definition, creation, design, and discontinuation of the pigeonholes, that is, the programs and departments of various kinds. Other important decisions here include the hiring and promotion of professionals and, in some cases, budgeting and the establishment and design of the interactive procedures themselves (if they do not fall under administrative fiat).

Decision making may be considered to involve the three phases of *identification* of the need for a decision, *development* of solutions, and *selection* of one of them. Identification seems to depend largely on individual initiative. Given the complexities of professional work and the rigidities of pigeonholing, change in this configuration is difficult to imagine without an initiating "sponsor" or "champion." Development may involve the same individual but often requires the efforts of collective task forces as well. And selection tends to be a fully interactive process, involving several layers of standing committees composed of professionals and administrators, and sometimes outsiders as well (such as government representatives). It is in this last phase that we find the full impact and complexity of mutual adjustment in the administration of professional organizations.

Models of Collective Choice

How do these interactive processes in fact work? Some writers have traditionally associated professional organizations with a *collegial* model, where decisions are made by a "community of individuals and groups, all of whom may have different roles and specialties, but who share common goals and objectives for the organization" (Taylor, 1983:18). *Common interest* is the guiding force, and decision making is therefore by consensus. Other writers instead propose a political model, in which the differences of interest groups are irreconcilable. Participants thus seek to serve their *self-interest,* and political factors become instrumental in determining outcomes.

Clearly, neither common interest nor self-interest will dominate decision processes all the time; some combination is naturally to be expected. Professionals may agree on goals yet conflict over how they should be achieved; alternatively, consensus can sometimes be achieved even where goals differ—Democrats do, after all, sometimes vote with Republicans in the U.S. Congress. In fact, we need to consider motivation, not just behavior, in order to distinguish collegiality from politics. Political success sometimes requires a collegial posture—one must cloak self-interest in the mantle of the common good. Likewise, collegial ends sometimes require political means. Thus, we should take as collegial any behavior that is *motivated* by a genuine concern for the good of the institution, and politics as any behavior driven fundamentally by self-interest (of the individual or his or her unit).

A third model that has been used to explain decision making in universities is the *garbage can.* Here decision making is characterized by "collections of choices looking for problems, issues and feelings looking for decision situations in which they may be aired, solutions looking for issues to which they might be an answer, and decision makers looking for work" (Cohen, March, and Olsen, 1972:1). Behavior is, in other words, nonpurposeful and often random, because goals are unclear and the means to achieve them problematic. Furthermore, participation is fluid because of the cost of time and energy. Thus, in place of the common interest of the collegial model and the self-interest of the political model, the garbage can model suggests a kind of *disinterest.*

The important question is not whether garbage can processes exist—we have all experienced them—but whether they matter. Do they apply to key issues or only to incidental ones? Of course, decisions that are not significant to anyone may well end up in the garbage can, so to speak. There is always someone with free time willing to challenge a proposal for the sake of so doing. But I have difficulty accepting that individuals to whom decisions are important do not invest the effort necessary to influence them. Thus, like common interest and self-interest, I conclude that disinterest neither dominates decision processes nor is absent from them.

Finally, *analysis* may be considered a fourth model of decision making. Here calculation is used, if not to select the best alternative, then at least to assess the acceptability of different ones. Such an approach seems consistent with the machine configuration, where a technostructure stands ready to calculate the costs and benefits of every proposal. But, in fact, analysis figures prominently in the professional configuration too, but here carried out mostly by professional operators themselves. Rational analysis structures arguments for communication and debate and enables champions and their opponents to support their respective positions. In fact, as each side seeks to pick holes in the position of the other, the real issues are more likely to emerge.

Thus, as indicated in Figure 2, the important collective decisions of the professional organization seem to be most influenced by collegial and political processes, with garbage can pressures encouraging a kind of haphazardness on one side (especially for less important decisions) and analytical interventions on the other side encouraging a certain rationality (serving as an invisible hand to keep the lid on the garbage can, so to speak!).

291

STRUCTURE AND
STRATEGY IN
PROFESSIONAL AND
INNOVATIVE
ORGANIZATIONS

Strategies in the Professional Organization

Thus, we find here a very different process of strategy making, and very different resulting strategies, compared with conventional (especially machine) organizations. While it may seem difficult to create strategies in these organizations, due to the fragmentation of activity, the politics, and the garbage can phenomenon, in fact the professional organization is inundated with strategies (meaning patterning in its actions). The standardization of skills encourages patterning, as do the pigeonholing process and the professional affiliations. Collegiality promotes consistency of behavior; even politics works to resist changing existing patterns. As for the garbage can model, perhaps it just represents the unexplained variance in the system; that is, whatever is not understood looks to the outside observer like organized anarchy.

Many different people get involved in the strategy-making process here, including administrators and the various professionals, individually and collectively, so that the resulting strategies can be very fragmented (at the limit, each professional pursues his or her own product-market strategy). There are, of course, forces that encourage some overall cohesion in strategy too: the common forces of administrative fiat, the broad negotiations that take place in the collective process (for example, on new tenure regulations in a university), even the forces of habit and tradition, at the limit ideology, that can pervade a professional organization (such as hiring certain kinds of people or favoring certain styles of teaching or of surgery).

Overall, the strategies of the professional organization tend to exhibit a remarkable degree of stability. Major reorientations in strategy—"strategic revolutions"—are discouraged by the fragmentation of activity and the influence of the individual professionals and their outside associates. But at a narrower level, change is ubiquitous. Inside tiny pigeonholes, services are continually being altered, procedure redesigned, and clientele shifted, while in the collective process, pigeonholes are constantly being added and rearranged. Thus, the professional organization is, paradoxically, extremely stable at the broadest level and in a state of perpetual change at the narrowest one.

SOME ISSUES ASSOCIATED WITH THE PROFESSIONAL ORGANIZATION

The professional organization is unique among the different configurations in answering two of the paramount needs of contemporary men and women. It is democratic, disseminating its power directly to its workers (at least those lucky enough to be professional). And it provides them with extensive autonomy, freeing them even from the need to coordinate closely with their colleagues. Thus, the professional has the best of both worlds. He or she is attached to an organization yet is free to serve clients in his or her own way, constrained only by the established standards of the profession.

The result is that professionals tend to emerge as highly motivated individuals, dedicated to their work and to the clients they serve. Unlike the machine organization, which places barriers between the operator and the client, this configuration removes them, allowing a personal relationship to develop. Moreover, autonomy enables the professionals to perfect their skills free of interference, as they repeat the same complex programs time after time.

But in these same characteristics, democracy and autonomy, lie the chief problems of the professional organization. For there is no evident way to control the work, outside of that exercised by the profession itself, no way to correct deficiencies that the professionals choose to overlook. What they tend to overlook are the problems of coordination, of discretion, and of innovation that arise in these configurations.

Problems of Coordination

The professional organization can coordinate effectively in its operating core only by relying on the standardization of skills. But that is a loose coordinating mechanism at best; it fails to cope with many of the needs that arise in these organizations. One need is to coordinate the work of professionals with that of support staffers. The professionals want to give the orders. But that can catch the support staffers between the vertical power of line authority and the horizontal power of professional expertise. Another need is to achieve overriding coordination among the professionals themselves. Professional organizations, at the limit, may be viewed as collections of independent individuals who come together only to draw on common resources and support services. Though the pigeonholing process facilitates this, some things inevitably fall through the cracks between the pigeonholes. But because the professional organization lacks any obvious coordinating mechanism to deal with these, they inevitably provoke a great deal of conflict. Much political blood is spilled in the continual reassessment of contingencies and programs that are either imperfectly conceived or artificially distinguished.

Problems of Discretion

Pigeonholing raises another serious problem. It focuses most of the discretion in the hands of single professionals, whose complex skills, no matter how standardized, require the exercise of considerable judgment. Such discretion works fine when professionals are competent and conscientious. But it plays havoc when they are not. Inevitably, some professionals are simply lazy or incompetent. Others confuse the needs of their clients with the skills of their trade. They thus concentrate on a favored program to the exclusion of all others (like the psychiatrist who thinks that all patients, indeed all people, need psychoanalysis). Clients incorrectly sent their way get mistreated (in both senses of that word).

Various factors confound efforts to deal with this inversion of means and ends. One is that professionals are notoriously reluctant to act against their own, for example, to censure irresponsible behavior through their professional associations. Another (which perhaps helps to explain the first) is the intrinsic difficulty of measuring the outputs of professional work. When psychiatrists cannot even define the words *cure* or *healthy,* how are they to prove that psychoanalysis is better for schizophrenics than is chemical therapy?

Discretion allows professionals to ignore not only the needs of their clients but also those of the organization itself. Many professionals focus their loyalty on their profession, not on the place where they happen to practice it. But professional organizations have needs for loyalty too—to support their overall strategies, to staff their administrative committees, to see them through conflicts with the professional associations. Cooperation is crucial to the functioning of the administrative structure, yet many professionals resist it furiously.

Problems of Innovation

In the professional organization, major innovation also depends on cooperation. Existing programs may be perfected by the single professional, but new ones usually cut across the established specialties—in essence, they require a rearrangement of the pigeonholes—and so call for collective action. As a result, the reluctance of the professionals to cooperate with each other and the complexity of the collective processes can produce resistance to innovation. These are, after all, professional *bureaucracies,* in essence, performance structures designed to perfect given programs in stable environments, not problem-solving structures to create new programs for unanticipated needs.

The problems of innovation in the professional organization find their roots in convergent thinking, in the deductive reasoning of the professional who sees the specific situation in terms of the general concept. That means new problems are forced into old pigeonholes, as is excellently illustrated in Spencer's comments: "All patients developing significant complications or death among our three hospitals . . . are reported to a central office with a narrative description of the sequence of events, with reports varying in length from a third to an entire page." And six to eight of these cases are discussed in the one-hour weekly "mortality-morbidity" conferences, including presentation of it by the surgeon and "questions and comments" by the audience (1978:1181). An "entire" page and ten minutes of discussion for a case with "significant complications"! Maybe that is enough to list the symptoms and slot them into pigeonholes. But it is hardly enough even to begin to think about creative solutions. As Lucy once told Charlie Brown, great art cannot be done in half an hour; it takes at least 45 minutes!

The fact is that great art and innovative problem solving require *inductive* reasoning—that is, the inference of the new general solution from the particular experience. And that kind of thinking is *divergent;* it breaks away from old routines or standards rather than perfecting existing ones. And that flies in the face of everything the professional organization is designed to do.

Public Responses to These Problems

What responses do the problems of coordination, discretion, and innovation evoke? Most commonly, those outside the profession see the problems as resulting from a lack of external control of the professional and the profession. So they do the obvious: try to control the work through other, more traditional means. One is direct supervision, which typically means imposing an intermediate level of supervision to watch over the professionals. But we already discussed why this cannot work for jobs that are complex. Another is to try to standardize the work or its outputs. But we also discussed why complex work cannot be formalized by rules, regulations, or measures of performance. All these types of controls really do, by transferring the responsibility for the service from the professional to the administrative structure, is destroy the effectiveness of the work. It is not the government that educates the student, not even the school system or the school itself; it is not the hospital that delivers the baby. These things are done by the individual professional. If that professional is incompetent, no plan or rule fashioned in the technostructure, no order from any administrator or government official, can ever make him or her competent. But such plans, rules, and orders can impede the competent professional from providing his or her service effectively.

Are there then no solutions for a society concerned about the performance of its professional organizations? Financial control of them and legislation against irresponsible professional behavior are obviously in order. But beyond that, solutions must grow from a recognition of professional work for what it is. Change in the professional organization does not *sweep* in from new administrators taking office to announce wide reforms, or from government officials intent on bringing the professionals under technocratic control. Rather, change *seeps* in through the slow process of changing the professionals—changing who enters the profession in the first place, what they learn in its professional schools (norms as well as skills and knowledge), and thereafter how they upgrade their skills. Where desired changes are resisted, society may be best off to call on its professionals' sense of public responsibility or, failing that, to bring pressure on the professional associations rather than on the professional bureaucracies.

293

STRUCTURE AND
STRATEGY IN
PROFESSIONAL AND
INNOVATIVE
ORGANIZATIONS

THE INNOVATIVE ORGANIZATION

By Henry Mintzberg

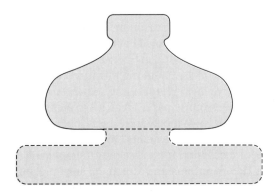

None of the organization forms so far discussed is capable of sophisticated innovation, the kind required of a high-technology research organization, an avant-garde film company, or a factory manufacturing complex prototypes. The entrepreneurial organization can certainly innovate, but only in relatively simple ways. The machine and professional organizations are performance, not problem-solving types, designed to perfect standardized programs, not to invent new ones. And although the diversified organization resolves some problem of strategic inflexibility found in the machine organization, as noted earlier it too is not a true innovator. A focus on control by standardizing outputs does not encourage innovation.

Sophisticated innovation requires a very different configuration, one that is able to fuse experts drawn from different disciplines into smoothly functioning ad hoc project teams. To borrow the word coined by Bennis and Slater in 1964 and later popularized in Alvin Toffler's *Future Shock* (1970), these are the *adhocracies* of our society.

THE BASIC STRUCTURE

Here again we have a distinct configuration of the attributes of design: highly organic structure, with little formalization of behavior; specialized jobs based on expert training; a tendency to group the specialists in functional units for housekeeping purposes but to deploy them in small project teams to do their work; a reliance on teams, on task forces, and on integrating managers of various sorts in order to encourage mutual adjustment, the key mechanism of coordination, within and between these teams; and considerable decentralization to and within these teams, which are located at various places in the organization and involve various mixtures of line managers and staff and operating experts.

To innovate means to break away from established patterns. Thus the innovative organization cannot rely on any form of standardization for coordination. In other words, it must avoid all the trappings of bureaucratic structure, notably sharp divisions

Adapted from The Structuring of Organizations (Prentice Hall, 1979), Chap. 21 on the adhocracy; on strategy formation from "Strategy Formation in an Adhocracy," coauthored with Alexandra McHugh, *Administrative Science Quarterly* (1985: 160–197), and "Strategy of Design: A Study of 'Architects in Co-Partnership,'" coauthored with Suzanne Otis, Jamal Shamsie, and James A. Waters, in J. Grant (ed.), *Strategic Management Frontiers* (JAI Press, 1988). A chapter similar to this one appeared in *Mintzberg on Management: Inside Our Strange World of Organizations* (Free Press, 1989).

of labor, extensive unit differentiation, highly formalized behaviors, and an emphasis on planning and control systems. Above all, it must remain flexible. A search for organigrams to illustrate this description elicited the following response from one corporation thought to have an adhocracy structure: "[W]e would prefer not to supply an organization chart, since it would change too quickly to serve any useful purpose." Of all the configurations, this one shows the least reverence for the classical principles of management, especially unity of command. Information and decision processes flow flexibly and informally, wherever they must, to promote innovation. And that means overriding the chain of authority if need be.

The entrepreneurial configuration also retains a flexible, organic structure, and so is likewise able to innovate. But that innovation is restricted to simple situations, ones easily comprehended by a single leader. Innovation of the sophisticated variety requires another kind of flexible structure, one that can draw together different forms of expertise. Thus the adhocracy must hire and give power to experts, people whose knowledge and skills have been highly developed in training programs. But unlike the professional organization, the adhocracy cannot rely on the standardized skills of its experts to achieve coordination, because that would discourage innovation. Rather, it must treat existing knowledge and skills as bases on which to combine and build new ones. Thus the adhocracy must break through the boundaries of conventional specialization and differentiation, which it does by assigning problems not to individual experts in preestablished pigeonholes but to multidisciplinary teams that merge their efforts. Each team forms around one specific project.

Despite organizing around market-based projects, the organization must still support and encourage particular types of specialized expertise. And so the adhocracy tends to use a matrix structure: Its experts are grouped in functional units for specialized housekeeping purposes—hiring, training, professional communication, and the like—but are then deployed in the project teams to carry out the basic work of innovation.

As for coordination in and between these project teams, as noted earlier standardization is precluded as a significant coordinating mechanism. The efforts must be innovative, not routine. So, too, is direct supervision precluded because of the complexity of the work: Coordination must be accomplished by those with the knowledge, namely the experts themselves, not those with just authority. That leaves just one of our coordinating mechanisms, mutual adjustment, which we consider foremost in adhocracy. And, to encourage this, the organization makes use of a whole set of liaison devices, liaison personnel and integrating managers of all kinds, in addition to the various teams and task forces.

The result is that managers abound in the adhocracy: functional managers, integrating managers, project managers. The last-named are particularly numerous, since the project teams must be small to encourage mutual adjustment among their members, and each, of course, needs a designated manager. The consequence is that "spans of control" found in adhocracy tend to be small. But the implication of this is misleading, because the term is suited to the machine, not the innovative configuration: The managers of adhocracy seldom "manage" in the usual sense of giving orders; instead, they spend a good deal of time acting in a liaison capacity, to coordinate the work laterally among the various teams and units.

With its reliance on highly trained experts, the adhocracy emerges as highly decentralized, in the "selective" sense. That means power over its decisions and actions is distributed to various places and at various levels according to the needs of the particular issue. In effect, power flows to wherever the relevant expertise happens to reside—among managers or specialists (or teams of those) in the line structure, the staff units, and the operating core.

To proceed with our discussion and to elaborate on how the innovative organization makes decisions and forms strategies, we need to distinguish two basic forms that it takes.

295

STRUCTURE AND
STRATEGY IN
PROFESSIONAL AND
INNOVATIVE
ORGANIZATIONS

The Operating Adhocracy

The *operating adhocracy* innovates and solves problems directly on behalf of its clients. Its multidisciplinary teams of experts often work under contract, as in the think-tank consulting firm, creative advertising agency, or manufacturer of engineering prototypes.

In fact, for every operating adhocracy, there is a corresponding professional bureaucracy, one that does similar work but with a narrower orientation. Faced with a client problem, the operating adhocracy engages in creative efforts to find a novel solution; the professional bureaucracy pigeonholes it into a known contingency to which it can apply a standard program. One engages in divergent thinking aimed at innovation, the other in convergent thinking aimed at perfection. Thus, one theater company might seek out new avant-garde plays to perform, while another might perfect its performance of Shakespeare year after year.

A key feature of the operating adhocracy is that its administrative and operating work tend to blend into a single effort. That is, in ad hoc project work it is difficult to separate the planning and design of the work from its execution. Both require the same spe-

FIGURE 1

The National Film Board of Canada: An Operating Adhocracy (circa 1975; used with permission)

* No lines shown on original organigram connecting Regional Programs to Studios or Filmmakers.

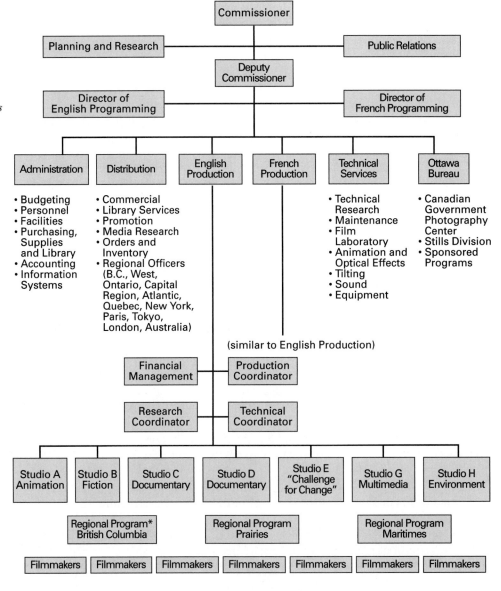

cialized skills, on a project-by-project basis. Thus it can be difficult to distinguish the middle levels of the organization from its operating core, since line managers and staff specialists may take their place alongside operating specialists on the project teams.

Figure 1 shows the organigram of the National Film Board of Canada, a classic operating adhocracy (even though it does produce a chart—one that changes frequently, it might be added). The Board is an agency of the Canadian federal government and produces mostly short films, many of them documentaries. At the time of this organigram, the characteristics of adhocracy were particularly in evidence: It shows a large number of support units as well as liaison positions (for example, research, technical, and production coordinators), with the operating core containing loose concurrent functional and market groupings, the latter by region as well as by type of film produced and, as can be seen, some not even connected to the line hierarchy!

The Administrative Adhocracy

The second type of adhocracy also functions with project teams, but toward a different end. Whereas the operating adhocracy undertakes projects to serve its clients, the *administrative adhocracy* undertakes projects to serve itself, to bring new facilities or activities on line, as in the administrative structure of a highly automated company. And in sharp contrast to the operating adhocracy, the administrative adhocracy makes a clear distinction between its administrative component and its operating core. That core is *truncated*—cut right off from the rest of the organization—so that the administrative component that remains can be structured as an adhocracy.

This truncation may take place in a number of ways. First, when the operations have to be machinelike and so could impede innovation in the administration (because of the associated need for control), it may be established as an independent organization. Second, the operating core may be done away with altogether—in effect, contracted out to other organizations. That leaves the organization free to concentrate on the development work, as did NASA during the Apollo project. A third form of truncation arises when the operating core becomes automated. This enables it to run itself, largely independent of the need for direct controls from the administrative component, leaving the latter free to structure itself as an adhocracy to bring new facilities on line or to modify old ones.

Oil companies, because of the high degree of automation of their production process, are in part at least drawn toward administrative adhocracy. Figure 2 shows the organigram for one oil company, reproduced exactly as presented by the company (except for modifications to mask its identity, done at the company's request). Note the domination of "Administration and Services," shown at the bottom of the chart; the operating functions, particularly "Production," are lost by comparison. Note also the description of the strategic apex in terms of standing committees instead of individual executives.

The Administrative Component of the Adhocracies

The important conclusion to be drawn from this discussion is that in both types of adhocracy the relation between the operating core and the administrative component is unlike that in any other configuration. In the administrative adhocracy, the operating core is truncated and becomes a relatively unimportant part of the organization; in the operating adhocracy, the two merge into a single entity. Either way, the need for traditional direct supervision is diminished, so managers derive their influence more from their expertise and interpersonal skills than from formal position. And that means the distinction between line and staff blurs. It no longer makes sense to distinguish those who have the formal power to decide from those who have only the informal right to ad-

297

STRUCTURE AND
STRATEGY IN
PROFESSIONAL AND
INNOVATIVE
ORGANIZATIONS

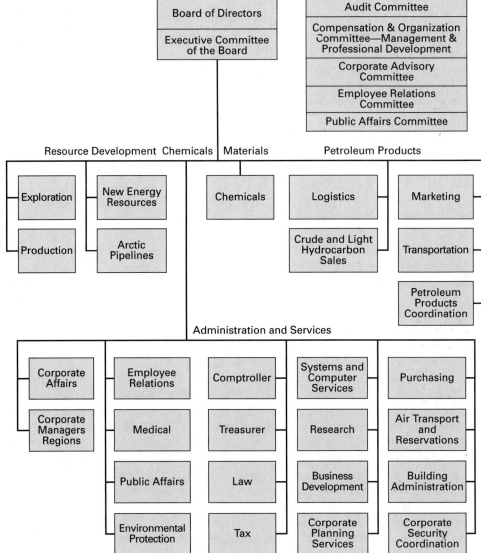

FIGURE 2
**Organigram of an Oil
Company: An
Administrative Adhocracy**

vise. Power over decision making in the adhocracy flows to anyone with the required expertise, regardless of position.

In fact, the support staff plays a key role in adhocracy, because that is where many of the experts reside (especially in administrative adhocracy). As suggested, however, that staff is not sharply differentiated from the other parts of the organization, not off to one side, to speak only when spoken to, as in the bureaucratic configurations. The other type of staff, however, the technostructure, is less important here, because the adhocracy does not rely for coordination on standards that it develops. Technostructure analysts may, of course, be used for some action planning and other forms of analysis—marketing research and economic forecasting, for example—but these analysts are as likely to take their place alongside the other specialists on the project teams as to stand back and design systems to control them.

To summarize, the administrative component of the adhocracy emerges as an organic mass of line managers and staff experts, combined with operators in the operating adhocracy, working together in ever-shifting relationships on ad hoc projects. Our logo figure at the start of this chapter shows adhocracy with its parts mingled together in one amorphous mass in the middle. In the operating adhocracy, that mass includes the middle line, support staff, technostructure, and operating core. Of these, the administrative adhocracy excludes just the operating core, which is truncated, as shown by the dotted section below the central mass. The reader will also note that the strategic apex of the figure is shown partly merged into the central mass as well, for reasons we shall present in our discussion of strategy formation.

299

STRUCTURE AND
STRATEGY IN
PROFESSIONAL AND
INNOVATIVE
ORGANIZATIONS

The Roles of the Strategic Apex

The top managers of the strategic apex of this configuration do not spend much time formulating explicit strategies (as we shall see). But they must spend a good deal of their time in the battles that ensue over strategic choices and in handling the many other disturbances that arise all over these fluid structures. The innovative configuration combines fluid working arrangements with power based on expertise, not authority. Together those breed aggressiveness and conflict. But the job of the managers here, at all levels, is not to bottle up that aggression and conflict so much as to channel them to productive ends. Thus, the managers of adhocracy must be masters of human relations, able to use persuasion, negotiation, coalition, reputation, and rapport to fuse the individualistic experts into smoothly functioning teams.

Top managers must also devote a good deal of time to monitoring the projects. Innovative project work is notoriously difficult to control. No MIS can be relied upon to provide complete, unambiguous results. So there must be careful personal monitoring of projects to ensure that they are completed according to specifications, on schedule and within budget (or, more likely, not excessively late and not too far in excess of cost estimates).

Perhaps the most important single role of the top management of this configuration (especially the operating adhocracy form) is liaison with the external environment. The other configurations tend to focus their attention on clearly defined markets and so are more or less assured of a steady flow of work. Not so the operating adhocracy, which lives from project to project and disappears when it can find no more. Since each project is different, the organization can never be sure where the next one will come from. So the top managers must devote a great deal of their time to ensuring a steady and balanced stream of incoming projects. That means developing liaison contacts with potential customers and negotiating contracts with them. Nowhere is this more clearly illustrated than in the consulting business, particularly where the approach is innovative. When a consultant becomes a partner in one of these firms, he or she normally hangs up the calculator and becomes virtually a full-time salesperson. It is a distinguishing characteristic of many an operating adhocracy that the selling function literally takes place at the strategic apex.

Project work poses related problems in the administrative adhocracy. Reeser asked a group of managers in three aerospace companies, "What are some of the human problems of project management?" Among the common answers: "[M]embers of the organization who are displaced because of the phasing out of [their] work . . . may have to wait a long time before they get another assignment at as high a level of responsibility" and "the temporary nature of the organization often necessitates 'make work' assignments for [these] displaced members." (1969:463) Thus senior managers must again concern themselves with a steady flow of projects, although in this case, internally generated.

CONDITIONS OF THE INNOVATIVE ORGANIZATION

This configuration is found in environments that are both dynamic and complex. A dynamic environment, being unpredictable, calls for organic structure; a complex one calls for decentralized structure. This configuration is the only type that provides both. Thus we tend to find the innovative organization wherever these conditions prevail, ranging from guerrilla warfare to space agencies. There appears to be no other way to fight a war in the jungle or to put the first man on the moon.

As we have noted for all the configurations, organizations that prefer particular structures also try to "choose" environments appropriate to them. This is especially clear in the case of the operating adhocracy. Advertising agencies and consulting firms that prefer to structure themselves as professional bureaucracies seek out stable environments; those that prefer the innovative form find environments that are dynamic, where the client needs are difficult and unpredictable.[1]

A number of organizations are drawn toward this configuration because of the dynamic conditions that result from very frequent product change. The extreme case is the unit producer, the manufacturing firm that custom-makes each of its products to order, as in the engineering company that produces prototypes or the fabricator of extremely expensive machinery. Because each customer order constitutes a new project, the organization is encouraged to structure itself as an operating adhocracy.

Some manufacturers of consumer goods operate in markets so competitive that they must be constantly changing their product offerings, even though each product may itself be mass produced. A company that records rock music would be a prime example, as would some cosmetic and pharmaceutical companies. Here again, dynamic conditions, when coupled with some complexity, drive the organization toward the innovative configuration, with the mass production operations truncated to allow for adhocracy in product development.

Youth is another condition often associated with this type of organization. That is because it is difficult to sustain any structure in a state of adhocracy for a long period—to keep behaviors from formalizing and thereby discouraging innovation. All kinds of forces drive the innovative configuration to bureaucratize itself as it ages. On the other hand, young organizations prefer naturally organic structures, since they must find their own ways and tend to be eager to innovate. Unless they are entrepreneurial, they tend to become intrapreneurial.

The operating adhocracy is particularly prone to a short life, since it faces a risky market which can quickly destroy it. The loss of one major contract can literally close it down overnight. But if some operating adhocracies have short lives because they fail, others have short lives because they succeed. Success over time encourages metamorphosis, driving the organization toward a more stable environment and a more bureaucratic structure. As it ages, the successful organization develops a reputation for what it does best. That encourages it to repeat certain activities, which may suit the employees who, themselves aging, may welcome more stability in their work. So operating adhocracy is driven over time toward professional bureaucracy to perfect the activities it does best, perhaps even toward the machine bureaucracy to exploit a single invention. The organization survives, but the configuration dies.

Administrative adhocracies typically live longer. They, too, feel the pressures to bureaucratize as they age, which can lead them to stop innovating or else to innovate in stereotyped ways and thereby to adopt bureaucratic structure. But this will not work if the organization functions in an industry that requires sophisticated innovation from all its participants. Since many of the industries where administrative adhocracies are

---

[1] I like to tell a story of the hospital patient with an appendix about to burst who presents himself to a hospital organized as an adhocracy: "Who wants to do another appendectomy? We're into livers now," as they go about exploring new procedures. But the patient returning from a trip to the jungle with a rare tropical disease had better beware of the hospital organized as a professional bureaucracy. A student came up to me after I once said this and explained how hospital doctors puzzled by her bloated stomach and not knowing what to do took out her appendix. Luckily, her problem resolved itself, some time later. Another time, a surgeon told me that his hospital no longer does appendectomies!

found do, organizations that survive in them tend to retain this configuration for long periods.

In recognition of the tendency for organizations to bureaucratize as they age, a variant of the innovative configuration has emerged—"the organizational equivalent of paper dresses or throw-away tissues" (Toffler, 1970:133)—which might be called the "temporary adhocracy." It draws together specialists from various organizations to carry out a project, and then it disbands. Temporary adhocracies are becoming increasingly common in modern society: the production group that performs a single play, the election campaign committee that promotes a single candidate, the guerrilla group that overthrows a single government, the Olympic committee that plans a single games. Related is what can be called the "mammoth project adhocracy," a giant temporary adhocracy that draws on thousands of experts for a number of years to carry out a single major task, the Manhattan Project of World War II being one famous example.

Sophisticated and automated technical systems also tend to drive organizations toward the administrative adhocracy. When an organization's technical system is sophisticated, it requires an elaborate, highly trained support staff, working in teams, to design or purchase, modify, and maintain the equipment. In other words, complex machinery requires specialists who have the knowledge, power, and flexible working arrangements to cope with it, which generally requires the organization to structure itself as an adhocracy.

Automation of a technical system can evoke even stronger forces in the same direction. That is why a machine organization that succeeds in automating its operating core tends to undergo a dramatic metamorphosis. The problem of motivating bored workers disappears, and with it goes the control mentality that permeates the structure; the distinction between line and staff blurs (machines being indifferent to who turns their knobs), which leads to another important reduction in conflict; the technostructure loses its influence, since control is built into the machinery by its own designers rather than having to be imposed on workers by the standards of the analysts. Overall, then, the administrative structure becomes more decentralized and organic, emerging as an adhocracy. Of course, for automated organizations with simple technical systems (as in the production of hand creams), the entrepreneurial configuration may suffice instead of the innovative one.

Fashion is most decidedly another condition of the innovative configuration. Every one of its characteristics is very much in vogue today: emphasis on expertise, organic structure, project teams, task forces, decentralization of power, matrix structure, sophisticated technical systems, automation, and young organizations. Thus, if the entrepreneurial and machine forms were earlier configurations, and the professional and the diversified forms yesterday's, then the innovative is clearly today's. This is the configuration for a population growing ever better educated and more specialized, yet under constant encouragement to adopt the "systems" approach—to view the world as an integrated whole instead of a collection of loosely coupled parts. It is the configuration for environments that are becoming more complex and more insistent on innovation, and for technical systems that are growing more sophisticated and more highly automated. It is the only configuration among our types appropriate for those who believe organizations must become at the same time more democratic and less bureaucratic.

Yet despite our current infatuation with it, adhocracy is not the structure for all organizations. Like all the others, it too has its place. And that place, as our examples make clear, seems to be in the new industries of our age—aerospace, electronics, think-tank consulting, research, advertising, filmmaking, petrochemicals—virtually all of which experienced their greatest development since World War II. The innovative adhocracy appears to be the configuration for the industries of the last half of the twentieth century.

301

STRUCTURE AND
STRATEGY IN
PROFESSIONAL AND
INNOVATIVE
ORGANIZATIONS

The structure of the innovative organization may seem unconventional, but its strategy making is even more so, upsetting virtually everything we have been taught to believe about that process.

Because the innovative organization must respond continuously to a complex, unpredictable environment, it cannot rely on deliberate strategy. In other words, it cannot predetermine precise patterns in its activities and then impose them on its work through some kind of formal planning process. Rather, many of its actions must be decided upon individually, according to the needs of the moment. It proceeds incrementally; to use Charles Lindblom's words, it prefers "continual nibbling" to a "good bite" (1968:25).

Here, then, the process is best thought of as strategy *formation,* because strategy is not formulated consciously in one place so much as formed implicitly by the specific actions taken in many places. That is why action planning cannot be extensively relied upon in these organizations: Any process that separates thinking from action—planning from execution, formalization from implementation—would impede the flexibility of the organization to respond creatively to its dynamic environment.

Strategy Formation in the Operating Adhocracy

In the operating adhocracy, a project organization never quite sure what it will do next, the strategy never really stabilizes totally but is responsive to new projects, which themselves involve the activities of a whole host of people. Take the example of the National Film Board. Among its most important strategies are those related to the content of the hundred or so mostly short, documentary-type films that it makes each year. Were the Board structured as a machine bureacracy, the word on what films to make would come down from on high. Instead, when we studied it some years ago, proposals for new films were submitted to a standing committee, which included elected filmmakers, marketing people, and the heads of production and programming—in other words, operators, line managers, and staff specialists. The chief executive had to approve the committee's choices, and usually did, but the vast majority of the proposals were initiated by the filmmakers and the executive producers lower down. Strategies formed as themes developed among these individual proposals. The operating adhocracy's strategy thus evolves continuously as all kinds of such decisions are made, each leaving its imprint on the strategy by creating a precedent or reinforcing an existing one.

Strategy Formation in the Administrative Adhocracy

Similar things can be said about the administrative adhocracy, although the strategy-making process is slightly neater there. That is because the organization tends to concentrate its attention on fewer projects, which involve more people. NASA's Apollo project, for example, involved most of its personnel for almost ten years.

Administrative adhocracies also need to give more attention to action planning, but of a loose kind—to specify perhaps the ends to be reached while leaving flexibility to work out the means en route. Again, therefore, it is only through the making of specific decisions—namely, those that determine which projects are undertaken and how these projects unfold—that strategies can evolve.

Strategies Nonetheless

With their activities so disjointed, one might wonder whether adhocracies (of either type) can form strategies (that is, patterns) at all. In fact, they do, at least at certain times.

At the Film Board, despite the little direction from the management, the content of films did converge on certain clear themes periodically and then diverge, in remarkably regular cycles. In the early 1940s, there was a focus on films related to the war effort. After the war, having lost that raison d'cêtre as well as its founding leader, the Board's films went off in all directions. They converged again in the mid-1950s around series of films for television, but by the late 1950s were again diverging widely. And in the mid-1960s and again in the early 1970s (with a brief period of divergence in between), the Board again showed a certain degree of convergence, this time on the themes of social commentary and experimentation.

This habit of cycling in and out of focus is quite unlike what takes place in the other configurations. In the machine organization especially, and somewhat in the entrepreneurial one, convergence proves much stronger and much longer (recall Volkswagenwerk's concentration on the Beetle for twenty years), while divergence tends to be very brief. The machine organization, in particular, cannot tolerate the ambiguity of change and so tries to leap from one strategic orientation to another. The innovative organization, in contrast, seems not only able to function at times without strategic focus, but positively to thrive on it. Perhaps that is the way it keeps itself innovative — by periodically cleansing itself of some of its existing strategic baggage.

The Varied Strategies of Adhocracy

Where do the strategies of adhocracy come from? While some may be imposed deliberately by the central management (as in staff cuts at the Film Board), most seem to emerge in a variety of other ways.

In some cases, a single ad hoc decision sets a precedent which evokes a pattern. That is how the National Film Board got into making series of films for television. While a debate raged over the issue, with management hesitant, one filmmaker slipped out and made one such series, and when many of his colleagues quickly followed suit, the organization suddenly found itself deeply, if unintentionally, committed to a major new strategy. It was, in effect, a strategy of spontaneous but implicit consensus on the part of its operating employees. In another case, even the initial precedent-setting decision wasn't deliberate. One film inadvertently ran longer than expected, it had to be distributed as a feature, the first for the organization, and as some other filmmakers took advantage of the precedent, a feature film strategy emerged.

Sometimes a strategy will be pursued in a pocket of an organization (perhaps in a clandestine manner, in a so-called "skunkworks"), which then later becomes more broadly organizational when the organization, in need of change and casting about for new strategies, seizes upon it. Some salesman has been pursuing a new market, or some engineer has developed a new product, and is ignored until the organization has need for some fresh strategic thinking. Then it finds it, not in the vision of its leaders or the procedures of its planners, not elsewhere in its industry, but hidden in the bowels of its own operations, developed through the learning of its workers.

What then becomes the role of the leadership of the innovative configuration in making strategy? If it cannot impose deliberate strategies, what does it do? The answer is that it manages patterns, seeking partial control over strategies but otherwise attempting to influence what happens to those strategies that do emerge lower down.

These are the organizations in which trying to manage strategy is a little like trying to drive an automobile without having your hands on the steering wheel. You can accelerate and brake but cannot determine direction. But there do remain important forms of control. First the leaders can manage the *process* of strategy-making if not the content of strategy. In other words, they can set up the structures to encourage certain kinds of activities and hire the people who themselves will carry out these activities. Second, they can provide general guidelines for strategy—what we have called *umbrella* strategies—seeking to define certain boundaries outside of which the specific patterns developed

303

STRUCTURE AND
STRATEGY IN
PROFESSIONAL AND
INNOVATIVE
ORGANIZATIONS

below should not stray. Then they can watch the patterns that do emerge and use the umbrella to decide which to encourage and which to discourage, remembering, however, that the umbrella can be shifted too.

A Grass-Roots Model of Strategy Formation

We can summarize this discussion in terms of a "grass-roots" model of strategy formation, comprising six points.

1. *Strategies grow initially like weeds in a garden, they are not cultivated like tomatoes in a hothouse.* In other words, the process of strategy formation can be overmanaged; sometimes it is more important to let patterns emerge than to force an artificial consistency upon an organization prematurely. The hothouse, if needed, can come later.

2. *These strategies can take root in all kinds of places, virtually anywhere people have the capacity to learn and the resources to support that capacity.* Sometimes an individual or unit in touch with a particular opportunity creates his, her, or its own pattern. This may happen inadvertently, when an initial action sets a precedent. Even senior managers can fall into strategies by experimenting with ideas until they converge on something that works (though the final result may appear to the observer to have been deliberately designed). At other times, a variety of actions converge on a strategic theme through the mutual adjustment of various people, whether gradually or spontaneously. And then the external environment can impose a pattern on an unsuspecting organization. The point is that organizations cannot always plan where their strategies will emerge, let alone plan the strategies themselves.

3. *Such strategies become organizational when they become collective, that is, when the patterns proliferate to pervade the behavior of the organization at large.* Weeds can proliferate and encompass a whole garden; then the conventional plants may look out of place. Likewise, emergent strategies can sometimes displace the existing deliberate ones. But, of course, what is a weed but a plant that wasn't expected? With a change of perspective, the emergent strategy, like the weed, can become what is valued (just as Europeans enjoy salads of the leaves of America's most notorious weed, the dandelion!).

4. *The processes of proliferation may be conscious but need not be; likewise they may be managed but need not be.* The processes by which the initial patterns work their way through the organization need not be consciously intended, by formal leaders or even informal ones. Patterns may simply spread by collective action, much as plants proliferate themselves. Of course, once strategies are recognized as valuable, the processes by which they proliferate can be managed, just as plants can be selectively propagated.

5. *New strategies, which may be emerging continuously, tend to pervade the organization during periods of change, which punctuate periods of more integrated continuity.* Put more simply, organizations, like gardens, may accept the biblical maxim of a time to sow and a time to reap (even though they can sometimes reap what they did not mean to sow). Periods of convergence, during which the organization exploits its prevalent, established strategies, tend to be interrupted periodically by periods of divergence, during which the organization experiments with and subsequently accepts new strategic themes. The blurring of the separation between these two types of periods may have the same effect on an organization that the blurring of the separation between sowing and reaping has on a garden—the destruction of the system's productive capacity.

6. *To manage this process is not to preconceive strategies but to recognize their emergence and intervene when appropriate.* A destructive weed, once noticed, is best uprooted immediately. But one that seems capable of bearing fruit is worth watching, indeed sometimes even worth building a hothouse around. To manage in this context is to create the climate within which a wide variety of strategies can grow (to establish flexible structures, develop appropriate processes, encourage supporting ideologies, and define guiding "umbrella" strategies) and then to watch what does in fact come up. The strategic initiatives that do come "up" may in fact originate anywhere, although often low down in the organization, where the detailed knowledge of products and markets resides. (In fact, to be successful in some organizations, these initiatives must be recognized by middle-level managers and "championed" by combining them with each other or with existing strategies before promoting them to the senior management.) In effect, the management encourages those initiatives that appear to have potential, otherwise it discourages them. But it must not be too quick to cut off the unexpected: Sometimes it is better to pretend not to notice an emerging pattern to allow it more time to unfold. Likewise, there are times when it makes sense to shift or enlarge an umbrella to encompass a new pattern—in other words, to let the organization adapt to the initiative rather than vice versa. Moreover, a management must know when to resist change for the sake of internal efficiency and when to promote it for the sake of external adaptation. In other words, it must sense when to exploit an established crop of strategies and when to encourage new strains to displace them. It is the excesses of either—failure to focus (running blind) or failure to change (bureaucratic momentum)—that most harms organizations.

I call this a "grass-roots" model because the strategies grow up from the base of the organization, rooted in the solid earth of its operations rather than the ethereal abstractions of its administration. (Even the strategic initiatives of the senior management itself are in this model rooted in its tangible involvement with the operations.)

Of course, the model is overstated. But no more so than the more widely accepted deliberate one, which we might call the "hothouse" model of strategy form*u*lation. Management theory must encompass both, perhaps more broadly labeled the *learning* model and the *planning* model, as well as a third, the *visionary* model.

I have discussed the learning model under the innovative configuration, the planning model under the machine configuration, and the visionary model under the entrepreneurial configuration. But in truth, all organizations need to mix these approaches in various ways at different times in their development. For example, our discussion of strategic change in the machine organization concluded, in effect, that they had to revert to the learning model for revitalization and the visionary model for turnaround. Of course, the visionary leader must learn, as must the learning organization evolve a kind of strategic vision, and both sometimes need planning to program the strategies they develop. And overall, no organization can function with strategies that are always and purely emergent; that would amount to a complete abdication of will and leadership, not to mention conscious thought. But none can function either with strategies that are always and purely deliberate; that would amount to an unwillingness to learn, a blindness to whatever is unexpected.

Environment Taking Precedence in the Innovative Organization

To conclude our discussion of strategy formation, as shown in Figure 3, in the innovative configuration it is the environment that takes precedence. It drives the organization, which responds continuously and eclectically, but does nevertheless achieve convergence during certain periods.[2] The formal leadership seeks somehow to influence both sides in this relationship, negotiating with the environment for support and attempting to impose some broad general (umbrella) guidelines on the organization.

If the strategist of the entrepreneurial organization is largely a concept attainer and that of the machine organization largely a planner, then the strategist of the innovative organization is largely a *pattern recognizer,* seeking to detect emerging patterns within and outside the strategic umbrella. Then strategies deemed unsuitable can be dis-

___
[2]We might take this convergence as the expression of an "organization's mind"—the focusing on a strategic theme as a result of the mutual adjustments among its many actors.

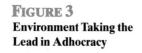

FIGURE 3
Environment Taking the
Lead in Adhocracy

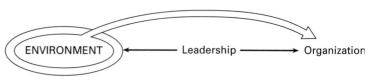

couraged while those that seem appropriate can be encouraged, even if that means moving the umbrella. Here, then, we may find the curious situation of leadership changing its intentions to fit the realized behavior of its organization. But that is curious only in the perspective of traditional management theory.

SOME ISSUES ASSOCIATED WITH THE INNOVATIVE ORGANIZATION

Three issues associated with the innovative configuration merit attention here: its ambiguities and the reactions of people who must live with them, its inefficiencies, and its propensity to make inappropriate transitions to other configurations.

Human Reactions to Ambiguity

Many people, especially creative ones, dislike both structural rigidity and the concentration of power. That leaves them only one configuration, the innovative, which is both organic and decentralized. Thus they find it a great place to work. In essence, adhocracy is the only structure for people who believe in more democracy with less bureaucracy.

But not everyone shares those values (not even everyone who professes to). Many people need order, and so prefer the machine or professional type of organization. They see adhocracy as a nice place to visit but no place to spend a career. Even dedicated members of adhocracies periodically get frustrated with this structure's fluidity, confusion, and ambiguity. "In these situations, all managers some of the time and many managers all the time, yearn for more definition and structure" (Burns and Stalker, 1966:122–123). The managers of innovative organizations report anxiety related to the eventual phaseout of projects; confusion as to who their boss is, whom to impress to get promoted; a lack of clarity in job definitions, authority relationships, and lines of communication; and intense competition for resources, recognition, and rewards (Reeser, 1969). This last point suggests another serious problem of ambiguity here, the politicization of these configurations. Combining its ambiguities with its interdependencies, the innovative form can emerge as a rather politicized and ruthless organization—supportive of the fit, as long as they remain fit, but destructive of the weak.

Problems of Efficiency

No configuration is better suited to solving complex, ill-structured problems than this one. None can match it for sophisticated innovation. Or, unfortunately, for the costs of that innovation. This is simply not an efficient way to function. Although it is ideally suited for the one-of-a-kind project, the innovative configuration is not competent at doing *ordinary* things. It is designed for the *extra*ordinary. The bureaucracies are all mass producers; they gain efficiency through standardization. The adhocracy is a custom producer, unable to standardize and so be efficient. It gains its effectiveness (innovation) at the price of efficiency.

One source of inefficiency lies in the unbalanced workload, mentioned earlier. It is almost impossible to keep the personnel of a project structure—high-priced specialists, it should be noted—busy on a steady basis. In January they may be working overtime with no hope of completing the new project on time; by May they may be playing cards for want of work.

But the real root of inefficiency is the high cost of communication. People talk a lot in these organizations; that is how they combine their knowledge to develop new ideas. But that takes time, a great deal of time. Faced with the need to make a decision in the machine organization, someone up above gives an order and that is that. Not so in the innovative one, where everyone must get into the act—managers of all kinds (functional, project, liaison), as well as all the specialists who believe their point of view should be represented. A meeting is called, probably to schedule another meeting, eventually to decide who should participate in the decision. The problem then gets defined and redefined, ideas for its solution get generated and debated, alliances build and fall around different solutions, until eventually everyone settles down to the hard bargaining over which one to adopt. Finally a decision emerges—that in itself is an accomplishment—although it is typically late and will probably be modified later.

The Dangers of Inappropriate Transition

Of course, one solution to the problems of ambiguity and inefficiency is to change the configuration. Employees no longer able to tolerate the ambiguity and customers fed up with the inefficiency may try to drive the organization to a more stable, bureaucratic form.

That is relatively easily done in the operating adhocracy, as noted earlier. The organization simply selects the set of standard programs it does best, reverting to the professional configuration, or else innovates one last time to find a lucrative market niche in which to mass produce, and then becomes a machine configuration. But those transitions, however easily effected, are not always appropriate. The organization came into being to solve problems imaginatively, not to apply standards indiscriminately. In many spheres, society has more mass producers than it needs; what it lacks are true problem solvers—the consulting firm that can handle a unique problem instead of applying a pat solution, the advertising agency that can come up with a novel campaign instead of the common imitation, the research laboratory that can make the really serious breakthrough instead of just modifying an existing design. The television networks seem to be classic examples of bureaucracies that provide largely standardized fare when the creativity of adhocracy is called for (except, perhaps, for the newsrooms and the specials, where an ad hoc orientation encourages more creativity).

The administrative adhocracy can run into more serious difficulties when it succumbs to the pressures to bureaucratize. It exists to innovate for itself, in its own industry. Unlike the operating adhocracy, it often cannot change orientation while remaining in the same industry. And so its conversion to the machine configuration (the natural transition for administrative adhocracy tired of perpetual change), by destroying the organization's ability to innovate, can eventually destroy the organization itself.

To reiterate a central theme of our discussion throughout this section: In general, there is no one best structure; in particular, there may be at a cost of something forgone, so long as the different attributes combine to form a coherent configuration that is consistent with the situation.

307

STRUCTURE AND
STRATEGY IN
PROFESSIONAL AND
INNOVATIVE
ORGANIZATIONS

By James Brian Quinn

Management observers frequently claim that small organizations are more innovative than large ones. But is this commonplace necessarily true? Some large enterprises are highly innovative. How do they do it? . . . This article [reports on a] $2\frac{1}{2}$ year worldwide study . . . [of] both well-documented small ventures and large U.S., Japanese, and European companies and programs selected for their innovation records. . . . More striking than the cultural differences among these companies are the similarities between innovative small and large organizations and among innovative organizations in different countries. Effective management of innovation seems much the same, regardless of national boundaries or scale of operations.

There are . . . many reasons why small companies appear to produce a disproportionate number of innovations. First, innovation occurs in a probabilistic setting. A company never knows whether a particular technical result can be achieved and whether it will succeed in the marketplace. For every new solution that succeeds, tens to hundreds fail. The sheer number of attempts—most by small-scale entrepreneurs—means that some ventures will survive. The 90% to 99% that fail are distributed widely throughout society and receive little notice.

On the other hand, a big company that wishes to move a concept from invention to the marketplace must absorb all potential failure costs itself. This risk may be socially or managerially intolerable, jeopardizing the many other products, projects, jobs, and communities the company supports. Even if its innovation is successful, a big company may face costs that newcomers do not bear, like converting existing operations and customer bases to the new solution.

By contrast, a new enterprise does not risk losing an existing investment base or cannibalizing customer franchises built at great expense. It does not have to change an internal culture that has successfully supported doing things another way or that has developed intellectual depth and belief in the technologies that led to past successes. Organized groups like labor unions, consumer advocates, and government bureaucracies rarely monitor and resist a small company's moves as they might a big company's. Finally, new companies do not face the psychological pain and the economic costs of laying off employees, shutting down plants and even communities, and displacing supplier relationships built with years of mutual commitment and effort. Such barriers to change in large organizations are real, important, and legitimate.

The complex products and systems that society expects large companies to undertake further compound the risks. Only big companies can develop new ships or locomotives; telecommunication networks; or systems for space, defense, air traffic control, hospital care, mass foods delivery, or nationwide computer interactions. These large-scale projects always carry more risk than single-product introductions. A billion-dollar development aircraft, for example, can fail if one inexpensive part in its 100,000 components fails.

Clearly, a single enterprise cannot by itself develop or produce all the parts needed by such large new systems. And communications among the various groups making design and production decisions on components are always incomplete. The probability of error increases exponentially with complexity, while the system innovator's control over decisions decreases significantly—further escalating potential error costs and risks. Such forces inhibit innovation in large organizations. But proper management can lessen these effects.

Originally published in the *Harvard Business Review* (May–June, 1985); winner of the McKinsey prize for the best article in the *Review* in 1985. Copyright © 1985 by the President and Fellows of Harvard College; all rights reserved. Reprinted with deletions by permission of the *Harvard Business Review*.

OF INVENTORS AND ENTREPRENEURS

A close look at innovative small enterprises reveals much about the successful management of innovation. Of course, not all innovations follow a single pattern. But my research—and other studies in combination—suggest that the following factors are crucial to the success of innovative small companies:

Need Orientation

Inventor-entrepreneurs tend to be "need or achievement oriented." They believe that if they "do the job better," rewards will follow. They may at first focus on their own view of market needs. But lacking resources, successful small entrepreneurs soon find that it pays to approach potential customers early, test their solutions in users' hands, learn from these interactions, and adapt designs rapidly. Many studies suggest that effective technological innovation develops hand-in-hand with customer demand (Von Hippel, 1982:117).

Experts and Fanatics

Company founders tend to be pioneers in their technologies and fanatics when it comes to solving problems. They are often described as "possessed" or "obsessed," working toward their objectives to the exclusion even of family or personal relationships. As both experts and fanatics, they perceive probabilities of success as higher than others do. And their commitment allows them to persevere despite the frustrations, ambiguities, and setbacks that always accompany major innovations.

Long Time Horizons

Their fanaticism may cause inventor-entrepreneurs to underestimate the obstacles and length of time to success. Time horizons for radical innovations make them essentially "irrational" from a present value viewpoint. In my sample, delays between invention and commercial production ranged from 3 to 25 years.[1] In the late 1930s, for example, industrial chemist Russell Marker was working on steroids called sapogenins when he discovered a technique that would degrade one of these, diosgenin, into the female sex hormone progesterone. By processing some ten tons of Mexican yams in rented and borrowed lab space, Marker finally extracted about four pounds of diosgenin and started a tiny business to produce steroids for the laboratory market. But it was not until 1962, over 23 years later, that Syntex, the company Marker founded, obtained FDA approval for its oral contraceptive.

For both psychological and practical reasons, inventor-entrepreneurs generally avoid early formal plans, proceed step-by-step, and sustain themselves by other income and the momentum of the small advances they achieve as they go along.

Low Early Costs

Innovators tend to work in homes, basements, warehouses, or low-rent facilities whenever possible. They incur few overhead costs; their limited resources go directly into

---

[1] A study at Battelle found an average of 19.2 years between invention and commercial production. Battelle Memorial Laboratories, "Science, Technology, and Innovation," Report to the National Science Foundation, 1973; also Dean (1974:13).

their projects. They pour nights, weekends, and "sweat capital" into their endeavors. They borrow whatever they can. They invent cheap equipment and prototype processes, often improving on what is available in the marketplace. If one approach fails, few people know; little time or money is lost. All this decreases the costs and risks facing a small operation and improves the present value of its potential success.

Multiple Approaches

Technology tends to advance through a series of random—often highly intuitive—insights frequently triggered by gratuitous interactions between the discoverer and the outside world. Only highly committed entrepreneurs can tolerate (and even enjoy) this chaos. They adopt solutions wherever they can be found, unencumbered by formal plans or PERT charts that would limit the range of their imaginations. When the odds of success are low, the participation and interaction of many motivated players increase the chance that one will succeed.

A recent study of initial public offerings made in 1962 shows that only 2% survived and still looked like worthwhile investments 20 years later.[2] Small-scale entrepreneurship looks efficient in part because history only records the survivors.

Flexibility and Quickness

Undeterred by committees, board approvals, and other bureaucratic delays, the inventor-entrepreneur can experiment, test, recycle, and try again with little time lost. Because technological progress depends largely on the number of successful experiments accomplished per unit of time, fast-moving small entrepreneurs can gain both timing and performance advantages over clumsier competitors. This responsiveness is often crucial in finding early markets for radical innovations where neither innovators, market researchers, nor users can quite visualize a product's real potential. For example, Edison's lights first appeared on ships and in baseball parks; Astroturf was intended to convert the flat roofs and asphalt playgrounds of city schools into more humane environments; and graphite and boron composites designed for aerospace unexpectedly found their largest markets in sporting goods. Entrepreneurs quickly adjusted their entry strategies to market feedback.

Incentives

Inventor-entrepreneurs can foresee tangible personal rewards if they are successful. Individuals often want to achieve a technical contribution, recognition, power, or sheer independence, as much as money. For the original, driven personalities who create significant innovations, few other paths offer such clear opportunities to fulfill all their economic, psychological, and career goals at once. Consequently, they do not panic or quit when others with solely monetary goals might.

Availability of Capital

One of America's great competitive advantages is its rich variety of sources to finance small, low-probability ventures. If entrepreneurs are turned down by one source, other sources can be sought in myriads of creative combinations.

Professionals involved in such financings have developed a characteristic approach to deal with the chaos and uncertainty of innovation. First, they evaluate a proposal's conceptual validity: If the technical problems can be solved, is there a real business there for someone and does it have a large upside potential? Next, they con-

---

[2]Business Economics Group, W. R. Grace & Co., 1983.

centrate on people: Is the team thoroughly committed and expert? Is it the best available? Only then do these financiers analyze specific financial estimates in depth. Even then, they recognize that actual outcomes generally depend on subjective factors, not numbers (Pence, 1982).

Timeliness, aggressiveness, commitment, quality of people, and the flexibility to attack opportunities not at first perceived are crucial. Downside risks are minimized, not by detailed controls, but by spreading risks among multiple projects, keeping early costs low, and gauging the tenacity, flexibility, and capability of the founders.

311

STRUCTURE AND
STRATEGY IN
PROFESSIONAL AND
INNOVATIVE
ORGANIZATIONS

LARGE-COMPANY BARRIERS TO INNOVATION

Less innovative companies and, unfortunately, most large corporations operate in a very different fashion. The most notable and common constraints on innovation in larger companies include the following:

Top Management Isolation

Many senior executives in big companies have little contact with conditions on the factory floor or with customers who might influence their thinking about technological innovation. Since risk perception is inversely related to familiarity and experience, financially oriented top managers are likely to perceive technological innovations as more problematic than acquisitions that may be just as risky but that will appear more familiar (Hayes and Garvin, 1982:70; Hayes and Abernathy, 1980:67).

Intolerance of Fanatics

Big companies often view entrepreneurial fanatics as embarrassments or troublemakers. Many major cities are now ringed by companies founded by these "nonteam" players—often to the regret of their former employers.

Short Time Horizons

The perceived corporate need to report a continuous stream of quarterly profits conflicts with the long time spans that major innovations normally require. Such pressures often make publicly owned companies favor quick marketing fixes, cost cutting, and acquisition strategies over process, product, or quality innovations that would yield much more in the long run.

Accounting Practices

By assessing all its direct, indirect, overhead, overtime, and service costs against a project, large corporations have much higher development expenses compared with entrepreneurs working in garages. A project in a big company can quickly become an exposed political target, its potential net present value may sink unacceptably, and an entry into small markets may not justify its sunk costs. An otherwise viable project may soon founder and disappear.

Excessive Rationalism

Managers in big companies often seek orderly advance through early market research studies or PERT planning. Rather than managing the inevitable chaos of innovation productively, these managers soon drive out the very things that lead to innovation in order to prove their announced plans.

Excessive Bureaucracy

In the name of efficiency, bureaucratic structures require many approvals and cause delays at every turn. Experiments that a small company can perform in hours may take days or weeks in large organizations. The interactive feedback that fosters innovation is lost, important time windows can be missed, and real costs and risks rise for the corporation.

Inappropriate Incentives

Reward and control systems in most big companies are designed to minimize surprises. Yet innovation, by definition, is full of surprises. It often disrupts well-laid plans, accepted power patterns, and entrenched organizational behavior at high costs to many. Few large companies make millionaires of those who create such disruptions, however profitable the innovations may turn out to be. When control systems neither penalize opportunities missed nor reward risks taken, the results are predictable.

HOW LARGE INNOVATIVE COMPANIES DO IT

Yet some big companies are continuously innovative. Although each such enterprise is distinctive, the successful big innovators I studied have developed techniques that emulate or improve on their smaller counterparts' practices. What are the most important patterns?

Atmosphere and Vision

Continuous innovation occurs largely because top executives appreciate innovation and manage their company's value system and atmosphere to support it. For example, Sony's founder, Masaru Ibuka, stated in the company's "Purposes of Incorporation" the goal of a "free, dynamic, and pleasant factory . . . where sincerely motivated personnel can exercise their technological skills to the highest level." Ibuka and Sony's chairman, Akio Morita, inculcated the "Sony spirit" through a series of unusual policies: hiring brilliant people with nontraditional skills (like an opera singer) for high management positions, promoting young people over their elders, designing a new type of living accommodation for workers, and providing visible awards for outstanding technical achievements.

Because familiarity can foster understanding and psychological comfort, engineering and scientific leaders are often those who create atmospheres supportive of innovation, especially in a company's early life. Executive vision is more important than a particular management background—as IBM, Genentech, AT&T, Merck, Elf Aquitaine, Pilkington, and others in my sample illustrate. CEOs of these companies value technology and include technical experts in their highest decision circles.

Innovative managements—whether technical or not—project clear long-term visions for their organizations that go beyond simple economic measures. . . . Genentech's original plan expresses [such a] vision: "We expect to be the first company to commercialize the [rDNA] technology, and we plan to build a major profitable corporation by manufacturing and marketing needed products that benefit mankind. The future uses of genetic engineering are far reaching and many. Any product produced by a living organism is eventually within the company's reach."

Such visions, vigorously supported, are not "management fluff," but have many practical implications.[3] They attract quality people to the company and give focus to their creative and entrepreneurial drives. When combined with sound internal operations, they help channel growth by concentrating attention on the actions that lead to profitability, rather than on profitability itself. Finally, these visions recognize a realistic time frame for innovation and attract the kind of investors who will support it.

313

STRUCTURE AND
STRATEGY IN
PROFESSIONAL AND
INNOVATIVE
ORGANIZATIONS

Orientation to the Market

Innovative companies tie their visions to the practical realities of the marketplace. Although each company uses techniques adapted to its own style and strategy, two elements are always present: a strong market orientation at the very top of the company and mechanisms to ensure interactions between technical and marketing people at lower levels. At Sony, for example, soon after technical people are hired, the company runs them through weeks of retail selling. Sony engineers become sensitive to the ways retail sales practices, product displays, and nonquantifiable customer preferences affect success. . . .

From top to bench levels in my sample's most innovative companies, managers focus primarily on seeking to anticipate and solve customers' emerging problems.

Small, Flat Organizations

The most innovative large companies in my sample try to keep the total organization flat and project teams small. Development teams normally include only 6 or 7 key people. This number seems to constitute a critical mass of skills while fostering maximum communication and commitment among members. According to research done by my colleague, Victor McGee, the number of channels of communication increases as $n[2^{n-1} - 1]$. Therefore:

For team size	=	1	2	3	4	5	6
Channels	=	1	2	9	28	75	186
		7	8	9	10	11	
		441	1016	2295	5110	11253	

Innovative companies also try to keep their operating divisions and total technical units small—below 400 people. Up to this number, only two layers of management are required to maintain a span of control over 7 people. In units much larger than 400, people quickly lose touch with the concept of their product or process, staffs and bureaucracies tend to grow, and projects may go through too many formal screens to survive. Since it takes a chain of yesses and only one no to kill a project, jeopardy multiplies as management layers increase.

Multiple Approaches

At first one cannot be sure which of several technical approaches will dominate a field. The history of technology is replete with accidents, mishaps, and chance meetings that allowed one approach or group to emerge rapidly over others. Leo Baekelund was looking for a synthetic shellac when he found Bakelite and started the modern plastics industry. At Syntex, researchers were not looking for an oral contraceptive when they

---

[3] Thomas J. Allen (1977) illustrates the enormous leverage provided such technology accessors (called "gatekeepers") in R&D organizations.

created 19-norprogesterone, the precursor to the active ingredient in half of all contraceptive pills. And the microcomputer was born because Intel's Ted Hoff "happened" to work on a complex calculator just when Digital Equipment Corporation's PDP8 architecture was fresh in his mind.

Such "accidents" are involved in almost all major technological advances. When theory can predict everything, a company has moved to a new stage, from development to production. Murphy's law works because engineers design for what they can foresee; hence what fails is what theory could not predict. And it is rare that the interactions of components and subsystems can be predicted over the lifetime of operations. For example, despite careful theoretical design work, the first high performance jet engine literally tore itself to pieces on its test stand, while others failed in unanticipated operating conditions (like an Iranian sandstorm).

Recognizing the inadequacies of theory, innovative enterprises seem to move faster from paper studies to physical testing than do noninnovative enterprises. When possible, they encourage several prototype programs to proceed in parallel. . . . Such redundancy helps the company cope with uncertainties in development, motivates people through competition, and improves the amount and quality of information available for making final choices on scale-ups or introductions.

Developmental Shoot-outs

Many companies structure shoot-outs among competing approaches only after they reach the prototype stages. They find this practice provides more objective information for making decisions, decreases risk by making choices that best reflect marketplace needs, and helps ensure that the winning option will move ahead with a committed team behind it. Although many managers worry that competing approaches may be inefficient, greater effectiveness in choosing the right solution easily outweighs duplication costs when the market rewards higher performance or when large volumes justify increased sophistication. Under these conditions, parallel development may prove less costly because it both improves the probability of success and reduces development time.

Perhaps the most difficult problem in managing competing projects lies in reintegrating the members of the losing team. If the company is expanding rapidly or if the successful project creates a growth opportunity, losing team members can work on another interesting program or sign on with the winning team as the project moves toward the marketplace. For the shoot-out system to work continuously, however, executives must create a climate that honors high-quality performance whether a project wins or loses, reinvolves people quickly in their technical specialties or in other projects, and accepts and expects rotation among tasks and groups. . . .

Skunkworks

Every highly innovative enterprise in my research sample emulated small company practices by using groups that functioned in a skunkworks style. Small teams of engineers, technicians, designers, and model makers were placed together with no intervening organizational or physical barriers to developing a new product from idea to commercial prototype stages. In innovative Japanese companies, top managers often worked hand in hand on projects with young engineers. Surprisingly, *ringi* decision making was not evident in these situations. Soichiro Honda was known for working directly on technical problems and emphasizing his technical points by shouting at his engineers or occasionally even hitting them with wrenches!

The skunkworks approach eliminates bureaucracies, allows fast, unfettered communications, permits rapid turnaround times for experiments, and instills a high level of group identity and loyalty. Interestingly, few successful groups in my research were structured in the classic "venture group" form, with a careful balancing of engineering, production, and marketing talents. Instead they acted on an old truism: introducing a new product or process to the world is like raising a healthy child—it needs a mother (champion) who loves it, a father (authority figure with resources) to support it, and pediatricians (specialists) to get it through difficult times. It may survive solely in the hands of specialists, but its chances of success are remote.

315

STRUCTURE AND
STRATEGY IN
PROFESSIONAL AND
INNOVATIVE
ORGANIZATIONS

Interactive Learning

Skunkworks are as close as most big companies can come to emulating the highly interactive and motivating learning environment that characterizes successful small ventures. But the best big innovators have gone even farther. Recognizing that the random, chaotic nature of technological change cuts across organizational and even institutional lines, these companies tap into multiple outside sources of technology as well as their customers' capabilities. Enormous external leverages are possible. No company can spend more than a small share of the world's $200 billion devoted to R&D. But like small entrepreneurs, big companies can have much of that total effort cheaply if they try.

In industries such as electronics, customers provide much of the innovation on new products. In other industries, such as textiles, materials or equipment suppliers provide the innovation. In still others, such as biotechnology, universities are dominant, while foreign sources strongly supplement industries such as controlled fusion. Many R&D units have strategies to develop information for trading with outside groups and have teams to cultivate these sources. Large Japanese companies have been notably effective at this. So have U.S. companies as diverse as Du Pont, AT&T, Apple Computer, and Genentech.

An increasing variety of creative relationships exist in which big companies participate—as joint venturers, consortium members, limited partners, guarantors of first markets, major academic funding sources, venture capitalists, spin-off equity holders, and so on. These rival the variety of inventive financing and networking structures that individual entrepreneurs have created.

Indeed, the innovative practices of small and large companies look ever more alike. This resemblance is especially striking in the interactions between companies and customers during development. Many experienced big companies are relying less on early market research and more on interactive development with lead customers. Hewlett-Packard, 3M, Sony, and Raychem frequently introduce radically new products through small teams that work closely with lead customers. These teams learn from their customers' needs and innovations, and rapidly modify designs and entry strategies based on this information.

Formal market analyses continue to be useful for extending product lines, but they are often misleading when applied to radical innovations. Market studies predicted that Haloid would never sell more than 5,000 xerographic machines, that Intel's microprocessor would never sell more than 10% as many units as there were minicomputers, and that Sony's transistor radios and miniature television sets would fail in the marketplace. At the same time, many eventual failures such as Ford's Edsel, IBM's FS system, and the supersonic transport were studied and planned exhaustively on paper, but lost contact with customers' real needs.

A STRATEGY FOR INNOVATION

The flexible management practices needed for major innovations often pose problems for established cultures in big companies. Yet there are reasonable steps managers in these companies can take. Innovation can be bred in a surprising variety of organizations, as many examples show. What are its key elements?

An Opportunity Orientation

In the 1981–1983 recession, many large companies cut back or closed plants as their "only available solution." Yet I repeatedly found that top managers in these companies took these actions without determining firsthand why their customers were buying from competitors, discerning what niches in their markets were growing, or tapping the innovations their own people had to solve problems. These managers foreclosed innumerable options by defining the issue as cost cutting rather than opportunity seeking. As one frustrated division manager in a manufacturing conglomerate put it: "If management doesn't actively seek or welcome technical opportunities, it sure won't hear about them."

By contrast, Intel met the challenge of the last recession with its "20% solution." The professional staff agreed to work one extra day a week to bring innovations to the marketplace earlier than planned. Despite the difficult times, Intel came out of the recession with several important new products ready to go—and it avoided layoffs.

Entrepreneurial companies recognize that they have almost unlimited access to capital and they structure their practices accordingly. They let it be known that if their people come up with good ideas, they can find the necessary capital—just as private venture capitalists or investment bankers find resources for small entrepreneurs.

Structuring for Innovation

Managers need to think carefully about how innovation fits into their strategy and structure their technology, skills, resources, and organizational commitments accordingly. A few examples suggest the variety of strategies and alignments possible:

> Hewlett-Packard and 3M develop product lines around a series of small, discrete, free-standing products. These companies form units that look like entrepreneurial start-ups. Each has a small team, led by a champion, in low-cost facilities. These companies allow many different proposals to come forward and test them as early as possible in the marketplace. They design control systems to spot significant losses on any single entry quickly. They look for high gains on a few winners and blend less successful, smaller entries into prosperous product lines.
>
> Other companies (like AT&T or the oil majors) have had to make large system investments to last for decades. These companies tend to make longterm needs forecasts. They often start several programs in parallel to be sure of selecting the right technologies. They then extensively test new technologies in use before making systemwide commitments. Often they sacrifice speed of entry for long-term low cost and reliability.
>
> Intel and Dewey & Almy, suppliers of highly technical specialties to EOMs, develop strong technical sales networks to discover and understand customer needs in depth. These companies try to have technical solutions designed into customers' products. Such companies have flexible applied technology groups working close to the marketplace. They also have quickly expandable plant facilities and a cutting edge technology (not necessarily basic research) group that allows rapid selection of currently available technologies.
>
> Dominant producers like IBM or Matsushita are often not the first to introduce new technologies. They do not want to disturb their successful product lines any sooner than necessary. As market demands become clear, these companies establish precise price-performance windows and form overlapping project teams to come up with the best answer for the marketplace. To decrease market risks, they use product shoot-outs as close to the market as possible. They develop extreme depth in production technologies to keep unit costs low from the outset. Finally, depending on the scale of the market entry, they have project teams report as close to the top as necessary to secure needed management attention and resources.
>
> Merck and Hoffman-LaRoche, basic research companies, maintain laboratories with better facilities, higher pay, and more freedom than most universities can afford. These companies leverage their internal spending through research grants, clinical grants, and re-

317

STRUCTURE AND
STRATEGY IN
PROFESSIONAL AND
INNOVATIVE
ORGANIZATIONS

search relationships with universities throughout the world. Before they invest $20 million to $50 million to clear a new drug, they must have reasonable assurance that they will be first in the marketplace. They take elaborate precautions to ensure that the new entry is safe and effective, and that it cannot be easily duplicated by others. Their structures are designed to be on the cutting edge of science, but conservative in animal testing, clinical evaluation, and production control.

These examples suggest some ways of linking innovation to strategy. Many other examples, of course, exist. Within a single company, individual divisions may have different strategic needs and hence different structures and practices. No single approach works well for all situations.

Complex Portfolio Planning

Perhaps the most difficult task for top managers is to balance the needs of existing lines against the needs of potential lines. This problem requires a portfolio strategy much more complex than the popular four-box Boston Consulting Group matrix found in most strategy texts. To allocate resources for innovation strategically, managers need to define the broad, long-term actions within and across divisions necessary to achieve their visions. They should determine which positions to hold at all costs, where to fall back, and where to expand initially and in the more distant future.

A company's strategy may often require investing more resources in current lines. But sufficient resources should also be invested in patterns that ensure intermediate and long-term growth; provide defenses against possible government, labor, competitive, or activist challenges; and generate needed organizational, technical, and external relations flexibilities to handle unforeseen opportunities or threats. Sophisticated portfolio planning within and among divisions can protect both current returns and future prospects—the two critical bases for that most cherished goal, high price/earnings ratios.

AN INCREMENTALIST APPROACH

Such managerial techniques can provide a strategic focus for innovation and help solve many of the timing, coordination, and motivation problems that plague large, bureaucratic organizations. Even more detailed planning techniques may help in guiding the development of the many small innovations that characterize any successful business. My research reveals, however, that few, if any, major innovations result from highly structured planning systems. [Why?] . . .

The innovative process is inherently incremental. As Thomas Hughes says, "Technological systems evolve through relatively small steps marked by an occasional stubborn obstacle and by constant random breakthroughs interacting across laboratories and borders" (Hughes, 1984:83). A forgotten hypothesis of Einstein's became the laser in Charles Townes's mind as he contemplated azaleas in Franklin Square. The structure of DNA followed a circuitous route through research in biology, organic chemistry, X-ray crystallography, and mathematics toward its Nobel prize–winning conception as a spiral staircase of [base pairs]. Such rambling trails are characteristic of virtually all major technological advances.

At the outset of the attack on a technical problem, an innovator often does not know whether his problem is tractable, what approach will prove best, and what concrete characteristics the solution will have if achieved. The logical route, therefore, is to follow several paths—though perhaps with varying degrees of intensity—until more information becomes available. Now knowing precisely where the solution will occur, wise managers establish the widest feasible network for finding and assessing alternative solutions. They keep many options open until one of them seems sure to win. Then they back it heavily.

Managing innovation is like a stud poker game, where one can play several hands. A player has some idea of the likely size of the pot at the beginning, knows the general but not the sure route to winning, buys one card (a project) at a time to gain information about probabilities and the size of the pot, closes hands as they become discouraging, and risks more only late in the hand as knowledge increases. . . .

Chaos within Guidelines

Effective managers of innovation channel and control its main directions. Like venture capitalists, they administer primarily by setting goals, selecting key people, and establishing a few critical limits and decision points for intervention rather than by implementing elaborate planning or control systems. As technology leads or market needs emerge, these managers set a few—most crucial—performance targets and limits. They allow their technical units to decide how to achieve these, subject to defined constraints and reviews at critical junctures.

Early bench-scale project managers may pursue various options, making little attempt at first to integrate each into a total program. Only after key variables are understood—and perhaps measured and demonstrated in lab models—can more precise planning be meaningful. Even then, many factors may remain unknown; chaos and competition can continue to thrive in the pursuit of the solution. At defined review points, however, only those options that can clear performance milestones may continue. . . .

Even after selecting the approaches to emphasize, innovative managers tend to continue a few others as smaller scale "side bets" or options. In a surprising number of cases, these alternatives prove winners when the planned option falls.

Recognizing the many demands entailed by successful programs, innovative companies find special ways to reward innovators. Sony gives "a small but significant" percentage of a new product's sales to its innovating teams. Pilkington, IBM, and 3M's top executives are often chosen from those who have headed successful new product entries. Intel lets its Magnetic Memory Group operate like a small company, with special performance rewards and simulated stock options. GE, Syntex, and United Technologies help internal innovators establish new companies and take equity positions in "nonrelated" product innovations.

Large companies do not have to make their innovators millionaires, but reward should be visible and significant. Fortunately, most engineers are happy with the incentives that Tracy Kidder (1981) calls "playing pinball"—giving widespread recognition to a job well done and the right to play in the next exciting game. Most innovative companies provide both. . . .

MATCH MANAGEMENT TO THE PROCESS

. . . Executives need to understand and accept the tumultuous realities of innovation, learn from the experiences of other companies, and adapt the most relevant features of these others to their own management practices and cultures. Many features of small company innovators are also applicable in big companies. With top-level understanding, vision, a commitment to customers and solutions, a genuine portfolio strategy, a flexible entrepreneurial atmosphere, and proper incentives for innovative champions, many more large companies can innovate to meet the severe demands of global competition.

CORPORATE-LEVEL STRATEGY AND STRUCTURE

This book has so far dealt with the business-level question, "What must we do to compete successfully in this industry?"[1] Each type of organizational configuration we have examined has followed a different process in answering that question. The entrepreneurial organization uses a strategy-making approach based on the vision of the entrepreneur. The machine organization uses planning during the stable periods in its environment but reverts to either the entrepreneurial or innovative process during more difficult times. The innovative organization's strategic process is based on intense team activity, while the professional organization arrives at patterns in its stream of action through a variety of means—individual professional judgment for the elaboration of the basic mission, administrative fiat for many support activities, and collective choice for the gray areas.

THE CORPORATE-LEVEL QUESTION

At the corporate level, the managers of firms must address a different question—"In which businesses should we compete?"[2] For firms that are in only one business, the vast majority, the business and corporate levels are the same. The distinction between levels is valid only for firms in, or considering entering, multiple businesses. Some people feel that the corporate-level question is the key question any business's management should ask, even at the outset.

But there is a real concern about the advisability of this view. We saw in Chapter Nine that most firms begin when entrepreneurs build on their technical skills and personal interests. Since these are almost by definition focused on one industry, is it truly a good idea to start with the corporate-level question? Probably not. Most businesses start small; only after a business firm has succeeded and grown do issues of geographical expansion, vertical integration, and especially diversification become important, or even relevant.[3] Firms will not even reach this stage if they are unsuccessful at the business level. Also, even in a diversified firm, the ultimate success of corporate strategy rests with the success of the firm's business units, only part of which will rest on their relationship with corporate headquarters.[4]

STAGES OF CORPORATE GROWTH AND DEVELOPMENT

Alfred Chandler found that firms in the United States historically tended to grow and develop in a distinctive pattern.[5] The first stage was the *single business.* Firms that were successful in their chosen business then went to the second stage —they *grew geographically domestically.* When they had exhausted their growth potential in the United States, these firms entered stage three—*vertical integration.* That is, they began supporting their core business by becoming their own suppliers (called *backward* or *upstream integration*) or their own customers (called *forward* or *downstream integration*). Fourth, these firms engaged in *diversification*—entering new businesses. Lastly, the largest U.S. firms *expanded their businesses internationally.*

Chandler's model is historically accurate, but it is also limited by the period he described—approximately 1870 through 1950. The United States market during that period was so large and so untapped that firms would naturally want to expand in the United States before going international. Hill and Jones have suggested a revised model with three stages.[6] Stage one is the single business. In stage two, firms may support their core businesses by vertically integrating, expanding globally, or both. In stage three, the firms diversify. This model is probably more accurate given the faster transport, faster communication, and greater global competition in the world today. As both these models suggest, answering the corporate-level question can take many forms, to which we now turn.

THE CONTENT OF CORPORATE-LEVEL STRATEGY

Single Business

As mentioned above, most firms answer the corporate-level question by being **single-business** firms. They try to find ways to make their core business distinctive, enabling them to achieve advantages in their competitive context. These firms have a core business, distinguished in differentiation and scope.

Single-business firms can focus all their resources on answering the business-level question. Often their managers will have an intimate knowledge of the industry. On the negative side, they may fail to take advantage of opportunities to support the core business through vertical integration or diversification.

Chain Integration

The first way for a firm to be in more than one business is through what many people call vertical integration; that is, producing its own inputs or disposing of its own outputs. In his reading later in this chapter, "Corporate Styles," Mintzberg questions why one would use the descriptive term "vertical" integration. He calls it **chain integration**, because it involves getting into businesses backward or foward in the operating chain.

To understand this, picture a chain of activities that begins with extraction of raw materials (e.g., mining iron ore, growing and harvesting corn), goes through various stages of processing, and ends with retail selling to consumers. Moving from the middle of this imaginary chain toward its beginning is **backward integration**. For example, a food processing firm might decide to operate its own ranches. Moving from the middle toward retailing is called **forward integration**, in our illustration, when the food processing firm opens hamburger shops in shopping malls. Of course, a firm could do both. Vertical integration involves very different businesses, not just different aspects of the same business. In our example, beef ranching is very different from food processing, which in turn is very different from hamburger retailing.

There are several possible benefits to chain integration, for example smoother planning, scheduling, and coordination of production to lower costs. Also, the market costs incurred in buying inputs or selling outputs may be eliminated, or even captured as added value, through chain integration. There are some possible disadvantages, too. During a period of rapid change, firms that invest heavily in technology to support chain integration may find themselves tied to obsolescent technology. Fluctuating demand creates problems for the schedules of chain-integrated operations. Perhaps the biggest problem is the higher level of investment required up and down the operating chain, possibly forcing the firm to bypass lower-cost external sources. A solution to this is **taper integration**,[7] which occurs when a firm purchases some of its inputs from outside suppliers and sells some of its outputs to independent distributors. This puts competitive pressure on the upstream or downstream units of the firm, forcing them to keep their cost structures in line.

Diversification

Other organizations, particularly large Fortune 500–type firms, answer the corporate-level question by **diversification**—being in multiple businesses that are not connected in the operating chain of the firm. Diversification is less clear-cut than it sounds. In a comprehensive study of diversification, Richard Rumelt found that firms may diversify in at least four ways, with differing levels of success in terms of corporate performance.[8] The first is the chain integration discussed above. Rumelt found that chain-integrated firms in his sample performed poorly. Most of them were large bureaucracies in mature industries, such as steel, that had succumbed to the disadvantages of chain integration discussed earlier.

The second type of diversification is **constrained diversification**, where new businesses are entered based on the firm's being able to build on existing skills. Some firms in his sample were "dominant-constrained," meaning that over 70 percent of their sales came from one large business unit. Others were "related-constrained," meaning that (1) no single business unit dominated the corporation, (2) the businesses were related to one another in some way, and (3) the businesses had been entered in the constrained way mentioned above.

The third kind of diversification is **linked diversification**, where the new businesses are not as strongly connected to previously existing skills; the firm might decide to enter and try to create or acquire new skills, in other words, find "links" to new skills and technology that it does not already have. As happened with constrained diversification, Rumelt found "dominant-linked" firms (one business unit with 70 percent or more of sales) and "related-linked" firms (no dominant business unit, but related businesses).

Lastly, Rumelt identified **unrelated diversification**, where the firm gets involved in new businesses which are entirely different, businesses that have no relationship to previous or current operations of the firm. These were divided into "unrelated passive" firms and "acquisitive conglomerates." The major difference between these two is that the aggressive firms were more active in making acquisitions during the period of Rumelt's study.

Rumelt found that corporate performance was less influenced by a firm's total level of diversification than by the way it got there. Specifically, he found that firms following a constrained diversification strategy were more successful than those following linked diversification. In his words, they enter "only those businesses that build upon, draw strength from, and enlarge some central strength or competence. While such firms frequently develop new products and enter new businesses, they are loath to invest in areas that are unfamiliar to management."[9] His message is clear—there is no problem with branching out, if the firm stays close to its central skills. This is what Peters and Waterman referred to as "stick to the knitting."[10]

THE ORGANIZATIONAL CONTEXT
OF CORPORATE-LEVEL STRATEGY

Mintzberg's second reading in this chapter, "The Diversified Organization," goes into great detail about structure in the typical diversified organization. The diversified organization is set of semi-autonomous units ("divisions") coupled with central administrative structure ("headquarters"). Divisions are created to serve distinct markets and are given control over the operating functions necessary to do so. Each may be a self-standing business, but headquarters *does* exist, distinguishing the diversified organization from a set of independent businesses. The prime coordination mechanism is the *standardization of outputs,* in this case typically financial outputs, when the central headquarters uses a standardized financial reporting system to control the divisions.

Mintzberg discusses the roles of headquarters in some detail. He also examines how the diversified organization drives its divisions toward a machine organization configuration. He then moves to what it is that motivates the creation of a diversified organization structure itself—market diversity. He argues that though there are three possible kinds of market diversity, the only one that leads to a classic diversified organization is product/service diversity.

Mintzberg then engages a debate over whether this form of organization has the economic benefits people claim. He thinks not. He examines the contributions of headquarters, and finds that it is not as much of a training ground for new general managers, nor as good at running a diverse company, as many argue. He criticizes the social performance of this type of organization as well, arguing that quantitative performance goals tend to drive out consideration of social goals. This problem is magnified, he argues, in large government agencies that adopt the diversified structure.

THE CONVENTIONAL APPROACH
TO CORPORATE-LEVEL STRATEGY

So far in this chapter we have examined the corporate-level question, describing the answers a firm might give, from the specific strategies it might adopt to the kind of structure it might use. But the question remains—how should a firm go about answering the corporate strategy question, particularly if it is already operating in many businesses and needs to know what to do with them?

A wing of the positioning school has been devoted to this issue for many years and has developed an elaborate set of analytical tools to help corporate strategists with it. We examine these tools in this section, along with a critique of them. Unfortunately for these tools, thinking has changed on the best way to answer the question, and the "old" tools are now being increasingly criticized. We examine the new way of thinking in the next section.

Portfolio Management

An individual investor may own a portfolio of particular stocks for a specific objective. It may be to maximize income, to minimize investment risk, or to maximize earnings growth. This concept has been extended to corporate strategy. In "portfolio management" approaches to corporate strategy, a firm may own a particular collection of businesses for a distinctive reason, for example, to maximize sales of the corporation (analogous to maximizing income), to smooth out cyclical cash flows from the different businesses (analogous to minimizing risk), or to maximize sales growth.

Boston Consulting Group (BCG) Matrix

The Boston Consulting Group (BCG) matrix was the first, and probably the easiest to understand, of the portfolio techniques.[11] It arrays a corporation's business units in a two-by-two matrix whose dimensions are market growth (low or high) and market share (low or high). Units with a high share of a low-growth market are called *cash cows,* because this kind of unit typically has a large positive cash flow. The Boston Consulting Group's advice for this kind of unit is to "milk" it for cash to transfer to other units that could use it more profitably. An example of the latter is a business with a low share of a high-growth market, called a *question mark.* The objective of portfolio techniques is to transfer cash from cash generators to cash needers. Here it means to feed the problem child enough cash so that it can become a *star*; that is, a unit with a high share of a high-growth market. Stars should be kept alive until the industry reaches its inevitable maturity, at which point it becomes a cash cow and throws off cash for other units, and so on. The last kind of unit in the BCG matrix is called a *dog*—it has a low share of a low-growth market. The BCG recommendation for dogs is to divest them. But research has shown that even these units can have at least a modest positive cash flow, and perhaps should be kept for this and other reasons.[12]

Problems with Portfolio Approaches

Some people have argued that portfolio techniques help managers analyze the activities of a diversified corporation, thereby helping them keep track of the diversity.[13] But as Michael Porter claims in his reading in this chapter, "From Competitive Advantage to Corporate Strategy," this type of abstract thinking about the activities of the business units is no substitute for industry-specific knowledge. Some people assert that the portfolio matrices give corporate managers insight into how to balance the corporation's diverse activities.[14] Porter counterargues that the balancing task is too complex. In reality what seems to happen is that a corporation gets too large, its managers having made mistakes by diversifying too broadly, and a new team comes in that pares the company down to a manageable size and scope. Some believe that portfolio approaches help corporate managers understand the implications of cash flows in diversified businesses.[15] Porter's response is that a corporate headquarters is no longer needed to supply capital for a sound strategy.

John Seeger, in an article entitled "Reversing the Images of BCG's Growth Share Matrix," adds some criticisms of his own.[16] He believes that portfolio approaches overemphasize the transfer of cash from cash producers to cash needers. Seeger is particularly articulate and colorful in his criticism of the idea that cash cows should be milked. He points out that cows can dry up if they are cloistered. Also, cows can give birth to calves only if they are managed properly; analogously, cash cows can spin off new ventures and new products.

Seeger is wary of "throwing money at the stars." The starlight we see in a telescope left its source long ago. The star may have burned down into a white dwarf; it may even have become a black hole, absorbing large quantities of resources and yielding little return.

Seeger doesn't like the advice of kicking the dogs either. Not all dogs are bad, he points out. Just as some dogs are warm, loving companions, so too some "dog" businesses can be used to keep competitors busy in some markets, and they can even be sources of cash for investment in other businesses.[17] The only category that Seeger likes in the BCG matrix is the question mark: it is the only one that requires management thought. Seeger's response is that *all* the categories require management thought!

A VALUE-CREATION APPROACH
TO CORPORATE-LEVEL STRATEGY

Michael Porter's reading in this chapter, "From Competitive Advantage to Corporate Strategy," articulates a value-creation approach to corporate strategy that is superior to the portfolio methods. Porter's approach prods managers into thinking in much more specific ways.

Porter begins with three basic premises. The first is that competition occurs at the business, not the corporate, level. Diversified corporations do not compete as corporations. Their corporate strategies must support (not hinder or dissipate) their business-level competitive strategies. The second premise is that diversification is not free—it inevitably adds costs and constraints to business units. This means that firms should be confident that a diversification move will be worthwhile, because they *can* be certain that it will increase costs. Porter's third basic premise is that shareholders can readily diversify themselves. They do not need corporate managers to do it for them. This implies that corporate managers must be assured that their diversification move will give shareholders some value that they could not obtain on their own.

Porter asserts that business units must be subjected to three tests. Ideally they would be applied *before* a corporation made an acquisition or started a new venture in a given industry. But they can be applied equally well to business units currently owned by the firm. The first test is *industry attractiveness*. The industries chosen for diversification must be structurally attractive or capable of being made attractive. Porter offers his Five Forces Model, which we discussed in detail in Chapter Four, to help assess industry attractiveness.

The second test is the *cost-of-entry* test. If the cost of getting into the new business is so high that all future profits are unable to pay it back, then the firm should consider not entering. If it is already in the industry, it should probably consider divesting the business unit, since it will never pay for itself. Acquisitions now take place in an increasingly efficient merger market; multiple bidders are commonplace, driving up the acquisition cost. In general, the more attractive a business, the higher its entry cost.

The third test of corporate strategy is the *better-off test*. Since competition occurs at the business level, this means one of two things. First is that the acquisition or new venture must become better able to compete effectively in its industry by virtue of its new ownership. The second is that the parent must gain something from the venture/acquisition that it can then diffuse throughout its other business units so that *they* can better compete.

In discussing this test, Porter makes a crucially important point: Diversifying risk is *not* something that makes business units or corporations better off. Shareholders can do it for themselves.

Porter discusses four approaches to corporate strategy. He does not like the first one, *portfolio management,* as we have already discussed. The second is *restructuring,* which occurs when a parent firm seeks out weak but high-potential firms, replaces the managements, and infuses needed cash, new strategies, or new technologies. If these measures work, the strengthened units are sold, because the parent can no longer add value. Restructuring passes all three tests of successful diversification—the cost of entry is low, the business units have unrealized potential, and they are better off after having been acquired.

The third and fourth concepts of corporate strategy are *transferring skills* and *sharing activities,* which emphasize the relationships *among* the business units. Corporations must get their business units to transfer value-creating skills among themselves, or to share value-creating activities.

Porter concludes that corporate strategy becomes more successful as it moves away from portfolio approaches and toward value-sharing activities, although the four concepts are not mutually exclusive. Successful corporate strategies tend to be ones where value-sharing is high, where the business units are in related fields, and where corporations make heavier-than-average use of start-ups and joint ventures. Porter believes that start-ups are less risky than acquisitions, although firms tend to prefer acquisition.

A COMPETENCY-BASED APPROACH TO CORPORATE-LEVEL STRATEGY

Prahalad and Hamel have articulated a view of the corporation that examines some of the same ideas as Porter, but from a somewhat different perspective.[18] Like him, they believe that competition occurs at the business level, but for them the roots of competitiveness are in **core competencies.** As Prahalad and Hamel describe them, core competencies are technical skills possessed by people scattered throughout an organization. Instead of a value chain, these authors conjure up a competency tree. The "roots" are the core competencies, which feed the "trunk" and "major limbs" of core products. These core products sustain the firm's business units by becoming components in their end products. For example, Casio has core competencies in miniaturization, microprocessor design, material science, and ultrathin precision casting. It uses these to make components (core products) such as thin plastic wafers and miniature microchips. Its business units can then combine these into credit-card–sized calculators, pocket televisions, and digital watches.

CONCLUSIONS ABOUT CORPORATE-LEVEL STRATEGY

The interesting thing about both the Porter and the Prahalad and Hamel views of corporate strategy is how much more interconnected a corporation needs to be than it did under the conventional views. There, business units were independent and were kept that way by fierce adherence to the doctrine of divisional autonomy. Whatever "stitching together" took place was typically limited to corporate headquarters' allocating cash among the businesses in its portfolio. Prahalad and Hamel, as well as Mintzberg, say that this view leads to a stifling of innovation. Independent business units feel no responsibility to contribute to the maintenance of a corporate-wide core competency, so they typically underinvest in them. Since they feel that they "own" their resources, especially competent people, they don't share them with other members of the portfolio. Both of these phenomena lead to less innovation.

Porter, Prahalad, and Hamel argue for a very different view of the corporation. It is knitted together in many ways. Porter urges active sharing of activities and skills in the various primary and support activities of the value chains of all of a corporation's business units. Prahalad and Hamel argue that a corporation should not even have a business unit unless it is marketing end products that use core products that are in turn based on core competencies that are the foundation of the entire corporation. All three authors see the corporation as something that *looks* diversified from the outside, but beneath the surface is alive with common activities and shared core skills.

NOTES TO CHAPTER TWELVE

1. Hofer, C. W., and D. Schendel, *Strategy Formulation: Analytical Concepts.* St. Paul: West Publishing, 1978.
2. Ibid.
3. Chandler, A. D., *Strategy and Structure: Chapters in the History of the Industrial Enterprise.* Cambridge, Mass.: M.I.T. Press, 1962.
4. Porter, M. E., "From Competitive Advantage to Corporate Strategy." *Harvard Business Review* (May–June 1987), pp. 43–59.
5. Chandler, *Strategy and Structure.*
6. Hill, C. W. L., and G. Jones, *Strategic Management: An Integrated Approach.* Boston: Houghton-Mifflin, 1992, pp. 202–3.
7. Harrigan, K. R., "Formulating Vertical Integration Strategies." *Academy of Management Review* 9 (1984): 638–52.
8. Rumelt, R., *Strategy, Structure and Economic Performance.* Boston: Harvard Business School, 1974.
9. Ibid., p. 123.
10. Peters, T. J., and R. H. Waterman, *In Search of Excellence.* New York: Harper & Row, 1982, Ch. 10.
11. Hedley, B., "Strategy and the Business Portfolio." *Long Range Planning* 10 (1977): 9–15.
12. Hambrick, D. C., I. C. Macmillan, and D. L. Day, "Strategic Attributes and Performance in the Four Cells of the BCG Matrix—A PIMS-based Analysis of Industrial-Product Businesses." *Academy of Management Journal* 25 (1982): 510–31.
13. Hill and Jones, *Strategic Management.*
14. Ibid.
15. Ibid.
16. Seeger, J., "Reversing the Images of BCG's Growth/Share Matrix." *Strategic Management Journal* 5 (1984): 93–97.
17. Hambrick, D. C., and I. C. Macmillan, "The Product Portfolio and Man's Best Friend." *California Management Review* 25 (Fall 1982): 84–95.
18. Prahalad, C. K., and G. Hamel, "The Core Competence of the Corporation." *Harvard Business Review* 68 (May–June 1990): 79–91.

READING | GENERIC STRATEGIES FOR EXTENDING AND RECONCEIVING THE CORE BUSINESS

By Henry Mintzberg

In Chapter Four we examined three generic strategies—locating, distinguishing, then elaborating the core business. These, especially the second one, are appropriate for the business level. After locating the core business in a given industry, the strategist answers the business-level question of "How do we compete successfully in this industry?" by distinguishing the core business along the dimensions of differentiation and scope.

Given a core business with a distinguishing competitive posture, in terms of differ-

Abbreviated version for this book of Henry Mintzberg, "Generic Strategies: Toward a Comprehensive Framework," in *Advances in Strategic Management,* vol. 5 (Greenwich, Conn.: JAI Press, 1988), pp. 1–67.

entiation and scope, we now come to the question of what strategies of a generic nature are available to extend or reconceive that core business. These are approaches designed to answer the corporate-level question, "What business should we be in?"

EXTENDING THE CORE BUSINESS

We come to strategies designed to take organizations beyond their core business. This can be done in so-called vertical or horizontal ways, as well as combinations of the two. "Vertical" means backward or forward in the operating chain, the strategy being known formally as "vertical integration," although why this has been designated vertical is difficult to understand, especially since the flow of product and the chain itself are almost always drawn horizontally! Hence this will here be labeled chain integration. "Horizontal" diversification (its own geometry no more evident), which will be called here just plain diversification, refers to encompassing within the organization other, parallel businesses, not in the same chain of operations.

CHAIN INTEGRATION STRATEGIES. Organizations can extend their operating chains downstream or upstream, encompassing within their own operations the activities of their customers on the delivery end or their suppliers on the sourcing end. In effect, they choose to "make" rather than to "buy" or sell. *Impartation* (Barreyre, 1984; Barreyre and Carle, 1983) is a label that has been proposed to describe the opposite strategy, where the organization chooses to buy what it previously made, or sell what it previously transferred.

DIVERSIFICATION STRATEGIES. *Diversification* refers to the entry into some business not in the same chain of operation. It may be *related* to some distinctive competence or asset of the core business itself (also called *concentric* diversification); otherwise, it is referred to as *unrelated* or *conglomerate,* diversification. In related diversification, there is evident potential synergy between the new business and the core one, based on a common facility, asset, channel, skill, even opportunity. Porter (1985:323–324) makes the distinction here between "intangible" and "tangible" relatedness. The former is based on some functional or managerial skill considered common across the businesses, as in a Philip Morris using its marketing capabilities in Kraft. The latter refers to businesses that actually "share activities in the value chain" (p. 323), for example, different products sold by the same sales force. It should be emphasized here that no matter what its basis, every related diversification is also fundamentally an unrelated one, as many diversifying organizations have discovered to their regret. That is, no matter what *is* common between two different businesses, many other things are not.

STRATEGIES OF ENTRY AND CONTROL. Chain integration or diversification may be achieved by *internal development* or *acquisition.* In other words, an organization can enter a new business by developing it itself or by buying an organization already in that business. Our little diagrams show the former as a circle growing out from the core business to envelope the new business, the latter as an arrow coming out from the core business to connect to the new but already established business. Both internal development and acquisition involve complete ownership and formal control of the diversified business. But there are a host of other possible strategies, as follows:

Strategies of Entry and Control

Full ownership and control
- Internal Development
- Acquisition

Partial ownership and control
- Majority, minority
- Partnership, including
  - Joint venture
  - Turnkey (temporary control)

Partial control without ownership
- Licensing
- Franchising
- Long-term contracting

COMBINED INTEGRATION-DIVERSIFICATION STRATEGIES. Among the most interesting are those strategies that combine chain integration with business diversification, sometimes leading organizations into whole networks of new businesses. *By-product diversification* involves selling off the by-products of the operating chain in separate markets, as when an airline offers its maintenance services to other carriers. The new activity amounts to a form of market development at some intermediate point in the operating chain. *Linked diversification* extends by-product diversification: one business simply leads to another, whether integrated "vertically" or diversified "horizontally." The organization pursues its operating chain upstream, downstream, sidestream; it exploits preproducts, end products, and by-products of its core products as well as of each other, ending up with a network of businesses, as illustrated in the case of a supermarket chain in Figure 1. *Crystalline diversification* pushes the previous strategy to the limit, so that it becomes difficult and perhaps irrelevant to distinguish integration from diversification, core activities from peripheral activities, closely related businesses from distantly related ones. What were once clear links in a few chains now metamorphose into what looks like a form of crystalline growth, as business after business gets added literally right and left as well as up and down. Here businesses tend to be related, at least initially, through internal development of core competences, as in the "coating and bonding technologies" that are common to so many of 3M's products.

FIGURE 1
Linked Diversification on a Time Scale — the Case of the Steinberg chain
From Mintzberg and Waters (1982:490).

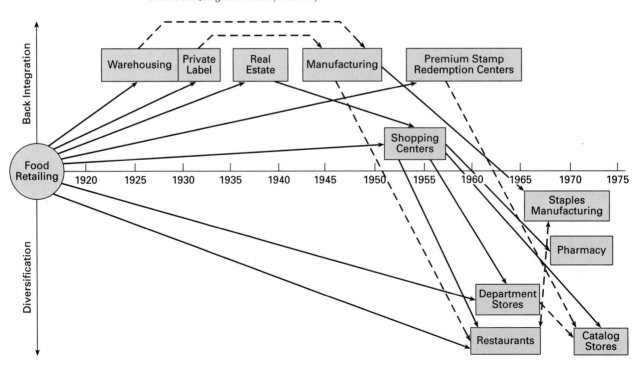

WITHDRAWAL STRATEGIES. Finally there are strategies that reverse all those of diversification: organizations cut back on the businesses they are in. "Exit" has been one popular label for this, withdrawal is another. Sometimes organizations *shrink* their activities, canceling long-term licenses, ceasing to sell by-products, reducing their crystalline networks. Other times they abandon or *liquidate* businesses (the opposite of internal development), or else they *divest* them (the opposite of acquisition).

RECONCEIVING THE CORE BUSINESS(ES)

It may seem strange to end a discussion of strategies of ever more elaborate development of a business with ones involving reconception of the business. But in one important sense, there is a logic to this: after a core business has been identified, distinguished, elaborated, and extended, there often follows the need not just to consolidate it but also to redefine it and reconfigure it—in essence, to reconceive it. As they develop, through all the waves of expansion, integration, diversification, and so on, some organizations lose a sense of themselves. Then reconception becomes the ultimate form of consolidation: rationalizing not just excesses in product offerings or markets segments or even new businesses, but all of these things together and more—the essence of the entire strategy itself. We can identify three basic reconception strategies:

BUSINESS REDEFINITION STRATEGY. A business, as Abell (1980) has pointed out, may be defined in a variety of ways—by the function it performs, the market it serves, the product it produces. All businesses have popular conceptions. Some are narrow and tangible, such as the canoe business, others broader and vague, such as the financial services business. All such definitions, no matter how tangible, are ultimately concepts that exist in the minds of actors and observers. It therefore becomes possible, with a little effort and imagination, to *redefine* a particular business—reconceive the "recipe" for how that business is conducted (Grinyer and Spender, 1979; Spender, 1989)—as Edwin Land did when he developed the Polaroid camera.[1]

BUSINESS RECOMBINATION STRATEGIES. As Porter notes, through the waves of diversification that swept American business in the 1960s and 1970s, "the concept of synergy has become widely regarded as passé"—a "nice idea" but one that rarely occurred in practice" (1985:317–318). Businesses were elements in a portfolio to be bought and sold, or, at best, grown and harvested. Deploring that conclusion, Porter devoted three chapters of his 1985 book to "horizontal strategy," which we shall refer to here (given our problems with the geometry of this field) as *business recombination* strategies—efforts to recombine different businesses in some way, at the limit to reconceive various businesses as one. Businesses can be recombined tangibly or only conceptually. The latter was encouraged by Levitt's "Marketing Myopia" (1960) article. By a stroke of the pen, railroads could be in the transportation business, ball bearing manufacturers in the friction reduction business. Realizing some practical change in behavior often proved much more difficult, however. But when some substantial basis exists for combining different activities, a strategy of business recombination can be very effective. There may never have been a transportation business, but 3M was able to draw on common tech-

---

[1] MacMillan refers to the business redefinition strategy as "reshaping the industry infrastructure" (1983:18), while Porter calls it "reconfiguration" (1985:519–523), although his notion of product *substitution,* (273–314) could sometimes also constitute a form of business redefinition.

nological capabilities to create a coating and bonding business.[2] Business recombination can also be more tangible, based on shared activities in the value chain, as in a strategy of *bundling,* where complementary products are sold together for a single price (e.g., automobile service with the new car). Of course, *unbundling* can be an equally viable strategy, such as selling "term" insurance free of any investment obligation. Carried to their logical extreme, the more tangible recombination strategies lead to a "systems view" of the business, where all products and services are conceived to be tightly interrelated.

CORE RELOCATION STRATEGIES. Finally we come full circle by closing the discussion where we began, on the location of the core business. An organization, in addition to having one or more strategic positions in a marketplace, tends to have what Jay Galbraith (1983) calls a single "center of gravity" (see his article in Chapter 6), some conceptual place where is concentrated not only its core skills but also its cultural heart, as in a Procter & Gamble focusing its efforts on "branded consumer products," each "sold primarily by advertising to the homemaker and managed by a brand manager" (1984:13). But as changes in strategic position take place, shifts can also take place in this center of gravity, in various ways. First, the organization can move *along the operating chain,* upstream or downstream, as did General Mills "from a flour miller to a related diversified provider of products for the homemaker"; eventually the company sold off its flour milling operation altogether (Galbraith, 1983:76). Second, there can be a shift *between dominant functions,* say from production to marketing. Third is the shift *to a new business,* whether or not at the same stage of the operating chain. Such shifts can be awfully demanding, simply because each industry is a culture with its own ways of thinking and acting. Finally, is the shift *to a new core theme,* as in the reorientation from a single function or product to a broader concept, for example when Procter & Gamble changed from being a soap company to being in the personal care business.

This brings us to the end of our discussion of generic strategies—our loop from locating a business to distinguishing it, elaborating it, extending it, and finally reconceiving it. We should close with the warning that while a framework of generic strategies may help to think about positioning an organization, use of it as a pat list may put that organization at a disadvantage against competitors that develop their strategies in more creative ways.

THE DIVERSIFIED ORGANIZATION

By Henry Mintzberg

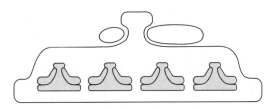

---

[2]Our suspicion, we should note, is that such labels often emerge after the fact, as the organization seeks a way to rationalize the diversification that has already taken place. In effect, the strategy is emergent. (See Chapter 1 on "Five Ps for Strategy.")

Adapted from *The Structuring of Organizations* (Prentice Hall, 1979), Chap. 20 on "The Divisionalized Form." A chapter similar to this appeared in *Mintzberg on Management: Inside Our Strange World of Organizations* (Free Press, 1989).

THE BASIC DIVISIONALIZED STRUCTURE

The diversified organization is not so much an integrated entity as a set of semiautonomous units coupled together by a central administrative structure. The units are generally called *divisions,* and the central administration, the *headquarters.* This is a widely used configuration in the private sector of the industrialized economy; the vast majority of the *Fortune* 500, America's largest corporations, use this structure or a variant of it. But, as we shall see, it is also found in other sectors as well.

In what is commonly called the "divisionalized" form of structure, units, called "divisions," are created to serve distinct markets and are given control over the operating functions necessary to do so, as shown in Figure 1. Each is therefore relatively free of direct control by headquarters or even of the need to coordinate activities with other divisions. Each, in other words, appears to be a self-standing business. Of course, none is. There *is* a headquarters, and it has a series of roles that distinguish this overall configuration from a collection of independent businesses providing the same set of products and services.

Roles of the Headquarters

Above all, the headquarters exercises performance control. It sets standards of achievement, generally in quantitative terms (such as return on investment or growth in sales), and then monitors the results. Coordination between headquarters and the divisions thus reduces largely to the standardization of outputs. Of course, there is some direct supervision—headquarters' managers have to have personal contact with and knowledge of the divisions. But that is largely circumscribed by the key assumption in this configuration that if the division managers are to be responsible for the performance of their divisions, they must have considerable autonomy to manage them as they see fit. Hence there is extensive delegation of authority from headquarters to the level of division manager.

Certain important tasks do, however, remain for the headquarters. One is to develop the overall *corporate* strategy, meaning to establish the portfolio of businesses in which the organization will operate. The headquarters establishes, acquires, divests, and

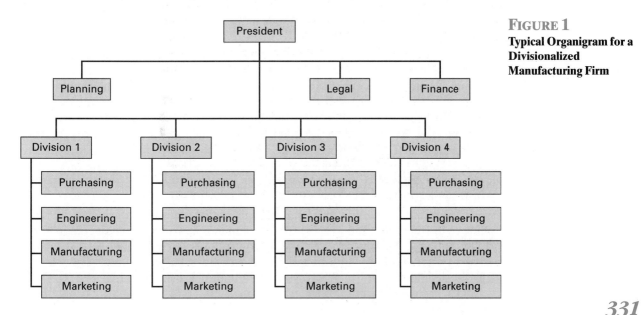

FIGURE 1
Typical Organigram for a Divisionalized Manufacturing Firm

closes down divisions in order to change its portfolio. Popular in the 1970s in this regard was the Boston Consulting Group's "growth share matrix," where corporate managers were supposed to allocate funds to divisions on the basis of their falling into the categories of dogs, cash cows, wildcats, and stars. But enthusiasm for that technique waned, perhaps mindful of Pope's warning that a little learning can be a dangerous thing.

Second, the headquarters manages the movement of funds between the divisions, taking the excess profits of some to support the greater growth potential of others. Third, of course, the headquarters, through its own technostructure, designs and operates the performance control system. Fourth, it appoints and therefore retains the right to replace the division managers. For a headquarters that does not directly manage any division, its most tangible power when the performance of a division lags—short of riding out an industry downturn or divesting the division—is to replace its leader. Finally, the headquarters provides certain support services that are common to all the divisions—a corporate public relations office or legal counsel, for example.

Structure of the Divisions

It has been common to label divisionalized organizations "decentralized." That is a reflection of how *certain* of them came to be, most notably Du Pont early in this century. When organizations that were structured functionally (for example, in departments of marketing, manufacturing, and engineering, etc.) diversified, they found that coordination of their different product lines across the functions became increasingly complicated. The central managers had to spend great amounts of time intervening to resolve disputes. But once these corporations switched to a divisionalized form of structure, where all the functions for a given business could be contained in a single unit dedicated to that business, management became much simpler. In effect, their structures became *more* decentralized, power over distinct businesses being delegated to the division managers.

But more decentralized does not mean *decentralized*. That word refers to the dispersal of decision-making power in an organization, and in many of the diversified corporations much of the power tended to remain with the few managers who ran the businesses. Indeed, the most famous case of divisionalization was one of relative *centralization:* Alfred P. Sloan introduced the divisionalized structure to General Motors in the 1920s to *reduce* the power of its autonomous business units, to impose systems of financial controls on what had been a largely unmanaged agglomeration of different automobile businesses.

In fact, I would argue that it is the *centralization* of power within the divisions that is most compatible with the divisionalized form of structure. In other words, the effect of having a headquarters over the divisions is to drive them toward the machine configuration, namely a structure of centralized bureaucracy. That is the structure most compatible with headquarters control, in my opinion. If true, this would seem to be an important point, because it means that the proliferation of the diversified configuration in many spheres—business, government, and the rest—has the effect of driving many suborganizations toward machine bureaucracy, even where that configuration may be inappropriate (school systems, for example, or government departments charged with innovative project work).

The explanation for this lies in the standardization of outputs, the key to the functioning of the divisionalized structure. Bear in mind the headquarters' dilemma: to respect divisional autonomy while exercising control over performance. This it seeks to resolve by after-the-fact monitoring of divisional results, based on clearly defined performance standards. But two main assumptions underlie such standards.

First, each division must be treated as a single integrated system with a single, consistent set of goals. In other words, although the divisions may be loosely coupled with each other, the assumption is that each is tightly coupled internally.[1]

Second, these goals must be operational ones, in other words, lend themselves to quantitative measurement. But in the less formal configurations—entrepreneurial and innovative—which are less stable, such performance standards are difficult to establish, while in the professional configuration, the complexity of the work makes it difficult to establish such standards. Moreover, while the entrepreneurial configuration may lend itself to being integrated around a single set of goals, the innovative and professional configurations do not. Thus, only the machine configuration of the major types fits comfortably into the conventional divisionalized structure, by virtue of its integration and its operational goals.

In fact, when organizations with another configuration are drawn under the umbrella of a divisionalized structure, they tend to be forced toward the machine bureaucratic form, to make them conform with *its* needs. How often have we heard stories of entrepreneurial firms recently acquired by conglomerates being descended upon by hordes of headquarters technocrats bemoaning the loose controls, the absence of organigrams, the informality of the systems? In many cases, of course, the very purpose of the acquisition was to do just this, tighten up the organization so that its strategies can be pursued more pervasively and systematically. But other times, the effect is to destroy the organization's basic strengths, sometimes including its flexibility and responsiveness. Similarly, how many times have we heard tell of government administrators complaining about being unable to control public hospitals or universities through conventional (meaning machine bureaucratic) planning systems?

This conclusion is, in fact, a prime manifestation of the hypothesis [discussed in Chapter 6] that concentrated external control of an organization has the effect of formalizing and centralizing its structure, in other words, of driving it toward the machine configuration. Headquarters' control of divisions is, of course, concentrated; indeed, when the diversified organization is itself a *closed system,* as I shall argue later many tend to be, then it is a most concentrated form of control. And, the effect of that control is to render the divisions its *instruments.*

There is, in fact, an interesting irony in this, in that the less society controls the overall diversified organization, the more the organization itself controls its individual units. The result is increased autonomy for the largest organizations coupled with decreased autonomy for their many activities.

To conclude this discussion of the basic structure, the diversified configuration is represented in the opening figure, symbolically in terms of our logo, as follows. Headquarters has three parts: a small strategic apex of top managers, a small technostructure to the left concerned with the design and operation of the performance control system, and a slightly larger staff support group to the right to provide support services common to all the divisions. Each of the divisions is shown below the headquarters as a machine configuration.

CONDITIONS OF THE DIVERSIFIED ORGANIZATION

While the diversified configuration may arise from the federation of different organizations, which come together under a common headquarters umbrella, more often it appears to be the structural response to a machine organization that has diversified its range of product or service offerings. In either case, it is the diversity of markets above

---

[1] Unless, of course, there is a second layer of divisionalization, which simply takes this conclusion down another level in the hierarchy.

all that drives an organization to use this configuration. An organization faced with a single integrated market simply cannot split itself into autonomous divisions; the one with distinct markets, however, has an incentive to create a unit to deal with each.

There are three main kinds of market diversity—product and service, client, and region. In theory, all three can lead to divisionalization. But when diversification is based on variations in clients or regions as opposed to products or services, divisionalization often turns out to be incomplete. With identical products or services in each region or for each group of clients, the headquarters is encouraged to maintain central control of certain critical functions, to ensure common operating standards for all the divisions. And that seriously reduces divisional autonomy, and so leads to a less than complete form of divisionalization.

Thus, one study found that insurance companies concentrate at headquarters the critical function of investment, and retailers concentrate that of purchasing, also controlling product range, pricing, and volume (Channon, 1975). One need only look at the individual outlets of a typical retail chain to recognize the absence of divisional autonomy: usually they all look alike. The same conclusion tends to hold for other businesses organized by regions, such as bakeries, breweries, cement producers, and soft drink bottlers: Their "divisions," distinguished only by geographical location, lack the autonomy normally associated with ones that produce distinct products or services.

What about the conditions of size? Although large size itself does not bring on divisionalization, surely it is not coincidental that most of America's largest corporations use some variant of this configuration. The fact is that as organizations grow large, they become inclined to diversify and then to divisionalize. One reason is protection: large organizations tend to be risk averse—they have too much to lose—and diversification spreads the risk. Another is that as firms grow large, they come to dominate their traditional market, and so must often find growth opportunities elsewhere, through diversification. Moreover, diversification feeds on itself. It creates a cadre of aggressive general managers, each running his or her own division, who push for further diversification and further growth. Thus, most of the giant corporations—with the exception of the "heavies," those with enormously high fixed-cost operating systems, such as the oil or aluminum producers—not only were able to reach their status by diversifying but also feel great pressures to continue to do so.

Age is another factor associated with this configuration, much like size. In larger organizations, the management runs out of places to expand in its traditional markets; in older ones, the managers sometimes get bored with the traditional markets and find diversion through diversification. Also, time brings new competitors into old markets, forcing the management to look elsewhere for growth opportunities.

As governments grow large, they too tend to adopt a kind of divisionalized structure. The central administrators, unable to control all the agencies and departments directly, settle for granting their managers considerable autonomy and then trying to control their results through planning and performance controls. Indeed, the "accountability" buzzword so often heard in governments these days reflects just this trend—to move closer to a divisionalized structure.

One can, in fact, view the entire government as a giant diversified configuration (admittedly an oversimplification, since all kinds of links exist among the departments), with its three main coordinating agencies corresponding to the three main forms of control used by the headquarters of the large corporation. The budgetary agency, technocratic in nature, concerns itself with performance control of the departments; the public service commission, also partly technocratic, concerns itself with the recruiting and training of government managers; and the executive office, top management in nature, reviews the principal proposals and initiatives of the departments.

In the preceding chapter, the communist state was described as a closed-system machine bureaucracy. But it may also be characterized as the ultimate closed system diversified configuration, with the various state enterprises and agencies its instruments, machine bureaucracies tightly regulated by the planning and control systems of the central government.

STAGES IN THE TRANSITION TO THE DIVERSIFIED ORGANIZATION

There has been a good deal of research on the transition of the corporation from the functional to the diversified form. Figure 2 and the discussion that follows borrow from this research to describe four stages in that transition.

At the top of Figure 2 is the pure *functional* structure, used by the corporation whose operating activities form one integrated, unbroken chain from purchasing through production to marketing and sales. Only the final output is sold to the customers.[2] Autonomy cannot, therefore, be granted to the units, so the organization tends to take on the form of one overall machine configuration.

As an integrated firm seeks wider markets, it may introduce a variety of new end products and so shift all the way to the pure diversified form. A less risky alternative, however, is to start by marketing its intermediate products on the open market. This in-

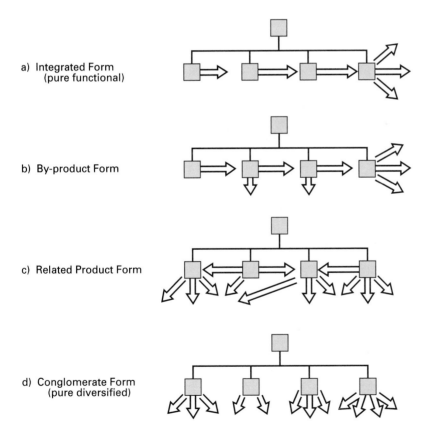

a) Integrated Form
   (pure functional)

b) By-product Form

c) Related Product Form

d) Conglomerate Form
   (pure diversified)

FIGURE 2
Stages in the Transition to the Pure Diversified Form

---

[2]It should be noted that this is in fact the definition of a functional structure: Each activity contributes just one step in a chain toward the creation of the final product. Thus, for example, engineering is a functionally organized unit in the firm that produces and markets its own designs, while it would be a market organized unit in a consulting firm that sells its design services, among other, directly to clients.

troduces small breaks in its processing chain, which in turn calls for a measure of divisionalization in its structure, giving rise to the *by-product* form. But because the processing chain remains more or less intact, central coordination must largely remain. Organizations that fall into this category tend to be vertically integrated, basing their operations on a single raw material, such as wood, oil, or aluminum, which they process to a variety of consumable end products. The example of Alcoa is shown in Figure 3.

Some corporations further diversify their by-product markets, breaking down their processing chain until what the divisions sell on the open market becomes more important than what they supply to each other. The organization then moves to the *related-product* form. For example, a firm manufacturing washing machines may set up a division to produce the motors. When the motor division sells more motors to outside customers than to its own sister division, a more serious form of divisionalization is called for. What typically holds the divisions of these firms together is some common thread among their products, perhaps a core skill or technology, perhaps a central market theme, as in a corporation such as 3M that likes to describe itself as being in the coating and bonding business. A good deal of the control over the specific product-market strategies can now revert to the divisions, such as research and development.

As a related-product firm expands into new markets or acquires other firms with less regard to a central strategic theme, the organization moves to the *conglomerate* form and so adopts a pure diversified configuration, the one described at the beginning of this reading. Each division serves its own markets, producing products unrelated to those of the other divisions—chinaware in one, steam shovels in a second, and so on.[3]

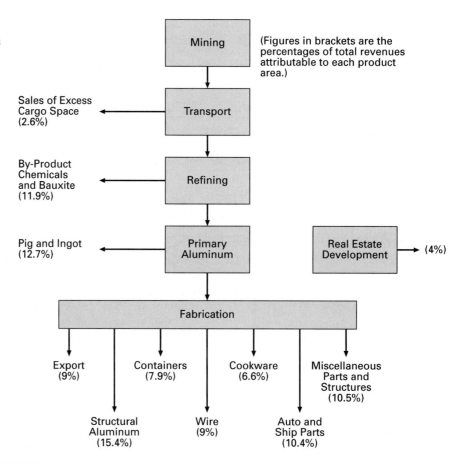

FIGURE 3

By-Product and End-Product Sales of Alcoa (from Rumelt, 1974:21)

Note: Percentages for 1969 prepared by Richard Rumelt from data in company's annual reports.

[3]I wrote this example here somewhat whimsically before I encountered a firm in Finland with divisions that actually produce, among other things, the world's largest icebreaker ships and fine pottery!

The result is that the headquarters planning and control system becomes simply a vehicle for regulating performance, and the headquarters staff can diminish to almost nothing—a few general and group managers supported by a few financial analysts with a minimum of support services.

SOME ISSUES ASSOCIATED WITH THE DIVERSIFIED ORGANIZATION

The Economic Advantages of Diversification?

It has been argued that the diversified configuration offers four basic advantages over the functional structure with integrated operations, namely an overall machine configuration. First, it encourages the efficient allocation of capital. Headquarters can choose where to put its money and so can concentrate on its strongest markets, milking the surpluses of some divisions to help others grow. Second, by opening up opportunities to run individual businesses, the diversified configuration helps to train general managers. Third, this configuration spreads its risk across different markets, whereas the focused machine bureaucracy has all its strategic eggs in one market basket, so to speak. Fourth, and perhaps most important, the diversified configuration is strategically responsive. The divisions can fine-tune their bureaucratic machines while the headquarters can concentrate on the strategic portfolio. It can acquire new businesses and divest itself of old, unproductive ones.

But is the single machine organization the correct basis of comparison? Is not the real alternative, at least from society's perspective, the taking of a further step along the same path, to the point of eliminating the headquarters altogether and allowing the divisions to function as independent organization? Beatrice Foods, described in a 1976 *Fortune* magazine article, had 397 different divisions (Martin, 1976). The issue is whether this arrangement was more efficient than 397 separate corporations.[4] In this regard, let us reconsider the four advantages discussed earlier.

In the diversified corporation, headquarters allocates the capital resources among the divisions. In the case of 397 independent corporations, the capital markets do that job instead. Which does it better? Studies suggest that the answer is not simple.

Some people, such as the economist Oliver Williamson (1975, 1985), have argued that the diversified organization may do a better job of allocating money because the capital markets are inefficient. Managers at headquarters who know their divisions can move the money around faster and more effectively. But others find that arrangement more costly and, in some ways, less flexible. Moyer (1970), for example, argued early on that conglomerates pay a premium above stock market prices to acquire businesses, whereas the independent investor need pay only small brokerage fees to diversify his or her own portfolio, and can do so easier and more flexibly. Moreover, that provides the investor with full information on all the businesses owned, whereas the diversified corporation provides only limited information to stockholders on the details inside its portfolio.

On the issue of management development, the question becomes whether the division managers receive better training and experience than they would as company presidents. The diversified organization is able to put on training courses and to rotate its managers to vary their experience; the independent firm is limited in those respects.

---

[4]The example of Beatrice was first written as presented here in the 1970s, when the company was the subject of a good deal of attention and praise in the business press. At the time of this revision, in 1988, the company is being disassembled. It seemed appropriate to leave the example as first presented, among other reasons to question the tendency to favor fashion over investigation in the business press.

But if, as the proponents of diversification claim, autonomy is the key to management development, then presumably the more autonomy the better. The division managers have a headquarters to lean on—and to be leaned on by. Company presidents, in contrast, are on their own to make their own mistakes and to learn from them.

On the third issue, risk, the argument from the diversified perspective is that the independent organization is vulnerable during periods of internal crisis or economic slump; conglomeration offers support to see individual businesses through such periods. The counter-argument, however, is that diversification may conceal bankruptcies, that ailing divisions are sometimes supported longer than necessary, whereas the market bankrupts the independent firm and is done with it. Moreover, just as diversification spreads the risk, so too does it spread the consequences of that risk. A single division cannot go bankrupt; the whole organization is legally responsible for its debts. So a massive enough problem in one division can pull down the whole organization. Loose coupling may turn out to be riskier than no coupling!

Finally, there is the issue of strategic responsiveness. Loosely coupled divisions may be more responsive than tightly coupled functions. But how responsive do they really prove to be? The answer appears to be negative: this configuration appears to inhibit, not encourage, the taking of strategic initiatives. The problem seems to lie, again, in its control system. It is designed to keep the carrot just the right distance in front of the divisional managers, encouraging them to strive for better and better financial performance. At the same time, however, it seems to dampen their inclination to innovate. It is that famous "bottom line" that creates the problem, encouraging short-term thinking and shortsightedness; attention is focused on the carrot just in front instead of the fields of vegetables beyond. As Bower has noted,

> [T]he risk to the division manager of a major innovation can be considerable if he is measured on short-run, year-to-year, earnings performance. The result is a tendency to avoid big risk bets, and the concomitant phenomenon that major new developments are, with few exceptions, made outside the major firms in the industry. Those exceptions tend to be single-product companies whose top managements are committed to true product leadership. . . . Instead, the diversified companies give us a steady diet of small incremental change. (1970:194)

Innovation requires entrepreneurship, or intrapreneurship, and these, as we have already argued, do not thrive under the diversified configuration. The entrepreneur takes his or her own risks to earn his or her own rewards; the intrapreneur (as we shall see) functions best in the loose structure of the innovative adhocracy. Indeed, many diversified corporations depend on those configurations for their strategic responsiveness, since they diversify not by innovating themselves but by acquiring the innovative results of independent firms. Of course, that may be their role—to exploit rather than create those innovations—but we should not, as a result, justify diversification on the basis of its innovative capacity.

The Contribution of Headquarters

To assess the effectiveness of conglomeration, it is necessary to assess what actual contribution the headquarters makes to the divisions. Since what the headquarters does in a diversified organization is otherwise performed by the various boards of directors of a set of independent firms, the question then becomes, what does a headquarters offer to the divisions that the independent board of directors of the autonomous organization does not?

One thing that neither can offer is the management of the individual business. Both are involved with it only on a part-time basis. The management is, therefore, logically left to the full-time managers, who have the required time and information.

Among the functions a headquarters *does* perform, as noted earlier, are the establishment of objectives for the divisions, the monitoring of their performance in terms of these objectives, and the maintenance of limited personal contacts with division managers, for example to approve large capital expenditures. Interestingly, those are also the responsibilities of the directors of the individual firm, at least in theory.

In practice, however, many boards of directors—notably, those of widely held corporations—do those things rather ineffectively, leaving business managements carte blanche to do what they like. Here, then, we seem to have a major advantage to the diversified configuration. It exists as an administrative mechanism to overcome another prominent weakness of the free-market system, the ineffective board.

There is a catch in this argument, however, for diversification by enhancing an organization's size and expanding its number of markets, renders the corporation more difficult to understand and so to control by its board of part-time directors. Moreover, as Moyer has noted, one common effect of conglomerate acquisition is to increase the number of shareholders, and so to make the corporation more widely held, and therefore less amenable to director control. Thus, the diversified configuration in some sense resolves a problem of its own making—it offers the control that its own existence has rendered difficult. Had the corporation remained in one business, it might have been more narrowly held and easier to understand, and so its directors might have been able to perform their functions more effectively. Diversification thus helped to create the problem that divisionalization is said to solve. Indeed, it is ironic that many a diversified corporation that does such a vigorous job of monitoring the performance of its own divisions is itself so poorly monitored by its own board of directors!

All of this suggests that large diversified organizations tend to be classic closed systems, powerful enough to seal themselves off from much external influence while able to exercise a good deal of control over not only their own divisions, as instruments, but also their external environments. For example, one study of all 5,995 directors of the *Fortune* 500 found that only 1.6 percent of them represented major shareholder interests (Smith, 1978) while another survey of 855 corporations found that 84 percent of them did not even formally require their directors to hold any stock at all! (Bacon, 1973:40).

What does happen when problems arise in a division? What can a headquarters do that various boards of directors cannot? The chairman of one major conglomerate told a meeting of the New York Society of Security Analysts, in reference to the headquarters vice presidents who oversee the divisions, that "it is not too difficult to coordinate five companies that are well run" (in Wrigley, 1970:V78). True enough. But what about five that are badly run? What could the small staff of administrators at a corporation's headquarters really do to correct problems in that firm's thirty operating divisions or in Beatrice's 397? The natural tendency to tighten the control screws does not usually help once the problem has manifested itself, nor does exercising close surveillance. As noted earlier, the headquarters managers cannot manage the divisions. Essentially, that leaves them with two choices. They can either replace the division manager, or they can divest the corporation of the division. Of course, a board of directors can also replace the management. Indeed, that seems to be its only real prerogative; the management does everything else.

On balance, then, the economic case for one headquarters versus a set of separate boards of directors appears to be mixed. It should, therefore, come as no surprise that one important study found that corporations with "controlled diversity" had better profits than those with conglomerate diversity (Rumelt, 1974). Overall, the pure diversified configuration (the conglomerate) may offer some advantages over a weak system of separate boards of directors and inefficient capital markets, but most of those advantages would probably disappear if certain problems in capital markets and boards of directors were rectified. And there is reason to argue, from a social no less than an economic standpoint, that society would be better off trying to correct fundamental inefficiencies in its economic system rather than encourage private administrative arrangements to circumvent them, as we shall now see.

The Social Performance of the Performance Control System

This configuration requires that headquarters control the divisions primarily by quantitative performance criteria, and that typically means financial ones—profit, sales growth, return on investment, and the like. The problem is that these performance measures often become virtual obsessions in the diversified organization, driving out goals that cannot be measured—product quality, pride in work, customers well served. In effect, the economic goals drive out the social ones. As the chief of a famous conglomerate once remarked, "We, in Textron, worship the god of New Worth" (in Wrigley, 1970:V86).

That would pose no problem if the social and economic consequences of decisions could easily be separated. Governments would look after the former, corporations the latter. But the fact is that the two are intertwined; every strategic decision of every large corporation involves both, largely inseparable. As a result, its control systems, by focusing on economic measures, drive the diversified organization to act in ways that are, at best, socially unresponsive, at worst, socially irresponsible. Forced to concentrate on the economic consequences of decisions, the division manager is driven to ignore their social consequences. (Indeed, that manager is also driven to ignore the intangible economic consequences as well, such as product quality or research effort, another manifestation of the problem of the short-term, bottom-line thinking mentioned earlier.) Thus, Bower found that "the best records in the race relations area are those of single-product companies whose strong top managements are deeply involved in the business" (1970:193).

Robert Ackerman, in a study carried out at the Harvard Business School, investigated this point. He found that social benefits such as "a rosier public image . . . pride among managers . . . an attractive posture for recruiting on campus" could not easily be measured and so could not be plugged into the performance control system. The result was that

> . . . the financial reporting system may actually inhibit social responsiveness. By focusing on economic performance, even with appropriate safeguards to protect against sacrificing long-term benefits, such a system directs energy and resources to achieving results measured in financial terms. It is the only game in town, so to speak, at least the only one with an official scoreboard. (1975:55, 56)

Headquarters managers who are concerned about legal liabilities or the public relations effects of decisions, or even ones personally interested in broader social issues, may be tempted to intervene directly in the divisions' decision-making process to ensure proper attention to social matters. But they are discouraged from doing so by this configuration's strict division of labor: divisional autonomy requires no meddling by the headquarters in specific business decisions.

As long as the screws of the performance control system are not turned too tight, the division managers may retain enough discretion to consider the social consequences of their actions, if they so choose. But when those screws are turned tight, as they often are in the diversified corporation with a bottom-line orientation, then the division managers wishing to keep their jobs may have no choice but to act socially unresponsively, if not actually irresponsibly. As Bower has noted of the General Electric price-fixing scandal of the 1960s, "a very severely managed system of reward and punishment that demanded yearly improvements in earnings, return and market share, applied indiscriminately to all divisions, yielded a situation which was—at the very least—conducive to collusion in the oligopolistic and mature electric equipment markets" (1970:193).

The Diversified Organization in the Public Sphere

Ironically, for a government intent on dealing with these social problems, solutions are indicated in the very arguments used to support the diversified configuration. Or so it would appear.

For example, if the administrative arrangements are efficient while the capital markets are not, then why should a government hesitate to interfere with the capital markets? And why shouldn't it use those same administrative arrangements to deal with the problems? If Beatrice Foods really can control those 397 divisions, then what is to stop Washington from believing it can control 397 Beatrices? After all, the capital markets don't much matter. In his book on "countervailing power," John Kenneth Galbraith (1952) argued that bigness in one sector, such as business, promotes bigness in other sectors, such as unions and government. That has already happened. How long before government pursues the logical next step and exercises direct controls?

While such steps may prove irresistible to some governments, the fact is that they will not resolve the problems of power concentration and social irresponsibility but rather will aggravate them, but not just in the ways usually assumed in Western economics. All the existing problems would simply be bumped up to another level, and there increase. By making use of the diversified configuration, government would magnify the problems of size. Moreover, government, like the corporation, would be driven to favor measurable economic goals over intangible social ones, and that would add to the problems of social irresponsibility—a phenomenon of which we have already seen a good deal in the public sector.

In fact, these problems would be worse in government, because its sphere is social, and so its goals are largely ill suited to performance control systems. In other words, many of the goals most important for the public sector—and this applies to not-for-profit organizations in spheres such as health and education as well—simply do not lend themselves to measurement, no matter how long and how hard public officials continue to try. And without measurement, the conventional diversified configuration cannot work.

There are, of course, other problems with the application of this form of organization in the public sphere. For example, government cannot divest itself of subunits quite so easily as can corporations. And public service regulations on appointments and the like, as well as a host of other rules, preclude the degree of division manager autonomy available in the private sector. (It is, in fact, these central rules and regulations that make governments resemble integrated machine configurations as much as loosely coupled diversified ones, and that undermine their efforts at "accountability.")

Thus, we conclude that, appearances and even trends notwithstanding, the diversified configuration is generally not suited to the public and not-for-profit sectors of society. Governments and other public-type institutions that wish to divisionalize to avoid centralized machine bureaucracy may often find the imposition of performance standards an artificial exercise. They may thus be better off trying to exercise control of their units in a different way. For example, they can select unit managers who reflect their desired values, or indoctrinate them in those values, and then let them manage freely, the control in effect being normative rather than quantitative. But managing ideology, even creating it in the first place, is no simple matter, especially in a highly diversified organization.

In Conclusion: A Structure on the Edge of a Cliff

Our discussion has led to a "damned if you do, damned if you don't" conclusion. The pure (conglomerate) diversified configuration emerges as an organization perched symbolically on the edge of the cliff, at the end of a long path. Ahead, it is one step away from disintegration—breaking up into separate organizations on the rocks below. Behind it is the way back to a more stable integration, in the form of the machine configuration at the start of that path. And ever hovering above is the eagle, representing the broader social control of the state, attracted by the organization's position on the edge of the cliff and waiting for the chance to pull it up to a higher cliff, perhaps more dangerous still. The edge of the cliff is an uncomfortable place to be, perhaps even a temporary one that must inevitably lead to disintegration on the rocks below, a trip to that cliff above, or a return to a safer resting place somewhere on that path behind.

READING — FROM COMPETITIVE ADVANTAGE TO CORPORATE STRATEGY

By Michael E. Porter

Corporate strategy, the overall plan for a diversified company, is both the darling and the stepchild of contemporary management practice—the darling because CEOs have been obsessed with diversification since the early 1960s, the stepchild because almost no consensus exists about what corporate strategy is, much less about how a company should formulate it.

A diversified company has two levels of strategy: business unit (or competitive) strategy and corporate (or companywide) strategy. Competitive strategy concerns how to create competitive advantage in each of the businesses in which a company competes. Corporate strategy concerns two different questions: what businesses the corporation should be in and how the corporate office should manage the array of business units.

Corporate strategy is what makes the corporate whole add up to more than the sum of its business unit parts.

The track record of corporate strategies has been dismal. I studied the diversification records of 33 large, prestigious U.S. companies over the 1950–1986 period and found that most of them had divested many more acquisitions than they had kept. The corporate strategies of most companies have dissipated instead of created shareholder value.

The need to rethink corporate strategy could hardly be more urgent. By taking over companies and breaking them up, corporate raiders thrive on failed corporate strategy. Fueled by junk bond financing and growing acceptability, raiders can expose any company to takeover, no matter how large or blue chip. . . .

A SOBER PICTURE

. . . My study of 33 companies, many of which have reputations for good management, is a unique look at the track record of major corporations. . . . Each company entered an average of 80 new industries and 27 new fields. Just over 70% of the new entries were acquisitions, 22% were start-ups, and 8% were joint ventures. IBM, Exxon, Du Pont, and 3M, for example, focused on startups, while ALCO Standard, Beatrice, and Sara Lee diversified almost solely through acquisitions. . . .

My data paint a sobering picture of the success ratio of these moves. . . . I found that on average corporations divested more than half their acquisitions in new industries and more than 60% of their acquisitions in entirely new fields. Fourteen companies left more than 70% of all the acquisitions they had made in new fields. The track record

Originally published in the *Harvard Business Review* (May–June 1987) and winner of the McKinsey Prize for the best in the Review in 1987. Copyright © 1987 by the President and Fellows of Harvard College; all rights reserved. Reprinted with deletions by permission of the Harvard Business Review.

in unrelated acquisitions is even worse—the average divestment rate is a startling 74%. Even a highly respected company like General Electric divested a very high percentage of its acquisitions, particularly those in new fields. . . . Some [companies] bear witness to the success of well-thought-out corporate strategies. Others, however, enjoy a lower rate simply because they have not faced up to their problem units and divested them. . . .

I would like to make one comment on the use of shareholder value to judge performance. Linking shareholder value quantitatively to diversification performance only works if you compare the shareholder value that is with the shareholder value that might have been without diversification. Because such a comparison is virtually impossible to make, my own measure of diversification success—the number of units retained by the company—seems to be as good an indicator as any of the contribution of diversification to corporate performance.

My data give a stark indication of the failure of corporate strategies.[1] Of the 33 companies, 6 had been taken over as my study was being completed. . . . Only the lawyers, investment bankers, and original sellers have prospered in most of these acquisitions, not the shareholders.

PREMISES OF CORPORATE STRATEGY

Any successful corporate strategy builds on a number of premises. These are facts of life about diversification. They cannot be altered, and when ignored, they explain in part why so many corporate strategies fail.

COMPETITION OCCURS AT THE BUSINESS UNIT LEVEL. Diversified companies do not compete; only their business units do. Unless a corporate strategy places primary attention on nurturing the success of each unit, the strategy will fail, no matter how elegantly constructed. Successful corporate strategy must grow out of and reinforce competitive strategy.

DIVERSIFICATION INEVITABLY ADDS COSTS AND CONSTRAINTS TO BUSINESS UNITS. Obvious costs such as the corporate overhead allocated to a unit may not be as important or subtle as the hidden costs and constraints. A business unit must explain its decisions to top management, spend time complying with planning and other corporate systems, live with parent company guidelines and personnel policies, and forgo the opportunity to motivate employees with direct equity ownership. These costs and constraints can be reduced but not entirely eliminated.

SHAREHOLDERS CAN READILY DIVERSIFY THEMSELVES. Shareholders can diversify their own portfolios of stocks by selecting those that best match their preferences and risk profiles (Salter and Weinhold, 1979). Shareholders can often diversify more cheaply than a corporation because they can buy shares at the market price and avoid hefty acquisition premiums.

These premises mean that corporate strategy cannot succeed unless it truly adds value—to business units by providing tangible benefits that offset the inherent costs of lost independence and to shareholders by diversifying in a way they could not replicate.

---

[1] Some recent evidence also supports the conclusion that acquired companies often suffer eroding performance after acquisition. See Frederick M. Scherer, "Mergers, Sell-Offs and Managerial Behavior," in *The Economics of Strategic Planning,* ed. Lacy Glenn Thomas (Lexington, MA: Lexington Books, 1986), p. 143, and David A. Ravenscraft and Frederick M. Scherer, "Mergers and Managerial Performance," paper presented at the Conference on Takeovers and Contests for Corporate Control, Columbia Law School, 1985.

To understand how to formulate corporate strategy, it is necessary to specify the conditions under which diversification will truly create shareholder value. These conditions can be summarized in three essential tests:

1. *The attractiveness test.* The industries chosen for diversification must be structurally attractive or capable of being made attractive.
2. *The cost-of-entry test.* The cost of entry must not capitalize all the future profits.
3. *The better-off test.* Either the new unit must gain competitive advantage from its link with the corporation or vice versa.

Of course, most companies will make certain that their proposed strategies pass some of these tests. But my study clearly shows that when companies ignored one or two of them, the strategic results were disastrous.

How Attractive Is the Industry?

In the long run, the rate of return available from competing in an industry is a function of its underlying structure [see Porter reading in Chapter Four]. An attractive industry with a high average return on investment will be difficult to enter because entry barriers are high, suppliers and buyers have only modest bargaining power, substitute products or services are few, and the rivalry among competitors is stable. An unattractive industry like steel will have structural flaws, including a plethora of substitute materials, powerful and price-sensitive buyers, and excessive rivalry caused by high fixed costs and a large group of competitors, many of whom are state supported.

Diversification cannot create shareholder value unless new industries have favorable structures that support returns exceeding the cost of capital. If the industry doesn't have such returns, the company must be able to restructure the industry or gain a sustainable competitive advantage that leads to returns well above the industry average. An industry need not be attractive before diversification. In fact, a company might benefit from entering before the industry shows its full potential. The diversification can then transform the industry's structure.

In my research, I often found companies had suspended the attractiveness test because they had a vague belief that the industry "fit" very closely with their own businesses. In the hope that the corporate "comfort" they felt would lead to a happy outcome, the companies ignored fundamentally poor industry structures. Unless the close fit allows substantial competitive advantage, however, such comfort will turn into pain when diversification results in poor returns. Royal Dutch Shell and other leading oil companies have had this unhappy experience in a number of chemicals businesses, where poor industry structures overcame the benefits of vertical integration and skills in process technology.

Another common reason for ignoring the attractiveness test is a low entry cost. Sometimes the buyer has an inside track or the owner is anxious to sell. Even if the price is actually low, however, a one-shot gain will not offset a perpetually poor business. Almost always, the company finds it must reinvest in the newly acquired unit, if only to replace fixed assets and fund working capital.

Diversifying companies are also prone to use rapid growth or other simple indicators as a proxy for a target industry's attractiveness. Many that rushed into fast-growing industries (personal computers, video games, and robotics, for example) were burned because they mistook early growth for long-term profit potential. Industries are profitable not because they are sexy or high tech; they are profitable only if their structures are attractive.

What Is the Cost of Entry?

Diversification cannot build shareholder value if the cost of entry into a new business eats up its expected returns. Strong market forces, however, are working to do just that. A company can enter new industries by acquisition or start-up. Acquisitions expose it to an increasingly efficient merger market. An acquirer beats the market if it pays a price not fully reflecting the prospects of the new unit. Yet multiple bidders are commonplace, information flows rapidly, and investment bankers and other intermediaries work aggressively to make the market as efficient as possible. In recent years, new financial instruments such as junk bonds have brought new buyers into the market and made even large companies vulnerable to takeover. Acquisition premiums are high and reflect the acquired company's future prospects—sometimes too well. Philip Morris paid more than four times book value for Seven-Up Company, for example. Simple arithmetic meant that profits had to more than quadruple to sustain the preacquisition ROI. Since there proved to be little Philip Morris could add in marketing prowess to the sophisticated marketing wars in the soft drink industry, the result was the unsatisfactory financial performance of Seven-Up and ultimately the decision to divest.

In a start-up, the company must overcome entry barriers. It's a real catch-22 situation, however, since attractive industries are attractive because their entry barriers are high. Bearing the full cost of the entry barriers might well dissipate any potential profits. Otherwise, other entrants to the industry would have already eroded its profitability.

In the excitement of finding an appealing new business, companies sometimes forget to apply the cost-of-entry test. The more attractive a new industry, the more expensive it is to get into.

Will the Business Be Better Off?

A corporation must bring some significant competitive advantage to the new unit, or the new unit must offer potential for significant advantage to the corporation. Sometimes, the benefits to the new unit accrue only once, near the time of entry, when the parent instigates a major overhaul of its strategy or installs a first-rate management team. Other diversification yields ongoing competitive advantage if the new unit can market its product, through the well-developed distribution system of its sister units, for instance. This is one of the important underpinnings of the merger of Baxter Travenol and American Hospital Supply.

When the benefit to the new unit comes only once, the parent company has no rationale for holding the new unit in its portfolio over the long term. Once the results of the one-time improvement are clear, the diversified company no longer adds value to offset the inevitable costs imposed on the unit. It is best to sell the unit and free up corporate resources.

The better-off test does not imply that diversifying corporate risk creates shareholder value in and of itself. Doing something for shareholders that they can do themselves is not a basis for corporate strategy. (Only in the case of a privately held company, in which the company's and the shareholder's risk are the same, is diversification to reduce risk valuable for its own sake.) Diversification of risk should only be a by-product of corporate strategy, not a prime motivator.

Executives ignore the better-off test most of all or deal with it through arm waving or trumped-up logic rather than hard strategic analysis. One reason is that they confuse company size with shareholder value. In the drive to run a bigger company, they lose sight of their real job. They may justify the suspension of the better-off test by pointing to the way they manage diversity. By cutting corporate staff to the bone and giving business units nearly complete autonomy, they believe they avoid the pitfalls. Such thinking misses the whole point of diversification, which is to create shareholder value rather than to avoid destroying it.

CONCEPTS OF CORPORATE STRATEGY

The three tests for successful diversification set the standards that any corporate strategy must meet; meeting them is so difficult that most diversification fails. Many companies lack a clear concept of corporate strategy to guide their diversification or pursue a concept that does not address the tests. Others fail because they implement a strategy poorly.

My study has helped me identify four concepts of corporate strategy that have been put into practice—portfolio management, restructuring, transferring skills, and sharing activities. While the concepts are not always mutually exclusive, each rests on a different mechanism by which the corporation creates shareholder value and each requires the diversified company to manage and organize itself in a different way. The first two require no connections among business units; the second two depend on them. . . . While all four concepts of strategy have succeeded under the right circumstances, today some make more sense than others. Ignoring any of the concepts is perhaps the quickest road to failure.

Portfolio Management

The concept of corporate strategy most in use is portfolio management, which is based primarily on diversification through acquisition. The corporation acquires sound, attractive companies with competent managers who agree to stay on. While acquired units do not have to be in the same industries as existing units, the best portfolio managers generally limit their range of businesses in some way, in part to limit the specific expertise needed by top management.

The acquired units are autonomous, and the teams that run them are compensated according to unit results. The corporation supplies capital and works with each to infuse it with professional management techniques. At the same time, top management provides objective and dispassionate review of business unit results. Portfolio managers categorize units by potential and regularly transfer resources from units that generate cash to those with high potential and cash needs. . . .

In most countries, the days when portfolio management was a valid concept of corporate strategy are past. In the face of increasingly well-developed capital markets, attractive companies with good managements show up on everyone's computer screen and attract top dollar in terms of acquisition premium. Simply contributing capital isn't contributing much. A sound strategy can easily be funded; small to medium-size companies don't need a munificent parent.

Other benefits have also eroded. Large companies no longer corner the market for professional management skills; in fact, more and more observers believe managers cannot necessarily run anything in the absence of industry-specific knowledge and experience. . . .

But it is the sheer complexity of the management task that has ultimately defeated even the best portfolio managers. As the size of the company grows, portfolio managers need to find more and more deals just to maintain growth. Supervising dozens or even hundreds of disparate units and under chain-letter pressures to add more, management begins to make mistakes. At the same time, the inevitable costs of being part of a diversified company take their toll and unit performance slides while the whole company's ROI turns downward. Eventually, a new management team is installed that initiates wholesale divestments and pares down the company to its core businesses. . . .

In developing countries, where large companies are few, capital markets are undeveloped, and professional management is scarce, portfolio management still works. But it is no longer a valid model for corporate strategy in advanced economies. . . . Portfolio management is no way to conduct corporate strategy.

Restructuring

Unlike its passive role as a portfolio manager, when it serves as banker and reviewer, a company that bases its strategy on restructuring becomes an active restructurer of business units. The new businesses are not necessarily related to existing units. All that is necessary is unrealized potential.

The restructuring strategy seeks out undeveloped, sick, or threatened organizations or industries on the threshold of significant change. The parent intervenes, frequently changing the unit management team, shifting strategy, or infusing the company with new technology. Then it may make follow-up acquisitions to build a critical mass and sell off unneeded or unconnected parts and thereby reduce the effective acquisition cost. The result is a strengthened company or a transformed industry. As a coda, the parent sells off the stronger unit once results are clear because the parent is no longer adding value, and top management decides that its attention should be directed elsewhere. . . .

When well implemented, the restructuring concept is sound, for it passes the three tests of successful diversification. The restructurer meets the cost-of-entry test through the types of company it acquires. It limits acquisition premiums by buying companies with problems and lackluster images or by buying into industries with as yet unforeseen potential. Intervention by the corporation clearly meets the better-off test. Provided that the target industries are structurally attractive, the restructuring model can create enormous shareholder value. . . . Ironically, many of today's restructurers are profiting from yesterday's portfolio management strategies.

To work, the restructuring strategy requires a corporate management team with the insight to spot undervalued companies or positions in industries ripe for transformation. The same insight is necessary to actually turn the units around even though they are in new and unfamiliar businesses. . . .

Perhaps the greatest pitfall . . . is that companies find it very hard to dispose of business units once they are restructured and performing well. . . .

Transferring Skills

The purpose of the first two concepts of corporate strategy is to create value through a company's relationship with each autonomous unit. The corporation's role is to be a selector, a banker, and an intervenor.

The last two concepts exploit the interrelationships between businesses. In articulating them, however, one comes face-to-face with the often ill-defined concept of synergy. If you believe the text of the countless corporate annual reports, just about anything is related to just about anything else! But imagined synergy is much more common than real synergy. GM's purchase of Hughes Aircraft simply because cars were going electronic and Hughes was an electronics concern demonstrates the folly of paper synergy. Such corporate relatedness is an ex post facto rationalization of a diversification undertaken for other reasons.

Even synergy that is clearly defined often fails to materialize. Instead of cooperating, business units often compete. A company that can define the synergies it is pursuing still faces significant organizational impediments in achieving them.

But the need to capture the benefits of relationships between businesses has never been more important. Technological and competitive developments already link many businesses and are creating new possibilities for competitive advantage. In such sectors as financial services, computing, office equipment, entertainment, and health care, interrelationships among previously distinct businesses are perhaps the central concern of strategy.

To understand the role of relatedness in corporate strategy, we must give new meaning to this often ill-defined idea. I have identified a good way to start—the value chain. [See pp. 96–98] Every business unit is a collection of discrete activities ranging from sales to accounting that allow it to compete. I call them value activities. It is at this level, not in the company as a whole, that the unit achieves competitive advantage.

I group these activities in nine categories. *Primary* activities create the product or service, deliver and market it, and provide after-sale support. The categories of primary activities are inbound logistics, operations, outbound logistics, marketing and sales, and service. *Support* activities provide the input and infrastructure that allow the primary activities to take place. The categories are company infrastructure, human resource management, technology development, and procurement.

The value chain defines the two types of interrelationships that may create synergy. The first is a company's ability to transfer skills or expertise among similar value chains. The second is the ability to share activities. Two business units, for example, can share the same sales force or logistics network.

The value chain helps expose the last two (and most important) concepts of corporate strategy. The transfer of skills among business units in the diversified company is the basis for one concept. While each business unit has a separate value chain, knowledge about how to perform activities is transferred among the units. For example, a toiletries business unit, expert in the marketing of convenience products, transmits ideas on new positioning concepts, promotional techniques, and packaging possibilities to a newly acquired unit that sells cough syrup. Newly entered industries can benefit from the expertise of existing units, and vice versa.

These opportunities arise when business units have similar buyers or channels, similar value activities like government relations or procurement, similarities in the broad configuration of the value chain (for example, managing a multisite service organization), or the same strategic concept (for example, low cost). Even though the units operate separately, such similarities allow the sharing of knowledge. . . .

Transferring skills leads to competitive advantage only if the similarities among businesses meet three conditions:

1. The activities involved in the businesses are similar enough that sharing expertise is meaningful. Broad similarities (marketing intensiveness, for example, or a common core process technology such as bending metal) are not a sufficient basis for diversification. The resulting ability to transfer skills is likely to have little impact on competitive advantage.

2. The transfer of skills involves activities important to competitive advantage. Transferring skills in peripheral activities such as government relations or real estate in consumer goods units may be beneficial but is not a basis for diversification.

3. The skills transferred represent a significant source of competitive advantage for the receiving unit. The expertise or skills to be transferred are both advanced and proprietary enough to be beyond the capabilities of competitors. . . .

Transferring skills meets the tests of diversification if the company truly mobilizes proprietary expertise across units. This makes certain the company can offset the acquisition premium or lower the cost of overcoming entry barriers.

The industries the company chooses for diversification must pass the attractiveness test. Even a close fit that reflects opportunities to transfer skills may not overcome poor industry structure. Opportunities to transfer skills, however, may help the company transform the structures of newly entered industries and send them in favorable directions.

The transfer of skills can be one time or ongoing. If the company exhausts opportunities to infuse new expertise into a unit after the initial post-acquisition period, the unit should ultimately be sold. . . .

By using both acquisitions and internal development, companies can build a transfer-of-skills strategy. The presence of a strong base of skills sometimes creates the possibility for internal entry instead of the acquisition of a going concern. Successful diversifiers that employ the concept of skills transfer may, however, often acquire a company in the target industry as a beachhead and then build on it with their internal expertise. By doing so, they can reduce some of the risks of internal entry and speed up the process. Two companies that have diversified using the transfer-of-skills concept are 3M and PepsiCo.

Sharing Activities

The fourth concept of corporate strategy is based on sharing activities in the value chains among business units. Procter & Gamble, for example, employs a common physical distribution system and sales force in both paper towels and disposable diapers. McKesson, a leading distribution company, will handle such diverse lines as pharmaceuticals and liquor through superwarehouses.

The ability to share activities is a potent basis for corporate strategy because sharing often enhances competitive advantage by lowering cost or raising differentiation. . . .

Sharing activities inevitably involves costs that the benefits must outweigh. One cost is the greater coordination required to manage a shared activity. More important is the need to compromise the design or performance of an activity so that it can be shared. A salesperson handling the products of two business units, for example, must operate in a way that is usually not what either unit would choose were it independent. And if compromise greatly erodes the unit's effectiveness, then sharing may reduce rather than enhance competitive advantage. . . .

Despite . . . pitfalls, opportunities to gain advantage from sharing activities have proliferated because of momentous developments in technology, deregulation, and competition. The infusion of electronics and information systems into many industries creates new opportunities to link businesses. . . .

Following the shared-activities model requires and organizational context in which business unit collaboration is encouraged and reinforced. Highly autonomous business units are inimical to such collaboration. The company must put into place a variety of what I call horizontal mechanisms—a strong sense of corporate identity, a clear corporate mission statement that emphasizes the importance of integrating business unit strategies, an incentive system that rewards more than just business unit results, cross-business-unit task forces, and other methods of integrating.

A corporate strategy based on shared activities clearly meets the better-off test because business units gain ongoing tangible advantages from others within the corporation. It also meets the cost-of-entry test by reducing the expense of surmounting the barriers to internal entry. Other bids for acquisitions that do not share opportunities will have lower reservation prices. Even widespread opportunities for sharing activities do not allow a company to suspend the attractiveness test, however. Many diversifiers have made the critical mistake of equating the close fit of a target industry with attractive diversification. Target industries must pass the strict requirement test of having an attractive structure as well as a close fit in opportunities if diversification is to ultimately succeed.

. . . Both the strategic logic and the experience of the companies I studied over the last decade suggest that a company will create shareholder value through diversification to a greater and greater extent as its strategy moves from portfolio management toward sharing activities. . . .

Each concept of corporate strategy is not mutually exclusive of those that come before, a potent advantage of the third and fourth concepts. A company can employ a restructuring strategy at the same time it transfers skills or shares activities. A strategy based on shared activities becomes more powerful if business units can also exchange skills. . . .

My study supports the soundness of basing a corporate strategy on the transfer of skills or shared activities. The data on the sample companies' diversification programs illustrate some important characteristics of successful diversifiers. They have made a disproportionately low percentage of unrelated acquisitions, *unrelated* being defined as having no clear opportunity to transfer skills or share important activities. . . . Even successful diversifiers such as 3M, IBM, and TRW have terrible records when they strayed into unrelated acquisitions. Successful acquirers diversify into fields, each of which is related to many others. Procter & Gamble and IBM, for example, operate in 18 and 19 interrelated fields respectively and so enjoy numerous opportunities to transfer skills and share activities.

Companies with the best acquisition records tend to make heavier-than-average use of start-ups and joint ventures. Most companies shy away from modes of entry besides acquisition. My results cast doubt on the conventional wisdom regarding start-ups. . . . successful companies often have very good records with start-up units, as 3M, P&G, Johnson & Johnson, IBM, and United Technologies illustrate. When a company has the internal strength to start up a unit, it can be safer and less costly to launch a company than to rely solely on an acquisition and then have to deal with the problem of integration. Japanese diversification histories support the soundness of start-up as an entry alternative.

My data also illustrate that none of the concepts of corporate strategy works when industry structure is poor or implementation is bad, no matter how related the industries are. Xerox acquired companies in related industries, but the businesses had poor structures and its skills were insufficient to provide enough competitive advantage to offset implementation problems.

An Action Program

. . . A company can choose a corporate strategy by:

1. Identifying the interrelationships among already existing business units. . . .
2. Selecting the core businesses that will be the foundation of the corporate strategy. . . .
3. Creating horizontal organizational mechanisms to facilitate interrelationships among the core businesses and lay the groundwork for future related diversification. . . .
4. Pursuing diversification opportunities that allow shared activities. . . .
5. Pursing diversification through the transfer of skills if opportunities for sharing activities are limited or exhausted. . . .
6. Pursuing a strategy restructuring if this fits the skills of management or no good opportunities exist for forging corporate interrelationships. . . .
7. Paying dividends so that the shareholders can be the portfolio managers. . . .

Creating a Corporate Theme

Defining a corporate theme is a good way to ensure that the corporation will create shareholder value. Having the right theme helps unite the efforts of business units and reinforces the ways they interrelate as well as guides the choice of new businesses to enter. NEC Corporation, with its "C&C" theme, provides a good example. NEC integrates its computer, semiconductor, telecommunications, and consumer electronics businesses by merging computers and communication.

It is all too easy to create a shallow corporate theme. CBS wants to be an "entertainment company," for example, and built a group of businesses related to leisure time. It entered such industries as toys, crafts, musical instruments, sports teams, and hi-fi retailing. While this corporate theme sounded good, close listening revealed its hollow ring. None of these businesses had any significant opportunity to share activities or transfer skills among themselves or with CBS's traditional broadcasting and record businesses. They were all sold, often at significant losses, except for a few of CBS's publishing-related units. Saddled with the worst acquisition record in my study, CBS has eroded the shareholder value created through its strong performance in broadcasting and records.

Moving from competitive strategy to corporate strategy is the business equivalent of passing through the Bermuda Triangle. The failure of corporate strategy reflects the fact that most diversified companies have failed to think in terms of how they really add value. A corporate strategy that truly enhances the competitive advantage of each business unit is the best defense against the corporate raider. With a sharper focus on the tests of diversification and the explicit choice of a clear concept of corporate strategy, companies' diversification track records from now on can look a lot different.

GLOBAL STRATEGY AND STRUCTURE

▼

In the previous chapter we examined some ways in which a firm can answer the corporate-level question—being in a single business, being in multiple businesses through chain (or vertical) integration, and being in multiple businesses through diversification. Each of these options deals with a firm that has decided to operate in one country (commonly called a domestic strategy). In this chapter we consider the decision about whether to operate in many parts of the world. Firms electing to do so have two basic options—multidomestic operation and global operation.[1]

INTERNATIONAL STRATEGY OPTIONS

Multidomestic and Global Strategies

As the name implies, a multidomestic strategy treats each country where a firm operates as a completely distinctive place. Firms assume that everything is different in the domestic economy of each country: Consumer tastes are different. Competitive conditions are different. Macroenvironmental conditions—political, economic, sociocultural, and technological—are seen to differ widely from country to country.

Firms respond to these differences by decentralizing their operations to each country or world region. Product offerings are tailored to the tastes in each country. Manufacturing is done in each country or at least *differs* for each country. Marketing may be the most decentralized of the functions, since it must directly address the distinctive needs in each country. What all this means is that competitive strategy for each country is in the hands of each country's national subsidiaries.

The assumptions underlying so-called "global strategy" are radically different. George Yip's reading in this chapter, "Global Strategy . . . in a World of Nations?" examines the forces for globalization by examining what he calls "globalization drivers." The first of these is *market drivers,* such as homogeneous customer needs, the existence of global customers and distribution channels, and the potential for transferring some marketing elements. There are also *cost drivers* such as economies of scale and scope, learning and experience, sourcing efficiencies, favorable logistics, differences among countries in costs and skills, and product development costs. Another set of drivers is *governmental drivers* such as favorable trade policies, compatible technical standards, and common marketing regulations. Lastly are the *competitive drivers,* which include interdependence among countries and globalized competitors.

The result of all this is a set of assumptions about the need for a broad approach. One assumption is that countries are essentially the same on the dimensions that matter. Other assumptions are that consumer tastes are homogeneous throughout the world and that competitive conditions are the same across the entire face of the planet. Political, economic, sociocultural, and technological factors do not differ significantly from place to place around the world, it is assumed.

Firms holding these assumptions operate accordingly. Products are standardized worldwide. Manufacturing is centralized in a limited number of locations, offering an optimal mix of the lowest costs and best skills. Marketing is centrally determined; products, pricing, promotion, and distribution are handled similarly around the world. Strategy in firms that choose a global approach is centrally determined and integrated across countries.

The strength of the multidomestic approach discussed later lies in its ability to recognize and address important differences across countries, to the extent that they do exist. Another strength is the relative organizational simplicity. Although having multiple country subsidiaries may *seem* complicated, the decentralization to each subsidiary allows the central staff to be small and coordination to be low: Most of the important decisions are made by the subsidiaries. Since each subsidiary is a self-contained unit that does not have to interact with other subsidiaries in other countries, except perhaps through market mechanisms, transfer pricing problems are greatly reduced.

The multidomestic approach has some weaknesses, though. Firms that use it cannot realize economies of scale in manufacturing and marketing as easily as global firms. Multidomestic firms have greater difficulty in sharing value-chain activities or transferring value-creating skills, both of which are crucial. And the multidomestic firm is at a disadvantage compared to the global firm that can launch coordinated competitive attacks against rival firms worldwide.

Sharing and transferring value-creating activities is much easier for a global firm. Fixed costs of production and new product development can be spread over worldwide production volume, realizing economies of scale. The cost economies mentioned above allow global firms to strive for worldwide cost leadership. Being integrated across countries also allows global firms to coordinate their competitive moves around the world. This permits them to use profits from one region or country to support competitive initiatives in other regions or countries.

But having standardized global products can make a firm vulnerable to smaller firms that target their products to local or regional tastes. Another problem is that global enterprises have significant burdens of organizational coordination. This problem can become especially difficult when rules cut across countries. Particularly onerous is transfer pricing. Multidomestic firms can rely on market control to decide pricing across their independent subsidiaries. Global firms must arrange transfer pricing among the various value-chain activities in which they are engaged around the world. As difficult as this is in one country, it is even more difficult internationally, especially when exchange rates fluctuate.

Thus firms must balance *pressures for global integration* against *pressures for local responsiveness.*[2] Yip recommends that firms manipulate a series of what he calls "global strategy levers," His reading examines these in detail. They include *market participation* choices (e.g., entering a locally unattractive market because of the global advantages gained), *product offering* choices (e.g., standardized or not), *value activity location* choices, alternative *marketing approaches,* and *competitive moves* (e.g., integration across countries, attacks in the home markets of competitors).

Incentives for globalization may often be offset by strong pressures for local responsiveness. For instance, the assumption of universal needs may be unfounded. Often there will be important differences in consumer tastes and preferences from country to country.[3] Countries differ widely in their infrastructures. Some have excellent transportation networks, others poor ones. Some have widespread television and radio broadcasting, others limited broadcasting. Many countries have incompatible electric utility service. Traditional practices may also differ, such as the Japanese preference for washing laundry in cold water or driving on the left side of the road.

Another pressure for local responsiveness is that distribution channels vary widely around the world. In some countries there are monopolies, or at least consolidation, in distribution; in others, distribution is fragmented. Also, some countries have layers of distribution between manufacturers and retailers, while others have few. Lastly, the demands of host governments may force firms to respond locally. Tariffs, quotas, and laws requiring certain percentages of local content all create this kind of pressure.

Bartlett and Ghosal[4] argue that firms are often required to respond to these two forces *simultaneously.* Thus they adopt a hybrid type of strategy that is a combination of multidomestic and global, which they call a *transnational strategy.* Caterpillar Tractor is a good example of this. It manufactures many component parts globally, realizing economies of scale. But it designs the components in a way that allows them to be assembled in different ways for different markets, and in different places. Both strategic moves increase Caterpillar's local responsiveness. On the service side, Caterpillar supports its products with a forty-eight hour, anywhere-in-the-world parts delivery guarantee to minimize expensive downtime for customers. This gives them a powerful global advantage.

GLOBAL ENTRY STRATEGIES

Whichever approach a firm chooses, it must also decide how to go about expanding globally. There are essentially five possibilities: exporting, licensing, franchising, joint ventures, and wholly owned subsidiaries. Each has its strong and weak points.

Exporting

Exporting is the way most firms get started in the global marketplace. They take some of their domestically produced goods and simply try to see if they can sell them in other countries. This is how Honda entered the U.S. motorcycle industry, as we saw in Pascale's Chapter 5 reading, "The Honda Effect." One advantage to exporting is that it allows the firms to avoid the costs of building production facilities in the importing country. Another is that exporting is consistent with global strategy; that is, manufacturing a standardized product in a central location.

One weakness of exporting is the other side of the strength just mentioned—the *home* location for production may not be the optimal one when compared with other locations around the world. Another weakness is that exporting can be burdened by high transportation costs. A third possible difficulty with exporting is tariffs and other trade barriers. Threats of U.S. import quotas and tariffs led many Japanese automobile manufacturers to reduce their use of exporting and to manufacture in the United States. Lastly, if an exporting company uses agents in its importing countries, there is no guarantee that those agents will serve the firm's best interests.

Licensing

A firm may wish to manufacture its products in another country but may be unwilling to spend the money and take the risks needed to do so. In this situation, it may grant a company in that country permission to manufacture the products locally, in return for a fee on each product sold. This is called *licensing;* the "home firm" is called the **licenser,** the foreign firm is its **licensee,** and the fee paid for each unit sold is called a **royalty.** Typically, the licensee bears the costs of setting up the host country manufacturing and marketing infrastructure. This is the first, and quite important, strength of licensing. Another is that the licensing firm does not have to bear the risks of operating in culturally, politically, and economically unfamiliar regions.

One drawback to licensing is that it fails to capitalize on the potential global economies of scale that might exist. This is related to a second problem with licensing— the licenser does not have tight control over operations in the licensee's country. Manufacturing may be poorly done, marketing may be sloppy, and coordinated strategic action is difficult, perhaps even impossible. Another major danger with licensing is that by sharing its core technology, a licenser risks giving away its distinctive competency.

Franchising

Licensing is favored by manufacturing firms. The analogue for service businesses, such as food service companies and hotels, is *franchising.* A **franchiser** sells rights to use its brand name to a **franchisee** in return for an up-front fee and an ongoing share of the franchisee's gross or profits. Because of the nature of service businesses, franchisers typically get their franchisees to agree to abide by strict rules of doing business. As in licensing, franchisers let franchisees bear the costs and risks of operating in foreign countries. Also, since economies of scale are less relevant in service businesses, franchising does not have licensing's cost disadvantages.

Like licensers, though, franchisers may have a problem with coordinating a worldwide competitive strategy. Similarly, their franchisees may not be as concerned as they are with quality and other features evoked by the brand name. The result could be a loss of worldwide reputation. One possible response to this problem is to establish subsidiaries, regionally or by country, whose only task is to monitor compliance with the franchising agreement.

Joint Ventures

When two or more companies join to form a new company jointly owned by them, it is called a *joint venture.* In the global context, this would typically be a home country firm (say, in the United States) forming a joint venture with a host country firm (say, in Japan). The objective of the home country firm would be to draw upon the host country firm's knowledge of local conditions (laws, customs, culture, etc.) to reduce its risk of entering the host country's markets. The host country firm is interested in the opportunity of gaining access to new technology and new products for sale in its home country.

This arrangement is the biggest strength of joint ventures. Another important advantage that two firms reduce the risk of doing business in the host country by each bearing part of that risk—the host firm is relieved of the burden of product development; the foreign firm is helped with its lack of knowledge of host-country conditions. A third advantage is that sometimes entry by a foreign firm alone would be impossible under local laws and restrictions. There is even some evidence that joint ventures are less likely to become targets of successful nationalization.[5]

The weakness of joint ventures are similar to those of licensing: Firms may create opportunities for their partners to gain control over core technology, and joint ventures are not as tightly controllable as wholly owned subsidiaries.

Wholly Owned Subsidiaries

If a firm is willing to bear the full risks, financial and otherwise, of operating in another country, it may elect to establish *wholly owned subsidiaries* in various countries. The full assumption of risk is this approach's largest disadvantage. Nevertheless, firms committed to a full-fledged global approach may find this strategy unavoidable, even if only to retain full control over a core technology.

Choosing an Entry Strategy

Hill and Jones offer some general guidelines for selecting an entry strategy.[6] Manufacturing firms needing to protect core technology should avoid licensing and joint ventures. If such firms wish to manufacture overseas, they should consider wholly owned subsidiaries. Service firms should consider franchising, preferably by creating a controlling subsidiary with a local joint venture partner. This provides local oversight, brings local knowledge to bear, and it often encouraged by local governments. Lastly, firms that wish to pursue an integrated global strategy would probably combine exporting with wholly owned subsidiaries. This would allow them to use their wholly owned subsidiaries to manufacture at lowest cost, while exporting from those production locations to anywhere in the world where their products are marketed. This arrangement allows tighter control and coordination than either join ventures or licensing does.

THE GLOBAL LOGIC OF STRATEGIC ALLIANCES

Kenichi Ohmae's reading in this chapter, "The Global Logic of Strategic Alliances," explores in depth another method for operating globally—strategic alliances. Since the reading is detailed, we will cover only the most important points here.

Ohmae urges managers to overcome their need for control and instead embrace the notion of alliances with other firms. He argues that three forces compel multinational firms to consider alliances. The first is the "Californiazation" of need—the idea that customers everywhere are looking for quality and good value. The second is that technology is so dispersed that no company can expect to control it; instead, companies must learn to manage multiple vendors. The third force is that almost all costs have become fixed, as opposed to variable. This may be somewhat true for manufacturing, for research and development, for development and maintenance of a brand name, and for information systems. The result is a need to boost sales to cover the fixed costs.

Ohmae does not like the various entry modes we have discussed above. They are too concerned with equity and control for his taste. He prefers relatively informal strategic alliances, which he characterizes as prudent no-equity-dependent arrangements for maximizing contributions to fixed costs. He compares them to marriages—no contract but a complementary sharing of skills and abilities. Ohmae expands on the benefits of this point in interesting detail.

GLOBAL STRUCTURE

Firms operating in multiple parts of the world need to design organizational structures to support the international strategy approach they have chosen. A firm that is engaged in exporting from one home base could meet its coordination needs with a *foreign operations department.* Diversified firms would have higher coordination needs—they would have to manage the exporting of several different product lines, perhaps to different areas of the world, and so on. Such a firm should probably adopt an *international division* to handle these activities. This division would become another division in the diversified structure.

The next level of complexity would be the establishment of *foreign subsidiaries.* These could be of two kinds. One, less complex, would be for the firms that are operating a multidomestic international strategy. Each subsidiary would be more-or-less autonomous, as we discussed earlier. The other, more complex, would be operated as part of a global enterprise. This would be placed in one location, but would perform some value-creating activity—manufacturing, marketing, R&D—for all of the firm's global locations. As mentioned earlier in this chapter, this type of foreign subsidiary comes with high organizational costs. This type of structure is what Galbraith and Kazanjian call an *international functional structure.*[7]

Corporations engaged in diverse international activity would most likely organize in a *global multinational structure.*[8] As Mintzberg showed in his reading in the previous chapter, diversified organizations tend to be sets of divisions, each of which is driven toward the machine organization type of configuration. The global multinational tends to be the same, except that the divisions are arrayed around the world. In other words, each division is an international structure operating in a single industry. It has plants, most likely wholly owned subsidiaries, in those places with the best mix of cost and skill. Each of its business units engages in global strategy in its respective industry. A variation on this structure is the *global SBU structure,* where a layer of regional management is added to ease coordination between the home office and its foreign subsidiaries.

For the transnational firm, which needs to balance local responsiveness and pressures for globalization, the structure of choice may be the *international matrix structure.* The product side of the matrix allows for economies of scale in production and research. The geographic side of the matrix allows strategy to be tailored for various countries and regions. In combination, local needs and global imperatives can be met, but at the cost of increased structural complexity.

NOTES TO CHAPTER THIRTEEN

1. For a detailed examination of these choices, see Prahalad, C. K., and Y. Doz, *The Multinational Mission: Balancing Local Demands and Global Vision.* New York: Free Press, 1987.

2. This section draws heavily from Prahalad and Doz, *The Multinational Mission.*

3. See Ohmae, K., "Managing in a Borderless World." *Harvard Business Review* 67 (May–June 1989): 152–61; and Bartlett, C., and S. Ghosal, "Managing across Borders: New Strategic Requirements." *Sloan Management Review* (Summer 1987), pp. 7–17.

4. Bartlett, C., and S. Ghosal, *Managing across Borders: The Transnational Solution.* Boston: Harvard Business School Press, 1989.

5. Bradley, D. G., "Managing Against Expropriation." *Harvard Business Review* 55 (July–August 1977): 75–83.

6. Hill, C. W. L., and G. Jones, *Strategic Management: An Integrated Approach.* Boston: Houghton-Mifflin, 1992, pp. 259–60.

7. Galbraith, J. R., and R. K. Kazanjian, *Strategy Implementation: Structure, Systems and Process, 2nd ed.* St. Paul: West Publishing, 1986, pp. 139–40.

8. Galbraith and Kazanjian, *Strategy Implementation.*

By George S. Yip

Whether to globalize, and how to globalize, have become two of the most burning strategy issues for managers around the world. Many forces are driving companies around the world to globalize by expanding their participation in foreign markets. Almost every product market in the major world economies—computers, fast food, nuts and bolts—has foreign competitors. Trade barriers are also falling; the recent United States/Canada trade agreement and the impending 1992 harmonization in the European Community are the two most dramatic examples. Japan is gradually opening up its long barricaded markets. Maturity in domestic markets is also driving companies to seek international expansion. This is particularly true of U.S. companies that, nourished by the huge domestic market, have typically lagged behind their European and Japanese rivals in internationalization.

Companies are also seeking to globalize by integrating their worldwide strategy. Such global integration contrasts with the multinational approach whereby companies set up country subsidiaries that design, produce, and market products or services tailored to local needs. This multinational model (also described as a "multidomestic strategy") is now in question (Hout et al., 1982). Several changes seem to increase the likelihood that, in some industries, a global strategy will be more successful than a multidomestic one. One of these changes, as argued forcefully and controversially by Levitt (1983) is the growing similarity of what citizens of different countries want to buy. Other changes include the reduction of tariff and nontariff barriers, technology investments that are becoming too expensive to amortize in one market only, and competitors that are globalizing the rules of the game.

Companies want to know how to globalize—in other words, expand market participation—and how to develop an integrated worldwide strategy. As depicted in Figure 1, three steps are essential in developing a total worldwide strategy:

- Developing the core strategy—the basis of sustainable competitive advantage. It is usually developed for the home country first.
- Internationalizing the core strategy through international expansion of activities and through adaptation.
- Globalizing the international strategy by integrating the strategy across countries.

Multinational companies know the first two steps well. They know the third step

FIGURE 1
Total Global Strategy

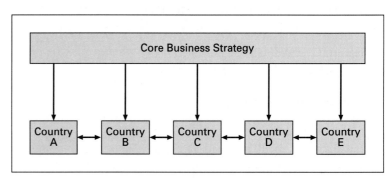

Develop Core Business Strategy

Internationalize the Strategy

Globalize the Strategy

Core Business Strategy

Country A — Country B — Country C — Country D — Country E

My framework, developed in this article, is based in part on M. E. Porter's (1986) pioneering work on global strategy. Bartlett and Ghoshal (1987) define a "transnational industry" that is somewhat similar to Porter's "global industry." Originally published in the *Sloan Management Review* (Fall 1989). Copyright © *Sloan Management Review* 1989; reprinted with deletions by permission of the *Review*.

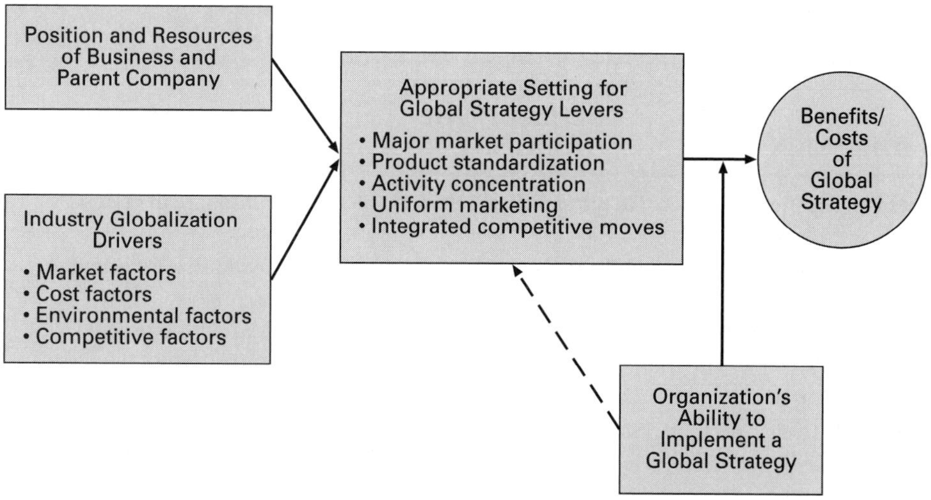

FIGURE 2
Framework of Global Strategy Forces

less well since globalization runs counter to the accepted wisdom of tailoring for national markets (Douglas and Wind, 1987).

This article makes a case for how a global strategy might work and directs managers toward opportunities to exploit globalization. It also presents the draw-backs and costs of globalization. Figure 2 lays out a framework for thinking through globalization issues.

Industry globalization drivers (underlying market, cost, and other industry conditions) are externally determined, while global strategy levers are choices available to the worldwide business. Drivers create the potential for a multinational business to achieve the benefits of global strategy. To achieve these benefits, a multinational business needs to set its *global strategy levers* (e.g., use of product standardization) appropriately to industry drivers, and to the position and resources of the business and its parent company. The organization's ability to implement the strategy affects how well the benefits can be achieved.

WHAT IS GLOBAL STRATEGY?

Setting strategy for a worldwide business requires making choices along a number of strategic dimensions. Table 1 lists five such dimensions or "global strategy levels" and their respective positions under a pure multidomestic strategy and a pure global strategy. Intermediate positions are, of course, feasible. For each dimension, a multidomestic strategy seeks to maximize worldwide performance by maximizing local competitive advantage, revenues, or profits; a global strategy seeks to maximize worldwide performance through sharing and integration.

Market Participation

In a multidomestic strategy, countries are selected on the basis of their stand-alone potential for revenues and profits. In a global strategy, countries need to be selected for their potential contribution to globalization benefits. This may mean entering a market that is unattractive in its own right, but has global strategic significance, such as the home market of a global competitor. Or it may mean building share in a limited number of key markets rather than undertaking more widespread coverage.... The Electrolux Group, the Swedish appliance giant, is pursuing a strategy of building significant share in major world markets. The company aims to be the first global appliance maker....

TABLE 1 **Globalization Dimensions/Global Strategy Levers**

DIMENSION	SETTING FOR PURE MULTIDOMESTIC STRATEGY	SETTING FOR PURE GLOBAL STRATEGY
Market Participation	No particular pattern	Significant share in major markets
Product Offering	Fully customized in each country	Fully standardized worldwide
Location of Value-Added Activities	All activities in each country	Concentrated—one activity in each (different) country
Marketing Approach	Local	Uniform worldwide
Competitive Moves	Stand-alone by country	Integrated across countries

Product Offering

In a multidomestic strategy, the products offered in each country are tailored to local needs. In a global strategy, the ideal is a standardized core product that requires minimal local adaptation. Cost reduction is usually the most important benefit of product standardization. . . . Differing worldwide needs can be met by adapting a standardized core product. In the early 1970s, sales of the Boeing 737 began to level off. Boeing turned to developing countries as an attractive new market, but found initially that its product did not fit the new environments. Because of the shortness of runways, their greater softness, and the lower technical expertise of their pilots, the planes tended to bounce a great deal. When the planes bounced on landing, the brakes failed. To fix this problem, Boeing modified the design by adding thrust to the engines, redesigning the wings and landing gear, and installing tires with lower pressure. These adaptations to a standardized core product enabled the 737 to become the best selling plane in history.

Location of Value Added Activities

In a multidomestic strategy, all or most of the value chain is reproduced in every country. In another type of international strategy—exporting—most of the value chain is kept in one country. In a global strategy, costs are reduced by breaking up the value chain so each activity may be conducted in a different country. . . .

Marketing Approach

In a multidomestic strategy, marketing is fully tailored for each country, being developed locally. In a global strategy, a uniform marketing approach is applied around the world, although not all elements of the marketing mix need be uniform. Unilever achieved great success with a fabric softener that used a globally common positioning, advertising theme, and symbol (a teddy bear), but a brand name that varied by country. Similarly, a product that serves a common need can be geographically expanded with a uniform marketing program, despite differences in marketing environments.

Competitive Moves

In a multidomestic strategy, the managers in each country make competitive moves without regard for what happens in other countries. In a global strategy, competitive moves are integrated across countries at the same time or in a systematic sequence: a competitor is attacked in one country in order to drain its resources for another country, or a competitive attack in one country is countered in a different country. Perhaps the best example is the counterattack in a competitor's home market as a parry to an attack on one's own home market. Integration of competitive strategy is rarely practiced, except perhaps by some Japanese companies.

Bridgestone Corporation, the Japanese tire manufacturer, tried to integrate its competitive moves in response to global consolidation by its major competitors. . . . These competitive actions forced Bridgestone to establish a presence in the major U.S. market in order to maintain its position in the world tire market. To this end, Bridgestone formed a joint venture to own and manage Firestone Corporation's worldwide tire business. This joint venture also allowed Bridgestone to gain access to Firestone's European plants.

BENEFITS OF A GLOBAL STRATEGY

Companies that use global strategy levers can achieve one or more of these benefits. . . .

- cost reductions
- improved quality of products and programs
- enhanced customer preference
- increased competitive leverage

Cost Reductions

An integrated global strategy can reduce worldwide costs in several ways. A company can increase the benefits from economies of scale by *pooling production or other activities* for two or more countries. Understanding the potential benefit of these economies of scale, Sony Corporation has concentrated its compact disc production in Terre Haute, Indiana, and Salzburg, Austria.

A second way to cut costs is by *exploiting lower factor costs* by moving manufacturing or other activities to low-cost countries. This approach has, of course, motivated the recent surge of offshore manufacturing, particularly by U.S. firms. For example, the Mexican side of the U.S.-Mexico border is now crowded with "maquiladoras"—manufacturing plants set up and run by U.S. companies using Mexican labor.

Global strategy can also cut costs by *exploiting flexibility.* A company with manufacturing locations in several countries can move production from location to location on short notice to take advantage of the lowest costs at a given time. Dow Chemical takes this approach to minimize the cost of producing chemicals. Dow uses a linear programming model that takes account of international differences in exchange rates, tax rates, and transportation and labor costs. The model comes up with the best mix of production volume by location for each planning period.

An integrated global strategy can also reduce costs by *enhancing bargaining power.* A company whose strategy allows for switching production among different countries greatly increases its bargaining power with suppliers, workers, and host governments. . . .

Improved Quality of Products and Programs

Under a global strategy, companies focus on a smaller number of products and programs than under a multidomestic strategy. This concentration can improve both product and program quality. Global focus is one reason for Japanese success in automobiles. Toyota markets a far smaller number of models around the world than does General Motors, even allowing for its unit sales being half that of General Motors's. . . .

Enhanced Customer Preference

Global availability, serviceability, and recognition can enhance customer preference through reinforcement. Soft drink and fast food companies are, of course, leading exponents of this strategy. Many suppliers of financial services, such as credit cards, must have a global presence because their service is travel related. . . .

Increased Competitive Leverage

A global strategy provides more points from which to attack and counterattack competitors. In an effort to prevent the Japanese from becoming a competitive nuisance in disposable syringes, Becton Dickinson, a major U.S. medical products company, decided to enter three markets in Japan's backyard. Becton entered the Hong Kong, Singapore, and Philippine markets to prevent further Japanese expansion (Var, 1986).

DRAWBACKS OF GLOBAL STRATEGY

Globalization can incur significant management costs through increased coordination, reporting requirements, and even added staff. It can also reduce the firm's effectiveness in individual countries if overcentralization hurts local motivation and morale. In addition, each global strategy lever has particular drawbacks.

A global strategy approach to *market participation* can incur an earlier or greater commitment to a market than is warranted on its own merits. Many American companies, such as Motorola, are struggling to penetrate Japanese markets, more in order to enhance their global competitive position than to make money in Japan for its own sake.

Product standardization can result in a product that does not entirely satisfy *any* customers. When companies first internationalize, they often offer their standard domestic product without adapting it for other countries, and suffer the consequences. . . .

A globally standardized product is designed for the global market but can seldom satisfy all needs in all countries. For instance, Canon, a Japanese company, sacrificed the ability to copy certain Japanese paper sizes when it first designed a photocopier for the global market.

Activity concentration distances customers and can result in lower responsiveness and flexibility. It also increases currency risk by incurring costs and revenues in different countries. Recently volatile exchange rates have required companies that concentrate their production to hedge their currency exposure.

Uniform marketing can reduce adaptation to local customer behavior. For example, the head office of British Airways mandated that every country use the "Manhattan Landing" television commercial developed by advertising agency Saatchi and Saatchi. While the commercial did win many awards, it has been criticized for using a visual image (New York City) that was not widely recognized in many countries.

Integrated competitive moves can mean sacrificing revenues, profits, or competitive position in individual countries, particularly when the subsidiary in one country is asked to attack a global competitor in order to send a signal or to divert that competitor's resources from another country.

FINDING THE BALANCE

The most successful worldwide strategies find a balance between overglobalizing and underglobalizing. The ideal strategy matches the level of strategy globalization to the globalization potential of the industry....

INDUSTRY GLOBALIZATION DRIVERS

To achieve the benefits of globalization, the managers of a worldwide business need to recognize when industry globalization drivers (industry conditions) provide the opportunity to use global strategy levers. These drivers can be grouped in four categories: market, cost, governmental, and competitive. Each industry globalization driver affects the potential use of global strategy levers....

Market Drivers

Market globalization drivers depend on customer behavior and the structure of distribution channels. These drivers affect the use of all five global strategy levers.

HOMOGENEOUS CUSTOMER NEEDS. When customers in different countries want essentially the same type of product or service (or can be so persuaded), opportunities arise to market a standardized product. Understanding which aspects of the product can be standardized and which should be customized is key. In addition, homogeneous needs make participation in a large number of markets easier because fewer different product offerings need to be developed and supported.

GLOBAL CUSTOMERS. Global customers buy on a centralized or coordinated basis for decentralized use. The existence of global customers both allows and requires a uniform marketing program. There are two types of global customers: national and multinational. A national global customer searches the world for suppliers but uses the purchased product or service in one country. National defense agencies are a good example. A multinational global customer also searches the world for suppliers, but uses the purchased product or service in many countries. The World Health Organization's purchase of medical products is an example. Multinational global customers are particularly challenging to serve and often require a global account management program....

GLOBAL CHANNELS. Analogous to global customers, channels of distribution may buy on a global or at least a regional basis. Global channels or middlemen are also important in exploiting differences in prices by buying at a lower price in one country and selling at a higher price in another country. Their presence makes it more necessary for a business to rationalize its worldwide pricing. Global channels are rare, but regionwide channels are increasing in number, particularly in European grocery distribution and retailing.

TRANSFERABLE MARKETING. The buying decision may be such that marketing elements, such as brand names and advertising, require little local adaptation. Such transferability enables firms to use uniform marketing strategies and facilitates expanded participation in markets. A worldwide business can also adapt its brand names and advertising campaigns to make them more transferable, or, even better, design global ones to start with. Offsetting risks include the blandness of uniformly acceptable brand names or advertising, and the vulnerability of relying on a single brand franchise.

Cost Drivers

Cost drivers depend on the economics of the business; they particularly affect activity concentration.

ECONOMIES OF SCALE AND SCOPE. A single-country market may not be large enough for the local business to achieve all possible economies of scale or scope. Scale at a given location can be increased through participation in multiple markets combined with product standardization or concentration of selected value activities. Corresponding risks include rigidity and vulnerability to disruption. . . .

LEARNING AND EXPERIENCE. Even if economies of scope and scale are exhausted, expanded market participation and activity concentration can accelerate the accumulation of learning and experience. The steeper the learning and experience curves, the greater the potential benefit will be. Managers should beware, though, of the usual danger in pursuing experience curve strategies—overaggressive pricing that destroyed not just the competition but the market as well. Prices get so low that profit is insufficient to sustain any competitor.

SOURCING EFFICIENCIES. Centralized purchasing of new materials can significantly lower costs. . . .

FAVORABLE LOGISTICS. A favorable ratio of sales value to transportation cost enhances the company's ability to concentrate production. Other logistical factors include nonperishability, the absence of time urgency, and little need for location close to customer facilities. . . .

DIFFERENCES IN COUNTRY COSTS AND SKILLS. Factor costs generally vary across countries; this is particularly true in certain industries. The availability of particular skills also varies. Concentration of activities in low-cost or high-skill countries can increase productivity and reduce costs, but managers need to anticipate the danger of training future offshore competitors. . . .

PRODUCT DEVELOPMENT COSTS. Product development costs can be reduced by developing a few global or regional products rather than many national products. The automobile industry is characterized by long product development periods and high product development costs. One reason for the high costs is duplication of effort across countries. The Ford Motor Company's "Centers of Excellence" program aims to reduce these duplicating efforts and to exploit the differing expertise of Ford specialists worldwide. As part of the concentrated effort, Ford of Europe is designing a common platform for all compacts, while Ford of North America is developing platforms for the replacement of the mid-sized Taurus and Sable. This concentration of design is estimated to save "hundreds of millions of dollars per model by eliminating duplicative efforts and saving on retooling factories" (*Business Week,* 1987).

Governmental Drivers

Government globalization drivers depend on the rules set by national governments and affect the use of all global strategy levers.

FAVORABLE TRADE POLICIES. Host governments affect globalization potential through import tariffs and quotas, nontariff barriers, export subsidies, local content requirements, currency and capital flow restrictions, and requirements on technology transfer. Host government policies can make it difficult to use the global levers of major market participation, product standardization, activity concentration, and uniform marketing; they also affect the integrated-competitive moves lever. . . .

COMPATIBLE TECHNICAL STANDARDS. Differences in technical standards, especially government-imposed standards, limit the extent to which products can be standardized. Often, standards are set with protectionism in mind. Motorola found that many of their electronics products were excluded from the Japanese market because these products operated at a higher frequency than was permitted in Japan.

COMMON MARKETING REGULATIONS. The marketing environment of individual countries affects the extent to which uniform global marketing approaches can be used. Certain types of media may be prohibited or restricted. For example, the United States is far more liberal than Europe about the kinds of advertising claims that can be made on television. The British authorities even veto the depiction of socially undesirable behavior. For example, British television authorities do not allow scenes of children pestering their parents to buy a product. . . .

Competitive Drivers

Market, cost, and governmental globalization drivers are essentially fixed for an industry at any given time. Competitors can play only a limited role in affecting these factors (although a sustained effort can bring about change, particularly in the case of consumer preferences). In contrast, competitive drivers are entirely in the realm of competitor choice. Competitors can raise the globalization potential of their industry and spur the need for a response on the global strategy levers.

INTERDEPENDENCE OF COUNTRIES. A competitor may create competitive interdependence among countries by pursuing a global strategy. The basic mechanism is through sharing of activities. When activities such as production are shared among countries, a competitor's market share in one country affects its scale and overall cost position in the shared activities. Changes in that scale and cost will affect its competitive position in all countries dependent on the shared activities. Less directly, customers may view market position in a lead country as an indicator of overall quality. Companies frequently promote a product as, for example, "the leading brand in the United States." Other competitors then need to respond via increased market participation, uniform marketing, or integrated competitive strategy to avoid a downward spiral of sequentially weakened positions in individual countries.

In the automobile industry, where economies of scale are significant and where sharing activities can lower costs, markets have significant competitive interdependence. As companies like Ford and Volkswagen concentrate production and become more cost competitive with the Japanese manufacturers, the Japanese are pressured to enter more markets so that increased production volume will lower costs. Whether conscious of this or not, Toyota has begun a concerted effort to penetrate the German market: between 1984 and 1987, Toyota doubled the number of cars produced for the German market.

GLOBALIZED COMPETITORS. More specifically, matching or preempting individual competitor moves may be necessary. These moves include expanding into or within major markets, being the first to introduce a standardized product, or being the first to use a uniform marketing program.

The need to preempt a global competitor can spur increased market participation. In 1986, Unilever, the European consumer products company, sought to increase its participation in the U.S. market by launching a hostile takeover bid for Richardson-Vicks Inc. Unilever's global archrival, Procter & Gamble, saw the threat to its home turf and outbid Unilever to capture Richardson-Vicks. With Richardson-Vicks's European system, P&G was able to greatly strengthen its European positioning. So Unilever's attempt to expand participation in a rival's home market backfired to allow the rival to expand participation in Unilever's home markets.

In summary, industry globalization drivers provide opportunities to use global strategy levers in many ways. Some industries, such as civil aircraft, can score high on most dimensions of globalization (Yoshino, 1986). Others, such as the cement industry, seem to be inherently local. But more and more industries are developing globalization potential. Even the food industry in Europe, renowned for its diversity of taste, is now a globalization target for major food multinationals.

Changes over Time

Finally, industry evolution plays a role. As each of the industry globalization drivers changes over time, so too will the appropriate global strategy change. For example, in the European major appliance industry, globalization forces seem to have reversed. In the late 1960s and early 1970s, a regional standardization strategy was successful for some key competitors (Levitt, 1983). But in the 1980s the situation appears to have turned around, and the most successful strategies seem to be national (Badenfuller et al., 1987).

In some cases, the actions of individual competitors can affect the direction and pace of change; competitors positioned to take advantage of globalization forces will want to hasten them. . . .

MORE THAN ONE STRATEGY IS VIABLE

Although they are powerful, industry globalization drivers do not dictate one formula for success. More than one type of international strategy can be viable in a given industry.

INDUSTRIES VARY ACROSS DRIVERS. No industry is high on every one of the many globalization drivers. A particular competitor may be in a strong position to exploit a driver that scores low on globalization. . . . The hotel industry provides examples both of successful global and successful local competitors.

GLOBAL EFFECTS ARE INCREMENTAL. Globalization drivers are not deterministic for a second reason: the appropriate use of strategy levers adds competitive advantage to existing sources. These other sources may allow individual competitors to thrive with international strategies that are mismatched with industry globalization drivers. For example, superior technology is a major source of competitive advantage in most industries, but can be quite independent of globalization drivers. A competitor with sufficiently superior technology can use it to offset globalization disadvantages.

BUSINESS AND PARENT COMPANY POSITION AND RESOURCES ARE CRUCIAL. The third reason that drivers are not deterministic is related to resources. A worldwide business may face industry drivers that strongly favor a global strategy. But global strategies are typically expensive to implement initially even though great cost savings and revenue gains should follow. High initial investments may be needed to expand within or into major markets, to develop standardized products, to relocate value activities, to create global brands, to create new organization units or coordination processes, and to implement other aspects of a global strategy. The strategic position of the business is also relevant. Even though a global strategy may improve the business's long-term strategic position, its immediate position may be so weak that resources should be devoted to short-term, country-by-country improvements. Despite the automobile industry's very strong globalization drivers, Chrysler Corporation had to deglobalize by selling off most of its international automotive businesses to avoid bankruptcy. Lastly, investing in nonglobal sources of competitive advantage, such as superior technology, may yield greater returns than global ones, such as centralized manufacturing.

ORGANIZATIONS HAVE LIMITATIONS. Finally, factors such as organization structure, management processes, people, and culture affect how well a desired global strategy can be implemented. Organizational differences among companies in the same industry can, or should, constrain the companies' pursuit of the same global strategy. . . .

THE GLOBAL LOGIC OF STRATEGIC ALLIANCES

READING

By Kenichi Ohmae

Companies are just beginning to learn what nations have always known: in a complex, uncertain world filled with dangerous opponents, it is best not to go it alone. Great powers operating across broad theaters of engagement have traditionally made common cause with others whose interests ran parallel with their own. No shame in that. Entente—the shrinking of an alliance—is a responsible part of every good strategist's repertoire. In today's competitive environment, this is also true for corporate managers.

But managers have been slow to experiment with genuinely strategic alliances. A joint venture here and there, yes, of course. A long-term contractual relationship, certainly. But the forging of entente, rarely. A real alliance compromises the fundamental independence of economic actors, and managers don't like that. After all, for them, management has come to mean total control. Alliances mean sharing control. The one precludes the other.

In stable competitive environments, this allergy to loss of control exacts little penalty. Not so, however, in a changeable world of rapidly globalizing markets and industries—a world of converging consumer tastes, rapidly spreading technology, escalating fixed costs, and growing protectionism. I'd go further. Globalization mandates alliances, make them absolutely essential to strategy. Uncomfortable, perhaps—but that's the way it is. Like it or not, the simultaneous developments that go under the name of globalization makes alliances—entente—necessary.

Why, then, the reluctance of so many companies either to experiment with alliances or to stick with them long enough to learn how to make them work? To some extent, both foot dragging and early exit are born of fear—that the alliance will turn out to be a Trojan horse that affords potential competitors easy access to home markets. But there is also an impression that alliances represent, at best, a convenience, a quick-and-dirty means of entry into foreign markets. These attitudes make managers skittish and impatient.

Unless you understand the long-run strategic value of entente, you will grow frustrated when it proves—as it must—not to be a cheap and easy way of responding to the uncertainties of globalization. If you expect more of your partners than is reasonable, you will blame them too quickly when things do not go as planned. Chances are your im-

Originally published in the *Harvard Business Review* (March–April 1989). Copyright 1989 by the President and Fellows of Harvard College; all rights reserved. Reprinted with deletions by permission of the *Harvard Business Review*.

patience will make you much less tolerant of them than you would be of your own subsidiary overseas.

When you expect convenience, you rarely have much patience for the messy demanding work of building a strong competitive position. Nor do you remember all the up-front overseas investments that you did *not* have to make. And without memory or patience, you risk precipitating exactly what you fear most: an unhappy or unsatisfied partner that decides to bow out of the alliance and try to tackle your markets on its own.

Alliances are not tools of convenience. They are important, even critical, instruments of serving customers in a global environment. Glaxo, the British pharmaceutical company, for example, did not want to establish a full business system in each country where it did business. Especially given its costly commitment to topflight R&D, it did not see how it could—or why it should—build an extensive sales and service network to cover all the hospitals in Japan and the United States. So it decided to link up with first-class partners in Japan, swap its best drugs with them, and focus its own resources on generating greater sales from its established network in Europe. *That* kind of value creation and delivery is what alliances make possible.

Few companies operating in the Triad of Japan, the United States, and Europe can offer such topflight levels of value to all their customers all the time all by themselves. They need partners. They need entente. They might wish things were otherwise. But deep down they know better. Or they should.

THE CALIFORNIAZATION OF NEED

To understand why alliances are a necessity and not just a fad or a fashion, you first have to understand *why* globalization makes them essential as vehicles for customer-oriented value.

The explanation begins with a central, demonstrable fact: the convergence of consumer needs and preferences. Whatever their nationality, consumers in the Triad increasingly receive the same information, seek the same kind of life-styles, and desire the same kinds of products. They all want the best products available, at the lowest prices possible. Everyone, in a sense, wants to live—and shop—in California.

Economic nationalism flourishes during election campaigns and infects what legislatures do and what particular interest groups ask for. But when individuals vote with their pocketbooks—when they walk into a store or showroom anywhere in the Triad—they leave behind the rhetoric and the mudslinging and the trappings of nationalism.

Do you write with a Waterman or a Mont Blanc pen or travel with a Vuitton suitcase because of national sentiments? Of course not. It does not matter if you live in Europe or Japan or the United States. You buy these pens or pieces of luggage because they represent the kind of value that you're looking for.

At the cash register, you don't care about country of origin or country of residence. You don't think about employment figures or trade deficits. You don't worry about where the product was made. It does not matter to you that a "British" sneaker by Reebok (now an American-owned company) was made in Korea, a German sneaker by Adidas in Taiwan, or a French ski by Rossignol in Spain. All you care about is the product's quality, price, design, value, and appeal to you as a consumer.

This is just as true for industrial customers. The market for IBM computers or Toshiba laptops is not defined by geographic borders but by the inherent appeal of the product to users, regardless of where they live. And with the proliferation of trade journals, trade shows, and electronic data bases, users have regular access to the same sources of product information. . . .

THE DISPERSION OF TECHNOLOGY

Today's products rely on so many different critical technologies that most companies can no longer maintain cutting-edge sophistication in all of them. The business software that made IBM PCs such an instant hit—1-2-3—was not, or course, an IBM product. It was a creation of Lotus Development Corporation. Most of the components in the popular-priced IBM PC itself were outsourced as well. IBM simply could not have developed the machine in anywhere near the time it did if it had tried to keep it 100% proprietary. In fact, the heart of IBM's accomplishment with the PC lay precisely in its decision—and its ability—to approach the development effort as a process of managing multiple external vendors. . . .

Naturally, they want to sell their products to as wide a range of customers as possible. Just as IBM needs to rely on an army of external vendors, so each vendor needs to sell to a broad array of customers. The inevitable result is the rapid dispersion of technology. No one company can do it all, simultaneously. No one company can keep all the relevant technologies in-house. . . . And that means no one can truly keep all critical technologies out of the hands of competitors around the globe. . . .

In short order, the technology becomes generally available, making time even more of a critical element in global strategy. Nothing stays proprietary for long. And no one player can master everything. Thus, operating globally means operating with partners—and that in turn means a further spread of technology.

THE IMPORTANCE OF FIXED COSTS

The convergence of customer need, together with this relentless dispersion of technology, has changed the logic by which managers have to steer. In the past, for example, you tried to build sustainable competitive advantage by establishing dominance in all of your business system's critical areas. You created barriers to entry where you could, locked away market share whenever possible, and used every bit of proprietary expertise, every collection of nonreplicable assets to shore up the wall separating you from competitors. The name of the game in most industries was simply beating the competition. If you discovered an ounce of advantage, you strengthened it with a pound of proprietary skill or knowledge. Then you used it to support the defensive wall you were building against competitors.

The forces of globalization turn this logic on its head. You can't meet the value-based needs of customers in the Triad entirely on your own. You can't do without the technology and skills of others. You can't even keep your own technology to yourself for very long. Having a superior technology is important, of course, but it is not sufficient to guarantee success in the market. Meeting customer needs is the key—no matter what the source of the technology. No wall you erect stands tall. No door you slam stays shut. And no road you follow is inexpensive.

To compete in the global arena, you have to incur—and somehow find a way to defray—immense fixed costs. You can't play a variable-cost game any more. You need partners who can help you amortize your fixed costs, and with them you need to define strategies that allow you to maximize the contribution to your fixed costs.

The evidence for this lesson is overwhelming. As automation has driven the labor content out of production, manufacturing has increasingly become a fixed-cost activity. And because the cost of developing breakthrough ideas and turning them into marketable products has skyrocketed, R&D has become a fixed cost too. . . .

In much the same way, building and maintaining a brand name is a fixed cost. For many products, a brand name has no value at all if brand recognition falls below certain levels.

Trying to save money on brand promotion makes no sense if what you're selling is a consumer "pull" product: you spend a little money but not enough to realize any "pull" benefits. And a half-baked, half-supported brand is worse than no brand at all. With some products, you can better use the same money to enhance commissions so that the sales force will push them. In branded competition, if you want to play, you have to ante up the fixed costs of doing so. . . .

You can also try to make some of these costs variable on your own. You can chase low-cost labor, for example, by moving production to developing countries, but that won't get you very far these days. In the past, you could make costs variable with your computers and management information systems by time-sharing. But experience has shown that you can't use time-sharing if you want a system that's dedicated to your own needs, a system capable of providing competitive advantage. So today, information technology is pretty much a fixed cost. Over the long term, of course, all these fixed costs become variable through adjustments in investments (capital expenditure) levels. But for the short term, they remain fixed. And the need to bolster contribution to them points in a single, clear direction: toward the forging of alliances to share fixed costs.

This is a fundamental change from the competitive world of 15 or even 10 years ago. And it demands a new logic for management action. In a variable-cost environment, the primary focus for managers is on boosting profits by reducing the cost of materials, wages, labor hours. In a fixed-cost environment, the focus switches to maximizing marginal contribution to fixed cost—that is, to boosting sales.

This new logic forces managers to amortize their fixed costs over a much larger market base—and this adds yet more fuel to the drive toward globalization. It also forces managers to rethink their strategies as they search for ways to maximize contribution to these fixed costs. Finally this logic mandates entente—alliances that both enable and facilitate global contribution-based strategies.

In practice, this means that if you don't have to invest in your own overseas sales force, you don't do it. If you run a pharmaceutical company with a good drug to distribute in Japan but no sales force to do it, find someone in Japan who also has a good product but no sales force in your country. You get double the profit by putting two strong drugs through your fixed-cost sales network, and so does your new ally. Why duplicate such huge expenses all down the line? Why go head-to-head? Why not join forces to maximize contribution to each other's fixed costs?

Maximizing the contribution to fixed costs does not come naturally. Tradition and pride make companies want to be the best at everything, to do everything themselves. But companies can no longer afford this solitary stance. . . .

DANGERS OF EQUITY

Global alliances are not the only valid mechanisms for boosting contribution to fixed costs. A strong brand umbrella can always cover additional products. You can always give heightened attention to, say, an expensive distribution system that you've already built in Japan or Europe. And there is always the possibility of buying a foreign company. Experience shows, however, that you should look hard—and early—at forging alliances. In a world of imperfect options, they are often the fastest, least risky, and most profitable way to go global.

You can expand brands and build up distribution yourself—you can do everything yourself—with enough time, money, and luck. But all three are in short supply. In particular, you simply do not have the time to establish new markets one-by-one throughout the Triad. . . . Today you have to be in all important markets simultaneously if you are going to keep competitors from establishing their positions. Globalization will not wait. You need alliances and you need them now. But not the traditional kind.

In the past, companies commonly approached international expansion by doing it on their own, acquiring others, or establishing joint ventures. Now, the latter two approaches carry important equity-related concerns. Let equity—the classic instrument of capitalism—into the picture, and you start to worry about control and return on investment. There is pressure to get money back fast for the money you put in and dividends from the paper you hold.

It's a reflex. The analysts expect it of you. So do the business press, colleagues, and stockholders. They'll nod politely when you talk about improved sales or long-term strategic benefits. But what everybody really wants in short order is chart-topping ROI. . . .

Managers must also overcome the popular misconception that total control increases chances of success. Companies that have enjoyed successful joint ventures for years can have things quickly go sour when they move to a literal equity- and contract-based mode of ownership. . . .

You can buy a company's equity, but you cannot buy the mind or the spirit or the initiative or the devotion of its people. Nor can you just go hire replacements. In different environments, the availability of key professional services—managerial, legal, and so on—varies considerably.

The lesson is painful but inescapable: having control does not necessarily mean a better managed company. You cannot manage a global company through control. In fact, control is the last resort. It's what you fall back on when everything else fails and you're willing to risk the demoralization of workers and managers.

This need for control is deeply rooted. . . . But good partnerships, like good marriages, don't work on the basis of ownership or control. It takes effort and commitment and enthusiasm from both sides if either is to realize the hoped-for benefits. You cannot own a successful partner any more than you can own a husband or wife.

In time, as the relationship between partners deepens and as mutual trust and confidence build, there may come a point when it no longer makes sense to remain two separate entities. Strategy, values, and culture might all match up so well that both sides want to finish the work of combination. . . .

An emphasis on control through equity, however, immediately poisons the relationship. Instead of focusing on contribution to fixed costs, one company imperialistically tells the other, "Look, I've got a big equity at stake in you. You don't give me all the dividends I want, so get busy and distribute my product. I'm not going to distribute yours, though. Remember, you work for me."

This kind of attitude problem prevents the development of intercompany management skills, which are critical for success in today's global environment. But these skills must be learned. . . .

Equity by itself is not the problem in building successful alliances. In Japan, we have a lot of "group companies," known as *keiretsu,* where an equity stake of, say, 3% to 5% keeps both partners interested in each other's welfare without threatening either's autonomy. Stopping that far short of a controlling position keeps the equity holder from treating the other company as if it were a subsidiary. Small equity investments like these may be the way to go.

Joint ventures may also work, but there are two obstacles that can trip them up. First, there is a contract, and contracts—even at their best—can only reflect an understanding of costs and markets and technologies at the moment companies sign them. When things change, as they always do, the partners don't really try to compromise and adjust. They look to the contract and start pointing fingers. After all managers are human. They are sweet on their own companies and tolerant of their own mistakes. Tolerance goes way down when partners cause mistakes.

The second problem with joint ventures is that parent companies behave as parents everywhere often do. They don't give their children the breathing space—or the time—they need to grow. Nor do they react too kindly when their children want to expand, especially if it's into areas the parents want to keep for themselves. "Keep your hands off" is the message they send, and that's not a good way to motivate anyone, let alone their own children.

This is not to say that joint ventures cannot work. Many work quite well. . . .

On balance, however, most parents are not so tolerant of their joint ventures' own ambitions. There have to be better ways to go global than a regular sacrifice of the first-born. There are.

Going global is what parents should do together—through alliances that address the issue of fixed costs. They work. Nissan distributes Volkswagens in Japan; Volkswagen sells Nissan's four-wheel drive cars in Europe. Mazda and Ford swap cars in the Triad; GM and Toyota both collaborate and compete in the United States and Australia. Continental Tyre, General Tire (now owned by Continental), Yokohama Rubber and Toyo Tire share R&D and swap production. In the United States, for example, General Tire supplies several Japanese transplants on behalf of Yokohama and Toyo, both of which supply tires on behalf of General and Continental to car companies in Japan. No equity changes hands.

In the pharmaceutical industry, where both ends of the business system (R&D and distribution) represent unusually high fixed costs, companies regularly allow their strong products to be distributed by (potential) competitors with excellent distribution systems in key foreign markets. . . .

The distribution of drugs is a labor- and relationship-intensive process. It takes a force of more than 1,000 detail people to have any real effect on Japanese medicine. Thus, unless you are committed to building and sustaining such a fixed cost in Japan, it makes sense to collaborate with someone who has such a force already in place—and who can reciprocate elsewhere in the Triad. . . .

There are more examples, but the pattern is obvious: a prudent, non-equity-dependent set of arrangements through which globally active companies can maximize the contribution to their fixed costs. No surprise here. These alliances are an important part of the way companies get back to strategy.

THE LOGIC OF ENTENTE

One clear change of mind necessary to make alliances work is a shift from a focus on ROI to a focus on ROS (return on sales). An ROS orientation means that managers will concern themselves with the ongoing business benefits of the alliance, not just sit around and wait for a healthy return on their initial investment. Indeed, equity investments almost always have an overtone of one company trying to control another with money. But few businesses succeed because of control. Most make it because of motivation, entrepreneurship, customer relationships, creativity, persistence, and attention to the "softer" aspect of organization, such as values and skills.

An alliance is a lot like a marriage. There may be no formal contract. There is no buying and selling of equity. There are few, if any, rigidly binding provisions. It is a loose, evolving kind of relationship. Sure, there are guidelines and expectations. But no one expects a precise, measured return on the initial commitment. Both partners bring to an alliance a faith that they will be stronger together than either would be separately. Both believe that each has unique skills, and functional abilities the other lacks. And both have to work diligently over time to make the union successful.

When one partner is weak or lazy or won't make an effort to explore what the two can do together, things can come apart. One-sidedness and asymmetry of effort and attention doom a relationship. If a wife goes out and becomes the family's breadwinner *and* does all the housework *and* raises the children *and* runs the errands *and* cooks the meals, sooner or later she will rebel. Quite right. If the husband were in the same position, he'd rebel too. As soon as either partner starts to feel that the situation is unfair or uneven, it will begin to come apart. Alliances are like that. They work only when the partners do.

It's hard work. It's all too easy for doubts to start to grow. A British whiskey company used a Japanese distributor until it felt it had gained enough experience to start its own sales operation in Japan. Japanese copier makers and automobile producers have done this to their U.S. partners. It happens. There's always the danger that a partner is not really in it for the long haul.

But the odds run the other way. There is a tremendous cost—and risk—in establishing your own distribution, logistics, manufacturing, sales, and R&D in every key market around the globe. It takes time to build skills in your own people and develop good relations with vendors and customers. Nine times out of ten, you will want to stay in the alliance. . . .

In practice, though, companies do start to have doubts. Say you've started up a Japanese alliance, not invested all that much, and been able to boost your production at home because of sales in Japan. Then you look at the actual cash flow from those sales, and it doesn't seem all that great. So you compare it with a competitor's results—a competitor that has gone into Japan entirely on its own. It's likely that you've forgotten how little effort you've put in when compared with the blood, sweat, and tears of your competitor. All you look at are the results.

All of a sudden you start to feel cheated; you remember every little inconvenience and frustration. You yield to the great temptation to compare apples with oranges, to moan about revenues while forgetting fixed costs. You start to question just how much the alliance is really doing for you.

It's a bit like going to a marriage counselor and complaining about the inconveniences of marriage because, had you not married, you could be dating anyone you like. You focus on what you think you're missing, on the inconveniences, and forget entirely about the benefits of being married. It's a psychological process. Alliance partners can easily fall into this kind of destructive pattern of thought, complaining about the annoyances of coordination, of working together, of not having free rein. They forget the benefits.

Actually, they forget to *look* for the benefits. And most accounting and control systems only make this worse. For instance, if you are running your own international sales operation in Japan, you know where to look for accurate measures of performance. You know how to read an income statement, figure out the return on invested capital, consolidate the performance of subsidiaries.

But when you're operating through a partner in Japan and you're asking yourself how that Japanese operation is doing, you forget to look for the benefits at home in the contribution to the fixed costs of R&D, manufacturing, and brand image. The financials don't highlight them; they usually don't even capture them. Most of the time, these contributions—like the extra production volume for OEM export—are simply invisible, below the line of sight.

Companies in the United States, in particular, often have large, dominate home-country operations. As a result, they report the revenues generated by imports from their overseas partners as their own domestic sales. In fact, they think of what they're doing not as importing but as managing procurement. Exports get recorded as overseas sales of the domestic divisions. In either case, the contribution of the foreign partner gets lost in the categories used by the U.S.-based accounting system.

It takes real dedication to track down the domestic benefit of a global alliance. And you're not even going to look for them if you spend all your time complaining. The relationship is never going to last. That's too bad, of course, if the alliance really does contribute something of value. But even when alliances are good, you can outgrow them. Needs change, and today's partner might not be the best or the most suitable tomorrow.

Financial institutions shift about like this all the time. If you're placing a major issue, you may need to tie up with a Swiss bank with deep pockets. If you need help with retail distribution, you may turn to Merrill Lynch or Shearson Lehman Hutton. In Japan, Nomura Securities may be the best partner because of its size and retail strength. You don't need to be good at everything yourself as long as you can find a partner who compensates for your weak points.

Managing multiple partners is more difficult in manufacturing industries but still quite doable. IBM in the United States has a few important allies; in Japan it has teamed up with just about everyone possible. (There has even been a book published in Japanese, entitled *IBM's Alliance Strategy in Japan.*) It has links with Ricoh in distribution and sales of low-end computers, with Nippon Steel in systems integration, with Fuji Bank in financial systems marketing, with OMRON in CIM, and with NTT in value-added networks. IBM is not a jack-of-all-trades. It has not made huge fixed-cost investments. In the eyes of Japanese customers, however, it has become an all-around player. No wonder IBM has achieved a major "insider" position in the fiercely competitive Japanese market, along with handsome sales ($7 billion in 1988) and profits ($1.2 billion).

Sure, individual partners may not last. Every business arrangement has its useful life. But maintaining a presence in Japan by means of alliances *is* a permanent endeavor, an enduring part of IBM's strategy. And acting as if current arrangements are permanent helps them last longer. Just like marriage. If you start cheating on day two, the whole thing gets shaky fast.

Why does the cheating start? You're already pretty far down the slippery slope when you say to yourself, "I've just signed this deal with so-and-so to distribute my products. I don't need to worry about that anymore as long as they send me my check on time." You're not holding up your half of the relationship. You're not working at it. More important, you're not trying to learn from it—or through it. You're not trying to grow, to get better as a partner. You've become a check casher, a coupon clipper. You start to imagine all sorts of grievances. And your eye starts to wander. . . .

A U.S. media company took 10% of the equity of a good ad agency in Japan. When the agency went public, the U.S. investor sold off 3% and made a lot of money over and above its original investment. It still had 7%. Then the stockholders started to complain. At Tokyo's crazy stock market prices, that 7% represented about $40 million that was just sitting in Japan without earning dividends. (The dividend payout ratio of Japanese companies is usually very low.) So the stockholders pushed management to sell off the rest and bring the money back to the United States, where they could get at least a money-market level of return. No growth, of course. No lasting position in the booming Japanese market. Just a onetime killing.

Much the same logic seems to lie behind the sale by several U.S.-based companies of their equity positions in Japanese joint ventures. McGraw-Hill (Nikkei-McGraw-Hill), General Electric (Toshiba), B.F. Goodrich (Yokohama Rubber), CBS (CBS-Sony), and Nabisco (Yamazaki-Nabisco), among others, have all realized handsome capital gains in this fashion. If they had not given up their participation in so lucrative a market as Japan, however, the value of their holdings would now be many times greater still. . . .

This kind of equity-based mind-set makes the eye wander. It sends the message that alliances are not a desirable—or effective—means of coping with the urgent and inescapable pressures of globalization or of becoming a genuine insider throughout the Triad market. It reinforces the short-term orientation of managers already hard-pressed by the uncertainties of a new global environment.

When a dispute occurs in a transnational joint venture, it often has overtones of nationalism, sometimes even racism. Stereotypes persist. "Americans just can't understand our market," complain some frustrated partners. "The Germans are too rigid," complain others. "Those mechanical Japanese may be smart at home, but they sure as hell are dumb around here." We've all heard the comments.

It does not take companies with radically different nationalities to have a "clash of cultures" in a joint venture. . . . Two corporate cultures rarely mesh well or smoothly. . . .

[W]e must recognize and accept the inescapable subtleties and difficulties of intercompany relationships. That is the essential starting point. Then we must focus not on contractual or equity-related issues but on the quality of the people at the interface between organizations. Finally, we must understand that success requires frequent, rapport-building meetings at at least three organizational levels: top management, staff, and line management at the working level.

This is hard, motivation-testing work. No matter what they say, however, many companies don't really care about extending their global reach. All they want is a harvesting of the global market. They are not interested in the hard work of serving customers around the world. They are interested in next quarter's ROI. They are not concerned with getting back to strategy or delivering long-term value or forging entente. They want a quickie. They want to feel good today and not have to work too hard tomorrow. They are not serious about going global or about the painstaking work of building and maintaining the alliances a global market demands.

Yet the relentless challenges of globalization will not go away. And properly managed alliances are among the best mechanisms that companies have found to bring strategy to bear on these challenges. In today's uncertain world, it is best not to go it alone.

. . . .

MANAGING CHANGE

▼

This chapter examines one of the most important processes in organizations—change. In Chapter Eleven we discussed a type of organization—innovative—whose essence is change. In this chapter we will explore change processes in a more general sense and how they affect strategy formation. One important theme of this chapter is that strategic change comes in two varieties. *Incremental change,* which we examined to some extent with the logical incrementalism model in Chapter Five, signifies a series of small alterations in how an organization carries out its activities. The small changes are intended to keep the organization in equilibrium as its environment undergoes gradual, evolutionary (which can eventually amount to revolutionary) change. *Radical change* connotes drastic modifications in a firm's frame of reference. It often results in a completely new equilibrium and a transformation of the entire organization.[1] As we will see below, both kinds of change are relevant to strategy formation but in different ways. We begin by examining some of the common elements in organizational change processes, typical barriers to change, and ideas for implementing change.

ORGANIZATIONAL CHANGE PROCESSES

Richard Daft has identified a five-step process for successful change in organizations.[2] First, someone in the organization must see a **need for change.** Managers or other organizational members gather information from external and internal sources. These possibly include, externally, customers, competitors, legislation, court decisions, regulations, consumer trends, and labor force trends, and, internally, employees and feedback from financial controls (e.g., posted losses on the income statement). By examining this information, members of the organization may perceive a gap between the firm's actual performance and its desired performance, which defines a need for change.

Next, someone in the organization has to generate an **idea** about how to make a needed change. People get ideas from external and internal sources. Some examples of external sources are suppliers (who might want to sell the firm a new kind of technology), professional associations (other firms in the same industry may have already solved a problem plaguing the firm), consultants, and the research literature (research and development departments in particular may get ideas from reading scholarly journals). Examples of internal sources are the creativity and inventiveness of the firm's members. The idea could be a new machine, a new way of managing, or a new product.

Then comes an **adoption** process, matching an idea to a perceived need. This could be the result of rational analysis, individual judgment by a powerful manager, or political bargaining.[3] Once adopted, the idea for change must undergo **implementation**. That is, people in a firm must actually try to use the idea and get others in the firm to do so as well. In other words, someone must try to make the change happen. We will say more about this below.

Lastly, to underpin adoption and implementation the firm must seriously commit its **resources**, including human energy, time, and financial resources. People must decide to devote themselves to drafting a coherent proposal for change, then must commit themselves to actually carrying out the change. All of this takes energy. Typically, change also takes time. Seeing the need, finding a good idea, going through the adoption process, recruiting interested people, and so forth, require lots of time. Money, especially if the idea requires large investments in new technology and machinery, is also a necessary ingredient in most change processes. As the firm goes through its learning process with the change, it may also make unavoidable mistakes that cost money. Even the best idea, intended to meet the most pressing need, will fail if the organization is not committed to allocating the resources needed to making the change effort succeed. We turn now to some of the barriers to change, and how they might be overcome.

IMPLEMENTING ORGANIZATIONAL CHANGE

In his Chapter Eleven reading, "Managing Innovation: Controlled Chaos," Quinn pointed to many of the barriers to change in large organizations: Top management may be isolated from things that would inform them of the need to change. Large organizations are typically intolerant of fanatics, who are often the real champions of change. Machine organizations have short time horizons, and their accounting practices may discourage risk taking and may even make it difficult to assess the benefits of changes. These are often excessively rational and process-oriented organizations, thus "red-tape" processes impede change.

Successful implementation in the face of these barriers starts with **diagnosing a true need for change**.[4] If members of the firm are not convinced that a change is needed, an enormous barrier will be created at the outset of the change process. Should that problem be successfully addressed, the change agents must **find an idea that fits the need**. Consistent with the idea that the firm must be serious about committing resources, the change effort will be greatly enhanced if there is **top management support**. As Quinn and Voyer argued in detail in their Chapter Five reading on logical incrementalism, chances for success are improved if change agents **design the change for incremental implementation**.

Anyone intending to create change in an organization should expect that there will be resistance. Accordingly, they must **develop plans to overcome resistance to change**. One way to do this has already been mentioned—**align the change with the needs and goals of its users**. Change agents should also make heavy use of **communication and education**. People who will be affected by a change will accept it more readily if they are educated about the true need for a change and kept fully informed about the consequences of it. The feedback received by the change agents from those who will be affected may also in many instances lead to improvements in the change process or even in the idea that is being implemented. Scholars have known for years that **participation**

and involvement by those affected will greatly reduce resistance to changes.[5] Only as a last resort should change agents use **force and coercion**.

One imaginative use of organizational resources that can facilitate change is to **create change teams**. Change teams foster excitement and energy among the people assigned to them. Change teams may also help change efforts by discouraging excess bureaucracy. Another creative and potentially powerful use of organizational resources is to **foster idea champions**. These are people who are deeply committed to the change idea. They see to it that the idea does not get lost in the bureaucracy and that technical activities are accomplished correctly and completely. Passionate idea champions are also invaluable in persuading others of the merits of a change.

STRATEGIC CHANGE

As we mentioned at the outset of this chapter, there are two kinds of organizational change—incremental and radical. Both are relevant and important to organizational strategy, but at different times and for different reasons. Tushman, Newman, and Romanelli's reading in this chapter, "Convergence and Upheaval: Managing the Unsteady Pace of Organizational Evolution," underscores this point. Their reading speaks eloquently and in detail of the phenomena of "converging change" and "frame-breaking change." Here, we examine their basic message.

Firms go through long periods where they make only incremental changes. These might be fine-tuning, for example, refining policies, developing personnel, and so forth. Or they might be incremental adjustments to the environment, for example, new and improved versions of existing products, entries into new markets, and so forth. These are long periods of converging change, when the firm can become more and more effective and efficient. But, as we implied above, these periods also foster stability and resistance to change of a more profound nature. These periods of convergence may be very functional, but only as long as there is no need for the organization to make major changes.

From time to time things occur that lead to short bursts of what Tushman and his coauthors call frame-breaking change. There may be significant discontinuities in the industry, for example, deregulation or substitute products. Or there may be major shifts in the product life cycle, as when an industry moves from growth to maturity. Sometimes the forces for frame-breaking change come from internal company dynamics, such as the death of a key person. "Frame-breaking changes," say these authors, "are revolutionary changes *of* the system as opposed to incremental changes *in* the system." There may be major reforms of mission and core values, significant alterations of power and status, and wholesale reorganization of the firm's structure, systems, and procedures. Significantly, frame-breaking change is often accompanied by changes in top management. The authors go into detail about the benefits of this phenomenon.

Tushman and his coauthors discuss some reasons why frame-breaking change must occur all at once. These include (1) the synergies that can be created in a new structure, (2) preventing pockets of resistance from getting organized, (3) releasing the pent-up forces favoring change, and (4) keeping the period of risk and uncertainty short by making implementation rapid. Top management must learn when to undergo frame-breaking change and when to stay with the relative stability of converging change. "Frame-breaking change is quite dysfunctional if the organization is successful and the environment is stable" say Tushman and his colleagues. "If, however, the organization is performing poorly and/or if the environment changes substantially, frame-breaking change is the only way to realign the organization with its competitive environment."

Tushman, Newman, and Romanelli claim that the vital tasks for those responsible for the welfare of organizations are: (1) to manage incremental change during convergent periods; (2) to have the vision to initiate and implement frame-breaking change prior to the competition; and (3) to mobilize an executive function which can initiate and implement both kinds of change.

RESPONDING TO CRISIS

Starbuck, Greve, and Hedberg's reading in this chapter, "Responding to Crisis," echoes some of these points, but with a different twist. The authors begin by reviewing the normal view of crises—events caused entirely by outside forces. In contrast, these authors point out that crises are more complex than that. They are interactions between severe environmental events, on the one hand, and deficiencies in the firm, on the other. Like Tushman and his colleagues, Starbuck and his coauthors believe that periods of great success can result in firms' creating programs that lessen sensitivity to their environments. They also maintain that the same processes that lead to success plant the seeds for failure.

Managers of such organizations are adept at explaining crises away. They rely heavily on accounting reports to show that only modest adjustments are needed. They fear rapid change, expecting it to produce undesirable consequences. The bad things that are happening are interpreted as coming from ill-advised, too-rapid changes. Starbuck and his colleagues point out that organizations encountering crises are like palaces—rigid, cohesive structures— perched on sandy mountaintops. In other words, they are like Mintzberg's machine organizations, tightly integrated and suffering from an inability to respond to changes in their environments. Like the previous authors concluded, Starbuck, Greve, and Hedberg argue that these structures must disintegrate before they are capable of being changed in necessary ways.

Crises are so difficult to handle once they start that the best way to "respond" to them is to evade them, and the authors offer several suggestions to do this. The first is to avoid excesses, especially excess rationality; a good way to accomplish this is to adopt countervailing prescriptions, such as encouraging dissenters even as they work toward consensus. The authors' second suggestion is to be ready to replace top managers, particularly if they are not able to see the need for drastic change. The third suggestion is to be aware of one's implicit assumptions, questioning them whenever possible. Fourth, firms should experiment with portfolios of new things while they are still affluent; once in crisis, resources may be unavailable.

Starbuck, Greve, and Hedberg then offer some specific advice to top managers, namely, that they should focus on managing ideology, instead of on the detailed physical and financial phenomena that will seem to cry out for their attention. They conclude by pointing out that the "Chinese symbol for crisis combines two simpler symbols, the symbol for danger and the one for opportunity. Crises are times of danger, but they are also times of opportunity. . . ."

TURNAROUND STRATEGIES

The previous reading advised firms to evade crisis, but the next and final reading in this chapter, Hofer's "Designing Turnaround Strategy," deals with how to respond to the most difficult kind of change situation—the firm that has failed to evade crisis and needs to be "turned around." Hofer offers some advice on how to select the proper kind of turnaround. He, like most of the previous authors, mentions that 90 percent of the time a turnaround is preceded by a change in top management. Hofer offers a distinction between strategic and operating turnarounds. He argues that a **strategic turnaround** involves one of three things: (1) moving from a smaller to a larger strategic group in the industry, (2) becoming more effective within the firm's current strategic group, or (3) moving to a smaller strategic group. Improved performance would be a *derivative* of one of these moves. Hofer mentions that most of the time strategic turnarounds should focus on greater market segmentation and on niche strategies. We will return to this point shortly.

Hofer then turns to the **operating turnaround**, which aims directly at performance enhancement. Operating turnarounds use one, or a combination, of three techniques: (1) increased revenue, (2) decreased costs, or (3) decreased assets. Hofer advises that firms close to the break-even point may be able to use cost cutting effectively, while firms far from break-even may have to rely on asset reduction. Firms that find themselves in between these positions will benefit from either a revenue-generating or an asset-reduction approach. The contingencies that will determine this choice are the longer-term potential of the firm and how critical its financial position is at the moment.

Turnaround Strategy: A Streamlined Model

Hofer admits in the reading that the terms he uses to describe operating turnarounds could also be used for strategic turnarounds. Hambrick and Shechter, in an article examining turnarounds in mature industrial-products businesses, assert that strategic and operating turnarounds may be indistinguishable except for their long-term intent.[6] Furthermore, they assert that Hofer's view of strategic turnarounds may boil down to "product/market refocusing."

Hambrick and Schecter thus suggest a slightly modified and streamlined model of turnaround strategy. They call the first set of approaches **efficiency-oriented turnaround techniques**. These are *cost-cutting* and *asset reduction*. As mentioned above, if a firm is only slightly below break-even, it may be able to get into the black by modestly cutting ordinary costs. Examples would be reducing electricity usage, cutting back on overtime pay, and finding cheaper sources of supply for raw materials or components. Firms that are well below break-even may have to consider getting rid of assets. Examples would be selling production plants or equipment and selling valuable but underused real estate. These two approaches can be used at the same time. Indeed, it may be impossible to use asset reduction without simultaneously cutting the costs associated with those assets.

Hambrick and Schecter also suggest two **entrepreneurially oriented turnaround techniques**. *Revenue generating* can be used when a firm is only slightly below break-even. An example would be inducing consumers to buy the firm's products by using coupons in the mail or newspapers or having the sales force make more frequent calls on certain kinds of customers. *Product/market refocusing* is more useful for firms further below break-even. Firms try to discover which of their products or markets have been the most lucrative. Then they increase their activity in those product segments or markets, abandoning or scaling back the less-successful ones.

NOTES FOR CHAPTER FOURTEEN

1. Meyer, A. D., J. B Goes, and G. R. Brooks, "Organizations in Disequilibrium: Environmental Jolts and Industry Revolutions." In *Organizational Change and Redesign,* eds. G. Huber and W. H. Glick. New York: Oxford University Press, 1992.

2. Daft, R. L., *Organization Theory and Design,* 4th ed. St. Paul: West Publishing, 1992, pp. 254–55.

3. Mintzberg, H., D. Raisinghani, and A. Theoret, "The Structure of Unstructured Decision Processes." *Administrative Science Quarterly* 21 (1976): 246–75.
4. The following discussion of implementation techniques is based on Daft, *Organization Theory and Design*, pp. 271–72.
5. Coch, L., and J. R. P. French, "Overcoming Resistance to Change." *Human Relations* 1 (1948): 512–33.
6. Hambrick, D., and S. M. Schecter, "Turnaround Strategies for Mature Industrial-Product Business units." *Academy of Management Journal* 26 (1984): 231–248.

CONVERGENCE AND UPHEAVAL: MANAGING THE UNSTEADY PACE OF ORGANIZATIONAL EVOLUTION

READING

By Michael L. Tushman, William H. Newman, and Elaine Romanelli

A snug fit of external opportunity, company strategy, and internal structure is a hallmark of successful companies. The real test of executive leadership, however, is in maintaining this alignment in the face of changing competitive conditions.

Consider the Polaroid or Caterpillar corporations. Both firms virtually dominated their respective industries for decades, only to be caught off guard by major environmental changes. The same strategic and organizational factors which were so effective for decades became the seeds of complacency and organization decline.

Recent studies of companies over long periods show that the most successful firms maintain a workable equilibrium for several years (or decades), but are also able to initiate and carry out sharp, widespread changes (referred to here as reorientations) when their environments shift. Such upheaval may bring renewed vigor to the enterprise. Less successful firms, on the other hand, get stuck in a particular pattern. The leaders of these firms either do not see the need for reorientation or they are unable to carry through the necessary frame-breaking changes. While not all reorientations succeed, those organizations which do not initiate reorientations as environments shift underperform.

This reading focuses on reasons why for long periods most companies make only incremental changes, and why they then need to make painful, discontinuous, system-wide shifts. We are particularly concerned with the role of executive leadership in managing this pattern of convergence punctuated by upheaval....

The task of managing incremental change, or convergence, differs sharply from managing frame-breaking change. Incremental change is compatible with the existing structure of a company and is reinforced over a period of years. In contrast, frame-breaking change is abrupt, painful to participants, and often resisted by the old guard. Forging these new strategy-structure-people-process consistencies and laying the basis for the next period of incremental change calls for distinctive skills.

Because the future health, and even survival, of a company or business unit is at stake, we need to take a closer look at the nature and consequences of convergent change and of differences imposed by frame-breaking change. We need to explore when and why these painful and risky revolutions interrupt previously successful patterns, and whether these discontinuities can be avoided and/or initiated prior to crisis. Finally, we need to examine what managers can and should do to guide their organizations through periods of convergence and upheaval over time....

The following discussion is based on the history of companies in many different industries, different countries, both large and small organizations, and organizations in various stages of their product class's life-cycle. We are dealing with a widespread phenomenon—not just a few dramatic sequences. Our research strongly suggests that the

Originally published in the *California Management Review* (Fall 1986). Copyright © 1986 by The Regents of the University of California. Reprinted with deletions by permission of the *Review.*

convergence/upheaval pattern occurs within departments at the business-unit level . . . and at the corporate level of analysis. . . . The problem of managing both convergent periods and upheaval is not just for the CEO, but necessarily involves general managers as well as functional managers.

PATTERNS IN ORGANIZATIONAL EVOLUTION: CONVERGENCE AND UPHEAVAL

Building on Strength: Periods of Convergence

Successful companies wisely stick to what works well. . . .

. . . convergence starts out with an effective dovetailing of strategy, structure, people, and processes. . . . The formal system includes decisions about grouping and linking resources as well as planning and control systems, rewards and evaluation procedures, and human resource management systems. The informal system includes core values, beliefs, norms, communication patterns, and actual decision-making and conflict resolution patterns. It is the whole fabric of structure, systems, people, and processes which must be suited to company strategy (Nadler and Tuchman, 1986).

As the fit between strategy, structure, people, and processes is never perfect, convergence is an ongoing process characterized by incremental change. Over time, in all companies studied, two types of converging changes were common: fine-tuning and incremental adaptations.

• **Converging Change: Fine-tuning.** Even with good strategy-structure-process fits, well-run companies seek even better ways of exploiting (and defending) their missions. Such effort typically deals with one or more of the following:

- *Refining* policies, methods, and procedures.
- *Creating specialized units and linking mechanisms* to permit increased volume and increased attention to unit quality and cost.
- *Developing personnel* especially suited to the present strategy—through improved selection and training, and tailoring reward systems to match strategic thrusts.
- Fostering individual and group *commitments* to the company mission and to the excellence of one's own department.
- Promoting *confidence* in the accepted norms, beliefs, and myths.
- *Clarifying* established roles, power, status, dependencies, and allocation mechanism

The fine-tuning fills out and elaborates the consistencies between strategy, structure, people, and processes. These incremental changes lead to an ever more interconnected (and therefore more stable) social system. Convergent periods fit the happy, stick-with-a-winner situations romanticized by Peters and Waterman (1982).

• **Converging Change: Incremental Adjustments to Environmental Shifts.** In addition to fine-tuning changes, minor shifts in the environment will call for some organizational response. Even the most conservative of organizations expect, even welcome, small changes which do not make too many waves.

A popular expression is that almost any organization can tolerate a "ten percent change." At any one time, only a few changes are being made; but these changes are still compatible with the prevailing structures, systems, and processes. Examples of such adjustments are an expansion in sales territory, a shift in emphasis among products in the product line, or improved processing technology in production.

The usual process of making changes of this sort is well known: wide acceptance of the need for change, openness to possible alternatives, objective examination of the pros and cons of each plausible alternative, participation of those directly affected in the preceding analysis, a market test or pilot operation where feasible, time to learn the new activities, established role models, known rewards for positive success, evaluation, and refinement.

The role of executive leadership during convergent periods is to reemphasize mission and core values and to delegate incremental decisions to middle-level managers. Note that the uncertainty created for people affected by such changes is well within tolerable limits. Opportunity is provided to anticipate and learn what is new, while most features of the structure remain unchanged.

The overall system adapts, but it is not transformed.

CONVERGING CHANGE: SOME CONSEQUENCES. For those companies whose strategies fit environmental conditions, convergence brings about better and better effectiveness. Incremental change is relatively easy to implement and ever more optimizes the consistencies between strategy, structure, people, and processes. At AT&T, for example, the period between 1913 and 1980 was one of ever more incremental change to further bolster the "Ma Bell" culture, systems, and structure all in service of developing the telephone network.

Convergent periods are, however, a double-edged sword. As organizations grow and become more successful, they develop internal forces for stability. Organization structures and systems become so interlinked that they only allow compatible changes. Further, over time, employees develop habits, patterned behaviors begin to take on values (e.g., "service is good"), and employees develop a sense of competence in knowing how to get work done within the system. These self-reinforcing patterns of behavior, norms, and values contribute to increased organizational momentum and complacency and, over time, to a sense of organizational history. This organizational history—epitomized by common stories, heroes, and standards—specifies "how we work here" and "what we hold important here."

This organizational momentum is profoundly functional as long as the organization's strategy is appropriate. The Ma Bell . . . culture, structure, and systems—and associated internal momentum—were critical to [the] organization's success. However, if (and when) strategy must change, this momentum cuts the other way. Organizational history is a source of tradition, precedent, and pride which are, in turn, anchors to the past. A proud history often restricts vigilant problem solving and may be a source of resistance to change.

When faced with environmental threat, organizations with strong momentum

- may not register the threat due to organization complacency and/or stunted external vigilance (e.g., the automobile or steel industries), or
- if the threat is recognized, the response is frequently heightened conformity to the status quo and/or increased commitment to "what we do best."

For example, the response of dominant firms to technological threat is frequently increased commitment to the obsolete technology (e.g., telegraph/telephone; vacuum tube/transistor; core/semiconductor memory). A paradoxical result of long periods of success may be heightened organizational complacency, decreased organizational flexibility, and a stunted ability to learn.

Converging change is a double-edged sword. Those very social and technical consistencies which are key sources of success may also be the seeds of failure if environments change. The longer the convergent periods, the greater these internal forces for stability. This momentum seems to be particularly accentuated in those most successful firms in a product class . . . in historically regulated organizations . . . or in organizations that have been traditionally shielded from competition. . . .

On Frame-Breaking Change

FORCES LEADING TO FRAME-BREAKING CHANGE. What, then, leads to frame-breaking change? Why defy tradition? Simply stated, frame-breaking change occurs in response to or, better yet, in anticipation of major environmental changes—changes which require more than incremental adjustments. The need for discontinuous change springs from one or a combination of the following:

• **Industry Discontinuities.** Sharp changes in legal, political, or technological conditions shift the basis of competition within industries. *Deregulation* has dramatically transformed the financial services and airlines industries. *Substitute product technologies* . . . or *substitute process technologies* . . . may transform the bases of competition within industries. Similarly, the emergence of industry standards, or *dominant designs* (such as the DC-3, IBM 360, or PDP-8) signal a shift in competition away from product innovation and towards increased process innovation. Finally, *major economic changes* (e.g., oil crises) and *legal shifts* (e.g., patent protection in biotechnology or trade/regulator barriers in pharmaceuticals or cigarettes) also directly affect bases of competition.

• **Product Life-cycle Shifts.** Over the course of a product class life cycle, different strategies are appropriate. In the emergence phase of a product class, competition is based on product innovation and performance, where in the maturity stage, competition centers on cost, volume, and efficiency. Shifts in patterns of demand alter key factors for success. For example, the demand and nature of competition for mini-computers, cellular telephones, wide-body aircraft, and bowling alley equipment was transformed as these products gained acceptance and their product classes evolved. Powerful international competition may compound these forces.

• **Internal Company Dynamics.** Entwined with these external forces are breaking points within the firm. Sheer size may require a basically new management design. For example, few inventor-entrepreneurs can tolerate the formality that is linked with large volume. . . . Key people die. Family investors may become more concerned with their inheritance taxes than with company development. Revised corporate portfolio strategy may sharply alter the role and resources assigned to business units or functional areas. Such pressures especially when coupled with external changes, may trigger frame-breaking change.

SCOPE OF FRAME-BREAKING CHANGE. Frame-breaking change is driven by shifts in business strategy. As strategy shifts so too must structure, people, and organizational processes. Quite unlike convergent change, frame-breaking reforms involve discontinuous changes throughout the organization. These bursts of change do not reinforce the existing system and are implemented rapidly. . . . Frame-breaking changes are revolutionary changes *of* the system as opposed to incremental changes *in* the system.

The following features are usually involved in frame-breaking change:

• **Reformed Mission and Core Values.** A strategy shift involves a new definition of company mission. Entering or withdrawing from an industry may be involved; at least the way the company expects to be outstanding is altered. . . .

• **Altered Power and Status.** Frame-breaking change always alters the distribution of power. Some groups lose in the shift while others gain. . . . These dramatically altered power distributions reflect shifts in bases of competition and resource allocation. A new strategy must be backed up with a shift in the balance of power and status.

• **Reorganization.** A new strategy requires a modification in structure, systems, and procedures. As strategic requirements shift, so too must the choice of organization form. A new direction calls for added activity in some areas and less in others. Changes in structure and systems are means to ensure that this reallocation of effort takes place. New structures and revised roles deliberately break business-as-usual behavior.

• **Revised Interaction Patterns.** The way people in the organization work together has to adapt during frame-breaking change. As strategy is different, new procedures, work flows, communication networks, and decision-making patterns must be established. With these changes in work flows and procedures must also come revised norms, informal decision-making/conflict-resolution procedures, and informal roles.

• **New Executives.** Frame-breaking change also involves new executives, usually brought in from outside the organization (or business unit) and placed in key managerial positions. Commitment to the new mission, energy to overcome prevailing inertia, and freedom from prior obligations are all needed to refocus the organization. A few exceptional members of the old guard may attempt to make this shift, but habits and expectations of their associations are difficult to break. New executives are most likely to provide both the necessary drive and an enhanced set of skills more appropriate for the new strategy. While the overall number of executive changes is usually relatively small, these new executives have substantial symbolic and substantive effects on the organization. . . .

WHY ALL AT ONCE? Frame-breaking change is revolutionary in that the shifts reshape the entire nature of the organization. Those more effective examples of frame-breaking change were implemented rapidly. . . . It appears that a piecemeal approach to frame-breaking changes gets bogged down in politics, individual resistance to change, and organizational inertia. . . . Frame-breaking change requires discontinuous shifts in strategy, structure, people, and processes concurrently—or at least in a short period of time. Reasons for rapid, simultaneous implementation include:

• *Synergy* within the new structure can be a powerful aid. New executives with a fresh mission, working in a redesigned organization with revised norms and values, backed up with power and status, provide strong reinforcement. The pieces of the revitalized organization pull together, as opposed to piecemeal change where one part of the new organization is out of synch with the old organization.

• *Pockets of resistance* have a chance to grow and develop when frame-breaking change is implemented slowly. The new mission, shifts in organization, and other frame-breaking changes upset the comfortable routines and precedent. Resistance to such fundamental change is natural. If frame-breaking change is implemented slowly, then individuals have a greater opportunity to undermine the changes and organizational inertia works to further stifle fundamental change.

• Typically, there is a *pent-up need for change.* During convergent periods, basic adjustments are postponed. Boat rocking is discouraged. Once constraints are relaxed, a variety of desirable improvements press for attention. The exhilaration and momentum of a fresh effort (and new team) make difficult moves more acceptable. Change is in fashion.

• Frame-breaking change is an inherently *risky and uncertain venture.* The longer the implementation period, the greater the period of uncertainty and instability. The most effective frame-breaking changes initiate the new strategy, structure, processes, and systems rapidly and begin the next period of stability and convergent change. The sooner fundamental uncertainty is removed, the better the chances of organizational survival and growth. While the pacing of change is important, the overall time to implement frame-breaking change will be contingent on the size and age of the organization.

PATTERNS IN ORGANIZATION EVOLUTION. This historical approach to organization evolution focuses on convergent periods punctuated by reorientation—discontinuous, organizationwide upheavals. The most effective firms take advantage of relatively long convergent periods. These periods of incremental change build on and take advantage of organization inertia. Frame-breaking change is quite dysfunctional if the organization is successful and the environment is stable. If, however, the organization is performing poorly and/or if the environment changes substantially, frame-breaking change is the only way to realign the organization with its competitive environment. Not all reorientations will be successful. . . . However, inaction in the face of performance crisis and/or environmental shifts is a certain recipe for failure.

Because reorientations are so disruptive and fraught with uncertainty, the more rapidly they are implemented, the more quickly the organization can reap the benefits of the following convergent period. High-performing firms initiate reorientations when environmental conditions shift and implement these reorientations rapidly. . . . Low-performing organizations either do not reorient or reorient all the time as they root around to find an effective alignment with environmental conditions. . . .

EXECUTIVE LEADERSHIP AND ORGANIZATION EVOLUTION

Executive leadership plays a key role in reinforcing systemwide momentum during convergent periods and in initiating and implementing bursts of change that characterize strategic reorientations. The nature of the leadership task differs sharply during these contrasting periods of organization evolution.

During convergent periods, the executive team focuses on *maintaining* congruence and fit within the organization. Because strategy, structure, processes, and systems are fundamentally sound, the myriad of incremental substantive decisions can be delegated to middle-level management, where direct expertise and information resides. The key role for executive leadership during convergent periods is to reemphasize strategy, mission, and core values and to keep a vigilant eye on external opportunities and/or threats.

Frame-breaking change, however, requires direct executive involvement in all aspects of the change. Given the enormity of the change and inherent internal forces for stability, executive leadership must be involved in the specification of strategy, structure, people, and organizational processes *and* in the development of implementation plans. . . .

The most effective executives in our studies foresaw the need for major change. They recognized the external threats and opportunities, and took bold steps to deal with them. . . . Indeed, by acting before being forced to do so, they had more time to plan their transitions.

Such visionary executive teams are the exceptions. Most frame-breaking change is postponed until a financial crisis forces drastic action. The momentum, and frequently the success, of convergent periods breeds reluctance to change. . . .

. . . most frame-breaking upheavals are managed by executives brought in from outside the company. The Columbia research program finds that externally recruited executives are more than three times more likely to initiate frame-breaking change than existing executive teams. Frame-breaking change was coupled with CEO succession in more than 80% of the cases. . . .

There are several reasons why a fresh set of executives are typically used in company transformations. The new executive team brings different skills and a fresh perspective. Often they arrive with a strong belief in the new mission. Moreover, they are unfettered by prior commitments linked to the status quo; instead, this new top team symbolizes the need for change. Excitement of a new challenge adds to the energy devoted to it.

We should note that many of the executives who could not, or would not, implement frame-breaking change went on to be quite successful in other organizations. . . . The stimulation of a fresh start and of jobs matched to personal competence applies to individuals as well as to organizations.

Although typical patterns for the when and who of frame-breaking change are clear—wait for a financial crisis and then bring in an outsider, along with a revised executive team, to revamp the company—this is clearly less than satisfactory for a particular organization. Clearly, some companies benefit from transforming themselves before a crisis forces them to do so, and a few exceptional executives have the vision and drive to reorient a business which they nurtured during its preceding period of convergence. The vital tasks are to manage incremental change during convergent periods; to have the vision to initiate and implement frame-breaking change prior to the competition; and to mobilize an executive which can initiate and implement both kinds of change.

CONCLUSION

. . . Managers should anticipate that when environments change sharply

- Frame-breaking change cannot be avoided. These discontinuous organizational changes will either be made proactively or initiated under crisis/turnaround conditions.
- Discontinuous changes need to be made in strategy, structure, people, and processes concurrently. Tentative change runs the risk of being smothered by individual, group, and organizational inertia.
- Frame-breaking change requires direct executive involvement in all aspects of the change, usually bolstered with new executives from outside the organization.
- There are no patterns in the sequence of frame-breaking changes, and not all strategies will be effective. Strategy and, in turn, structure, systems, and processes must meet industry-specific competitive issues.

Finally, our historical analysis of organizations highlights the following issues for executive leadership:

- Need to manage for balance, consistency, or fit during convergent period.
- Need to be vigilant for environmental shifts in order to anticipate the need for frame-breaking change.
- Need to manage effectively incremental as well as frame-breaking change.
- Need to build (or rebuild) a top team to help initiate and implement frame-breaking change.
- Need to develop core values which can be used as an anchor as organizations evolve through frame-breaking changes (e.g., IBM, Hewlett-Packard).
- Need to develop and use organizational history as a way to infuse pride in an organization's past and for its future.
- Need to bolster technical, social, and conceptual skills with visionary skills. Visionary skills add energy, direction, and excitement so critical during frame-breaking change. . . .

RESPONDING TO CRISIS

READING

By William H. Starbuck, Arent Greve, and Bo L. T. Hedberg

For nearly 50 years, Facit was regarded as a successful manufacturer of business machines and office furnishings. Facit grew until it operated factories in twenty cities and it maintained sales units in fifteen countries. Employment reached 14,000. Suddenly, this success metamorphosed into impending disaster. For three consecutive years, gross profits were negative and employment and sales declined. Plants were closed or sold.

Originally published in the *Journal of Business Administration* (Spring 1978). Reprinted with deletions by permission of the *Journal of Business Administration*.

Again and again, top managers were replaced and the managerial hierarchy was reorganized. Consultants were called in: they recommended that more operations should be closed and more employees should be fired. But after numerous meetings, the top managers could not decide whether to do what the consultants recommended. . . .

Facit . . . exemplifies organizations which encounter crises. Crises are times of danger, times when some actions lead toward organizational failure. . . .

Based on several case studies of organizations facing crises, this article explains what makes some organizations especially prone to encounter crises, it describes how organizations typically react to crises, and it prescribes how organizations ought to cope with crises.

WHY DO CRISES OCCUR?

One initial conjecture was that crises originate as threatening events in organizations' environments. A competing conjecture was that crises originate from defects within organizations themselves. Analyses of actual crises suggest that both conjectures are partly true and both are partly false. Organizations facing crises do perceive the crises as having originated in their environments. For example, Facit's top managers attributed many difficulties to temporary depressions of the firm's economic environment, and they often complained about the fierceness of market competition. At first, Facit's top managers thought that electronic calculators would replace mechanical calculators only very gradually; later, they saw electronic calculators as a technological revolution that was progressing too quickly for Facit to adapt to it (Starbuck and Hedberg, 1977).

And it was, in fact, true that national economic growth was sometimes faster and sometimes slower. There were indeed competing firms that were wooing Facit's customers. Electronic calculators actually did challenge and ultimately replace mechanical calculators. So the observations of Facit's top managers had bases in reality. But one would have to be quite gullible to accept such reasons as completely explaining Facit's crises.

Organizations' perceptions are never totally accurate. Organizations decide, sometimes explicitly but often implicitly, to observe some aspects of their environments and to ignore other aspects. They also interpret, in terms of their current goals, methods and competences, what they do observe. Such interpretation is evident in the statements about electronic calculators by Facit's top managers.

There are special reasons to question the perceptions of the top managers in organizations facing crises. If crises result partly from defects within organizations, these defects could distort the organizations' perceptions. Because distorted perceptions appear in all organizations, it may be overstatement to say that distorted perceptions are alone sufficient to cause crises. However, perceptual distortions do seem to contribute to crises by leading organizations to take no actions or inappropriate actions. . . .

Defects in organizations not only affect perceptions; they also affect the realities that are there to be perceived. Organizational defects are translated into environmental realities when organizations choose their immediate environments—by choosing suppliers, product characteristics, technologies or geographic locations—or when they manipulate their environments—by advertising, training employees, conducting research or negotiating cooperative agreements (Starbuck, 1976). . . .

Learning to Fail

Talk of organizational defects can, however, easily create misimpressions about the differences between those organizations which encounter crises and those which avoid crises. The organizations which encounter crises do not have qualitatively unusual characteristics, and they are not fundamentally abnormal. Probably the great majority of organizations have the potential to work themselves into crises, and the processes which produce crises are substantially identical with the processes which produce successes (Hedberg et al., 1976).

LEARNING/PROGRAMMING

These ironies arise from how organizations learn and from how they use their successes. The key process for organizational learning is programming: when organizations observe that certain activities appear to succeed, they crystallize these activities as standardized programs. These programs are built into the formalized roles assigned to organizations' members. Both programs and roles make activities consistent across different people and across different times. Programs generate activities that resemble those leading to good results in the past, and they do so efficiently. Organizations respond quickly to most environmental events because these events activate previously learned programs. Programs also loosen organizations' connections to their environments. Because environmental events fall into equivalence classes according to which programs they activate, organizations fail to perceive many of the small differences among environmental events. Because organizations indoctrinate their members and train them to perform roles, organizations fail to accommodate or utilize many of the differences among members who are recruited at various times in diverse locations (Nystrom et al., 1976).

Programming often facilitates success, and success always fosters programming. Success also produces slack resources and opportunities for buffering—both of which allow organizations to loosen their connections to their environments (Cyert and March, 1963; Thompson, 1967). Customers are clustered into equivalence classes, and products are standardized. Raw materials and products are stored in inventories, work activities are smoothed, and work schedules are stretched out into the future. Programs and roles are added rather frequently and discarded less frequently. Technologies are frozen by means of large capital investments. . . .

Programming, buffering, and slack resources are tools that cut on two sides. On one side, these tools enable organizations to act autonomously—to choose among alternative environments, to take risks, to experiment, to construct new environmental alternatives—and autonomous actions are generally prerequisites for outstanding successes. But on the other side, these tools render organizations less sensitive to environmental events. Organizations become less able to perceive what is happening, so they fantasize about their environments, and it may happen that realities intrude only occasionally and marginally on these fantasies. Organizations also become less able to respond to the environmental events they do perceive. . . .

WHAT REACTIONS DO CRISES EVOKE?

Explaining Crises Away

It seems that conventional accounting reports, and the ideology asserting that such reports should be bases for action, are among organizations' major liabilities. The more seriously organizations attend to their accounting reports, the more likely they are to encounter crises, and the more difficulty they have coping with crises.

Accounting reports are intentionally historical: at best they indicate what happened during the previous quarter, and even recent reports are strongly influenced by purchases of goods and equipment dating back many years and by inventories of unsalable products and obsolete components. The formats of accounting reports change very slowly. Accounting reports also intentionally focus upon formalized measures of well observed phenomena; the measures are always numerical, the importances of phenomena are appraised in monetary units, and the observations are programmatic. Much of the content in every report is ritualized irrelevance.

. . . The organizations which take their accounting reports very seriously are assuming that their worlds change slowly—that precedents are relevant to today's actions, that tomorrow's environments will look much like yesterday's, that current programs and methods are only slightly faulty at most (Hedberg and Jönsson, 1978; Thompson, 1967). Such organizations devote few resources to monitoring and interpreting unexpected environmental events; they do not tolerate redundant, ostensibly inessential activities; they guide their development by means of systematic long-range planning. . . .

All of these characteristics make it difficult for organizations to see unanticipated threats and opportunities. Many unanticipated events are never perceived at all; others are only perceived after they have been developing for some time. Then when unanticipated events are perceived, these characteristics introduce perceptual errors. One consequence is that organizations overlook the earliest signs that crises are developing. . . .

Those organizations which are strongly wedded to their pasts, naturally enough, fear rapid changes. They expect abrupt changes to produce undesirable consequences. This logic is often reversed when undesirable events occur: the undesirable events are hypothesized to be the consequences of rapid changes. The early signs of crises are attributed to the organizations' injudicious efforts to change—new markets, capital investments, inexperienced personnel, or product innovations. Such interpretations imply that no remedies are needed beyond prudent moderation, because performances will improve automatically as operations stabilize.

The idea that organizations ought to be stable structures also fosters another rationalization for early signs of crises—that poor performances result from transient environmental pressures such as economic recessions, seasonal variations in consumption, or competitors' foolish maneuvers. This rationale implies that no major strategic reorientations are called for; to the contrary, the current strategic experiments ought to terminate. Organizations decide that temporary belt-tightening is needed, together with some centralization of control and restraints on wasteful entrepreneurial ventures, but these are portrayed as beneficial changes that focus attention on what is essential (Beer, 1974; Nystrom et al., 1976; Thompson, 1967). . . .

. . . Managers who have helped to formulate strategies . . . resist strategic reorientations in order to retain power and status, and they try to persuade themselves and others that their strategies are appropriate . . . [they] may launch propaganda campaigns that deny the existence of crises. These propaganda efforts always include distortions of accounting reports: accounting periods are lengthened, depreciation charges are suspended, gains from sales or reevaluations of assets are included with operating profits. . . .

Facit's top managers made numerous efforts to persuade stockholders, employees, and the public that no crises existed, that the crisis was not serious, or that the crisis had ended. When poor performance first intruded into Facit's accounting reports, the top managers explained that this poor performance was the temporary product of currency devaluations and fierce competition. "Facit is well equipped to meet future competition. . . . Improvement is underway, but has not affected this year's outcome." Later, as the crisis deepened, Facit's managing director was replaced several times: each new managing director reported sadly that the situation was actually worse than his predecessor had publicly admitted, but he was happy to be able to announce that the nadir had been passed and the future looked rosy. Again and again, Facit's top managers announced that their firm was in sound condition and that improved performances were imminent; the chairman of the board and the managing director made such announcements even while they were secretly negotiating to sell the firm. After two years of serious difficulties, when plants were being closed, when hundreds of employees were losing their jobs, and when the top managers were privately in despair, the top managers announced that they intended to expand Facit's product line by sixty percent (Starbuck and Hedberg, 1977). . . .

Living in Collapsing Palaces

The organizations which encounter crises resemble palaces perched on mountaintops that are crumbling from erosion. Like palaces, these organizations are rigid, cohesive structures that integrate elegant components. Although their flawless harmonies make organizational palaces look completely rational—indeed, beautiful—to observers who are inside them, observers standing outside can see that the beauty and harmony rest upon eroding grounds.

Organizational palaces are rigid because their components mesh so snugly and reinforce their neighbors. Perceptions, goals, capabilities, methods, personnel, products, and capital equipment are like stone blocks and wooden beams that interlock and brace each other. There are no chinks, no gaps, and no protruding beams because careful reason has guided every expansion and remodeling. Rationality is solidified in integrated forms that are very difficult to move: the components which blend smoothly in one arrangement fit badly in another, components which mesh tightly must be moved simultaneously, and movements fracture tight junctions. So the inhabitants' first reactions to crises are to maintain their palaces intact—they shore up shaky foundations, strengthen points of stress, and patch up cracks—and their palaces remain sitting beautifully on eroding mountaintops.

However, shoring up affords only temporary remedies against crumbling mountains, and eventually, the palaces themselves start falling apart. People begin to see that the top managers have been making faulty predictions: doubts arise that the top managers know how to cope with the crises, and the top managers usually end up looking like incompetent liars. Idealism and commitments to organizational goals fade; cynicism and opportunism grow; uncertainty escalates (Jönsson and Lundin, 1977; Kahn et al., 1964; Vickers, 1959). But cuts and reorganizations stir up power struggles that undermine cooperation. . . .

Two or three years after Facit's crisis became obvious, the top managers reached a state of paralysis. The managerial hierarchy had been reorganized repeatedly. Several small plants had been closed, and the main office-furnishings plant had been sold. But the situation had continued to get worse and worse. . . .

At this point, Electrolux bought Facit and achieved a dramatic turnaround. Eighthundred employees were laid off right away, but these people were being rehired within three months. It was discovered that Facit possessed a large, unfilled demand for typewriters: a mechanical-calculator plant was converted to typewriters, and the typewriter plants were expanded. The demand for office furnishings was also found to exceed production capacity. Facit's research had developed electronic calculators, small computers, and computer terminals which had never been marketed aggressively; substantial demands existed for these products. During the second year after Electrolux stepped in, Facit's employment went up 10%, production increased 25%, and Facit earned a profit.

Facit's turnaround was made possible by the disintegration that preceded it. The impediments to learning usually grow very strong in organizations. Because organizations are intricate, they fear that changes would produce unforeseen disadvantages. Because organizations are logically integrated, they expect changes to initiate cascades of further changes. Because organizations are rational, they buttress their current programs and roles with justifying analyses. These impediments to learning grow strongest in the organizational palaces that emphasize rational analyses, reliable information, and logical consistency. Palaces have to be taken apart before they can be moved to new locations, and organizations have to unlearn what they now know before they can learn new knowledge. Organizations have to lose confidence in their old leaders before they will listen to new leaders. Organizations have to abandon their old goals before they will adopt new goals. Organizations have to reject their perceptual filters before they will notice events they previously overlooked. Organizations have to see that their old methods do not work before they will invent and use new methods (Cyert and March, 1963; Hedberg, 1981; Nystrom et al., 1976).

Unfortunately, crisis-ridden organizations may learn that their old methods do not work, and yet they may not learn new methods which do work.

HOW TO COPE WITH CRISES

Crises are dangerous, by definition. After crises have fully developed, organizations face serious risks of failure. To eliminate these risks is often difficult, and the remedies bring pain to some people. Consequently, the best way to cope with crises is to evade them.

Avoiding Excesses

. . . case studies suggest that many organizations adhere too strictly to those prescriptions which favor rationality, reliability, formality, logical consistency, planning, agreement, stability, hierarchical control and efficiency. All of these properties can bring benefits when they appear in moderation: organizations need some rationality, some formality, some stability, and so on. But excessive emphases on these properties turn organizations into palaces—palaces on eroding mountaintops. Organizations also need moderate amounts of irrationality, unreliability, informality, inconsistency, spontaneity, dissension, instability, delegation of responsibility, and inefficiency. These properties help to keep perceptions sharp, they disrupt complacency, and they nurture experimentation and evolutionary change (Hedberg et al., 1976; Miller and Mintzberg, 1974).

One sensible operating rule is that whenever organizations adopt one prescription, they should adopt a second prescription which contradicts the first. Contradictory prescriptions remind organizations that each prescription is a misleading oversimplification that ought not be carried to excess. For example, organizations should work toward consensus, but they should also encourage dissenters to speak out; organizations should try to exploit their strategic strengths, but they should also try to eliminate their strategic weaknesses; organizations should formulate plans, but they should also take advantage of unforeseen opportunities and they should combat unforeseen threats. It is as if each prescription presses down one pan of a balance: matched pairs of prescriptions can offset each other and keep a balance level. . . .

But balancing prescriptions is a defensive tactic that cannot rescue the organizations which already face crises. These organizations have been defending themselves— unsuccessfully—too long; they need to go on the offensive. The remainder of this article

prescribes how organizations can terminate their crises and begin to rebuild themselves in viable forms.

Replacing Top Managers

When Electrolux took over Facit, it promptly fired all of Facit's top managers. This is exactly what Electrolux should have done. If Electrolux had not taken such drastic action, its intervention would probably have failed. . . .

Indiscriminate replacements of entire groups of top managers are evidently essential to bringing organizations out of crises. The veteran top managers ought to be replaced even if they are all competent people who are trying their best and even if the newcomers have no more ability, and less direct expertise, than the veterans. . . .

[In crises,] remedies are needed urgently. Perhaps the greatest need is for dramatic acts symbolizing the end of disintegration and the beginning of regeneration. Because propaganda and deceit have been rife, these symbolic acts have to be such that even skeptical observers can see they are sincere acts; and because the top managers represent both past strategies and past attempts to deceive, these symbolic acts have to punish the top managers. In addition, however, the organizations need new perceptions of reality, fresh strategic ideas, and revitalization. Since no one really knows what strategies will succeed, new strategies have to be discovered experimentally. Experimenting depends upon enthusiasm and willingness to take risks; people must have confidence their organizations can surmount new challenges and exploit discoveries. Experimenting also depends upon seeing aspects of reality which have been unseen and upon evaluating performances by criteria that differ from past criteria. . . .

. . . replacements of one or two top managers at a time are not enough. Such gradual replacements happen spontaneously while crisis-ridden organizations are disintegrating: if gradual replacements were sufficient to end crises, the crises would already have ended. But when top managers are replaced gradually, the newcomers are injected into ongoing, cohesive groups of veterans, and the newcomers exert little influence on these groups, whereas the groups exert much influence on the newcomers.

Group cohesion also impedes the veteran's own efforts to adopt remedies. Each member of a group is constrained by the other members' expectations, and cohesion draws these constraints tight. A group as a whole may bind itself to its current methods even though everyone in the group is individually ready to change; when a group includes one or two members who actively resist change, these resisters can control what happens. . . .

Rejecting Implicit Assumptions

One reason groups of top managers find change difficult is that many of the assumptions underlying their perceptions and behaviors are implicit ones. Explicit assumptions can be readily identified and discussed, so people can challenge these assumptions and perhaps alter them. But implicit assumptions may never be seen by the people who make them, and these unseen assumptions may persist indefinitely. . . .

Experimenting with Portfolios

. . . In order to escape from crises, organizations have to invest in new markets, new products, new technologies, new methods of operating, or new people. Diversification plays the same role in these investments as it does in other investments: expected returns are traded for protection against mistaken predictions. . . .

But crisis-ridden organizations find it difficult to pursue several alternatives simultaneously because they lack resources. Not many organizations start to develop alternatives while they are still [affluent]. . . .

Managing Ideology

Top managers are often the villains of crises. They are the real villains insofar as they steer their organizations into crises and insofar as they intensify crises by delaying actions or taking inappropriate actions. And they are symbolic villains who have to be replaced before crises end. But top managers are also the heroes when their organizations escape from crises. They receive the plaudits, and they largely deserve the plaudits because their actions have been the crucial ones.

Sometimes top managers contribute to escapes from crises by inventing new methods and strategies. Top managers have the best chance to do this effectively in small organizations . . . because small organizations do not make sharp demarcations among managers at different levels and they do not sharply distinguish managers from staff analysts. However, even in small organizations, the top managers should beware of relying on their own strategy-making skills. In large organizations where top management is a specialized occupation, it is generally a mistake for the top managers to act as strategy makers. . . .

. . . when top managers are occupied with strategy making, they are not doing the more important work which is their special responsibility: managing ideology. The low-level and middle managers do attend to ideological phenomena to some extent, but they focus their attentions upon visible, physical phenomena—the uses of machines, manual and clerical work, flows of materials, conferences, reports, planning documents such as schedules and blueprints, or workers' complaints. Top managers have the complementary responsibility: although they have to attend to visible, physical phenomena to some extent, they should concentrate their attentions on ideological phenomena such as morale, enthusiasm, beliefs, goals, values, and ideas. Managing ideology is very difficult because it is so indirect—like trying to steer a ship by describing the harbor toward which the ship should sail. But managing ideology is also very important because ideological phenomena exert such powerful effects upon the visible, physical phenomena.

Electrolux's turnaround of Facit was wrought almost entirely by managing ideology (Starbuck and Hedberg, 1977). Except for the replacements of top managers, Electrolux left Facit's organization largely alone. Electrolux did loan Facit approximately two million dollars so that actions would not have to be taken solely out of financial exigency, but this was a small sum in relation to the size of the company. What Electrolux did was to reconceptualize Facit and Facit's environment. Electronic calculators were no longer a technological revolution that was leaving Facit behind: Facit was making and selling electronic calculators. Typewriters and office furnishing became key product lines instead of sidelines to calculators. Competition stopped being a threat and became a stimulus. As Electrolux's managing director put it: "Hard competition is a challenge; there is no reason to withdraw." A newspaper remarked: "Although everything looks different today, the company is still more or less managed by the same people who were in charge of the company during the sequence of crises. It is now very difficult to find enough people to recruit for the factories. . . . All the present products emanate from the former Facit organization, but still, the situation has changed drastically." . . .

Facit . . . [is an organization that has] rediscovered the truth of an ancient, Chinese insight. The Chinese symbol for crisis combines two simpler symbols, the symbol for danger and the one for opportunity. Crises are times of danger, but they are also times of opportunity. . . .

DESIGNING TURNAROUND STRATEGIES

By Charles W. Hofer

At some time in their history, most successful organizations suffer stagnation or decline in their performance. . . . Nevertheless, the Western ethic that "one must grow or die" causes psychological problems in such instances, much as the onset of middle age does in many individuals. . . .

This article will discuss turnarounds and turnaround strategies in business organizations. . . . [It will examine] turnarounds at the business-unit level. Its focus will be prescriptive rather than descriptive. Specifically, it will (1) analyze the nature of business-level turnaround situations, (2) discuss the types of turnaround strategies that are possible at this level, (3) present an analytical framework for deciding what type of turnaround strategy should be used in particular situations, and (4) discuss how to design and implement the various aspects of the indicated turnaround strategy.

THE NATURE OF TURNAROUND SITUATIONS

There are two factors that are important in describing turnaround situations. They are (1) the areas of organizational performance affected and (2) the time criticality of the turnaround situation.

In terms of organizational performance, the types of turnarounds that have been pursued and studied most frequently are those involving declines in organizational efficiency and/or profitability. Such declines usually have been measured by declining net income after taxes, although net cash flow and earnings per share have also been used.

The types of turnaround receiving next highest priority have been those involving stagnation or declines in organizational size or growth. The reason for such attention derives partly from the obvious link between size, growth, and net income, partly from the Western myth that one must grow or die, and partly from research findings linking profitability to relative market share. . . .

The third type of turnarounds to receive substantial management attention in the 1980s have been those involving poor organizational asset utilization. Such turnaround efforts have not received as much publicity or research attention as the first two, however, primarily because they have been pursued by firms that are performing reasonably well in terms of profits and growth. Thus, poor performance with respect to asset utilization does not *appear* to pose the same threat to organizational or management survival as poor performance in the former areas. Furthermore, such asset utilization turnaround strategies usually have not been discussed by the firms pursuing them outside of their management councils, primarily for competitive reasons. Asset utilization turnarounds are likely to receive far greater attention from top management in the late 1980s and early 1990s than they have to date, however, because the combination of reasonable profits and poor asset utilization provides an open invitation to corporate takeover and greenmail specialists. . . . Despite (or perhaps because of) such threats, it is still likely that most asset utilization turnaround efforts will continue to be pursued with a low profile.

The second characteristic of turnaround situations that is important to the design of effective turnaround strategies is the time criticality of the firm's current situation. If

Copyright © 1986 by Charles W. Hofer. Reproduced with deletions by permission of the author. This paper is a revision of "Turnaround Strategies" by Charles W. Hofer, originally published in W. F. Glueck, *Business Policy and Strategic Management,* 3rd ed., McGraw-Hill, 1980.

there is imminent danger to survival, it is almost always necessary to make an operational response to the situation in the near term even though a strategic response may eventually follow. The reason for this is the lengthy time delay that usually exists between the taking of a strategic action and the response that accompanies it. When the threat to organizational survival is not imminent (i.e., when there is some time to respond in a variety of ways), then it is possible to "customize" the turnaround strategy to the specific situation involved.

TYPES OF TURNAROUND STRATEGIES

There are two broad types of turnaround strategies that may be followed at the business-unit level: strategic turnarounds and operating turnarounds.

Strategic turnarounds are of two types: those that involve a change in the organization's strategy for competing in the same business, and those that involve entering a new business or businesses. The latter involve questions of corporation portfolio strategy and will not be discussed further here. Strategies for saving the existing business may be further subdivided according to the nature of the competitive position change desired, and by the core skills and competitive weapons around which the strategy is built. Most such strategic turnarounds can be classified into one of three categories:

1. Those that seek to move to a larger strategic group in the industry involved
2. Those that seek to compete more effectively within the business' existing strategic group through the use of different (or substantially modified) competitive weapons and core skills
3. Those that seek to move to a smaller strategic group in the industry involved

In terms of competitive weapons and core skills, most strategic turnarounds involve switches in the ways firms seek to achieve differentiation or cost effectiveness, rather than switches from a differentiation strategy to a cost effectiveness strategy, or vice versa.

Operating turnarounds are usually one of four types, none of which involves changing the firm's business-level strategy. These are nonstrategic turnarounds that emphasize: (1) increased revenues, (2) decreased costs, (3) decreased assets, or (4) a balanced combination of two or more of the preceding options. It should be noted that these categories could also be used to describe strategic turnarounds. In strategic turnarounds, though, the focus is on the strategy changes sought, with the performance produced being a derivative of the strategy change. In operating turnarounds, by contrast, the focus is on the performance targets, and any actions that can achieve them are to be considered whether they make good long-run strategic sense or not.

In practice, the distinction between strategic and operating actions and turnarounds becomes blurred because actions that substantially decrease assets also often require a change in strategy to be most effective, and so on. The distinction is still relevant, however, because of the different priorities attached to short-term versus long-term actions and trade-offs in the two types of strategies.

SELECTING THE TYPE OF TURNAROUND STRATEGY TO BE FOLLOWED

In trying to decide what type of turnaround strategy should be pursued in a particular situation, three questions should be asked:

1. Is the business worth saving? More specifically, can the business be made profitable in the long run, or is it better to liquidate or divest it now? And, if it is worth saving, then,

2. What is the current operating health of the business?

3. What is the current strategic health of the business?

Although one occasionally encounters turnarounds that involve long time horizons, the vast majority of turnaround situations involve severe constraints on the time available for action. In fact, in most turnaround situations there is some imminent danger to the firm's survival. For this reason, one must first check the current operating health of the business as longer-term considerations will be irrelevant if the firm goes bankrupt in the near term. For this same reason, the first step in assessing a firm's current operating health is an analysis of its current financial condition. The purpose of such analysis is to determine: (1) how probable it is that the firm may go bankrupt in the near term, (2) how much time it has to make needed changes before it goes bankrupt, (3) the magnitude of the turnaround needed to avoid bankruptcy, and (4) the financial resources that could be raised in the short term to aid in the battle. Once this analysis is completed, similar analyses must be conducted of the firm's current market, technological, and production positions in order to complete the determination of its current operating health.

After these analyses are completed, the task of selecting the optimal type of turnaround strategy can begin. In general, such optimal strategies will depend on the firm's current operating and strategic health. . . . If both are weak, then liquidation is probably the best option unless the firm has no other businesses in which it could invest. In the latter case, a combined operating/strategic turnaround with very tight controls might be possible. With a weak operating position and a moderate or strong strategic position, an operating turnaround strategy is usually needed, although divesture is also reasonable if the corporation has other businesses in which it might invest.

When the business is strong operationally but weak strategically, then a strategic turnaround is almost always indicated although the firm may have a grace period in which to decide what it will do. When both operating and strategic health are strong, turnaround strategies are seldom needed unless it is to improve asset utilization, which may sometimes lag. The approach to use for improving asset utilization in such cases will normally depend on the firm's current strategic health.

Once a business has selected the type of broad turnaround strategy it should use, that is, strategic or operating, it then needs to select the more specific aspects of its turnaround strategy. The details of these action plans will depend, of course, on the exact nature of the industry in which the business competes and on its strengths and weaknesses vis-à-vis its major competitors in that industry.

THE NEED FOR NEW TOP MANAGEMENT

Before discussing any specific turnaround options, though, one nearly universal generalization must be made. It is the "fact" that almost all successful turnarounds require the replacement of the business's current top management. There is, of course, no law written in stone that says a firm's current top management team cannot supervise a successful turnaround. Usually, however, the old management has such a strong set of beliefs about how to run the business in question, many of which must be wrong for the current problems to have arisen, that the only way to get a new view of the situation is to bring in new top management. There will, of course, be some exceptions to this generalization as there are to all generalizations. Nonetheless, in over 95% of the cases cited by Kami and Ross (1973) and by Schendel, Patton, and Riggs (1976), a change in top management did accompany a successful turnaround. Thus, one can say that a successful turnaround will require, almost without exception, either a change in top management or a substantial change in the behavior of the existing management team. Moreover, increasing evidence from the experiences of General Electric and other similar multi-industry companies indicates that different general managers are skilled at different types of tasks. Consequently, the new top management team should be selected to the degree possible with the skills appropriate to the type of turnaround strategy that will need to be followed. For instance, an entrepreneurial strategist should be chosen if a high-growth, strategic turnaround is to be pursued, while a hard-nosed, experienced cost cutter should be selected if an operating turnaround with a major cost-reduction effort is to be pursued.

STRATEGIC TURNAROUNDS

Strategic turnarounds are appropriate when the business has an average or strong current operating position, but a lost position strategically. Although it is possible that the business could be weak in its strategic technological, production, or financial positions (situations which usually produce declines in profits and ROI) but not its market share, such is not usually the case. Instead, most strategic turnarounds involve situations in which there has been a major decline in both sales and share position, and possibly even a change in the strategic group in which the business competes. Consequently, the principal method of differentiating among strategic turnarounds is according to the magnitude of the share reversal or strategic group change sought. Three options are possible: (1) a maintenance of the business's current share and/or strategic group position accompanied by a refocusing of the business on one or more easily defensible product-market segments or niches within the strategic group selected; (2) one-level shifts in share and strategic group position,[1] that is, movement from a dropout position to a follower position or from a follower position to a competitor position or from a competitor position to a leader position; or (3) two-level shifts in share and strategic group position, that is, from a dropout position to a competitor position or from a follower position to a leader position.

Usually, however, two-level shifts in share and strategic group position, or even one-level shifts that involve attempting to secure the leadership position, are not possible unless the business has unusual strategic resources that it has failed to exploit as well as access to discretionary strategic funds 50 to 100% more than it could normally generate on its own. (One such source is a corporate parent that is willing to fund heavy investments in areas of relative competitive advantage over moderately long periods of time, such as Phillip Morris was willing to do with Miller's.) The only other times when shifts of such magnitude are possible are (1) when the current leader slips, (2) when there is a major change in stage of product-market evolution, or (3) when the turnaround firm is the former leader who had recently fallen.

Normally, therefore, the choice of a strategic turnaround strategy is between a one-level shift in share and strategic group position (which might involve moving from fifth, sixth, or seventh position to a second, third, or fourth position in the industry), and a segmentation or niche strategy within the business' current strategic group. Again, unless the business has unusual resources or there is a shift in stage of product-market evolution, the segmentation/niche type strategy will normally be more profitable in terms of ROI, earnings per share, and other similar asset utilization measures of organizational

---

[1] Theoretically it would be possible, at least in some industries, to make a one-level shift in share position within the *same* strategic group. Practically, however, almost all efforts to achieve one- or two-level shifts in share position require a change in the strategic group in which the business competes.

performance. However, segmentation/niche strategies usually provide little or no opportunity for eventually seizing leadership in the industry involved and will usually produce lower total dollar sales and net income than a successful one-level share and strategic group shifting turnaround strategy—unless the segments selected for the new focus grow substantially. Most businesses, therefore, usually try strategic turnarounds that involve seeking higher dollar sales through one-level shifts in share and strategic group position, with a possible, even though remote, opportunity for seizing leadership should competitors slip or environmental challenges change.

Optimally, a strategic turnaround should attempt to combine the best features of both these approaches; that is, it should seek segmentation, but in such a way that overall sales and share would increase because of the strategic position or group change. Such an optimum strategic turnaround is usually not possible, however, unless there is a newly emerging segment to the market, and even then the turnaround business must be able to develop superior products for that segment, as well as upgrading its competences in the other functional areas important for serving that segment. Moreover, to be able to maintain any headstart it might get on its competitors, the firm involved needs to be able to differentiate itself from its key competitors in some relatively enduring way—a most difficult task if its competitors have superior resources.

The major conclusion that can be drawn from industry practice to date is that too much attention is given to strategic turnarounds that involve one-level increases in share and strategic group position, and not enough to strategic turnarounds that involve segmentation and niche hunting.

OPERATING TURNAROUNDS

There are four different types of operating turnaround strategies that are possible:

1. Revenue-increasing strategies
2. Cost-cutting strategies
3. Asset-reduction strategies
4. Combination strategies

While these turnaround strategies might seem to correspond in some ways to the three different types of strategic turnarounds noted above, attempts to make such a correspondence are really misleading since the correspondence is more one of results than of means, and as a consequence, usually exists only in the short term. A comparison of a typical strategic turnaround involving a one-level shift in the strategic group in which the firm competes with a typical revenue-increasing operating turnaround should help illustrate the differences. In the former instance, the business involved would normally develop a new line of products, alter the basic character of its production system, invest heavily in R&D, possibly even change its methods of distribution, and be slightly overstaffed in anticipation of future growth. In addition, that growth would start slowly since the efforts being undertaken are long-term ones. Later, however, the growth rate would take off for a period of several years before it slowed as the firm reached its new position.

In a typical revenue-generating operating turnaround, however, the firm would keep its existing line of products, although it might supplement these with products that it used to make but had discontinued—provided there was some indication this action would boost current sales. Also, the business might produce some products totally unrelated to its principal business if these required little start-up expense and helped utilize its facilities more fully in the short-term. In addition, both R&D and staffing would be at moderate or low levels relative to sales, while some major marketing efforts, such as price cutting, increased advertising, or increased direct sales calls, would be undertaken to stimulate current sales. One other difference would also exist. In a strategic turnaround designed to move a business to a larger strategic group, few activities would be undertaken that were not directly related to the business's long-term strategic thrust. At the same time, substantial attention would be given to *all* of the key success factors critical to the future health of the business. In a revenue-increasing operating turnaround, by contrast, almost total attention would be focused on short-term, revenue-generating actions with little or no attention to the other areas of the business. Moreover, several of the revenue-generating actions undertaken in such an operating turnaround might have no bearing on the long-term strategic health of the business. In short, strategic and operating turnarounds are really substantially different in character, even though there sometimes appears to be a similarity in the short-term results they produce.

Because of the primary focus on short-term operating actions, the first step in any operating turnaround should be to identify the resources and skills that the business will need to implement its long-term strategy so that these can be protected in the short-term action program that will follow. Once these resources have been identified, the type of operating turnaround strategy to be followed should be selected based primarily on the firm's current break-even position. . . .

If the firm is close to its current break-even point . . . but has high direct labor costs, high fixed expenses, or limited financial resources, then cost-cutting turnaround strategies are usually preferable because moderately large short-term decreases in fixed costs are usually possible and because cost-cutting actions take effect more quickly than revenue-generating actions. On the other hand, if the business is extremely far below its break-even point . . . then the only viable option is usually an asset-reduction turnaround strategy, especially if the business is close to bankruptcy. . . . If the firm's sales fall between the above ranges . . . then the most effective operating turnarounds usually involve revenue-generating or asset-reduction strategies, because in such circumstances there is usually no way to reduce costs sufficiently to reach a new break-even, and time and resources are typically not adequate to attempt a combination turnaround strategy. The choice between revenue-generating and asset-reduction strategies in such situations depends primarily on the longer-term potential of the business after turnaround, and the criticalness of the firm's current financial position. . . .

No matter what type of operating turnaround strategy is followed, though, the limited financial resources and time urgency associated with most operational turnaround situations require that particular attention be given to all actions that will have a major cash flow impact on the business in the short term. As a consequence, actions such as collecting receivables, cutting inventories, increasing prices when possible, focusing on high-margin products, stretching payables, decreasing wastage, and selling off surplus assets should almost always be pursued. . . .

SUMMARY AND CONCLUSIONS

Before closing, three other points deserve repeating. First, before starting any turnaround, an explicit calculation should be made to determine whether the turnaround effort will be worth it. Too often firms embark on turnaround efforts as a knee-jerk reaction to the myth that nothing can be worse than failure, that is, liquidation. Such is not the case, though, and in many instances, stockholders, employees, and other organizational stakeholders would be better served if management faced up to the true prospects and benefits of long-run survival and decided to liquidate the business for what it is worth now.

Second, before embarking on a strategic turnaround, an explicit investigation should be made of the conditions in the industry involved, and, in particular, of its competitive structure and stage of evolution. The reason for such analysis is quite simple. It is that industry structure is not uniformly flexible at all points in time. Thus, there are times when strategic changes abound within an industry. During such periods, shifts in relative competitive position occur moderately often. Consequently, during such times strategic turnarounds are relatively easy and inexpensive. At other times, however, it is almost impossible to make major shifts in competitive position with the resources available to most firms in the industry. During these periods, strategic turnarounds should not be attempted unless the organization has access to substantial outside resources or unless there are special circumstances, such as a competitor asleep at the switch, that provide unique opportunities in an otherwise barren situation.

Finally, it should be noted that the ideas presented in this article are based on limited research and study. It is, therefore, likely that some of them will be modified (or elaborated on) by future research.

C H A P T E R   1 5

THINKING STRATEGICALLY

What does it mean to think strategically? As we discussed in previous chapters, in the dominant, prescriptive approach, strategic thinking is related to one of three things. First came design, the idea that strategy formation is a conceptual process based on the skill of a powerful strategic manager. Then came planning—strategic thinking became design guided by formal techniques. The third and most contemporary of the prescriptive approaches, the positioning school, has implied that strategic thinking is a matter of rigorous analysis, using tools such as the five forces of competition or the value chain. In this chapter we examine other perspectives on strategic thinking that offer alternate perspectives to the ones cited above.

STRATEGIC THINKING IN AN ENACTED WORLD

The standard prescriptive view is that strategy, formulated by design, formal procedure, or analysis, describes an organization's adaptive response to the environment it faces. Smircich and Stubbart question this view in their article, "Strategic Management in an Enacted World."[1] They begin their criticism with the most fundamental part of the prescriptive concept—the very existence of organizational environments. There are three ways of thinking about organizational environments, they assert. The first is that environments are *objective* and unambiguously "real." The second is that environments are objectively real, but ambiguous; they become *perceived* phenomena, understood only in incomplete ways. The last way of thinking about environments is that they are *enacted* or socially constructed domains. This means that they are the result of how managers and other organizational members use language, ideas, and concepts while trying to understand and interpret the field of objects and events swirling around the firm.[2]

Each of these views has different implications for strategic thinking and action. Objective environments severely constrain strategic managers, who must simply deal with them as they are. Perceived environments lead to a focus on solving the problems of flawed understanding—if only managers could improve their understanding, in this

view, the organization would be better able to cope with the environment's difficulties. Enacted environments are more liberating to strategic thinking. Enactment encourages people to realize that relating to and understanding the environment can be a flexible and creative process. Strategic managers do not face "hard reality" so much as deal with a sphere of experience that can be understood and perhaps even shaped.

What *Is* an Organizational Environment?

The enactment perspective implies a different way of strategic thinking, which Smircich and Stubbart translate into three suggestions for strategists. The first is to *abandon the prescription that organizations should adapt to their environments.* This prescription is rooted in the "backward-looking" bias in much mainstream strategic theory. It is always easy in 20/20 hindsight to say that a firm should have done such-and-such to adapt itself better to its environment. But strategic managers live in the present and are concerned about what the future will bring. They need to know what they should do *now,* and the prescriptive view does not give them much guidance. One can only tell that a response was adaptive *after the fact.* If managers take any particular actions to adapt to existing conditions, those very actions will alter the conditions. For example, if every firm in an industry hastens to take advantage of a strategic opening, the opening disappears.

The events and situations facing a firm are always subject to multiple interpretations. When the incumbent firms and other actors in an industry (suppliers and buyers, for example) act differently, because they interpret the events and situations differently, the relationships among those events and situations will change. The industry will always be in a state of flux as the various firms take action. In Smircich and Stubbart's view, the "environment" is not making people act in certain ways; instead, through their actions, people *create* or *enact* what they think of as the environment. As a result, strategic managers have an opportunity to give the members of their organizations novel and interesting frameworks and interpretations with which to understand this "environment." These could in turn lead to novel and interesting strategic initiatives.

Rethink SWOT Analysis

Smircich and Stubbart's second suggestion is to *rethink constraints, threats, and opportunities* i.e. the familiar SWOT (Strength, Weakness, Opportunity, and Threat) analysis. There is evidence that the managers of firms in an industry will, over time and because of formal and informal discussions, create "industry wisdom."[3] The latter is the conventional thinking in an industry about what does and does not work, which products will or will not sell, and so on. Karl Weick has pointed out that industry wisdom can become a powerful shaper of strategic thinking in an industry, so powerful that its underlying assumptions are never tested. By not testing assumptions, industry members suffer from "collective ignorance"[4] of their own making. "What everyone knows" about an industry can become an opportunity for those who do not know. Smircich and Stubbart give the example of Philip Morris' introduction of a "diet beer," Miller Lite. After acquiring Miller Brewing, Philip Morris did not "know," unlike its experienced competitors in the brewing industry, that a diet beer could not sell. Philip Morris' testing of that assumption led to the most successful product innovation in the history of brewing and helped Miller Brewing rise from the doldrums to second place in the brewing industry.

These phenomena suggest a powerful prescription for strategic thinking—managers should look to themselves and their actions (and inactions) for the source of their troubles. As we saw in the Starbuck, Greve, and Hedberg reading, "Responding to Crisis," in the previous chapter, the source of an organization's crisis is often found in the thinking patterns of top managers and others in the organization. Smircich and Stubbart suggest that strategic managers should reflect on the ways in which their actions create and sustain their particular organizational results. Strategic managers should try to hold a *dual perspective*—transcending their current situation while simultaneously understanding their actions within their system of meaning, which should be kept open to reflection and reassessment. Doing this will allow strategic managers to challenge apparent limits and test new possibilities for organizational action.

A Different Role for Strategic Managers

Smircich and Stubbart's third suggestion is to *think differently about the role of the strategic manager.* They reject the designer-planner-organizer model of strategist so popular in the prescriptive approaches. The interpretive perspective sees the strategic manager's task as a combination of imagination, creativity, and art, very much like the craftsperson of Mintzberg's reading, "Crafting Strategy," in Chapter Five. People in organizations face a continuous stream of experiences every day. They need help in understanding that experience. Strategic managers can help by defining relevant and irrelevant categories of experience, by providing a vision to account for events and experiences, and by helping the members create a culture that nurtures splendid meanings. Many of Smircich and Stubbart's themes and suggestions are echoed by other scholars of strategy, as we will see below.

STRATEGIC THINKING: STRATEGIC INTENT AND CORE COMPETENCIES

In their article, "Strategic Intent," Hamel and Prahalad take a pragmatic look at the same territory covered by Smircich and Stubbart, but from a different perspective.[5] Hamel and Prahalad's objective was to understand how small Japanese firms like Honda, Komatsu, and Canon were able, during the 1960s, 1970s, and 1980s, to overcome their larger American and European rivals such as General Motors, Caterpillar, and Xerox. They found that Western and Eastern strategists followed very different models of strategic thinking. To use the words of Smircich and Stubbart, Hamel and Prahalad found that Western and Eastern firms had enacted different ways of forming strategy.

The Western Model of Strategic Thinking

The model used by American and European managers centered on the problem of sustaining a strategic match among the firm's many businesses or functions. In other words, they used the familiar prescriptive approaches we discussed earlier in this text. This model stressed that firms must restrain their ambitions to correspond to available resources, they must search for advantages that are inherently sustainable, and they must look for niches unserved by more powerful competitors.

This model handled risk by building a balanced portfolio of businesses, some of which generated cash, some of which consumed cash. We have also seen this, a form of corporate-level strategic portfolio management, earlier in this text in Chapter Twelve. The relatedness of the business units was typically defined in terms of common products, distribution channels, and customers. To support their portfolio approach, the Western firms observed by Hamel and Prahalad typically used Strategic Business Unit (SBU) organizational structures, that is, they allocated resources to product/market divisions. Each unit in the portfolio was assumed to own all the critical resources and skills it needed to succeed with its business-level strategy.

All firms must find a way to achieve consistency up and down the hierarchy from corporate level through business level to the functional level. These firms achieved consistency between the corporate and business levels by forcing conformity to financial objectives. The structure discussed by Hamel and Prahalad resembles the model Mintzberg presented in his reading, "The Diversified Organization," in Chapter Twelve. These firms achieved consistency between the business and functional levels by tightly restricting the *means* used to implement strategy. These include rules, procedures, and market definitions. In other words, at the business level the firms adopted Mintzberg's *machine organization* configuration. Lastly, supporting what Smircich and Stubbart pointed out, these firms also sought consistency by adhering to accepted industry practices.

The Eastern Model of Strategic Thinking

The basic emphasis of the Eastern model is not strategic fit. Instead, it is on finding an answer to the problem of how to leverage meager resources to attain seemingly unreachable goals. It stresses the need to speed up organizational learning so that the firm can build new advantages more quickly than competitors. Rather than seek niches, Eastern firms try to find new industry rules that could erode the advantages of their competitors. This is reminiscent of Smircich and Stubbart's suggestion that strategic managers should seek new interpretations.

Eastern-model firms, like Western-model firms, allocate resources to business units, but a critical difference is that they also allocate resources to core competencies that cut across all product/market business units.[6] Their managers try to track these investments across the entire corporation, so that the actions of individual business units do not undermine or prevent investment in future developments. Structures differ from those of Western firms. They handle consistency between the corporate and business levels by focusing on a particular strategic intent.

Hamel and Prahalad defined strategic intent as "an obsession with winning at all levels of the organization . . . sustained . . . over the 10- to 20-year quest for global leadership."[7] Consistency between the business and functional levels comes from the guidance given by intermediate-term challenges or objectives. An added feature of this process is that employees are encouraged to devise the means by which those objectives can be met. Both the corporate-level strategic intent and the business-level challenges are examples of what Mintzberg earlier called *umbrella strategy*—articulated guidelines that allow strategies to "deliberately emerge" within bounds.

Competitive Innovation

Hamel and Prahalad think that the preoccupation with planning and analysis in the mainstream prescriptive models leads strategic thinkers to ask the wrong questions. They point out that planners typically ask, "How will next year be different?" The implication is that, armed with that information, the strategist will know what to do. This is strongly reminiscent of Smircich and Stubbart's notion of *objective* or *perceived environment*—just find out what is going on, and the answer should become apparent.

Hamel and Prahalad assert that a better question is, "What must we do differently next year to get closer to our strategic intent?" This question is much more consistent with Smircich and Stubbart's advice that managers should examine what it is they *do,* not what is supposedly going on in the environment. The attitude embedded in the question could yield a novel way of thinking about the world, one that gives the firm more advantages. Hamel and Prahalad almost put it in Smircich and Stubbart's terms: "The essence of strategy lies in creating tomorrow's competitive advantages faster than competitors mimic the ones you possess today. . . . An organization's capacity to improve existing skills and learn new ones is the most defensible competitive advantage of all."[8] They call this *competitive innovation.*

CARRYING OUT COMPETITIVE INNOVATION. Hamel and Prahalad suggest four approaches to competitive innovation. First, firms should try to *create layers of advantage.* More sources of competitive advantage mean less risk in competitive battles. A typical pattern is to start with relatively nondefensible advantages such as low wage costs, followed by a move to more-defensible advantages such as higher quality and reliability, ending with very defensible strategies such as well-known global brands. The layers are sources not only of strength in competitive arenas but also for learning new competencies. Since management and innovation are *synthesis-oriented* activities, the more pieces there are to put together, the better.

Borrowing from the "castle" metaphor used by Starbuck and his colleagues in the previous chapter, Hamel and Prahalad suggest that firms innovate competitively by a *search for loose bricks.* Loose bricks are market niches left underdefended by large competitors. Managers should have "few orthodoxies" about how to break into these loose brick markets. If many different kinds of openings exist in various countries, for example, firms should try to exploit them in as many ways as necessary. In saying that managers should have few orthodoxies, Hamel and Prahalad are again clearly calling for challenging industry wisdom.

Hamel and Prahalad define their third approach—*changing the terms of engagement*—as "refusing to accept the front runner's definition of industry and segment boundaries."[9] This is directly related to the enactment view. An example is how Kodak and IBM once tried to compete with Xerox by copying the latter's business system—the same segmentation, products, distribution, service, and pricing. They failed. Canon competed by using a very different system—standardized parts to reduce costs, a different distribution system, and radically different service and marketing approaches. They succeeded. This experience causes Hamel and Prahalad to draw an interesting distinction between "barriers to entry" and "barriers to imitation." IBM and Kodak found the barriers to *imitation* high; Canon found the barriers to *entry* were sharply reduced once the rules of the game were altered.

The authors point out that "a successful competitor is likely to be wedded to a 'recipe' for success. That's why the most effective weapon new competitors possess is probably a clean sheet of paper. And why an incumbent's greatest vulnerability is its belief in accepted practice."[10] All of this evokes the idea, discussed above, about how strategic thinkers get stuck in particular patterns of thinking, and how they should take a fresh look at the ways that business should be done in the industry.

The fourth approach to competitive innovation is another mind-stretcher—*competing through collaboration.* Licensing, joint ventures, and other forms of collaboration all can be used to gain competitive advantages of one sort or another. For example, Hamel and Prahalad found a Japanese firm that formed joint ventures with many European competitors of its largest European rival, quickly multiplying its advantages in the resulting "battle by proxy." They observed that another way to use collaboration is to compete by "hijacking" development efforts: A firm competes with its rival in mature products but forms a joint venture with the rival, agreeing to manufacture more advanced products for the rival to market under its label. The firm hopes that the rival will (1) take the offer and (2) cut back its investment in the development of the advanced products. The authors reported that this scenario often happened; the result was short-term gain for the larger rival, followed by long-term inability to innovate. Lastly, a firm can use collaboration to measure the strengths and weaknesses of its rivals, which was a prime motivator for Toyota in its joint venture with General Motors, and for Mazda in its venture with Ford.

Strategy "Recipes"

Hamel and Prahalad argue that the many tools of formal strategic planning have hurt the firms that use them. The tools limit the number of options that firms will consider,

and, echoing Mintzberg's critique of planning in Chapter Ten, they yield predictable strategies that rivals easily decode. The authors say that "strategy 'recipes' limit opportunities for competitive innovation. . . . Too often strategy is seen as a positioning exercise in which options are tested by how they fit existing industry structure. . . . The strategist's goal is not to find a niche within the existing industry space but to create new space that is uniquely suited to the company's own strengths, space that is off the map."[11]

Strategic Thinking at the Corporate Level

In their "Strategic Intent" article and in their other article, "The Core Competence of the Corporation,"[12] to which we referred in Chapter Twelve, Hamel and Prahalad develop a distinctive perspective about corporate-level strategy, too. Decentralization, which usually accompanies the Strategic Business Unit (SBU) structure popular in the West, is seductive because it puts decision making in the hands of those closest to the information needed to make decisions and eases the burden on corporate headquarters. But there are problems.

The managers of independent SBUs may not make the wisest investment decisions from the *corporate* standpoint. They may "de-skill" the company by outsourcing components, giving it a short-term advantage at the cost of failing to develop deeply embedded skills. Treating upstream component-manufacturers within the corporation as cost centers may lead to disincentives to invest in them, resulting in the same de-skilling outcome, along with an "upskilling" for the outside suppliers, which they may translate into competitive advantages later.

Lastly, as we saw in Chapter Twelve, the divisionalized organization typically uses a performance control system based on some form of standardized financial output, such as return on investment. As we saw in the earlier chapter, this can lead to what Prahalad and Hamel call "denominator management"; that is, reducing the denominator (investment) of the return on investment ratio. Combining this with the tendency of diversified organizations to move middle managers around as a "management development" tool yields a management cadre that "looks to the numbers" and lacks knowledge about the nuances of the various businesses in which the corporation operates.

What is needed to overcome these problems, according to Prahalad and Hamel, is a more intense effort by top management to add value: "Economies of scope may be as important as economies of scale in entering global markets. But capturing economies of scope demands interbusiness coordination that only top management can provide."[13] Unfortunately, top managers in diversified organizations all too often abdicate their value-adding function, preferring to optimize cash flows and balance the portfolio, as we discussed in Chapter Twelve.

Strategic Thinking by Everyone

Hamel and Prahalad conclude their distinctive look at the strategy process with a discussion of who should be involved in it. They review the dominant view that strategy is formulated by top management and then implemented by those at lower levels of the corporation. They argue that this dichotomy thwarts competitiveness because it fosters an elitist view of strategy making. This elitist view demotivates and reduces the power of most members of the organization. It also makes it more difficult to produce creative strategies for two reasons. First, a small group of supposedly elite managers and planners is not large or diverse enough to challenge prevailing wisdom. It is more likely to be stuck in the industry's conventional mind-set. Second, creative strategies seldom emerge from the annual planning ritual, as we saw in Chapter Ten. Planning extrapolates the past into the future.

Hamel and Prahalad conclude by urging managers to be less cautious. The challenge for top managers is to revitalize the corporation by developing faith in its ability to deliver on difficult goals, by motivating its members to take on that challenge, and by focusing its attention long enough to let its members internalize new core competencies.

STRATEGIC THINKING AND THE LEARNING ORGANIZATION

In his book *The Fifth Discipline: The Art and Practice of the Learning Organization,*[14] Peter Senge discusses how to create "organizations where people continually expand their capacity to create the results they truly desire, where new and expansive patterns of thinking are nurtured, where collective aspiration is set free, and where people are continually learning how to learn together."[15] He calls these "learning organizations," and, since we have been discussing the need for firms to learn how to innovate more quickly than their rivals, his ideas are clearly related to strategic thinking.

Senge identifies five "learning disciplines" that undergird the learning organization. The first is **personal mastery**, "the discipline of continually clarifying and deepening our personal vision, of focusing our energies, of developing patience, and of seeing reality objectively."[16] Senge believes that individuals and organizations need each other to succeed at learning. Therefore, from the organizational and the individual standpoints, it is important for each member of an organization to develop himself or herself as fully as possible. The idea of personal mastery fits well with Prahalad and Hamel's notion that people who are "competency carriers" should be kept fresh, current, and excited.[17]

Senge's second discipline is **mental models**, "deeply ingrained assumptions, generalizations, or even pictures or images that influence how we understand the world and how we take action."[18] This discipline is a way for organizational members to do what Smircich and Stubbart suggested: to realize that they even *have* mental models and to become more reflective and knowledgeable about their ways of interpreting the world.

The third discipline is **building shared vision**, "the capacity to hold a shared picture of the future we seek to create."[19] The idea behind a shared vision is to foster genuine commitment and enrollment, not merely compliance. This discipline is closely related to Hamel and Prahalad's notion of "strategic intent," the creation of a compelling obsession that can drive achievement ("results we truly desire") in a firm for a long period.

Senge's fourth discipline is **team learning**. He points out that frequently we see groups in organizations whose individual members are very intelligent, but whose collective efforts seem unwise. Senge believes that the capacity of an organization to learn is constrained by the capacity of its teams to learn, because "teams, not individuals, are the fundamental learning unit in modern organizations."[20] Senge says that "the discipline of team learning starts with 'dialogue,' the capacity of the members of a team to suspend assumptions and enter into a genuine 'thinking together.' To the Greeks *dialogos* meant a free-flowing of meaning through a group, allowing the group to discover insights not attainable individually."[21] Obviously, engaging in dialogue in this sense is very close to the kind of interpretive freedom and suspension of assumptions advocated by Smircich and Stubbart.

The fifth discipline is **systems thinking**, the idea that organizations are wholistic patterns of interconnected parts. It is the fifth discipline, according to Senge, because it is the one "that integrates the disciplines, fusing them into a coherent body of theory and practice."[22] Senge describes systems thinking in great detail in his book, including an examination of what he calls "system archtypes," interconnected loops of factors that appear often in a variety of organizational and other systemic contexts. Space does not permit an in-depth examination of Senge's thinking about systems, but we will examine what he calls the "laws of the fifth discipline."

The Laws of the Fifth Discipline[23]

The first law of systems thinking is that *today's problems come from yesterday's "solutions."* Things that companies do often set off ripples in their systems that do not have consequences until much time has passed. By the time the consequences show up, no one makes the connection to the earlier action. A good example is the Western management practices that Hamel and Prahalad criticized. The portfolio and SBU approaches were the "solutions" of their time, but ultimately they led to de-skilling and weakened competitive ability. The second law is *the harder you push, the harder the system pushes back*. This is called "compensating feedback." A business example would be a firm that drops its price and spends more on advertising to boost the sales of a sagging product. This might boost sales temporarily, but the lower revenues might lead the firm to cut corners to compensate. Soon its quality starts to decline, and it loses even more customers. It may be better to take a deeper look at the system, making changes that have a more profound, but perhaps delayed, effect. In our example, the answer may be to improve product quality and patiently wait for its benefits.

Law three is that *behavior grows better before it grows worse.* This is the idea that compensating feedback has a built-in lag. In the example given above, the price-dropping and increased advertising *do* boost sales. The long-run problem of declining quality and fewer customers does not surface until much later. *The easy way out usually leads back in* is the fourth law. This is the idea that firms push harder and harder on the solutions with which they are already familiar, whether they work or not. Typically they do not work, and the problem persists.

The fifth law of systems thinking is that *the cure can be worse than the disease.* Often, organizations try a short-term solution that works, but then find that they need to try it again, only sooner. Before long, they are applying the "solution" almost always; they are addicted to it. The short-term improvement has led to a long-term dependency. This is so common in systems, Senge says, that it has its own technical term—"Shifting the burden to the intervenor." A common example in business is shifting the burden to consultants, instead of training managers to solve problems themselves. Hamel and Prahalad noticed another variation on this: Firms that outsourced components to become competitive in the short run found themselves unable to innovate in the long run, becoming even more dependent on their suppliers.

The sixth law of systems thinking is another counterintuitive one: *Faster is slower.* Senge points out that most systems, be they people or business organizations, have optimal growth rates. Attempts to speed up the rate of growth of a business may seem to work in the short run. But in the long run the organization may be unable to sustain the growth and may even have to shrink back down to its former size or smaller. In trying to go faster, the company has, when measured over a longer period, gone more slowly.

Most of us assume that when we see a problem, its cause occurred recently and nearby. We assume that cause and effect are close in time and space. Unfortunately, as the seventh law of systems thinking tells us, *cause and effect are not closely related in time and space.* Complex systems are so intricate, so interconnected, and have so many lags, that the "cause" of any given problem that is occurring may not have happened recently or anywhere near the problem. Hamel and Prahalad again provide an example: The decline of American business that we see in the 1990s began in the 1950s and 1960s, when firms stopped investing in their core competencies.

The difficulty of matching effect to cause may discourage some strategic systems thinkers. Serge rekindles hope by offering the eighth law: *Small changes can produce big results—but the areas of highest leverage are often the least obvious.* Because cause and effect are not in close spatial or temporal proximity, people who look at systems have a difficult time finding areas of leverage. Senge offers some interesting advice to make the task a bit easier: "There are no simple rules for finding high-leverage changes, but there are ways of thinking that make it more likely. Learning to see underlying 'structures' rather than 'events' is a starting point. . . . Thinking in terms of processes of change rather than 'snapshots' is another."[24] In the first suggestion, Senge is urging managers to think of whole systems, not just isolated events that they produce. In the second, he urges a dynamic, not static, view, urging managers to trace through the loops of the system. Senge expands on this in the ninth and tenth laws.

Because managers tend to think in terms of snapshots, they believe that many things are impossible. An example is the commonly accepted relationship between reduced cost and quality. Many believe that these two are incompatible, that quality automatically means higher cost, and that lower cost automatically means lower quality. But the ninth law of systems thinking says that *you can have your cake and eat it too—but not at once.* In other words, you can have high quality *and* low cost, but only over time, as the system matures. For example, total quality management (TQM) initiatives have tended to reduce costs, but only gradually. The up-front costs of implementing the system, switching to a different inventory method, training workers in TQM, and so forth are offset only bit-by-bit as the firm learns a better way of operating.

As Mintzberg mentioned in "Crafting Strategy" in Chapter Five, management theory has a bias toward analysis; that is, recommending to managers that they split large problems into smaller pieces. Unfortunately, the tenth law is that *dividing an elephant in half does not produce two small elephants.* Living systems, such as companies, have integrity. Their character depends on the whole. This is the logic of Prahalad and Hamel's recommendations to managers of diversified corporations. To add value, those managers must oversee the process of resource allocation to core competencies across the full panoply of the corporation's business units. Historical overreliance on the SBU structure had led to some business units failing to keep investment in core competencies high enough, because they felt no responsibility to the corporate whole.

There is no blame is the eleventh, and last, law of systems thinking. By this Senge means that it is foolish to assign blame to outside factors, something at which, unfortunately, many managers have become adept. He agrees with Smircich and Stubbart when he says, "Systems thinking shows us that there is no outside; that you and the cause of your problems are part of a single system."[25] This is also reminiscent of a main point made by Starbuck, Greve, and Hedberg—crises are rooted in the interaction between events in the environment and weaknesses in the firm. The "environment" and the "firm" are parts of the same system.

STRATEGIC THINKING: ACTION OR ANALYSIS?

Tom Peters makes many points in his reading in this chapter, "Strategy Follows Structure: Developing Distinctive Skills," that relate to the points made by Smircich and Stubbart, Hamel and Prahalad, and Senge. We touch on only the most important here.

Peters starts by saying that execution is strategy, by which he means that mundane execution is almost invariably the "secret" behind the success of excellent companies. Top performers have a package of distinctive skills that they execute flawlessly and repeatedly. Excellent performance is rooted in three organizational skills. The first is **providing high quality and service**. The success of U.S. firms during the early postwar period led them to take their eye off the ball of service and quality. Also, the mentality associated with low cost production channeled firms into situations where they lost their edge. **Continuous innovation** is the second basic skill. This is reminiscent of Hamel and

Prahalad's notion of competitive innovation. It is also consistent with the material on innovative organizations from Chapter Eleven.

Also reminiscent of innovative organizations is Peter's third skill—**all hands**. This means the active involvement and participation by all members of the firm. This evokes Hamel and Prahalad's notion that everyone must be involved, from the earliest possible stages, in carrying out strategic intent.

Also like Prahalad and Hamel, Peters suggests that the key to strategic thinking lies in *skills.* Top managers must become creators or shapers or keepers of skills. Peters spends some time criticizing planning processes, even at companies, such as General Electric, where planning ruled supreme. He concludes that passion can lead to failures, but firms have no choice. Experience shows that firms cannot plan their way to certain success.

THE MYTH OF THE WELL-EDUCATED MANAGER

The final reading in this text is "Myth of the Well-Educated Manager," by J. Sterling Livingston. You will no doubt find it provocative reading, because Livingston's basic argument is that management education reduces a person's chances of being an effective manager. At the very least, Livingston argues, scholastic achievement is no yardstick for potential success as a manager. Highly educated people fail partly because they do not learn what they need to do their jobs effectively. What do they need to learn, in Livingston's opinion?

Managers need to learn **problem solving**, something at which business schools excel. Unfortunately, this preoccupation with problem solving overdevelops analytical ability, while we have seen that management typically involves synthesis. Managers also need to learn **problem finding**, a much more important skill. This is because problems in practice never come pre-packaged and identified. Management education does a poor job, in Livingston's opinion, at teaching this skill. Even more important is the third skill, **opportunity finding**. Finding a problem and solving it only returns the organization to normalcy. Success is attained by exploiting opportunities that move the organization to a new level. This skill is often avoided in management education. Lastly, managers need to find their **natural management style**—learning to act in ways consistent with their unique personalities. Livingston concludes that experience is the key to the practitioner's skill, and this is something that management schools cannot provide.

Livingston then goes on to identify the characteristics needed in the potential manager. The first is **the need to manage**; only those who have a strong desire to influence the performance of others and who get genuine satisfaction from doing so can learn to manage effectively. The second is **the need for power**; psychologists have found that effective managers in complex organizations are high in the need for power. Lastly, good managers must have **the capacity for empathy**. This means being able to cope with the emotional reactions that inevitably occur when people work together in an organization. One cannot allow oneself to relate to people only on an intellectual or cognitive level. One cannot become "emotion-blind."

Livingston concludes that many people are not learning, either from education or from experience, what they need to be effective managers. This is partly because crucial management skills are not taught in management programs, partly because the people are not taught properly in their jobs, and partly because what *is* taught in management programs is misleading. Managerial aspirants must be taught to learn from their own firsthand experience. At the end of a formal education in management, this is advice well worth heeding.

CONCLUSIONS ABOUT STRATEGIC THINKING

What themes have emerged in this chapter about strategic thinking? We suggest the following:

1. Open up thinking. It seems that the prerequisite for good strategic thinking is to think more freely about what the organization is facing. Smircich and Stubbart point out that the very existence of an objective environment is something that managers should question. Senge suggests that managers should become more aware of the mental models that guide their actions. Hamel and Prahalad exhort managers to "have few orthodoxies" when looking for "loose bricks" in the strategies of competitors. They point out the distinction between barriers to imitation (which can be high) and barriers to entry (which can be low if management thinks of new ways to sidestep them). They even suggest the seemingly paradoxical "cooperate to compete."

Opening up thinking, according to Smircich and Stubbart, includes questioning industry wisdom. This is reflected in all of Hamel and Prahalad's suggestions noted above, along with their explicit warning about the folly of trying to follow industry recipes.

2. Realize where problems come from. All these authors, in their own way, assert that the problems faced by firms are the result of their own actions. Making competitive moves will provoke responses that may haunt a firm eventually. The same is true, perhaps more so, for *failing* to make competitive moves. We saw this in Peters' reading, where planning inhibits firms from maintaining their awareness of the importance of quality and service. We also saw it in Hamel and Prahalad's thesis that failure to invest in core skills leads to eventual competitive weakness. The idea that an organization is the source of its own problems was explicitly articulated in Senge's eleventh law—don't blame anybody because everybody is part of the same system.

3. Think long-term. Almost all of Senge's laws of systems thinking were based on the idea that systems always change over the long term. Anything done now *will* have long-term consequences. The problem is that when those consequences finally occur, no one remembers the actions that made those consequences happen. So when a firm takes an action now, it must think through what that action might yield at some future date. Remember, too, that actions taken to make things better in the long run will take a long time to have an effect. Strategic thinking requires patience, one of Senge's attributes of personal mastery.

4. Keep active and keep learning. All the authors reviewed in this chapter prefer acting and learning over planning and analyzing. Learning to innovate continuously and looking for opportunities to apply what has been learned and created are the best ways to sustain competitive advantage. This was clearly Hamel and Prahalad's message. In doing these things, firms must view themselves as whole system. Instead of being a patchwork of business units, firms should base themselves on core skills that cut across all business units and lead to core products that can be applied by several business units in their end products.

5. Manage culture and process. A good way to reconcile the seeming contradiction between the last two points is to use umbrella strategy, where only the broad outlines of the firm's long term strategic direction are spelled out. The innovative energies of the firm's members are then allowed to roam freely within those boundaries, with strategy emerging from all the action. This is similar in spirit to Hamel and Prahalad's notion of strategic intent, and Smircich and Stubbart's idea that top managers should shape culture, symbolism, and meaning. Hamel and Prahalad suggest something more akin to process strategy when they urge top management to add value to corporate strategy by actively orchestrating investment in core competencies across all business units.

6. Open up who does the thinking. Virtually everyone cited in this chapter has suggested that the days of elite strategy formulation are over. Thinking is much more effective when it is done by many minds, not just one. Peters called this "all hands." Hamel and Prahalad talked about the benefits of many minds and viewpoints, and the demotivation and disempowerment of elitist strategy formulation. Senge discussed the value of team learning, calling teams the basic learning unit of the modern organization. In an earlier chapter, Mintzberg discussed the benefits to innovation of having many people engaged in mutual adjustment, working on problems of innovation. Of all the themes in this chapter, perhaps this one is the most important. Organizations need to have their people think and learn to form good strategy, and thinking and learning are more powerful when they harness the energies of everyone in the organization. This is the essence of the strategy process.

NOTES TO CHAPTER FIFTEEN

1. This section draws heavily from Smircich, L., and C. Stubbart, "Strategic Management in an Enacted World." *Academy of Management Review* (1985), pp. 724–36.
2. For a full discussion of the enactment view of organizational environments, see Weick, K. E., *The Social Psychology of Organizing,* 2nd ed. Reading, Mass.: Addison-Wesley, 1979.
3. Huff, A. S., "Industry Influences on Strategy Reformulation." *Strategic Management Journal* 3 (1982): 119–31.
4. Weick, *The Social Psychology of Organizing.*
5. This section draws heavily from Hamel, G., and C. K. Prahalad, "Strategic Intent." *Harvard Business Review* 67 (May–June 1989): 63–76.
6. Prahalad, C. K., and G. Hamel, "The Core Competence of the Corporation." *Harvard Business Review* 68 (May–June 1990): 79–91.
7. Hamel and Prahalad, "Strategic Intent," p. 64.
8. Hamel and Prahalad, "Strategic Intent," p. 69.
9. Hamel and Prahalad, "Strategic Intent," p. 70.
10. Hamel and Prahalad, "Strategic Intent," p. 71.
11. Hamel and Prahalad, "Strategic Intent," p. 72–73.
12. Prahalad and Hamel, "The Core Competence of the Corporation."
13. Hamel and Prahalad, "Strategic Intent," p. 74.
14. Senge, P. M., *The Fifth Discipline: The Art and Practice of the Learning Organization.* New York: Doubleday/Currency, 1990.
15. Ibid., p. 3.
16. Senge, *The Fifth Discipline,* p. 7
17. Prahalad and Hamel, "The Core Competence of the Corporation."
18. Senge, *The Fifth Discipline,* p. 8.
19. Senge, *The Fifth Discipline,* p. 9.
20. Senge, *The Fifth Discipline,* p. 10.
21. Ibid.
22. Senge, *The Fifth Discipline,* p. 12.
23. This section is based on Chapter Four of Senge, *The Fifth Discipline.*
24. Senge, *The Fifth Discipline,* p. 65.
25. Senge, *The Fifth Discipline,* p. 67.

STRATEGY FOLLOWS STRUCTURE: DEVELOPING DISTINCTIVE SKILLS

By Thomas J. Peters

. . . strategy follows structure. Distinctive organizational performance, for good or ill, is almost entirely a function of deeply engrained repertoires. The organization, within its marketplace, *is* the way it *acts* from moment to moment—not the way it thinks it *might* act or *ought* to act. Larry Greiner recently noted,

> Strategy evolves from inside the organization—not from its future environment. . . . Strategy is a deeply engrained and continuing pattern of management behavior that gives direction to the organization—not a manipulable and controllable mechanism that can easily be changed from one year to the next. Strategy is a nonrational concept stemming from the informal values, traditions, and norms of behavior held by the firm's managers and employees—not rational, formal, logical, conscious and predetermined thought processes engaged in by top executives. Strategy emerges out of the cumulative effect of many informal actions and decisions taken daily over the years by many employees—not a "one shot" statement developed exclusively by top management for distribution to the organization. (1983:13)

Of course we understand, at one level, exactly what Greiner is saying; few would disagree with it. At the same time, however, we more often than not manage as if the principal variable at our command—in order to bring about an adjustment to a changing environment—is the "strategy lever."

EXECUTION IS STRATEGY

SAS (Scandinavian Air System) [in the early 1980s] completed a monumental "strategic turnaround." In a period of 18 months, amid the worst recession in 40 years, it went from a position of losing $10 million a year to making $70 million a year (on $2 billion in sales), and virtually the entire turnaround came at the direct expense of such superb performers as SwissAir and Lufthansa. The "strategy" (he calls it "vision") of SAS's Jan Carlzon was "to become the premiere business person's airline." Carlzon is the first to admit that it is a "garden variety" vision: "It's everyone's aspiration. The difference was, we executed." Carlzon describes SAS as having shifted focus from "an aircraft orientation" to a "customer orientation," adding that, "SAS *is* the personal contact of one person in the market and one person at SAS." He sees SAS as "50 million 'moments of truth' per year, during each of which we have an opportunity to be distinctive." That number is arrived at by calculating that SAS has 10 million customers per year, each one comes in contact with five SAS employees on average, which leads to a product of 50 million "opportunities."

Perdue Farms sells chickens. In the face of economists' predictions for over 50 consecutive years (according to Frank Perdue), Perdue Farms has built a three-quarter-billion-dollar business. Margins exceed that of its competitors by 700 or 800%. . . . Frank Perdue argues, and a careful analysis of his organization would lead one to argue, that his magic is simple: "If you believe there's absolutely no limit to quality [remember we're talking about roasters, not Ferraris] and you engage in every business dealing with total integrity, the rest [profit, growth, share] will follow automatically. . . ."

A colleague of mine once said, "Execution *is* strategy." The secret to success of the

Originally published in the *California Management Review* (Spring 1984). Copyright © 1984 by The Regents of the University of California. Reprinted with deletions by permission of the *Review.*

so-called excellent companies that Bob Waterman and I looked at, and the ones that I have looked at since, is almost invariably mundane execution. The examples—small and large, basic industry or growth industry—are too numerous to mention: Tupperware, Mary Kay, Stew Leonard's, Mrs. Field's Cookies, W. L. Gore, McDonald's, Mars, Perdue Farms, Frito-Lay, Hewlett-Packard, IBM, and on it goes.

My reason for belaboring this point is to suggest that, above all, the top performers—school, hospital, sports team, business—are a *package of distinctive skills.* In most cases, one particularly distinctive strength—innovation at 3M, J&J, or Hewlett-Packard; service at IBM, McDonald's, Frito-Lay, or Disney; quality at Perdue Farms, Procter & Gamble, Mars, or Maytag—and the distinctive skill—which in all cases is a product of some variation of "50 million moments of truth a year"—are a virtual unassailable barrier to competitor entry or serious encroachment. David Ogilvy quotes Mies van der Rohe as saying of architecture, "God is in the details" (1983:101). Jan Carlzon of SAS puts it this way, "We do not wish to do one thing a thousand percent better, we wish to do a thousand things one percent better." Francis G. (Buck) Rodgers, IBM's corporate marketing vice-president, made a parallel remark, "Above all we want a reputation for doing the little things well." And a long-term observer of Procter & Gamble noted, "They are so thorough, it's boring." The very fact that excellence has a "thousand thousand little things" as its source makes the word "unassailable" (as in "an unassailable barrier to entry") plausible. No trick, no device, no sleight of hand, no capital expenditure will close the gap for the also rans.

DISTINCTIVE COMPETENCE: THE FORGOTTEN TRAIL

The focus on execution, on distinctive competence is indeed not new. Philip Selznick, as far as I can determine, talked about it first:

> The term "organization" suggests a certain bareness, a lean, no-nonsense system of consciously coordinated activities. It refers to an *expendable tool,* a rational instrument engineered to do a job. An "institution," on the other hand, is more nearly a natural product of social needs and pressures—a responsive adaptive organism. The terms institution, organizational character, and distinctive competence all refer to the same basic process—the transformation of an engineered, technical arrangement of building blocks into a purposive social organization. (1957:5)

Early thinking about strategy, which was the focus of my MBA schooling a dozen years ago at Stanford, was driven by the industry standard: Edmund P. Learned and others's (1965) textbook, *Business Policy.* The focus of strategy making at that point was clearly on analyzing and building distinctive competences.

In the years since Selznick and Learned and others, the focus on distinctive competence has been downgraded. Analysis of strategic position within a competitive system has all but butted out concern with the boring details of execution (which sum up to that elusive competence). Presumably the "people types" (the OB faculty) take care of such mundane stuff. The experience curve, portfolio manipulation, competitive cost position analysis, and the like have reigned supreme for the last decade or so.

I have no problem with the usefulness of any of these tools. Each is vital, and a few of them, indeed, were used very thoughtfully or regularly just a dozen years ago. However, we seem to have moved (rushed?) from a position of "implementation without thought" (analyzing structures on the basis of span of control, rather than on the basis of external forces) to "thought without implementation." We have reached a wretched position in which Stanford, annually voted by the business school deans as America's leading business school (and thus the world's), has only *three* of 91 elective

MBA courses focusing on the making (manufacturing policy) or selling (sales management) functions of business.[1] This distortion of priorities was poignantly brought home to me late last school year. A local reporter attended my last class (an elective based on *In Search of Excellence*) and asked my students if the course had been useful. One student, quoted in the subsequent article, tried to say the very most complimentary thing he could: "It's great. Tom teaches all that soft, intangible stuff—innovation, quality, customer service—that's not found in the hard P&L or balance statements." Soft? Hard? Has that youngster got it straight or backwards—is there a problem here? . . .

As best I can determine, there are only *three* truly distinctive "skill packages" . . .

TOTAL CUSTOMER SATISFACTION. . . . As Ted Levitt begins in his . . . very readable book, *The Marketing Imagination,* "There is no such thing as a commodity" (1983:72). The often slavish devotion to the experience curve effect is not responsible for our forgetting all of this counter evidence, to be sure. Making more (selling at a lower price to gain share) in order to achieve a barrier to entry via lowest subsequent industry cost is certainly not a bad idea. It's a great one. But the difficulty seems to be the unintended resultant *mind-set.* As one chief executive officer noted to me, "We act as if cost—and thus price—is the only variable available these days. In our hell bent rush to get cost down, we have given all too short shrift to quality and service. So we wake up, at best, with a great share and a lousy product. It's almost always a precarious position that can't be sustained." Also, I suspect, the relative ease of gaining dominant market position—first in the United States, and then overseas—by most American corporations in the 1950s through the 1970s (pre-OPEC, pre-Japan) led institutions to take their eye off the service and quality ball. The focus was simply on making a lot of it for ever-hungry markets. Moreover, this led to the executive suite dominance by financially trained executive-administrators, and the absence of people who were closer to the product (and thus the importance of quality and service)—namely, salespersons, designers, and manufacturers. . . .

CONTINUOUS INNOVATION. The second basic skill trait is the ability to constantly innovate. Virtually all innovations—from miracle drugs, to computers, to airplanes, to bag size changes at Frito-Lay, to menu item additions at McDonald's—come from the wrong person, in the wrong division, of the wrong company, in the wrong industry, for the wrong reason, at the wrong time, with the wrong set of end-users. The assumption behind most planning systems, particularly the highly articulated strategic planning systems of the seventies, was that we could plan our way to new market successes. The reality differs greatly. Even at the mecca of planning systems, General Electric, the batting average of strategic planning was woefully low. In the 1970s (when planners were regularly observed walking on water at Fairfield), GE's major innovative, internally generated business successes—for example, aircraft engines, the credit business, plastics, and the information services company—came solely as a product of committed, somewhat irrational (assumed, inside, to be crazy) champions. When Jack Welch became GE's chairman in 1980—ending a 30-year reign by accountants—he moved to enhance entrepreneurship. One of his first steps was to reduce the corporate planning staff by more than 80 percent. The most truly innovative companies—Hewlett-Packard, the Raychem Corporation, 3M, Johnson & Johnson, PepsiCo, and the like—clearly depend upon a thoroughly innovative climate. Radical decentralization marks Johnson & Johnson. Both J&J and IBM (via its new Independent Business Unit structure) gives the innovating unit a Board of Directors with an explicit charter to "ignore the strictures of formal planning systems and to keep the bureaucrats out of the hair of the inventors." 3M is simply a collection of skunkworks. . . .

---

[1] "Course Descriptions for Electives Taught in the 1983–84 Academic Year," Stanford University Graduate School of Business. [Peters later adds that 34 courses focus on accounting, finance, and decision analysis.]

... A most unlikely vital company is U.S. Shoe, yet the entrepreneurial vigor of this billion-and-a-half-dollar company is extraordinary. A recent *Fortune* article attributed its success to "superior market segmentation." The next issue of *Fortune* carried a letter to the editor from the son of the founder which rebutted that argument: "My father's real contribution was not superior market segmentation. Rather, he created a beautiful corporate culture which encouraged risk taking. . . ."

ALL HANDS. The third and final regularly found skill variable is the sine qua non that goes hand in glove with the first two. Superior customer service, quality, and courtesy (total customer satisfaction) is not a product of the executive suite—it's an all hands effort. Constant innovation from multiple centers is similarly not the domain of a handful of brilliant thinkers at the top. Thus, virtually all of these institutions put at the head of their corporate philosophies a bone-deep belief in the dignity and worth and creative potential of *all* their people. Said one successful Silicon Valley chief executive officer recently, "I'll tell you who my number one marketing person is. It's that man or woman on the loading dock who decides *not* to *drop* the box into the back of the truck." Said another, "Doesn't it follow that if you wish your people to treat your customers with courtesy that you must treat your people with courtesy?" Many sign up for these three virtues, but only the truly distinguished companies seem to practice them regularly.

COMMON THREAD: THE ADAPTIVE ORGANISM

These three skills—and these three alone—are virtually the *only* effective sources of sustainable, long-term competitive advantage. Notice that each suggests the essence of an adaptive organism. The organization that provides high perceived value—service, quality, courtesy—invariably does so by constantly listening and adapting to its customers' needs. The innovative company is similarly radically focused on the outside world. And the expectation that all people will contribute creatively to their jobs—receptionist and product designer alike—means similarly that each person is a source of external probing and a basis for constant renewal, fulfillment, and adaptation. These organizations, then, are alive and are excited—in both the "attuned" and the "enthusiastic" sense of that word. Moreover, such organizations are in the process of constant redefinition. The shared values surrounding these skills—customer listening and serving, constant innovation, and expecting all people to contribute—are rigid. But, paradoxically, the rigid values/skills are in service of constant externally focused adaptation and growth.

The excellent companies—chicken makers to computer makers—use their skills as the basis for continually reinventing adaptive strategies—usually on a decentralized basis—to permit them to compete effectively in both mature and volatile youthful markets. Skills, in a word, *drive* strategy in the best companies.

SKILLS VERSUS STRATEGY

I tend to see the word strategy, in the sense that it's currently taught in the business schools (or practiced by the leading consultants), as *not* having much meaning at the corporate or sector level at all, but as being the appropriate domain of the strategic business unit or other form of decentralized unit (the IBU at IBM, the division of Hewlett-Packard or J&J, the merchant organization at Macy's). To return to our 7-S model, this is the classic case for what we have constantly called "soft is hard." The driving variable in the model, which creates the preconditions for *effective* strategizing, is, above all, skills. Strategy is the dependent variable, operable at a lower level in the business.

We view the constantly innovating, constantly customer-serving organization as one that continually *discovers* new markets and new opportunities. The notion of the learning organization, the adapting organization, the discovering organization, reigns supreme. . . . By contrast, we watch the traditional "strategists" fall into the abyss time and again. Because a market looks good on paper, they believe the company should take it on. Yet they invariably underestimate the executional effort (skill base) required to do extremely well at *anything*.

PROACTIVE LEADERSHIP

If there is some sense to all the above, what then is the leader's role? If not master strategist, then what? He or she becomes, above all, a creator or shaper or keeper of skills. . . .

Above all the leader's role becomes proactive rather than reactive. . . . The important people are those that view their prime role as protecting the champions from the silliness of inertial bureaucracies. . . . Sam Walton, founder of the remarkably successful WalMart Corporation, says, "The best ideas have always come and will always come from the clerks. The point is to seek them out, to listen, and to act. . . .

ENTHUSIASTS, PASSION, AND FAITH

Let's really stray afield from the world of traditional definitions of strategy formulation. Ray Kroc says, "You gotta be able to see the beauty in a hamburger bun." Recall that Debbie Fields of Mrs. Field's Cookies says, "I am not a business woman, I am a cookie person." Sam Walton loves retailing. From Steve Jobs to Famous Amos, the creators of effective organizations are unabashed *enthusiasts*. Bill Hewlett and Dave Packard had a passion for their machines. Herman Lay had a passion for his potatoes. Forrest Mars loved factories. Marvin Bower of McKinsey loved his clients. John Madden loved linebackers. The love was transmitted and transmuted into excitement, passion, enthusiasm, energy. These virtues infected an entire organization. They created the adaptive organization—the organization aimed externally, yet depending upon the full utilization of each of its people. This seemingly simple-minded definition of effective strategy for the ages even holds in mature organizations. The fervor with which Procter & Gamble revered quality has now been passed down through many generations. The "salesman's bias" of an IBM and 3M has similarly been maintained several generations beyond the founder. The passionate belief that the dominant skill reigns supreme is at the heart of business success. . . .

So where does all this leave us? The world of experience curves, portfolios, and 4-24 box matrices has led us badly astray. George Gilder notes in *Wealth and Poverty,*

> Economists who attempt to banish chance through methods of rational management also banish the only source of human triumph. The inventor who never acts until statistics affirm his choice, the businessman who waits until the market is proven—all are doomed to mediocrity by their trust in a spurious rationality. (1981:264)

The devilish problem is that there is nothing wrong with any of these strategy tools. In fact, each one is helpful! I think of the same thing in the area of quality: quality circles, automation, and statistical quality control are extraordinarily powerful tools—

but *if and only if* a bone-deep belief in quality comes first. Given the 145-year tradition at Procter & Gamble, the tools are then helpful. Absent the faith, passion, belief, value, and skill, the tools become just one more manifestation of bureaucracy—another attempt to patch a fundamental flaw with a bureaucratic band-aid. . . .

But we should never forget for a moment that the analytic models are not neutral. Any analyst worth his salt, with anything from a decision tree to a portfolio analysis, can shoot down any idea. Analysts are well-trained naysayers, professional naysayers. Yet it turns out that only passion, faith, and enthusiasm win. Passion can also lead to losses—many of them, of that there is no doubt. Yet there is no alternative. We simply can't plan our way to certain success. John Naisbitt, *Megatrends* author, asserts: "Strategic planning turned out to be an orderly, rational way to efficiently ride over the edge of the cliff." I think he's not far off. Above all, the winning companies that we've observed—small and large, regulated or unregulated, mature or new—are ruled by somewhat channeled passion in pursuit of distinctive skill building and maintenance.

MYTH OF THE WELL-EDUCATED MANAGER

READING

By J. Sterling Livingston

How effectively a manager will perform on the job cannot be predicted by the number of degrees he holds, the grades he receives in school, or the formal management education programs he attends. Academic achievement is not a valid yardstick to use in measuring managerial potential. Indeed, if academic achievement is equated with success in business, the well-educated manager is a myth.

Managers are not taught in formal education programs what they most need to know to build successful careers in management. Unless they acquire through their own experience the knowledge and skills that are vital to their effectiveness, they are not likely to advance far up the organizational ladder.

Although an implicit objective of all formal management education is to assist managers to learn from their own experience, much management education is, in fact, miseducation because it arrests or distorts the ability of managerial aspirants to grow as they gain experience. Fast learners in the classroom often, therefore, become slow learners in their executive suite.

Men who hold advanced degrees in management are among the most sought after of all university graduates. Measured in terms of starting salaries, they are among the elite. Perhaps no further proof of the value of management education is needed. Being highly educated pays in business, at least initially. But how much formal education contributes to a manager's effectiveness and to his subsequent career progress is another matter.

Professor Lewis B. Ward (1970) of the Harvard Business School has found that the median salaries of graduates of that institution's MBA program plateau approximately 15 years after they enter business and, on the average, do not increase significantly thereafter. While the incomes of a few MBA degree holders continue to rise dramatically, the career growth of most of them levels off just at the time men who are destined for top management typically show their greatest rate of advancement.

Equally revealing is the finding that men who attend Harvard's Advanced Management Program (AMP) after having had approximately 15 years of business experience, but who—for the most part—have had no formal education in management, earn almost a third more, on the average, than men who hold MBA degrees from Harvard and other leading business schools.

Originally published in the *Harvard Business Review* (January–February 1971). Copyright © by the President and Fellows of Harvard College; all rights reserved. Reprinted with deletions by permission of the *Harvard Business Review*.

Thus the arrested career progress of MBA degree holders strongly suggests that men who get to the top in management have developed skills that are not taught in formal management education programs and may be difficult for many highly educated men to learn on the job. . . .

UNRELIABLE YARDSTICKS

Lack of correlation between scholastic standing and success in business may be surprising to those who place a premium on academic achievement. But grades in neither undergraduate nor graduate school predict how well an individual will perform in management.

After studying the career records of nearly 1,000 graduates of the Harvard Business School, for example, Professor Gordon L. Marshall concluded that "academic success and business achievement have relatively little association with each other" (Marshall, 1964). In reaching this conclusion, he sought without success to find a correlation between grades and such measures of achievement as title, salary, and a person's own satisfaction with his career progress. (Only in the case of grades in elective courses was a significant correlation found.)

Clearly, what a student learns about management in graduate school, as measured by the grades he receives, does not equip him to build a successful career in business.

Scholastic standing in undergraduate school is an equally unreliable guide to an individual's management potential. Professor Eugene E. Jennings of the University of Michigan has conducted research which shows that "the routes to the top are apt to hold just as many or more men who graduated below the highest one third of their college class than above (on a per capita basis)" (1967:21).

A great many executives who mistakenly believe that grades are a valid measure of leadership potential have expressed concern over the fact that fewer and fewer of those "top-third" graduates from the better-known colleges and universities are embarking on careers in business. What these executives do not recognize, however, is that academic ability does not assure that an individual will be able to learn what he needs to know to build a career in fields that involve leading, changing, developing, or working with people.

Overreliance on scholastic learning ability undoubtedly has caused leading universities and business organizations to reject a high percentage of those who have had the greatest potential for creativity and growth in nonacademic careers.

This probability is underscored by an informal study conducted in 1958 by W. B. Bender, Dean of Admissions at Harvard College. He first selected the names of 50 graduates of the Harvard class of 1928 who had been nominated for signal honors because of their outstanding accomplishments in their chosen careers. Then he examined the credentials they presented to Harvard College at the time of their admission. He found that if the admission standards used in 1958 had been in effect in 1928, two thirds of these men would have been turned down. (The proportion who would have been turned down under today's standards would have been even higher.)

In questioning the wisdom of the increased emphasis placed on scholastic standing and intelligence test scores, Dean Bender asked, "Do we really know what we are doing?"[1]

---

[1] Quoted in Anthony G. Athos and Lewis B. Ward, "Corporations and College Recruiting: A Study of Perceptions" (unpublished study prepared for the Division of Research, Harvard Business School), p. 14.

There seems to be little room for doubt that business schools and business organizations which rely on scholastic standing, intelligence test scores, and grades as measures of managerial potential are using unreliable yardsticks.

Career Consequences

. . . ARRESTED PROGRESS AND TURNOVER. Belief in the myth of the well-educated manager has caused many employers to have unrealistic performance expectations of university graduates and has led many employees with outstanding scholastic records to overestimate the value of their formal education. As a consequence, men who hold degrees in business administration—especially those with advanced degrees in management—have found it surprisingly difficult to make the transition from academic to business life. An increasing number of them have failed to perform up to expectations and have not progressed at the rate they expected.

The end result is that turnover among them has been increasing for two decades as more and more of them have been changing employers in search of a job they hope they "can make a career of." And it is revealing that turnover rates among men with advanced degrees from the leading schools of management appear to be among the highest in industry.

As Professor Edgar H. Schein of the Massachusetts Institute of Technology's Sloan School of Management reports, the attrition "rate among highly educated men and women runs higher, on the average, than among blue-collar workers hired out of the hard-core unemployed. The rate may be highest among people coming out of the better-known schools" (1969:95). Thus over half the graduates of MIT's master's program in management change jobs in the first three years, Schein further reports, and "by the fifth year, 73% have moved on at least once and some are on their third and fourth jobs" (p. 90).

Personnel records of a sample of large companies I have studied similarly revealed that turnover among men holding master's degrees in management from well-known schools was over 50% in the first five years of employment, a rate of attrition that was among the highest of any group of employees in the companies surveyed.

The much publicized notion that the young "mobile managers" who move from company to company are an exceptionally able breed of new executives and that "job-hopping has become a badge of competence" is highly misleading. While a small percentage of those who change employers are competent managers, most of the men who leave their jobs have mediocre to poor records of performance. They leave not so much because the grass is greener on the other side of the fence, but because it definitely is brown on their side. My research indicates that most of them quit either because their career progress has not met their expectations or because their opportunities for promotion are not promising.

In studying the career progress of young management-level employees of an operating company of the American Telephone & Telegraph Company, Professors David E. Berlew and Douglas T. Hall of MIT found that "men who consistently fail to meet company expectations are more likely to leave the organization than are those who turn in stronger performances" (1964:36).

I have reached a similar conclusion after studying attrition among recent management graduates employed in several large industrial companies. Disappointing performance appraisals by superiors is the main reason why young men change employers.

"One myth," explains Schein, "is that the graduate leaves his first company merely for a higher salary. But the MIT data indicate that those who have moved on do not earn more than those who have stayed put" (p. 90). Surveys of reunion classes at the Harvard Business School similarly indicate that men who stay with their first employer generally earn more than those who change jobs. Job-hopping is not an easy road to high income; rather, it usually is a sign of arrested career progress, often because of mediocre or poor performance on the job.

WHAT MANAGERS MUST LEARN

One reason why highly educated men fail to build successful careers in management is that they do not learn from their formal education what they need to know to perform their jobs effectively. In fact, the tasks that are the most important in getting results usually are left to be learned on the job, where few managers ever master them simply because no one teaches them how.

Formal management education programs typically emphasize the development of problem-solving and decision-making skills, for instance, but give little attention to the development of skills required to find the problems that need to be solved, to plan for the attainment of desired results, or to carry out operating plans once they are made. Success in real life depends on how well a person is able to find and exploit the opportunities that are available to him, and, at the same time, discover and deal with potential serious problems before they become critical.

Problem Solving

Preoccupation with problem solving and decision making in formal management education programs tend to distort managerial growth because it overdevelops an individual's analytical ability, but leaves his ability to take action and to get things done underdeveloped. The behavior required to solve problems that already have been discovered and to make decisions based on facts gathered by someone else is quite different from that required to perform other functions of management.

On the one hand, problem solving and decision making in the classroom require what psychologists call "respondent behavior." It is this type of behavior that enables a person to get high grades on examinations, even though he may never use in later life what he has learned in school.

On the other hand, success and fulfillment in work demand a different kind of behavior which psychologists have labeled "operant behavior." Finding problems and opportunities, initiating action, and following through to attain desired results require the exercise of operant behavior, which is neither measured by examinations nor developed by discussing in the classroom what someone else should do. Operant behavior can be developed only by doing what needs to be done.

Instruction in problem solving and decision making all too often leads to "analysis paralysis" because managerial aspirants are required only to explain and defend their reasoning, not to carry out their decisions or even to plan realistically for their implementations. Problem solving in the classroom often is dealt with, moreover, as an entirely rational process, which, of course, it hardly ever is.

As Professor Harry Levinson of the Harvard Business School points out: "The greatest difficulty people have in solving problems is the fact that emotion makes it hard for them to see and deal with their problems objectively" (1070:109–110).

Rarely do managers learn in formal education programs how to maintain an appropriate psychological distance from their problems so that their judgments are not clouded by their emotions. Management graduates, as a consequence, suffer their worst trauma in business when they discover that rational solutions to problems are not enough; they must also somehow cope with human emotions in order to get results.

Problem Finding

The shortcomings of instruction in problem solving, while important, are not as significant as the failure to teach problem finding. As the research of Norman H. Mackworth of the Institute of Personality Assessment and Research, University of California, has revealed "the distinction between the problem-solver and the problem-finder is vital" (1969:242).

Problem finding, Mackworth points out, is more important than problem solving and involves cognitive processes that are very different from problem solving and much more complex. The most gifted problem finders, he has discovered, rarely have outstanding scholastic records, and those who do excel academically rarely are the most effective problem finders. . . .

. . . the [skill managers] need cannot be developed merely by analyzing problems discovered by someone else; rather, it must be acquired by observing firsthand what is taking place in business. While the analytical skills needed for problem solving are important, more crucial to managerial success are the perceptual skills needed to identify problems long before evidence of them can be found by even the most advanced management information system. Since these perceptual skills are extremely difficult to develop in the classroom, they are now largely left to be developed on the job.

Opportunity Finding

A manager's problem-finding ability is exceeded in importance only by his opportunity-finding ability. Results in business, Peter F. Drucker reminds us, are obtained by exploiting opportunities, not by solving problems. Here is how he puts it:

> All one can hope to get by solving a problem is to restore normality. All one can hope, at best, is to eliminate a restriction on the capacity of the business to obtain results. The results themselves must come from the exploitation of opportunities. . . . "Maximization of opportunities" is a meaningful, indeed a precise, definition of the entrepreneurial job. It implies that effectiveness rather than efficiency is essential in business. The pertinent question is not how to do things right, but how to find the right things to do, and to concentrate resources and efforts on them. (1964:5).

Managers who lack the skill needed to find those opportunities that will yield the greatest results, not uncommonly spend their time doing the wrong things. But opportunity-finding skill, like problem-finding skill, must be acquired through direct personal experience on the job.

This is not to say that the techniques of opportunity finding and problem finding cannot be taught in formal management education programs, even though they rarely are. But the behavior required to use these techniques successfully can be developed only through actual practice.

A manager cannot learn how to find opportunities or problems without doing it. The doing is essential to the learning. Lectures, case discussions, or text books alone are of limited value in developing ability to find opportunities and problems. Guided practice in finding them in real business situations is the only method that will make a manager skillful in identifying the right things to do.

Natural Management Style

Opportunities are not exploited and problems are not solved, however, until someone takes action and gets the desired results. Managers who are unable to produce effective results on the job invariably fail to build successful careers. But they cannot learn what they most need to know either by studying modern management theories or by discussing in the classroom what someone else should do to get results.

Management is a highly individualized art. What style works well for one manager in a particular situation may not produce the desired results for another manager in a similar situation, or even for the same manager in a different situation. There is no one best way for all managers to manage in all situations. Every manager must discover for himself, therefore, what works and what does not work for him in different situations. He cannot become effective merely by adopting the practices or the managerial style of someone else. He must develop his own natural style and follow practices that are consistent with his own personality.

What all managers need to learn is that to be successful they must manage in a way that is consistent with their unique personalities. When a manager "behaves in ways which do not fit his personality," as Rensis Likert's managerial research has shown, "his behavior is apt to communicate to his subordinates something quite different from what he intends. Subordinates usually view such behavior with suspicion and distrust" (1969:90).

Managers who adopt artificial styles or follow practices that are not consistent with their own personalities are likely not only to be distrusted, but also to be ineffective. It is the men who display the "greatest individuality in managerial behavior," as Edwin E. Ghiselli's studies of managerial talent show, who in general are the ones "judged to be best managers" (1969:236).

Managers rarely are taught how to manage in ways that are consistent with their own personalities. In many formal education and training programs, they are in fact taught that they must follow a prescribed set of practices and adopt either a "consultative" or "participative" style in order to get the "highest productivity, lowest costs, and best performance" (Likert, 1969:11).

The effectiveness of managers whose personalities do not fit these styles often is impaired and their development arrested. Those who adopt artificial styles typically are seen as counterfeit managers who lack individuality and natural styles of their own.

Managers who are taught by the case method of instruction learn that there is no one best way to manage and no one managerial style that is infallible. But unlike students of medicine, students of management rarely are exposed to "real" people or to "live" cases in programs conducted either in universities or in industry.

They study written case histories that describe problems or opportunities discovered by someone else, which they discuss, but do nothing about. What they learn about supervising other people is largely secondhand. Their knowledge is derived from the discussion of what someone else should do about the human problems of "paper people" whose emotional reactions, motives, and behavior have been described for them by scholars who may have observed and advised managers, but who usually have never taken responsibility for getting results in a business organization.

Since taking action and accepting responsibility for the consequences are not a part of their formal training, they neither discover for themselves what does—and what does not—work in practice nor develop a natural managerial style that is consistent with their own unique personalities. Managers cannot discover what practices are effective for them until they are in a position to decide for themselves what needs to be done in a specific situation, and to take responsibility both for getting it done and for the consequences of their actions.

Elton Mayo, whose thinking has had a profound impact on what managers are taught but not on how they are taught, observed a quarter of a century ago that studies in the social sciences do not develop any "skill that is directly useful in human situations" (1945:19). He added that he did not believe a useful skill could be developed until a person takes "responsibility for what happens in particular human situations—individual or group. A good bridge player does not merely conduct post mortem discussions of the play in a hand of contract; he takes responsibility for playing it" (p. 32).

Experience is the key to the practitioner's skill. And until a manager learns from his own firsthand experience on the job how to take action and how to gain the willing cooperation of others in achieving desired results, he is not likely to advance very far up the managerial ladder.

NEEDED CHARACTERISTICS

Although there are no born natural leaders, relatively few men ever develop into effective managers or executives. Most, in fact, fail to learn even from their own experience what they need to know to manage other people successfully. What, then, are the characteristics of men who learn to manage effectively?

The answer to the question consists of three ingredients: (1) the need to manage, (2) the need for power, and (3) the capacity for empathy. In this section of the article, I shall discuss each of these characteristics in some detail.

The Need to Manage

This first part of the answer to the question is deceptively simple: only those men who have a strong desire to influence the performance of others and who get genuine satisfaction from doing so can learn to manage effectively. No man is likely to learn how unless he really wants to take responsibility for the productivity of others, and enjoys developing and stimulating them to achieve better results.

Many men who aspire to high-level managerial positions are not motivated to manage. They are motivated to earn high salaries and to attain high status, but they are not motivated to get effective results through others. They expect to gain great satisfaction from the income and prestige associated with executive positions in important enterprises, but they do not expect to gain much satisfaction from the achievements of their subordinates. Although their aspirations are high, their motivation to supervise other people is low.

A major reason why highly educated and ambitious men do not learn how to develop successful managerial careers is that they lack the "will to manage." The "*way* to manage," as Marvin Bower has observed, usually can be found if there is the "*will* to manage." But if a person lacks the desire, he "will not devote the time, energy, and thought required to find the way to manage" (1966:6).

No one is likely to sustain for long the effort required to get high productivity from others unless he has a strong psychological need to influence their performance. The need to manage is a crucial factor, therefore, in determining whether a person will learn and apply in practice what is necessary to get effective results on the job.

High grades in school and outstanding performance as an accountant, an engineer, or a salesman reveal how able and willing a person is to perform tasks he has been assigned. But an outstanding record as an individual performer does not indicate whether that person is able or willing to get other people to excel at the same tasks. Outstanding scholars often make poor teachers, excellent engineers often are unable to supervise the work of other engineers, and successful salesmen often are ineffective sales managers.

Indeed, men who are outstanding individual performers not uncommonly become "do-it-yourself" managers. Although they are able and willing to do the job themselves, they lack the motivation and temperament to get it done by others. They may excel as individual performers and may even have good records as first-line managers. But they rarely advance far up the organizational hierarchy because, no matter how hard they try, they cannot make up through their own efforts for mediocre or poor performance by large numbers of subordinates.

Universities and business organizations that select managerial candidates on the basis of their records as individual performers often pick the wrong men to develop as managers. These men may get satisfaction from their own outstanding performance, but unless they are able to improve the productivity of other people, they are not likely to become successful managers.

Fewer and fewer men who hold advanced degrees in management want to take responsibility for getting results through others. More and more of them are attracted to jobs that permit them to act in the detached role of the consultant or specialized expert, a role described by John W. Gardner (1965) as the one preferred increasingly by university graduates. . . .

As Charlie Brown prophetically observed in a "Peanuts" cartoon strip in which he is standing on the pitcher's mound surrounded by his players, all of whom are telling him what to do at a critical point in a baseball game: "The world is filled with people who are anxious to act in an advisory capacity." Educational institutions are turning out scholars, scientists, and experts who are anxious to act as advisers, but they are producing few men who are eager to lead or take responsibility for the performance of others.

Most management graduates prefer staff positions in headquarters to line positions in the field or factory. More and more of them want jobs that will enable them to use their analytical ability rather than their supervisory ability. Fewer and fewer are willing to make the sacrifices required to learn management from the bottom up; increasingly, they hope to step in at the top from positions where they observe, analyze, and advise but do not have personal responsibility for results. Their aspirations are high, but their need to take responsibility for the productivity of other people is low.

The tendency for men who hold advanced degrees in management to take staff jobs and to stay in these positions too long makes it difficult for them to develop the supervisory skills they need to advance within their companies. Men who fail to gain direct experience as line managers in the first few years of their careers commonly do not acquire the capabilities they need to manage other managers and to sustain their upward progress past middle age.

"A man who performs nonmanagerial tasks five years or more," as Jennings discovered, "has a decidedly greater improbability of becoming a high wage earner. High salaries are being paid to manage managers (1967:15). This may well explain in part why the median salaries of Harvard Business School graduates plateau just at the time they might be expected to move up into the ranks of top management.

The Need for Power

Psychologists once believed that the motive that caused men to strive to attain high-level managerial positions was the "need for achievement." But now they believe it is the "need for power," which is the second part of the answer to the question: What are the characteristics of men who learn to manage effectively? . . .

Power seekers can be counted on to strive hard to reach positions where they can exercise authority over large numbers of people. Individual performers who lack this drive are not likely to act in ways that will enable them to advance far up the managerial ladder. They usually scorn company politics and devote their energies to other types of activities that are more satisfying to them. But, to prevail in the competitive struggle to attain and hold high-level positions in management, a person's desire for prestige and high income must be reinforced by the satisfaction he gets or expects to get from exercising the power and authority of a high office.

The competitive battle to advance within an organization, as Levinson points out, is much like playing "King of the Hill" (1969:53). Unless a person enjoys playing that game, he is likely to tire of it and give up the struggle for control of the top of the hill. The power game is a part of management, and it is played best by those who enjoy it most.

The power drive that carries men to the top also accounts for their tendency to use authoritative rather than consultative or participative methods of management. But to expect otherwise is not realistic. Few men who strive hard to gain and hold positions of power can be expected to be permissive, particularly if their authority is challenged.

Since their satisfaction comes from the exercise of authority, they are not likely to share much of it with lower-level managers who eventually will replace them, even though most high-level executives try diligently to avoid the appearance of being authoritarian. It is equally natural for ambitious lower-level managers who have a high need for power themselves to believe that better results would be achieved if top management shared more authority with them, even though they, in turn, do not share much of it with their subordinates.

One of the least rational acts of business organizations is that of hiring managers who have a high need to exercise authority, and then teaching them that authoritative methods are wrong and that they should be consultative or participative. It is a serious mistake to teach managers that they should adopt styles that are artificial and inconsistent with their unique personalities. Yet this is precisely what a large number of business organizations are doing; and it explains, in part, why their management development programs are not effective.

What managerial aspirants should be taught is how to exercise their authority in a way that is appropriate to the characteristics of the situation and the people involved. Above all, they need to learn that the real source of their power is their own knowledge and skill, and the strength of their own personalities, not the authority conferred on them by their positions. They need to know that overreliance on the traditional authority of their official positions is likely to be fatal to their career aspirations because the effectiveness of this kind of authority is declining everywhere—in the home, in the church, and in the state as well as in business.

More than authority to hire, promote, and fire is required to get superior results from most subordinates. To be effective, managers must possess the authority that comes with knowledge and skill, and be able to exercise the charismatic authority that is derived from their own personalities.

When they lack the knowledge or skill required to perform the work, they need to know how to share their traditional authority with those who know what has to be done to get results. When they lack the charisma needed to get the willing cooperation of those on whom they depend for performance, they must be able to share their traditional authority with the informal leaders of the group, if any exist.

But when they know what has to be done and have the skill and personality to get it done, they must exercise their traditional authority in whatever way is necessary to get the results they desire. Since a leader cannot avoid the exercise of authority, he must understand the nature and limitations of it, and be able to use it in an appropriate manner. Equally important, he must avoid trying to exercise authority he does not, in fact, possess.

The Capacity for Empathy

Mark Van Doren once observed that an educated man is one "who is able to use the intellect he was born with: the intellect, and whatever else is important" (1967:13). At the top of the list of "whatever else is important" is the third characteristic necessary in order to manage other people successfully. Namely, it is the capacity for empathy or the ability to cope with the emotional reactions that inevitably occur when people work together in an organization.

Many men who have more than enough abstract intelligence to learn the methods and techniques of management fail because their affinity with other people is almost entirely intellectual or cognitive. They may have "intellectual empathy" but may not be able to sense or identify the unverbalized emotional feelings which strongly influence human behavior (Paul, 1967:155). They are emotion-blind just as some men are color-blind.

Such men lack what Normal L. Paul describes as "affective empathy" (p. 155). And since they cannot recognize unexpressed emotional feelings, they are unable to learn from their own experience how to cope with the emotional reactions that are crucial in gaining the willing cooperation of other people.

Many men who hold advanced degrees in management are emotion-blind. As Schein has found, they often are "mired in the code of rationality" and, as a consequence, "undergo a rude shock" on their first jobs (p. 92). After interviewing dozens of recent graduates of the Sloan School of Management at MIT, Schein reported that "they talk like logical men who have stumbled into a cell of irrational souls," and he added,

> At an emotional level, ex-students resent the human emotions that make a company untidy. . . . [Few] can accept without pain the reality of the organization's human side. Most try to wish it away, rather than work in and around it. . . . If a graduate happens to have the capacity to accept, maybe to love, human organization, this gift seems directly related to his potential as a manager or executive" (p. 90).

Whether managers can be taught in the classroom how to cope with human emotions is a moot point. There is little reason to believe that what is now taught in psychology classes, human relations seminars, and sensitivity training programs is of much help to men who are "mired in the code of rationality" and who lack "affective empathy."

Objective research has shown that efforts to sensitize supervisors to the feelings of others not only often have failed to improve performance, but in some cases have made the situation worse than it was before (see Fleishmann et al., 1955). Supervisors who are unable "to tune in empathically" on the emotional feelings aroused on the job are not likely to improve their ability to emphathize with others in the classroom (Paul, pp. 150–157).

Indeed, extended classroom discussions about what other people should do to cope with emotional situations may well inhibit rather than stimulate the development of the ability of managers to cope with the emotional reactions they experience on the job.

CONCLUSION

Many highly intelligent and ambitious men are not learning from either their formal education or their own experience what they most need to know to build successful careers in management.

Their failure is due, in part, to the fact that many crucial managerial tasks are not taught in management education programs but are left to be learned on the job, where few managers ever master them because no one teaches them how. It also is due, in part, to the fact that what takes place in the classroom often is miseducation that inhibits their ability to learn from their experience. Commonly, they learn theories of management that cannot be applied successfully in practice, a limitation many of them discover only through the direct experience of becoming a line executive and meeting personally the problems involved.

Some men become confused about the exercise of authority because they are taught only about the traditional authority a manager derives from his official position—a type of authority that is declining in effectiveness everywhere. A great many become inoculated with an "antileadership vaccine" that arouses within them intense negative feelings about authoritarian leaders, even though a leader cannot avoid the exercise of authority any more than he can avoid the responsibility for what happens to his organization.

Since these highly educated men do not learn how to exercise authority derived from their own knowledge and skill or from the charisma of their own personalities, more and more of them avoid responsibility for the productivity of others by taking jobs that enable them to act in the detached role of the consultant or specialized expert. Still others impair their effectiveness by adopting artificial managerial styles that are not consistent with their own unique personalities but give them the appearance of being "consultative" or "participative," an image they believe is helpful to their advancement up the managerial ladder.

Some managers who have the intelligence required to learn what they need to know fail because they lack "whatever else is important," especially "affective empathy" and the need to develop and stimulate the productivity of other people. But the main reason many highly educated men do not build successful managerial careers is that they are not able to learn from their own firsthand experience what they need to know to gain the willing cooperation of other people. Since they have not learned how to observe their environment firsthand or to assess feedback from their actions, they are poorly prepared to learn and grow as they gain experience.

Alfred North Whitehead once observed that "the secondhandedness of the learned world is the secret of its mediocrity" (Whitehead, 1929:79). Until managerial aspirants are taught to learn from their own firsthand experience, formal management education will remain secondhanded. And its secondhandedness is the real reason why the well-educated manager is a myth.

EDWARD MARSHALL BOEHM, INC.

JAMES BRIAN QUINN, *Tuck School Dartmouth College*

Edward Marshall Boehm—a farmer, veterinarian, and nature lover living near New York City—was convinced by his wife and friends to translate some of his clay animal sculptures into pieces for possible sale to the gift and art markets. Boehm recognized that porcelain was the best medium for portraying his creations because of its translucent beauty, permanence, and fidelity of color as well as form. But the finest of the porcelains, hard paste porcelain, was largely a secret art about which little technical literature existed. Boehm studied this art relentlessly, absorbing whatever knowledge artbooks, museums, and the few U.S. ceramic factories offered. Then after months of experimentation in a dingy Trenton (N.J.) basement, Boehm and some chemist friends developed a porcelain clay equal to the finest in the world.

Next Boehm had to master the complex art of porcelain manufacture. Each piece of porcelain sculpture is a technical as well as artistic challenge. A 52-step process is required to convert a plasticine sculpture into a completed porcelain piece. For example, one major creation took 509 mold sections to make 151 parts, and consumed 8 tons of plaster in the molds. Sculptural detail included 60,000 individually carved feather barbs. Each creation had to be kiln-fired to 2400° where heat could change a graceful detail into a twisted mass. Then it had to be painted, often in successive layers, and perhaps fired repeatedly to anneal delicate colors. No American had excelled in hard paste porcelains. And when Boehm's creations first appeared no one understood the quality of the porcelain or even believed it was hard paste porcelain.

But Boehm began to create in porcelain what he knew and loved best, nature—particularly the more delicate forms of animals, birds, and flowers. In his art

Boehm tried "to capture that special moment and setting which conveys the character, charm, and loveliness of a bird or animal in its natural habitat." After selling his early creations for several years during her lunch hours, his talented wife, Helen, left an outstanding opthalmic marketing career to "peddle" Boehm's porcelains full time. Soon Mrs. Boehm's extraordinary merchandising skills, promotional touch, and sense for the art market began to pay off. People liked Boehm's horses and dogs, but bought his birds. And Boehm agreeably complied, striving for ever greater perfection on ever more exotic and natural bird creations.

By 1968 some Boehm porcelains (especially birds) had become recognized as collectors items. An extremely complex piece like "Fondo Marino" might sell for $28,500 at retail, and might command much more upon resale. Edward Marshall Boehm, then 55—though flattered by his products' commercial success—considered his art primarily an expression of his love for nature. He felt the ornithological importance of portraying vanishing species like U.S. prairie chickens with fidelity and traveled to remote areas to bring back live samples of rare tropical birds for study and later rendering into porcelain. A single company, Minton China, was the exclusive distributor of Boehm products to some 175 retail outlets in the U.S. Boehm's line included (1) its "Fledgling" series of smaller somewhat simpler pieces, usually selling for less than $100, (2) its profitable middle series of complex sculptures like the "Snowy Owl" (see picture) selling from $800 to $5,000, and (3) its special artistic pieces (like "Fondo Marino"

Case copyright © 1976 by James Brian Quinn.

The generous cooperation of Edward Marshall Boehm, Inc. is gratefully acknowledged.

or "Ivory Billed Woodpeckers") which might sell initially for over $20,000.

Individual Boehm porcelains were increasingly being recognized as outstanding artistic creations and sought by some sophisticated collectors. Production of such designs might be sold out for years in advance, but it was difficult to anticipate which pieces might achieve this distinction. Many of the company's past policies no longer seemed appropriate. And the Boehms wanted to further position the company for the long run. When asked what they wanted from the company, they would respond, "to make the world aware of Mr. Boehm's artistic talent, to help world wildlife causes by creating appreciation and protection for threatened species, and to build a continuing business that could make them comfortably wealthy, perhaps millionaires." No one goal had great precedence over the others.

QUESTIONS

1. What strategy should the Boehms follow?
2. Why?

Snowy Owl
Courtesy of Edward Marshall Boehm, Inc.

E & J Gallo Winery

JAMES BRIAN QUINN, *Tuck School Dartmouth College*

"The winemaker is a warrior" begins an old Italian poem. For nearly 50 years, the two sons of an Italian immigrant have taken those words to heart. Ever since they pooled $5,900 in capital to set up their winery in Modesto, California, in 1933, the brothers have managed their enterprise with a discipline, precision, and success that few companies enjoy. But, in the late 1980s, Ernest and Julio, then in their 70s, had to worry about the future of their remarkable concern. In 1986, *Fortune* magazine published a rare and insightful article on the company. The article, quoted almost in its entirety, follows.

A Will to Dominate

When it comes to business, the brothers Ernest and Julio Gallo brook neither waste nor weakness. Just ask the scores of companies, large and small, that over the past five decades have made the mistake of venturing onto their turf. [Despite their ages, Ernest and Julio Gallo] have not lost their desperate will to dominate. ... What is Gallo's secret? "A constant striving for perfection in every aspect of our business," says Ernest. That may sound self-serving, but it is in large part true. Plainly put, Ernest and Julio are better at the nuts and bolts of the wine business than anyone else in the world. They are more resourceful, more thorough, more exacting. And they are not afraid to exercise their power over grape growers, distributors, or anyone else. "I sometimes feel like an Olympic runner who gets mad at his coach," says David Terk, an independent distributor in Abilene, Texas. "Gallo pushes so hard you end up working more than you want."

Not that the Gallos face no challenges. The most unusual by far comes from their younger brother, Joseph, 66. In a drama worthy of the wine-country soap opera *Falcon Crest,* Joseph is suing for a one-third interest in the winery. He claims that the winery is an outgrowth of their father's wine-grape business and that his big brothers cheated him out of his rightful inheritance.

Ernest and Julio's other problems are more mundane. The national obsession with fitness and the crackdown on drunken driving have had a sobering effect on wine production, Gallo included. Americans drank 6.5% less table wine in 1985 than in 1984 and will probably cut consumption 5% more this year, according to *Impact,* an industry newsletter. The wine industry's smartest response to the new abstinence is coolers, fruity beverages with a splash of wine and roughly the alcohol content of beer. Gallo, in typical fashion, has outsmarted everyone: its year-old cooler, Bartles & Jaymes, is number one.

Further challenges come from another trend among wine drinkers—the swing to pricey table wines made from the finest grapes. Americans are demanding better quality than ever before, and premium wines have raised their share of the $8.3-billion-a-year business from 8% in 1980 to 20% today. Gallo sells more premium wine than any other producer, but its growth in this category is limited because it lacks snob appeal. The name *Gallo,* which means "rooster" in Italian, is associated with screw tops and bottles in paper bags (from its earlier marketing history). The brothers are

Case copyright © 1989 James Brian Quinn.

This case was prepared from secondary sources only with the help of Professor Richard D'Aveni. Research associate on this case was Penny C. Paquette. Materials reproduced by special permission from "How Gallo Crushes The Competition," by Jaclyn Fierman, September 1, 1986. Copyright © 1986 *Fortune* magazine.

battling to upgrade their image with the same vengeance they bring to every war they wage.

For now they can take heart in making the most, if not the best, wine in the world. The joke goes that Gallo spills more than anyone else sells. The truth is not far off. Last year Gallo shipped over 150 million gallons of wine, according to the *Gomberg-Fredrikson Report,* an authoritative industry newsletter. Its most popular brands are Chablis Blanc, Hearty Burgundy, Carlo Rossi, and other low-priced jug wines, which together account for a commanding 31% of the volume in that end of the market. The brothers also sell more champagne (André), brandy (E&J), sherry, vermouth, and port than anyone else. All told, they buy roughly 30% of California's annual wine-grape harvest and produce one of every four bottles of wine sold in the United States.

They also squeeze profits from the wine business while others come up dry. The winery is privately owned by Ernest, Julio, and their fecund families—between them the brothers have 4 children, 20 grandchildren, and 6 great-grandchildren. Three children, a son-in-law, and 4 grandchildren work for the company, but share little of Ernest and Julio's power. . . . [Ernest and Julio] keep financial details tightly corked. Based on interviews with dozens of current and former employees, industry experts, and competitors, *Fortune* estimated that Gallo earns at least $50 million a year on sales of roughly $1 billion. By comparison, Seagram, the nation's largest distillery and second-largest winery, booked roughly $350 million in wine revenues [in 1984] and lost money on its best-selling table wines, Paul Masson and Taylor California Cellars. Gallo's other main competitors, Almadén, owned by National Distillers & Chemical Corp., and Inglenook, owned by Heublein, are making money, but not much.

Private ownership and staggering volume contribute to Gallo's success. The company can wrest market share from competitors by settling for paper-thin margins and occasional losses that stockholders of publicly held companies might not tolerate for long. Moreover, Gallo does not have disparate claims on its resources and can devote all its energy to wine. "Unlike our major competition," says Ernest, "wine is our only business."

[Few] other companies could afford to replicate the degree of vertical integration Gallo has built up over the years. The brothers own Fairbanks Trucking Co., one of the largest intrastate truckers in California. Its 200 semis and 500 trailers are constantly hauling wine out of Modesto and raw materials back in—including sand from around the state and lime from Gallo's quarry east of Sacramento. Alone among wine producers, Gallo makes bottles—2 million a day—and its Midcal Aluminum Co. spews out screw tops as fast as the bottles are filled.

Crusher Power

Most of the country's 1,300 or so wineries concentrate on production to the neglect of marketing. They entrust their fate with consumers to independent distributors who work for several competing producers. Most distributors, in turn, figure their job is done once they take orders and make deliveries to grocery and liquor stores. Gallo, by contrast, participates in every aspect of selling short of whispering in the ear of each imbiber. The company owns its distributors in about a dozen markets and probably would buy many of the more than 300 independents who handle its wines if laws in most states did not prohibit doing so.

Gallo's power elicits emotions from admiration to hate from just about everyone touched by it. "The hate part," says a Sonoma Valley grower, "is getting rejected by Gallo at the crusher"—the place where growers bring their grapes to be graded, sold, and eventually crushed into juice and fermented. Distributors feel hatred or something near it if they are unceremoniously dumped, as many have been for failing to satisfy Ernest's demanding requirements. Competitors hate being singled out as the next rival to be vanquished. Says a cowed Stuart Bewley, who helped start California Cooler five years ago, "They aim all their guns at once." Bewley's brand was the market leader in wine coolers until Gallo stormed into the business. Bewley sold California Cooler to Brown-Forman (in 1984) but still manages the operation. Yet even competitors thank the Gallos for expanding the wine market. While the Gallos may not make the world's best wine, they have lifted the U.S. standard for low-priced table wine well above that served in Italy or France.

A Divided Kingdom

E & J Gallo Winery is a divided kingdom. Julio is president and oversees production. Big brother Ernest is chairman and rules over marketing, sales, and distribution. The two steer clear of each other, conducting business on separate floors. "We don't have everyday contact," says Julio, whose domain is the first floor at the neoclassic headquarters some natives call Parthenon West. Ernest holds court upstairs. The brothers mesh well despite the division: Julio's goal is to make more wine than Ernest can sell, Ernest's to sell more than Julio can make.

Thick fingered and full faced, Julio aptly describes himself as a farmer at heart. "I like to walk in the fields with the old-timers," he says. "I feel at home in the vineyards." Make no mistake, though, Julio is a patrician farmer, dressed not in overalls and work boots but in linen trousers and slightly scuffed wing tips. His office is elegantly appointed, with a solid oak desk and inlaid wooden artworks depicting harvest scenes in the French countryside. His modern ranch house down the road from the winery is festooned with images of grapes, from jade carvings along the walls to the silverware and place mats on his table.

Ernest conducts business in a setting cluttered with mementos not from the fields but from the world of selling. He has a framed *New Yorker* cartoon that shows two couples drinking wine in a restaurant. The caption reads: "Surprisingly good, isn't it? It's Gallo. Mort and I simply got tired of being snobs." Expressions of fierce pride abound from the Gallo-green crushed-velvet couch to an ambitious collection of glass, metal, and ceramic statuettes of *galli.* Paler, grittier, and less courtly than his brother, Ernest cares little for social or decorative amenities. "We don't socialize much," says the more affable Julio. "There's not much to talk about."

Ernest wouldn't waste time schmoozing anyway. He would rather interrogate than converse. He bridles when questioned and has the habit of answering with questions of his own. He is after all the information he can get and is intolerant when someone does not deliver. "If you try to cover up, he'll expose you," says George Frank, who directed Gallo's East Coast sales for three decades and retired last year.

Ernest's employees toil much harder than most because they know the boss will try to catch them off guard. "I never knew if he was checking on the market-place or on me," says Frank. On frequent trips around the country, Ernest orders a distributor to pick him up at eight in the morning, map in hand. Mindful of neither distance nor direction, he points to several towns where he wants to check the positioning of his products in stores. "Ernest doesn't want you to take him on a tour," says Laurence Weinstein, a distributor in Madison, Wisconsin. "If he sees you turning left, he'll tell you to turn right."

The distributors behave more like family members than independents because most owe their success to the winery. "Ernest picked distributors who were hungry," says Frank. "They knew if they failed with Gallo, they might be out on the street." Once Ernest chooses a distributor, he or his troops plan strategy with him down to the last detail, analyzing traffic patterns in every store in the district and the number of Gallo cases each should stock.

A Regimented Distribution System

Ernest encourages distributors to hire a separate sales force to sell his products alone. When Texas distributor David Terk decided it wasn't worth the extra money to employ a special Gallo team, he and Ernest severed ties. Terk eventually came around to Gallo's way of thinking and has been reinstated. "If you follow Ernest's advice," Terk says, "he'll make you rich." Ernest also tries to persuade distributors to sell his wines exclusively. "We never told distributors to throw out Gallo competitors," says Frank. "But we might have asked them how they planned to do justice if they carried two competing brands."

The Federal Trade Commission objected to that friendly persuasion 10 years ago, charging Gallo with unfair competition. Gallo signed a consent order that prohibited it from punishing distributors for selling competing brands and from requiring them to disclose sales figures. The FTC set aside the order three years ago after Gallo argued that the market had grown more competitive and that the order was giving other wine makers an unfair advantage: they were freed to set up exclusive deals with distributors.

Now that Gallo can regiment its distributors once again, it rarely hears a grumble out of them. One bold exception: Ohio distributor Bernard Rutman sued Gallo last year, alleging that the company violated antitrust laws when it dumped him for no good reason after 40 years of loyal service. Without Gallo products, which Rutman referred to as "call items" or "door openers," he lost several retail accounts. Rutman claimed that Gallo's action had reduced competition because he could no longer afford the sales force needed to sell a broad range of products. Gallo fought the charges and won, arguing that it was not the winery's responsibility to open doors for competitors. Rutman is appealing.

Ernest finds distributors who will open doors for *him.* Aggressive salesmen are crucial to Gallo's success because they are the winery's link to retailers, and retailers have the last crack at influencing consumers. "Seagram," concedes Edgar Bronfman Jr., "has typically pushed everything to the distributor and left it to him to deal with the stores." Ernest makes certain that his distributors deal with the stores like no others. They build floor displays, lift cases, and dust the bottles on the shelves. "If you turn your back on a Gallo salesman," says a manager of a San Francisco liquor store, "he'll turn the place into a Gallo outlet."

Gallo leaves nothing to chance—and very little to the imagination. Required reading and rereading for new salesmen is Gallo's 300-page training manual.

More graphic than the *Kama Sutra*, it describes and diagrams every conceivable angle of the wine business. "As a sales representative of Gallo wine," the tome begins, "you are the man that Ernest and Julio Gallo depend on to sell retailers the merchandising ideas that sell Gallo wine to consumers."

What follow are 16 dizzying chapters, each ending with a quiz. A section on how to display Gallo products in stores spells out which items to place at eye level (the most highly advertised ones) and which to position above the belt (impulse items). Another details how much shelf space Gallo brands should occupy (seven feet on each of five shelves, the largest area the eye can easily scan). Maintaining shelves the Gallo way requires a ten-point checklist (No. 7: "Wherever there is a decided price advantage in buying a larger size, the larger size should be placed to the right of the smaller size.") The "complete sales call" would be incomplete unless all ten steps from another checklist were taken (No. 6: "It's time to think . . . you should know what you'd like to say and how you're going to say it to *this* retailer.").

Among the trove of sales tips: "An off-color joke may be great if you're selling pornography, but it's a little difficult to use this opener . . . to sell the retailer on cold-box placement for wine." The retail world is made up of six types of buyers, the manual explains. They range from "the silent type (he just listens)" to "the aggressive type (he's looking for a fight)." If you run into the silent type, "avoid embarrassing questions." When you meet up with an aggressive one, "let him win the battle, but you win the war."

Gallo hasn't lost a war yet. Even Coca-Cola, no wimp at marketing, surrendered in 1983 after six years of butting barrels with the wine Goliath. When Coke got into the wine business in 1977, consumption had been rising 7% a year. But that trend soon fizzled. The profit margins Coke was used to in soda never materialized for wine, not even close. By the time Coke sold its Wine Spectrum unit to Seagram for more than $200 million, it had overpromoted and underpriced its Taylor California Cellars.

From Plebeian to Snob

Pleasing the plebeian palate in Podunk used to be all that mattered in the wine business, and no one did that better than Gallo. But today even Podunk has wine snobs. Having to prove themselves all over again is a nasty twist of fate for the Gallos, who have devoted decades to upgrading everyday drinking wine for Americans. "We have varietals we think are the very best," Julio insists. Not Chateau Lafite, to be sure, but

certainly respectable. Some wine connoisseurs compare Gallo's varietals to competing brands that sell for twice as much.

The screw-top stigma hurts, but the Gallo brothers learned early how bitter the wine business can be. They got their first taste as young boys, toiling in their father Joseph's Modesto vineyard in their spare time. After Julio finished high school and Ernest graduated from Modesto Junior College, they worked full time for their father. "He believed in hard work and no play," says Julio. "None at all."

An immigrant from the Piedmont region in northwest Italy, Joseph Gallo was a small-time grape grower and shipper. Prohibition did not put him out of work: the government permitted wine for medicinal and religious use. But the Depression took a tragic toll. The Gallo business almost went under, and in the spring of 1933 Joseph shot his wife and reportedly chased Ernest and Julio across his fields waving a shotgun. After they escaped, Joseph killed himself. Ernest is reminded of the tragedy daily: his childhood residence, a stucco house with a pillared porch, is on the road from the winery to his present home, a modest bungalow with a security guard out front. Julio relived the horror years later when his second son, Philip, then a teenager, committed suicide.

Prohibition ended the same year that their parents died, and the Gallos, then in their early 20s, decided to switch from growing grapes to producing wine. Problem was, they had no idea how to make the stuff. They found instructions in two thin pamphlets in the Modesto Public Library and, with $5,900.23 to their names, burst out of the post-Prohibition starting gate with 600 other newly formed wineries. "My confidence," recalls Ernest, "was unlimited."

Finding customers was the next hurdle, and Ernest was born with an instinct for that. A Chicago distributor wrote to newly licensed California wineries, inviting them to send him samples. Ernest went the extra mile. He boarded a plane for Chicago, met the man at his office, and sold him 6,000 gallons at 50 cents a gallon. Ernest continued east and sold the rest of the first year's production for a profit of $34,000. The Gallos initially sold wine in bulk to bottlers, but in 1938 they started doing their own bottling under the Gallo label, a far more profitable venture. Sales grew unabated for years.

"Success in life," says the insular Ernest, "depends on who your parents were and what circumstances you grew up in." Hard work was Joseph Gallo's ethic, and it became Ernest's as well. Driving himself and others is a survival instinct for Ernest. But perhaps because his father ultimately failed, Ernest also believes that hard work alone is not enough. "It boils down to luck," he says of his and Julio's success. "Circumstances could have been otherwise."

Growing with Thunder

As luck would have it, the Gallos had their first phenomenal success with a high-alcohol, lemon-flavored beverage they began selling in the late 1950s. A radio jingle sent the stuff to the top of the charts on skid rows across the country: "What the word? Thunderbird. How's it sold? Good and cold. What's the jive? Bird's alive. What's the price? Thirty-twice." But Thunderbird also left Gallo with a gutter image it has been hard pressed to shake.

Each in his own way, the Gallos are fighting to change that. Julio may be more easygoing than Ernest, but he is no pushover when it comes to getting what he wants from growers. Says Frank, Gallo's former East Coast executive: "He works with grapes as if he's pursuing the Holy Grail." With the help of graduates from California's top oenology schools, Julio has experimented with hundreds of varieties over the years. In the 1960s he made an unprecedented offer of 15-year contracts to growers who would rip up their vineyards and replant better grapes. Julio got his better grapes, and he also got an assured supply of his most essential raw material. Unlike small wineries, which grow the bulk of their grapes, Gallo buys more than 95 percent of the grapes it crushes.

Growing for Gallo is a mixed blessing. The 1,500 Gallo growers know they have a home for their grapes every season because Gallo's needs are so vast. But they are never sure how much they will get paid until they get to one of Gallo's three grape-crushing and fermenting operations: the Frei Brothers winery in Sonoma County, which Gallo bought from the Frei family in 1977, or the Livingston and Fresno plants in San Joaquin Valley. If grapes do not meet standards for Gallo's top-quality wines—handpicked, the right color, the proper acid and sugar balance—the winery downgrades them for use in other products and slashes the price. The *Healdsburg Tribune,* a newspaper in Sonoma County, has condemned the Gallos and called for state regulation of grading. An editorial claimed growers had been victimized by "sudden devaluation or outright rejection of their grapes, always with the company's take-it-or-leave-it attitude. . . . Most growers have little choice but to take it."

One who chose not to take it was Steven Sommer, a Sonoma grower who filed a grievance with the California Department of Agriculture in 1984 after Gallo downgraded most of his 50-ton harvest from $475 a ton to $275. Gallo claimed the grapes were off color and therefore would not yield flavorful wine. "It was just the way the sun was shining on them," Sommer insisted. The state ruled in Gallo's favor: since the growers had no written contract stating otherwise, Gallo had the right to judge grapes however it chose. Sommer's protest served a purpose, though. Gallo now gives one-year contracts in Sonoma County that spell out its standards. "The old-timers always did business on a handshake," says Julio. "The young growers want things in writing." Sommer has gone into business for himself, producing wine from the grapes he grows.

Julio insists on rigorous standards in Modesto, where all Gallo products are blended, bottled, and tasted every morning at 11 o'clock. Gallo was among the first producers to store wine in stainless steel containers instead of the usual redwood or concrete casks that can breed bad-tasting bacteria. Like giant thermos bottles, tanks at Gallo's three crushers and at the Modesto headquarters protect 300 million gallons of wine from the searing heat. Passers-by could easily mistake the Modesto plant for an oil refinery. There's no sign anywhere that says Gallo. "We know where the place is," Julio explains.

The refinery image is a sore point with Julio. "It was never my ambition to run the biggest winery in the world," he says. "It doesn't impress me at all." Unlike other wineries, Gallo offers no tours to the public. [Although Gallo has a 3-million-gallon underground cask facility], changing Gallo's image is really an above-ground proposition, and Ernest is throwing more than $40 million into advertising this year to get the quality message to consumers. . . . It features sensuous, slow-moving images of ethnic weddings, sunlit vineyards, and crystal goblets, to a mesmerizing score by Vangelis, the Academy Award–winning composer for the movie *Chariots of Fire.*

The new image is being crafted by Hal Riney, a San Francisco ad man with an agency bearing his name. Riney is also the genius behind those fictional farmers, Frank Bartles and Ed Jaymes, who told us in their early ads about how they put their orchard and vineyard together to make a premium wine cooler. "So Ed took out a second on his house," says poker-faced Frank, "and wrote to Harvard for an MBA." The pair was recently seen in New York City eating "big doughnuts" (the locals call them bagels).

Bartles & Jaymes has hurtled to the top of a high heap—there are over 100 coolers on the market. Cooler sales reached almost 40 million cases in 1984, and Marvin Shanken, publisher of *Impact,* predicted that consumption could swell to 90 million cases and constitute a third of the total wine market by 1990. The wine in most coolers is made from the cheapest grapes, and initially the mix was far more profitable than straight wine. But in typical fashion, Gallo devastated everyone else's profit margins when it entered the war. "We've had to double our ad spending and put our products on promotion a lot more often," says California Cooler's Bewley. Another major accomplishment for Riney has been getting along with Ernest Gallo. Before Riney, scores of agencies tried and failed to hack Ernest's ways. That kind of turnover is legendary at Gallo. A few employees, like Frank, stay forever, but many leave after a few years with whatever tricks they've managed to learn from one of America's best marketing minds.

A Generation Gap

A long-time Gallo executive puts his finger on a problem this has caused: "There's a whole level missing at Gallo in terms of age." The Gallos will not tolerate being crossed, even by family. Their battle with brother Joseph, who raises cattle and grows grapes, started when Joseph began selling cheese under the Gallo name. Ernest and Julio claimed Joseph was violating their trademark and, they say, offered him a royalty-free license to use the name. When Joseph refused, Ernest and Julio sued him for trademark infringement.

Joseph's lawyer says his research for that suit led to the discovery that the trademark dated back to the father's business. He then researched the father's estate to determine whether Joseph, who was 13 when his father killed himself, was an heir to the trademark. That search, the lawyer says, led to the discoveries that Joseph had inherited an interest in the father's business and that E & J Winery is an outgrowth of that business. Ernest and Julio say Joseph's claim is ridiculous, and that they started the winery with their own savings.

Ernest tries to recruit Ivy Leaguers and young MBAs—nearly all of them men. "We look for creativity, compatibility, and a sense of urgency," he says. But he doesn't give the whiz kids room to grow. Gallo graduates say the most frustrating thing about Ernest is his insistence on keeping everything secret. "I never saw a profit-and-loss statement," says Diana Kelleher, 39, who was marketing manager for several products in the early 1980s and one of the few women executives at Gallo. "Ernest wouldn't tell anyone the cost of raw materials, overhead, or packaging." Kelleher now runs a Los Angeles consulting firm.

Julio has begun to pass his scepter: His son, Robert, 52, and son-in-law, James Coleman, 50, oversee much of the day-to-day production. Ernest refuses to give anyone an aerial view of his part of the kingdom.

Both his sons, David, 47, and Joseph, 45, work on his side of the business, but neither is heir apparent. Though both graduated from Notre Dame and Joseph has an MBA from Stanford, they lack their father's drive and authority. Those who have worked closely with the family say that Joseph's judgment is uneven and David's behavior occasionally bizarre.

But if Ernest's sons are less prepared to run Gallo than they should be, the problem may have more to do with his management style than their deficiencies. Ernest claims he wants people to be daring, yet his intimidating manner usually produces sycophants. He governs by a committee consisting of his sons and a handful of top executives. On most policy matters, Ernest goes around the table and asks each man for his opinion. But he usually fails to elicit their best because they try to second-guess him. Ernest cannot bear to relinquish control. The deep-rooted need to hold on is understandable: in his world, events can get so wildly out of control that they produce the tragedies of his youth. Call his style shortsighted, even paranoid. Rest assured, though, Ernest has figured out how to sell Gallo products from the grave. He probably is well along on a manual outlining every conceivable war that could break out in the wine world and ten steps to win each one."

THE CHANGING WINE MARKET

Although the U.S. market is growing, the U.S. total consumption of wines is still only sixth in the world, behind much smaller countries like Spain, Italy, and Argentina (see Exhibit 1). Moreover, the United States is a poor ninth in terms of per capita wine consumption among major countries, fortieth if all countries are included.

Production of wine has always been an international phenomenon (see Exhibit 2). France leads the world in quality wine exports, although individual wines from other areas (including a strong new representation from California) enjoy excellent individual reputations. Such wines usually come from individual vineyards, although starting in the mid-1970s, there were innumerable attempts to reproduce the qualities of the great wines—particularly French wines—by using the same varieties of grapes and similar soil conditions. Although the French have dominated with the concept of the "varietal" wines—those made from only one grape variety—the idea is beginning to spread to other areas. The Italians, in particular, are beginning to specialize, exploiting certain well-regarded grape stocks, their favorable growing climate, and low-cost labor.

New technology has also begun to affect the industry. Until recently, mass-produced wines were simply not stable enough to be transportable and had to be drunk within a few months of fermentation. Wines had to be aged in wood, distilled to kill destructive bacteria, or sweet enough to cope with storage and transport. However, modern technologies of wine processing and storage allow world transport of most varieties. But nearly half the cost of most imported wines is in excise duties and local taxes. Customs duties on wine in developed countries are generally specific to the particular wine and increase with the gradations of the wine and whether it is imported in bottles or bulk containers.

Many changes in technology have to do with the development of special grape varieties designed to appeal to the palates of modern consumers. The French call these varieties "noble," but they tend to be less productive per acre than some of the stronger wine grapes, yielding fewer grapes after more attention has been paid to them. Nevertheless, it is the fermentation process that has changed most. White dry wines formerly tended to be unstable unless they were treated with sulfur. The California industry, however, pioneered a revolution in which the juice is fermented at relatively cool temperatures in cylinders made of stainless steel. The temperature is much easier to control than in traditional wooden vats. And the wine can be kept firmly insulated from the air by means of inert gases. For red wines, tradition dictated that they be kept in wood storage for several years to stand the strains of travel and further storage. This led to stronger, tougher wines which provided energy for the drinker. Now stainless steel, temperature- and atmosphere-controlled tanks, and careful measurement and control of the fermentation process allow production and shipment virtually anywhere for markets in which lightness is preferred, fruitiness is desirable, and nourishment is tertiary. (See Exhibit 3.)

The American Market

The American market for imported wines is the world's largest and most competitive. While wines were long the beverage of the elite, the large emerging class of professional people and the extended travel habits of Americans have led to a broad geographic and income distribution for imported wines. As the 1980s began, wine consumption was growing in the United States at an annual rate of 6–7%, with estimates for the 1985–1990 era being an average of 6.7% against an earlier growth rate of less than 4%. Wine purchases were growing at over twice the rate for soft drinks and beer, while sales of distilled spirits remained static. The U.S. wine industry responded by producing high-quality "jug wines" on a massive scale at prices which importers found hard to match. A number of well-to-do Californians also formed new boutique wineries to satisfy the emerging tastes for distinctiveness. Nevertheless, imports took over an increasing share of the total American market. In 1960 they accounted for 7% of the market, 10% in 1970, and 21% in 1980. By 1985 the figure was over 25%. The new market was still dominated by some very large players. In 1985 the approximate market shares were as follows:

E & J Gallo	26.1%
Seagram and Sons	8.3%
Canandaigua	5.4%
Brown Forman	5.1%
National Distillers	4.0%
Heublein	3.7%
Imports	25.0% (approx.)
All others	22.6% (approx.)

Source: Compiled from *Fortune,* September 1, 1986, and import data modified from world data sources.

An estimated 7% of the U.S. population consumed nearly two-thirds of all table wines sold, and nearly half these people lived in five states: California, New York, Florida, Illinois, and Texas. However, table wine was becoming much more widespread geographically in the mid-1980s. A saying persisted that "every time an old bourbon drinker dies, two wine drinkers come of age." The wine and spirits industry journal, *Impact,* estimated that per capita consumption would reach 5.4 gallons a year by 1990, translating into a sales increase of about 80% over the entire decade. While the mid- and low-priced wine markets became more competitive, the premium segment, which accounted for approximately 10% of the $5.5 billion California wine industry, boomed at a 12% growth rate. However, the resulting rush by the boutique vintners to satisfy this market produced a scattered and often inconsistent offering. Consumers who had earlier embraced common, inexpensive wines began to move to these wines, to imported beers, and to wine coolers. Growth of low-priced California wines had flattened since 1980 and actually fell 5% in 1985. In the mid-1980s, the U.S. wine-producing industry was beginning to undergo many mergers and consolidations as firms moved for

scale economies and as foreign wineries and producers sought expanded access to U.S. distribution. For many, the industry was notoriously lacking in profits. As one executive of Christian Brothers said, "You want to know how to make a small fortune in the wine business? Start with a large one."

QUESTIONS

1. Why did Ernest and Julio Gallo choose their particular strategy? What are the strengths and weaknesses of their past strategy?

2. What important environmental and business changes must Gallo Winery deal with in the near future? What strategic alternatives exist?

3. If you were a consultant to the Gallos, how would you approach the issues of strategy implementation posed by the new strategy?

4. If you were competing against the Gallos, what actions would you take? What specific actions should the Gallos take in the near future? Why?

EXHIBIT 1
Wine Consumption Comparison by Country

Source: "A Difficult Vintage: A special survey,"
The Economist, December 24, 1983.

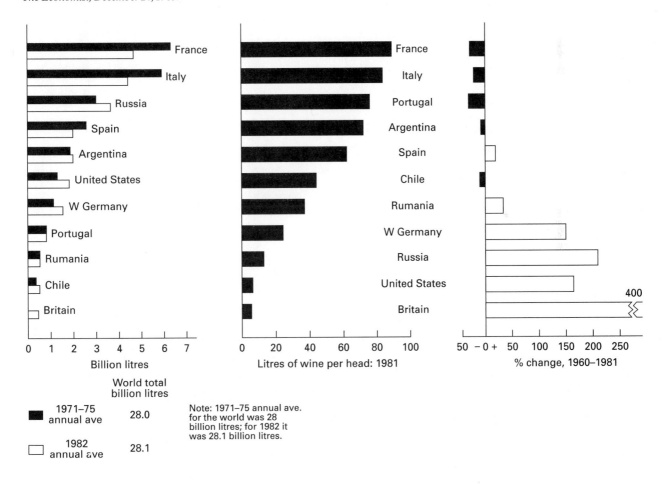

	World total billion litres
1971–75 annual ave	28.0
1982 annual ave	28.1

Note: 1971–75 annual ave. for the world was 28 billion litres; for 1982 it was 28.1 billion litres.

439

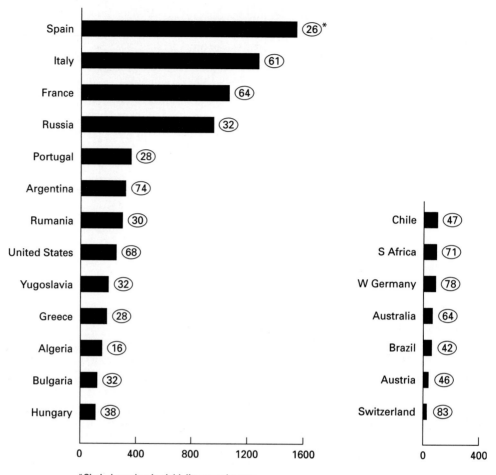

EXHIBIT 2

The Big Producers. Area in Production: 1982 (in thousands of hectares)

Source: "A Difficult Vintage: A special survey," The Economist, December 24, 1983.

*Circled number is yield, litres per hectare

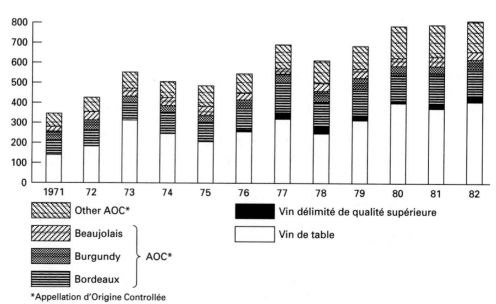

EXHIBIT 3

Defying all Comers. French Wine Exports: in Millions of Litres.

Source: "A Difficult Vintage: A special survey," The Economist, December 24, 1983.

Other AOC*

Beaujolais

Burgundy

Bordeaux

} AOC*

Vin délimité de qualité supérieure

Vin de table

*Appellation d'Origine Controllée

GENERAL MILLS, INC.

JAMES BRIAN QUINN, *Tuck School Dartmouth College*

In 1866, Mr. C. C. Washburn constructed a flour mill on the banks of the Mississippi River near Minneapolis. From these beginnings grew General Mills, the premier flour miller in the United States until it voluntarily sold approximately half its milling capacity in the mid-1960s. By the mid-1980s this and other strategic shifts had changed General Mills into a highly diversified consumer products company on the *Fortune* 100 list. How did these events occur? And what did they portend for the future of this once conservative, middle western, flour milling enterprise?

EARLY HISTORY

In 1928 Washburn Crosby's President, James Ford Bell, began to realize that the network of grain and flour mills he had merged to become General Mills was not going to have the kind of profitability he wanted for the company's future. He began to focus General Mills on more controllable, high-margin, consumer items, starting one of the country's first research operations dedicated to new product development. Bisquick, the nation's first prepared mix, grew from this effort in 1931, as did Cheerios, the world's first ready-to-eat oat cereal in 1941. By then major marketing efforts had made General Mills into the largest flour miller in the United States and its trade names—Wheaties (cereals), Gold Medal (flour), and Betty Crocker (mixes)—into household words.

The War, Electronics, and Chemicals

Then during World War II, General Mills diversified almost by accident into any field—lens coatings, sandbags, electronics, materials testing equipment, and torpedo direction devices—that helped support the war effort while keeping its own highly skilled technical teams intact. After the war it tried to use these same skills in small consumer appliances and started a line of coffee makers, toasters, pressure cookers, and steam irons in 1946. But General Mills soon discovered that it lacked the marketing ability and the trade outlets to compete with larger companies like GE and Westinghouse. And consumer appliances were sold off in 1954.

NEW DIRECTIONS

At about this time, a new management team joined the company, headed by General Edwin W. Rawlings, a dynamic, forceful man who had risen rapidly in the wartime Army Air Force to become one of the youngest four star generals in the nation's history.

Case copyright © 1989 by James Brian Quinn. Research associates—Penny C. Paquette and Allie J. Quinn.

Material is partly drawn from an earlier case written by James Brian Quinn and Mariann Jelinek. The generous cooperation of General Mills, Inc. is gratefully acknowledged.

The Changes Begin—Close Outs and Divestitures

Rawlings began to probe many of the areas that had concerned his predecessors—notably the commodity nature of the company's businesses and the wild and unpredictable swings caused by its dependency on grains and milling. At first he did this through a series of informal presentations. Later these became more formalized Management Operations Reviews—MORs as they were called—to reevaluate all aspects of the company's business.

In short order, General Mills sold off its Magnaflux Division to Champion Spark Plug Co., closed selected foods operations in Mexico and England (major soybean plants, various oil seed operations), and—perhaps most important—got out of the electronics business in 1964. All of this was backdrop for the most traumatic decision in General Mills' history. By the early 1960s worldwide overcapacity in flour milling was rampant. But the company had a strong internal need for flour, both for its institutional customers and for its consumer products like layer cakes and Bisquick.

Eventually, General Mills did not leave commodity (bakery) flour entirely. The consumer flour business was profitable enough to keep, but quite seasonal. Therefore the company maintained enough of a presence in bakery flour to even out the peaks and valleys of flour production and demand. The decision made in 1964 took the better part of a year and struck at the very heart of General Mills—no longer to be the world's largest flour miller.

Consumer Products

As milling capacity decreased to half its former size, the company's product mix changed markedly. And packaged foods soon provided some 75% of General Mills' total sales. About this time, General Rawlings announced a growth goal of 10% per year. And many shared the view that the central focus for expansion should be in *consumer products,* beginning with foods. As an executive commented,

> It made a lot of sense to us. . . . Here was a business—consumer products beginning with family flour, and progressing to cereals, cake mixes, and so on—that had showed a history of steady growth. With our marketing ability, it was obvious that we could control our own destiny to a degree, there. . . . The philosophy was, "We're already there, and obviously we can sell things to the consumer. That's where our strength is."

General Mills' first nonfood consumer acquisition was Rainbow Crafts (a manufacturer of creative toys, including Play Doh), purchased in October 1965. An executive vice president of the Chemicals Division during this period recalled that the "toy and craft" involvement began almost casually, but quickly led to other things,

> It seems to me that somebody came up with the idea that, "Look, there's a little company down in Cincinnati that makes Play Doh, and it's available." To my knowledge, it came to us. I don't think we found it. Rainbow Crafts just happened to be there, it happened to be a good idea, and we happened to get it. Then we started a real search (internally and externally) into other-than-food consumer areas. These quickly extended into the craft, game, toy, fashion, and jewelry businesses—all broad consumer lines other than food.

As background for this wider diversification program, the Acquisitions Group performed a major review of the consumer product industries of the United States. From this it distilled some six areas of major interest. These were: specialty retailing; restaurants; fashions; furniture; travel; and crafts, games, and toys. These investigations helped refine the company's acquisition criteria. Eventually, these criteria became to acquire consumer product or service companies: in low-technology fields, with the possibility of a brand franchise, growing faster than gross national product, in fragmented industries, in industries with at least $300 million total potential, and with the possibility of significant earnings-per-share impact. The intention was to build up a position over a period of time through acquisition of smaller units, rather than acquiring large single units.

The acquisition group presented these criteria and candidate industries to the Executive Council in fall 1967. It sanctioned looking into several industries further. The first of these was the fashion industry. The acquisition group then went through a full segmentation of that industry by customer age, type of product, price, style, distribution techniques, and so on. Following a full field investigation of some 200 companies, a few attractive and available candidates were brought in to top management. Even then, further education was needed. For example, one of the primary fashion candidates quickly left after he was asked in a top management interview to describe his five-year planning processes. He commented, "They really don't understand this industry, do they?" However, within a short while, these sorts of problems receded. One executive later recalled,

As part of the process, we did a very interesting thing, a sort of popularity contest. In effect each member ranked the presented areas in the order they thought we ought to consider them for diversification. As you might expect, the winners of the popularity contest were those most closely related to our existing businesses. The restaurant business got the most votes, the apparel industry very few. The next year was spent studying these industries and developing fairly comprehensive strategies for getting into them. . . . But many of the top managers were still not comfortable with the idea of investing significant amounts of money in unrelated new areas.

Nevertheless, in 1967 Craftmaster Corporation (maker of paint-by-number oil painting sets and other craft and hobby kits) was acquired, as was Kenner Products Corporation (maker of a broad line of innovative toys). Then in 1968, General Mills added Parker Brothers (makers of Monopoly and other games) and Model Products Corporation.

THE McFARLAND YEARS

A prime mover in all this, Mr. James P. McFarland, was named president and chief operating officer in December 1967 to succeed General Rawlings, with Rawlings continuing as CEO. A 40 year veteran with General Mills, Jim McFarland had risen through marketing and general management positions in the Flour, Grocery Products, and later Consumer Products Divisions. *The Wall Street Journal* described him as "a man who had done well in every job he has been given." McFarland continued the strategy of making acquisitions in related areas, with Jesse Jones (maker of sausage and other meat specialties) and Gorton Corporation (a processor of seafoods) in 1968 and other Consumer Foods acquisitions on the Continent, in the United Kingdom, and Canada.

In addition, McFarland created a New Ventures Group "to form entrepreneurial teams that will conceive and develop new areas of profit growth." Acquisitions were stepped up with Monocraft Products (jewelry), Dexter Thread Mills (mail order crafts), Knothe Brothers (sleepwear), Donruss Co. (bubble gum), and David Crystal, Inc. (apparel) being added. Named Chief Executive Officer in 1969, Mr. McFarland could report the largest annual sales increase in the company's history, 18%—and a profit increase of 15%.

Establishing a Corporate Identity

Soon McFarland began a broad-based review of the company's overall direction. His own view was that the company should move from the assortment of businesses in which it then operated to "a family of businesses" which would offer more growth potential and possess greater balance. But he decided that the company's key managers should actively participate in this decision.

McFarland began by stating, for the first time, a corporate "mission." He felt that the real talent of the company rested in "its ability to market consumer products and/or services for which a brand franchise could be developed." Although the company had adequate skills in research, manufacturing, and technology, its critical edge lay in its marketing capability. The broad mission developed for General Mills became "to discern consumer wants and needs and convert those into products and services for which it could develop markets and a brand franchise."

The next step was to further develop, test, and communicate these concepts within the organization. McFarland took some 30–35 top managers "for a three-day retreat up north" which became known as the "goodness to greatness" conference. The company already had some broad financial and growth goals. The whole group first reviewed these and decided they still seemed appropriate. Next Mr. McFarland broke the total unit up into groups of 6 to 8 people. On the first day he asked them to define, "What are the characteristics of a great company?" Each group considered this from the viewpoint of stockholders, employees, suppliers, the public, and society—and reported back:

> Among characteristics agreed upon as keys to corporate greatness were: "A well-defined corporate purpose"; "A growth corporation in key leading indicators, including particularly earnings per share, sales and an overall increase in market penetration"; "An intense desire for greatness"; "An unusually high degree of creativity and innovation"; "The look of greatness, achieved through flair and imaginative and effective communication"; "Diversification," and "A participative, responsible internal climate."

The second day's discussions were devoted—in the same format—to the company's strengths and weaknesses relative to the defined posture of "greatness." The third day focused on how to overcome the company's weaknesses and move from being a "very good company" toward being a "great company." At the end of each day, the whole group came together and tried to reach a broad consensus through further discussions. The Planning Director then distilled and summarized this consensus for the record. These meetings led to certain fundamental conclusions. In Mr. McFarland's words,

> We had this strong desire to grow. But the feeling was that we were not involved in enough areas of growth—industries or business activities of natural growth. We either had to go against the trends or be absolutely miracle-makers within our fields. Therefore, we decided that we should undertake and develop some new areas of activity. . . . There were also some more subjective elements [in our conclusions]; that we needed more flair in our business, more get up and go, and so on.

The "Comfort Factor"

Until 1969, most acquisitions, domestically and internationally, had been in the foods area. Some non-foods businesses appealed to management more than others. "The closer an item was to the core of the business, the more comfortable they would feel." Cosmetics were considered closer to foods than apparels. Broadcasting was closer than furniture because the company itself was spending so much on TV advertising. The company justified the consideration of non-food areas because of its deep seated faith in its ability to market consumer products to the homemaker and her family. This perception evolved into a "loose strategy" over a period of time through the interaction of key management personnel. Out of this came two thrusts. One was to expand in food-related sectors. The other was to develop new growth centers based on General Mills' marketing skills directed essentially at the homemaker. There was a strong informal feeling that the great majority of the company's resources should be used to expand in the food related areas.

Two Thrusts

Almost the reverse occurred. Over the next five years General Mills invested something like $400 million in new businesses, and the majority were not closely related to foods. A Direct Marketing Division was formed to include LeeWards Creative Crafts, Eddie Bauer (sports equipment and leisure wear), and The Talbots (fine clothing), all with both mail order and retail stores. And General Mills' fashion activities expanded to include Monet costume jewelry; Kimberly

Knitwear; Picato; Alligator Company; Lord Jeff Knitting Company; and the Foot-Joy Company.

There were two main reasons why acquisitions were primarily outside the food area. First, the company was unable to continually develop good acquisition candidates in many food related sectors. The field was highly competitive, and acquisition opportunities tended to be marginal—that is, they either were not market leaders or their cost was prohibitive. Second, when candidate companies were strong in some areas, FTC restrictions prevented the company from acquiring them. In addition, there were two organizations whose sole responsibility was to find and develop new opportunities in the non-food sector. There was a strong bias for these groups to find interesting candidates, and they did.

Still in this same era, General Mills became vitally interested in the "away-from-home eating" market. Red Lobster Inns were acquired in January 1970. Betty Crocker Pie Shops—in the Minneapolis area—opened to feature a broad line of quality, fresh-baked pies. Betty Crocker Tree House restaurants were opened in four cities. And General Mills opened fish and chip shops in Arizona and take-out chicken shops in Britain. The Corporate Controller commented on General Mills' restaurant activities:

> Data indicated that more and more meals were being eaten away from home. Being a food company, we felt that we should and could participate [successfully] in this segment . . . Red Lobster Inns were acquired on a performance contract basis. And it was one of the best performance contracts we ever had. There were only about 6 outlets in the entire chain and they were all in central Florida. What we really acquired was three people who deeply understood the restaurant business—that is, the basic mathematics of that business. The real key to satisfactory return is capital turnover. They had built their restaurants so the sales/investment ratio was about 1.5 to 1. With inflation and the more or less sunk cost in investment, you can't go anywhere but up on returns.

Various executives noted that the company could start small in the restaurant business and use a "roll out" concept—that is, expand successful chains in discreet units, duplicating a local success in new geographical areas, with very little risk after the first few were proved. While the Red Lobster Inns proved successful, other efforts did not. Three of the four chains started internally were liquidated.

A Dazzling Array

By the mid-1970s General Mills businesses had proliferated into a fairly dazzling array. Table 1 shows how rapid growth was and how all this was financed. But some segments were not meeting profit goals. And others were competing for the same markets and resources.

The company had entered five new industries. Simultaneously, rising capital costs and the cash demands of many growing businesses made the Board of Directors and many securities analysts increasingly nervous. The company responded with two major steps. First, management changed its publicly stated strategy to one of consolidating the industries into which it diversified. Second, it placed new emphasis on internal growth as opposed to growth from external sources.

TABLE 1 Income Statement *(in $ millions)*

	1967	1969	1971	1973	1975	1977
Sales	628	885	1120	1662*	2309*	2909*
COGS	401	579	724	1010	1532	1786
Depreciation	14	23	27	35	42	48
Net income	30	38	44	66	76	117
Total assets	367	622	750	909	1206	1447
Long-term debt	92	214	252	214	305	276
Common equity	194	281	329	426	560	725

* Restated for pooling of interest.

Source: Data drawn from various annual reports of General Mills, Inc.

An All-Weather Company

Soon, however, acquisitions did continue with Harris Stamp, International Incentives, Feldbacher Backwarenfabrik (Austrian pretzels), David Reid, Bowers and Ruddy Galleries, General Interiors Corp., Clipper Games (Holland), Wallpapers-to-Go, and York Steak House Systems, Inc. becoming major acquisitions. By 1977 General Mills, Inc. (GMI), had some 95 operating subsidiaries in which it held total or major equity positions. Some 30–35% of GMI's business came from non-foods products; its management had decided not to increase the ratio further for fear that General Mills would be considered a "conglomerate" and its P/E ratios would suffer accordingly.

During Mr. McFarland's eight years as Chief Executive Officer the company had grown spectacularly as shown below.

By 1977 top managers were confident that General Mills had developed into an "all weather" company, able—more than ever before—to maintain growth despite the buffets of politics, the economy, or other external environments. In spring 1977, as Mr. McFarland stepped down as chairman, General Mills signed a letter of intent to sell off its Chemical Division for $75 million, the last of the early post–World War II diversifications. Mr. McFarland said,

> We've gone through the wage and price controls period. We've gone through the recession. We went through the boom. We've gone through the energy crisis, and—I think because of our planning process and our understanding of our business—we've been able to maintain growth. We should constantly position ourselves to be a truly "all-weather growth company."
>
> I always believed that one of my greatest responsibilities as Chief Executive Officer was not only to use our physical facilities well, but more importantly, our human resources. For each individual, this meant to make a spot where he could effectively at least start things, implement them, and innovate. The more you use the thoughts of your vital organization, your human resources, the better off you are.

	1977	1969	1977 AS % OF 1969
Sales	$2,209M	$885M	328
Total assets	1,447M	662	232
Net income	117M	36.2M	323
Earnings per share	2.36	.89	265
Stock prices	$26\frac{1}{2}–35\frac{1}{2}$	$15\frac{3}{4}–2\frac{3}{4}$	165

Source: Data drawn from company's annual reports and various public sources.

A NEW MANAGEMENT FOR A NEW ERA

E. Robert Kinney became chairman of General Mills in early 1977. Mr. Kinney had come to GMI when it bought Gorton Corp. Prior to that time Kinney had built two small companies into thriving enterprises. Although not in General Mills' Midwest tradition, Kinney's "good gutsy Maine business sense"[1] fit well with General Mills' philosophy. Kinney had moved through several operations positions before becoming its chief financial officer and later president. Although General Rawlings and Mr. McFarland are given most credit for repositioning General Mills, Mr. Kinney continued the entrepreneurial flair that had characterized General Mills' preceding decades. During his five years as CEO, General Mills grew from $2.65 billion to $4.85 billion in sales at an annual average rate of 12.9%. Mr. Kinney further developed the basic strategies of his predecessors—primarily emphasizing and extending the successful and fast growing Consumer Foods and Restaurant lines. But much also happened in the Toys Group. The company gained the "galaxywide" rights to market products based on the Star Wars movies which it parlayed into a $100 million a year enterprise. In another arena, General Mills' Izod line suddenly became fashionable, and sales skyrocketed.

Organizationally, Kinney continued to maintain very loose reins on his subsidiary managements, a policy which was obviously favored by the various entrepreneurs who had sold their burgeoning businesses to General Mills and stayed on to make them grow rapidly with seemingly limitless cash.[2] However, by 1981 many of the original founders of General Mills' subsidiaries had retired, died, or gone on to other endeavors, including Darden of Red Lobster, Chernow of Monet, the Talbots, Feighner of Tom's Foods, the Hoffmans of Wallpapers-to-Go, Grayson of York Steak Houses, and Gallardo of Casa Gallardo.

After a short but successful reign, in April 1981 Kinney handed the mantle of CEO on to Mr. Bruce Atwater, a 23-year veteran of General Mills and president and COO since 1977. *Forbes,* which had disparaged General Mills' earlier diversification attempts in the mid-1970s as "disastrous," noted that "General Mills had doubled its return on equity and its earnings growth rates to 17.9% and 15.3%, respectively, and was now near the top of its industry."[3] While almost half of GMI's sales and earnings in fiscal year 1982 came from its four major areas of diversification—restaurants, toys and crafts, fashion goods, and specialty retailing—45% of its growth over the last decade had come from new products and services developed internally and only 10% from new acquisitions. Between 1967 and 1979 non-food acquisitions had cost General Mills some $335 million and 3.5 million shares, about the price of one good-sized acquisition, but in 1981 they contributed $2 billion in sales and $184 million in operating profits.

Interestingly, 13 of GMI's older (over 25 years) food lines tripled their volume in the same decade to some $2 billion, by responding rapidly and shrewdly to changing consumer tastes (low-calorie foods, specialty cake mixes, "healthy" breakfast cereals, and so on). With this strong base, Mr. Atwater predicated sales would double in five years to $8 billion and capital spending would rise to $1.4 billion. "Unlike some consumer companies we have more growth opportunities than we have capital to devote to growth."[3]

Managers and Entrepreneurs

In September 1981, *Business Week* noted,

> This year for the first time, General Mills is imposing stringent financial controls and restrictions on its once nearly autonomous subsidiary chiefs. . . . The corporation has increased internal working capital charges to 13% from 7%. And it has launched a study of the feasibility of taking a "balance sheet approach" to financial management that would look at the cost of financing fixed assets and would force each subsidiary to simulate intracompany dividends. . . . "We want the managers to look at after-tax results, not just pre-tax profits," explains Jane Evans.[2]

With Mr. Atwater firmly in charge, the company was reorganized with two vice-chairmen—one responsible for the Consumer Foods Group and the other the Fashion, Toys, Specialty Retailing, and Restaurant Groups. While wanting to avoid the evils of overcontrol, Mr. Atwater noted, "You've got to do things differently when you reach a certain size, or you're going to suffer." In the *1981 Annual Report* he noted,

> [Our strategy] demands intelligent and responsive employees who stay in close touch with the consumer. Employees of this caliber are also necessary to support our management philosophy of decentralized growth centers. A combination of decentralized operations, a strong financial reporting system, and heavy emphasis on long range planning are the basic elements of our strategy.

As the entrepreneurial founders of many of General Mills' business were replaced—often by managers who had progressed upward through the Consumer Foods Group—the product management system that worked so well in Consumer Foods was being adapted to nonfood areas as well. *Fortune* noted some of the impacts as follows, "While the product management system does create champions and encourages or at least rewards risk taking to some degree, it is also a relatively cumbersome process-oriented system in which the annual product plan follows a formula and the most common frustration of product managers themselves is how long it takes to get their proposed actions through the system."[4]

Mr. Atwater emphasized "we're trying to get things done as close to the market as we can. The object is to make running a General Mills Company as much like running a free standing business as possible." Nevertheless, *Business Week* noted in 1981,

> For some of the entrepreneurial managers, the jury remains out on whether General Mills will make good on

its implied promise to keep strategic planning within the individual companies' domains. To them, the answer revolves around whether the corporate parent will remain as willing to accept variations in financial goals and performance as it said. "When you were by yourself, you set the standards," sums up Foot-Joy's Tarlow. "Here the standards are set and they're largely General Mills' standards."[2]

But like many other companies, General Mills had its problems with its entrepreneurs, too. When its Kimberly Division's founder had insisted that the division stick with its money-losing knitted products line, there were no experts in General Mills willing to second guess him. Ultimately, General Mills had to liquidate the operation when the division head's "knits strategy" caused excessive losses. In 1985, General Mills' very sophisticated management was still concerned with the problems of how to best utilize, motivate, and control a highly decentralized entrepreneurial management system.

A Long-Term Viewpoint

Nevertheless, General Mills had an important tradition of risk taking and patience in developing its enterprises. Tenacity in the face of problems had long permeated the Consumer Foods area where Atwater commented, "We judge people not on whether a product succeeded or failed, but on how well they approached the marketplace."[3] He also said, "We are long-term people . . . when we are convinced that consumer demand exists for a product, we constantly refine the product until it achieves marketing success. We never cut and run."[4] Applied to non-food areas this philosophy led to patience with such troublesome subsidiaries as Ship n' Shore, which plunged into the red in 1979 when it bet wrong on the potential popularity of Quiana, a synthetic silk. "I told them it would take two years to turn around Ship n' Shore, and there was no pressure (to speed that up)," said Stanley Gillette, the subsidiary's president.[2]

Atwater's style brought with it a new dedication to planning, careful market analyses, and targeted acquisitions programs. When *Dun's* selected General Mills as one of its five best managed companies, it stated, "Behind General Mills' success is its mastery of consumer marketing. It exhaustively researches the market potential of every new product considered, and, once the decision to go ahead is made, puts the product in the hands of a product manager whose single assignment is to make it a success. Management plows big bucks into its development and promotion and sticks with it until it turns a profit."[5] But flexibility

was also needed. At the 1983 Annual Meeting Mr. Atwater added,

> General Mills intends to continue "our necessarily risk-oriented marketing activities" to execute its strategy of balanced diversification, aggressive consumer marketing, and entry into adjacent businesses. An overly cautious marketing approach would enable our competitors to move ahead more rapidly than General Mills in developing opportunities. On the other hand, a risk-oriented marketing approach inevitably results in a certain number of initiatives that don't work out. But, what the consumer wants and needs (and competitor's offerings) continually change. This is why it is far more risky to stay with the status quo than to continually experiment with changes and improvements.[6]

THE MID-1980s

1981 through early 1984 were hard years for the US. economy. And General Mills whose growth was intimately tied to consumer spending experienced a slower rise in sales. Nevertheless, return on average equity met or exceeded stated corporate goals, dividends per share continued to be raised, and earnings per share continued their 22-year record of increase. Within the five industry groups, however, unforeseen problems cropped up and were reflected in group level financial results. (See exhibits for a summary of group performance for the fiscal years 1979 through 1984.)

Consumer Foods led the company forward with its strategy of increased market share and profit growth in its traditional brands, introduction of meaningful new products in established categories, entry or creation of carefully selected new markets through internal development or acquisition, and concentration on productivity improvements in all areas. The other four groups each faltered, leading one analyst to comment that "A principal strength of General Mills has been its ability to diversify outside the consumer food business . . . This diversification is now being tested."[7]

The Restaurant Group which by 1984 accounted for nearly 20% of the company's sales was hard hit by a sudden decline in the Red Lobster chain's popularity and customer counts. As far back as 1982, research indicated to Joe Lee (manager of Red Lobster's first outlet and now the Restaurant Group president) that consumers were interested in a more casual dining experience, as well as lighter fresh food, and a greater variety of price points. "The research was telling him one thing; the Red Lobster books said something else.

Doing very well—in the first year of the recession—hid the believability of the research. With 370 restaurants you didn't want to do the wrong thing," said Lee.[8]

During fiscal 1984 the company began a $100 million chainwide remodeling program and curtailed further expansion of Red Lobster until the remodeling was finished and earnings improved. The other four restaurants'—York Steak House, Casa Gallardo (Mexican foods), Daryll's (casual style, diverse menu), and Good Earth—concepts were constantly modified during this period with continuous expansion and improving results. Mr. Lee's philosophy—placing maximum responsibility and autonomy close to the restaurant—seemed to pay dividends. "Once Joe approves a plan, he lets the presidents do whatever is necessary to implement it," said one executive. But Lee also held personal quarterly meetings and had short monthly reports from each of his key people. He spent much of his time visiting individual restaurants around the country. "I've got to have a feel of the business myself. I can't get that in an office. I want to see what is actually happening in the restaurants and with the customers." Said an executive, "If Joe heard of a new restaurant concept or a new type of dishwasher, he would go miles out of his way to see it for himself. He almost got killed once when his airplane crash landed in Newfoundland because he wanted to visit his shrimp supplier personally." With high energy and standards, Lee had set a target of doubling his restaurants between 1982 and 1985.[9]

The Toy Group had suffered heavily from Parker Brothers entry into the video game market—which promptly went into a tailspin beginning in 1983. In 1982, its first year in the video business, Parker Brothers racked up earnings of $20 million on sales of $74 million. With such an auspicious start, the company geared up to produce $225 million of cartridges in fiscal 1983. Instead, it had to settle for revenues of $117 million and a loss.[8] Luckily, Parker had adopted basically a "software only" strategy and was able to scale down its operations and stem its losses somewhat. And the success of Star Wars toys and its line of licensed character products, Strawberry Shortcake and the Care Bears, balanced off its video game problems and some currency woes caused by its Mexican operations. In 1985 Parker and the entire Toys Group were trying hard to define how to recapture their lost volume and exploit the complex home entertainment marketplace.

The Fashion Group's Izod/LaCoste—while relatively small when acquired—had become the mainstay of GMI's fashion lines. Capitalizing on increased consumer interest in physical fitness, General Mills built Izod's alligator into a highly profitable symbol of quality and broadened its product line into a full range of leisure wear. At first the problem was to produce enough of Izod's classic shirt (the 2058) to meet orders. Izod's Ivy League look became the "sport shirt of choice" in the *Preppy Handbook* craze of the early 1980s, and competition copied the alligator concept and style with wild abandon. But it was Izod's failure to adapt its prep styles into other variations or a total "look" of shirts, pants, accessories (etc.) that gave others a chance to muscle out shelf space in retail stores. Under this impact, the Izod line began a steady decline in 1982. As Jane Evans, then the executive vice president of Fashion, said,

> "I think it is important to remember that fashion came to Izod. It was not because of anything we did as far as changing the shirt. All of a sudden we were reclassified as being a "fashion line.' We didn't understand the implications of that." While some 20% of all knit shirts were brought by fad conscious teenage girls, Evans maintained, "Izod had no interest in chasing the juniors." She said flatly, "That is a huge business, it's a dangerous business, and it's not one we'll ever go after.[8]

The mainstream of GMI's David Crystal line—dressy sportswear geared to suburban activities—also proved to be out of tune with apparel market trends, as had Kimberly's double knit and synthetic fabrics.[10] While recognizing General Mills' impressive record and historical strengths, *The Wall Street Journal* summarized certain concerns as follows:

> The manner in which senior management disclosed Izod's problems also raises questions about how well it tracks General Mills' diverse operating units. Analysts say the Izod episode disclosed other potential problems: (1) Management's staple food heritage may prevent it from adapting to the faster paced marketing needs of nonfoods businesses ... Fashion isn't like Wheaties and Cheerios. When you turn the key in the morning, you know you're going to sell cereals. But in the rag business, every day is really a new day. (2) The company's formal reporting systems may keep management in the dark until it's too late. And (3) entrepreneurship may be frustrated by great reliance on research and what one analyst calls "a typical large company monthly review that looks at all the numbers. I'm not sure that breeds the kind of creativity you need to run a business," he says.[11]

Specialty Retailing had been developed by General Mills using "consumer trend analysis" to identify new distribution channels for conventional consumer products—chiefly mail-order marketing. The Talbots brought GMI into the fashion retailing market with a substantial mail-order volume. First The Talbots' mail-order sales were extended out of The Talbots' traditional New England markets. Then as new customer loyalties developed, they were exploited with additional retail outlets in selected new areas. Eddie Bauer (quality, down-insulated outdoor gear) followed the same strategy. And both brought General Mills into the new telecommuncations, computer, and in-home shopping markets.

Overall in Specialty Retailing there were some success stories and some problems. The Talbots, Eddie Bauer, Lee Wards retail operations, and Pennsylvania House furniture lines were gradually expanded and doing well. But Lee Wards Creative Crafts mail-order business and two other furniture operations experienced serious setbacks and were eventually divested. And overall Specialty Retailing results were hurt by (1) the collapse of the Collectibles business, which was sold in 1983; (2) the sharp downturn in the housing market and hence sales at Wallpapers-to-Go outlets (these were either sold or remodeled and repositioned as full-service decorating stores); and (3) Wild West Stores' failure to react to changes in jeans fashions (The Wild West stores closed down and reopened as We Are Sportswear outlets in 1982–1984).

How Long Is the Primrose Path?

1984 may have been a watershed year for General Mills. Despite selling off its snack foods operation (Tom's Food) which increased its fiscal 1984 operating profits by more than $100 million, net earnings were down $11.7 million from 1983. Earnings per share would have been down also, except that the company bought back 3.2 million shares of common stock on the open market. Security analysts, most of whom had been as confident as management of the company's ability to correct its problems and continue its winning strategy, began in late 1984 to ask such questions as, "How long is the primrose path? Are the problems ahead or being put behind?" At General Mills Annual Meeting in September 1984, Mr. Atwater said that while Izod was troubled, it would "break even" for the fiscal year ending May 1985. But only a few weeks later he conceded that Izod would have a loss of millions of dollars and could take a 5 cent per share bite out of earnings.[11] This incident created a concern that General Mills might have some fundamental problems to grapple with before it resumed its strong recent growth history.

QUESTIONS

1. Evaluate General Mills' implementation of its diversification program. To what extent can such a program be truly planned? How? How permanent can a strategy be in this kind of company? Why?

2. What are the main portfolio issues facing General Mills at the end of the case? What should it do about these?

3. What kind of organization and control systems should General Mills adopt? Why? How should it evaluate and reward managers in its various entrepreneurial endeavors? In its more mature lines?

EXHIBIT 1 General Mills, Inc.—Business Segment Data, 1980–1984

FISCAL YEAR	SALES ($ MILLIONS)	PERCENT OF TOTAL SALES	PRE-TAX OPERATING PROFITS AFTER REDEPLOYMENT ($ MILLIONS)	PROFITS AS PERCENT OF SALES	RETURN ON IDENTIFIABLE ASSETS	CAPITAL EXPENDITURES ($ MILLIONS)	DEPRECIATION EXPENSE ($ MILLIONS)
Consumer Foods							
1980	$2,218.8	53.2%	$210.5	9.5%	27.7%	$ 80.6	$33.6
1981	2,514.6	51.8	217.7	8.7	25.9	95.7	40.6
1982	2,707.4	51.0	263.0	9.7	28.9	96.2	46.6
1983	2,792.6	50.3	268.2	9.6	27.3	123.8	51.9
1984	2,713.4	48.4	383.0	14.1	41.0	130.3	53.9
Restaurants							
1980	525.7	12.6	52.7	10.0	19.6	49.8	14.3
1981	704.0	14.5	75.3	10.7	19.9	85.1	19.7
1982	839.4	15.8	79.2	9.4	16.0	122.4	24.4
1983	984.5	17.7	80.0	8.1	14.0	107.6	30.6
1984	1,079.7	19.3	37.3	3.5	6.4	82.3	34.7
Toys							
1980	647.0	15.5	60.1	9.3	13.6	34.7	19.2
1981	674.3	13.9	70.6	10.5	17.6	28.6	22.9
1982	654.8	12.3	79.2	12.1	19.6	30.6	20.7
1983	728.3	13.1	104.6	14.4	23.2	39.3	22.8
1984	782.7	14.0	51.0	6.5	9.4	36.3	22.2
Fashion							
1980	442.5	10.1	43.7	10.3	18.9	5.2	3.9
1981	580.5	12.0	87.5	15.1	27.0	14.4	5.0
1982	657.3	12.4	101.7	15.5	28.2	13.4	6.0
1983	616.3	11.1	75.9	12.3	21.9	17.3	6.2
1984	587.4	10.5	37.9	6.5	9.7	16.3	7.3
Specialty Retailing							
1980	365.3	8.5	26.4	7.4	14.5	19.3	4.1
1981	379.0	7.8	13.2	3.5	5.5	19.2	5.2
1982	453.2	8.5	(11.9)	−2.6	−4.6	21.8	7.7
1983	429.1	7.7	16.1	3.8	6.7	17.1	9.1
1984	437.6	7.8	(10.9)	−2.5	−5.2	14.3	9.2

Source of Raw Data: General Mills, Inc., *Annual Report,* 1980–1984.

EXHIBIT 2 **General Mills, Inc., and Subsidiaries. Five-Year Financial Summary—Before Restatements (As Reported), 1980–1984** *(amounts in millions, except per share data)*

	MAY 27, 1984	MAY 29, 1983	MAY 30, 1982	MAY 31, 1981	MAY 25, 1980
Operating Results					
Earnings per share[a]	$ 4.98	$ 4.89	$ 4.46	$ 3.90	$ 3.37
Return on average equity	19.0%	19.9%	19.1%	18.2%[b]	17.6%[b]
Dividends per share[a]	$ 2.04	1.84	1.64	1.44	1.28
Sales	$ 5,600.8	5,550.8	5,312.1	4,852.4	4,170.3
Costs and expenses:					
Cost of sales, exclusive of items below	$ 3,165.9	3,123.3	3,081.6	2,936.9	2,578.5
Selling, general, and administrative[c]	$ 1,841.7	1,831.6	1,635.5	1,384.0	1,145.5
Depreciation and amortization	$ 133.1	127.5	113.2	99.5	81.1
Interest	$ 61.4	58.7	75.1	57.6	48.6
Earnings before income taxes	$ 398.7	409.7	406.7	374.4	316.6
Net earnings	$ 233.4	245.1	225.5	196.6	170.0
Net earnings as a percent of sales	4.2%	4.4%	4.2%	4.1%	4.1%
Weighted average number of common shares[a][d]	46.9	50.1	50.6	50.4	50.5
Taxes (income, payroll, property, etc.) per share[a]	$ 6.22	5.70	5.88	5.99	4.66
Financial Position					
Total assets	$ 2,858.1	2,943.9	2,701.7	2,301.3	2,012.4
Land, buildings, and equipment, net	$ 1,229.4	1,197.5	1,054.1	920.6	747.5
Working capital at year end	$ 244.5	235.6	210.7	337.3	416.3
Long-term debt, excluding current portion	$ 362.6	464.0	331.9	348.6	377.5
Stockholders' equity	$ 1,224.6	1,227.4	1,232.2	1,145.4	1,020.7
Stockholders' equity per share[a]	$ 27.03	25.68	24.50	22.75	20.32
Other Statistics					
Working capital provided from operations	$ 348.3	401.6	353.6	317.8	262.7
Total dividends	$ 96.0	92.7	82.3	72.3	64.4
Gross capital expenditures	$ 282.4	308.0	287.3	246.6	196.5
Research and development	$ 63.5	60.6	53.8	45.4	44.4
Advertising media expenditures	$ 349.6	336.2	284.9	222.0	213.1
Wages, salaries, and employee benefits	$ 1,121.6	1,115.2	1,028.4	907.0	781.2
Number of employees	80,297	81,186	75,893	71,225	66,032
Accumulated LIFO charge	$ 79.7	79.7	75.5	73.7	60.3
Common stock price range[a]	$ 57$\frac{1}{8}$– 41$\frac{5}{8}$	$ 57$\frac{3}{4}$– 38$\frac{5}{8}$	$ 42$\frac{1}{8}$– 32$\frac{5}{8}$	$ 35$\frac{3}{4}$– 23$\frac{3}{8}$	$ 28$\frac{1}{4}$– 19$\frac{1}{4}$

[a] Years prior to fiscal 1976 have been adjusted for the two-for-one stock split in October 1975.

[b] Amounts not restated for vacation accrual accounting change made in fiscal 1982.

[c] Includes redeployment gains or losses.

[d] Years prior to fiscal 1983 include common share equivalents.

Source: General Mills, Inc., *Annual Report,* 1980–1984.

EXHIBIT 3 General Mills, Inc. Operating Income 1980–1985 ($ in millions, except earnings per share)

	1980	1981	% CHANGE	1982	% CHANGE	1983	% CHANGE	1984E	% CHANGE	1985E	% CHANGE
Food Processing											
Cereals and granola products	$ 90.0	$ 99.7	+ 10.8%	$128.2	+ 28.6%	$131.2	+ 2.3%	$152.0	+ 15.9%	$165.0	+ 8.6%
Snacks	38.0	40.0	+ 5.3	44.0	+ 10.0	46.0	+ 4.6	18.0	– 60.9	21.0	+ 16.7
Flour baking mixes and desserts	55.0	52.0	– 5.5	59.0	+ 13.5	57.0	– 3.4	60.0	+ 5.3	63.0	5.0
Frozen and refrigerated products	6.0	3.0	– 50.0	8.0	+166.7	10.0	+ 25.0	13.0	+ 30.0	17.0	+ 30.8
Consumer flour and commercial	21.5	23.0	+ 7.0	24.0	+ 4.4	24.0	–0–	27.0	+ 12.5	29.0	+ 7.4
Total	$210.5	$217.7	+ 3.4	$263.2	+ 20.9	$268.2	+ 1.9	$270.0	+ 0.7	$295.0	+ 9.3
Restaurants											
Red Lobster	$ 46.0	$ 70.0	+ 52.2	$ 74.2	+ 6.0	$ 73.0	– 1.6	$ 64.0	– 12.3	$ 70.0	+ 9.4
York Steak Houses	10.0	11.0	+ 10.0	12.5	+ 13.6	13.0	+ 4.0	14.0	+ 7.7	15.0	+ 7.1
Other	(3.3)	(5.7)	+ 72.7	(7.5)	+ 31.6	(6.0)	– 20.0	(3.0)	– 50.0	–0–	NM
Total	$ 52.7	$ 75.3	+ 42.9	$ 79.2	+ 5.2	$ 80.0	+ 1.0	$ 75.0	– 6.2	$ 85.0	+ 13.3
Crafts, Games, and Toys											
Parker Brothers	$ 26.0	$ 28.0	+ 7.7	$ 18.0	– 35.7	$ 43.6	+142.2	$ 10.0	– 77.1	$ 20.0	+100.0
Kenner	24.0	26.0	+ 8.3	39.0	+ 50.0	46.0	+ 18.0	50.0	+ 8.7	60.0	+ 20.0
Fundimensions	–0–	3.0	NM	4.0	+ 33.0	(3.0)	NM	(2.0)	– 33.3	3.0	NM
International	10.1	13.6	+ 34.7	18.2	+ 33.8	18.0	– 1.1	15.0	– 16.7	17.0	+ 13.3
Total	$60.1	$ 70.6	+ 17.5	$ 79.2	+ 12.2	$104.6	+ 32.1	$ 73.0	– 30.2	$100.0	+ 37.0
Apparel and Accessories											
David Crystal	$ 31.0	$ 62.5	+101.6	$ 60.0	– 4.0	$ 45.0	– 25.0	$ 27.0	– 40.0	$ 25.0	– 7.4
Monet	21.7	25.0	+ 15.2	25.0	–0–	21.9	– 12.4	23.0	+ 5.0	25.0	+ 8.7
Ship n' Shore and Other	(9.0)	–0–	NM	16.7	NM	9.0	– 46.1	10.0	+ 11.1	12.0	+ 20.0
Total	$ 43.7	$ 87.5	+100.2	$101.7	+ 16.2	$ 75.9	– 25.4	$ 60.0	– 21.0	$ 62.0	+ 3.3
Specialty retailing	26.4	13.2	– 50.0	(11.9)	NM	16.1	NM	28.0	+ 73.9	38.0	+ 35.7
Total operating profits	$393.4	$464.3	+ 18.0	$511.4	+ 10.1	$544.8	+ 6.5	$506.0	– 7.2	$580.0	+ 14.6
Unallocated expenses	28.2	32.3	+ 14.5	29.6	– 8.4	76.4[1]	+158.1	45.0	– 41.1	50.0	+ 11.1
Interest expense	48.6	57.6	+ 18.5	75.1	+ 30.4	58.7	– 21.8	60.0	+ 2.2	65.0	+ 8.3
Pretax income	316.6	374.4	+ 18.3	406.7	+ 8.6	409.7	+ 0.7	401.0	– 2.2	465.0	+ 15.9
Taxes	146.6	177.8	+ 21.3	181.2	+ 1.9	164.6	– 9.2	168.3	+ 2.2	204.5	+ 21.5
Net income	$170.0	$196.6	+ 15.6	$225.5	+ 14.7	$245.1	+ 8.7	$232.7	– 5.1	$260.5	+ 11.9
Average shares (millions)	50.4	50.4	–0–	50.6	+ 0.4	50.1	– 1.0	47.0	– 6.2	46.5	– 1.1
Earnings per share	$ 3.37	$ 3.90	+ 15.7	$ 4.46	+ 14.4	$ 4.89	+ 9.6	$ 4.95	+ 1.2	$ 5.60	+ 13.1

E—First Boston Corporation estimates.

[1] Includes $12 million of TRASOP and $15 million of currency translation losses.

Source: First Boston Corporation, *Research Progress Report*, April 3, 1984.

EXHIBIT 4 **Family Spending Patterns by Age of Head of Household: Percentage of Average Annual Expenditures by Product Category**

ITEM	AVERAGE ALL FAMILIES	UNDER 25	25–34	35–44	45–54	55–64	65 AND OVER
Food	19.4%	11.5%	15.9%	21.6%	20.5%	20.3%	22.8%
At home	17.0	9.1	13.3	18.7	18.0	18.1	21.1
Away from home	2.2	1.9	2.3	2.6	2.2	1.9	1.5
Other	0.2	0.5	0.3	0.3	0.3	0.3	0.2
Alcoholic Beverages	1.0	1.2	1.2	0.9	0.9	0.9	0.6
Tobacco	1.6	1.7	1.6	1.6	1.7	1.8	1.2
Housing	25.4	31.4	29.1	23.9	21.8	22.7	28.7
Shelter	16.2	24.5	20.3	15.2	13.4	12.9	15.8
Utilities	5.3	3.4	4.6	5.2	5.2	5.7	7.4
Other	3.9	3.5	4.2	3.5	3.2	4.0	5.5
Furnishings	5.1	5.4	6.1	5.6	4.7	4.3	4.0
Appliances	1.3	1.6	1.5	1.3	1.1	1.1	1.1
Furniture	1.8	2.3	2.4	2.1	1.6	1.2	1.1
Other	2.0	1.5	2.2	2.2	2.0	2.0	1.8
Clothing and Accessories	8.3	8.3	8.6	9.2	8.6	7.7	6.4
Men/boys	2.7	2.6	3.0	3.3	3.0	2.4	1.5
Women/girls	4.0	3.4	3.7	4.5	4.3	3.9	3.6
Materials, etc.	1.6	2.3	1.9	1.4	1.3	1.4	1.3
Transportation	20.2	25.5	20.1	19.2	22.0	21.3	14.9
Automobile	19.6	25.0	19.6	18.6	21.3	20.7	14.1
Other	0.6	0.5	0.5	0.6	0.7	0.6	0.8
Medical Care	6.1	3.8	5.1	5.1	5.7	7.0	10.2
Health insurance	2.5	1.6	2.0	1.9	2.2	3.0	4.8
Uninsured expense	3.6	2.2	3.1	3.2	3.5	4.0	5.4
Personal Care	1.3	0.5	0.8	1.2	1.4	1.7	1.7
Recreation	8.3	8.6	8.7	8.3	8.0	8.5	7.2
Vacation	3.1	2.0	2.6	2.6	3.1	3.8	4.0
Other	5.2	6.6	6.1	5.7	4.9	4.7	3.2
Reading	1.9	1.1	1.4	1.8	3.1	2.1	0.8
Other	1.3	0.9	1.2	1.4	1.4	1.6	1.4

Source: Equity Research, E. F. Hutton and Company, Inc., May 9, 1983.

EXHIBIT 5 Estimated Retail Food Dollar Sales, 1980–1982 *($ millions)*

CATEGORY	Industry			General Mills			Estimated Market Share		
	1982	1981	1980	1982	1981	1980	1982	1981	1980
Dry Packaged Foods									
RTE cereal	$3,260.0	$3,200.0	$2,420.0	$ 665.0	$ 610.0	$ 490.0	23.0%	19.1%	20.2%
Desserts	1,100.0	1,000.0	828.0	410.0	375.0	300.0	39.3	37.5	36.2
Family flour	460.0	470.0	427.0	155.0	160.0	180.0	33.7	34.0	41.2
Instant potatoes	190.0	195.0	140.0	90.0	60.0	50.0	47.4	30.8	35.7
Portable bars (granola)	220.0	200.0	104.0	145.0	110.0	45.0	65.9	55.0	43.3
Biscuit mixes	125.0	110.0	104.0	105.0	100.0	75.0	84.0	90.9	72.1
Helper dinners and casseroles	110.0	110.0	84.0	75.0	100.0	58.0	68.2	90.9	69.0
	$5,465.0	$5,285.0	$4,107.0	$1,645.0	$1,515.0	$1,198.0	30.1%	28.7%	29.2%
Frozen Foods									
Processed fish	$ 650.0	$ 650.0	$ 646.0	$ 130.0	$ 150.0	$ 140.0	20.0%	23.1%	21.7%
Pizza	780.0	950.0	667.0	50.0	40.0	25.0	6.4	4.2	3.7
	$1,430.0	$1,600.0	$1,313.0	$ 180.0	$ 190.0	$ 165.0	12.6	11.9	12.6
Refrigerated									
Yogurt	$ 550.0	$ 525.0	$ 450.0	$ 100.0	$ 80.0	$ 30.0	18.2%	15.2%	6.7%
TOTAL	$7,445.0	$7,410.0	$5,870.0	$1,925.0	$1,785.0	$1,393.0	25.8%	24.1%	23.7%

Note: European, Canadian, Foodservice and Commercial flour and seafood sales represent the remainder of annual sales.

Source: Equity Research, E. F. Hutton and Company, Inc., May 9, 1983.

EXHIBIT 6

Other Market Statistics. Sales of Toys/Games by Major Categories, 1978–1982 *(in millions of dollars—based on manufacturers' prices)*

CATEGORY	1978	1979	1980	1981	1982
Dolls and accessories	$308	$288	$308	$ 395	$ 600
Games and puzzles	534	539	601	634	569
Preschool toys and playsets	365	388	386	404	376
Electronic games (nonvideo)	112	375	476	276	371
Video games	—	—	455	1,090	2,068
Stuffed animals and puppets	243	244	268	307	282
Unpowered toy cars, trucks, boats, and planes	155	190	256	331	279
Riding toys (excluding street bicycles)	154	178	176	230	254
Space toys	187	192	167	186	158

Source: Toy Manufacturers of America in "Basic Analysis—Leisure Time," Standard & Poor's *Industry Surveys,* October 13, 1983.

Food-Away-From-Home Market, 1981–1983 *(food and drink sales, in billions of dollars)*

MARKET	R1981	R1982	% CHG. 1981–82	E1983
Commercial feeding				
Restaurants, lunchrooms	$ 39.3	$ 42.0	6.9%	$ 45.4
Limited menu restaurants	30.8	33.7	9.4	37.3
Bars and taverns	8.3	8.7	4.8	9.2
Hotel and motel restaurants	6.9	7.4	7.2	8.1
Cafeterias	2.3	2.4	4.3	2.6
Other	18.2	18.6	2.2	19.9
Total	$105.8	$112.8	6.6	122.5
Institutional feeding	18.6	19.6	5.4	20.7
Military feeding	0.7	0.7	—	0.8
Grand total	$125.1	$133.1	6.4	$144.0

E   estimated, R   revised.

Source: National Restaurant Association in "Basic Analysis—Retailing," Standard & Poor's *Industry Surveys,* January 26, 1984.

EXHIBIT 6 (Continued)

Child Population in the United States, 1983–1990 *(in thousands)*

AGE	1983	1985	% CHANGE 1983–85	1990	% CHANGE 1983–90
Under 5	17,846	18,453	+3.4%	19,198	+ 7.6%
5–9	15,960	16,611	+4.1	18,591	+16.5
10–14	17,768	16,797	−5.5	16,793	−5.5

Source: U.S. Department of Commerce, Bureau of the Census in "Current Analysis—Leisure Time," Standard & Poor's *Industry Surveys,* August 9, 1984.

Birth Statistics, 1970–1990E *(in thousands)*

YEAR	NUMBER OF BIRTHS	NUMBER OF FIRST BIRTHS	FIRST BIRTHS AS % OF TOTAL BIRTHS
1990E	3,849,000	—	—
1985E	3,826,000	—	—
1984E	3,788,000	—	—
1983E	3,614,000	—	—
1982E	3,704,000	—	—
1981	3,629,238	1,553,665	42.81
1980	3,612,258	1,545,604	42.79
1979	3,494,396	1,479,260	42.33
1978	3,333,279	1,401,491	42.05
1977	3,326,632	1,387,143	41.70
1976	3,167,788	1,324,811	41.82
1975	3,144,198	1,319,126	41.95
1974	3,159,958	1,314,194	41.59
1973	3,136,965	1,243,358	39.64
1972	3,258,411	1,289,257	39.57
1971	3,555,970	1,375,668	38.69
1970	3,731,386	1,430,680	38.34

Source: U.S. Department of Commerce, Bureau of the Census in "Current Analysis—Leisure Time," Standard & Poor's *Industry Surveys,* August 9, 1984.

EXHIBIT 7 **Comparative Financials, 1982**

	REVENUES ($ BILLIONS)	RETURN ON ASSETS	RETURN ON SALES
Food Processing			
Beatrice	$ 9.19	0.9%	0.5%
Borden, Inc.	4.11	6.6	4.0
Campbell Soup	2.95	8.3	5.1
Carnation Co.	3.38	11.4	5.6
Consolidated Foods	6.04	6.6	2.5
Dart & Kraft	10.00	6.9	3.5
General Foods	8.25	6.9	3.5
General Mills	5.55	8.9	4.4
H. J. Heinz	3.74	9.9	5.7
International Multifoods	1.11	7.5	3.2
Kellogg Co.	2.37	17.7	9.6
Nabisco Brands	5.87	8.4	5.4
Pillsbury Co.	3.68	5.8	3.8
Quaker Oats	2.71	8.1	4.4
Ralston Purina	4.80	4.4	1.9
Toys			
Coleco Ind.	$ 0.51	23.3%	8.8%
Milton Bradley Co.	0.36	6.4	5.3
Restaurants			
Chart House	$ 0.38	6.3%	4.9%
Denny's, Inc.	0.96	6.4	3.8
Victoria Station	0.11	NM	—
Apparel Manufacturers			
Manhattan Ind.	$ 0.40	4.3%	1.9%
Philips-Van Heusen	0.46	4.1	1.9
Warnaco	0.50	8.5	4.7

Source: Data compiled from various analyses in Standard & Poor's *Industry Surveys.*

IBM (A): The System/360 Decision

JAMES BRIAN QUINN, *Tuck School Dartmouth College*

The decision by the management of the International Business Machines Corp. to produce a new family of computers, called the System/360, was one of the most crucial and portentous—as well as perhaps the riskiest—business judgments of recent times. The decision committed IBM to laying out money in sums that read like the federal budget—some $5 billion over a period of four years. To launch the 360, IBM was forced into sweeping organizational changes, with executives rising and falling with the changing tides of battle. The very character of this large and influential company was significantly altered by the ordeal of the 360, and the way it thought about itself changed, too. Bob Evans, the line manager who had the major responsibility for designing this gamble of a corporate lifetime, was only half joking when he said: "We called this project 'You bet your company.' "

Evans insisted that the 360 "was a damn good risk, and a lot less risk than it would have been to do anything else, or to do nothing at all," and there is a lot of evidence to support him. . . . A long stride ahead in the technology of computers in commercial use was taken by the 360. So sweeping were the implications that it required ten years before there was enough data to evaluate the wisdom of the whole undertaking.

The new System/360 was intended to obsolete virtually all other existing computers—including those being offered by IBM itself. Thus, the first and most extraordinary point to note about this decision was that it involved a challenge to the marketing structure of the computer industry—an industry that the challenger itself had dominated overwhelmingly for nearly a decade. It was roughly as though General Motors had decided to scrap its existing makes and models and offer in their place one new line of cars, covering the entire spectrum of demand, with a radically redesigned engine and an exotic fuel. . . .

[In 1966] there were perhaps 35,000 computers in use, and it was estimated that there would be 85,000 by 1975. IBM sat astride this exploding market, accounting for something like two-thirds of the worldwide business—that is, the dollar value of general-purpose computers then installed or on order. IBM's share of this market [in 1965] represented about 77% of the company's $3.6 billion gross revenues [and $477 million of profits].

Several separate but interrelated steps were involved in the launching of System/360. Each one of the steps involved major difficulties, and taking them all meant that IBM was accepting a staggering challenge to its management capabilities. First, the 360 depended heavily on microcircuitry, an advance technology in the field of computers. In a 1952 vacuum-tube model of IBM's first generation of computers, there were about 2,000 components per cubic foot. In a second-generation machine, which used transistors instead of tubes, the figure was 5,000 per cubic foot. The System/360 model 75 computer, using hybrid microcircuitry, involved 30,000 components per cubic foot. The old vacuum-tube computer could perform approximately

Case compilation copyright © 1983 by James Brian Quinn. All sections drawn from a two-part series: T. A. Wise, "IBM's $5 Billion Gamble," and "The Rocky Road to the Marketplace," *Fortune*, September–October 1966. Copyright © 1966 Time, Inc. All rights reserved to original copyright holder. Reproduced by permission. Questions at end added by Professor Quinn. Verb tenses have been edited to clarify time relationships. Minor sections have been deleted (. . .) when peripheral.

2,500 multiplications per second; the 360 model 75 was designed to perform 375,000 per second. The cost of carrying out 100,000 computations on the first-generation model was $1.38; the 360 reduced the cost to $3\frac{1}{2}$ cents.

The second step was the provision for compatibility—that is, as the users' computer requirements grew they could move up from one machine to another without having to discard or rewrite already existing programs. Limited compatibility had already been achieved by IBM, and by some of its competitors too, for that matter, on machines of similar design but different power. But it had never been achieved on a broad line of computers with a wide range of powers, and achieving this compatibility depended as much on developing compatible programs or "software" as it did on the hardware. All the auxiliary machines—"peripheral equipment" as they are called in the trade—had to be designed so that they could feed information into or receive information from the central processing unit; this meant that the equipment had to have timing, voltage, and signal levels matching those of the central unit. In computerese, the peripheral equipment was to have "standard interface." The head of one competing computer manufacturing company acknowledges that at the time of the System/360 announcement he regarded the IBM decision as sheer folly and doubted that IBM would be able to produce or deliver a line that was completely compatible.

Finally—and this was the boldest and most perilous part of the plan—it was decided that six main units of the 360 line, originally designated models 30, 40, 50, 62, and 70, should be announced and made available simultaneously. (Models at the lower and higher ends of the line were to be announced later.) This meant that all parts of the company would have to adhere to a meticulous schedule.

UP IN MANUFACTURING, DOWN IN CASH

The effort involved in the program was enormous. IBM spent over half a billion dollars on research and development programs associated with the 360. This involved a tremendous hunt for talent: by the end of 1966, one-third of IBM's 190,000 employees had been hired since the new program was announced. Between that time, April 7, 1964, and the end of 1967, the company opened five new plants in the United States and abroad and had budgeted a total of $4.5 billion for rental machines, plant, and equipment. Not even the Manhattan Project, which produced the atomic bomb in World War II, cost so much (the government's costs up to Hiroshima are reckoned at $2 billion), nor, probably, had any other privately financed commercial project in history.

Such an effort changed IBM's nature in several ways:

> The company, which was essentially an assembler of computer components and a business-service organization, became a major manufacturing concern as well. It became the world's largest maker of integrated circuits, producing an estimated 150 million of the hybrid variety annually in the late 1960s.
>
> After some ambivalence, IBM abandoned any notion that it was simply another American company with a large foreign operation. The view now is that IBM is a fully integrated international company, in which the managers of overseas units are presumed to have the same capabilities and responsibilities as those in the U.S. The company's World Trade subsidiary stopped trying to develop its own computers; instead, it marketed the 360 overseas, and helped in the engineering and manufacturing of the 360.
>
> The company's table of organization was restructured significantly at least three times during the 360's development cycle. Several new divisions and their executives emerged, while others suffered total or partial eclipse. An old maxim of the IBM organization was that few men rose to line executive positions unless they had spent some time selling. A new group of technically oriented executives came to the forefront for the first time, diluting some of the traditional power of the marketing men in the corporation.

The Missionaries and the Scientists

Oddly enough, the upheaval at IBM went largely unnoticed. The company was able to make itself over more or less in private. It was able to do so partly because IBM is so widely assumed to be an organization in which the unexpected simply doesn't happen. Outsiders viewing IBM presume it to be a model of rationality and order—a presumption related to the company's products which are, of course, instruments that enable (and require) their users to think clearly about management.

This image of IBM, moreover, had been furthered over the years by the styles of the two Watsons. Tom Watson, Sr., combined an intense devotion to disciplined thinking with formal, rather Victorian attitudes about conduct, clothes, and courtesy. The senior Watson's hostility toward drinking, and his demand that employees dedicate themselves totally to the welfare of the corporation, created a kind of evangelical atmosphere. When Tom Watson, Jr., took over from his father in 1956, the manner and style shifted somewhat, but the missionary zeal remained—now overlaid by a new dedication to the disciplines of science. The overlay reinforced the image of IBM as a chillingly efficient organization, one in which plans were developed logically and executed with crisp efficiency. It was hard to envision the company in a gambling role.

The dimensions of the 360 gamble are difficult to state precisely. The company's executives, who are men used to thinking of risks and payoffs in hard quantitative terms, insist that no meaningful figure could ever be put on the gamble—that is, on the odds that the program would be brought off on schedule, or on the costs involved if it failed.

Outsailing the Boss

At the time, it scarcely seemed that any gamble at all was necessary. IBM was way out ahead of the competition, and looked as if it could continue smoothly in its old ways forever. Below the surface, though, IBM's organization didn't fit the changing markets so neatly anymore, and there really was, in Evans's phrase, a risk involved in doing nothing.

No one understood this more thoroughly, or with more sense of urgency, than one of the principal decision makers of the company, T. Vincent Learson. His entire career at IBM, which began in 1935, had been concerned with getting new products to market. In 1954 he was tapped by young Tom Watson as the man to spearhead the company's first big entry into the commercial computer field—with the 702 and 705 models. His success led to his promotion to vice president and group executive in 1956. In 1959 he took over both of the company's computer development and manufacturing operations, the General Products Division and the Data Systems Division.

Learson stood 6 foot 6 and was a tough and forceful personality. When he was managing any major IBM program, he tended to be impatient with staff reports and committees, and to operate outside the conventional chain of command; if he wanted to know why a program was behind schedule, he was apt to call directly on an executive at a much lower level who might help him find out. But he often operated indirectly, too, organizing major management changes without his own hands being visible to the men involved. Though he lacked the formal scientific background that is taken for granted in many areas of IBM, Learson had a reputation as a searching and persistent questioner about any proposals brought before him; executives who had not done their homework might find their presentations falling apart under his questions—and might also find that he would continue the inquisition in a way that made their failure an object lesson to any spectators. And Learson was the most vigorous supporter of the company's attitude that a salesman who had lost an order without exhausting all the resources the company had to back him up deserved to be drawn and quartered.

At IBM, Learson was known as demanding, domineering, and direct—given to calling people anywhere in the company to find out firsthand what was going on. But Learson was also known as a friendly and whimsical man who was IBM's number one cheerleader. He delighted in showing up unannounced, whether in a hospital to cheer up one of his sick secretaries or at a retirement dinner in Boston for a lady who ran a course in keypunching there when Learson was a young salesman. For all the diverging views of Learson, the man, as a top executive the degree of loyalty that Learson inspired was remarkable. Said one former executive, who was forced out of IBM, "I admire the man. He's like General Patton—someone you follow into battle."

Learson's personal competitiveness was something of a legend at IBM. It was significantly demonstrated in the Newport-to-Bermuda yacht race, in which Learson entered his own boat, the Thunderbird. He boned up on the history of the race in past years, and managed to get a navigator who had been on a winning boat three different times. He also persuaded Bill Lapworth, the famous boat designer, to be a crewman. Learson traveled personally to California to get one of the best spinnaker men available. All these competitive efforts were especially fascinating to the people at IBM because Tom Watson, Jr., also had an entry in the Bermuda race; he'd, in fact, been competing in it for years. Before the race Watson goodhumoredly warned Learson at a board meeting that he'd better not win if he expected to stay at IBM. Learson's answer was not recorded. But Learson won the race. Watson's Palowan finished twenty-fourth on corrected time.

When Learson took over the computer group he found himself supervising two major engineering centers that had been competing with each other for some time. The General Products Division's facility in Endicott, New York, produced the low-priced 1401 model, by far the most popular of all IBM's computers—or of anyone else's to that date; something like 10,000 of them had been installed by the mid-

1960s. Meanwhile, the Data Systems Division in Poughkeepsie made the more glamorous 7000 series, of which the 7090 was the most powerful. Originally, IBM had intended that the two centers operate in separate markets, but as computer prices came down in the late 1950s and as more versions of each model were offered, their markets came to overlap—and they entered a period in which they were increasingly penetrating each other's markets, heightening the feeling of rivalry. Each had its own development program, although any decision to produce or market a new computer, of course, had to be ratified at corporate headquarters. The rivalry between the two divisions was to become an element in, and be exacerbated by, the decision to produce the 360.

Both the 1401 and the 7000 series were selling well in 1960. But computer engineers and architects are a restless breed; they are apt to be thinking of improvements in design or circuitry five minutes after the specifications of their latest machines are frozen. In the General Products Division, most such thinking in 1960 and 1961 was long term; it was assumed that the 1401 would be on the market until about 1968. The thinking at the Data Systems Division concerned both long-range and more immediate matters.

A $20 Million Stretch

One of the immediate matters was the division's "Stretch" computer, which was already on the market but having difficulties. The computer had been designed to dwarf all others in size and power, and it was priced around $13,500,000. But it never met more than 70 percent of the promised specifications, and not many of them were sold. In May 1961, Tom Watson made the decision that the price of Stretch should be cut to $8 million to match the value of its performance—at which level Stretch was plainly uneconomic to produce. He had to make the decision, it happened, just before he was to fly to California and address an industry group on the subject of progress in the computer field.

Before he left for the coast, an annoyed Watson made a few tart remarks about the folly of getting involved in large and overambitious projects that you couldn't deliver on. In his speech, he admitted that Stretch was a flop. "Our greatest mistake in Stretch," he said, "is that we walked up to the plate and pointed at the left-field stands. When we swung, it was not a homer but a hard line drive to the outfield. We're going to be a good deal more careful about what we promise

in the future." Soon after he returned the program was quietly shelved; only seven of the machines were ultimately put in operation. IBM's overall loss on the program was about $20 million.

The Stretch fiasco had two consequences. One was that the company practically ignored the giant-computer field during the next two years—and thereby enabled Control Data to get a sizable headstart in the market. Customers were principally government and university research centers, where the most complex scientific problems are tackled and computers of tremendous power are required. Eventually, in 1963, Watson pointed out that his strictures against overambitious projects had not been meant to exclude IBM from this scientific market, and the company later tried to get back into it. Its entry was to be the 360–90, the most powerful machine of the new line.

A second consequence of the Stretch fiasco was that Learson and the men under him, especially those in the Data Systems Division, were under special pressure to be certain that the next big project was thought out more carefully and that it worked exactly as promised. As it happened, the project the division had in mind in 1960–1961 was a fairly ambitious one: it was for a line of computers, tentatively called the 8000 series, that would replace the 7000 series, and would also provide a limited measure of compatibility among the four models projected. The 8000 series was based on transistor technology, and therefore still belonged to the second generation; however, there had been so much recent progress in circuitry design and transistor performance that the series had considerably more capability than anything being offered by IBM at that time.

The principal sponsor of the 8000 concept was Fred Brooks, head of systems planning for the Poughkeepsie division. An imaginative, enthusiastic 29-year-old North Carolinian with a considerable measure of southern charm, Brooks became completely dedicated to the concept of the new series, and beginning in late 1960 he began trying to enlist support for it. He had a major opportunity to make his case for the 8000 program at a briefing for the division's management, which was held at Poughkeepsie in January 1961.

By all accounts, he performed well: he was relaxed, confident, informed on every aspect of the technology involved, and persuasive about the need for a change. Data Systems' existing product line, he argued, was a mixed bag. The capability of some models overlapped that of others, while still other capabilities were unavailable in any model. The 8000 series would end all this confusion. One machine was already built, cost estimates and a market forecast had been made, a pricing schedule had been completed, and Brooks proposed announcing the series late that year or early in 1962. It could be the division's basic product line until 1968, he added. Most of Brooks' audience found his case entirely persuasive.

Enter the Man from Headquarters

Learson, however, was not ready to be sold so easily. The problems with Stretch must have been on his mind, and probably tended to make him look hard at any big new proposals. Beyond that, he was skeptical that the 8000 series would minimize the confusion in the division's product line, and he wondered whether the concept might not even contribute to the confusion. Learson had received a long memorandum from his chief assistant, Don Spaulding, on the general subject of equipment proliferation. Spaulding argued that there were already too many different computers in existence, and that they required too many supporting programs and too much peripheral equipment; some drastic simplification of the industry's merchandise was called for.

With these thoughts in mind, Learson was not persuaded that Brooks' concept was taking IBM in the right direction. Finally, he was not persuaded that the company should again invest heavily in second-generation technology. Along with a group of computer users, he had recently attended a special course on industrial dynamics that was being given at the Massachusetts Institute of Technology. Much of the discussion had been over his head, he later recalled, but from what his classmates were saying he came away with the clear conviction that computer applications would soon be expanding rapidly, and that what was needed was a bold move away from "record keeping" and toward more sophisticated business applications.

There was soon direct evidence of Learson's skepticism about the 8000 series. Shortly after the briefing Bob Evans, who was then manager of processing systems in the General Products Division, was dispatched to Poughkeepsie as head of Data Systems' planning and development. He brought along a number of men who had worked with him in Endicott. Given the rivalry between the two divisions, it is not very surprising that he received a cool welcome. His subsequent attitude toward the 8000 concept ensured that his relations with Brooks would stay cool.

Evans made several different criticisms of the concept. The main one was that the proposed line was "nonhomogeneous"—that is, it was not designed throughout to combine scientific and business applications. Further, he contended that it lacked sufficient compatibility within the line. It would compound the proliferation problem. He also argued that it was time to turn to the technologies associated with integrated circuits.

Blood on the Floor

For various reasons, including timing, Brooks was opposed, and he and Evans fought bitterly for several months. At one point Evans called him and quietly mentioned that Brooks was getting a raise in salary. Brooks started to utter a few words of thanks when Evans said flatly, "I want you to know I had nothing to do with it."

In March 1961, Brooks had a chance to make a presentation to the corporate management committee, a group that included Tom Watson, his brother, A. K. Watson, who headed the World Trade Corp., Albert Williams, who was then president of the corporation (later chairman of the executive committee), and Learson. Brooks made another effective presentation, and for a while he and his allies thought that the 8000 might be approved after all.

But early in May it became clear that Evans was the winner. His victory was formalized in a meeting, at the Gideon Putnam Hotel in Saratoga, of all the key people who had worked on the 8000. There, on May 15, Evans announced that the 8000 project was dead and that he now had the tough job of reassigning them all to other tasks. In the words of one participant, "There was blood all over the floor."

Evans now outlined some new programs for the Data Systems Division. His short-term program called for an extension of the 7000 line, both upward and downward. At the lower end of the line there would be two new models, the 7040 and 7044. At the upper end there would be a 7094 and a 7094 II. This program was generally noncontroversial, except for the fact that the 7044 had almost exactly the same capabilities as a computer called Scamp, which was being proposed by another part of IBM. It would obviously make no sense to build both computers; and, as it happened, Scamp had some powerful support.

Scamp was a small scientific computer developed originally for the European market. Its principal designer was John Fairclough, a young man (he was then 30) working in the World Trade Corp.'s Hursley Laboratory, sixty miles southwest of London. The subsidiary had a sizable stake in Scamp. It had been trying for many years to produce a computer tailored to the needs of its own markets, but had repeatedly failed, and had therefore been obliged to sell American-made machines overseas.

But Scamp looked especially promising, and the subsidiary's executives, including Fairclough and A. K. Watson, were confident that it would meet American standards. It had previously tested well and attracted a fair amount of attention in IBM's American laboratories. Evans himself came to Hursley to look at it, and was impressed. But its similarity to the 7044 finally took Fairclough and some associates to the United States to test their machine against a 7044 prototype.

Mere Equality Won't Do

As things turned out, Scamp did about as well as the 7044—but, also as things turned out, that wasn't good enough. Evans and Learson were resolved to stretch out the 7000 line, but opposed to anything that would add to proliferation. In principle, A. K. Watson, who had always run World Trade as a kind of personal fiefdom, could have stepped in and ordered the production of Scamp on his own authority. In practice, he decided the argument against proliferation was a valid one. And so, in the end, he personally gave the order to drop Scamp. Fairclough got the news one day soon after he had returned to England, and he found himself with a sizable staff that had to be reassigned. He says that he considered resigning, but instead worked off his annoyance by sipping Scotch and brooding much of the night.

Evans and Learson had also agreed that Data Systems should try its hand at designing a computer line that would blanket the market. The General Products Division was asked to play a role in the new design, but its response was lukewarm, so the bulk of the work at this stage fell to Data Systems. The project was dubbed NPL, for new product line; the name System/360 was not settled on until much later. To head the project, Evans selected his old adversary Brooks—a move that surprised a large number of IBM executives, including Brooks himself.

Still smarting over the loss of the 8000 project, and suspicious that the NPL was just a "window-dressing" operation, Brooks accepted the job only tentatively. To work with him, and apparently to ensure the NPL did not end up as the 8000 under a new name, Evans brought Gene Amdahl, a crack designer whom the company had called on to work on several earlier

computers. However, Amdahl's influence was offset by That of another designer, Gerrit Blaauw, a veteran and past supporter of the 8000 project. Brooks' group received enough money to show that the company took NPL seriously (the first-year appropriation was $3,800,000), but Amdahl and Blaauw disagreed on design concepts, and the project floundered until November 1961.

Even to the trained eye IBM's main divisions appeared to be in excellent health in the summer of 1961. The General Products Division, according to Evans, was "fat and dumb and happy" in the lower end of the market, selling the 1401 at a furious rate, and still feeling secure about its line through about 1968. The World Trade Corp. was growing rapidly, although it had suffered its third major setback on getting a computer line of its own. The Data Systems Division was extending its old 7000 line to meet the competition, and working on the NPL.

THE PROLIFERATING PRODUCTS

But it was around this time that Tom Watson and Learson—then a group executive vice president, and nominally at least working under Albert Williams, the company president—developed several large concerns. There was the absence of any clear, overall concept of the company's product line; 15 or 20 different engineering groups scattered throughout the company were generating different computer products, and while the products were in most cases superior, the proliferation was putting overwhelming strains on the company's ability to supply programming for customers. The view at the top was that IBM required some major changes if it expected to stay ahead in the computer market when the third generation came along.

Between August and October 1961, Watson and Learson initiated a number of dialogues with their divisional lieutenants in an effort to define a strategy for the new era. By the end of October, though, neither of them believed that any strategy was coming into focus. At this point Learson made a crucial decision. He decided to set up a special committee, composed of representatives from every major segment of the company, to formulate some policy guidance. The committee was called SPREAD—an acronym for systems programming, research, engineering, and development. Its chairman was John Haanstra, then a vice president of the General Products Division. There were 12 other members, including Evans, Brooks, and Fairclough.

The SPREAD Committee—Fall 1961

The SPREAD Committee was conducted informally, but with a good amount of spirited discussion. For the same purposes it broke up into separate committees, such as one on programming capability. Haanstra, as one member put it, acted as a hammer on the committee anvil, forcing ideas into debate and demanding definitions. Still, there was some feeling that Haanstra was bothered by the fact that the group was heavily represented by "big machine"–oriented men.

The progress of the committee during November was steady, but it was also, in Learson's view, "hellishly slow." Suddenly Haanstra found himself promoted to the presidency of the General Products Division and Bob Evans took over as chairman of SPREAD. The committee meetings were held in the New Englander Motor Hotel, just north of Stamford, Connecticut. In effect, although not quite literally, Learson locked the doors and told the members that they couldn't get out until they had reached some conclusions.

While Evans accelerated the pace of the sessions somewhat, Fred Brooks increasingly emerged as the man who was shaping the direction of the committee recommendations. This was not very surprising, for he and his group had had a headstart in thinking out many of the issues. By December 28, 1961, the SPREAD Committee had hammered out an 80-page statement of its recommendations. On January 4, 1962, the committee amplified the report for the benefit of the 50 top executives of the corporation.

Brooks was assigned the role of principal speaker on this occasion. The presentation was split into several parts and took an entire day. The main points of the report were:

> There was a definite need for a single, compatible family of computers ranging from one with the smallest existing core memory, which would be below the 1401 line, to one as powerful as IBM's biggest—at that time the 7094. In fact, the needs were said to extend beyond the IBM range, but the report expressed doubt that compatibility could be extended that far.
>
> The new line should not be aimed simply at replacing the popular 1401 or 7000 series, but at opening up whole new fields of computer applications. At that time compatibility between those machines and the new line was not judged to be of major importance, because the original timetable on the appearance of the

various members of the new family of computers stretched out for several years.

The System/360 must have both business and scientific applications. This dual purpose was a difficult assignment because commercial machines accept large amounts of data but have little manipulative ability, while scientific machines work on relatively small quantities of data that are endlessly manipulated. To achieve duality the report decided that each machine in the new line would be made available with core memories of varying sizes. In addition, the machine would provide a variety of technical and esoteric features to handle both scientific and commercial assignments.

Information input and output equipment, and all other peripheral equipment, must have "standard interface"—so that various types and sizes of peripheral equipment could be hitched to the main computer without missing a beat. This too was to become an important feature of the new line.

Learson recalled the reaction when the presentation ended. "There were all sorts of people up there and while it wasn't received too well, there were no real objections. So I said to them, 'All right, we'll do it.' The problem was, they thought it was too grandiose. The report said we'd have to spend $125 million on programming the system at a time when we were spending only about $10 million a year for programming. Everybody said you just couldn't spend that amount. The job just looked too big to the marketing people, the financial people, and the engineers. Everyone recognized it was a gigantic task that would mean all our resources were tied up in one project—and we knew that for a long time we wouldn't be getting anything out of it."

APRIL 1964—PUBLIC ANNOUNCEMENT

When Tom Watson, Jr., made what he called "the most important product announcement in the company's history," he created quite a stir. International Business Machines is not a corporation given to making earth-shaking pronouncements casually, and the declaration that it was launching an entirely new computer line, the System/360, was headline news. The elaborate logistics that IBM worked out in order to get maximum press coverage—besides a huge assembly at Poughkeepsie, IBM staged press conferences on the same day in 62 cities in the United States and in 14 foreign countries—underscored its view of the importance of the event. And the fact that the move until then had been a closely guarded secret added an engaging element of sur-

prise. . . . In the scattered locations where IBM plans, builds, and sells its products, there was, on that evening of April 7, 1964, a certain amount of dancing in the streets. . . .

But the managerial and organizational changes that were brought about by the company's struggle to settle on, and then to produce and market, the new line [had very long-term] effects. In each of these several aspects, past, present, and future were closely intertwined.

The Rising Cost of Asking Questions

No part of the whole adventure of launching System/360 was as tough, as stubborn, or as enduring as the programming. Early in 1966, talking to a group of IBM customers, Tom Watson, Jr., said ruefully: "We are investing nearly as much in System/360 programming as we are in the entire development of System/360 hardware. A few months ago the bill for 1966 was going to be $40 million. I asked Vin Learson last night before I left what he thought it would be for 1966 and he said $50 million. Twenty-four hours later I met Watts Humphrey, who is in charge of programming production, in the hall here and said, 'Is this figure about right? Can I use it?' He said it's going to be $60 million. You can see that if I keep asking questions we won't pay a dividend this year."

Watson's concern about programming went back to the beginnings of the System/360 affair. By late 1962 he was sufficiently aware of the proportions of the question to invite the eight top executives of IBM to his ski lodge in Stowe, Vermont, for a three-day session on programming. The session was conducted by Fred Brooks, the corporate manager for the design of the 360 project, and other experts; they went into the programming in considerable detail. While the matter can become highly technical, in general IBM's objective was to devise an "operating system" for its computer line, so that the computers would schedule themselves, without manual interruption, and would be kept working continuously at or near their capacity. At the time it announced System/360, IBM promised future users that it would supply them with such a command system.

Delivery on that promise was agonizingly difficult. Even though Tom Watson and the other top executives knew the critical importance of programming, the size of the job was seriously underestimated. The difficulty of coordinating the work of hundreds of programmers was enormous. The operating system IBM was striving for required the company to work out many new ideas and approaches; as one company executive said, "We were trying to schedule inventions, which is a dangerous thing to do in a committed project." Customers came up with more extensive programming tasks than the company had expected, and there were inevitable delays and slowdowns. The difficulties of programming prevented some users from getting the full benefits from their new machines for years. The company didn't have most of the bugs out of the larger systems' programming until at least mid-1967—well behind its expectations.

The Cold Realities of Choice

In technology, IBM was also breaking new ground. During the formative years of the decisions about the technology of System/360, a lengthy report on the subject was prepared by the ad hoc Logic Committee, headed by Erich Bloch, a specialist in circuitry for IBM. Eventually, the Logic Committee report led to the company's formal commitment to a new hybrid kind of integrated-circuit technology—a move that, like many other aspects of the 360 decision, is still criticized by some people in the computer industry, both inside and outside of IBM.

The move, though, was hardly made in haste. The whole computer industry had raced through two phases of electronic technology—vacuum tubes and transistors—between 1951 and 1960. By the late 1950s it was becoming apparent that further technological changes of sweeping importance were in the offing. At that time, however, IBM was not very much of a force in scientific research, its strengths lying in the assembling and marketing of computers, not in their advanced concepts. The company's management at the time had the wit to recognize the nature of the corporate deficiency, and to see the importance of correcting it. In 1956, IBM hired Dr. Emanuel Piore, formerly chief scientist of U.S. naval research. Piore became IBM's director of research and a major figure in the technological direction that the company finally chose for its System/360.

In the end, the choice narrowed to two technologies. One was monolithic integrated circuitry: putting all the elements of a circuit—transistors, resistors, and diodes—on one chip at one time. The other was hybrid integrated circuitry—IBM rather densely termed it "solid logic technology"—which means making transistors and diodes separately and then soldering them into place. In 1961 the Logic Committee decided that the production of monolithic circuits in great quantities would be risky, and in any case would not meet the schedule for any new line of computers to be marketed by 1964.

There was little opposition to this recommendation initially, except among a few engineering purists. Later, however, the opposition strengthened. The purists believed that monolithic circuits were sure to come, and that the company in a few years would find itself frozen into a technology that might be obsolete before the investment could be recovered. However, the Logic Committee's recommendation on the hybrid approach was accepted; since that time, Watson has referred to the acceptance as "the most fortunate decision we ever made."

THE SECRETS CIRCUITS HIDE

The decision to move into hybrid integrated technology accelerated IBM's push into component manufacturing, a basic change in the character of the company. In the day of vacuum tubes and transistors, IBM had designed the components for its circuits, ordered them from other companies (a principal supplier: Texas Instruments), then assembled them to its own specifications. But with the new circuitry, those specifications would have to be built into the components from the outset. "Too much proprietary information was involved in circuitry production," said Watson. "Unless we did it ourselves, we could be turning over some of the essentials of our business to another company. We had no intention of doing that." In addition, of course, IBM saw no reason why it should not capture some of the profit from the manufacturing that it was creating on such a large scale.

The company's turn to a new technology jibed neatly with a previous decision made in 1960 by Watson at the urging of the man who was then IBM president, Al Williams, that the company should move into component manufacturing. By the time the decision to go into hybrid circuits was made, IBM already had started putting together a component manufacturing division. Its general manager was John Gibson, a Johns Hopkins Ph.D. in electrical engineering. Under Gibson, the new division won the authority, hitherto divided among other divisions of the company, to designate and to buy the components for computer hardware, along with a new authority to manufacture them when Gibson thought it appropriate.

This new assignment of responsibility was resented by managers in the Data Systems and General Products divisions, since it represented a limitation of their authority. Also, they protested that they would be unable to compare the price and quality of inhouse components with those made by an outside supplier if they lost their independence of action. But Vincent Learson, then group executive vice president, feared that if they kept their independence they would continue to make purchases outside the company, and that IBM as a consequence would have no market for its own component output. He therefore put the power of decision in Gibson's hands. IBM's board, in effect, ruled in Gibson's favor when, in 1962, it authorized the construction of a new manufacturing plant, and the purchase of its automatic equipment, at a cost of over $100 million.

Systems Design: Worldwide

While IBM was making up its corporate mind about the technology for System/360, the delegation of specific responsibilities was going ahead. Learson designated Bob Evans, now head of the Federal Systems Division, to manage the giant undertaking. Under Evans, Fred Brooks was put in charge of all the System/360 work being done at Poughkeepsie, where four of the original models were designed; he was also made manager of the overall design of the central processors. The plant at Endicott was given the job of designing the model 30, successor to the popular 1401, which had been developed there. And John Fairclough, a systems designer at World Trade, was assigned to design the model 40 at the IBM lab at Hursley, England.

Out of the Hursley experience came an interesting byproduct that had significant implications for IBM's future. With different labs engaged in the 360 design, it was vital to provide for virtually instant communication between them. IBM therefore leased a special transatlantic line between its home offices and the engineers in England, and later in Germany. The international engineering group was woven together with considerable effectiveness, giving IBM the justifiable claim that the 360 computer was probably the first product of truly international design.

In a Tug-of-War, Enough Rope to Hang Yourself

Even in a corporation inured to change, people resist change. By 1963, with the important decisions on the 360 being implemented, excitement about the new product line began to spread through the corporation—at least among those who were privy to the secret. But this rising pitch of interest by no means meant that the struggle inside the company was settled. The new family of computers cut across all the old lines of authority and upset all the old divisions. The System/360 concepts plunged IBM into an organizational upheaval.

Resistance came in only a mild form from the World Trade Corp., whose long-time boss was A. K. Watson, Tom's brother. World Trade managers always thought of European markets as very different from those in the United States, and as requiring special considerations that U.S. designers would not give them. Initially they had reservations about the concept of a single computer family, which they thought of as fitted only to U.S. needs. But when IBM laboratories in Europe were included in the formulation of the design of some of the 360 models, the grumblings from World Trade were muted. Later A. K. Watson was made vice chairman of the corporation and Gilbert Jones, formerly the head of domestic marketing of computers for the company, took over World Trade. These moves further integrated the domestic and foreign operations, and gave World Trade assurance that its voice would be heard at the top level of the corporation.

The General Products Division, for its part, really bristled with hostility. Its output, after all, accounted for two-thirds of the company's revenues for data processing. It had a popular and profitable product in the field, the 1401, which the 360 threatened to replace. The executive in charge of General Products, John Haanstra, fought against some phases of the 360 program. Haanstra thought the new line would hit his division hard. He was concerned, from the time the System/360 program was approved, about the possibility that it would undermine his division's profits. Specifically, he feared that the cost of providing compatibility in the lower end of the 360 line (which would be General Products' responsibility) might price the machines out of the market. Later he was to develop some more elaborate arguments against the program.

Long after the company's SPREAD Committee had outlined the System/360 concept, and it had been endorsed by IBM's top management, there were numerous development efforts going on inside the company that offered continuing alternatives to the concept—and they were taken seriously enough, in some cases, so that there were fights for jurisdiction over them. Early in 1963, for example, there was a row over development work at IBM's San Jose Laboratory, which belonged to the General Products Division. It turned out that San Jose—which had been explicitly told to stop the work—was still developing a low-power machine similar to the one being worked on in World Trade's German lab. When he heard about the continuing effort, A. K. Watson went to the lab, along with Emanuel Piore, and seems to have angrily restated his demand that San Jose cut it out. Some people from San Jose were then transferred to Germany to work on the German machine, and the General Products effort was stopped. In the curious way of organizations, though, things turned out well enough in the end; the German machine proved to be a good one, and the Americans who came into the project contributed a lot to its salability. With some adaptations, the machine was finally incorporated into the 360 line, and, as the model 20 it later sold better than probably any other in the series.

TOP MANAGEMENT SHIFTS

In the fall of 1963, Tom Watson . . . made some new management assignments that reflected the impact of the 360 program on the corporation. Learson was shifted away from supervising product development and given responsibility for marketing, this being the next phase of the 360 program. Gibson took over Learson's former responsibilities. The increasing development of IBM into a homogeneous international organization was reflected in the move up of A. K. Watson from World Trade to corporate vice chairman. He was succeeded by Gilbert Jones, former head of domestic marketing. Piore became a group vice president in charge of research and several other activities.

One reason for Watson's interest in speeding up the 360 program in late 1963 was an increasing awareness that the IBM product line was running out of steam. The company was barely reaching its sales goals in this period. Some of this slowdown, no doubt, was due to mounting rumors about the new line. But there was another, critical reason for the slowdown: major customers were seeking ways of linking separate data-processing operations on a national basis, and IBM had limited capability along that line. Finally, IBM got a distinctly unpleasant shock in December 1963, when the Honeywell Corp. announced a new computer. Its model 200 had been designed along the same lines as the 1401—a fact Honeywell cheerfully acknowledged—but it used newer, faster, and cheaper transistors than the 1401 and was therefore priced 30 percent below the IBM model. To make matters worse, Honeywell's engineers had figured out a means by which customers interested in reprogramming from an IBM 1401 to a Honeywell 200 could do so inexpensively. The vulnerability of the 1401 line was obvious, and so was the company's need for the new line of computers.

It was around this time that some IBM executives began to argue seriously for simultaneous introduction of the whole 360 family. There were several advantages to the move. One was that it would have a tremendous public relations impact and demonstrate the distinctive nature of IBM's new undertaking. Customers would have a clear picture of where and how they could grow with the computer product line, and so would be more inclined to wait for it. Finally, there might be an antitrust problem in introducing the various 360 models sequentially. The Justice Department might feel that an IBM salesman was improperly taking away competitors' business if he urged customers not to buy their products because of an impending announcement of his own company's new model. IBM had long had a company policy under which no employee was allowed to tell a customer of any new product not formally announced by the management. (Several employees have, in fact, been fired or disciplined for violating the rule.) Announcing the whole 360 line at once would dispose of the problem.

Learson Stages a Shoot-Out

Beginning in late 1963, then, the idea of announcing and marketing the 360 family all at once gained increasing support. At the same time, by making the 360 program tougher to achieve, the idea gave Haanstra some new arguments against the program. His opposition now centered on two main points. First, he argued that the General Products manufacturing organization would be under pressure to build in a couple of years enough units of the model 30 to replace a field inventory of the 1401 that had been installed over a five-year period. He said that IBM was in danger of acquiring a huge backlog, one representing perhaps two or three years' output, and that competitors, able to deliver in a year or less, would steal business away.

But Haanstra's argument was countered to some extent by a group of resourceful IBM engineers. They believed that the so-called "read-only" storage device could be adapted to make the 360–30 compatible with the 1401. The read-only technique, which involved the storing of permanent electronic instructions in the computer, could be adapted to make the model 30 act

like a 1401 in many respects: the computer would be slowed down, but the user would be able to employ his 1401 programs. IBM executives had earlier been exposed to a read-only device by John Fairclough, the head of World Trade's Hursley Laboratory in England, when he was trying (unsuccessfully) to win corporate approval for his Scamp computer.

Could the device really be used to meet Haanstra's objections to the 360–30? To find out, Learson staged a "shoot-out" in January 1964, between the 1401-S and the model 30. The test proved that the model 30, "emulating" the 1401, could already operate at 80% of the speed of the 1401-S—and could improve that figure with other adaptations. That was good enough for Learson. He notified Watson that he was ready to go, and said that he favored announcing the whole System/360 family at once.

"Going . . . Going . . . Gone!"

Haanstra was still not convinced. He persisted in his view that his manufacturing organization probably could not gear up to meet the production demand adequately. On March 18 and 19, a final "risk-assessment" session was held at Yorktown Heights to review once again every debatable point of the program. Tom Watson, Jr., President Al Williams, and 30 top executives of the corporation attended. This was to be the last chance for the unpersuaded to state their doubts or objections on any aspect of the new program—patent protection, policy on computer returns, the company's ability to hire and train an enormous new work force in the time allotted, and so on. Haanstra himself was conspicuously absent from this session. In February he had been relieved of his responsibilities as president of the General Products Division and assigned to special duty—monitoring a project to investigate the possibility of IBM's getting into magnetic tape. (He later became a vice president of the Federal Systems Division.) At the end of the risk-assessment meeting, Watson seemed satisfied that all the objections to the 360 had been met. Al Williams, who had been presiding, stood up before the group, asked if there were any last dissents, and then, getting no response, dramatically intoned, "Going . . . going . . . gone!"

The April 7, 1964 announcement of the program unveiled details of six separate compatible computer machines; their memories would be interchangeable, so that a total of nineteen different combinations would be available. The peripheral equipment was to consist of forty different input and output devices, including printers, optical scanners, and high-speed tape drives. Delivery of the new machines would start in April 1965.

The Nature of the Risk

The basic announcement of the new line brought a mixed reaction from the competition. The implication that the 360 line would make obsolete all earlier equipment was derided and minimized by some rival manufacturers, who seized every opportunity to argue that the move was less significant than it appeared ... [or claimed it was unfeasible or uneconomic for customers].

But some of the competition was concerned enough about the System/360 to respond to its challenge on a large scale. During the summer of 1964, General Electric announced that its 600 line of computers would have time-sharing capabilities. The full import of this announcement hit IBM that fall, when MIT, prime target of several computer manufacturers, announced that it would buy a G.E. machine. IBM had worked on a time-sharing program back in 1960 but had abandoned the idea when the cost of the terminals involved seemed to make it uneconomic. G.E.'s success caught IBM off base and in 1964 and 1965 it was scrambling madly to provide the same capability in the 360 line. Late in 1964, RCA announced it would use pure monolithic integrated circuitry (i.e., as opposed to IBM's hybrid circuitry) in some models of its new Spectra 70 line. This development probably led to a certain amount of soul-searching at IBM.

In the end, ... the company felt that the turn to monolithic circuitry did not involve capabilities that threatened the 360 line; furthermore, if and when monolithic circuitry ever did prove to have decisive advantages over IBM's hybrid circuitry, the company was prepared—the computers themselves and some three quarters of the component manufacturing equipment could be adapted fairly inexpensively to monolithics. As for time sharing, any anxieties IBM had about that were eased in March 1965, when Watts Humphrey, a systems expert who had been given the assignment of meeting the time-sharing challenge, got the job done. ...

IBM announced additions to the 360 line in 1964 and 1965. One was the model 90, a supercomputer type, designed to be competitive with Control Data's 6800. Another was the 360–44, designed for special scientific purposes. Also, there was the 360–67, a large time-sharing machine. Another, the 360–20, represented a pioneering push into the low end of the mar-

ket. None of these were fully compatible with the models originally announced, but they were considered part of the 360 family.

System/360 underwent many changes after the concept was originally brought forth back in 1962 and even after Watson's announcement in 1964. More central processors were later offered in the 360 line; some of them had memories that were much faster than those originally offered. The number of input-output machines [increased several times]. ...

"Major Reshufflements"

IBM had several managers trying to keep the 360 program on track in 1964–1965. Gibson, who had succeeded Learson in the job, was replaced late in 1964. His successor, Paul Knaplund, lasted about another year. ... In 1965 there was one item of unalloyed bad news: the company had suffered heavy setbacks at the high end of the 360 line—that is, in its efforts to bring forth a great supercomputer in the tradition of Stretch. In 1964 it wrote off $15 million worth of parts and equipment developed specifically for the 360–90.

There were signs at about this time that the 360 program was still generating other reshufflements of divisions and personnel. Dr. Piore had been freed from operational duties and responsibilities and given a license to roam the company checking on just about all technical activities. Some of his former duties were placed in a division headed by Eugene Fubini, a former Assistant Secretary of Defense and the Pentagon's deputy director of research and engineering before he joined IBM in 1965. Fubini was one of the first outsiders ever brought into the company at such a high executive level. Another change represented a comeback for Stephen Dunwell, who had managed the Stretch program and had been made the goat for its expensive failure to perform as advertised. When IBM got into the 360 program, its technical group discovered that the work done on Stretch was immensely valuable to them; and Watson personally gave Dunwell an award as an IBM fellow (which entitled him to work with IBM backing, for five years, on any project of his choosing).

In 1971 58-year-old Tom Watson, Jr., slowed by poor health, turned over the chairmanship of the company to T. Vincent Learson. While Learson was taking on the top job, computer makers were rattled by a recession and shaken by a series of corporate crises. 1970–1972 saw General Electric Co. and RCA withdraw from the field, cutting the number of U.S. computer makers from nine to seven. The industry was struck by a backlash from oversold customers, a new generation of computers, and a switch in government expenditures away from R&D and toward social services. Customers became sales resistant and cost conscious.

Business Week commented,

> The Learson era in the computer business promises to be vastly different from the preceding two decades of frantic growth, during which IBM's yearly revenues increased more than thirty-fold—from $226 million in 1951 to $8.2 billion this year. The outlook for the industry is for a lower rate of growth from a bigger base. But the growth will still be a very healthy 10% to 12% annually, depending on the state of the general economy. If IBM merely holds its present share of the market, this pace of growth would mean annual increments in its revenues of around half a billion dollars. . . .

On his sixtieth birthday in 1972, T. V. Learson surprised nearly everyone by announcing his retirement after only 18 months as chairman. Said Learson, "We believe very strongly that in a business as technical and competitive as this, the interests of IBM will be best served by management teams of younger upcoming men and women. . . ." Learson's successor as chairman, 52-year-old Frank Cary, was a quieter and more amiable executive, yet few observers felt the management shuffle heralded any significant departure from the vigorous marketing oriented practices of the Learson era.

QUESTIONS

1. What stimulated the change in strategy at the time of the 360? Evaluate the process by which change was brought about.
2. Evaluate Mr. Learson as a change manager. Why does he act this way?
3. How could other companies have taken advantage of IBM's 360 strategy? What should IBM do about these?

SONY CORPORATION

JAMES BRIAN QUINN, *Tuck School Dartmouth College*

Sony Corporation began in the rubble and chaos of Japan at the end of World War II. Its first quarters were a small corner room of a burned out department store in Tokyo's Ginza district. Masaru Ibuka (age 37) had brought along seven young engineers to start "some sort of electronics laboratory or enterprise." His earlier company, Japan Precision Instrument Co., had supplied vacuum tube voltmeters and other instruments to the now defunct war effort, and Mr. Ibuka felt an obligation to provide continued work for his people. "We realized we could not compete against companies already in existence and against products in which they specialized. We started with the basic concept that we had to do something that no other company had done before."

From these inauspicious beginnings sprang one of the world's most innovative companies with worldwide sales in 1982 of $4.53 billion. In a nation not then known for product innovation, what had led to Sony's unique capabilities? Could its successful past policies survive the ferocious competitive atmosphere of the mid-1980s? A brief history of several of Sony's most important innovations provides an interesting basis for analysis.

MEAGER BEGINNINGS

Ibuka wanted to apply a mix of electronics and engineering to the consumer field, but Japan's banks and markets were anything but encouraging to a tiny upstart with no consumer experience. In August 1945, the group's first problem was to find something to sell. The small group considered anything: bean paste soup, slide rules, an electric rice cooker Ibuka invented. Despite widespread fuel shortages, some electricity existed. Ibuka thought there was a genuine "need" for the innovative aluminum cooker. Technically it worked well—if the water levels and the rice were just right—but none sold. So Ibuka's team began to repair or modify wartime radios for a music and news hungry city. This barely enabled the company to survive as Ibuka slowly depleted his meager savings to keep his people employed during the first arduous year.

Then Akio Morita joined the company. He had been associated with Ibuka on thermal guidance and nocturnal vision projects during the war and had seen an article about his friend's shortwave adaptor and electronic repair business in October 1945. Though there was little money for a salary, Ibuka conveyed his missionary feelings about making electronics technology available to a peacetime civilian Japan. The talented Morita took a faculty appointment at the Tokyo Institute of Technology, but contributed part of his time to Ibuka's small company.

The Young Team

Like Ibuka, Morita had been an inveterate tinkerer as a child and was a descendant of a leading samurai family.

Case copyright © 1986 by James Brian Quinn. Research associates—Penny C. Paquette and Roger Wellington.

The generous support of the Adolf H. Lundin Professorship at the International Management Institute, Geneva, Switzerland, is gratefully acknowledged. The generous cooperation of Sony Corporation is gratefully acknowledged.

As a student at Waseda University, Ibuka had won patents and international awards for a system to transmit sound by modulating neon light. Morita had ghost written articles for his professors at Osaka Imperial University where he had specialized in electronics. But there the similarities ended. Ibuka had failed his employment examination for a large Japanese electric company and only got his first job through the intervention of a friend. Morita's family company awaited him whenever he was ready.

Ibuka was passionate about invention, a humanist, a dreamer in many ways. Morita was a realist who had been trained in business by his father since birth. Ibuka had little interest in accounting and the intricacies of marketing. Morita was an administrator, as well as an enthusiastic, outgoing man who could charm or spellbind an audience. The two became the closest of friends.

Early Capitalization

When Morita decided to leave the University, Ibuka took an all-night train ride to persuade the elder Morita to let his son join the fledgling company. At first the senior Morita was not impressed. Later he not only acquiesced, but invested his own funds in the new firm. The banks were reluctant to lend even short-term money, so operating funds were constantly begged from the senior Morita and from personal friends. Eventually the elder Mr. Morita became the company's largest shareholder.

On May 7, 1946, the company was formally incorporated as Tokyo Telecommunications Engineering Co. (TTK being the Japanese acronym). Since companies capitalized at over 200,000 yen encountered more difficult incorporation regulations, TTK listed the company at 198,000 yen—$500-600 in exchange value—which was not much of an exaggeration.

The Purposes of Incorporation were listed in the Prospectus along with the new company's "Management Policies." Both of these remarkable statements—little changed since then—are shown in Exhibit 1. In 1983 Sony's Chairman Morita restated some of these basic principles:

> Young people who join our company next year will stay for 25 years. So that means for them the company should be prosperous for that period. All the top people feel responsible that the company live a long, long time, rather than making a big current profit to make a very large bonus. That's why we don't pay bonuses to executives. We pay bonuses to employees because we

like for the employees to feel and participate in the company's results.

> Every year, when we receive our new graduate employees, I like to make a little speech to them. Now you have become a Sony employee. You will spend the most brilliant time of your life here. Nobody can live twice. This is the only life you can have, so I want you to become happy at Sony. If you don't feel happy, you better go out and change your job. But if you decide to stay with us, you must devote yourself to make your life happy and also to make your colleagues happy. People work together here for all of us in mutual benefit, mutual interest.*

Expansion with Umbrellas

When TTK surpassed its breakeven volume (primarily making voltmeters), Ibuka poured the cash flows into the introduction of an electrically heated cushion he had invented. TTK sold several hundred. Then Ibuka invented and produced a resonating sound generator that allowed operators trained with military telegraph equipment to hear their usual "dots and dashes" instead of the disconcerting "clicking" of the civilian systems. The American Occupation Forces (rebuilding Japan's destroyed communications systems to American standards) encountered some of TTK's equipment and were so impressed with its sophistication and quality that they began to order from the tiny company. By then TTK had expanded into some shacks in the Shinagawa district that were so dilapidated that executives had to use umbrellas during rainstorms. Nevertheless, Ibuka insisted on such rigorous design and quality standards that TTK—through clever use of a carefully developed supplier network—was soon performing almost all of Japan Broadcasting Network's (NHK's) revisions, converting its equipment to modern standards and building industrial and commercial electronic devices for other companies.

But TTK had no consumer products. Ibuka seriously considered a wire recorder, first introduced by the military in World War II. Japan's Dr. Kenzo Nagai held some key patents on the wire recorder, the device would be unique in consumer markets, and TTK had the proper skills to produce it. Ibuka was just about to commit his best resources to an onslaught on the wire recorder. Then one day as he was visiting the offices of NHK, a member of the Occupation Forces showed him a tape recorder from the United States, and history was made.

---

* All quotations not footnoted came from personal interviews with Professor Quinn.

THE TAPE RECORDER

Tape recorders were unheard of in Japan—there wasn't even a word for them. Ibuka's team quickly checked the available patents and found Dr. Nagai held a key one here as well. They rapidly purchased the rights to it, knowing they had the magnetic and electrical skills to make a good machine. But there was little published information about either magnetic tapes or recorders. In Japan there was no plastic available to produce tape and no way to acquire any plastic through Japan's stringent import regulations. The TTK team tried cellophane; it stretched. They tried paper—Ibuka made tapes in his kitchen from rice paper and a paste of boiled rice—its edges caught and broke. Finally, Morita got a cousin in a paper manufacturing company to prepare a batch of specially calendered paper with a slick surface.

Ibuka's group had to develop special techniques to cut the paper, hold it, and coat it uniformly with magnetic powder. They had to compensate for the less controllable paper base by designing extra quality into the circuitry, recording head, feed systems, and amplifiers in the recorder. It was a great struggle. The accounting manager constantly warned they were spending too much; they could bankrupt the company. Morita kept saying, "Be a little more patient and we will make a fortune." Finally after many months they created not just a new concept in tapes, but a new recorder, a new testing technology, and their own complete tape coating machine. Sony became perhaps the first company in the world to make the entire range of products from tapes to recorders, skills involving nearly a dozen basic technologies. In late 1949 they made their first unit, the G-type recorder, weighing over 100 pounds and selling for $400.

But would the device sell? Neither Ibuka nor Morita had marketing experience. After many months of effort the first unit sold to an *oden* shop—a kind of Japanese pub where people came to eat, sing, and talk noisily. Technically the expensive, cumbersome device performed well, but no one quite knew what to do with it. Ibuka's response was to take all his top engineers to an inn and work night and day to reduce the recorder's cost by 50% and to improve its size, weight, and portability. The result was a concept for a suitcase enclosed recorder at a reasonable price—and at less than one-half the G-type's weight.

As markets—at first to record NHK's English language programs for use in schools—opened, 3M began to sell its excellent magnetic tape to Japanese broadcasters and other large users. TTK tried to negotiate a license and reached a financially very attractive proposition. But in exchange for the license, 3M insisted that TTK drop its recorder manufacturing. After much consideration Morita and Ibuka said no, wanting no outside control over their product line. But this also meant TTK was now in competition with a much larger and very sophisticated world competitor, a very difficult situation for the young company.

TRANSISTOR RADIOS

In 1952 Ibuka went to the United States to explore possible markets for his tape recorder. While he was there, a U.S. friend told him that Western Electric was ready to license its transistor patent for the first time. Ibuka investigated, but when he heard the price was $25,000, he left the United States knowing the price was too much for TTK. Ibuka worried as he made the long trip home. He was convinced the transistor would revolutionize electronics, though no one then realized how. As he pondered what to do, another concern came into place. He had hired a number of young physicists. "Would tape recorders be challenge enough for them, motivate them to use their best abilities, or let them grow to their full potentials?" Ibuka was convinced they could not.

"A Pocketable Radio"

By the time Mr. Ibuka reached Tokyo, his questions had crystalized into a strategy to keep his people and his company growing. A short time later he announced, "We're going to use the transistor to make radios small enough so that each individual can carry them for his own use, but with a receiving ability that will enable civilization to reach areas that have no electric power." At that time "portable radios" weighed 10–20 pounds, were briefcase sized, and had batteries that lasted only a few hours. Ibuka spoke of a "pocketable transistor radio." But no one had applied transistors to radios—or much of anything else. The thought of a quality radio the size of a cigarette pack seemed almost beyond belief.

But Kazuo Iwama, a young geophysicist with no knowledge of transistors, was fired by Ibuka's enthusiasm. He left his job as tape recorder production head to lead the transistor task force. Morita had negotiated a license agreement with Western Electric whereunder the $25,000 patent was credited against potential future royalties. But the Ministry of International Trade and Industry (MITI) had to approve the release of the $25,000 in foreign currency. MITI was furious. If the big Japanese companies weren't interested in transistors, why should MITI support TTK? And why hadn't TTK come to MITI before any negotiations? They delayed approval for months until Ibuka's persuasiveness finally prevailed in early 1954.

Ibuka and Iwama immediately left for the United States, where they found that no one had achieved satisfactory yields on the high-frequency transistors needed for radio. Even lower-frequency transistors for hearing aids sold for $150–500. Ibuka and Iwama visited all the U.S. laboratories and plants they could, sending detailed letters to Iwama's task force each night. Months passed as the task force tried to reach the high frequencies needed for radio and the production yields required for commercial exploitation. Again the financial stability of the company was at risk as transistor program costs grew. Only an expanding tape recorder market kept it going.

Shock and a Market

Then came a shock. Texas Instruments announced the world's first transistorized radio, produced for Regency Co. In early 1955 TTK's team pulled out all stops, moving with what they had. In August they put their first radio on display. It was about $4" \times 8" \times 1\frac{1}{2}"$. They set a goal of 10,000 transistor radios in the first year and achieved 8,000. "The success of Sony is," said Iwama later, "that we produced a little less than was required. When there is enough, the market is saturated." Still Ibuka wanted a "pocketable radio." Despite the skepticism of marketing experts who thought the product would be too small, squeaky, and unreliable, Ibuka pushed on. TTK's component suppliers refused to modify their standard product lines, which were largely copied from world designs. They too were doubtful of the product's success. Ibuka single-handedly persuaded them to go ahead by offering Sony's technical support and production guidance. It was a momentous change for Japan. Japanese manufacturers had to become truly independent of foreign technology for perhaps the first time. In March 1957 the "pocketable" Type 63 radio was introduced using almost exclusively Japanese know-how. Since the Type 63 was still slightly larger than a shirt pocket, Sony made special shirts into which they would fit. Over a million Type 63s were soon sold.

Once the principle was proved, the bigger companies moved in. TTK changed its name to Sony, derived from the Latin sonis (for sound). The name had been carefully chosen to be simple, recognizable, and pronounceable in many languages. The Sony name became almost generic for transistor radios. "Sunny" and "Somy" trade names appeared and were fought off. Meanwhile, Sony had a two- to three-year technology lead and moved on to provide the world's first transistorized shortwave and FM receivers for consumers.

THE SONY SPIRIT

By now Sony was becoming known as a maverick among Japanese companies. It was not bound up in the traditions of older companies and relied as little as possible on the government or banks. Morita and Ibuka could make fast decisions, unhindered by the formalities of the ringi method of consensus building found in most larger companies. Over a single lunch Morita reached agreement with CBS for Sony to distribute CBS records in Japan. As the company grew at an amazing pace, it hired senior people away from other concerns—a practice frowned on by more traditional Japanese companies.

Some of the executives' backgrounds were unusual. Ibuka convinced Dr. Kikuchi, Sony's research head, to leave MITI after 26 years there. Shigeru Kobayashi was recruited from the printing industry, given charge of an ailing semiconductor plant, and told "do what you want." Norio Ohga—a music major destined to become a major opera baritone—was recruited upon his graduation from the university. He remained a consultant to Sony as he rose to operatic fame. When he returned from the stage—with no business training—he was made head of the tape recorder plant and rose to be a top board member of Sony. Morita and Ibuka always looked first for talent, not someone "to fill a job." Then with full trust they gave their selections a free hand. "I never knew what hidden abilities I had until I came to Sony," commented one of many so treated.

"Do Something Creative"

Sony's personnel grew over ten times in the 1950s and four times in the 1960s. Many of its personnel policies derived from its original goal to "establish an ideal factory—free, dynamic, and pleasant." To Ibuka this meant "to have fixed production and budgetary requirements but within these limits to give Sony employees the freedom to do what they want. This way we draw on their deepest creative potentials."[1]

Many more specific policies flowed from the remarkable experiences of Shigeru Kobayashi who took over Sony's Atsugi plant after its brief—and only—strike in 1961. Ibuka told Kobayashi, who knew nothing about semiconductor technology, "You are free to do there whatever you like. Try to do something truly creative." Kobayashi soon concluded the plant's problems derived from people feeling themselves insignificant there, what he called "a small pebble complex." He thought essential trust had been destroyed because management had tried to set up contrived Western methods for measuring output, increasing efficiency, and motivating people.

To eliminate cafeteria lines and to build trust Kobayashi removed all cashier attendants, letting people voluntarily place their meal coupons in appropriate boxes. He shut down the forbidding dormitories used by most Japanese companies then, built small prefabricated homes where a few employees could live together, and gave employees full autonomy over their premises. This had never been done in Japan. Next he eliminated time clocks, and created autonomy for Sony's recreation groups, moving away from the carefully controlled company teams so common in Japan.

Cells and Trust

Then Kobayashi developed a series of vertical and horizontal interconnecting teams or "cells" in the plant. Each was a specialized unit that could take charge of its own work. In these small (2 to 20 person) cells, workers could more easily develop a team spirit and help each other. Each cell would respond to input from all other cells above, below, on its sides. The cell would determine what methods to follow and evaluate its own output. Orders did not flow from above. Management's job was to assist the cells, to help them solve problems, to set overall goals, and to praise superior performances, while the cells were to control specific tasks at the workplace and group levels. The specifics of Kobayashi's "cell" system are different in each plant now, but the spirit and values it conveys continue.

In most areas, all new employees—whether law graduates or finance specialists—must spend several months on the production line learning to appreciate the company's products, practices, and culture. All engineers and scientists hired still must work in sales for several weeks or months. Promising people are shifted every two to three years to new areas to expand their knowledge and to identify their abilities for promotion. Typically workers learn several processes and are switched among tasks to keep up their interest. Production lines may be purposely segmented so they can be restructured rapidly if product mixes change. Rewards flow not to individuals, but to groups.

Morita recently said, "The best way to train a person is to give him authority. . . . We tell our young people: don't be afraid to make a mistake, but don't make the same mistake twice. If you think it is good for the company, do it. If something is wrong, I'm the man who should be accused. As CEO it's my job to take on the critics from the outside. For example, this year [1983] our profits are down, I tell my management, don't you worry about that, just do your job right."

Unlike other Japanese companies where seniority determines responsibility, young Sony employees were loaded with work and responsibility. But there was a complex "godfather system" in which a high executive watched over and specifically trained younger talent. A new executive interacted almost daily with his corporate mentor and received sophisticated insights and a corporate perspective. Mr. Morita expressed the overall philosophy this way, "Sony motivates executives not with special compensation systems but by giving them joy in achievement, challenge, pride, and a sense of recognition."

TUMMY AND OTHER TELEVISIONS

As its pocketable radio business boomed, Sony turned to all transistorized television. At first Sony's system could only drive small picture tubes, 5–8" across, but not the larger tubes then popular. When Ibuka proposed to introduce a "mini-TV," the market experts again said, "It will never sell. RCA tried it and failed. The market wants big screens." Undeterred, Ibuka introduced an 8" set in Japan (May 1960) and in the United States (June 1961). Again the road to the marketplace was complex and difficult, but Ibuka's "tummy television" sets became eminently successful.

During this rapid growth period Mr. Morita moved his family to New York so that Sony's top management would know the U.S. market, not through statistics, but through intuition. Although his wife and children could not speak English at first, he insisted that they meet and entertain Americans, enter American camps and schools. Their acculturation was rapid. Morita, himself, often helped sweep out the shabby rat-infested offices of Sony Corp. of America (Sonam), and worked 16-hour days and 7-day weeks. While joining in menial tasks, the distinguished Morita pushed Sonam to be the highest quality U.S. company. He insisted on "establishing proper servicing before distribution" and spent money to import more service engineers, rather than allowing Sonam to move into more acceptable sales headquarters in New York.

When offered a chance by a leading U.S. radio manufacturer to rebrand Sony transistor radios and have them introduced under the American company's well-accepted 50-year-old name, Morita refused. When asked how he could turn down the benefits of a fast start and 50 years' experience, Morita replied, "This is the first year of our 50 years' experience. If we do not do things ourselves, 50 years from now we will not be a great company like yours today."

"No Fun in Copying"

By 1964 color television had begun to take over the U.S. market. After some diverse experimentation, virtually every color manufacturer operated under RCA's "shadow mask" system using a triangle of three electron guns and a grid of tiny color "dots" to create color. But Ibuka said, "I could see no fun in merely copying their excellent system." In 1961 Ibuka had seen the Chromatron tube invented by Dr. O. E. Lawrence (world famous physicist and developer of the first cyclotron). The tube used a series of phosphor "stripes" to generate color, was potentially much simpler to manufacture than the shadow mask, and produced about three times the brightness of the RCA system. Sony had introduced the Chromatron in Japan, but it was plagued with defects, service costs were crushing, and losses were mounting daily on the product. Sonam was stridently pressing for a color system to sell in the United States—using the shadow mask.

Then some General Electric representatives came to license Sony a tube with three electron guns in line, not in the triangular configuration of the shadow mask. No one wanted after all their frustrations to be a mere licensee of a U.S. company, but Sony began investigating this and other possibilities. Engineering morale reached a low in the fall of 1966 after the GE approach. Ibuka came to the labs every day counseling, suggesting, experimenting, encouraging. He started small teams on different approaches in parallel and developed the backup technology for each. He quickly switched engineers from one project to another as roadblocks or leads developed for each alternative.

Ibuka said, "We must produce a product of our own. There is nothing more pitiable than a man who can't or doesn't dream. Dreams give direction and purpose to life, without which life would be mere drudgery." During this difficult period, Morita himself feared for the financial viability of the company, yet he had to calm his dealers. "Business should be considered in ten-year cycles," he explained. "If we wait and develop a unique product, we may start several years later, but we will be stronger than all the others in 10 years."

Then toward the end of 1966, a young engineer, Miyaoka, made a mistake while experimenting. Using a single gun and three cathodes, he had produced a blurred picture. "But it was a picture"—and a new concept. Intuitively, Ibuka recognized the promise of this approach and said, "This is it. This is the system to go with."

Ibuka became the project manager himself. His team often worked all night, taking a few hours off to rest on the sofa. By February they thought they had a better picture than the RCA tube, but for months they had problems with electron acceleration and control. Repeatedly experiments failed, and the engineers despaired. Finally, on October 16, 1967, the new "Trinitron" system really worked for the first time. It was a totally unique concept—using phosphor stripes, a one gun, three-beam system, and a vertical stripe aperture grille—in a market dominated worldwide by the shadow mask system.

In April Ibuka announced the Trinitron's availability in six months. The program's production head, Yoshida, didn't think that schedule was possible. He pleaded and convinced Ibuka to limit the size of the screen to 12" because of fears that the Trinitron's glass bulb might fail in larger sizes. Again teams worked until they lost track of night and day. But after 6 months the first sets rolled off the assembly line. And within a year, the Trinitron dominated the small-screen market in Japan. After at first dismissing its added brightness as a function of its small 12" size—"a clever marketing ploy" said U.S. competitors—the U.S. market responded. The Trinitron earned the first Emmy in the United States ever given to a product innovation. Although named for the prize himself, Ibuka saw that his key engineers shared in it. Sony could not catch up with world demand for the fabulously successful Trinitron until the late 1970s.

VIDEO TAPE RECORDERS

A final example, the video tape recorder (VTR), offers other insights about Sony's management of innovation. The first practical VTR, the Quadruplex, was introduced by Ampex in 1956. It set the standard for commercial television broadcasting for almost 20 years. NHK, Japan's national television network, bought a Quadruplex and (along with MITI) encouraged electronics manufacturers' engineers to become familiar with it. The "Quad" cost about $60,000 and was a complex machine filling several closet-sized equipment racks. In 1958, $3\frac{1}{2}$ months after Mr. Ibuka first saw the Ampex machine, a team under Dr. Nobutshu Kihara and Mr. K. Iwama completed an operating prototype using similar principles.

All the leading (six or seven) Japanese consumer electronics companies launched major VTR programs. In the United States, Ampex expanded its line into professional and industrial units. Philips dominated similar markets in Europe, but ignored consumer markets—perhaps because its VTR business was housed in a division with no consumer lines. No American consumer electronics company invested significantly in VTRs until after 1970, in part because their attention was riveted on surviving the 1950s and 1960s shakeout in the large U.S. TV market.

Sony Gears Up

Dr. Kihara, who headed Sony's VTR program, would later figure prominently in many of Sony's other famous innovations. When asked how Sony approached such radical innovations Dr. Kihara noted, "Mr. Ibuka would often come in with the 'seed or hint' of an idea and ask him to 'try it out.'" For example, shortly after Dr. Kihara had helped build the first VTR prototype (which would have to be priced at about 20 million yen or $55,000) Ibuka said, "We want to make commercial video recorders, can you develop one that will sell for 2 million yen ($5,500)?" After Kihara did that, Ibuka said, "Now can we make a color recorder for the home at 200,000 yen ($550)?" The complex sequence that ensued led to Sony's early preeminence in the home VTR market.

Sony's first commercial machine (in 1963) lacked Ampex's fidelity, but was one-twentieth of its size and sold for less than one-quarter of its $60,000 price. By 1965 Sony had the compact CV-2000 for $600, operating reel to reel in black and white to high commercial standards. Its U-Matic machine, the first video cassette recorder, became quite successful in commercial color markets in 1972 at $1,100. But Sony's target was the home market; its product was to be the legendary Betamax.

Early Stages

When did it all start? Mr. Ibuka says, "Around 1951–1952 I started to conceive of something called the video tape recorder; but at that time there was no TV broadcasting in Japan, there was no source to record

from. Then we started the transistor radio project, and assigned all our engineers and technicians to it. So we stopped the video tape program until 1958, when Ampex began to deliver its video tape recorder. If we had worked on it steadily, I believe we would have been able to produce the tape recorder first. Within $3\frac{1}{2}$ months (after seeing the Ampex machine) we got an image. Ampex had invented a four-head machine. We invented the one-head machine. We developed our own system. I specifically ordered Sony engineers not to develop a broadcasting machine. Many engineers wanted to imitate the Ampex machine and make a good business in the broadcast field. I strongly ordered that we would make a $500 home machine."

The first all-transistorized VTR was the Sony PV100, a two-head 2" tape machine. The biggest customers were an American medical X-ray company and American Airlines—to monitor landings. In 1965 Sony introduced its first home use VTR, the CV-2000. No formal market research studies were made. "After our experience with the micro-TV, I didn't believe the marketing research people. Merchandising and marketing people cannot envision a market that doesn't exist."

Mr. Ibuka continued, "We decided that the video tape recorder must be a cassette type. Our experience in audio said that open reel types were not good in the home market. We succeeded with the U-Matic, which was the first video cassette recorder in the world. When we decided on the U-Matic (U format) standard, Japan Victor and Matsushita agreed on it. We supplied our technology to both companies. Shortly after, we were able to come up with the Beta form of recording which is a helical system using all the space on the tape. All the relevant technologies were invented by us. We asked Matsushita to join us in that standard. But they had a license to operate with our original patent. So they denied us."

Instead, Matsushita changed the size of their cassettes for their VHS format (which depended in part on Sony's patents) so they could record twice as long, two hours. Other Japanese companies went to potential Japanese and American manufacturers to get them to join in their (VHS) standard, not Beta. They even convinced MITI to ask Sony to make the VHS format the national standard. But Sony already had some 200,000 recorders and many tapes in the marketplace. As one of the many alternatives it had looked at, Sony had actually tried the VHS format and was convinced that its BETA—meaning "full coverage" in Japanese—format was much superior. Sony stayed with the Beta system while many other Japanese companies and American consumer electronic companies adopted VHS. Zenith was the main U.S. exception.

The Design Approach

Dr. Kihara said, "My group started ten different major test options or approaches. Within these we developed two or three alternatives for each subsystem. . . . Much of the development process was trial and error. We did not have formal written plans. . . . For example, we developed a loading system with one reel and a leader, not two reels. We developed another where the wind up drum was inside the cassette. We developed the U-loading system, the M-loading system. We developed single heads, double heads, the skip system, and the asimuth system for reading and writing on the tapes. And so on. By taking the best of each option we ultimately developed Betamax."

In 1982 a development team member said, "Kihara was in charge of what kind of developments would be pursued, what systems to use. At Sony development moves fast. We make quick—but not rash—decisions. Kihara makes the decisions himself." This was reiterated. "Kihara believes there are only a few people directly involved in a new technology who have adequate information or knowledge about that technology. With new products one must create a new market. Not many people know how these new markets will develop, what a product can do, how well it will function, how it could be used by customers." Says Dr. Kihara, "We have never been told by Morita or Ibuka 'this product's sales will be this big or must make this much money.' "

"In my engineering intuition, something interesting comes to mind. I look at the unique things I can do. . . . I don't want to be a copycat. I want to be first, number one. I don't worry about marketing figures. At other companies, top executives expect their top engineers to do managerial chores. Here they do not. They give me a lot of time for development work."

"Produce Something New, Unique"

Dr. Kihara continued, "Most companies make profit the first priority. Sony's primary mission is to produce something new, unique, and innovative for the enhancement of people's lives. Technical people report right to the top of the organization. There is no formal technical committee, but many joint discussions. I like to make 'surprising reports' to Mr. Morita and Ibuka. If an idea is merely under development, I don't report it. After I obtain a working model, then I report it to Morita and Ibuka. I like to surprise the top. In the early development stages, there are typically only 5 or 6 people involved on a project team; for example in the Mavica camera there were 7 to 8. We work together until we have made a model. After we get the go ahead, the project may be expanded to perhaps 30 people."

At Sony there were no specific budgets for individual projects. Kihara reported to Morita once a year on his total budget. But most individual projects in Kihara's group were kept "beneath the surface," hidden in detail even from Morita and Ibuka. Dr. Kihara met with his younger engineers in a prolonged session at least every two months. Said Kihara, "I try to transfer my technical knowhow and to cultivate an atmosphere of innovation. The best reward system for a young engineer is the joy he gets from making products that are used and sold. The rate of new products from this area is the highest in the company. This gives the group confidence and satisfaction. Sometimes there may be some bonuses involved, but this is not as important as other things."

Research to Production

Sony consciously rotates its engineers to other divisions and back to engineering. In many large Japanese companies technology is transferred by drawings, prototypes, or production models. But in Sony people from other areas join the development team directly. They are trained on the spot by Research and Development people. Those most suited for production will go on with the project into production. This practice leaves a vacuum in development which can be filled by new people who infuse the department with fresh blood and ideas.

Dr. Kikuchi, director of research, said, "Everyone at the top has a strong interest in engineering and scientific problems and encourages people below to talk to them. And it is easy for us to talk to them. Even Sony's business people must talk technical languages, not just finance."

In 1982 Sony's President Iwama and Chairman Morita still visited the R&D labs frequently as did now honorary chairman, Ibuka. "Mr. Morita frequently telephones or brings in ideas from around the world on how to apply physics in new ways. And Mr. Ibuka visits many places in Sony randomly. After playing golf near the research center, he will drop in at the laboratory. He wants to see things, touch things. Recently he went to the laboratory and touched his tongue to a new tape compound, to taste it, to see what it was. He leaves people very excited."

There were monthly meetings between the top board and the technical section heads. But there was little calculation of projected financial ratios or returns for particular projects. Dr. Kikuchi said, "We as management must define the problems, but only with sufficient specificity to leave many directions open for technical work. The goal must be clear. It may not be expressed numerically. At first there may not even be a date attached. But it must be clear and not change easily. We let the technical leaders choose the approaches."

"Periodically, I give a crystal award' for highly evaluated work. Even if a team has lost a competition within Sony, we will still give them a crystal award if their quality of work is especially good. . . . We also may give engineers a certain percentage of a new product's first year's sales if their ideas had particular merit. The amount of money is significant, but not huge."

THE WALKMAN AND MAVICA

Through 1982, Sony continued its innovative ways. In the early 1980s two new products offered interesting examples of Sony's innovation capabilities, the Walkman sound system and the Mavica all-electronic still camera system.

As had happened so often before, the idea for Walkman (a compact cassette player with small earphones for highly portable listening) came from Ibuka and Morita. Mr. Morita, who purposely visited places where young people congregated, found that they wanted to listen to music on a very personal basis, especially if the sound was loud rock music. He also thought—as an avid golfer—that sportsmen would like a high-quality portable sound system. He gave the engineers a target of developing small high-quality earphones and a simple light tape player. When the marketing people heard of the project, they did not think such a system would sell well. They wanted to make the cassette record as well as play. Morita said, "No, Keep it small and simple." Despite marketing's skepticism, Mr. Morita was confident that there was a big market for the new concept. The Walkman sold out instantly upon introduction.

The Mavica Still Camera

In the fall of 1981, Sony had announced its revolutionary Mavica all-electronic camera for shooting still pictures. Exhibit 3 describes the way the system operated. The camera used no film or chemical developing processes. Images were recorded on a small magnetic disk called Mavipak and could be viewed immediately on a home TV set through a specially designed playback unit. The system also had a color printer called the Mavigraph which could electronically produce hard copy prints from the video signals developed by the Mavica.

The key technical developments for the system were (1) an electronic recording technique using very-high-density magnetic disks (developed in the 1960s by Sony), (2) the development of very high-quality charged couple devices (CCDs), which converted the optical image coming through the lens of the camera into a series of electrically charged spots on a semiconductor, and (3) the creation of high-density circuit boards small enough to operate the complex camera. Then the problem was to bring these together with optics into a quality system. Again there had been no market analysis on the project. "This was one of my dreams come true," said Kihara, "I wanted it to happen regardless of the marketplace."

Dr. Kihara said, "We got the original idea for the electronic still camera 25 years ago. But the technology did not exist to make it practical." Mr. Iwama, who later became president of Sony, had started the original research on the CCD around 1970. He judged the CCD to be a very important technology and backed it as one of the largest research projects Sony had in the 1970s. By 1982 the CCD was a small semiconductor device (about the size of a fingernail) on which several 100,000 individual pickup dots could convert optically focused light into individual electrical pulses.

Information from the CCD could be transferred directly to a magnetic storage device (disk or semiconductor RAM) from which the original image could be later retrieved, electronically enhanced, or eliminated to make room for another image. The resolution of individual pictures was of course limited by the density of information the camera could pick up and store. A color picture from a regular camera using regular instant film would contain about 100 million bits of information. CCDs, in 1981 could pick up about 200,000 bits of information for the same-sized black and white picture. But the density of information CCDs could pick up was doubling every two to three years, and image processing software could improve the picture's appearance even more. Electronically enhanced pictures from a 600,000-bit source would be difficult for the eye to discern from a regular film photograph.

The Mavica was no larger than a conventional 35mm single-lens reflex camera. Once its pictures were recorded on the Mavipak (or only on part of it), the disk could be removed from the camera and then inserted again with no fear of recording a new picture over a previous picture. Since the Mavipak could be erased, the memory disk could be used repeatedly with no deterioration of picture or color quality. Even small children could load a Mavipak into the camera. In 1982 a Mavipak memory medium could record 50 still color pictures. But this technology was rapidly advancing as well.

Dr. Kihara said, "Although the basic technologies were developed over the last 15 years, the real origin of the Mavica was October 1980. At that time I could see that all the technologies were available to make the idea concrete. We put a small team of seven to eight people on it. In August 1981 we unveiled the product. I did not talk to Mr. Ibuka about the Mavica in concrete form until winter 1980–1981 when I showed him the circuit board. Even then Ibuka didn't think it could be done. But we introduced the product with essentially the same circuit board." At one stage Mr. Ibuka had actually said the project should be stopped, but Dr. Kihara told his team to go ahead anyway. Dr. Kihara said Mr. Ibuka was "very fair" in his appraisal of the ultimate result.

The first official announcement of the Mavica system underlined its radical potentials: "Sony's new magnetic video still camera uses no photographic film and therefore does not require developing and printing processes which are indispensable to conventional chemical photography. This new still video camera represents an epic-making innovation in the history of still photography. For more than 104 years since the invention by Daguerre of France, there has been no fundamental change in the concept and technology of photography."

The Mavica Marketplace

The Mavica camera would move into a marketplace that was yet to be defined. Projected prices in Japan were $650 for the camera, $220 for the playback unit, and $2.60 for each magnetic disk. No price was initially announced for the printer, but it was expected to cost approximately $800–$1,000. The Mavica could also be used as a video camera. By attaching it to a portable Sony video tape recorder, one could make video films. Images could also be transmitted electronically over telephone lines. In addition, the Mavigraph allowed one to make hard copies of the graphics created on the Sony computer system, other compatible computer systems, and certain imaging equipment like Xrays, CAT scanners, or commercial graphic arts devices. While the initial image on a standard U.S. television set would be limited to the 350 horizontal lines on the tube, high-resolution screens of 1,500 lines were expected in the near future.

The investment community responded cautiously, but positively, concerning the product's impact.

In its investment report, E. F. Hutton said, "In Hutton's view, the so-called photography industry is in the path of a tidal wave of digital electronic technology. In recent decades, digital electronics has revolutionized many industries that had been based on nonelectronic processes. And the processing display of scenes/images may become one of the most important uses of digital electronics yet seen. . . . The lion's share of the [photographic] industry profits have been from the sale of consumables (photographic film, paper, and chemicals) as opposed to hardware. The consumables are chemical based, reasonably proprietary, highly profitable—with film and paper made by the mile and sold by the millimeter."[2]

In its report on the photographic and imaging industry, Smith Barney noted,

- Recent developments, including the rapid growth of electronic home movies, have raised concerns about the impact of electronic imaging on current consumer photographic systems. . . .
- Silver halide technology [which currently dominates consumer imaging] will continue to improve in film sensitivity and sharpness, and hardware will become more compact, reliable, and convenient.
- We expect electronic cameras and other hardware to be more expensive than their silver halide counterparts, but the electronic consumables or recording media will be less costly to use.
- We project a total market for consumer electronic imaging of about $4–5 billion in 1990, accounting for about 39% of total consumer imaging expenditures.[3]

Electronics had already begun to erode the Super 8 movie camera marketplace: Smith Barney summarized shipments of Super 8 movie cameras as follows:

Super 8MM Movie Cameras

YEAR	SHIPMENTS (IN THOUSANDS)
1962	838
1967	1027
1972	1043
1977	609
1978	525
1979	280
1980	230
1981	180
1982	100 (est.)

Smith Barney further estimated that "approximately 11.5 billion conventional exposures, including color negative, slide, and black-and-white films, will require the purchase of about $1.2 billion of conventional film in 1984. Developing and printing will come to about $3 billion in the same year [with reprints and enlargements adding another $0.3 billion]. In addition to nearly $150 million for instant cameras, consumers will spend about $700 million in 1984 for 900 million instant exposures. . . . The [total] still photographic market in 1984 [will be] about $8.3 billion."[4] While the U.S. consumer would expend approximately $9.1 billion in 1984 for still photography and movies (both conventional and video), the worldwide market was estimated to be about $23 billion.

In responding to the Sony announcement, Kodak's president, Mr. Chandler, said, "People like color prints, . . . more than 85% of the amateur pictures taken are prints, rather than slides, up from about 66% 10 years ago. Traditional still photographs provide better images than those from electronic cameras, which at present can be viewed only over a television screen."[5] In October 1982, Kodak demonstrated a TV display device for displaying developed negatives from its disc cameras. This unit, informally dubbed the EkTViewer, used a 350,000-element CCD chip and provided a good-quality image on television. With a 2–1 zoom device, the unit allowed cropping into any quadrant of the original image with little loss of resolution. Kodak said the display unit would probably be priced around $300–400. Others speculated that commercial extensions of the EkTViewer could allow zooming, cropping, focus adjustments, contrast changes, and shifts in color balance on the monitor. The commercial units were forecast to handle both disc and 35mm films, but would probably cost well over $1,000.

Polaroid had taken equity positions in a number of smaller companies in the high-density magnetic recording, fiber optics, ink jet printing, and continuous tone color film recording fields. Polaroid's Palette, which sold for about $1,500, was the most successful color film recorder/printer introduced in the early 1980s. This system allowed the user to output digital images from IBM, Apple, and DEC PC's and record them on either instant print or 135 film.

Several Japanese competitors were also working on similar electronic camera and print systems, but none would divulge details. Canon said that it might have an electronic camera "in 2–3 years—but maybe not for 10 years." Even Sony's chairman Morita conceded that the initial Mavica posed little threat to conventional 35 millimeter cameras, but thought the Mavica would "open up a new market." Mr. Webster of Kodak further observed, "if you tie [the Mavica] in with the work that Sony and others are doing in high definition television—with a picture that has twice as many elements in both directions, or 4 times the current resolution—then you would be getting into the realm of what would compete with 35 millimeter and Polaroid cameras." In addition, as its resolution problems were resolved, Mavica might offer substantial cost advantages for the consumer. Estimated costs for the Mavica would be only 5–10 cents per picture against 80 cents for a Polaroid shot, or 42 cents for a pocket 110 shot on Kodak film. Even then, such prices assumed that silver costs would stay around $15 an ounce and not suddenly balloon as they recently had to around $48 an ounce.

Estimated U.S. retail still camera sales were as follows:

Estimated Domestic Retail Still Camera Sales
(units and $ in millions)

	1984	1983	1984	1983
Disc	5.2	4.9	$ 230	$ 225
Cartridge (110 and 126)	3.2	3.6	65	80
Instant	3.8	3.6	145	125
35 Range-finder	3.0	2.4	375	310
35 SLR	2.6	2.7	585	635
Other	0.1	0.1	80	80
	17.9	17.3	$1480	$1455

Source: P. J. Enderlin, Smith Barney, Harris Upham & Co., Inc., Electronic Imaging—Impact on Consumer Photography, December 20, 1984.

The biggest trend in camera sales was the growth of 35mm cameras from about 3% of the amateur market in the late 1970s to over 50% in the early 1980s. Much of this gain had come at the expense of instant cameras. This reflected the impact of the lower cost, more convenient, more compact, and more reliable equipment introduced and heavily promoted by its Japanese manufacturers. The best 35mm films far exceeded the resolving power of the human eye—and film performance had recently been accelerating its already impressive historical rate of improvement.

Initially magnetic disks would offer sufficient capability to store electronic images. Kodak's 5.25" floppy disk could hold 3.3 megabytes. However, 3M estimated that with magneto-optics, a similar-size disk could hold 600 megabytes on each side. This technology was under rapid development. In estimating the potential markets for the Mavica, the sales patterns of video cassette recorders and color video cameras are instructive. See the accompanying tables.

U.S. Color Video Camera Market, 1979–1985E

YEAR	(UNITS 000)	YEAR-END PENETRATION % OF HOUSEHOLDS
1979	61	.1
1980	115	.3
1981	190	.5
1982	296	.9
1983	414	1.3
1984E	500	1.9
1985E	700	2.6

Source: P. J. Enderlin, Smith Barney, Harris Upham & Co., Inc., Electronic Imaging—Impact on Consumer Photography, December 20, 1984.

U.S. Video Cassette Recorder Market Sales to Dealers, 1975–1985E *(units 000)*

YEAR	PORTABLE -(*)	TABLE MODEL	TOTAL	YEAR-END PENETRATION % OF HOUSEHOLDS
1975			20	0.03
1977			209	0.3
1980			805	2.4
1981			1,361	4.0
1982	436	1,599	2,035	6.4
1983	750	3,341	4,091	11.1
1984E	1,000	6,000	7,000	19.1
1985E	1,200	6,800	8,000	28.2

(*)Includes camcorders.

Smith Barney estimated the breakdown of the 1984 and 1990 markets as follows:

Domestic Consumer Electronic Imaging Market, 1984 vs. 1990 *($ billions)*

	1990	1984
Still photography		
Silver halide	$11.0	$8.3
Electronic	1.0	0
Movies		
Silver halide	0	.1
Electronic	3.5	.7
Total consumer imaging	$15.5	$9.1
Total electronic	$ 4.5	$ .7
% electronic	29%	8%

Source: P. J. Enderlin, Smith Barney, Harris Upham & Co., Inc., Electronic Imaging—Impact on Consumer Photography, December 20, 1984.

As the mid 1980s emerged, most experts predicted a genuine revolution in the photographic and imaging industries led by new electronic and electro-optical technologies. The question was where Mavica would fit into this revolution and how each of the major players would respond to the challenge?

At this same time Sony was again about to pioneer with the first introduction of a compact disk (laser optical) audio record player which could record 100 billion bits of information on its 5" disk and a small 8mm hand-held video camera (CAMCORDER) which could threaten all existing amateur (Super 8) film systems.

ISSUES FOR THE FUTURE

Despite these exciting developments, Sony's financial performance slowed markedly in the mid '80s. Mr. Morita, under fire from the press and investment analysts, had to review Sony's posture in the light of changing world electronic markets and determine how to position the company and its newest cluster of revolutionary products for the 1990s. Exhibit 4 shows Sony's mid 1980s financial position and product portfolio. Exhibit 5 shows the basic Mavica system and its potential extensions. The Polaroid case offers additional information on camera and imaging markets.

QUESTIONS

1. What are the most critical policies and practices which made Sony so innovative as a company? Can they be transferred to other companies? What problems do they pose for Sony?

2. How does Sony compare and contrast with conventional views of "the Japanese management style"? How did it compare and contrast with the American approach to "entrepreneurship" when it was a small company?

3. What overall strategy should Sony have followed in the late '80s? Why?

4. How should Mavica fit into that strategy? What should be the specific strategy for introduction of Mavica? Why?

EXHIBIT 1
Sony Corporation

PURPOSES OF INCORPORATION

- The establishment of an ideal factory—free, dynamic, and pleasant—where technical personnel of sincere motivation can exercise their technological skills to the highest levels.

- Dynamic activities in technology and production for the reconstruction of Japan and the elevation of the nation's culture.

- Prompt application of the highly advanced technology developed during the war in various sectors to the life of the general public.

- Making rapidly into commercial products the superior research results of universities and research institutes, which are worth applying to the daily lives of the public.

MANAGEMENT POLICIES

- We shall eliminate any untoward profit-seeking, shall constantly emphasize activities of real substance, and shall not seek expansion of size for the sake of size.

- Rather, we shall seek a compact size of operation through which the path of technology and business activities can advance in areas that large enterprises, because of their size, cannot enter.

- We shall be as selective as possible in our products and will even welcome technological difficulties. We shall focus on highly sophisticated technical products that have great usefulness in society, regardless of the quantity involved. Moreover, we shall avoid the formal demarcation between electricity and mechanics, and shall create our own unique products coordinating the two fields with a determination that other companies cannot overtake.

- Utilizing to the utmost the unique features of our firm, which shall be known and trusted among the acquaintances in the business and technical worlds, we shall open up through mutual cooperation our production and sales channels and our acquisition of supplies to an extent equal to those of large business organizations.

- We shall guide and foster subcontracting factories in directions that will help them become independently operable and shall strive to expand and strengthen the pattern of mutual help with such factories.

- Personnel shall be carefully selected, and the firm shall be comprised of as small a number as feasible. We shall avoid mere formal position levels and shall place our main emphasis on ability, performance, and personal character, so that each individual can show the best in ability and skill.

Source: Sony Corporation of America.

EXHIBIT 2 Milestones in VTR Product Development

MARKET	MODEL	COMPANY	DATE OF COMMERCIAL INTRODUCTION	TAPE WIDTH*	TAPE UTILIZATION (SQ. FT./HOUR)	PRICE (IN CONSTANT 1967 $)
Broadcast	VR–1000	AMPEX	1956	2"	747	$60,000
Professional	VR–1500	AMPEX	1962	2"	375	12,000
Industrial	PV–100	SONY	1962	2"	212	13,000
Industrial/professional	EL–3400	PHILIPS	1964	1"	188	3,500
Industrial/professional	CV–2000	SONY	1965	$\frac{1}{2}$"	90	600
Industrial/professional	N–1500	PHILIPS	1972	$\frac{1}{2}$"	70	1,150
Industrial/professional	U-Matic	SONY	1972	$\frac{3}{4}$"	70	1,100
Consumer	Betamax	SONY	1975	$\frac{1}{2}$"	20	850
Consumer	VHS	JVC	1976	$\frac{1}{2}$"	16	790
Consumer	VR2020	PHILIPS	1980	$\frac{1}{2}$"	6	520

* From 1972 onward, all models used cassettes instead of open reels and all used high-energy tape.

Source: Sony company records.

EXHIBIT 3
Perspective View of Mavica

Source: Sony Corporation.

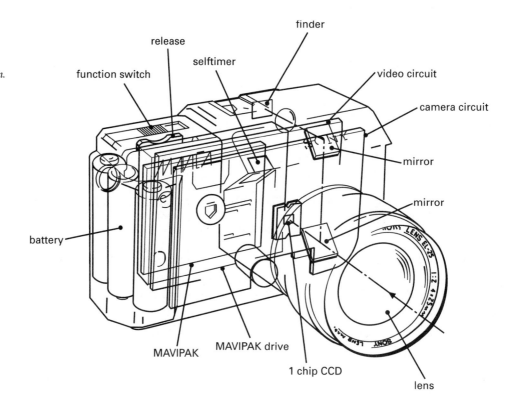

484

EXHIBIT 4 Sony Corporation (Sony Kabushiki Kaisha) Financials
Consolidated Ten-Year Summary, 1973–1982

Millions of yen except per share amounts (thousands of U.S. dollars except per share amounts)

	1982	1981	1980	1979	1978	1977	1976	1975	1974	1973
Net sales										
Overseas	¥829,665/ $3,372,622	¥744,775	¥610,545	¥394,554	¥320,085	¥310,721	¥272,455	¥224,248	¥198,939	¥148,653
Domestic	¥284,157/ $1,155,110	306,266	282,218	248,901	214,832	195,303	191,073	185,362	198,112	165,408
Total	¥1,113,822/ $4,527,732	1,051,041	892,763	643,455	534,917	506,024	463,528	409,610	397,051	314,061
Operating income	¥109,584/ $445,464	142,589	117,245	74,719	30,766	56,445	61,974	42,644	53,880	48,079
Income before income taxes	¥85,542/ $347,732	132,731	116,748	41,272	52,378	64,363	64,388	39,187	46,414	49,159
Income taxes	¥45,871/ $186,468	69,652	53,026	26,960	29,387	32,985	35,625	22,415	23,693	24,656
Net income	¥45,820/ $186,260	66,901	68,643	17,716	25,874	34,898	30,926	16,893	22,518	25,134
Per depositary share	¥198.67/ $0.81	291.67	318.34	82.16	120.00	161.85	143.42	78.34	106.55	121.40
Depreciation	¥48,229/ $196,053	32,421	24,703	20,086	15,844	12,992	10,778	10,850	10,298	7,586
Net working capital	¥195,240/ $793,859	181,362	137,188	84,265	97,272	89,162	90,840	89,296	64,612	38,892
Capital investment (additions to fixed assets)	¥112,091/ $455,654	98,089	48,715	38,916	37,604	33,732	16,169	12,468	25,878	35,825
Shareholders' equity	¥474,592/ $1,929,236	425,765	325,523	263,349	251,024	230,541	201,034	174,421	160,115	119,988
Per depositary share	¥2,057.72/ $8.36	1,856.20	1,509.67	1,221.33	1,164.17	1,069.18	932.33	808.91	757.66	579.56
Total assets	¥1,240,355/ $5,042,093	1,152,655	877,413	763,907	618,854	552,138	509,859	423,123	416,681	344,194
Average number of shares (in thousands of shares)	230,639	229,375	215,625	215,625	215,625	215,625	215,625	215,625	211,328	207,031
Number of issued shares (as of end of fiscal year)	230,714	230,625	215,625	215,625	215,625	215,625	215,625	172,500	172,500	132,500
Number of employees	43,126	38,555	32,821	30,607	27,112	25,881	22,713	22,108	21,635	20,600

Notes: (1) Each Depository Share represents 1 share of Common Stock. Per share amounts are based on the average number of shares outstanding during each period, adjusted for all stock distributions. (2) 1981 amounts have been restated using FASB 52, as described in Note 1 of Notes to Consolidated Financial Statements. (3) U.S. dollar amounts for fiscal 1982 are translated for convenience from yen at the rate of ¥246 = U.S. $1, the Tokyo foreign exchange market rate as of December 14, 1982, as described in Note 3 of Notes to Consolidated Financial Statements.

Source: Sony Corporation, *Annual Report*, 1982.

EXHIBIT 4
(Continued)

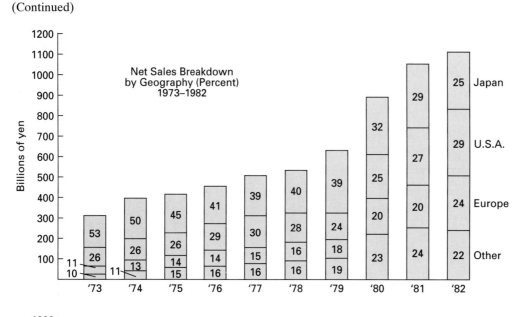

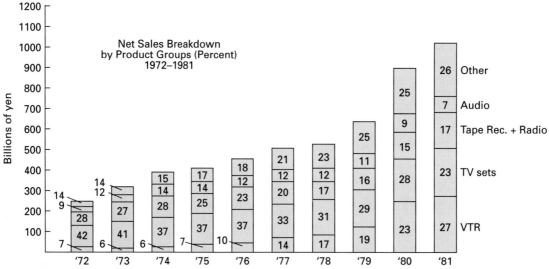

Note: In 1982 Sony changed its product groupings as follows: (1) Video Equipment (VTRs, video cameras, video tapes*, etc.); (2) Television Sets (color, black and white, projection*, etc.); (3) Audio Equipment (Hi-Fi audio products, tape recorders and radios, audio tapes*, etc.); (4) Others (Business Machines, etc.). The starred items were previously in the "Other" category. In 1982 Sony provided the following net sales breakdown by product groups:

	PERCENT OF NET SALES			
	VIDEO	TV	AUDIO	OTHER
1981	34	26	29	11
1982	43	23	23	11

Source: Sony Corporation, SEC Form 20F, 1981 and 1982.

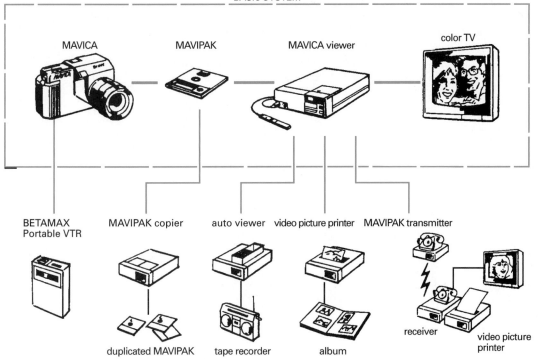

BASIC SYSTEM

MAVICA   MAVIPAK   MAVICA viewer   color TV

BETAMAX Portable VTR   MAVIPAK copier   auto viewer   video picture printer   MAVIPAK transmitter

duplicated MAVIPAK   tape recorder   album   receiver   video picture printer

EXHIBIT 5   **Mavica System**

Source: Sony Corporation.

487

W. L. Gore & Associates, Inc.

Frank Shipper, *Salisbury State University*
Charles C. Manz, *Arizona State University*

"To make money and have fun."
W. L. Gore

THE FIRST DAY ON THE JOB

On July 26, 1976 Jack Dougherty, a newly minted M.B.A. from the College of William and Mary bursting with resolve, dressed in a dark blue suit, reported to his first day at W. L. Gore & Associates. He presented himself to Bill Gore, shook hands firmly, looked him in the eye, and said he was ready for anything.

What happened next was one thing for which Jack was not ready. Gore replied, "That's fine, Jack, fine. Why don't you look around and find something you'd like to do." Three frustrating weeks later he found that something, dressed in jeans, loading fabric into the mouth of a machine that laminates the company's patented GORE-TEX membrane to fabric. By 1982, Jack had become responsible for all advertising and marketing in the fabrics group. This story is part of the folklore that is heard over and over about W. L. Gore. Today the process is slightly more structured. New Associates take a journey through the business before settling into their own positions, regardless of the specific position for which they are hired. A new sales Associate in the Fabric Division may spend six weeks rotating through different areas before beginning to concentrate on sales and marketing. Among other things he may learn is how GORE-TEX fabric is

made; what it can and cannot do; how Gore handles customer complaints; and how it makes its investment decisions.

Anita McBride related her early experience at W. L. Gore & Associates this way:

> Before I came to Gore I had worked for a structured organization and I came here, and for the first month it was fairly structured because I was going through training and this is what we do and this is how Gore is and all of that, and I went to Flagstaff for that training. After a month I came down to Phoenix and my sponsor said, "Well, here's your office," it's a wonderful office and, "Here's your desk," and walked away. And I thought now what do I do, you know? I was waiting for a memo or something, or a job description. Finally after another month I was so frustrated, I felt what have I gotten myself into and so I went to my sponsor and I said "What the heck do you want from me? I need something from you," and he said, "If you don't know what you're supposed to do, examine your commitment, and opportunities."

BACKGROUND

W. L. Gore & Associates is a company that evolved from the late Wilbert L. Gore's experiences personally,

Case by Frank Shipper, Salisbury State University, and Charles C. Manz, Arizona State University. Copyright 1992.

The authors gratefully acknowledge the assistance of Anita McBride, Trish Hearn, and Dave McCarter, W. L. Gore Associates who shared their personal experiences as well as ensured that the case accurately reflected the Gore company and culture.

organizationally and technically. He was born in Meridian, Idaho (near Boise) in 1912. He claimed that by age six he had become an avid hiker in the Wasatch Mountain Range in Utah. In those mountains, at a church camp, he met Genevieve, his future wife. She is called Vieve by everyone. In 1935, they got married; in their eyes, it was a partnership. He would make breakfast and she would make lunch. The partnership lasted a lifetime.

Gore received both a Bachelor of Sciences degree in chemical engineering in 1933 and a Masters of Sciences in Physical Chemistry in 1935 from the University of Utah. He began his professional career at American Smelting and Refining in 1936. He moved to Remington Arms Company in 1941. He moved once again to E. I. DuPont de Nemours in 1945. He held positions of research supervisor and head of operations research. While at DuPont he worked on a team to develop applications for polytetrafluoroethylene, frequently referred to as PTFE in the scientific community and known as "Teflon" by DuPont's consumers. (It is known by consumers under other names from other companies.) On this team Wilbert Gore, called Bill by everyone, felt a sense of excited commitment, personal fulfillment, and self-direction. He followed the development of computers and transistors and felt that PTFE had the ideal insulating characteristics for use with such equipment.

He tried a number of ways to make a PTFE coated ribbon cable without success. A breakthrough came in his home basement laboratory. He was explaining the problem to his son, Bob. Bob saw some PTFE sealant tape made by 3M and asked his father, "Why don't you try this tape?" His father then explained to his son that everyone knows you cannot bond PTFE to itself. Bob went on to bed.

Bill Gore remained in his basement lab and proceeded to try what everyone knew would not work. At about 4 a.m., he woke up his son waving a small piece of cable around saying excitedly, "It works, it works." The following night father and son returned to the basement lab to make ribbon cable coated with PTFE.

For the next four months Bill Gore tried to persuade DuPont to make a new product—PTFE coated ribbon cable. By this time in his career Bill Gore knew some of the decision makers at DuPont. After talking to a number of decision makers it became clear that DuPont wanted to remain a supplier of raw materials and not a fabricator.

Bill began to discuss with his wife, Vieve, the possibility of starting their own insulated wire and cable business. On January 1, 1958, their wedding anniversary, they founded W. L. Gore & Associates. The basement of their home served as their first facility. After finishing dinner on their anniversary, Vieve turned to her husband of 23 years and said, "Well, let's clear up the dishes, go downstairs, and get to work." They viewed this as another partnership.

Bill Gore was 45 years old with five children to support when he left DuPont. He left behind a career of 17 years, and a good and secure salary. To finance the first two years of the business they mortgaged their house and took $4000 from savings. All of their friends told them not to do it.

The first few years were rough. In lieu of salary some of their employees accepted room and board in the Gore home. At one point 11 Associates[1] were living and working under one roof. The order which was almost lost that put the company on a profitable footing came from the City of Denver's water department. One afternoon, Vieve answered a phone call while sifting PTFE powder. The caller indicated that he was interested in the ribbon cable, but wanted to ask some technical questions. Bill was out running some errands. The caller asked for the product manager. Vieve explained that he was out at the moment. Next he asked for the sales manager and finally, the president. Vieve explained that they were also out. The caller became outraged and hollered, "What kind of company is this anyway?" With a little diplomacy the Gores were able eventually to secure an order for $100,000. This order put the company over the hump and it began to take off.

W. L. Gore & Associates has continued to grow and develop new products primarily derived from PTFE, including its best known product, GORE-TEX fabric.[2] In 1986, Bill Gore died while backpacking in the Wind River Mountains of Wyoming. Before he died he had become chairman and, his son Bob had become president, a position he continues to occupy. Vieve remains as the only other officer, secretary-treasurer.

THE OPERATING COMPANY

W. L. Gore & Associates is a company without titles, hierarchy, or any of the conventional structures associated with enterprises of its size. The titles of president and secretary-treasurer are used only because they are required by the laws of incorporation. In addition, Gore is not a company that prohibits a corporate wide mission or code of ethics statement, but neither does

Gore require or prohibit business units from developing such statements for themselves. Thus, the Associates of some business units who have felt a need for such statements have developed them for themselves. The majority of business units within Gore do not have such statements. When questioned about this issue one Associate stated, "The company belief is that (1) its four basic operating principles cover ethical practices required of people in business; (2) it will not tolerate illegal practices." Gore's management style has been referred to as un-management. The organization has been guided by Bill's experiences on teams at DuPont and has evolved as needed.

For example, in 1965 W. L. Gore & Associates was a thriving and growing company with a facility on Paper Mill Road in Newark, Delaware with about 200 Associates. One warm Monday morning in the summer, Bill Gore was taking his usual walk through the plant. All of a sudden he realized that he did not know everyone in the plant. The team had become too big. As a result, the company has a policy that no facility will have over 150–200 Associates. Thus was born the expansion policy of "Get big by staying small." The purpose of maintaining small plants is to accentuate a close-knit and interpersonal atmosphere.

Today, W. L. Gore & Associates consists of 44 plants worldwide with over 5300 Associates. In some cases the plants are clustered together on the same site as in Flagstaff, Arizona with four plants on the same site. Twenty-seven of those plants are in the United States and 17 are overseas. Gore overseas plants are located in Scotland, Germany, France, and Japan, manufacturing electronics, medical, industrial, and fabric products.

Gore electronic products are found in unconventional places where conventional products will not do. In space shuttles, for example, Gore wire and cable assemblies withstood the heat of ignition and the cold of space. In addition, they are found in fast computers, transmitting signals at up to 93% of the speed of light. Gore cables are even underground, in oil drilling operations, and undersea, on submarines that require superior microwave signal equipment and no-fail cables that can survive high pressure. The Gore electronic products division has a history of anticipating future customer needs with innovative products. Gore electronic products are well known in industry for their ability to last under adverse conditions.

In the medical arena, GORE-TEX expanded PTFE is considered an ideal replacement for human tissue in many situations. In patients suffering from cardiovascular disease, the diseased portion of arteries are often replaced by tubes of expanded PTFE that are strong, biocompatible, and able to carry blood at arterial pressures. Gore has a dominant share in this market. Other Gore medical products include patches that can literally mend broken hearts by patching holes and repairing aneurysms, a synthetic knee ligament that provides stability by replacing the natural anterior cruciate ligament, and sutures that allow for tissue attachment and offer the surgeon silk-like handling coupled with extreme strength. In 1985, W. L. Gore & Associates, Inc. won Britain's Prince Philip Award for Polymers in the Service of Mankind. The award recognized especially the life-saving achievements of the Gore medical products team.

The industrial products division produces a number of products including sealants; filter bags, cartridges, and clothes; and coatings. These products tend to have specialized and critical applications. Gore's reputation for quality appears to influence the industrial purchasers of these products.

The Gore fabrics division, which is the largest division, supplies laminates to manufacturers of foul weather gear, ski wear, running suits, footwear, gloves, and hunting and fishing garments. Fire fighters and U.S. Navy pilots wear GORE-TEX fabric gear. So do some Olympic athletes. And the U.S. Army has adopted a total garment system built around a GORE-TEX fabric component.

GORE-TEX membrane has nine billion pores randomly dotting each square inch and is feather light. Each pore is 700 times larger than a water vapor molecule, yet thousands of times smaller than a water droplet. Wind and water cannot penetrate the pores, but perspiration can escape. As a result, fabrics bonded with GORE-TEX membrane are waterproof, windproof, and breathable. The laminated fabrics bring protection from the elements to a variety of products—from survival gear to high-fashion rain wear. Recently, other manufacturers including 3M have brought out products to compete with GORE-TEX fabrics. Gore, however, continues to have a commanding share of this market.

Bill Gore wanted to avoid smothering the company in thick layers of formal "management." He felt that they stifled individual creativity. As the company grew, he knew that a way had to be devised to assist new people to get started and to follow their progress. This was seen as particularly important when it came to compensation. W. L. Gore & Associates has developed what they call their "sponsor" program to meet these needs. When people apply to Gore, they are initially screened by personnel specialists as in most companies.

For those who meet the basic criteria, there are interviews with other Associates. Before anyone is hired, an Associate must agree to be their sponsor. The sponsor is to take a personal interest in the new Associate's contributions, problems, and goals. The sponsor is both a coach and an advocate. The sponsor tracks the new Associate's progress, helping and encouraging, dealing with weaknesses and concentrating on strengths. Sponsoring is not a short-term commitment. All Associates have sponsors and many have more than one. When individuals are hired initially, they will have a sponsor in their immediate work area. If they move to another area, they will have a sponsor in that work area. As Associates' responsibilities grow they may acquire additional sponsors.

Because the sponsoring program looks beyond conventional views of what makes a good Associate, some anomalies occur in the hiring practices. Bill Gore has proudly told the story of "a very young man" of 84 who walked in, applied, and spent five very good years with the company. The individual had 30 years of experience in the industry before joining Gore. His other Associates had no problems accepting him, but the personnel computer did. It insisted that his age was 48. The individual success stories at Gore come from diverse backgrounds.

An internal memo by Bill Gore described three kinds of sponsorship expected and how they might work as follows:

1. The sponsor who helps a new Associate *get started* on this job. Also, the sponsor who helps a present Associate get started on a new job (starting sponsor).
2. The sponsor who sees to it the Associate being sponsored *gets credit* and recognition for contributions and accomplishments (advocate sponsor).
3. The sponsor who sees to it that the Associate being sponsored is *fairly paid* for contributions to the success of the enterprise (compensation sponsor).

   A single sponsor can perform any one or all three kinds of sponsorship. A sponsor is a friend and an Associate. All the supportive aspects of the friendship are also present. Often (perhaps usually) two Associates sponsor each other as advocates.

In addition to the sponsor program Gore Associates are asked to follow four guiding principles:

1. Try to be fair.
2. Use your freedom to grow.
3. Make your own commitments, and keep them.
4. Consult with other Associates prior to any action that may adversely affect the reputation or financial stability of the company.

The four principles are often referred to as Fairness, Freedom, Commitment and Waterline. The waterline terminology is drawn from an analogy to ships. If someone pokes a hole in a boat above the waterline, the boat will be in relatively little real danger. If someone, however, pokes a hole below the waterline, the boat is in immediate danger of sinking.

The operating principles were put to a test in 1978. By this time the word about the qualities of GORE-TEX fabric were being spread throughout the recreational and outdoor markets. Production and shipment had begun in volume. At first a few complaints were heard. Next some of the clothing started coming back. Finally, much of the clothing was being returned. The trouble was that the GORE-TEX fabric was leaking. Waterproof was one of the two major properties responsible for GORE-TEX fabric's success. The company's reputation and credibility were on the line.

Peter W. Gilson who led Gore's fabric division says, "It was an incredible crisis for us at that point. We were really starting to attract attention, we were taking off—and then this." Peter and a number of his Associates in the next few months made a number of those below the waterline decisions.

First, the researchers determined that oils in human sweat were responsible for clogging the pores in the GORE-TEX fabric and altering the surface tension of the membrane. Thus, water could pass through. They also discovered that a good washing could restore the waterproof property. At first this solution known as the "Ivory Snow Solution" was accepted.

A single letter from "Butch," a mountain guide in the Sierras, changed the company's position. Butch wrote how he had been leading a group and, "My parka leaked and my life was in danger." As Gilson says, "That scared the hell out of us. Clearly our solution was no solution at all to someone on a mountain top." All of the products were recalled. As Gilson says, "We bought back, at our own expense, a fortune in pipeline material. Anything that was in the stores, at the manufacturers, or anywhere else in the pipeline."

In the meantime, Bob Gore and other Associates set out to develop a permanent fix. One month later, a second generation GORE-TEX fabric had been developed. Gilson, furthermore, told dealers that if at any time a customer returned a leaky parka, they should replace it and bill the company. The replacement program alone cost Gore roughly $4 million.

FIGURE 1
The Lattice Structure

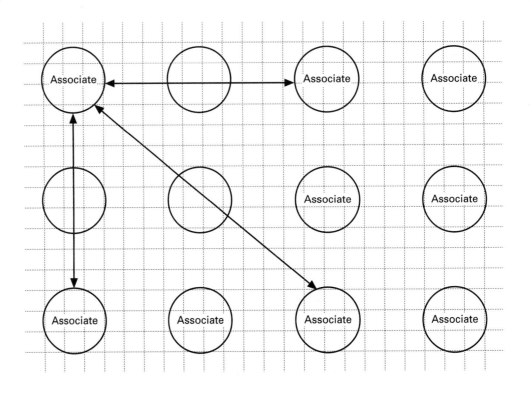

ORGANIZATIONAL STRUCTURE

W. L. Gore & Associates has not only been described as un-managed, but also as unstructured. Bill Gore referred to the structure as a lattice organization. A lattice structure is portrayed in Figure 1. The characteristics of this structure are:

1. Lines of communication are direct—person to person—with no intermediary
2. No fixed or assigned authority
3. Sponsors, not bosses
4. Natural leadership defined by followership
5. Objectives are set by those who must "make them happen"
6. Tasks and functions organized through commitments.

The structure within the lattice is described by the people at Gore as complex and evolves from interpersonal interactions, self-commitment to group-known responsibilities, natural leadership, and group-imposed discipline.

Bill Gore once explained this structure by saying, "Every successful organization has an underground lattice. It's where the news spreads like lightning, where

people can go around the organization to get things done." Another description of what is occurring within the lattice structure is constant cross-area teams—the equivalent of quality circles going on all the time. When a puzzled interviewer told Bill that he was having trouble understanding how planning and accountability worked, Bill replied with a grin, "So am I. You ask me how it works, every which way."

The lattice structure does have some similarities to traditional management structures. For instance, a group of 30 to 40 Associates who make up an advisory group meets every six months to review marketing, sales, and production plans. As Bill Gore has conceded, "The abdication of titles and rankings can never be 100%."

One thing that might strike an outsider in the meetings and the other places in Gore organization is the informality and amount of humor. Meetings tend to be only as long as necessary. As Trish Hearn, an Associate in Newark, Delaware, said, "No one feels a need to pontificate." Words such as "responsibilities" and "commitments," are, however, commonly heard. This is an organization that seems to take what it does very seriously, but its members do not take themselves too seriously.

Gore, for a company of its size, may have the shortest organizational pyramid. The pyramid consists of Bob Gore, the late Bill Gore's son, as President, and

Vieve, Bill Gore's widow, as secretary-treasurer. All the other members of the Gore organization are referred to as Associates. Words such as employees, subordinates, and managers are taboo in the Gore culture.

Gore does not have any managers, but it does have many leaders. Bill Gore described in an internal memo the kinds of leadership and the role of leadership as follows:

1. The Associate who is recognized by a team as having a special knowledge, or experience (for example, this could be a chemist, computer expert, machine operator, salesman, engineer, lawyer). This kind of leader gives the team *guidance in a special area.*

2. The Associate the team looks to for coordination of individual activities in order to achieve the agreed upon objectives of the team. The role of this leader is to persuade team members to *make the commitments* necessary for success (commitment seeker).

3. The Associate who proposes necessary objectives and activities and seeks agreement and team *consensus on objectives.* This leader is perceived by the team members as having a good grasp of how the objectives of the team fit in with the broad objective of the enterprise. This kind of leader is often also the "commitment seeking" leader in 2. above.

4. The leader who evaluates relative contribution of team members (in consultation with other sponsors) and reports these contribution evaluations to a compensation committee. This leader may also participate in the compensation committee on relative contribution and pay and *reports changes in compensation* to individual Associates. This leader is then also a compensation sponsor.

5. The leader who coordinates the research, manufacturing and marketing of one product type within a business, interacting with team leaders and individual Associates who have commitments regarding the product type. These leaders are usually called *product specialists.* They are respected for their knowledge and dedication to their products.

6. *Plant leaders* who help coordinate activities of people within a plant.

7. *Business leaders* who help coordinate activities of people in a business.

8. *Functional leaders* who help coordinate activities of people in a "functional" area.

9. *Corporate leaders* who help coordinate activities of people in different businesses and functions and who try to promote communication and cooperation among all Associates.

10. *Intrapreneuring Associates* who *organize new teams* for new businesses, new products, new processes, new devices, new marketing efforts, new or better methods of all kinds. These leaders invite other Associates to "sign up" for their project.

It is clear that leadership is widespread in our lattice organization and that it is continually changing and evolving. The situation that leaders are frequently *also* sponsors should not confuse that these are different activities and responsibilities.

Leaders are not authoritarians, managers of people, or supervisors who tell us what to do or forbid us doing things; nor are they "parents" to whom we transfer our own self-responsibility. However, they do often advise us of the consequences of actions we have done or propose to do. Our actions result in contributions, or lack of contribution, to the success of our enterprise. Our pay depends on the magnitude of our contributions. This is the basic discipline of our lattice organization.

Many other aspects are arranged along egalitarian lines. The parking lot does not have any reserved parking spaces except for customers and the handicapped. There is only one area in each plant in which to eat. The lunchroom in each new plant is designed to be a focal point for Associate interaction. As Dave McCarter of Phoenix explains, "The design is no accident. The lunchroom in Flagstaff has a fireplace in the middle. We want people to like to be here." The location of the plant is also no accident. Sites are selected based on transportation access, a nearby university, beautiful surroundings, and climate appeal. Land cost is never a primary consideration. McCarter justifies the selection by stating, "Expanding is not costly in the long-run. The loss of money is what you make happen by stymieing people into a box."

Not all people function well under such a system, especially initially. For those accustomed to a more structured work environment, there are adjustment problems. As Bill Gore said, "All our lives most of us have been told what to do, and some people don't know how to respond when asked to do something—and have the very real option of saying no—on their job. It's the new Associate's responsibility to find out what he or she can do for the good of the operation." The vast majority of the new Associates, after some initial floundering, adapt quickly.

For those who require more structured working conditions and cannot adapt, Gore's flexible work place is not for them. According to Bill for those few, "It's an unhappy situation, both for the Associate and the sponsor. If there is no contribution, there is no paycheck."

As Anita McBride, an Associate in Phoenix, says, "It's not for everybody. People ask me do we have turnover, and yes we do have turnover. What you're seeing looks like utopia, but it also looks extreme. If you finally figure the system it can be real exciting. If you can't handle it you gotta go. Probably by your own choice, because you're going to be so frustrated."

In rare cases an Associate "is trying to be unfair,"

in Bill's own words. In one case the problem was chronic absenteeism and in the other the individual was caught stealing. "When that happens, all hell breaks loose," said Bill Gore. "We can get damned authoritarian when we have to."

Over the years, Gore & Associates have faced a number of unionization drives. The company neither tries to dissuade an Associate from attending an organizational meeting nor retaliates when flyers are passed out. Each attempt has been unsuccessful. None of the plants have been organized to date. Bill believed that no need exists for third-party representation under the lattice structure. He asked the question, "Why would Associates join a union when they own the company? It seems rather absurd."

Overall, the Associates appear to have responded positively to the Gore system of un-management and un-structure. Bill estimated the year before he died that, "The profit per Associate is double" that of DuPont.

The lattice structure is not without its critics. As Bill Gore stated, "I'm told from time to time that a lattice organization can't meet a crisis well because it takes too long to reach a consensus when there are no bosses. But this isn't true. Actually, a lattice, by its very nature works particularly well in a crisis. A lot of useless effort is avoided because there is no rigid management hierarchy to conquer before you can attack a problem."

The lattice has been put to the test on a number of occasions. For example, in 1975, Dr. Charles Campbell, the University of Pittsburgh's senior resident, reported that a GORE-TEX arterial graft had developed an aneurysm. An aneurysm is a bubble-like protrusion that is life-threatening. If it continues to expand, it will explode. Obviously, this kind of problem has to be solved quickly and permanently.

Within only a few days of Dr. Campbell's first report, he flew to Newark to present his findings to Bill and Bob Gore and a few other Associates. The meeting lasted two hours. Dan Hubis, a former policeman, who had joined Gore to develop new production methods, had an idea before the meeting was over. He returned to his work area to try some different production techniques. After only three hours and twelve tries, he had developed a permanent solution. In other words, in three hours a potentially damaging problem to both patients and the company was resolved. Furthermore, Hubis's redesigned graft has gone on to win widespread acceptance in the medical community.

Other critics have been outsiders who had problems with the idea of no titles. Sarah Clifton, an Associate at the Flagstaff facility, was being pressed by some outsiders as to what her title was. She made one up and had it printed on some business cards—SUPREME COMMANDER. When Bill Gore learned what she did, he loved it and recounted the story to others.

Another critic, Eric Reynolds, founder of Marmot Mountain Works Ltd. of Grand Junction, Colorado, and a major Gore customer, "I think the lattice has its problems with the day-to-day nitty-gritty of getting things done on time and out the door. I don't think Bill realizes how the lattice system affects customers. I mean after you've established a relationship with someone about product quality, you can call up one day and suddenly find that someone new to you is handling your problem. It's frustrating to find a lack of continuity." He goes on to say, "But I have to admit that I've personally seen at Gore remarkable examples of people coming out of nowhere and excelling."

Bill Gore was asked a number of times if the lattice structure could be used by other companies. His answer was, "No. For example, established companies would find it very difficult to use the lattice. Too many hierarchies would be destroyed. When you remove titles and positions and allow people to follow who they want, it may very well be someone other than the person who has been in charge. The lattice works for us, but it's always evolving. You have to expect problems." He maintained that the lattice system works best when put in place in start-up companies by dynamic entrepreneurs.

RESEARCH AND DEVELOPMENT

Research and development, like everything else at Gore, are unstructured. There is no formal Research and Development Department. Yet the company holds many patents, although most inventions are held as proprietary or trade secrets. Any Associate can ask for a piece of raw PTFE, known as a silly worm, with which to experiment. Bill Gore believed that all people had it within themselves to be creative.

The best way to understand how research and development works is to see how inventiveness has previously occurred at Gore. By 1969, the wire and cable division was facing increased competition. Bill Gore began to look for a way to straighten out the PTFE molecules. As he said, "I figured out that if we ever unfold those molecules, get them to stretch out straight, we'd have a tremendous new kind of material." He thought that if PTFE could be stretched, air could be introduced into its molecular structure. The result would be greater volume per pound of raw material without affecting performance. Thus, fabricating costs would be reduced and the profit margins would be increased. Going about this search in a scientific manner with his son, Bob, the Gores heated rods of PTFE to various temperatures and then slowly stretched them. Regardless of the temperature or how carefully they stretched them the rods broke.

Working alone late one night in 1969 after countless failures, Bob in frustration yanked at one of the rods violently. To his surprise, it did not break. He tried it again and again with the same results.

The next morning Bob demonstrated his breakthrough to his father, but not without some drama. As Bill Gore recalled, "Bob wanted to surprise me so he took a rod and stretched it slowly. Naturally, it broke. Then he pretended to get mad. He grabbed another rod and said, 'Oh the hell with this,' and gave it a pull. It didn't break—he'd done it." The new arrangement of molecules changed not only the wire and cable division, but led to the development of GORE-TEX fabric and what is now the largest division at Gore, plus a host of other products.

Initial field-testing of GORE-TEX fabric was conducted by Bill and Vieve in the summer of 1970. Vieve made a hand-sewn tent out of patches of GORE-TEX fabric. They took it on their annual camping trip to the Wind River Mountains in Wyoming. The very first night in the wilderness, they encountered a hail storm. The hail tore holes in the top of the tent, but the bottom filled up like a bathtub from the rain. As Bill Gore stated, "At least we knew from all the water that the tent was waterproof. We just need to make it stronger, so it could withstand hail."

The second largest division began on the ski slopes of Colorado. Bill was skiing with his friend Dr. Ben Eiseman of the Denver General Hospital. As Bill Gore told the story, "We were just about to start a run when I absentmindedly pulled a small tubular section of GORE-TEX out of my pocket and looked at it. 'What is that stuff?' Ben asked. So I told him about its properties. 'Feels great,' he said, 'What do you use it for?' 'Got no idea,' I said. 'Well give it to me,' he said, 'and I'll try it in a vascular graft on a pig.' Two weeks later, he called me up. Ben was pretty excited. 'Bill,' he said, 'I put it in a pig and it works. What do I do now?' I told him to get together with Pete Cooper in our Flagstaff plant, and let them figure it out." Now hundreds of thousands of people throughout the world walk around with GORE-TEX vascular grafts.

Every Associate is encouraged to think, experiment, and follow a potentially profitable idea to its conclusion. For example, at a plant in Newark, Delaware, a machine that wraps thousands of feet of wire a day was designed by Fred L. Eldreth, an Associate with a third grade education. The design was done over a weekend. Many other Associates have contributed their ideas through both product and process breakthroughs.

Without a Research and Development Department innovations and creativity work very well at Gore & Associates. The year before he died, Bill Gore claimed that, "The creativity, the number of patent applications and innovative products is triple . . ." that of DuPont.

ASSOCIATE DEVELOPMENT

As Ron Hill, an Associate in Newark, said, Gore " . . . will work with Associates who want to advance themselves." Associates are offered many in-house training opportunities. They do tend to be technical and engineering focused because of the type of organization Gore is, but the company also offers in-house programs in leadership development. In addition, the company has cooperative programs with their Associates to obtain training through universities and other outside providers. Gore will pick up most of the costs for the Associates. The emphasis in Associate development, as in many parts of Gore, is that the Associate must take the initiative.

PRODUCTS

The products that Gore makes are arranged into four divisions—electronics, medical, industrial, and fabrics. The Electronic Products Division produces wire and cable for various demanding applications in aerospace, defense, computers, and telecommunications. The wire and cable products have earned a reputation for unequaled reliability. Most of the wire and cable is used where conventional cables cannot operate. For example, Gore wire and cable assemblies were used in the space shuttle Columbia because they would stand the heat of ignition and the cold of space. Gore wire was used in the moon vehicle shuttle that scooped up samples of moon rocks and Gore's microwave coaxial assemblies have opened new horizons in microwave technology. Back on earth, the electrical wire products help make the world's fastest computers possible because electrical signals can travel through them at up to 93% of the speed of light. Because of the physical properties of the GORE-TEX material used in their construction, the electronic products are used extensively in defense systems, electronic switching for telephone systems, scientific and industrial instrumentation, microwave communications and industrial robotics. Reliability is a watchword for all Gore products.

In medical products, reliability is literally a matter of life and death. GORE-TEX expanded PTFE is an ideal material used to combat cardiovascular disease. When human arteries are seriously damaged or plugged with deposits that interrupt the flow of blood, the diseased portions can often be replaced with GORE-TEX artificial arteries. GORE-TEX arteries and patches are not rejected by the body because the patient's own tissues grow into the graft's open porous spaces. GORE-TEX vascular grafts come in many sizes to restore circulation to all areas of the body. They have saved limbs from amputation and saved lives. Some of the tiniest grafts relieve pulmonary problems in newborns. GORE-TEX expanded PTFE is also used to help people with kidney disease. Associates are developing a variety of surgical reinforcing membranes, known as GORE-TEX cardiovascular patches, which can literally mend broken hearts, by patching holes and repairing aneurysms.

Through the waterproof Fabrics Division, Gore technology has traveled to the roof of the world on the backs of renowned mountaineers. GORE-TEX fabric is waterproof and windproof, yet breathable. Those features have qualified GORE-TEX fabric as essential gear for mountaineers and adventurers facing extremely harsh environments. The PTFE membrane blocks wind and water, but allows sweat to escape. That makes GORE-TEX fabric ideal for anyone who works or plays hard in foul weather. Backpackers have discovered that a single lightweight GORE-TEX fabric shell will replace a poplin jacket and a rain suit, and dramatically out-perform both. Skiers, sailors, runners, bicyclists, hunters, fishermen and other outdoor enthusiasts have also become big customers of garments made of GORE-TEX fabric. General sportswear, as well as women's fashion footwear and handwear, of GORE-TEX fabric are as functional as they are beautiful. Boots and gloves, both for work and recreation, are waterproof thanks to GORE-TEX liners. GORE-TEX garments are even becoming standard items issued to many military personnel. Wetsuits, parkas, pants, headgear, gloves and boots keep the troops warm and dry in foul weather missions. Other demanding jobs also require the protection of GORE-TEX fabric because of its unique combination of chemical and physical properties.

The GORE-TEX fibers products, like the fabrics, end up in some pretty tough places. The outer protective layer of the NASA's spacesuit is woven from GORE-TEX fibers. GORE-TEX fibers are in many ways the ultimate in synthetic fibers. They are impervious to sunlight, chemicals, heat and cold. They are strong and uniquely resistant to abrasion.

Industrial filtration products, such as GORE-TEX filter bags, reduce air pollution and recover valuable solids from gases and liquids more completely than alternatives; they also do it more economically. They could make coal burning plants completely smoke free, contributing to a cleaner environment. Other divisions also serve the needs of industry.

Industrial Products Division also produces joint sealant, a flexible cord of porous PTFE that can be applied as a gasket to the most complex shapes, sealing them to prevent leakage of corrosive chemicals, even at extreme temperature and pressure. Steam valves packed with GORE-TEX valve stem packing are guaranteed for the life of the valve when used properly.

The coatings division applies layers of PTFE to steel castings and other metal articles by a patented process. Called Fluroshield[3] protective coatings, this fluorocarbon polymer protects processing vessels in the production of corrosive chemicals.

GORE-TEX microfiltration products are used in medical devices, pharmaceutical manufacturing, and chemical processing. These membranes remove bacteria and other microorganisms from air or liquids, making them sterile and bacteria-free.

COMPENSATION

Compensation at W. L. Gore & Associates takes three forms—salary, profit sharing, and an Associates' Stock Ownership Program (ASOP).[4] Entry level salary is in the middle for comparable jobs. According to Sally Gore, daughter-in-law of the founder, "We do not feel we need to be the highest paid. We never try to steal people away from other companies with salary. We want them to come here because of the opportunities for growth and the unique work environment." Associates' salaries are reviewed at least once a year and more commonly twice a year. The reviews are conducted by a compensation team for most workers in the facility in which they work. The sponsors for all Associates act as their advocate during this review process. Prior to meeting with the compensation committee the sponsor checks with customers or whoever uses the results of the person's work to find out what contribution has been made. In addition, the evaluation team will consider the Associate's leadership ability, willingness to help others to develop to their fullest.

Besides salaries W. L. Gore & Associates has profit sharing and ASOP plans for all Associates. Profit sharing typically occurs twice a year, but is profitability dependent. The amount is also dependent on time in service and annual rate of pay. In addition, the firm buys company stock equivalent to 15% of the Associates' annual income and places it in an (ASOP) retirement fund. Thus, an Associate becomes a stockholder after being at Gore for one year. Bill wanted all Associates to feel that they are themselves the owners.

The principle of commitment is seen as a two-way street. W. L. Gore & Associates tries to avoid layoffs. Instead of cutting pay, which is seen at Gore as disastrous to morale, the company has used a system of temporary transfers within a plant or cluster of plants, and voluntary layoffs.

MARKETING STRATEGY

Gore's marketing strategy is based on making the determination that it can offer the best valued products to a marketplace, that people in that marketplace appreciate what it manufactures, and that Gore can become a leader in that area of expertise. The operating procedures used to implement the strategy follow the same principles as other functions at Gore.

First, the marketing of a product revolves around a leader who is referred to as a product champion. According to Dave McCarter, "You marry your technology with the interests of your champions as you got to have champions for all these things no matter what. And that's the key element within our company. The product champion, or I should say without a product champion you can't do much anyway, so it is individually driven. If you get a person interested in a particular market or a particular product for the marketplace, then there is no stopping them."

Second, a product champion is responsible for marketing the product through commitments with sales representatives. Again according to Dave McCarter, "We have no quota system. Our marketing and our sales people make their own commitments as to what their forecasts are. There is no person sitting around telling them that that is not high enough, you have to increase it by 10 percent, or whatever somebody feels is necessary. You are expected to meet your commitment, which is your forecast, but nobody is going to tell you to change it. . . . There is no order of command, no chain involved. These are groups of independent people who come together to make unified commitments to do something and sometimes when they can't make those agreements . . . You may pass up a market place, . . . but that's o.k. because there's much more advantage when the team decides to do something."

Third, the sales representatives are on salary. They are not on commission. They participate in the profit sharing and ASOP plans in which all other Associates participate.

As in other areas of Gore, the individual success stories come from diverse backgrounds. Dave McCarter related one of these success stories as follows:

I interviewed Sam one day. I didn't even know why I was interviewing him actually. Sam was retired from AT&T. After 25 years, he took the golden parachute, and went down to Sun Lakes to play golf. He played golf a few months and got tired of that. He was selling life insurance.

I sat reading the application; his technical background interested me. . . . He had managed an engineering department with 600 people. He'd managed manufacturing plants for AT&T and had a great wealth of experience at AT&T. He said, "I'm retired. I like to play golf but I just can't do it every day so I want to do something else. Do you have something around here I can do?" I was thinking to myself, this is one of these guys I would sure like to hire but I don't know what I would do with him. The thing that triggered me was the fact that he said he sold insurance and here is a guy with a high degree of technical background selling insurance. He had marketing experience, international marketing experience. So, the bell went off in my head that we were trying to introduce a new product into the marketplace that was a hydrocarbon leak protection cable. You can bury it in the ground and in a matter of seconds it could detect a hydrocarbon (gasoline, etc.). I had a couple of other guys working on it who hadn't been very successful with marketing it. We were having a hard time finding a customer. Well, I thought that kind of a product would be like selling insurance. If you think about it, why should you protect your tanks? It's an insurance policy that things are not leaking into the environment. That has implications, big time monetary. So, actually, I said, "Why don't you come back Monday? I have just the thing for you." So he did. We hired him; he went to work, a very energetic guy. Certainly a champion of the product, he picked right up on it, ran with it single handed. . . . Now it's a growing business. It certainly is a valuable one too for the environment.

In the implementation of its marketing strategy, Gore relies on cooperative and word-of-mouth advertising. Cooperative advertising is especially used to promote GORE-TEX fabric products. Those products are sold through a number of clothing manufacturers and distributors, including Apparel Technologies, Lands End, Austin Reed, Timberland, Woolrich, North Face, Grandoe, and Michelle Jaffe. Gore engages in cooperative advertising because the Associates believe positive experiences with any one product will carry over to purchases of other and more GORE-TEX fabric products. Apparently, this strategy is paying off. Richard Zuckerwar, President of The Grandoe Corporation, said about his company's introduction of GORE-TEX gloves, "Sports activists have had the benefit of GORE-TEX gloves to protect their hands from the elements. . . . With this handsome collection of gloves . . . you can have warm, dry hands without sacrificing style."

The power of informal marketing techniques extends beyond consumer products. According to Dave McCarter, "In the technical end of the business, company reputation probably is most important. You have to have a good reputation with your company." He went on to say that without a good reputation, a company's products would not be considered seriously by many industrial customers. In other words, the sale is often made before the representative calls. Using its marketing strategies, Gore has been very successful in securing a market leadership position in a number of areas ranging from waterproof outdoor clothing to vascular grafts.

FINANCIAL INFORMATION

W. L. Gore is a closely held private corporation. Financial information is as closely guarded as proprietary information on products and processes. About 90% of the stock is owned by Associates who work at Gore.

According to Shanti Mehta, an Associate, Gore's return on assets and sales rank it among the top 10% of the Fortune 500 companies. According to another source, W. L. Gore & Associates is working just fine by any financial measure. It has had 31 straight years of profitability and positive return on equity. The compounded growth rate for revenues at W. L. Gore & Associates from 1969–1989 was over 18% discounted for inflation.[5] In 1969 total sales were about $6 million and in 1990, $660 million. This growth has been financed without debt.

PUBLIC SOURCES OF INFORMATION

Aburdene, Patricia, and John Nasbitt, *Re-inventing the Corporation,* New York: Warner Books, 1985.

Angrist, S. W., "Classless Capitalists," *Forbes,* May 9, 1983, pp. 123–24.

Franlesca, L., "Dry and Cool," *Forbes,* August 27, 1984, p. 126.

Hoerr, J., "A Company Where Everybody Is the Boss," *Business Week,* April 15, 1985, p. 98.

Levering, Robert, *The 100 Best Companies to Work for in America,* Chapter on W. L. Gore & Associates, Inc.

McKendrick, Joseph, "The Employees as Entrepreneur," *Management World,* January 1985, p. 12–13.

Milne, M. J., "The Gorey Details," *Management Review,* March 1985, pp. 16–17.

Price, Kathy, "Firm Thrives Without Boss," *AZ Republic,* February 2, 1986.

Posner, B. G., "The First Day on the Job," *Inc.,* June 1986, pp. 73–75.

Rhodes, Lucien, "The Un-manager," *Inc.,* August 1982, p. 34.

Simmons, J., "People Managing Themselves: Un-management at W. L. Gore Inc." *The Journal for Quality and Participation,* December 1987, pp. 14–19.

"The Future Workplace," *Management Review,* July 1986, p. 22–23.

Trachtenberg, J. A., "Give Them Stormy Weather," *Forbes,* March 24, 1986, Vol. 137, No. 6, pp. 172–74.

Ward, Alex, "An All-Weather Idea," *The New York Times Magazine,* November 10, 1985, Sec. 6.

Weber, Joseph, "No Bosses. And Even 'Leaders' Can't Give Orders," *Business Week,* December 10, 1990, pp. 196–97.

"Wilbert L. Gore," *Industry Week,* October 17, 1983, pp. 48–49.

NATIONAL WESTMINSTER BANK USA

CHARLES SMITH, *Hofstra University*

INTRODUCTION

When Bill Knowles, then an executive vice president at Bankers Trust, New York, was first called by a corporate headhunter in 1981 with an offer to become the chief executive officer (CEO) of National Bank of North America (NBNA), Knowles said he wasn't interested.

Two years earlier, NBNA had been acquired by National Westminster Bank Group, a London-based international financial institution with assets of more than $110 billion. NBNA was the result of more than 20 mergers and acquisitions in the 1950's and 60's, structured around MeadowBrook National Bank, a well-run bank that had built a strong presence on Long Island and expanded into New York City and Westchester. However, over a period of many years, NBNA was reputed to have become bureaucratic, depersonalized and lacking in direction.

Knowles' initial response had no doubt been influenced by how NBNA had been known to be a marginal bank in the very competitive New York marketplace. No doubt his hesitation was reinforced by his strong roots in Bankers Trust, where he was well compensated, recognized as successful, and having as secure a career position as one can ask for.

However, Knowles was intrigued by NBNA's need for strategic planning and cultural redirection, and understood that its new parent bank would be willing to give him a relatively free hand and the space he needed to run things as he saw fit.

Eventually he reconsidered the offer and ac-

cepted the job, later confessing that he was also excited by the challenge of a "David and Goliath" situation: NBNA being eleventh in size among New York City banks and heading for direct competition in some markets with Chase, Chemical Bank and Citibank, the industry's giants. He had a hope, which has since become a conviction, that the bank could become a dynamic organization, a good place to work, and that it would outperform its competitors in target markets.

THE EARLY DAYS: SYSTEMS IN PLACE AND INITIAL CHANGES

In his first few months at NBNA, Knowles listened and observed. For one thing, he found himself with a lot of good people and saw some changes already under way. But he also found that the bank badly needed a clear mission, and a strong corporate culture. Its markets needed to be defined more clearly, and, from the customers' perspective, working with the bank needed to become simpler and more straightforward. The bank was run through a complex set of checks and balances, and most decisions were made by committees that met almost continuously. A bureaucratic system allowed for little risk-taking and encouraged political behavior,

This case was prepared by Dr. Charles Smith, Hofstra University.

This case was written based upon information furnished publicly and via interview with William T. Knowles of National Westminster Bank USA. The author wishes to thank NatWest USA for their cooperation, and to indicate that the information here is presented for classroom discussion rather than to illustrate effective or ineffective handling of an administrative situation.

while control was in the hands of the auditors and staff functionaries.

NatWest USA President Bob Wallace recalled some of the early problems:

> ... Our good calling officers were frustrated by rules that seemed designed to guard the bank against its own customers. Endless procedural crosschecks made it difficult to put a loan on the books. The emphasis had been on control, rather than on service, and line officers couldn't present the bank nor themselves in a positive manner. There were attitude problems. In one instance, a senior officer held up approval of a floor plan for the relocation of his division until he succeeded in adding three feet to his own office. Little kingdoms flourished. There was poor communication between groups, even when it was necessary for the conduct of business. Information was viewed as a source of power and wasn't shared freely.
>
> Clerical employees got no consideration at all. Several of us were shown the site of a processing operation. It was a room without windows, with inadequate lighting, and the paint was peeling off the walls. The officer in charge took pride that it had a low occupancy expense, and was shocked when we told him it would have to be corrected immediately.
>
> ... Coming in late and leaving early were not causes for reprimand and counseling. Arriving late for meetings had become the standard because they never started on time anyway. There was no sense of urgency.
>
> ... In some areas, form was more important than substance. The best example was a system purchased to track officer calls on customers. It offered many features, including grouping customers by geographic area, sales size and the success of the calling effort. However, the bank had only bought the module that accounted for the actual number of calls made, using information from the system for employee performance reviews. It didn't take a genius to realize that what mattered was number of calls made, rather than the results (of the calls). The system, needless to say, got an early burial.
>
> ... all of our contacts with the calling officers convinced us that they did not have a winning mentality. They questioned the value of bringing in new business. They assumed that if we had won the business away from another bank, it had to be tainted. There were no rewards for introducing a new relationship to the bank. ... (but there were certainly penalties if something went wrong.)

Nevertheless, Knowles did find some positive elements with which to work. The new ownership held to its hands-off policy, and provided support and encouragement. Also, there were talented people in the organization who knew how to get things done despite the rules, and who later became valued contributors to the new culture.

Bill Knowles' first task was to describe the values and mores he felt should be operative. He prepared a detailed statement of mission and strategy he hoped would be understandable and relevant at every level in the organization. The statement identified a two-phase transition strategy, intended to first install a solid infrastructure, then build a consistently profitable and competitive bank. In a departure from the past, the bank would concentrate on clearly defined markets, rather than endeavor to be a full-service operation. (The present Statement of Mission and Values is found in Exhibit 1.)

The Statement of Mission and Strategy set goals for return on assets (ROA) and return on equity (ROE), at levels that would make NatWest USA's performance comparable to its competitors, who were identified then as Irving Trust, The Bank of New York, Marine Midland and European American Bank.

In the mission statement, Knowles emphasized the need to gain respect in the financial community, develop first-class talent, become more efficient and cost-conscious, push decision-making downward, and develop group effectiveness, cooperation and team spirit.

By identifying core businesses and setting financial goals, Knowles had set a standard by which success could be measured, and established a timeframe within which the goals could be reached. These goals would put NatWest at the high end of New York banks.

Some thought the new CEO appeared overly optimistic. At a time when the only earnings on the bank's income statement were coming from tax credits, Knowles was calling for a benchmark ROA of .60% by 1987. The benchmark for ROA was reached in 1985—two years ahead of target—and surpassed in 1986. A comparison to 1981 when Knowles accepted the CEO post indicates the extent of the change—return on assets then was .22%.[1]

With markets well defined and staff functions altered and reduced, the bank set forth strategies to achieve new objectives. The major changes focused on two areas: developing a high-quality management team and developing a customer-orientation emphasizing profitability rather than growth.

Knowles felt that a complete transformation of NatWest's internal culture was crucial to building a more customer-oriented bank. In his 1981 mission statement, he called for synergy, a less parochial focus on profit-center earnings, and the willingness of management to lead by example.

He communicated a sense of urgency, stressing that changes in corporate culture had to start at the top.

Decision making was to be pushed down the line and pleasing customers, instead of bank examiners, was underscored as paramount.

MANAGEMENT TRANSITIONS

In the 1981 statement, Knowles also tackled the sensitive issue of management personnel changes—changes necessary for more effective functioning and instilling a new culture. He felt senior-management needed more qualified people, and recognized the need to go outside to find new managers. He recalls:

> . . . I was very open with the staff about this. I said we were going to have to go outside because we were just too big a bank to be competitive without introducing additional talent. I said I would try to get it over with as quickly as possible, but that I needed a window of about a year to accomplish it. At the end of the year, we were able to limit outside hires to primarily specialists, tax lawyers, etc.

The following was part of his public statement, excerpted from the August, 1981 Statement of Mission and Strategy:

> . . . The single most important element that will enable us to compete more effectively in the future than we have in the past is people. We have to be uncompromising in insisting on first-class talent, because if we don't have it, or grow it, we cannot move up. Neither our name nor our ownership can compensate for less than top-flight personnel who perform in a superior way.
>
> . . . As a first step, therefore, we are identifying the 50 to 60 key jobs in the organization and determining if the incumbent either is or can operate at a superior performance level. If not, changes will be made. This does not imply a cold or heavy-handed approach to people. On the contrary, we should always conduct ourselves so as to demonstrate respect and compassion in our dealings with our staff. It does mean, however, that we will be rigorous in setting goals and measuring results, and rewarding those who can do the job or making changes where results are not satisfactory.
>
> . . . Once the 50–60 key jobs are filled by people who meet high standards of performance as professionals and/or managers, they will serve as role models, and we will then attempt to build the organization by recruiting trainees and advancing people already here. We want to move away from the habit of going outside to fill our senior and even semi-senior positions. This will have to be done for a while longer, but our goal is to "grow on our own" in time.

Building from the Top Down

The grooming of the management team became the main focus of the transition.

Knowles had the freedom to choose his principal partners: one, to be the bank's chief operating officer (COO), the other, to be the liaison with the NatWest parent organization. As COO, he brought in Bob Wallace, who had been CEO of an Oregon bank owned by a holding company. John Gale was brought in as the liaison, and the three formed a partnership, under the heading Office of the Chairman, that, according to Knowles, ". . . is based on trust, informality and candor . . . We've developed into a team that represents the values we wanted to see projected throughout the bank."

Knowles, Wallace and Gale meet every Monday before their individual sector meetings, and also meet off-site at dinner every few weeks to discuss what is going on in their respective sectors.

The Office of the Chairman saw the selection of people as the key to success. They agreed that all outside hires, as well as internal promotions, had to "buy into" the new value system, and they have held firmly to their standards.

Wallace recalled that, in their internal process, they found outstanding people a couple of levels down in the organization, people who'd gone unrecognized before, but who were able to flourish in the changing environment.

Some jobs did have to be filled from outside, and all three members of the Office of the Chairman interviewed candidates for positions at levels of vice presidents and above. In each case, they looked for people with compatible values. Wallace describes the selection and promotion criteria:

> . . . We want people who are team players who want to work in an atmosphere of openness and caring. We may have made some mistakes with the professional skills of people brought in, but never on their values.
>
> . . . At every opportunity, we promoted people who would be seen by their peers as apolitical. One of the first tasks was to pick four division heads for our United States Group. We reviewed the candidates, their qualifications, and chose the candidates who hadn't run a "campaign" for the job. This and other promotions gave a clear signal that politics were out.

Developing a Customer Orientation

Selection of the management team took place simultaneously with the bank's development of competitive strategies based on customer service. Wallace was instrumental in setting the tone for this aspect of the transition:

> . . . First, we had to get a good grip on the bank's strengths and weaknesses. We quickly concluded that the bank's senior officers should get out in the marketplace to sample our customer's attitudes, and evaluate the skill-level of our lending officers. While what follows may seem a litany of what was wrong with the bank, let me assure you that we were encouraged by the good things we found, including some excellent talent among our line officers.

> But. . . . we found product deficiencies that put us at a competitive disadvantage. . . . And we were troubled by the lack of value placed on the contact with customers.

> For example, I once asked the head of one division to coordinate his calling with mine. He told me that would be easy, because he didn't call on customers. He viewed himself purely as an administrator, and he added that the bank knew that when he was hired. Unfortunately, while his statement was extreme, it was not inconsistent with the feelings of others. We had to show by example that customer contact was the most important job at the bank.

> The three members of the Office of the Chairman emphasized their desire to make calls on customers. At first, we would be taken on safe calls where the customer wouldn't embarrass the officer or the bank by telling stories of inadequate levels of service. But before long, there was less screening of the names we called on. We are still calling on customers wherever it will do the most good in marketing the bank. More to the point, it is (now) recognized throughout the bank that you don't graduate from customer contact. It's the most important thing we do.

> When we became serious about developing a customer-oriented atmosphere, changes were dramatic. It was like a dam breaking. We were literally flooded with information on why customers found us a difficult bank to deal with. On some of my early calls, I had found a key symptom of disregard for service. Officers simply did not listen to customers. Therefore, they never found out what customers wanted from the bank. Some of our officers acted as if they'd been sent in on a mission, and the customers better not get in their way. Today, one of the primary thrusts of our sales training is learning to listen. In addition, we have worked hard to change how people think about customer service. We emphasized that everyone in the bank has customers to serve; the support people's customers are the line people, and the line people, in turn, have external customers. It took repeated emphasis, but I think today most people have their priorities in order.

Changes Slow in Coming

Somewhat ironically, a lack of products had forced the bank's officers to develop extraordinary skills in the only area they had available to them: lending. Several parts of the bank were successful, driven by the ability to outperform competitors and to structure difficult credit transactions. In the area of lending, NatWest could function effectively because it was one area where officers did not have to depend upon the performance of others in the organization.

In spite of an initial euphoria changes seemed, to many, slow to come. Ed McDougal, formerly a line head and now executive vice president for Human Resources, recalled that his excitement when joining NatWest carried him a few months, but was dampened when he saw how attempts at action and decision-making were continually swamped in bureaucracy. McDougal recalls:

> . . . I found basically four types of people in the bank at that time. There were the cynics who said "This too shall pass." There were the skeptics who said "I'm all for it, but it will never work." Both of these groups suffered from a genuine inferiority complex about NBNA. The third group was a small corps of leaders who said "Believe it." And finally we had a bunch of supporters who said "Why No?" Many were young, and lacked experience. But they were smart, energetic and ambitious, and had a real can-do attitude. In my opinion, we needed to convert the skeptics and develop the can-do people.

McDougal also recalled an informal talk with Knowles that kept him from becoming too discouraged. McDougal was then at a mid-manager's level, five levels down in the organization. When Knowles would drop in once in a while at NatWest's midtown headquarters, he'd ask how things were going. McDougal would express his frustrations, and Knowles would encourage him and also share his own frustrations. Once he told McDougal, "You keep pushing from the bottom, and I'll keep pushing from the top. Someday, we'll meet in the middle."

When McDougal was finally promoted to department head, he began his push. One particular frustration for him was the lack of credit approval authority at the line level. The charter for his department said that the minimum loan the department could make was $250,000, yet the largest loan anyone could approve, himself included, was $250,000. In effect, despite being solely accountable for growing a loan portfolio, McDougal or his staff couldn't make any loans without someone else's approval.

It was clear the time had come to stop focusing on just the problems and get on with the job at hand. As McDougal said:

> . . . I was tired of hearing about our limited product line and our cumbersome credit approval process. The time had come to do business and to celebrate some victo-

ries. It was September (1982). We were in our budgeting cycle, and we put together a budget for 1983 that showed a 15% loan growth despite a three-year history of no growth. Also in September, as a tangible demonstration of our confidence and resolve, we scheduled a party for November, to celebrate the victories we would have over the next two-and-a-half months. There were some skeptics, but we did have our victory party, and we had something to celebrate. In fact, our portfolio grew by over 25% in 1983 without sacrificing quality or profitability standards.

... My function at that time was to be a teacher of credit and marketing, and we tried to use mistakes as a springboard to learn, and not an excuse to punish. I saw myself as a role model, confidence builder, cheerleader and facilitator. I learned how to use the bureaucracy to slow down the imposition of new rules, regulations and controls, and how to avoid it to get the job done.

As slow as the process was, changes were clearly happening. Success stories began to replace complaints and the bank began to openly celebrate these successes. When a deal was completed, a senior person would make a point of saying "good job." Wallace noted that people in the bank responded immediately to the much-needed praise.

A good example that change for the better was manifesting itself was seen in the way NatWest USA handled a new problem. In an effort to build volume, the bank had accepted greater domestic risks than it should have. This, on top of an emerging international debt crisis, resulted in an overall asset quality in 1983 that was not as good as had been expected. Bob Wallace noted:

> ... The bank had good enough credit people to deal with the situation quickly. We evaluated the problem loans, devised strategies and set out to make corrections. The plan worked, and today our asset quality is among the best of the New York banks. Best of all, it was accomplished without enormous write-offs. But solving the asset quality problem had an additional benefit. It demonstrated clearly that we were working as a team. It showed that we were more interested in solutions than in pointing the finger. It proved that we were becoming a different bank.

Flexibility was enhanced at NatWest when the authority for lending was pushed down in the organization, allowing lending departments to make loans of up to $2 million without outside approval. McDougal noted the significance of this event and some of the critical events that followed:

> No one ever believed it could happen. This was the first significant sign to the line units that the bureaucracy was in retreat. The symbolism went well beyond the actual impact. A new core of leaders had made it happen.

But the biggest signpost was yet to come. The bank had waited until September, 1983, until it was reasonably sure that it would show its third consecutive year of increased earnings, before taking on a name which would identify it with our parent. To celebrate the new name and our success to date, the bank held a party for the entire staff, a party complete with excellent food, music and a 15-minute sound-and-slide show that actually had people cheering. This was not NBNA, it was NatWest USA. There was a euphoria throughout the whole bank that lasted for weeks. Even when it finally wore away, morale was at a new, higher plateau. The bank had been permanently lifted by this one gala celebration.

Anecdotes about successes increasingly replaced jokes about failure. Stories of teamwork replaced some of the legends about the idiosyncrasies of individuals. At our victory party, we invited all branch managers to attend. Now, understand, our business customers were primarily medium-sized companies scattered over the five boroughs of New York. They used our branches to make deposits, cash checks and bring documents. Many saw the local branch manager more often than they saw the account officer. But the branch managers were rarely thanked for their efforts. They felt that they were not appreciated. The only time they ever heard from us was when the customers felt they didn't receive the service they were entitled to. Inviting the managers to our party to thank them for their help in serving our customers seemed like a little thing at the time, but it created a bond which enhanced our ability to serve our customers.

(In addition), my predecessor had started a tradition of a quarterly profit improvement awards. We (in middle-market lending) decided to give the award to an assistant branch manager who had referred us a large piece of business. The branch people were ecstatic. It was unheard of that a branch person would receive an award from another group.

The Human Resource Function

McDougal was promoted in 1984 to executive vice president and head of Human Resources. With the fervor of a crusader, Ed took responsibility for the staff meetings, audiovisual presentations and gala celebrations that continue to repeat over and over again the desire for change as stated in the original mission statement. McDougal's recollection of this period indicates the importance of the Human Resources Group and his role in the transition:

> My first priority as head of Human Resources was to have a team. We had many people who were competent from a professional/technical point of view, but effectiveness was hampered by a lack of teamwork. It wasn't a fun place to work. I told the department heads at our first group management meeting that I had never worked in a place for very long where I didn't have a

good time, and I didn't expect to start here. That was the only threat I ever issued. From then on we met regularly to discuss all issues.

One of the first major tasks of the group management was to create a strategic plan for Human Resources. In effect, we needed to create a vision of our future. A vision we all shared, and would work cooperatively to reach. We launched this planning process not through some technical preparation, but rather by spending three days together, off site, learning how to work together. Our next step was to create a statement of values and beliefs for the Human Resources Group. And it was only at this point that we began the process of creating a strategic plan. That plan served as a basis for providing increasingly higher levels of service to our customers, the employees and managers of the bank.

From the bank's perspective, we went through the process in the spring of 1985 of creating a statement of values for the overall organization. This involved a series of meetings with teams composed of members of the Office of the Chairman, executive vice presidents, all senior vice presidents, and a representative group of eight people, male and female, black and white, vice president to secretary. The final result is a statement of values (see Exhibit 1) which spells out how it is appropriate to act within the bank. This statement of values was presented to all the employees of the organization during a series of 11 breakfasts, conducted in Westchester, New York and Long Island. The presenters were all the senior and executive officers of the bank.

The final event which stands out in my mind is the bank's second victory celebration. Shortly after I became the head of Human Resources, Bill Knowles said we needed an occasion to have another employee party. The occasion became the launching of the bank's new quality effort. This, along with our success to date, suggested the name "Just the Beginning." In October of 1985, we held a series of "Just the Beginning" parties throughout the bank. Once again, they were a rousing success and lifted the morale of almost everyone in the organization. But there is one anecdote about the "Just the Beginning" parties which I think is a fitting story to close.

One of our Division Heads who managed people on off-shifts asked if we could have one of the parties other than at night when many of her people could not attend. These were employees who often felt ignored. So we held a sit-down luncheon with music and dancing, and concluded with the unveiling of a lavish dessert table. An older woman, whom I had never met before, grabbed my elbow as we walked up to the dessert table and said this reminded her of a wedding reception. Kiddingly I said, "Well, you're really our bride today." She looked at me and said, almost with tears in her eyes, "I feel like royalty." Nothing in my entire time in the bank has ever brought home to me more how people can be made to feel special.

At a conference on organizational development, in the fall of 1986, NatWest USA presented a history of its transformation process since the 1981 changeover.

In closing remarks, Ed McDougal and Bob Wallace expressed their perceptions of how far the bank had come. McDougal noted:

> We are a successful organization. We have done it by acting in a way that is consistent with values originally outlined in our mission statement, now codified in a statement of values. The challenges ahead of us are greater than the challenges behind. But we are prepared to meet them with a formula for success. There may still be some cynics, but most of the skeptics have been converted, and the core of believers is much larger. The younger people are still mostly here, four years older, and when they see our success to date, still say, "Why not?" I report directly to Bill (Knowles), which says something about the role Human Resources plays in the organization. Bill and Bob (Wallace) had both talked to me at the time of the change. They said they were looking for someone who was practical, yet sensitive. They wanted the function to have credibility within the bank, and have a customer orientation. I also took it as the ultimate confirmation of a management style.

McDougal's views are consistent with Wallace's:

> We now have an organization whose strengths are apparent. We have a marketing organization based on customer requirements and input from our own officers. Systems and operations areas now work in partnerships with line areas, because of the leadership provided by those who head these groups.
>
> When something we put in place didn't work, it was changed. We were able to prove by example that there was not pride of authorship or a penalty for an innovation that didn't work. And people began to realize that there was more fun in accomplishing an objective than in trying to find out who to blame. We in the Office of the Chairman continue to walk around, to meet with customers and seek information wherever we can. People realize that there is no penalty for speaking their mind.
>
> My own experience (illustrates) the atmosphere . . . When Bill (Knowles) and I were looking at whether I could make a contribution, he said he was looking for a full partner. I knew he meant that, but I also know that somebody has to run the store. Well, after five years, I can honestly say that the three of us in the Office of the Chairman have a partnership. We trust, respect and like each other and, maybe more importantly, we feel free to disagree with each other. It's worked for us, and I think it has worked for the whole bank. We are all proud to be part of a winning team.

Summary: Some Candid Observations by the CEO

With changes apparent and financial statements that tell a story of success in many areas, there are still problems and challenges in NatWest's efforts to differentiate itself and to reach its goals. In an interview with the casewriter, Bill Knowles frankly expressed his concerns and hopes:

We're now finding that we have got to work through, but also around the system to try to enrich the environment down below, to unleash the energies that are there. There are still supervisors who grew up in the old school, who use knowledge as power, who feel threatened, who will not permit their people to advance their careers by seeking positions elsewhere in the bank.

ABOUT BUREAUCRACY:

What did disappear, fairly quickly, was the committees. There were committees for everything. All the executive vice presidents met to decide the salaries, the computer systems questions, real estate questions, loan questions. It was like the knights would consider everything, whether they had expertise or not in the particular thing.

What didn't go away, and what we had a couple of false starts on, was the clutter in the system. This was because of the mergers, sticking 23 banks together so quickly, and the self-protective mentality that had grown up here. It was very hierarchical.

The clutter was incredibly hard to disassemble. Those vines had grown around all the pipes and wires and furniture, and it was just impossible to pull out. We established a clutter committee to monitor the process. It's like weeding a garden, you cannot do it in 10 minutes. It takes a long time, and you have to pick the weeds out one at a time. We are still doing it, and we still have a six-part-form mentality in some places, where we still cannot think simply.

The people in our organization are intelligent and honest. If you catch a dishonest person you deal with that, but you don't set up a whole mechanism to protect yourself from the odd, random event.

We tried to change the whole fundamental philosophical basis of the organization, and say "Hey, wait a minute, why in God's name do I have to sign a form that I received a report? If I received it, I received it, and if I didn't receive it, I didn't receive it.

There are still vestiges, and they stick out more now, and we can laugh at them a little.

ON BRINGING QUALITY TO THE WORKPLACE:

I gave a talk to the Long Island and New York City chapters of Young Presidents Organization. They were primarily presidents of mid-sized companies. The talk was on quality as the way that America could regain competitiveness in the world marketplace. That is more possible with companies like our bank and their companies, because there isn't so much bureaucracy. The middle-market companies of the country (there are close to 800,000 of them) could effect quality and bring back the quality that is good for our society and that we have lost so much of.

. . . . I don't know that it is profound, but I am committed to quality as the only way out. Not only for this bank, but for our society as a whole. The Far Eastern economies are providing much better quality in everything, from electronics to gasoline stations. We have now put our entire staff through quality training, one- or two-day training on the techniques of quality and what is expected.

. . . . We have staff parties, establish what we hope and believe in. So that if there is a bad cell at the bank, at least the people know that that is deviant, that that is not the norm. They know they are in a rotten branch, for example, and the chances are that they know somebody who is in a good branch, or who came from a good branch, and that the bank's management stands on the side of making it the way it ought to be.

. . . . Everybody wants to send good news up, particularly because we have been so strong in articulating the kind of environment, the quality that we want. Anything that comes up that doesn't sound that way is considered bad news. So we have to be extremely careful to get the truth through, rather than just something that matches what we put out.

. . . . It is paradoxical, it almost works against you. I think the answer is just to keep digging at it. Digging at it at the most junior levels of command, going down and talking to them. Also, we have what we call a video magazine and once a quarter we have a tape that talks about quality successes and quality barriers.

DEALING WITH THE ISOLATION OF THE MANAGER:

I deal with the isolation just by being informal and walking around, I have breakfast with the officers on all levels. We also have an endless series of excuses to get together for meetings and parties here. I mean, I have been to eight events here in the last three weeks with 50 or 60 officers, and it's rare if I don't know who they are. I walk around and try to see everybody in the non-branch staff at Christmas, to wish them a good holiday. I probably see 2500 to 3000, out of the 4500, and the executive vice presidents do too.

You have to go breaking down isolation, and that only lasts so long, and you have to do it again. It'll just grow back, that's natural.

ON BASIC STRATEGY:

This has really been the story of trying to make a bank competitive by narrowing its mission, its focus, and trying to achieve superiority in the area of commodity services by working through people. Because all services are the same in the businesses we are in. It's like insurance companies. If I asked you to identify the differences among them, you can't. Nobody could name the difference between banks either. So what we've got to do is to work very hard to take a representative sample of our society, which is our employees, and somehow to work with them in delivery of "faceless" services and try to do something special.[2]

What we're doing now is having the "Executive Vice

President of the Week." For a week, on a rotating basis, an executive vice president takes all the complaint calls that come into the bank, the "let me speak to the president calls." This means the EVP's are getting calls about their peers and about the organizations of other EVP's, and it saves complainers from being battered around by a dozen or so people before they get an answer.

THE CEO'S PERSONAL PHILOSOPHY:

In our society, in the business sector of our society and, I'm sure, in other sectors as well, people are driven by the attractiveness, the appeal, of putting their stamp on something, or effecting a change that will be identified with them, putting their imprimatur on something. People go to work to do that—they don't go to work to earn a paycheck. There is a self-pride that says "I did that, I was associated with that, I was on the team that installed this." Just so that they are a part of something that is significant. I think that's what really motivates me, but I also think it's what motivates others. And for me, putting my stamp on something, not just in profit terms but in human terms as well. I have a feeling that there is a power in the ability of a staff to produce when they are committed to doing something that makes sense to them—if they can see [the mission] is productive in terms of profit and the environment is conducive to letting them put their stamp on something worthwhile.

When what you do is make it fun. Make it enjoyable to be in that environment. That's part of the compensation and part of the benefits. It's more style.

Work should be fun. . . . if you go out and sample 6 out of 10 people here, they'll tell you work is tough, it's not fun, but four will tell you yes, it's fun. There is that slice. If we can make that five next year and six the next year, we're on our way.

Whether it's NatWest or some other organization, it's important to keep in mind what that organization is there for, what you are there to do. An organization left on its own will run off in different directions, because of the natural desire to experiment and grow and change. Unless that is properly channeled all the time, it will grow in a lot of directions and all those energies need to be focused on something that you and they really want. The biggest change around here is not so much what I have done, or anyone has done. The biggest turnaround here is to see what the people are doing translated into something the marketplace values—and that is profit. Can you imagine how disheartening, how debilitating it is to work very hard and to end up in a losing enterprise? That is how this organization once was—good people working hard, and it coming out all wrong.

When most people ask "What's wrong with this place?" the answer is usually communication, teamwork. But have you ever heard of any place, any organizational system that was perfect? I think we have to work hard to keep on the track we are on now, keep at it all the time.

THE STATEMENT OF VALUES

The Statement of Values provides the philosophical foundation for all we do. It is our credo, our system of fundamental beliefs.

As National Westminster Bank USA we share values which both support our Mission Statement and commit us to excellence in fulfilling the needs of our customers, the communities we serve, our parent organizations and ourselves.

Customers Our customers are the foundation of our business. We listen to their needs and respond in a manner which is timely, straightforward and courteous. We earn our future with them through leadership in quality and service.

Communities The prosperity and well-being of the communities in which we live and work are fundamental to our long-term success.

Therefore, we commit to serve them by providing leadership and support which enrich the overall quality of life.

Parent The National Westminster Bank Group has entrusted us with capital and its good name. We commit to invest these resources prudently, to earn a superior return and to work in partnership with our parent to enhance its worldwide structure.

Ourselves We, the employees, are the strength of the Bank and the source of its character. We work together to foster an open environment where trust and caring prevail. Pride and enjoyment come from commitment, leadership by example and accomplishment. We encourage personal growth and ensure opportunity based upon performance.

We recognize our individual responsibility to uphold these values, and in turn to enhance the Bank's reputation which is rooted in integrity, achievement and quality.

THE MISSION STATEMENT

The Mission Statement is the strategic translation of the Statement of Values. It is more specific, converting the value system into goals and programs.

Mission As the principal banking vehicle of the NatWest Group in the United States, our mission is to serve the overall marketing and operational requirements of the Group in this country. In doing so, we achieve profitable growth and an enhanced reputation.

To fulfill this mission we must continue to see ourselves not as full-service, across-the-board competitor of the largest money-center banks in every market, but rather as a significant competitor in what we regard as our core businesses. In addition, we must continue to develop the considerable potential for synergy that exists with our parent, in international markets as well as in this country.

Customers We are in four core businesses. In each of these core markets two fundamental precepts apply: our commitment to relationship banking and the essential responsibility of our support units to provide high-quality, low-cost service.

EXHIBIT 1
(Continued)

Consumer In this market, an area of traditional strength, we seek a stable and increasing source of core deposits that can be invested at an acceptable spread. We are relatively well-positioned for this with a sizable branch network, including offices in some key locations in New York City and substantial coverage in the desirable suburban counties surrounding it.

We will compete not by attempting to gain market share through the introduction of product breakthroughs, but by offering superior personal service, coupled with a competitive line of both deposit and consumer credit products introduced in a timely manner.

Commercial lending and deposit responsibility for companies with sales of up to $10 million is an important element of our consumer business. Commercial business adds a significant dimension to what was formerly a purely retail approach, and is aimed at enabling us to use our branch system more efficiently.

Middle Market The Middle Market continues to be one of the natural markets for NatWest USA. By our definition, it consists of companies with annual sales ranging between $10 million and $250 million, located primarily within a 100-mile radius of New York City, as well as companies on a selective basis throughout the country wherever we can serve them effectively. We compete by meeting the credit needs of customers in a responsive and flexible manner, and by bringing specialty services—particularly Trust, Treasury, Cash Management and Trade Finance—to middle-market companies in a more effective way than do other major banks.

Corporate Together with our parent, we have developed a rational and effective way for the Group to approach the enormous corporate market on a national basis. NatWest PLC is responsible for multinational companies and for servicing certain specialized-industry customers on behalf of London. Other than these, NatWest USA is responsible for the national market. We address this on a niche basis, both as to industry and geography, through our network of regional offices. Here again, our specialized support services—Cash Management, Trust, Treasury and Trade Finance—play a key role in our ability to compete effectively against money-center as well as regional banks.

International While we will continue to service the well-established and profitable public and quasi-public sectors, our mission in International is to increasingly concentrate on activities that more directly serve the offshore needs of our domestic customer base. These are principally credit and non-credit transactions that facilitate foreign trade.

Further, we will continue to build on our strengths in correspondent banking, and from that base expand selectively into private sector lending if margins are acceptable. Our areas of particular expertise are Latin America and the Far East. In Europe, we utilize the capabilities of our parent to a greater extent. Our international strategy reflects, in a complementary way, our role within the world-wide coverage of the NatWest Group.

Communities We derive business and our profits from the communities in which we operate. Therefore, we acknowledge a responsibility to invest in those communities to keep them vigorous and attractive. This goes beyond mere compli-

EXHIBIT 1
(Continued)

ance with the Community Reinvestment Act. It involves active participation by our staff, as well as direct financial support.

Parent Because we have been entrusted with our parent's name, we have a responsibility to enhance its reputation in all we do, as well as to achieve a superior financial return.

We expect to achieve this year—two years ahead of schedule—the 60-basis-point return on assets (ROA) goal set forth in the original 1981 Mission Statement. Our new goal is 70 basis points by 1988. In comparing our performance, we continue to regard Bank of New York, Marine Midland and European American Bank as our peers.

Our quality effort is directly related both to achieving our new ROA goal and to enhancing the reputation of our parent.

Ourselves The internal environment we seek, as outlined in the Statement of Values, rests on a set of strategies, policies and programs that are fundamental in our Bank:

- An uncompromising insistence on quality people.
- A pay-for-performance policy which has application Bank-wide as well as individually.
- A standard of excellence in communications.
- A lean organizational structure, free of redundant staff layers, to encourage individual initiative and decision making.
- A willingness by supervisors and managers to be judged on how well they foster the desired environment in their areas.

Quality Program Quality represents the everyday expression of our value system. It is the means by which we carry out the strategies and goals set forth in the Mission Statement.

The Bank's commitment to quality is thoroughgoing and long-term. It is how we intend to differentiate ourselves and, at the same time, achieve a cost advantage over our competitors. In addition, customers, are willing to pay a premium for high-quality services.

Customers The everyday things we do to better serve customers are obvious, but they bear repeating. These actions apply to everyone because, even where there is no direct customer contact, everything we do is related to serving customers:

- We listen to our customers to determine their needs and then attempt to fill those needs.
- We respond in a thoughtful, professional and timely manner.
- We deliver our products and services error free and in a consistent manner.
- We price our products and services fairly.
- We are always respectful and courteous.
- We do our work in essential staff areas as cost effectively as possible, because we invest our principal resources in customer-driven activities.

Communities In all our community activities we seek to reflect the Bank's commitment to quality and excellence while helping others.

This is a dimension of our job that goes beyond day-to-day duties. It involves

EXHIBIT 1
(Continued)

community service: giving generously to United Way, donating blood, taking leadership roles in significant community organizations.

We furnish substantial community support on the corporate level as well. Our contributions budget has grown each year and provides major funding for education, health care, community welfare and the arts. In addition, we have chosen to direct significant portions of our Corporate Communications budget to sponsorship of quality arts projects.

Parent Superior quality in everything we do is the only way to meet the dual responsibility we have to our parent of enhancing its reputation and meeting our financial goals.

High-quality work is key to enhancing the NatWest name. But it is also critical to achieving our new financial goal, because we must do this by improving margins rather than by expanding assets. Quality banking involves several things:

- Wider lending and investing spreads.
- Increased fee and service-charge income, which can be expected if we deliver quality products consistently.
- Expanded demand deposits.
- Higher credit quality, resulting in lower credit costs and fewer non-performing loans and charge-offs.
- Reduced tax liability

An additional element that enhances our reputation as a quality institution and ensures that we achieve our goals is consistent prudence both in the extension of credit and in our asset/liability management activities.

Ourselves The competence, dedication and hard work of our staff are the essential ingredients in our success. We need quality people. Therefore, we are very selective in hiring, and take training and promotion from within very seriously.

We closely monitor salary and benefit trends and seek to be fully competitive, increasing compensation levels in relation to those of our peers as the performance of the Bank improves. On an individual level, we reward according to the contribution.

We have developed a variety of programs to improve communication: an expanded NewsBeam, staff and management bulletins, staff meetings, special surveys and the like. We constantly seek new ways to increase communication at all levels of the Bank.

We encourage leadership by example, creating an environment that is caring, trusting, fair and enjoyable.

By doing quality work, each of us contributes directly to achieving the Bank's goals. In the process, we also foster a stimulating work environment and enhance our individual well-being.

Financial Highlights
(dollar amounts in thousands)

	1987	1986	1985	1984	1983
For the Year					
Net Interest Income	$ 394,125	$ 371,104	$ 336,175	$ 283,699	$ 234,878
Provision for Loan Losses	349,400	57,400	51,500	44,400	31,000
Non-Interest Income	130,109	110,020	96,187	81,494	61,745
Operating Expenses	352,574	322,638	292,978	255,276	222,808
Net Income (Loss)	(212,008)	67,673	54,575	40,062	25,332
At Year-End					
Assets	$11,539,277	$11,080,016	$9,796,328	$8,726,726	$7,470,847
Loans	8,216,356	7,363,751	6,415,038	5,679,582	4,631,661
Deposits:					
Core	6,372,288	6,174,877	5,145,869	4,642,772	3,578,957
Other	3,166,725	2,609,434	2,764,292	2,376,446	2,167,288
Equity Capital	409,036	621,044	554,443	504,534	498,067

*[The notes accompanying these statements, found in NatWest USA's 1987 Annual Report, are important for fair
and complete interpretation of financial condition.]*

EXHIBIT 2
(continued)

Consolidated Statement of Operation

(amounts in thousands)

	Year Ended December 31		
	1987	**1986**	**1985**
Interest Income			
Loans	$ 740,775	$680,964	$665,170
Investment securities			
U.S. Treasury and Federal agencies	71,683	69,622	66,339
State and municipal	52,346	55,940	29,426
Other	4,464	1,247	1,100
Trading account	1,553	6,220	4,588
Deposits with banks, Federal funds sold and securities purchased under agreements to resell	53,867	52,484	68,177
Total Interest Income	924,688	866,477	834,800
Interest Expense			
Deposits (Note D)	435,424	399,530	438,027
Borrowed funds (Note E)	94,842	95,459	60,131
Long-term debt (Notes F and H)	297	384	467
Total Interest Expense	530,563	495,373	498,625
Net Interest Income	394,125	371,104	336,175
Provision for loan losses (Note B)	349,400	57,400	51,500
Net Interest Income After Provision for Loan Losses	44,725	313,704	284,675
Non-Interest Income			
Service charges on deposit accounts	37,049	33,027	30,469
Letter of credit and acceptance fees	19,583	16,394	13,659
Credit card fees	14,897	14,933	14,252
Syndication and other loan related fees	13,740	5,481	2,715
Investment securities gains	4,926	7,890	8,762
Other	39,914	32,295	26,330
Total Non-Interest Income	130,109	110,020	96,187
Operating Expenses			
Salaries and benefits (Note J)	205,074	190,390	173,725
Supplies and services	48,677	43,811	40,833
Net occupancy (Notes C, H and K)	33,839	30,618	26,659
Business development	24,472	18,386	17,154
Equipment (Notes C and K)	24,447	21,735	18,816
Other	16,065	127,698	15,791
Total Operating Expenses	352,574	322,638	292,978
Income (Loss) Before Income Taxes	(177,740)	101,086	87,884
Provision for income taxes (Note G)	34,268	33,413	33,309
Net Income (Loss)	$(212,008)	$ 67,673	$ 54,575

Consolidated Statement of Condition
(amounts in thousands except share amounts)

EXHIBIT 2
(continued)

	December 31	
	1987	**1986**
Assets		
Cash and due from banks (Note K)	$ 582,220	$ 677,574
Interest bearing deposits with banks	646,618	578,026
Investment securities (Notes A and K)		
U.S. Treasury and Federal agencies	919,395	813,760
State and municipal	734,693	837,811
Other	155,648	25,867
Total (approximate market value of $1,787,723 and $1,724,036)	1,809,736	1,677,438
Trading account	44,560	95,791
Federal funds sold and securities purchased under agreements to resell	6,936	23,213
Loans, less unearned income of $85,348 and $60,464	8,216,356	7,363,751
Allowance for loan losses	(407,790)	(112,299)
Loans—net (Notes B and K)	7,808,566	7,251,452
Premises and equipment—net (Notes C, F and H)	236,606	235,276
Due from customers on acceptances	249,752	365,935
Other assets	154,283	175,311
Total Assets	$11,539,277	$11,080,016
Liabilities and Equity Capital		
Deposits (Note D)		
Demand	$2,114,470	$2,427,387
Retail savings and time	4,257,818	3,747,490
Other domestic time	1,335,644	983,570
Foreign office	1,831,081	1,625,864
Total	9,539,013	8,784,311
Borrowed funds (Note E)		
Federal funds purchased	618,140	677,957
Securities sold under agreements to repurchase	263,220	177,103
Other	312,740	313,569
Total	1,194,100	1,168,629
Acceptances outstanding	252,668	372,399
Accounts payable and accrued liabilities (Note G)	139,733	126,983
Long-term debt (Note F)	4,727	6,650
Total Liabilities	11,130,241	10,458,972
Equity Capital (Notes I and M)		
Common stock, $5 par value:	38,376	38,376
Authorized 7,773,867 shares; issued and outstanding 7,675,138 shares		
Surplus	238,657	238,657
Undivided profits	132,003	344,011
Total Equity Capital	409,036	621,044
Total Liabilities and Equity Capital	$11,539,277	$11,080,016

EXHIBIT 2
(continued)

Composition of Loan Portfolio *(amounts in thousands)*

| | DECEMBER 31 | | | | |
	1987	1986	1985	1984	1983
Domestic					
Commercial, financial, and agricultural	$5,377,938	$4,415,500	$3,630,686	$2,749,054	$1,758,653
Real estate construction	125,672	110,102	164,578	168,586	131,689
Real estate mortgage and warehouse	816,102	967,586	691,940	715,493	718,044
Installment loans to individuals	696,797	587,973	541,440	446,149	362,115
Other loans to individuals	177,576	162,174	205,899	135,214	79,793
Lease financing	29,581	21,345	23,676	23,561	4,106
Other	114,257	96,210	39,424	96,014	31,499
Total Domestic	7,337,923	6,360,890	5,297,643	4,334,071	3,085,899
Foreign					
Governments and official institutions	472,009	464,163	435,079	440,823	485,695
Banks and other financial institutions	284,859	348,768	368,934	438,525	508,451
Commercial and industrial	206,477	249,645	358,018	506,332	580,391
Other	436	749	1,624	811	1,090
Total Foreign	963,781	1,063,325	1,163,655	1,386,491	1,575,627
Less: Unearned income	85,348	60,464	46,260	40,980	29,865
Total Loans	$8,216,356	$7,363,751	$6,415,038	$5,679,582	$4,631,661

Maturities of Loans *(amounts in thousands)*

| | December 31, 1987 | | | |
	TOTAL	DUE BEFORE ONE YEAR	DUE IN ONE TO FIVE YEARS	DUE AFTER FIVE YEARS
Commercial, financial, agricultural and other	$5,492,195	$3,006,427	$1,887,733	$598,035
Real estate construction	125,672	33,931	85,797	5,944
Foreign	963,781	577,506	166,249	220,026
Total	6,581,648	3,617,864	2,139,779	824,005
Loans with interest-sensitive rates	6,131,510	3,518,861	1,870,741	741,908
Loans with fixed rates	450,138	99,003	269,038	82,097
Total	$6,581,648	$3,617,864	$2,139,779	$824,005

Excludes real estate mortgage and warehouse loans, loans to individuals and lease financing loans.

Cross-Border Outstandings *(amounts in thousands)*

EXHIBIT 2
(continued)

	GOVERNMENTS AND OFFICIAL INSTITUTIONS	BANKS AND OTHER FINANCIAL INSTITUTIONS	COMMERCIAL AND INDUSTRIAL	TOTAL
December 31, 1987				
Argentina	$ 96,313	$ 23,997	$13,553	$133,863
Brazil	87,579	120,901	250	208,730
Mexico	102,608	9,303	16,858	128,769
December 31, 1986				
Argentina	$ 83,976	$ 30,350	$12,823	$127,149
Brazil	88,167	115,799	267	204,233
Mexico	93,623	9,280	18,727	121,630
December 31, 1985				
Argentina	$ 69,223	$ 40,936	$10,500	$120,659
Brazil	73,827	125,706	767	200,300
France		104,771		104,771
Mexico	96,464	4,131	20,466	121,061
South Korea	40,265	63,459	22,730	126,454

The above schedule discloses cross-border outstandings (loans, acceptances, interest bearing deposits with banks, accrued interest receivable and other interest bearing investments) due from borrowers in each foreign country where such outstandings exceed 1.00 percent of total assets.

At December 31, 1987, 1986 and 1985, countries whose total outstandings were individually between .75 and 1.00 percent of total assets are as follows:

    1987—France and Japan, totaling $197.7 million.

    1986—Chile, France, South Korea and Venezuela, totaling $362.4 million.

    1985—Canada, Chile and Venezuela, totaling $267.3 million.

Exhibit 2
(continued)

Changes in Cross-Border Outstandings

(amounts in millions)

	Argentina		Brazil		Mexico	
	1987	**1986**	**1987**	**1986**	**1987**	**1986**
Aggregate outstandings at January 1	$127.1	$120.7	$204.2	$200.3	$121.6	$121.1
Net change in short-term outstandings	(2.0)	.2	6.7	5.0		5.1
Changes in other outstandings:						
Additional outstandings	7.5	3.9	1.8		8.6	
Interest income accrued	10.9	8.5	4.0	14.9	8.8	11.0
Collections of: Principal	(.2)				(1.1)	(1.2)
Accrued interest	(9.4)	(6.2)	(4.5)	(15.1)	(8.5)	(13.4)
Other changes			(3.5)	(.9)	(.6)	(1.0)
Aggregate outstandings at December 31	$133.9	$127.1	$208.7	$204.2	$128.8	$121.6

The following restructurings occurred during 1987 and 1986

(amounts in millions)

	Argentina	Brazil	Mexico
	1987	**1986**	**1986**
Amount restructured	$124.2	$13.8	$80.7
Weighted average year of maturity			
(including any grace periods): Pre-restructuring	1992	1985	1998
Post-restructuring	2004	1993	2004
Weighted average interest rate: Pre-restructuring	Prime+	Prime+	Prime+
	2% on $20.0	$1^3/_4$%	$1^1/_8$% on $14.6
	LIBOR+		LIBOR+
	$1^1/_8$% on $104.2		$1^1/_8$% on $66.1
Post-restructuring	LIBOR+	LIBOR+	LIBOR+
	$^{13}/_{16}$%	$1^1/_8$%	$^{13}/_{16}$%

The above schedule discloses changes in the period and restructuring information for those countries experiencing liquidity problems with outstandings greater than 1.00 percent of total assets.

In early 1988, once regulatory approvals have been obtained, First Jersey will join the National Westminster Bank Group as an affiliate of a newly formed holding company, to be named National Westminster Bancorp. The other banking subsidiary will be National Westminster Bank USA, headquartered across the Hudson River in New York City.

NatWest USA: In Perspective

National Westminster Bank USA traces its origins to the charter of The First National Bank of Freeport, established in 1905, under which NatWest USA operates today. After a series of mergers, the bank became known as National Bank of North America (NBNA). In 1979, NBNA was acquired by the National Westminster Bank Group. In September 1983, the bank changed its name to National Westminster Bank USA, and in June 1984 dedicated National Westminster Bank Center, the 30-story corporate headquarters at 175 Water Street near Manhattan's South Street Seaport.

Values, Mission, Commitment to Quality

From that office and others, NatWest USA's 4,600 employees supply a full range of banking services to corporate and individual customers. In doing so, they work within a framework of values and goals spelled out in a publication titled "The NatWest Way: Our Values, Mission and Commitment to Quality," which has been distributed to all employees.

The statement outlines business goals, strategies and a commitment to excellence in responding to the needs of customers, communities, the parent organization and the bank's employees. This commitment includes a comprehensive quality improvement program, through which the bank is working to differentiate itself in the marketplace. The program makes quality the focus for each staff member and has an impact on every aspect of the bank's operations.

Customer Service

Those operations include four lending areas (the Community Banking, New York City, Regional and United States groups), and five support areas (the Technology & Processing, Financial & Planning, Credit Policy & Administration, Human Resources, and Administration groups). The bank's Treasury group supports the line areas and is responsible for asset and liability management, brokerage sales and services, and trading. The bank also has Marketing and Corporate Trust divisions.

Two subsidiaries were also formed in 1986. They are NatWest USA Credit Corporation, which offers asset-based financing to medium-sized companies, and NatWest USA Capital Corporation, a small business investment corporation (SBIC).

NatWest USA serves its retail customers through a 135-branch network and a network of automated teller machines, called Teller Beam, in New York City, Westchester County and Long Island. Teller Beam is part of the NYCE (New York Cash Exchange) network of automated teller machines and the nationwide CIRRUS network. NatWest USA is a founding member of NYCE, which was established in 1984.

Retail customers are also served by the bank's Consumer Credit division,

Exhibit 3
A Recent Profile of NatWest USA

Exhibit 3
(Continued)

which offers VISA, MasterCard and Gold MasterCard, as well as a full line of consumer credit products. Individuals whose net worth is $1 million or more may also take advantage of the personalized financial services offered by the bank's Private Banking department, through offices in Manhattan and Great Neck, Long Island. This department offers opportunities for cross-selling bank products, an important aspect of doing business at NatWest USA.

NatWest USA's other specialties include lending to middle-market corporate customers in the printing, textile and apparel, diamond and jewelry, publishing and real estate industries, particularly in New York City. Nationwide, NatWest USA specializes in meeting the financial needs of the health services, media, utilities and leasing industries.

The bank also concentrates on geographic niches, lending to middle-market corporate customers in the tri-state area outside of New York City. Large corporate and middle-market customers outside the tri-state area are served by representative offices and an Edge Act Office in Miami. NatWest USA's international division serves the international needs of the bank's domestic customers.

Two major staff areas provide key support to the bank's lending groups. They are the Administration and Technology & Processing groups. Administration encompasses the Legal, Auditing, Loan Review, Consulting Services and General Services divisions.

Two separate groups, Systems and Operations, were recently combined to form Technology & Processing. This restructuring was done to open the door to new opportunities and to further enhance customer service.

COMMUNITY INVOLVEMENT

NatWest USA recognizes that the prosperity and well-being of the communities that it serves are fundamental to its long-term success. Therefore it is committed to serve them by providing leadership and support which enrich the overall quality of life.

NatWest USA encourages voluntarism, is a leading supporter of United Way and has a substantial corporate contributions program. Also, the bank has developed a far-reaching "Arts in the Community" program which, this summer, won a Presidential Citation as part of the White House Program on Private Sector Initiatives, and awards in 1985 and 1987 from Business Committee for the Arts.

Major "Arts in the Community" events have included concerts by Luciano Pavarotti and Placido Domingo, and numerous concerts in Carnegie Hall. The bank also sponsors a wide range of arts events in local communities, such as concerts by Long Island Concerts Pops, American Concert Band, New Orchestra of Westchester and Brooklyn Philharmonic.

In addition to "Arts in the Community" sponsorships, other community involvement includes employee participation in walk-a-thons and other civic functions, as well as bank sponsorship of events to benefit organizations such as the American Heart Association and Special Olympics. In all, NatWest USA was involved in 107 community events in the past year.

Among the community events sponsored by the bank are several concerned with education. Through its "Outstanding Young Achiever" award program, the bank recognized and gave financial awards to outstanding seniors at 22 New York metropolitan area high schools. And in connection with its sponsorships of PBS broadcasts, NatWest USA develops and sends teaching kits to music teachers to encourage interest in the arts among students.

EXHIBIT 3
(Continued)

During the past four quarters, as part of the NatWest USA "Speakers in Your Community" program, bank representatives have given 102 speeches on financial topics—an average of one every three working days—to business, civic and service organizations important to the bank.

This strong commitment to the community reflects the bank's Statement of Mission, Values and Commitment to Quality, and contributes to its growth.

The National Westminster Bank Group, headquartered in London, is among the largest, most profitable financial institutions in the world, with total assets of more than $120 billion and more than 90,000 employees worldwide. Including subsidiary companies, the Group has operations in 36 countries.

EXHIBIT 4
Market Research at NATWEST USA

The Marketing Department at NATWEST USA provided research indicative of the degree to which the firm has been able to achieve its goal of differentiation via quality programs and other strategic and cultural changes. Representatives noted that the true test for NATWEST USA is the degree to which any organizational changes translated into changing perceptions by customers, i.e., whether customers feel that they are receiving more valuable products and information, and whether they feel confident about the bank and positive about the treatment received from it. It was observed that the types of changes that NATWEST USA is seeking are very long term, and the full effects of programs implemented will have to be evaluated over a number of years into the future. Nevertheless, studies conducted thus far provide glimpses of the effects of NATWEST USA's efforts and of areas where further improvement is necessary.

The sheer amount of market research at NATWEST USA is impressive—in the past two years alone, several major research studies have been carried out, conducted both by internal researchers and outside agencies. Each of the studies utilized sophisticated experimental designs with control groups, standard statistical sampling and data collection via interview, survey and customer "shopping" techniques (in which researchers acted as customers and "bought" products and services).

The following describes and summarizes the conclusions of three major studies:

THE MIDDLE MARKET STUDY

The Middle Market Study, concluded in March, 1986, examined the financial behavior, needs and attitudes of middle market companies operating nationwide, and also examined NATWEST USA's competitive position within the Tri-State region of New York, New Jersey and Connecticut. This study, along with the Commercial Banking Study (described below), provided current market research on the bulk of NATWEST USA's business community markets. The "middle market" study covered firms with sales between $50–250 million and the "commercial market" study covered firms between $5–50 million.

The Middle Market Study indicated that the middle market is dominated by manufacturing (50%) and wholesale trade (27%) businesses. The manufacturing industry was described as a "huge, attractive market, but also the most competitive market segment." The wholesale trade industry, while less competitive for banking services, also uses fewer banks and fewer services. Yet the companies in the wholesale trade have the greatest demand for borrowing, both in terms of the

519

EXHIBIT 4
(Continued)

percentage of firms in the industry that borrow as well as the amounts that they seek. The retail trade and the manufacturing industry also have heavy concentrations of borrowers.

The intense competition in the middle market is evidenced by the fact that most companies use four banks and are, on the average, actively solicited by four new banks as well. The research concluded that the intense competition "underscores the importance of staying actively involved in customer relationships, of having targeted calling programs and of making effective calls on companies." It was observed that customers are becoming increasingly involved in their bank relationships and that this trend will continue. More companies want to know exactly where they stand with their banks and want the details of their agreements in writing. The trend is reflected in the three areas of changes in recent years that middle market customers consistently reported:

1. More calls are being made by bankers' representatives.
2. More is being asked of the banks.
3. A greater participation of company's treasury staff is present in initiating and maintaining a relationship with a bank.

With regard to bank selection issues, the study indicated that the vice president of finance was the officer most often responsible for selection of a bank as a service provider. The key selection criteria was described as "the company's overall relationship with the bank", an overall relationship seen as more important than specifics such as loan terms and conditions. The specific terms do take on greater importance with certain issues, such as with respect to data processing services, leveraged buyout/acquisition loans, foreign exchange and trade services. For firms dealing internationally, the study indicated that the key criteria for selection of a bank for international services is the presence of an existing domestic relationship and a bank's international service capabilities.

The study also indicated that the financial strength of the bank is a very important concern to the middle market companies. Utilizing annual reports, accounting and financial officers of the middle market companies evaluate the financial condition of the banks they use and the banks that solicit them.

Useful findings resulted when researchers asked the customers what types of things affected their view of the "importance" of a bank to their business, and what factors improved the relationships of the companies with their banks. Banks were found to increase in importance to middle market companies to the degree they are willing to lend, provide account officer service and have competitive loan pricing. The bank's relationship with the company was found to improve with the introduction of new ideas and new services, the interest of the servicing bank in company information, the improvement of quality and frequency of the bank's visits. Conversely, failures in these same areas, in terms of not keeping up to date with new ideas and possible services to offer, not calling often enough and not understanding the company's decision making processes detracted from the company's relationship. The most serious mistake, from the point of view of the customers, was the bank not being thoroughly familiar with the company being serviced.

The Middle Market Study concluded that, in the Tri-State Region, NATWEST USA is an important competitor, with 12% market concentration and positioned similarly to Marine Midland, Bank of New York and Irving Trust. Most of its customers consider NATWEST USA to be a principal bank (i.e.,

EXHIBIT 4
(Continued)

one of the banks they use most for domestic banking services) and $\frac{1}{3}$ use NATWEST USA as their overall lead bank. NATWEST USA's customers and prospects are most heavily penetrated by the other four major banks.

With regard to customer calling, the study indicated that 78% of NATWEST USA's prospects were called on more frequently by at least one or more competitors than they were called upon by NATWEST USA. However, NATWEST USA's customer calls were found to be highly effective in gaining new business, and more effective overall when compared to the competition.

In light of this information, the researchers concluded that NATWEST USA should segment the middle market and made recommendations on reallocating the bank's resources to the most desirable segments.

THE COMMERCIAL BANKING STUDY

The Commercial Banking Study was concluded in August, 1986 and examined similar issues as did the Middle Market Study but with respect to companies with annual sales of between $5,000,000 and $50,000,000.

The Commercial Banking Study focused on the nine county New York area where NATWEST USA's principal commercial market is located (Bronx, Kings, Nassau, New York, Queens, Richmond, Rockland, Suffolk and Westchester). This study indicated that NATWEST USA is a major competitor in the commercial banking market. The bank is tied with Chase Manhattan in terms of market share, in fourth position behind Chemical Bank, Manufacturers Hanover and Citibank.

Interviews with the commercial market customers indicated that NATWEST USA's account officers and top management are doing an excellent job in terms of visiting and serving the commercial market customers. A high proportion of customers are called on regularly and interactions are perceived as highly effective.

NATWEST USA is viewed as a credit provider to the commercial banking market, having a higher proportion of borrowing customers than most of the competition and a credit policy that is viewed more favorably than that of its competition. NATWEST USA's non-credit services are also viewed favorably by the overall market, but ratings varied significantly among different sales size segments. NATWEST USA's strongest non-credit service is in the area of cash management.

While the Banker's Trust acquisition clearly positioned NATWEST USA as a major competitor, the Commercial Market Study emphasized that, in order to maintain the bank's market position, prospect calling efforts should be improved.

THE BRANCH SHOPPING STUDY

The Branch Shopping Study, concluded in January, 1987, was undertaken to determine how the customer was treated and how the customer perceived a NATWEST USA branch when they came in to open an account or inquire about the bank's services. The study placed emphasis on perceptions of bank employees' behavior and knowledge and attitudes when approached by customers under varying circumstances. The study also compared appearance of the branches and the presence and quality of sales efforts between NATWEST USA and their competitive counterparts across different regions.

The Branch Shopping Study differed from the usual types of research

EXHIBIT 4
(Continued)

wherein an interviewer obtained opinions from respondents. In this study, a researcher approached the NATWEST USA branch representative as a "shopper" and recorded opinions and experiences resulting from the contact. The "shopper" either came into a branch to open a checking account or cash a check and inquire about high interest bearing checking accounts.

In the case where a checking account was opened, shoppers were instructed not to specify the type of checking account they wanted to open, in an effort to see if branch representatives mentioned or discussed and explained the types of accounts available, explained about service charges and types of checks available, and counseled shoppers about appropriate accounts for them.

In the case where the customers came in to cash a check, they proceeded to the teller lines. They were instructed not to endorse the check prior to seeing the teller. They took note of any inappropriate behavior displayed by the tellers as well as the procedures followed by them. After the check was cashed, shoppers asked if the bank offered high interest checking accounts. This procedure was designed to measure the ability of the tellers to service customers and provide information about products and services offered by the institution.

Approximately two hundred account opening and check cashing transactions were evaluated, two thirds of which were with NATWEST USA branches and the remaining third with the branches of competitors. The study was completed over a two month period in late 1986.

The focus of data analysis was on overall "quality of service" measured in terms of the sales skills of tellers and representatives (defined as knowledge of service, ability to listen, ability to communicate, responsiveness to inquiry, credibility and salesmanship), interpersonal skills (courtesy, friendliness, attitude and establishment of rapport) and personal attributes (professional appearance, organization, promptness, business-like manner and efficiency). An overall measure of satisfaction with the total shopping experience was included in the measure of quality.

The Branch Shopping Study's main conclusions were as follows:

1. Overall, NATWEST USA branch personnel are performing equal to, and, at times, better than the personnel of competitors in terms of quality of service they are providing. The study found that 66% of the shoppers were either extremely or very satisfied with NATWEST USA, while only 59% were satisfied with competitor branch personnel (Table A.1).

2. The level of quality equal to competitors was found for both types of transactions studied (Table A.2). NATWEST USA representatives scored at least as high as competitors on courtesy and friendliness and higher on attitude and the initial establishment of rapport (Table A.3). The perceptions of these interpersonal skills varied significantly across the NATWEST USA operating regions and by the type of transaction studied (Table A.4).

3. In terms of the ratings of personal attributes of tellers and branch representatives, NATWEST USA was rated equal to or higher than their competitors in terms of efficiency, professional appearance, promptness, organization and business-like attitudes. Professional appearance and organizational skills rated highest for NATWEST USA representatives in comparison to the competition (Table A.5).

4. The Branch Shopping Study compared certain measures to a similar study conducted in 1983. NATWEST USA has apparently improved in the areas of product knowledge and sales-related skills, but not in customer relations skills. Another comparison to the 1983 Study indicated an interesting dynamic taking place with regard to pressures upon bank personnel at peak times. Differences in the quality of service were noted in the current study between busy and non-busy hours, while the 1983 Study had not perceived such differences. Interestingly, the differences noted in

Exhibit 4
(Continued)

the present study were not in the direction that might be expected. Service at NATWEST USA branches was found to be slightly better during the busy hours, and the study speculated that greater efficiency may arise at the peak times out of necessity.

5. Concerning branch environments, the study indicated that the interior and exterior environments for both NATWEST USA and its competition are in excellent condition. The average waiting time in NATWEST USA branches was found to be lower than the average for other banks. (Table A.6).

TABLE A.1 NatWest USA Branch Shopping Study: Satisfaction with Service Provided by Personnel—Overall by Total Bank

| | NATWEST USA | Competition | | |
		TOTAL	COMMERCIAL	THRIFT
(BASE: TOTAL TRANSACTIONS)	(259) %	(128) %	(104) %	(24) %
Extremely Satisfied	23	21	23	⑫
Very Satisfied	43	38	34	58
Neither Satisfied Nor Dissatisfied	28	30	34	13
Not Too Satisfied	5	10	8	17
Not at All Satisfied	1	—	—	—
No Response	—	1	1	—

□ = significantly higher
○ = significantly lower

EXHIBIT 4
(Continued)

TABLE A.2 NatWest USA Branch Shopping Study: Satisfaction with Service Provided by Personnel—Overall by Transaction

(BASE: TOTAL TRANSACTIONS)	Opening a Checking Account		Cashing a Check and High Interest Bearing Account Inquiry	
	NAT. WEST (130) %	COMP (64) %	NAT. WEST (129) %	COMP (64) %
Extremely Satisfied	25	27	22	16
Very Satisfied	46	33	40	44
Neither Satisfied Nor Dissatisfied	22	25	33	34
Not Too Satisfied	5	14	5	6
Not at All Satisfied	1	—	—	—
No Response	1	1	—	—

TABLE A.3 NatWest USA Branch Shopping Study: Ratings of Branch Representatives on Interpersonal Skills (Percentage of Shoppers Rating "Extremely Satisfied") by Total Bank

(BASE: TOTAL TRANSACTIONS)	NATWEST USA (259) %	Competition		
		TOTAL (128) %	COMMERCIAL (104) %	THRIFT (24) %
Courtesy	46	47	48	43
Friendliness	41	42	43	41
Attitude	36	31	31	31
Establishing Rapport	28	26	27	24

EXHIBIT 4
(Continued)

TABLE A.4 NatWest USA Branch Shopping Study: Ratings of Branch Representatives on Interpersonal Skills (Percentage of Shoppers Rating "Extremely Satisfied") by Transaction

	Opening a Checking Account		Cashing a Check And High Interest Bearing Account Inquiry	
(BASE: TOTAL TRANSACTIONS)	NAT. WEST (130) %	COMP (64) %	NAT. WEST (129) %	COMP (64) %
Courtesy	53	51	39	42
Friendliness	45	44	35	41
Attitude	44	31	29	31
Establishing Rapport	35	32	22	20

TABLE A.5 NatWest USA Branch Shopping Study: Ratings of Branch Representatives on Personal Attributes (Percentage of Shoppers Rating "Extremely Satisfied") by Total Bank

		Competition		
(BASE: TOTAL TRANSACTIONS)	NATWEST USA (259) %	TOTAL (128) %	COMMERCIAL (104) %	THRIFT (24) %
Efficiency	42	38	39	33
Professional Appearance	40	32	32	34
Promptness	37	37	40	28
Organization	32	24	24	25
Business-Like	31	26	25	29

□ = significantly higher
O = significantly lower

EXHIBIT 4
(Continued)

TABLE A.6 NatWest USA Branch Shopping Study: Branch Environment—Total Transaction Time

(BASE: TOTAL TRANSACTIONS)	NATWEST USA (259) %	Competition		
		TOTAL (128) %	COMMERCIAL (104) %	THRIFT (24) %
Less Than 10 Minutes	26	30	32	17
10–19 Minutes	42	27	27	29
20–29 Minutes	24	29	31	21
30–39 Minutes	6	9	9	8
40 or More Minutes	2	5	1	25
Average Waiting Time (in Minutes)	15.1	17.1	15.4	24.3

□ = significantly higher

○ = significantly lower

PEET, RUSS, ANDERSON & DETROIT (PRA&D)

JAMES BRIAN QUINN, *Tuck School Dartmouth College*

▼

The accounting profession, which had long been very stable and predictable, began changing dramatically during the 1970s and 1980s. First, the merger boom of the 1970s cut the ranks of publicly owned corporations normally served by the Big Eight accounting firms. The audit fee from a merged firm was usually about 65% of the combined fees the two firms had paid independently. While this saved the client companies substantial amounts, it cut dramatically into the fees of the accounting firms.

Then in the late 1970s the Federal Trade Commission (FTC), seeking to increase competition in the accounting profession, forced the profession to eliminate its self-imposed strictures against advertising and the solicitation of other firms' clients. Client corporations quickly learned they could radically reduce audit fees by replacing their auditors every few years. Reputation and long-standing client ties were no longer enough to attract or hold clients, or to shield accounting firms from price competition. As firms began actively courting competitors' clients, they also aggressively sought ways to cut their internal costs and to provide new client services. This led to substantial investments in computer and other technologies designed to reduce—or gain higher yields from—the high-priced labor involved in an audit. It also promoted further diversification into management consulting, tax counseling, systems design, and other services.

INDUSTRY STRUCTURE

Despite such efforts, *The Public Accounting Report* stated that revenues at the eight largest firms grew a total of only 22% from 1982–1985, down from 40% over the preceding two-year span. But accounting revenues rose only 14%; the biggest gains in the early 1980s came from consulting fees, up 33%. Simultaneously, net income per partner was being depressed by diminishing ratios of professional staff to partners (caused by the decreased demand in the audit area for ordinary "number crunchers"), by lower utilization rates (because more professional hours had to be spent on non-chargeable activities such as marketing or practice development as it was called in the industry), and by the increasing cost of recruiting and retaining the higher-quality professional staff firms now needed. So intense were the pressures on revenues that one of the larger firms took the unprecedented step of pushing out or retiring 10% of its partners.

Smaller and medium-sized firms either developed specialized niches or merged to broaden their services, gain expertise, or gain necessary economies of scale. In the mid-1980s some of the larger firms had even merged to gain the worldwide sales and expertise demanded by their large multinational clients. As such mergers increasingly divided the remaining members of the Big Eight from the smaller firms, their greater scale and potentials began raising antitrust issues.

The 1982 *Census of Service Industries* reported some 49,000 U.S. accounting firms, with revenues totaling $14.6 billion. The Big Eight among these firms (then Arthur Andersen; Peat Marwick; Ernst &

Case copyright © 1989, James Brian Quinn. This case was developed by Penny Paquette under the guidance of Professor Quinn.

Disguised name of a real firm. Internal figures of PRA&D have been adjusted by constants in each exhibit.

Whinney; Coopers & Lybrand; Price Waterhouse; Arthur Young; Touche Ross; and Deloitte, Haskins, & Sells) earned more than 28% of all industry revenues, while the 12 largest firms received 32% of the total. Less than 3% of all firms had revenues of more than $1 million in 1982, and less than 1% had revenues exceeding $2.5 million. The Big Eight firms had an estimated $3.8 billion in non-U.S. billings in 1984, and foreign billings accounted for at least 25% of total billings for each of the Big Eight. (See Appendix A for a profile of the largest accounting firms.) Their international operations, originally established primarily to serve U.S.-based multinationals, tended to be organized abroad as loose collections of largely autonomous partnerships. Smaller accounting firms conducted considerably less international business. Table 1 breaks out revenues by type of service for the U.S. accounting profession as a whole and for a typical Big Eight firm in 1982. The size, number, ranking, and names of the largest accounting concerns actually shifted substantially as the 1980s emerged.

A study by the Congressional Research Service found that in 1980 clients of the then Big Eight accounted for 94% of all sales, 94% of all profits, 90% of all income taxes paid, 94% of all people employed, and 94% of all assets owned by New York Stock Exchange members. The eight to ten largest CPA firms tended to handle the preponderance of all *Fortune* 500 companies' business, but smaller companies and numerous not-for-profits and governmental organizations were also among their clients. Larger clients purchased tax and consulting services well in excess of what they spent on audits. But in the mid-1980s only about a fifth of the Big Eight's revenues were from nonaudit services.

TABLE 1 **1982 Revenues by Type for Accounting Firms**

TYPE OF SERVICE	U.S. ACCOUNTING PROFESSION AVERAGE	TYPICAL BIG EIGHT FIRM
Accounting/ auditing	50.8%	50–75%
Tax preparation and consulting	26.8	15–25
Bookkeeping	11.9	
Management advisory	8.2	10–30
Other	2.4	

Source: Office of Technology Assessment, *Trade in Services,* OTA-ITE-316, September 1988, p. 48.

TRENDS IN THE PROFESSION

The main focus of the profession's diversification efforts had been into management advisory or consulting services which in the United States yielded profit margins of about 20%, almost three times that on standard audits. While consulting competitors complained about unfair competition from auditing firms, the firms themselves felt that the experience they gained as auditors made them better consultants for their clients and that consulting improved the quality of their audits by helping them know more about their clients. The profession maintained that it had erected a careful "Chinese wall" between their auditing and consulting functions and cited the fact that only 10–40% of their audit clients ended up as consulting clients. But criticism was mounting against CPA firms for moving into specific areas of consulting some thought bordered on "conflicts of interest" with the objectivity needed in the auditing side of the business. For example, Peat Marwick had bought a major share in a public relations firm; Arthur Andersen had become a major factor in the asset-appraisal business; and Deloitte, Haskins, & Sells and Touche Ross were putting increased emphasis on consulting for investment bankers in corporate mergers, reorganizations, and bankruptcies. Others wondered openly whether an audit unit could really offer an unbiased appraisal of a system, major project, or decision its consulting group had recommended.

Aggravating matters was the fact that consultants in most firms were paid a bit more than auditors, and the disparate nature of the two activities often led to a culture clash. Public accountants had taken rigorous professional training and examinations to be certified as public accountants. They had to be not only knowledgeable about and adhere to the regulations of government bodies affecting financial and reporting matters but to the rules of the profession as interpreted by Generally Accepted Accounting Principles (GAAP) and the SEC in its Financial Accounting Standards Board (FASB) rulings. They had their own professional journals and looked to their professional colleagues for support and movement elsewhere in the industry.

The conflicts of this professionalism with the more freewheeling style of the consultants was further exacerbated by the partnership form that CPA firms followed. Accountants from the firms' earlier history usually dominated the partnership numerically. Consultants, who typically were not CPAs, could only be quasi-partners in that portion of the firm certifying audits. And disproportions between audit and consulting fees affected one group's willingness to share incomes and investments with the other. How these conflicts—and the power relationships they involved—could be resolved was an open question in the late 1980s.

Even so, the FTC was pushing for further sweeping changes in the professional codes which governed the accounting profession. The FTC was proposing that accountants would soon be free to draw contingent fees from sums recovered for clients as a result of audit work done in lawsuits, to accept commissions from the sellers of financial products the accountants had reviewed or recommended to customers, and to form private or even publicly held companies to process regular bookkeeping and accounting transactions for clients. The traditional partnership form the profession had adopted had made partners "fully and personally responsible" for their firm's CPA certifications and opinions. Many accountants were concerned that such moves would convert public accounting from its previous status as a "profession" with responsibilities beyond mere commercial concerns into "just another business." While the industry was fighting the FTC's efforts to promote harmful competition and to protect its image as a profession, legal actions against auditing firms had mounted, and most of the Big Eight had faced at least one potentially devastating lawsuit. Firms were hard pressed to get enough malpractice insurance to cover possible losses.

PRA&D POSITION

In the mid-1980s Peet, Russ, Anderson, & Detroit (PRA&D) sought to adjust its strategic position to respond to these changes in its industry and to the new global business environment it faced. PRA&D was among the largest and most prestigious of the public accounting firms. It was heavily represented among both manufacturing and service clients in the United States and in international markets. Well respected and conservative, PRA&D had so far moved cautiously in terms of diversification and marketing aggressiveness, but had developed strong consulting, tax, and systems units. PRA&D's headquarters were in a major Atlantic seaboard city, but it had branches or affiliates in most large U.S., European, Asian, Latin American, and Pacific Rim cities as well. Its past organization had given extensive autonomy to its partners in each local branch. But its central office had exerted strong policy controls in most functional areas, particularly those

dealing with audit, tax, and ethical standards. Despite the presence of a Management Committee—elected by the partnership and usually containing the top functional and branch heads of the firm—PRA&D's Managing Partner, Henry Johnson, exercised very significant influence throughout the firm because of his personality and highly respected professional skills.

In 1989, concerned about the developing fragmentation resulting from its many specialized activities, its continued growth, and PRA&D's necessarily localized presence in so many different geographical areas, Mr. Johnson began to worry about how to reorganize and reposition his firm in light of the new competitive pressures. He wanted to establish a more focused organization and operating philosophy to deal with the complexities the firm then faced.

A considerable amount of self-analysis over the last two years had convinced the Management Committee that the 1980s' rapid rates of change, intense competition, new technology development, and needs for specialized skills would increase rather than decline. PRA&D felt it was well positioned in some market segments (notably with large traditional multinational manufacturers) and not as well in others (particularly smaller and mid-sized services companies). As a mid-sized member of the then Big Eight, PRA&D did not have the resources to develop a dominating presence in all areas. The gap in size between PRA&D and its largest competitors was already significant, and if past growth rates continued, the gap would increase in the future.

PRA&D's commitment to providing high-quality professional services through autonomous professional partners was fundamental to its culture. The firm had enjoyed well-deserved strengths in terms of its name recognition and its reputation for quality, integrity, and service, especially to its large clients. The latter were rather widely distributed both geographically and by industry classification. However, PRA&D felt it lacked partner presence in many business segments and in some geographical areas which were likely to be important to its future. Over the last several years, growth pressures had been so great that the Management Committee was beginning to doubt whether there were an adequate number of partners to pursue its former highly decentralized strategy in the future. PRA&D's resources seemed spread among many smaller practice units, making it difficult to concentrate resources on a single client's needs, and indeed to provide the full array of services it wished in many markets.

Because of its highly decentralized partnership structure, PRA&D had often placed more emphasis on current profitability than on long-term investments in many of the growing areas of accounting and consulting. Although its client listings in the *Fortune* 500 was high relative to its competitors, there was some concern whether the firm was growing with the new clients who would become the next generation of *Fortune* 500 companies. Because of its highly decentralized structure and management philosophy, PRA&D found it difficult to develop the levels of specialization some of its stronger competitors had. As a consequence, PRA&D was suffering from lower billing rates and profitability in some key growth areas, especially in specialized industries like health care, financial services, and high-technology manufacturing. In the past, PRA&D had grown primarily by developing new business at its local geographic offices and by attempting to give each office the capability to deliver PRA&D's full range to all types of clients in its area.

While this strategy was extremely successful into the late 1970s, fragmentation and lack of coordination had become serious problems by the late 1980s. Only a few offices had the resources to carry out a full-service strategy across the full range of businesses in their areas. Because PRA&D was smaller than some of its major competitors, it had fewer partners, and its partnership skills were being badly stretched to meet the increasingly wide array of customer needs. Most of PRA&D's geographical offices and professional services were still very highly regarded in the industry, especially among its existing clients. However, it was becoming ever more difficult for its partners to find the time to generate new business or to focus on new emerging markets in any coordinated way across the United States—much less PRA&D's many international markets.

A MARKET-DRIVEN STRATEGY

Intuitively, Mr. Johnson and the Management Committee strongly preferred a "market-driven strategy," focusing PRA&D's efforts on the services, delivery needs, and specialized capabilities key growth markets would demand in the future. However, they were concerned that PRA&D did not have enough partners or associates in its development pipeline (1) to maintain its existing customer base with the kind of quality for which PRA&D was known and (2) to simultaneously develop new "key growth markets." Although they had generally risen through PRA&D's auditing ranks, most members of its Management Committee recognized that the increasing complexities of the CPA mar-

ket place required greater specialization on many professional disciplines in their practice (like taxes, mergers, international regulations, and computer systems) as well as on the needs of specific types of clients (like not-for-profit, government, consortia, financial services, etc. groups). They also recognized that many organizational and incentive changes would be essential to shift PRA&D from its traditional stance into a market-driven enterprise.

ORGANIZATION AND INCENTIVE ISSUES

In the past, PRA&D's partners had been primarily rewarded based upon the profitability and growth their particular geographical office generated. No special incentives existed to develop specific new markets or to cooperate with other offices on a large *Fortune* 500 client's audit which might need staffing support in their geographic area, yet be coordinated by a Practice Partner in another area. The local practice office and the disciplines (like audit, tax, or systems) within the office were the central organizational units in PRA&D. Regional, industry specialist, and other "specialized practice units" were generally subordinate to the practice offices. However, there had been much discussion about the desirability of centralizing some of the disciplines more or developing Regional Partners who would work with all the other partners in a designated geographical area. As envisioned, the Regional Partners would have primary responsibility (rather than simply a coordinating role) for regionwide strategy, planning, market development, and emphasis, and the allocation of many personnel and financial resources. The Regional Partners (reporting to the Management Committee) would be responsible for balancing the goals and needs of all "practice units" and geographical areas within their region into a consolidated strategy. Together, they would be responsible for drawing up a firmwide strategy and operating plan extending at least three years into the future. Although the development of such Regional Partners had been considered for some time, the concept had not been implemented.

The basic problem of organizing PRA&D—as with other major accounting firms—revolved around some very complex coordination and incentive issues. Within PRA&D there were at least seven levels of organization which needed to interact: (1) *Specialized Practice Units* focused on special issues, like government contracting, acquisitions and mergers, bankruptcies, or employee benefits and pensions; (2) *Industry*

Specialists Units focused on particular industries like health care, law, retailing, minerals, or energy development; (3) *Practice Offices* having coordinative responsibilities for all local audit, law, systems, and specialized services activities; (4) *Regional Offices* which—if implemented—would be under a Regional Partner responsible for coordination, supervision, and operating performance of the overall practice within a large geographical area; (5) *Activity Partners* at both the national and major city offices, responsible for tax, systems, or management consulting services; (6) *Audit* or *Practice Partners* who coordinated large audits or consulting projects nationwide (or globally) and often had continuing responsibilities for client relationships with that customer; (7) the *Managing Partner* (and *Management Committee*) elected by all full partners.

COMMUNICATION AND COORDINATION AMONG GROUPS

Within PRA&D, as in other major accounting firms, the Management Consulting activity had grown rapidly. Although not as large as its biggest competitors in management consulting, PRA&D had developed a fine reputation for professional consulting. However, it had been unable to obtain substantial synergies between its Accounting and Management Consulting groups. At first, PRA&D had hoped that each group would be able to build the other's business by recognizing particular skills in its sister organization and recommending to clients that they enquire about PRA&D's capabilities in those areas. For example, an auditor might see a genuine inventory control problem developing in a client firm and suggest PRA&D Consulting's excellent inventory control group to work on it. Similarly, PRA&D's Consulting Group might develop an acquisition strategy for a client and recommend some of PRA&D Accounting's very sophisticated services at key junctures for the client. For a variety of reasons, this type of relationship had not developed well.

However, it had proved to be equally difficult for PRA&D to transfer specialized knowledge even within its Accounting Group or its Management Consulting Group. For example, the Accounting Group might develop an extremely sophisticated solution to a complex problem in Seattle, but other PRA&D offices might never hear about the solution. The Chicago Accounting Office might identify interesting new growth areas among high-technology or services companies in its

area or develop a superb sales methodology for generating new clients. But such information was rarely effectively transmitted to or exploited by other offices. The Management Committee was deeply concerned that the firm was losing substantial profits by not utilizing its full capabilities and solutions to problems which existed inside PRA&D. The firm's highly decentralized, partner-centered, operating philosophy had dictated that all plans—for goals, client service activities, office or departmental operations be generated "bottom up." The Management Committee was concerned that these plans were not properly coordinated across the entire firm, nor did they serve well as the basis for PRA&D's most important strategic decisions: partner evaluation, business development, and partner deployment.

The Management Committee was also concerned that its current methodology of awarding partnership shares exacerbated local offices' independence, and hindered their coordination with others' activities. It also encouraged development of specialization at local levels, where it was difficult to find enough clients to justify the critical mass of people necessary to develop a specialty in real depth. Finally, it was extremely difficult to move a highly qualified specialist—or a partner with strongly developed client contacts—from one local office to another, either temporarily or permanently. Such people often had very strong personal preferences for a particular job location. In addition, they tended to be major contributors to local profitability. Consequently, practice offices were reluctant to transfer such people to other locations, or to lend them for any substantial period of time. And individuals hesitated to move to another location where they would lose income or partnership shares while they rebuilt their contacts and billing capabilities in the new area.

The reverse problem often occurred when another office asked a local practice office for support on a large client audit or consulting project which had a division or activity in its area. The local office might have its resources entirely deployed against its own high-priority client base, and be reluctant to take top-rated people from those clients to support another office's project. There were also great difficulties in stimulating local partners to invest substantial amounts of time or money in developing new skill sets or specialties which might not bring profits to their local office for many years. And, finally, many partners tended to resist investment in technologies (especially those they could not directly control) which were not immediately or solely related to their own particular practice's development and profitability. These were common problems for many CPA firms. But PRA&D, which had very sophisticated systems people and techniques for serving clients, had been slower than others to develop the coordinated computer, management information, incentives, and networking systems needed for its own operations.

The Management Committee was deeply aware of these problems and perplexed by them. Many of the specialist, practice, and local partners also shared these concerns, although many others were less worried. Because enough partners had been making very high incomes and were quite comfortable with existing practices, it had been extraordinarily difficult to develop an integrated strategy which could focus PRA&D's enormous potentials on selected markets either in the United States or worldwide.

QUESTIONS

1. What major strategic options exist for PRA&D? How can PRA&D evaluate those options effectively given the diverse interests of its various internal constituencies? What strategy would you recommend and why?

2. How does strategy in this professional environment differ from that in other fields? How does the interaction of Management Consulting, Accounting, and other specialist groups affect the decision?

3. What problems would you foresee in implementing your strategy? Specifically, how should PRA&D deal with these?

APPENDIX A—PROFILE OF THE MAJOR ACCOUNTING FIRMS

Growth and Source of International versus U.S. Revenues, 1977 and 1986

	U.S. versus Total Revenues		Comp. Annual Growth Rate 1977–1986		TREND IN GEOGRAPHIC EMPHASIS
FIRM	1977	1986	WORLDWIDE	U.S.	
Peat Marwick Main	71%	52%	20%	16%	Overseas
Arthur Andersen	75	76	16	16	Balanced
Coopers & Lybrand	52	56	14	15	Domestic
Price Waterhouse	51	53	12	13	Domestic
PRA&D	50	52	10	14	Overseas
Ernst & Whinney	74	68	15	14	Overseas
Arthur Young & Co.	54	47	15	13	Overseas
Touche Ross & Co.	53	53	14	14	Balanced
Deloitte, Haskins	54	55	12	12	Balanced

Source: 1977 figures from P. Bernstein, "Competition Comes to Accounting," *Fortune,* July 17, 1978; and 1986 figures from *Public Accounting Report,* as cited in "Peat Marwick and KMG Main Agree to Merge," *The Wall Street Journal,* September 4, 1986.

1986 Relative Market Positions International versus U.S.

FIRM	World Wide		United States	
	REVENUES ($ MILLIONS)	RELATIVE POSITION	REVENUES ($ MILLIONS)	RELATIVE POSITION
Peat Marwick Main	$2,700	1.5	$1,400	1.0
Arthur Andersen	1,800	1.2	1,360	1.5
Coopers & Lybrand	1,550	1.1	865	1.2
PRA&D	1,450	1.0	790	1.1
Price Waterhouse	1,400	1.0	742	1.2
Ernst & Whinney	1,360	1.0	930	1.1
Arthur Young & Co.	1,330	1.2	625	1.0
Touche Ross & Co.	1,120	1.0	590	2.4
Deloitte, Haskins & Sells	1,100	2.6	610	1.0

Note: Relative market positions are calculated by dividing a firm's revenues by those of the next largest competitor.

Source: 1976 revenues from *Public Accounting Report,* as cited in "Peat Marwick and KMG Main Agree to Merge," *The Wall Street Journal,* September 4, 1986.

Consulting Practices of Major CPA Firms

FIRM	1987 WORLDWIDE CONSULTING REVENUES ($ MILLIONS)	% OF TOTAL REVENUES WORLDWIDE	NUMBER OF CONSULTANTS
Arthur Andersen	$838	36%	9,639
Peat Marwick Main	438	13	4,700
PRA&D	390	20	3,750
Coopers & Lybrand	381	18	4,712
Ernst & Whinney	374	21	3,255
Price Waterhouse	345	20	4,300
Touche Ross & Co.	248	17	2,142
Deloitte, Haskins & Sells	209	14	2,271
Arthur Young & Co.	204	12	2,443

Source: Consultants News and *Bowman's Accounting Report,* in "Cutting the Pie," *The Wall Street Journal,* July 26, 1988.

MICROSOFT CORPORATION

GEORGE W. DANFORTH, ROBERT N. MCGRATH,
GARY J. CASTROGIORANNI, *all of Louisiana State University*

▼

Microsoft began in 1975 in the midst of great excitement and anticipation among American back-room computer hobbyists who began to foresee the advent of microcomputers made possible by the development of the microprocessor. Until then, computers were very large, usually filling an entire room, and thus computer enthusiasts were forced to buy expensive computer time on mainframes. But microprocessor technology was rapidly advancing, and pockets of young computer enthusiasts watched eagerly, waiting for the pivotal breakthrough that would launch a revolution.

Shortly after Intel announced development of the 8080 chip in 1974, the December issue of *Popular Mechanics* featured the Altair, the world's first microcomputer, produced by a small company called MITS (Micro Instrumentation and Telemetry Systems). Finding practical applications for the Altair was extremely difficult though because it required the user to be technically proficient with programming in machine language, a skill only the most gifted possessed.

One week after reading the article on the Altair, two nineteen-year-old computer buffs, Paul Allen and Bill Gates, called MITS and claimed to have written a program that would allow the Altair to be programmed in BASIC, a programming language that had been used on larger computers. Two months later, in February 1975, they successfully demonstrated their program at a MITS laboratory in Albuquerque. In July 1975, Gates and Allen formed a partnership called Microsoft (short for Microcomputer Software) with the intent of developing computer languages for the Altair and other microcomputers that were sure to follow. Microsoft's first contract was to develop BASIC for the Altair.

MS-DOS

In 1980, IBM covertly decided to enter the burgeoning microcomputer industry. At this time, IBM contacted Microsoft and asked if it could write a BASIC program to reside in the permanent memory of an 8-bit computer. IBM also asked Microsoft to furnish languages for the machine to include FORTRAN, Pascal, and COBOL. In order to do this, Microsoft had to gain access to operating system software. While BASIC had its own operating system embedded within itself, the other languages worked under CP/M, which was then the dominant operating system in the industry and was produced by Digital Research. Both Gates and IBM representatives approached Digital Research about supplying CP/M as the operating system for the IBM machines, but Digital balked because IBM insisted on extremely restrictive contract provisions. Gates was disappointed. He had hoped to gain access to Digital's CP/M for the 8086 chip which was then in development. Then, Microsoft could have adapted their languages to the emergent operating system.

Until then, Digital Research had developed operating systems and Microsoft had focused on program

Case copyright © 1992 by George W. Danforth. Case by George W. Danforth, Robert N. McGrath, and Gary J. Castrogiovanni, Louisiana State University. Copyright 1992, George W. Danforth.

ming languages, and both had respected the other's domain. A year earlier, Digital Research had violated this implied understanding by adding languages to its catalog. Microsoft's relationship with Digital Research was disintegrating.

Bill Gates decided on a bold move. He told IBM that Microsoft could not only supply the languages for the IBM machine, but also the operating system. IBM, now irritated by the inflexibility of Digital Research, accepted.

Microsoft's contract to supply the IBM operating system started a battle with Digital Research over which company would supply the dominant operating system in the industry. Many proponents of CP/M argued that, as the industry standard, CP/M was best for linking existing languages, applications software, and hardware. Nonetheless, less than a year following the announcement of the IBM-PC, numerous microcomputer manufacturers signed contracts with Microsoft to include MS-DOS (the Microsoft operation system) as their hardware's resident operating system. If a major player like IBM was entering the market, it was highly likely that application software programmers would write programs that were compatible with the IBM system. If a manufacturer's machine could not run popular applications programs, customers would not buy it.

In 1983, Lotus released what was to be the most popular applications software ever produced, an electronic spreadsheet program called Lotus 1-2-3. Lotus 1-2-3 was written for and operated only under MS-DOS. Largely because of the phenomenal demand for 1-2-3, MS-DOS was used by over 80 percent of all users in 1984. By 1986, half of Microsoft's annual revenues of $61 million came from the sale of MS-DOS.

Although Microsoft had made short shrift of Digital Research in the MS-DOS – CP/M battle, there is little doubt that its remarkable success was the result of MS-DOS's affiliation with the IBM name. CP/M was by all standards an excellent operating system, and nearly all software and hardware were tuned into it. It was the quick and powerful emergence of the IBM-PC that catapulted MS-DOS and Microsoft into success. The IBM-PC quickly became the industry standard machine, forcing other manufacturers to make machines that were compatible with the IBM system. Ninety-nine percent of IBM compatibles carried MS-DOS as their operating system.

Digital Research learned a costly lesson. Whether a company produced hardware, operating systems, languages, or applications software, its product had to be positioned so as to be included in the dominant configuration of these products. Customers bought hardware that was capable of running certain programs, and likewise bought software that would run on the particular machine they owned. Understanding this interdependence between microcomputers and various types of software was the key to positioning both hardware and software in the market. Holding a commanding position in operating systems software, Microsoft turned its attention to applications software.

THE ELECTRONIC SPREADSHEET

In the early 1980s, many computer companies did not believe that microcomputers held significant potential for business applications. Then, the appearance of the first electronic spreadsheet, called VisiCalc, met a specific and powerful business need. Previously, managers interested in calculating solutions to complex problems had been forced to either spend hours using a calculator or to get company computer personnel to write a specific program for the company mainframe. VisiCalc enabled managers to define their model and run countless alternative solutions. Initially, the program could be run only on an Apple II (and this was a primary determinant of the Apple II's success). It was later adapted to run on the IBM-PC. Another spreadsheet program, SuperCalc, was developed by Sorcim to run on CP/M systems. There was little doubt that the advent of spreadsheets heralded a boom in hardware and software sales to businesses.

When Gates and Allen decided to enter the applications software market in 1980, the spreadsheet was a logical starting point. Because there was no hardware standard at the time, Microsoft's strategy was to develop a spreadsheet that could be ported to as many different machines as possible. The two dominant spreadsheet programs were limited in this respect. VisiCalc could not run under the CP/M operating system, and SuperCalc could not operate on Apple IIs. Gates decided to develop a spreadsheet that was ported to all the operating systems on the market, including CP/M, Apple DOS, Unix, and of course MS-DOS.

While Microsoft was developing its spreadsheet, dubbed Multiplan, IBM placed great pressure on Microsoft to ensure that the new spreadsheet could run on its limited 64K PC models. Gates acquiesced to the computer giant, sacrificing many design attributes in order to keep in the good graces of Microsoft's primary customer.

When released in late 1982, Multiplan met with some initial success but then was quickly eclipsed by Lotus 1-2-3 in 1983. Unlike Multiplan, 1-2-3 was aimed at 256K machines and reflected the richness of capability that the increased RAM afforded. Sales of Lotus 1-2-3 took off. In 1982, Lotus 1-2-3 settled into the number one selling software spot, a position it held for the following six years. With the extraordinary success of 1-2-3, Lotus became the top maker of software in 1982 having annual sales of $157 million compared to $125 million for Microsoft.

Microsoft had made a costly mistake. By agreeing to IBM's request that Multiplan be operable on 64K machines, Microsoft had been blind to the growing demand for more powerful, high-end machines and their associated software. Interestingly, IBM's sales of 256K PCs skyrocketed that year. IBM felt that 1-2-3 had done for the IBM-PC what VisiCalc had done for the Apple II.

However, the Multiplan project was not a complete loss. Although 1-2-3 had taken firm control of the U.S. spreadsheet market, accounting for 80 percent of all sales in 1986, Microsoft had adeptly positioned Multiplan in Europe. In 1982, Microsoft began to adapt Multiplan to each of the European languages. In addition, Gates decided to open up subsidiaries in each of their three major European markets—England, France, and Germany. Multiplan's ability to run on many different systems proved to be a great advantage. Unlike the U.S. market, IBM-PCs and compatibles did not dominate in Europe. Apple controlled 50 percent of the market and Commodore 30 percent.

When IBM arrived in Europe in 1984, its PC included Multiplan rather than Lotus 1-2-3. By the time Lotus brought 1-2-3 to Europe in 1985, it was too late. In 1987, while Lotus 1-2-3 held 80 percent of the American spreadsheet market to Multiplan's 6 percent, Multiplan dominated the European market, accounting for 60 percent in Germany and 90 percent in France.

Because Multiplan was so successful overseas, Microsoft continued to distribute it. But Bill Gates would not forget why the package had failed in the U.S. and 1-2-3 had succeeded instead.

WORD PROCESSING

In 1983, Microsoft launched its offensive on a second front, word processing. At that time, WordStar, developed by MicroPro, was the most popular word processing software. The Microsoft designers believed they could best WordStar by including in their program a number of additional characteristics. Microsoft Word would be the first word processing software that displayed bold-type, underlining, italics, subscripts, and superscripts on the screen. In addition, the screen could be divided into windows, allowing the user to work with more than one text at a time. Instead of requiring the user to format each text individually, Word would offer style sheets which stored formats created by the user for repeated use. Lastly, Word would be capable of printing out in any of the fonts available in the state-of-the-art laser printers.

Word was introduced to the U.S. market in a novel way. Demonstration copies which would do everything but save or print files were sent out at great expense to the 100,000 subscribers of PC World in its November 1983 special edition. Although many newspapers lauded the unique and imaginative marketing technique employed by Microsoft, Word was greeted with a marginal response. The word processing program, although extremely powerful, proved to be too complex for the average user. Subsequent improved versions in 1984 and 1985 steadily increased sales. However, Microsoft was again beaten out, this time by a small software publisher called WordPerfect.

WordPerfect was jointly founded by a computer science professor and his student in 1979. The company's only employees were a group of students that helped with distribution tasks. Yet the fledgling enterprise was able to differentiate its program through a heavy emphasis on service. WordPerfect provided free telephone support to customers and followed up every inquiry until the customer was satisfied.

While Microsoft spent millions promoting Word, WordPerfect avoided sophisticated promotional campaigns, building a loyal following by word of mouth. Microsoft was at a loss as to how to respond to WordPerfect's ingenious grassroots campaign. WordPerfect's sales grew steadily and quickly. In 1986, it became the top selling word processing software. Info Corp listed the top selling word processing programs for 1986 as follows:

1. WordPerfect	31%
2. WordStar	16%
3. IBM VisiOn	13%
4. pfs:Write and Multimate	12%
5. Word	11%

Word was losing out to WordPerfect and others for a very different reason than Multiplan had lost to Lotus

1-2-3. Multiplan failed in the U.S. because Microsoft was coerced by IBM into gauging the program for IBM's low-end machines. Word was losing because Microsoft, in its zeal to create the most powerful word processing program available, had failed to consider the full array of user needs.

Just as the success of Multiplan was resurrected by turning to the European market, so too would Word fare better there. When Word arrived in France in 1984 with mixed reviews, WordStar and Textor, produced by a French company, were already well positioned. Gates and his European staff decided on a three pronged penetration strategy. First, to encourage distributors to sell Word, Microsoft France provided distributors with free training and a free copy of Word. Second, Microsoft arranged to have all retailer demonstrations of Hewlett Packard's new LaserJet printer performed using Word. Lastly, Microsoft France persuaded many printer manufacturers to promote Word because of its ability to port to sophisticated, high-end multifont printers. Michael Lacombe, CEO of Microsoft France, explained:

> When a client would go to a retailer and asked to see how Word worked with a printer, in 95 percent of the cases, the distributor would not be able to answer the question. We visited all the printer manufacturers and sold them on the idea of a Microsoft Word binder with several pages of printing samples.

As a result of this aggressive marketing effort, Word began making inroads into the French market in 1985. After a much-refined Word 3.0 was released in April 1986, sales of Word rose fast. In 1987, it was the highest selling word processing software in France with sales of 28,700 copies compared to 10,300 for IBM VisiOn, 7000 for Textor, 3,800 for WordPerfect, and 3,300 for WordStar.

While Microsoft had again created a phenomenal success in Europe with a program that had been unsuccessful in the U.S., the great improvements made in the 3.0 version of Word also substantially increased its U.S. market share. In this version, the previous problems experienced by users in learning Word were solved by what was then an ingenious solution. Included with all 3.0 versions of Word was a step-by-step on-line tutorial that replaced the traditional user's manual. U.S. sales of Word climbed substantially. By 1989, Word's sales had reached 650,000 compared to 937,000 of Word-Perfect. Although Word was by many standards a superior product, WordPerfect had firmly established itself as the word processing software of choice for PC users. Once customers learned and grew comfortable with a program, it was often difficult and costly for them to switch.

While Microsoft was having difficulty capturing market share with its earlier versions of Word in 1984 and 1985, it was working feverishly on a Word program for the Apple Macintosh computer which was the only substantial challenger to the IBM standard. When Word for the MAC was released in 1985 there were no other word processing programs available for the Macintosh except Apple's own software, called Mac-Write, which was included with the sale of each machine. Although Word for the MAC had some bugs, it began to gather a following among Macintosh users. When the 3.0 version was released in 1986, it was a tremendous success. By 1988, with annual sales of 250,000 copies, it was second only to the PC versions of WordPerfect and Word. WordPerfect released its own version for the Macintosh in 1988, but it was too late. As WordPerfect had beaten Microsoft to the U.S. PC market, so had Microsoft preempted WordPerfect in the Macintosh market. When Word version 4.0 was released in 1989, 100,000 copies were sold immediately, confirming Word's preeminence with the Macintosh.

GRAPHICAL USER INTERFACES

Although the IBM-PC was the best selling microcomputer in the industry and was copied by a great number of other manufacturers, the Apple Macintosh surpassed all others in user friendliness because of Apple's unique work with graphical user interfaces. While users of IBM-PCs and compatibles had to interact with their machines using learned text commands such as erase, the Macintosh user employed a mouse to connect icons or simple images on the screen. For instance, instead of typing the command, erase, the MAC user could use a mouse to point to a file icon and pull it to an icon of a trash can. Both Gates and Apple co-founder Steve Jobs believed that the future of microcomputing was in graphical interface technology because it made computers extremely user-friendly, opening up the world of computers to the most unsophisticated user.

In 1981, Apple asked Microsoft to write applications programs for the Macintosh, realizing that the availability of high demand software could determine the success of the Macintosh just as the popularity of VisiCalc had launched the Apple II. Microsoft and Apple began a close collaboration aimed at designing an optimum match between the Macintosh configuration and Microsoft's applications programs. The agreement specified that Microsoft versions of Multiplan,

Chart, and File would be shipped with each Macintosh machine, and that Microsoft could not publish software with a graphical user interface until one year after the Macintosh was released or December 1983 at the latest.

In the following years, Microsoft enjoyed tremendous success with its Macintosh applications programs. In addition to Word for the MAC, Microsoft's new spreadsheet program, Excel, sold at a rapid rate, beating out Lotus's new integrated software called Jazz. In 1986, Microsoft sold 160,000 copies of Excel to MAC users compared to 10,000 copies of Lotus's Jazz. By 1989l, Lotus had decided to stay away from the Macintosh market altogether. Microsoft's success with Macintosh users made it the number one developer of applications software for the first time. The key lesson learned from Microsoft's experience in the Macintosh market was that Microsoft's primary competitive advantage was in graphical user interfaces. As it was clear that the PC market would inevitably move toward graphical interface technology, Microsoft appeared to be in a commanding position to expand its influence in the development of software for that market.

WINDOWS

Windows was Microsoft's attempt to change MS-DOS into a graphical user interface. Although IBM had been successful in setting its hardware and operating system (MS-DOS) as industry standards, no such standardization applied to PC applications software. Each applications program written for the PC was unique in the method demanded to modify or print a file. In addition, the popular PC applications programs communicated with printers differently. Different printers demanded different intermediary programs called drivers to enable printers to receive data from applications. Consequently, when a customer bought a copy of a particular applications software, she often received as many as a dozen diskettes, only one of which carried the applications program. The extra diskettes contained drivers to adapt the program to various printers.

To address this problem, Microsoft decided in 1981 to develop a program that would act as a layer between the operating system and applications software, interpreting the particular communications requirements of the printer and monitor being used. The second purpose of this program would be to place a graphical interface over MS-DOS that would standardize the appearance of applications so that they would share common commands for such actions as modifying texts or printing files.

While Microsoft was working on their graphical interface, dubbed Windows, other companies began to develop their own versions. VisiCorp, for example, released VisiOn in 1983. More perturbing, however, was that some industry analysts were speculating that IBM was working on its own version of a graphical interface. In the past, powerful IBM had largely looked to Microsoft to develop the software for its PC; however Gates suspected that IBM wanted to grab a piece of the highly lucrative software market for itself. Past dealings with Big Blue proved that the computer giant was intent on expanding its control to include standardization of the entire computer configuration to include not only hardware but also software. When IBM announced in 1983 that it was releasing TopView, a graphical interface to rest on top of DOS, it was a clear signal that IBM was no longer content to remain in the domain of hardware. This action by IBM, although disturbing to Microsoft, was not at all surprising. The computer industry in general was characterized by Machiavellian moves and countermoves. While companies were often dependent on others to develop and position their products into a dominant or advantageous hardware-software configuration, collaborative efforts and contracts were usually characterized by ulterior motives and covert countervailing thrusts.

Recognizing that IBM was attempting to squeeze Microsoft out of future software sales, Gates acted quickly. He contacted the manufacturers of IBM compatible computers and tried to persuade them to follow Microsoft's lead with Windows, and thus isolate IBM. A large group of IBM compatible manufacturers did not want IBM to further monopolize standards and were amenable to waiting for Microsoft's version of Windows rather than following IBM's lead by including TopView with its machines. Although they were competitors, many software companies also pledged their support to Microsoft Windows. The support of Lotus was particularly appreciated as it was the primary supplier of applications software for the PC and compatibles. It was apparent that they did not relish the thought of a stronger, more influential IBM and were willing to accept Microsoft's lead to prevent it. The software publishers were also confident that Microsoft would create an interface environment into which they could easily port their applications programs. IBM, on the other hand, had released a version of TopView configured in such a way that, if successful, would give Big Blue a significant advantage in the development of future applications.

Gates's success in this effort would prove critical

to the success of Windows. He had never hesitated to play hardball in the past with larger, more powerful companies. While some criticized Gates as an opportunist, others saw him as an astute and resolute visionary.

The Windows project was characterized by lengthy and embarrassing delays. Although Gates announced the imminent release of Windows in 1983, it did not hit the market until November of 1985. Over twenty software publishers had to delay their Windows ported applications software. By 1985, most of these companies had put all Windows associated software projects on hold. Nevertheless, shortly after its introduction, Windows was a great success. After sales exceeded 1 million copies of Windows, the 2.0 version was released in 1987. This version offered a user interface that was very similar to that of the Macintosh. When Microsoft released its PC version of Excel that same year, Windows's credibility increased even more, and PC manufacturers began positioning their machines against Apple's Macintosh.

THE APPLE LAWSUIT

On March 17, 1988, Apple announced that it was suing Microsoft over Windows 2.03 and Hewlett Packard over New Wave, its graphical interface environment. What made the announcement particularly unsavory to Gates was that he had just seen the CEO of Apple, John Sculley, and no mention was made of it. Apple announced the news of the suit to the press before notifying Microsoft.

Apple argued that it had spent millions creating a distinctive visual interface which had become the Macintosh's distinguishing feature and that Microsoft had illegally copied the "look and feel" of their Macintosh. Microsoft countered that its 1985 contract with Apple granted it license to use the visual interface already included in six Microsoft programs, and that this license implicitly covered the 1987 version, Windows 2.03. In July of 1989, Judge Schwarzer dropped 179 of the 189 items that Apple had argued were copyright violations. The ten remaining items were related to the use of certain icons and overlapping windows in Windows 2.03. In February of 1990, Judge Walker of the Federal District Court of San Francisco took over the case. He had previously ruled against Xerox in their suit against Apple over the same copyrights. In March 1990, Walker ruled that the portions of 2.03 under debate were not covered by the 1985 agreement between Apple and Microsoft. As of late 1991, the case is still in

litigation. If Apple should lose the case, it would also lose a competitive advantage in terms of distinctive visual interface. If Microsoft should lose, it might have to take all current versions of Windows off the market and pay royalties on past sales to Apple.

A DISTINCTIVE ORGANIZATION

Computer programming is an activity dominated by the young. It is also an extremely intense activity that demands absolute focused concentration on the part of the programmer for extended periods of time. The software industry can be characterized as competition between groups of minds. It is an utterly innovative industry in which relatively little resources are spent on anything but the support of the imaginative process.

Finding its genesis in the early days of Microsoft, when Gates and Allen and a small coterie of programmers literally worked and slept at work for weeks at a time under incredible pressure, the Microsoft culture has jelled into its present and unique form. The working atmosphere at Microsoft counterbalances the intensity of activity with an offbeat emphasis on an unstructured and informal environment. Working hours are extraordinarily flexible. Dress and appearance are extremely casual. Many programmers work in bare feet. It is not unknown for a team of programmers working in an intense project to take a break at 3 A.M. and spend thirty minutes making considerable racket with their electric guitars and synthesizers.

The present Microsoft complex in Redmond, Washington, looks more like a college campus than the headquarters of a Fortune 500 company. It can be almost surrealistic. Most of the 5200 employees have offices with windows. The courtyards adjoining the principle structures are often rife with the activity of employees juggling, riding unicycles, or playing various musical instruments.

Microsoft employs many people from foreign countries, giving the company grounds an international flavor. Some of these employees work on the many foreign translations of Microsoft's software. Others are simply many of the best programmers in the world that Microsoft attracts to its fold.

Microsoft hires the very best and hardest working programmers, and then allows them wide discretion in their work. When hiring, Microsoft cares little about a candidate's formal education or experience. After all, neither Bill Gates nor Paul Allen ever graduated from college. No matter how lofty an applicant's credentials appear to be, she is not hired until she has been thoroughly questioned on programming knowledge and skills. Charles Simonyi, chief architect of the development groups for Multiplan, Word, and Excel, insisted for some time on personally interviewing each applicant. He explained:

> There are a lot of formulas for making a good candidate into a good programmer. We hire talented people. I don't know how they got their talent and I don't care. But they are talented. From then on, there is a hell of a lot the environment can do.

Microsoft employees earn relatively modest salaries, compared to the rest of the industry. Bill Gates himself has never earned more than $175,000 in salary per year (he is, however, a billionaire due to his 35 percent share of Microsoft stock). Employee turnover is about 8 percent, well below the industry standard.

Microsoft is loosely structured. Programmers are usually assigned to small project teams. Gates explains that "it takes a small team to do it right. When we started Excel, we had five people working on it, including myself. We have seven people working on it today." Communications at Microsoft are open. Everyone is tied together in a vast electronic network, and anyone can send a message to anyone else via electronic mail regardless of relative status.

One of the keys to Microsoft's success is that it attracts the finest programmers in the industry and creates an environment that not only pleases and retains employees but is also conducive to high computer programming productivity. No amount of financial might can make a software company successful. There are no apparent economies of scale to be realized. The primary asset that determines success or failure of a software company is the creativity and performance of its people.

POSITIONING FOR THE 90s

In 1987, Microsoft began collaborating with IBM on the development of a new operating system called OS/2 and a new, more powerful graphical interface named Presentation Manager. In late 1989, IBM released OS/2 version 1.2 for IBM-PCs. Microsoft released OS/2 version 1.21 for IBM-compatible machines in mid-1990. Sales of OS/2 have been far lower than hoped.

Many industry observers consider OS/2 the inevitable replacement of DOS; however, DOS version 5.0 was released in 1991, fueling speculation and confusion as to which direction Microsoft was leading the industry in. In fact, IBM appears to believe it was double-crossed. When the introduction of OS/2 went poorly, Microsoft continued to upgrade and push MS-DOS and Windows, at the expense of OS/2 and Presentation Manager. IBM has since taken over the majority of the development on OS/2 and distanced itself from Microsoft.

In June of 1991, IBM and Apple began a joint venture to develop an entirely new PC standard in which they will control the rights to the operating system and the microprocessor. This cooperation between the two largest microcomputer manufacturers could have a tremendous effect on the software industry. If IBM and Apple are successful in developing and controlling a new industry standard operating system, Microsoft's would lose its preeminent position in the industry. Right now, nearly all applications programs written are ported through Microsoft's MS-DOS/ Windows environment, enabling Microsoft to determine the direction and makeup of future computer applications. If the IBM-Apple initiative proves successful, Microsoft could be placed in the unfamiliar position of following another company's lead for the first time in its history.

The IBM–Apple venture is not a sure bet, though. The advanced technology they are working on is extraordinarily complex, and the risks are high for both companies. John Sculley, CEO of Apple, has said: "This is something only Apple and IBM could pull off. Still, it's a big gamble, and we're betting our whole company on it." Another concern is that the radically different cultures of the two manufacturers and their historical disdain for one another may make progress difficult.

In addition, Microsoft still holds significant sway over the applications development efforts of other software companies. Over time, customers have made significant investments in hardware and software that operate in the MS-DOS/Windows environment. It is questionable whether software publishers or customers would make wholesale changes so readily.

Bill Gates comments:

> Sure, we're being attacked on all sides, but that's nothing new. Customers will vote on all of this. I think ours will thank us for preserving their current investment in PCs, while improving that technology. That has always been our strategy.

1. What were the critical factors in Microsoft's past success? Trace the crucial interactions with its customers and competitors. How can these patterns be applied in the future?

2. What are the major differences in strategic management in a company like Microsoft versus an Intel, IBM, or Sony? The major similarities? How does one form a strategy in this environment? What are the key trends Microsoft must deal with?

3. What are the critical factors in managing software development? How can one leverage intellect in these enterprises? How does an industry or competitive analysis shift in these enterprises? What are the keys to strategy in the future? What would you do to respond to the new joint venture between IBM and Apple?

"The Future of the PC," *Fortune,* August 26, 1991, pp. 40–49.

"How Bill Gates Keeps the Magic Going," *Fortune,* June 18, 1990, pp. 82–89.

"IBM, Apple in Pact to Control Desktop Standard," *Computerworld,* July 8, 1991, pp. 1, 102–103.

Ichbiah, D. & Knepper, S., *The Making of Microsoft* (Rocklin, CA; Prima Publishing, 1991).

"It's Grab Your Partner Time For Software Makers," *Business Week,* February 8, 1988, pp. 86–88.

"PCs: What the Future Holds," *Business Week,* August 12, 1991, pp. 58–64.

"Redrawing the Map: Will IBM/Apple Alliance Shift the Balance of Power," *InfoWorld,* July 22, 1991, pp. 44–436.

"Software: The New Driving Force," *Business Week,* February 27, 1984, pp. 74–98.

EXHIBIT 1 Five Year Summary of Microsoft's Financial Performance

DATE	SALES ($000)	NET INCOME	EPS
1990	1,183,466	279,186	2.34
1989	803,530	170,538	1.52
1988	590,827	123,908	1.11
1987	345,890	71,878	0.65
1986	197,514	39,254	0.39
GROWTH RATE (%)	56.4	63.3	56.5

Source: *Compact Disclosure* (Information Database), Disclosure, Inc.

EXHIBIT 2 Three Year Summary of Microsoft's International Revenues

(IN THOUSANDS)	1990	1989	1988
European Operations	$363,294	$212,018	$144,825
Other International Operations	102,522	72,456	46,874
Export	184,433	153,787	90,537
Total International Revenues	$650,249	$438,261	$282,256
Percentage of Total Revenues	54.9%	54.5%	447.8%

Source: *Compact Disclosure* (Information Database), Disclosure, Inc.

EXHIBIT 3 **Microsoft's Earnings per Share Growth (Actual and Future Estimates)**

| | Microsoft vs. Industry EPS Growth Rates | | | | P/E |
	LAST 5 YRS ACTUAL (%)	91/92 (%)	92/93 (%)	NEXT 5 YEARS	ON 92 EPS
Microsoft	51.8	35.1	23.8	27.7	26.5
Industry	9.3	30.6	25.7	20.4	21.3
S&P 500	6.5	1.7	17.5	7.8	17.7
Microsoft/Industry	5.6	1.1	0.9	1.4	1.2
Microsoft/S&P 500	8.0	21.1	1.4	3.5	1.5

THE BOSTON YWCA: 1991

DONNA M. GALLO, *University of Massachusetts, Amherst*
BARBARA GOTTFRIED, *Bentley College*
ALAN HOFFMAN, *Bentley College*

▼

In the summer of 1991 Mary Kinsell, controller and chief financial officer for the Boston YWCA, briefed her successor, Carolyn Rosen, and Marti Wilson-Taylor, the YWCA's new Executive Director. Deeply aware of the organization's financial crisis, Kinsell noted that the past twenty years had created many difficulties for the once predominant Boston YWCA. Especially pressing was the need to seek out new sources of funding because of significant cuts in federal funding to non-profits, increased demand and competition in the fitness and day-care industries, and increased real estate costs. In addition, the YWCA faced questions about how to deal with several aging YWCA buildings, located in prime neighborhoods of Boston but unmodernized and slowly deteriorating. Ms. Kinsell warned, "The Boston YWCA is like a dowager from an old Boston family that has seen better days: it is 'building rich' and 'cash poor.' Leveraging equity from its buildings is difficult and making operations generate enough cash flow to maintain the buildings seems almost impossible." The YWCA must now meet these challenges or it will be forced to cut back its activities, and may even face bankruptcy.

THE FIRST 100 YEARS

The Young Women's Christian Association (YWCA) is a non-profit organization whose original mission was "To provide for the physical, moral, and spiritual welfare of young women in Boston." For more than twelve decades it has done just that: meeting the changing needs of women in the community by providing services, opportunities, and support in an environment of shared sisterhood.

In 1866, a group of affluent women formed the Boston Young Women's Christian Association to rent rooms to women and children whom the Industrial Revolution had forced to leave their failing farms for work in city factories. Not only were their working conditions deplorable, but their living conditions consisted almost entirely of unsafe slums and unsanitary tenements. The Boston YWCA offered a clean, safe alternative to these living conditions, as well as recreation, companionship, and an employment referral network for women. The success of the facility led to the opening of the Berkeley Residence (40 Berkeley Street, Boston) in 1884, with accommodations for 200 residents and an employment and training bureau. It also housed the first YWCA gymnasium in America, a crucial part of its mission to "empower women through fitness, health care, and independent employment opportunities." At this early date in the YWCA's history, most of the funding for the YWCA's facilities and services was raised by wealthy women patrons both through their family connections and from among their friends and acquaintances. From its inception, the YWCA, unlike the larger, more well-known, and more aggressive YMCA, which easily garnered bank loans and donations, had to struggle to fund its projects.

Case by Donna M. Gallo, Boston College, and Barbara Gottfried and Alan Hoffman, Bentley College.

In the ensuing decades, the Boston YWCA opened *The School of Domestic Science* to train women as institutional housekeepers and managers, and started a secretarial training program, and other training and educational programs for women. In 1911, the Boston YWCA became affiliated with the other YWCA's in the United States. By this time, the YWCA was no longer merely a philanthropic association run by upper class women for women of a lower class, but an association of working women meeting the needs of other working women in the home and in the marketplace. Nevertheless, the continued support of wealthy patrons was crucial to the YWCA's viability as a community resource.

In the early 1920s, the "Y" initiated a capital campaign under the slogan, "Every Girl Needs the YWCA," to raise funds for another building. Over one million dollars in contributions was received by subscription from among donors of both the middle and upper classes, and in 1927 ground was broken at the corner of Clarendon and Stuart Streets for the Boston YWCA's new headquarters. The new building, including recreational facilities, a swimming pool, classrooms, meeting rooms, and offices for the staff, was dedicated in 1929 and has served as headquarters for the association ever since.

During World War II, the YWCA contributed to the war effort by sponsoring educational lectures and forums such as "Fix-It-Yourself" for the wives of servicemen, offering housing to women doing war work, and providing recreation and entertainment to men and women in the armed services. During this time the YWCA continued to be managed and funded primarily by women, for women.

After the war, YWCA administrators made a concerted effort to reach out to immigrant women. An interracial charter was adopted at the national convention which called for the integration and participation of minority groups in every aspect of the association, the community, and the nation. In addition, rapid postwar population growth in the suburbs west of Boston led to the opening in 1964 of the West Suburban Branch of the "Y" in Natick, Massachusetts, 20 miles west of Boston. The Natick "Y" focused its energies on the needs and wants of the suburban women and their children. Additionally, advocates formed a lobbying group, the YWCA Public Affairs Committee, to focus on the areas of housing and family planning, and to call attention to the needs of those women, especially mothers, that were not being met by traditional social service organizations.

Throughout its first 100 years, the Boston YWCA, staffed and funded almost entirely by women, worked to empower women by helping them take charge of their lives, plan for their futures, and become economically independent and self-supporting.

RECENT HISTORY

In 1866, the Boston YWCA became the first YWCA in the nation. Today we are part of the oldest and largest women's organization in the world, serving all people regardless of sex, race, religion or income. Our One Imperative is the elimination of racism.

Mary L. Reed
Former Executive Director, 1986

The 1960s were a time of social and cultural upheaval, especially with regard to civil rights, the movement whose goal was equality for all races. In support of the civil rights movement, the YWCA made a commitment to fight racism and integrate its programs and services at every level, initiating a special two-year action plan in 1963. The operating budget for the plan provided for two staff members and support services to become more involved with other community groups working in the areas of fair housing, voter registration, and literacy programs. In 1967, the YWCA's first black president, Mrs. Robert W. Clayton was elected at the National Convention. In 1968 the Boston YWCA opened Aswalos house in Dorchester, Massachusetts, especially to meet the needs of women in the inner city. As a fitting ending to the 1960s, the *One Imperative,* "To eliminate racism wherever it exists and by any means necessary," was adopted and added to the statement of purpose as the philosophical basis for the YWCA in coming years.

Although fighting racism remained important, in the 1970s the YWCA shifted its attention to issues raised by the changing roles of women in American society. The 1960s and 1970s were decades of the revival and growth of feminist movement in the United States and throughout the world. The social and political arena in which the Boston and other YWCA's were operating was changing rapidly. More and more women were working outside the home while raising children. The number of women living at or near the poverty level was on the rise. Classes and programs at the YWCA had to be redesigned to meet changing demands. For instance, the "Y" offered instruction in survival skills for urban living; but more radically, because non-traditional jobs for women were on the rise, in 1977 the "Y" launched its first non-traditional training program, funded by the federal government, to train women to work in the construction industry. Thus, in the 1970s, federal, state and local governments became increasingly involved in social welfare, whereas in the past these needs had been met by private charitable and voluntary organizations. At the same time that the YWCA began to rely more on government funding and less on private donations, the YWCA's Board of Directors in the 1960s and 1970s changed to reflect the racial and class diversity of the women in the communities the YWCA served. While the new Board members helped the YWCA to respond effectively to the immediate needs of the inner city community, they lost touch with the monied constituency which had formerly been the YWCA's base of support, and that monied constituency in turn shifted its attention and support to other causes.

THE CHANGING ENVIRONMENT

The late 1970s saw a dramatic rise in the number of unwed mothers, teen pregnancy, and teen parenting. At the same time, more and more state and federal funds became available for social programs, and many non-profits directed their energies to establishing themselves as vendors or service providers to win government contracts. The Boston YWCA became a major vendor in the areas of child care, employment training, teen services, and domestic abuse programming. As a result of the YWCA's strong advocacy efforts, major federal and state contracts were awarded to the YWCA for further study of issues related to teen pregnancy. However, the YWCA's redirecting of its efforts toward securing government funding significantly eroded its base of private support, especially among those upper crust women who had, for generations, been the primary source of funds for the YWCA in Boston, and the YWCA which had for a long time been one of a few non-profits, became one of many contending for the same funds.

As the decade came to a close, the outlook for the Boston YWCA began to shift. Given the community's growing need for services and their own aging facilities, the management team of the Boston YWCA realized they would have to make some tough decisions about allocating funds that were beginning to get more scarce. If they were to decide that a major outlay of cash or large loans for facilities were necessary, they would have to pull funds from the programs and services the association provided to the community at a time when the need for community services was greater than ever and funds for these services were scarcer than they had been for some time. However, if the YWCA's management team continued to allocate funds for services and programs while making only minimal allocations for facility maintenance, they risked incurring the cost either of major repairs further down the line, or the serious deterioration of their major assets. Though the management team did not want to lose sight of the YWCA's commitment to the women and children in the community, the "Y's" financial crisis would require foresight, careful planning, and some hard choices.

THE ECONOMIC CRUNCH

In the early 1980s the need for social services grew, increasing the number of non-profit organizations competing for the same funds. At the same time the Reagan Administration cut back federal funding, and non-profits were forced to go back to raising funds through private donations, grants, bequests, and the United Way. The mid-1980s, however, were prosperous years, especially in the Boston area. Individuals and companies gave more generously than in past years to non-profits, and in response to the limited availability of federal funds for social services during the Reagan era, non-profits increasingly directed their resources to funding everything from homeless shelters and food pantries to drug and alcohol rehabilitation centers.

However, the economic downturn in late 1987 immediately cut into the funding flow for non-profits. Corporations and the general public became more discerning about where they directed their charitable contributions. Many people lost their jobs; a high debt lifestyle caught up with others; in short, people's disposable income dropped off. It became increasingly difficult to raise the funds necessary to keep up the facilities and to provide the services the community continued to demand. As the economy worsened, the need for services increased proportionately and at a more rapid rate than the Boston YWCA had ever witnessed. At the same time, the YWCA had to contend both with its old "mainstream" image in the face of the proliferation of more "chic" non-profits such as homeless shelters, battered women's shelters or "safe houses," etc. and with the growing mis-perception of the YWCA as an organization run primarily by women of color for women of color.

The climate for the banking industry in Boston during the late 1980s also altered dramatically. Many banks were in financial trouble and those that had lent freely in the mid-1980s now scrutinized every loan request and rejected a large majority of those they received. Funds for capital improvements and construction were not looked upon favorably by most Boston area banks; and money to fund new projects and large renovations became nearly impossible to obtain. These negative trends have only worsened so far in the 1990s, as the YWCA faces the absolute necessity of making some hard decisions regarding the allocation of its shrinking resources.

SOURCES OF FUNDING

Revenue for the Boston YWCA comes from three sources:

1. *Support Funds*—funds from the United Way of Massachusetts Bay, contributions, grants, legacies, and bequests.
2. *Operating Revenue*—money from program fees, government sponsored programs, membership dues, housing and food services.
3. *Non-Operating Revenue*—income from leasing of office space to outside concerns, investment income, and net realized gain on investments. The table below shows the percentage each has contributed to the total revenue for the past 5 years.

Percentage Breakdown—Sources of Funding

	1985	1986	1987	1988	1989	1990
Support Funds	22%	22%	23%	21%	24%	33%
Operating Revenue	67%	66%	65%	67%	63%	54%
Non-Operating Revenue	11%	12%	12%	12%	13%	13%

From 1985 to 1989 the United Way accounted for 70–80% of the support funds revenue. But like all non-profit organizations in the late 1980s, the United Way was under fire for its operational procedures and found itself in a fiercely competitive fundraising environment. The United Way anticipated a 30% drop in fundraising for 1991, which would affect all the agencies it funded, including the Boston YWCA. At the same time, operating revenues for the YWCA dropped off in 1990 as well, so that more, rather than less support funding was needed to operate. Since support funding is expected to continue to decrease in the next three to five years, the Boston YWCA must discover new sources of funding to maintain its services and meet its operational expenses.

FACILITIES

In 1987, the Boston YWCA was operating from four facilities in neighborhoods of Boston and one in a western suburb of the city. During 1987, the Boston Redevelopment Authority, a commission which oversees all real estate development in the city, awarded a parcel of land to the YWCA for $1.00 on which to build a new facility as part of the city's redevelopment plan. The new facility would replace the old Dorchester YWCA, Aswalos House, which a grant would then convert to transitional housing for unwed mothers and their children. Since the YWCA now had a new parcel of land, and other existing facilities in need of maintenance and repair, the management team embarked on a three-year study to analyze its programs and services, and its properties. Most importantly, they decided to implement an aggressive renovation schedule designed to modernize all facilities, to protect the value of the YWCA's major assets, its buildings.

As part of this renovation, repair, and maintenance program, the association's management team had to perform a thorough review of its programs and services. The programs most beneficial to the agency in terms of revenue and those the community had the greatest need for had to be assessed for future expectations of growth and space requirements. New programs would have to be accommodated and those programs that were no longer financially feasible or in demand would have to be eliminated. The management team planned to complete their research and decision-making prior to implementing any expansion or renovation of the buildings.

I. West Suburban Program Center

When the YWCA expanded, and opened a branch in Natick, Massachusetts, a suburb located twenty miles west of Boston in 1964, it bought a building which quickly became inadequate to the YWCA's needs, and in 1981 the center moved to a new facility. The resources for women at this branch were designed to serve its suburban constituency, and included programs for women re-entering the job market after years of parenting, training programs for displaced workers, spousal and family abuse programs, divorce support groups, and counseling for women suffering from breast cancer. However, in 1988, after much research and years of restructuring the services offered at the West Suburban Program Center, its inability to support itself financially through its operations led to a decision to close down the facility.

II. Aswalos House

Aswalos House, located in Dorcester, Massachusetts, an urban center within the jurisdiction of the City of Boston, was originally opened in 1968. Until 1989, it housed an After School Enrichment Program and a Teen Development Program which offered training for word processing and clerical work, and GED preparation courses. Later, Aswalos House added a program for teen mothers.

In 1989, the receipt of a $100,000 HUD grant transformed Aswalos House into transitional housing for teenage mothers and their children, and existing programs were transferred to other facilities. Originally the programs were to be transferred to the new Dorchester Branch planned for the parcel acquired from the City of Boston. However, that parcel was never developed because development costs were estimated at $1.5 million–$2 million, but the YWCA was only able to raise $300,000. Consequently, the parcel of land was returned to the City of Boston.

The new Aswalos House for teen mothers opened in October 1990, and provided transitional housing for ten mothers and their children. Prospective occupants have to be between sixteen and twenty and demonstrate severe financial need. Counseling services are provided, and a staff case worker arranges for schooling and job training for the teenagers. In addition, a staff housing advocate coordinates permanent housing for the mothers and their children.

Half the expense of running the facility is covered by a federal grant to the Boston YWCA. The remaining half is made up by fees paid by the teen mothers from their welfare income, and by contributions from the United Way and private donations.

III. YWCA Child Care Center

The YWCA Child Care Center is rather inconveniently located in downtown Boston on the fringe of the commercial district, and is rented rather than owned by the YWCA. To be licensed as a day care center in the Commonwealth of Massachusetts, it had to undergo extensive renovations. The owner of the property contributed a substantial portion of the cost of the renova-

tion work, and the balance of the expense was covered by a private grant so that no loans were necessary to complete the project.

The center, a licensed pre-school, provides daycare for fifty children at fees of $110 a week per toddler and $150 a week per child for children under 3. Some scholarships are available for families who are unable to pay. When the center first opened, many of its clients were on state-funded day care vouchers. Participation has now dropped considerably, however, because a significant percentage of state-funded day care vouchers were cut from the state budget. To compensate for the loss of clients, the center went into the infant care business, caring for children from 6 months to 2 years, but it continues to run at less than capacity.

IV. The Berkeley Residence

The Berkeley Residence was opened in 1884 in downtown Boston to serve as housing for women of all ages. Originally there was housing for one hundred residents, an employment and training bureau, and a gymnasium, the first in the country for women. In 1907, 35 rooms and a meeting hall were added to the facility.

In 1985 the Berkeley Residence was cited by Boston's Building Code Department because it did not meet current safety and fire codes of the city or the Commonwealth. Major repairs and renovations estimated at $1 million were necessary to bring the building up to healthy, safe, and legal standards. In 1986, a construction loan for the full amount was secured at 10% interest amortized over 25 years. Once the project was completed, payments would come to approximately $100,000 annually. Work began in 1988. Repairs were needed to the infrastructure of the building, and included a conversion from oil heat to gas, a sprinkler system and smoke detector system wired throughout the building, new elevators, as well as many other repairs and maintenance work of a less costly nature. Tenants were not displaced during construction, a major concern at the beginning of the project's planning stage.

After completion of the renovation work in the spring of 1991, the facility now rents 215 rooms which provide long-term and short-term housing for women of all ages. The Berkeley Residence offers inexpensive rent and meals, an answering service, and maid service. Other services located at the facility include a referral network for jobs and services, social services, tourist information, and emergency services. The building is open and staffed 24 hours a day, 7 days a week, providing safe, secure housing at reasonable rates for single women in the city.

V. Boston YWCA Headquarters at 140 Clarendon Street

Constructed between 1927 and 1929, the headquarters for the Boston YWCA is advantageously located at the corners of Clarendon and Stuart Streets on the edge of one of the city's most prestigious retail districts, Newbury and Boylston streets and Copley Place in the heart of Boston's Back Bay business district. The area offers the finest in upscale retail stores and desirable office space, including the John Hancock Building and the Prudential Center. The Clarendon Headquarters, a 13-story brick and steel building, sits on approximately 13,860 square feet of land and includes approximately 167,400 square feet of space. It currently houses the YWCA administration offices, the Parlin House Apartments, the Melnea Cass Branch of the YWCA, and several commercial tenants. The Melnea Cass Branch operates health and fitness facilities which include a swimming pool and employment training programs. The Parlin Apartments occupy floors 9–13 and are comprised of studio, one- and two-bedroom apartments rented at market rates.

The building has not been significantly renovated since its completion in 1929, and no longer complies with city and state building codes. In 1987, the building elevators desperately needed repairs at an estimated cost of $270,000. The building also needs a new sprinkler system to insure the safety of its residents and tenants and to bring the building up to code. The Parlin Apartments also require major renovations to achieve an acceptable standard of safety, appearance, and comfort. The Apartments currently use common electric meters, and need to be rewired so tenants can control the electricity to their individual units, and pay accordingly. The YWCA's administrative offices also require improvements and repairs.

The health and fitness facilities also require significant repairs, updating, and renovation. Old, dreary locker rooms are unattractive to current and potential members, and a larger men's locker room is needed to accommodate male members. In addition, to keep up with new trends in the fitness industry, the YWCA needs to refurbish its space for aerobics classes and purchase new weight training equipment. During this time, the YWCA has also been forced to close the pool for repairs, and the pool building itself needs significant exterior work. Cost estimates for the work on the pool and pool building are in excess of $200,000. At the same time, a decrease in demand for health and fitness clubs and an increase in competition in both the day-care and health and fitness industries has had a negative effect on revenues for this facility.

Because the YWCA's Clarendon headquarters is in such a state of disrepair, it has become very costly to maintain and operate the building. In years past, the Board of Directors has chosen to funnel their scarce available resources into their programs rather than into general repairs and maintenance of the facilities, with the result that the building at 140 Clarendon Street is currently running at a net loss in excess of $200,000 a year.

In 1988 a certified appraiser valued the Clarendon property at $16 million. (However, the real estate market in the Boston area has since declined significantly.) The Boston YWCA's Board of Directors then sought a $7 million loan for the proposed renovations from several major Boston area banking and financial institutions, but most of these institutions did not respond favorably to the loan request. While there were a number of valid reasons for the banks' refusing to loan the YWCA the funds necessary for the renovations, including the YWCA's own uncertainty about how the changes would affect revenues, that the YWCA is a women's organization without connections in the "old-boy" network of the banking establishment contributed to the YWCA's lack of financial credibility. Finally, although the Clarendon building's excess value would cover the loan to value ratio, the banks raised serious questions about whether the YWCA's existing and potential cash flow could meet the debt service obligation.

The executive committee of the Boston YWCA is now faced with a serious dilemma. It must decide what to do with a deteriorating facility that not only serves as its headquarters, but also as a flagship of services offered by all the area YWCA's. After several years of study, review, and debate they are considering the following options for the Clarendon headquarters:

1. Sell the building with a guaranteed lease back for its facilities and offices.
2. Sell the building to an interested local insurance company and rent space for the administrative offices in a nearby office building.
3. Bring in an equity partner to fund the renovations for a percentage of ownership in the facility.
4. Continue with minimal renovations and operate as they have in the past.

INCREASING COMPETITION IN FITNESS SERVICES

In 1989, the management team of the Boston YWCA hired a consulting firm to review their Health Promotion Services division, housed at 140 Clarendon Street, one of the YWCA's primary sources of both operating revenue and expense, and to assist them in finding ways to enhance this branch of their services. The consultants surveyed current, former, and potential members about the strengths and weaknesses of the YWCA's Health Promotion Services including appearance, cleanliness, scheduling, products (i.e., equipment, classes, swimming pool, etc.), and overall management of the facility. This study also noted that there is considerable competition from the following vendors in the area of health and fitness:

1. Bally's Holiday Fitness Centers
2. Healthworks
3. Fitcorp
4. BostonSports
5. SkyClub
6. The Mount Auburn Club
7. Nautilus Plus
8. Fitness International
9. Fitness First
10. The Club at Charles River Park
11. Mike's Gym
12. Fitness Unlimited
13. Gold's Gym

The health club marketplace is, for the most part, a standardized industry in terms of the products and services offered at the various facilities. Most clubs offer free weights, weight equipment, exercise and aerobics classes, locker rooms, and showers with towels available. During the 1980s many new health clubs opened and the health club market became increasingly competitive. These clubs went to great expense to promote elaborate grand openings and fund extensive advertising campaigns to attract new members. The consultants' study found that fifteen other health and fitness facilities within the city are in direct competition with the YWCA. However, among the competition, the YWCA does fill a unique niche because it is affordable, strongly emphasizes fitness in a non-competitive and non-commercial environment, appeals to a diverse cross-section of people, and is conveniently located. Other clubs are perceived as more commercial and competitive than the YWCA, with a greater emphasis on social interaction and frills such as saunas, racquetball and squash courts, eating facilities, etc. A comparison of the YWCA's Heath Promotion Services to other health clubs in the city shows the YWCA to be in a price range somewhere between the commercial clubs and the no-frills gymnasiums. The commercial clubs range from $800–$1200 a year, plus a one-time

initiation fee of from $100–$1200; the no-frills gymnasiums range from $300–$400 per year; and the YWCA costs between $420 and $600 a year, plus an annual membership fee of $35.

The YWCA is comparable in size to the competition, but its space is not as well laid out as at other clubs. Most of the other clubs are air-conditioned but the YWCA isn't, and its membership drops significantly during the summer months, while for other clubs summer is the peak season. The YWCA also ranked behind the top four clubs in cleanliness, and members noted that its dreary atmosphere contributed to their sense of its uncleanliness. The YWCA's weight lifting equipment and weight machines are not quite up to the standards of the competition and the YWCA lacks the staffing and supervision other clubs provide. On the other hand, the YWCA can boast a swimming pool, an indoor track, and day care. Only one other club has a pool that comes close in size to the YWCA's, and only two other clubs offer indoor tracks or day care.

According to the consultants' study, current users of the YWCA's Health Promotion Services joined because the YWCA is convenient, provides a caring environment that promotes interaction, and is relatively inexpensive. A current user profile revealed that members are generally seeking a health and fitness experience for themselves as individuals rather than a social atmosphere and that what mattered to them additionally was sensible class schedules, adequate staffing, communication with the members, timely information, affordable pricing, an atmosphere without pressure, and an open, caring, and diverse environment. The complaint most often cited among current users was the lack of communication with members with regard to scheduling changes for classes, changes in the hours of operation, class cancellations, pool closings, and changes in procedures and policies of the club. Other factors that concerned current members were: lack of cleanliness, dreary appearance, small men's locker room, poor management of the staff, poor management of class capacity, inadequate maintenance of equipment, poor scheduling, poor layout of the facility, and the lack of public relations and advertising to attract new members.

Former members were also surveyed to determine why they did not renew. Their reasons mirrored the complaints of current members:

- Poor communications with members
- Equipment breakdowns
- Untimely equipment repairs
- Poor upkeep/cleanliness
- Poor ventilation

- Dreary appearance
- Dissatisfaction with staff (no personal attention)
- Rigid schedules
- Lack of air conditioning
- Overall deterioration of the facility

The study also concluded that marketing and promotion of the Health Promotion Services is minimal, with little effort put into attracting new members, making it nearly invisible in the community.

Marti Wilson-Taylor, the new executive director, and Carolyn Rosen, the new chief financial officer, quickly realized as they took control of the Boston YWCA in 1991 that several major decisions concerning the YWCA's physical facilities and programs and services had to be made. However, first and foremost, it was necessary for them to determine the strategic direction of the YWCA for the remainder of the decade. In an environment of increasing competition and shrinking resources the challenge facing them is great.

EXHIBIT 1

Detailed Analysis of YWCA Revenues 1991

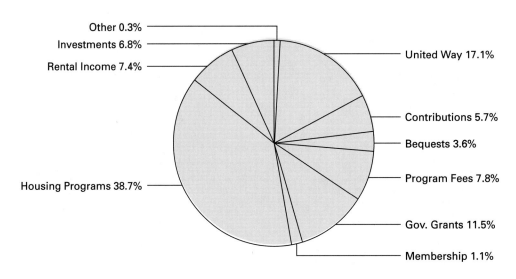

Other 0.3%
Investments 6.8%
Rental Income 7.4%
Housing Programs 38.7%
United Way 17.1%
Contributions 5.7%
Bequests 3.6%
Program Fees 7.8%
Gov. Grants 11.5%
Membership 1.1%

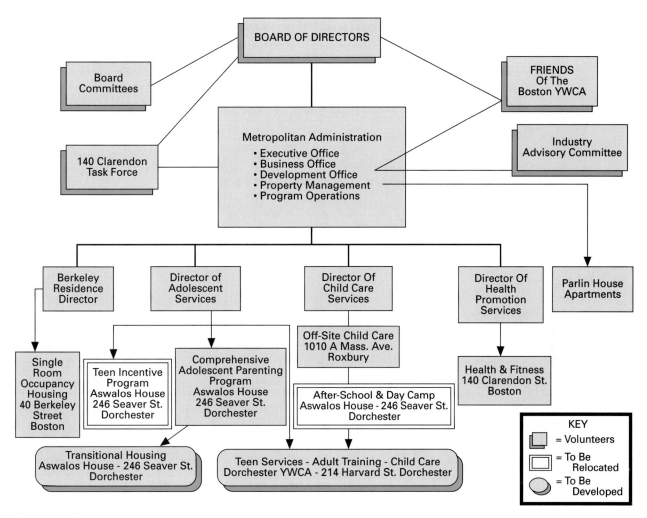

BOARD OF DIRECTORS

Board Committees

FRIENDS Of The Boston YWCA

140 Clarendon Task Force

Industry Advisory Committee

Metropolitan Administration
• Executive Office
• Business Office
• Development Office
• Property Management
• Program Operations

Berkeley Residence Director

Director of Adolescent Services

Director Of Child Care Services

Director Of Health Promotion Services

Parlin House Apartments

Off-Site Child Care 1010 A Mass. Ave. Roxbury

Health & Fitness 140 Clarendon St. Boston

Single Room Occupancy Housing 40 Berkeley Street Boston

Teen Incentive Program Aswalos House 246 Seaver St. Dorchester

Comprehensive Adolescent Parenting Program Aswalos House 246 Seaver St. Dorchester

After-School & Day Camp Aswalos House - 246 Seaver St. Dorchester

Transitional Housing Aswalos House - 246 Seaver St. Dorchester

Teen Services - Adult Training - Child Care Dorchester YWCA - 214 Harvard St. Dorchester

KEY
= Volunteers
= To Be Relocated
= To Be Developed

EXHIBIT 2
Boston YWCA—1991. Table of Organization

551

EXHIBIT 3 Boston YWCA. Statement of Support and Revenue, Expenses, Capital Additions, and Changes in Fund Balances. Year ended June 30, 1991 (with comparative totals for the year ended June 30, 1990).

	CURRENT FUND	PLANT FUND	ENDOWMENT FUND	JUNE 30, 1991 TOTALS	JUNE 30, 1990 TOTALS
Support and Revenue					
Support:					
United Way	$ 703,643	—	—	703,643	713,500
Contributions and grants	233,264	—	—	233,264	197,700
Legacies and bequests	150,386	—	—	150,386	537,540
	1,087,293	—	—	1,087,293	1,448,740
Operating revenue:					
Program fees	320,611	—	—	320,611	355,170
Government-sponsored programs	471,615	—	—	471,615	411,050
Membership	45,674	—	—	45,674	71,579
Housing and food service	1,589,587	—	—	1,589,587	1,586,553
	2,427,487	—	—	2,427,487	2,424,352
Non-operating revenue:					
Rental income	302,641	—	—	302,641	298,036
Investment income	278,982	—	—	278,982	244,224
Net realized gain on investments	41,392	—	—	41,392	2,308
Other revenue	7,967	—	—	7,967	43,790
	630,982	—	—	630,982	588,358
Total support and revenue	4,145,762	—	—	4,145,762	4,461,450
Expenses					
Program services:					
Aswalos House	250,621	14,782	—	265,403	384,776
Berkeley Residence	1,053,131	86,465	—	1,139,596	1,054,106
Cass Branch	1,216,544	128,673	—	1,345,217	1,394,075
Childcare	422,411	2,030	—	424,441	344,011
Harvard	6,132	—	—	6,132	—
	2,948,839	231,950	—	3,180,789	3,176,968
Supporting services:					
General and administration	632,657	15,364	—	648,021	793,861
Fundraising	287,448	6,981	—	294,429	135,978
	920,105	22,345	—	942,450	929,839
Total expenses	3,868,944	254,295	—	4,123,239	4,106,807
Excess (deficiency) of support and revenue over expenses before capital additions	$ 276,818	(254,295)	—	22,523	354,643

EXHIBIT 3 (continued)

	CURRENT FUND	PLANT FUND	ENDOWMENT FUND	JUNE 30, 1991 TOTALS	JUNE 30, 1990 TOTALS
Capital Additions					
Grants and gifts	106,495	38,985	—	145,480	314,798
Investment income	—	5,529	65,598	71,127	68,018
Net realized gain on investment transactions	—	—	72,577	72,577	63,874
Write-off of deferred charges	—	—	—	—	(305,312)
Loss on sale of asset	—	—	—	—	(11,856)
Total capital additions	106,495	44,514	138,175	289,184	129,522
Excess (deficiency) of support and revenue over expenses after capital additions	383,313	(209,781)	138,175	311,707	484,165
Fund balances, beginning of year	1,379,040	1,486,053	3,042,128	5,907,221	5,423,056
Transfers between funds:					
Plant acquisition	(274,155)	274,155	—	—	—
Principal repayment on loan payable to endowment fund	(143,841)	143,841	—	—	—
Permanent fund transfer	346,908	(346,908)	—	—	—
	(71,088)	71,088	—	—	—
Fund balances, end of year	$ 1,691,265	1,347,360	3,180,303	6,218,928	5,907,221

	CURRENT FUND	PLANT FUND	ENDOWMENT FUND	JUNE 30, 1991 TOTALS	JUNE 30, 1990 TOTALS
Assets					
Current assets:					
Cash	$ 137,469	66,292	—	203,761	110,684
Cash in escrow and security deposits	40,642	—	—	40,642	37,932
Accounts receivable, (less allowance for doubtful accounts of $3,500 in 1991 and $2,687 in 1990)	102,334	—	—	102,334	166,245
Supplies and prepaid expenses	54,452	—	—	54,452	73,613
Total current assets	334,897	66,292	—	401, 189	388,474
Pooled investments	1,793,198	—	3,180,303	4,973,501	4,775,252
Land, buildings and equipment, net	—	2,147,155	—	2,147,155	1,869,963
Deferred charges	—	349,638	—	349,638	349,638
	1,793,198	2,496,793	3,180,303	7,470,294	6,994,853
	$2,128,095	2,563,085	3,180,303	7,871,483	7,383,327
Liabilities and Fund Balances (Deficit)					
Current liabilities:					
Current maturities of long-term notes payable	—	18,979	—	18,979	17,524
Accounts payable and accrued expenses	254,757	—	—	254,757	201,581
Deferred revenue	182,073	—	—	182,073	202,717
Total current liabilities	436,830	18,979	—	455,809	421,822
Long-term notes payable, less current maturities	—	1,196,746	—	1,196,746	910,443
Loan payable to endowment fund	—	—	—	—	143,841
Total liabilities	436,830	1,215,725	—	1,652,555	1,476,106
Fund balances (deficit):					
Unrestricted:					
Designated by governing board to function as endowment	1,507,135	—	—	1,507,135	1,453,867
Undesignated	(101,933)	—	—	(101,933)	(354,084)
	1,405,202	—	—	1,405,202	1,099,783
Restricted—nonexpendable	286,063	223,798	3,180,303	3,690,164	3,545,183
Net investment in plant	—	1,123,562	—	1,123,562	1,262,255
Total fund balances	1,691,265	1,347,360	3,180,303	6,218,928	5,907,221
	$2,128,095	2,563,085	3,180,303	7,871,483	7,383,327

CADBURY SCHWEPPES, PLC

FRANZ T. LORKE, JAMES COMBS,
GARY CASTROGIOVANNI, *all of Louisiana State University*

▼

All large (food) companies have broken out of their product boundaries. They are no longer the bread, beer, meat, milk or confectionery companies they were a relatively short time ago—they are food and drink companies. (Smith, Child, & Rowlinson, 1990: 9)

Sir Adrian Cadbury, Chairman, (retired)
Cadbury Schweppes, PLC.

In the early 1990s, Cadbury Schweppes, PLC embodied the archetypical modern food conglomerate. With extensive international operations in confectionery products and soft drinks, the company maintained a diversified global presence. Although Cadbury had enjoyed a relatively stable competitive environment through much of the company's history, contemporary developments in the international arena presented Cadbury management with many different and critical challenges.

The History of Cadbury

The company began in 1831 when John Cadbury began processing cocoa and chocolate in the United Kingdom (U.K.) to be used in beverages. In 1847, the company became Cadbury Brothers, and in 1866, it enjoyed its first major achievement when the second generation of Cadburys found a better way to process cocoa. By using an imported cocoa press to remove unpalatable cocoa butter from the company's hot cocoa drink mix instead of adding large quantities of sweeteners, Cadbury capitalized on a growing public concern for adulterated food.

The company further prospered when it later found that cocoa butter could be used in recipes for edible chocolates. In 1905, Cadbury introduced Cadbury Dairy Milk (CDM) as a challenge to Swiss firms' virtual monopoly in British milk chocolate sales. A year later, the firm scored another success with the introduction of a new hot chocolate drink mix, Bournville Cocoa. These two brands provided much of the impetus for Cadbury's early prosperity (Jones, 1986).

Cadbury faced rather benign competition throughout many of the firm's early years. In fact, at one point, Cadbury provided inputs for the U.K. operations of the American firm, Mars, Inc. (Smith, Child, and Rowlinson, 1990). Cadbury also formed trade associations with its U.K. counterparts, J. S. Fry and Rowntree & Co., for the purpose of, among other things, reducing uncertainty in cocoa prices. The company later merged financial interests with J. S. Fry, but spurned offers to consolidate with Rowntree in 1921 and 1930 (Jones, 1986).

Facing growing protectionist threats in overseas markets following World War I, Cadbury began manufacturing outside the U.K., primarily in Commonwealth countries (see Figure 1). This international growth was also prompted by increasing competition. For example, by 1932 Cadbury management considered the Swiss company, Nestlé, as their primary competitor in the international arena (Jones, 1986).

Case Copyright 1992, Franz T. Lohrke
Case by Franz T. Lohrke, James Combs, and Gary Castrogiovanni, all of Louisiana State University.

FIGURE 1 **Cadbury's Foreign Direct Investment**
Source: Jones, 1986.

| 1914–1918 | 1921 | | 1930 | 1933 | 1937 | | 1939–1945 |
| World War I | Australia | | New Zealand | Ireland | South Africa | | World War II |

In 1969, Cadbury merged with Schweppes, the worldwide maker of soft drinks and mixers. The merger offered both companies an array of advantages, both defensive and offensive. First of all, both companies faced potential takeover threats from larger firms, so the merger placed the new company in a better defensive posture to ward off unwanted suitors. On the offensive side, the marriage allowed the new company to compete better on a worldwide scale. Cadbury had invested primarily in Commonwealth countries, and Schweppes had branched out into Europe and North America, so the new company enjoyed greater geographic dispersion. The increased international presence also allowed the company to defray product development costs over a wider geographic base. Furthermore, the new company enjoyed greater bargaining power from suppliers. For example, following the merger, Cadbury Schweppes became the largest U.K. purchaser of sugar (Smith, Child, & Rowlinson, 1990).

The British confectionery companies historically pursued a different strategy than their American counterparts. While U.S. companies, such as Mars, Inc., manufactured narrow product lines and employed centralized production, Cadbury maintained 237 confectionery products until World War II forced the company to scale back to 29. While faced with a lack of intense competition, Cadbury's brand proliferation strategy could be undertaken. As rivalry heated up in the mid-1970s, though, Cadbury's share of the U.K. chocolate market fell from 31.1 percent to 26.2 between 1975 and 1977. Management then began to realize that the lower cost, American-style strategy of rationalized product lines and centralized production provided the only viable means to compete (Child & Smith, 1987).

Cadbury had long been famous for its unique management style. "Cadburyism" drew influence from the founders' Quaker heritage, providing for worker welfare and harmonious community relations. Following Cadbury's reorientation toward core products and rationalized production, though, the company's old management style underwent a transformation. Confectionery manufacturing personnel were reduced from 8,565 to 4,508 between 1978 and 1985 (Child & Smith, 1987). In the process, management's traditional close relationship with workers, which had been built through years of maintaining employment stability, began to erode as worker reduction became a professed goal of Cadbury executives.

The Environment

As is the case with several products in the food industry, many of Cadbury's product lines enjoyed very long product life cycles. (See Table 1 for assorted confectionery products of Cadbury and its rivals.) Food and beverage companies derived substantial benefit from their long-established products, such as Cadbury's CDM bar, and the occasional new product introductions required little in the way of technological investment. The food companies, therefore, competed primarily by seeking cost reduction through process improvements such as automation, by finding alternative inputs to replace expensive cocoa, and by introducing creative packaging and marketing (Child & Smith, 1987).

Successful new product introductions remained sporadic, and many of the most successful confectionery products, such as Mars Bar and Rowntree's Kit Kat, had been around since the 1930s (Tisdall, 1982). Some unsatisfied demand seemed to persist, however, as was evidenced by Rowntree's successful 1976 launch of its Yorkie bar, Mars' profitable introduction of Twix a few years later, Cadbury's notable 1984 launch in the U.K. of its Whispa bar, and Hershey's 1988 introduction of Bar None (Weber, 1989).

Nevertheless, new brand introductions required immense investments in development and marketing costs with only limited possibilities for success. For instance, various research suggests that approximately 60 percent of new food product introductions have been withdrawn inside of five years, and this figure may be an underestimate (Smith, Child, & Rowlinson, 1990). Consequently, established brands with customer loyalty represented crucial assets for food and beverage companies.

TABLE 1 Assorted Major Brand Names of Cadbury Schweppes and Its Confectionery Competition

Cadbury Schweppes:
Cadbury Dairy Milk (CDM)	Whole Nut
Milk Tray	Roses
Crunchie	Fruit and Nut
Whispa	Trebor

Nestlé:
Nestlé Crunch bar	Polo
Kit Kat	Quality Street
Smarties	Yorkie
After Eight	Aero
Rolo	Black Magic
Dairy Box	Fruit Pastilles
Butterfinger	Baby Ruth

M&M/Mars, Inc.:
Mars Bar	Galaxy
Twix	Maltesers
Bounty	Milky Way
M&Ms	Snickers

Hersheys:
Hershey Bar	Reese's Peanut
Hershey Kisses	Butter Cup
Mounds	Reese's Pieces
Almond Joy	

Phillip Morris:
- Milka
- Tobler One
- E. J. Brachs candy

Modern Cadbury-Schweppes

Expansion was key to Cadbury's plans to improve its international position. Chief Executive Officer Dominic Cadbury commented, "If you're not operating in terms of world market share, you're unlikely to have the investment needed to support your brands" (Borrus, Sassen, & Harris, 1986: 132). In 1986, Cadbury shared third place in the world with Rowntree and Hershey, each having approximately 5 percent of the market. Nestlé held second place with about 7.5 percent, while Mars dominated internationally with approximately 13 percent (van de Vliet, 1986: 44–45).

To generate its necessary worldwide expansion, Cadbury had two primary markets in which to gain positions. Enjoying a dominant position in its home market, the company realized that the United States and the remaining countries of the European Economic Community (those besides the U.K.) provided critical markets for a worldwide standing. According to Terry Organ, director of international confectionery, "Rightly or wrongly . . . we decided to tackle the U.S.

first" (van de Vliet, 1986: 45). Earlier, Cadbury had taken steps toward competing more vigorously in the U.S. by acquiring Peter Paul in 1978. By 1980, however, the company still controlled only about 3.5 percent of the U.S. confectionery market, far eclipsed by its bigger rivals, Hershey and Mars.

Cadbury did not have sufficient size to employ the sales force of its competitors. The company, therefore, had to rely on food brokers to push products to wholesalers, which left the firm far removed from the consumer. Further, the company could be easily outspent in advertising by its two larger rivals (Borrus, et al., 1986).

To compound problems, the company also committed two marketing blunders in the U.S. market. When Cadbury introduced Whispa, the company's marketing success of the decade in the U.K., management did not realize that distribution channels in the U.S. were longer than in the U.K. Consequently, the candy bars aged seven to nine months by the time they reached test markets in New England, and consumers reacted accordingly.

The company's second mistake occurred following an effort to standardize its candy bar size across countries. When Cadbury first introduced its CDM bar in the U.S., the bar commanded a higher price than its U.S. rivals. Since CDM was also larger than U.S. competitors' regular bars, consumers were willing to pay a little extra. When Cadbury reduced the size, management discovered that given the choice between CDM and American confectionery products of equal size and price, U.S. consumers usually chose the more familiar American products (van de Vliet, 1986). According to one former Cadbury executive, "What happened in the U.S. was a gigantic, gargantuan cock-up, and the fact that London (Cadbury headquarters) did not know what was happening is a sheer disgrace" (Gofton, 1986: 20).

Not all the news from the other side of the Atlantic was bad for the U.K. company, however. Although Peter Paul Cadbury only commanded a small slice of the market, some products such as Coconut Mounds and York Peppermint Patties dominated their segments. Cadbury's Creme Eggs also enjoyed seasonal success. Moreover, the company's acquisition of Canada Dry from R. J. Reynolds provided Cadbury Schweppes with a strong position in the carbonated mixers market in the U.S. and many other countries (see Table 2 for U.S. market shares). For example, although Cadbury Schweppes only commanded about a 3 percent market share in the $43 billion U.S. soft drink industry, the company sold Canada Dry, the number one ginger ale and club soda in the U.S., and

TABLE 2 Top Five Soft Drink Companies in United States (percent of total market)

	1986	1987	1988	1989	1990
Coca-Cola, Co.	39.8	39.9	39.8	40.0	40.4
Classic	19.1	19.8	19.9	19.5	19.4
Diet Coke	7.2	7.7	8.1	8.8	9.1
Sprite	3.6	3.6	3.6	3.6	3.6
PepsiCo	30.6	30.8	31.3	31.7	31.8
Pepsi-Cola	18.6	18.6	18.4	17.8	17.3
Diet Pepsi	4.4	4.8	5.2	5.7	6.2
Mountain Dew	3.0	3.3	3.4	3.6	3.8
Dr. Pepper	4.8	5.0	5.3	5.6	5.8
Dr. Pepper	3.9	4.0	4.3	4.6	4.8
Diet Dr. Pepper	.4	.4	.4	.4	.4
Seven-Up	5.0	5.1	4.7	4.3	4.0
7-Up	3.5	3.4	3.1	3.0	2.9
Diet 7-Up	1.4	1.0	1.0	.9	.9
Cadbury Schweppes	4.2	3.7	3.5	3.1	3.2
Canada Dry	1.4	1.4	1.4	1.3	1.2
Sunkist	.9	.7	.7	.7	.7
Schweppes prod.	.5	.5	.5	.6	.6
Crush	1.4	1.0	.8	.6	.6
Total Market Share of Top Five	84.5	84.5	84.5	84.6	85.2

Source: *Standard and Poor's Industry Surveys*, 1991.

TABLE 3 Top Five Companies in the $8 Billion U.S. Confectionery Market (percent of total market)

1980		1988	
COMPANY	MARKET SHARE	COMPANY	MARKET SHARE
Mars	17.0	Hershey	20.5
Hershey	15.3	Mars	18.5
Nabisco	7.1	Jacobs Suchard	6.7
E. J. Brachs	6.4	Nestlé	6.7
Peter Paul/Cadbury	3.5	Leaf	5.6

Source: Weber, 1989.

market remained dominated by family-owned firms and suffered from overcapacity (van de Vliet, 1986). Successful expansion in the EEC, however, was crucial to Cadbury's remaining a dominant player in the worldwide food and beverage industries.

Contemporary Challenges

The 1990s brought about radical shifts in the industries in which Cadbury Schweppes competed. First, corporate leaders (and stock markets) discovered that food and beverage enterprises with established brand names were not mundane investments offering only lackluster financial returns. Purchasing popular brands or taking over companies that had portfolios full of well known products often provided a safer and more economical avenue for growth than attempting to develop entirely new products. In 1985, for instance, Philip Morris acquired General Foods for $5.75 billion, approximately three times book value, while R. J. Reynolds laid out $4.9 billion for Nabisco Brands (van de Vliet, 1986).

These attempts to acquire popular brands were also dictated by dramatic industry-wide changes which altered the nature of competition faced by the international food and beverage enterprises. First, the push by the 12 countries of the European Economic Community (EEC) to remove trade barriers among the member nations by 1992 sparked a buying frenzy of European food companies with established brand names (see Table 4 for a comparison of the North American and EEC market). Many non-European companies feared that the EEC would eventually increase tariff barriers for products from outside the Community, which could have effectively closed foreign companies out of the market. This anticipation of "Fortress Europe" sent companies without EEC operations scurrying to acquire European enterprises.

Schweppes, the leading tonic water in the American market (Winters, 1990). Additionally, the cola giants, Coca-Cola and PepsiCo, did not (as yet) vigorously market products in segments dominated by Cadbury Schweppes. Overall, though, the company faced an uphill struggle in many segments of the U.S. market.

In an effort to remedy some of the company's problems in the U.S. confectionery market, Cadbury decided to sell its manufacturing assets to Hershey in 1988, catapulting the Pennsylvania company to the dominant position in the U.S. market (see Table 3). Cadbury also granted Hershey licenses to manufacture and sell its Peter Paul products including Mounds, Almond Joy, and York Peppermint Patties. Under this arrangement, Cadbury gained the benefit of Hershey's marketing muscle behind the Peter Paul products (Swarns & Toran, 1988).

Cadbury faced additional challenges to building market share in the European Economic Community (EEC). Schweppes' beverages enjoyed success on the Continent (Borrus, et al., 1986), but Europe's confectionery industry proved difficult to break into since the

TABLE 4 **The United States (U.S.) and the European Economic Community (EEC)**

	U.S.	EEC
Population	243.8 million	323.6 million
Gross National Product (GNP) (in 1987 $U.S.)	4.436 trillion	3.782 trillion
Per capita GNP	$18,200	$11,690
Inflation	3.7%	3.1%
Unemployment	6.1%	11.0%

Note: EEC members include the U.K. (England, Scotland, Wales, Northern Ireland), Ireland, Denmark, Germany, France, Belgium, the Netherlands, Luxembourg, Portugal, Spain, Italy, and Greece.

Source: House, 1989.

Second, the common perception that only the largest companies in most industries would survive in Europe as well as internationally contributed to the takeover hysteria. To become big quickly, companies began aggressively acquiring rival food companies. For example, Nestlé scored a major victory in July 1988 when it outbid its Swiss counterpart, Jacob Suchard, to acquire Cadbury's long time U.K. competitor, Rowntree. In the process, Nestlé moved from a minor status in the EEC confectionery market into a first place duel with Mars. In the U.K. market, Nestlé's acquisition positioned the company in a second place battle with Mars and within striking distance of first place Cadbury (*Mergers and Acquisitions,* 1989). In January 1992, Nestlé also attempted to continue its acquisition binge by launching a hostile takeover bid for the French mineral water company, Source Perrier.

Other major food conglomerates, such as Phillip Morris (U.S.) and Unilever Group (U.K./Netherlands) were also rumored to be on the prowl for acquisitions in Europe (Browning & Studer, 1992). These heavyweights not only presented medium-sized food and beverage companies like Cadbury with increased competition in the marketplace, they also represented potential bidders in any acquisitions attempted by Cadbury. This increased competition threatened to drive up acquisition prices through cutthroat bidding for popular brand names. In fact, as the takeover battles became more heated, stock market analysts speculated that Cadbury and other medium-sized companies could find themselves targets of acquisition attempts (Browning & Studer, 1992).

The European food and beverage industries were undergoing other changes along with the acquisition binges. At the end of the food and beverage distribution pipeline, for example, many European supermar-

kets were also consolidating. In April 1990, eight EEC grocery chains formed an alliance to combine buying power and promote house brands. As these supermarket companies combined forces, they greatly enhanced their bargaining power against the food and beverage companies. This increased power threatened future profits of food and beverage companies since the grocery chains' ability to demand price concessions from the companies was enhanced by the stores' consolidation. Furthermore, since supermarkets only wanted to carry the top two or three brands for each product type, food and beverage companies faced the option of acquiring popular brands or risking lost shelf space in stores (Templeman & Melcher, 1990).

In response to these massive changes in the industry, Cadbury also began acquiring name brand products and searching for strategic alliances. In 1986, for example, the company decided to end its bottling agreement with Pepsi to form a joint venture with Coke in the U.K. (Gofton, 1986). In 1990, Cadbury purchased the European soft drink operations of Source Perrier (Templeman & Melcher, 1990), and in 1991, the company formed a joint venture with Appolinarus Brunnen AG, a German bottler of sparkling water.

With the competitive environment heating up, Cadbury management faced a number of crucial questions. Could the company continue to compete independently against the food and beverage megacorporations that were forming or should Cadbury merge with another company before being faced with a hostile takeover attempt? Did Cadbury have the resources to acquire more brand names or should management continue to investigate the joint venture route? Should the company reduce emphasis on Europe and instead attempt to exploit new opportunities in the underdeveloped Asian market? Whatever Cadbury Schweppes management decided to do, it had to move quickly. The choices of popular name brand food and beverage products on the table were being cleared away fast.

TABLE 5 **Food Sales—Europe (Including the U.K.)**

Nestlé	$15.1 billion
Unilever	12.2
Phillip Morris*	8.0
BSN	7.8
Mars	4.1
Cadbury Schweppes	3.1

* Includes Jacobs Suchard

Source: Templeman & Melcher, 1990.

TABLE 6 Cadbury Schweppes' 1990 Worldwide Sales (In £ million*)

REGION	TOTAL SALES	CONFECTIONERY	BEVERAGES
United Kingdom	1,476.0	715.4	760.6
Continental Europe	638.0	195.6	442.4
Americas	403.7	18.3	373.5
Pacific Rim	495.5#	N/A	N/A
Africa and other	132.9	91.2	8.8

*1 £ = $1.93

#Sales primarily in Australia/New Zealand

N/A: not available

Note: Total Sales will not always equal Confectionery plus Beverages. In the U.S. (Americas region), for example, Cadbury Schweppes also generated sales from its Mott's subsidiary.

Source: Compact Disclosure; *The Wall Street Journal.*

TABLE 7 Cadbury Schweppes Financials (In £ 000)

BALANCE SHEET FISCAL YEAR ENDING	12/29/90	12/30/89	12/31/88
Assets			
Cash	62,600	57,400	41,300
Marketable Securities	118,000	33,300	200,700
Receivables	554,100	548,200	434,500
Inventories	328,200	334,800	253,400
TOTAL CURRENT ASSETS	1,062,900	973,700	929,900
Net Prop, Plant, Equip.	978,800	822,500	602,200
Other Long Term Assets	320,700	332,600	20,700
TOTAL ASSETS	2,362,400	2,128,800	1,552,800
Liabilities			
Notes Payable	60,100	57,400	92,200
Accounts Payable	272,100	263,900	409,500
Current Capital Leases	76,200	76,300	21,900
Accrued Expenses	320,900	305,900	52,100
Income Taxes	78,200	95,800	81,800
Other Current Liab.	154,700	143,600	118,800
TOTAL CURRENT LIAB.	962,200	942,900	776,300
Long Term Debt	407,900	381,400	124,700
Other Long Term Liab.	108,401	124,000	74,600
TOTAL LIABILITIES	1,478,500	1,448,300	975,600
Preferred Stock	300	N/A	3,300
Net Common Stock	174,400	173,600	150,400
Capital Surplus	95,800	36,700	33,000
Retained Earnings	115,800	167,600	88,800
Miscellaneous	381,600	217,400	210,500
TOTAL SHAREHOLDERS EQ.	767,900	595,300	486,000
Minority Interest	116,000	85,200	91,200
TOTAL LIAB. & NET WORTH	2,362,400	2,128,800	1,552,800
1 £ =	$1.93	$1.61	$1.81

EXHIBIT 7 (continued)

INCOME STATEMENT (IN £ 000) FISCAL YEAR ENDING	12/29/90	12/30/89	12/31/88
Net Sales	3,146,100	2,766,700	2,381,600
Cost of Goods Sold	1,738,400	1,596,900	1,365,000
GROSS PROFIT	1,407,700	1,179,800	1,016,600
Sell Gen & Admin Exp.	1,074,700	907,500	787,800
INCOME BEFORE INT & TAX	333,000	272,300	228,800
Non-Operating Inc.	3,800	3,100	4,400
Interest Expense	57,200	31,100	17,500
Income Before Taxes	279,600	244,300	215,700
Taxes & Misc. Expenses	100,200	85,500	75,200
Income Before Ex. Items	179,400	157,800	140,500
Extraordinary Items	N/A	15,200	28,400
NET INCOME	179,400	173,000	168,900
1 £ =	$1.93	$1.61	$1.81

N/A: not applicable

Source: Compact Disclosure; *The Wall Street Journal.*

REFERENCES

Borrus, A., Sassen, J., & Harris, M. A. 1986. Why Cadbury Schweppes looks sweet to the raiders. *Business Week,* January 13: 132–133.

Browning, E. S., & Studer, M. 1992. Nestlé and Indosuez launch hostile bid for Perrier in contest with Agnellis. *The Wall Street Journal,* January 21: A3.

Child, J., & Smith, C. 1987. The context and process of organizational transformation—Cadbury Limited in its sector. *Journal of Management Studies,* 24: 565–593.

Gofton, K. 1986. Has Cadbury got his finger on the button? *Marketing,* July 31: 20–25.

House, K. E. 1989. The 90's & Beyond: The U. S. stands to retain its global leadership. *The Wall Street Journal,* January 23: A8.

Jones, G. 1986. The chocolate multinationals: Cadbury, Fry and Rowntree 1918–1939. In G. Jones (Ed.), *British Multinationals: Origins, Management and Performance:* 96–118. Brookfield, VT: Gower Publishing Co.

Mergers and Acquisitions. 1989. The Nestlé-Rowntree deal: Bitter battle, sweet result. September–October: 66–67.

Smith, C., Child, J. & Rowlinson, M. 1990. *Reshaping work: The Cadbury experience.* Cambridge: Cambridge University Press.

Standard and Poor's Industry Surveys. 1991. Food, beverages, and tobacco. June 27: F23–F27.

Swarns, R. L., & Toran, B. 1988. Hershey to buy U.S. business from Cadbury. *The Wall Street Journal,* July 25: 30.

Templeman, J., & Melcher, R. A. 1990. Supermarket Darwinism: The survival of the fattest. *Business Week,* July 9: 42.

Tisdall, P. 1982. Chocolate soldiers clash. *Marketing,* July 29: 30–34.

van de Vliet, A. 1986. Bittersweet at Cadbury. *Management Today,* March: 42–49.

The Wall Street Journal. Various issues.

Weber, J. 1989. Why Hershey is smacking its lips. *Business Week,* October 30: 140.

Winters, P. 1990. Cadbury Schweppes' plan: Skirt cola giants. *Advertising Age,* August 13: 22–23.

ZAYRE CORPORATION (A)

JAMES BRIAN QUINN, *Tuck School Dartmouth College*

▼

Discount retailing for broad ranges of nonfoods merchandise really began in the 1950s. The first stores—like Arlan's, Two Guys from Harrison, Kings, and J. M. Fields—moved into cheap vacated warehouse or mill spaces. Early discounters tended to be individual entrepreneurs with an intuitive sense of the new U.S. marketplace. Family sizes were exploding in the postwar baby boom; U.S. manufacturing efficiencies were creating millions of new jobs; the purchasing power of the working and middle classes had ballooned; national advertising media were stimulating widespread brand recognition and standardized tastes; and the automobile facilitated mobility, suburbanization, and mass purchasing on a scale never possible before. In 1956 Zayre Corporation became the first company to exploit these trends by building a complete newly constructed retail discount store and chain specially designed for self-service sales of general merchandise.

DISCOUNTERS TAKE OVER

The large department stores, which were then the dominant form of retail merchandising, ignored discounters at first. Most responded by upgrading their locations, displays, and services—and raising margins to cover the added costs. The three great national department store chains each reacted differently. Sears undertook an awesome branch rollout into the suburbs, aimed at the price-conscious middle income market. J. C. Penney followed suit on a later and smaller scale. Montgomery Ward, anticipating a postwar recession, froze its posture, hoarded cash, and went into decline.

In the early-to-mid-1960s S. S. Kresge and Woolworth's abandoned their early variety-store format (open counters, small items in jumbled displays) to build the Kmart and Woolco chains with a large range of merchandise and more sophisticated presentation. And discount sales boomed:

YEAR	NUMBER OF STORES	DISCOUNT SALES
1960	1,329	$ 2 billion
1970	5,000	19 billion
1980	8,300	45 billion
1984	8,600	56 billion

Discounters' 1984 sales represented 48% of all retail general merchandising sales. While there were several major shakeouts on the way, the top seven chains increasingly concentrated their share of the market from $11 billion in 1974, to $21 billion in 1978, to $34 billion in 1983. In New England, discounting accounted for an incredible 72% of full-line general merchandise sales, with five of the nation's largest 15 discounters headquartered there. Many of the top names of expansionary 1970s had essentially disappeared—including Woolco, Grants, Korvettes, Mammoth Marts, Two Guys, and Kings. Zayre Corp. had not only survived the rugged shakeout which had occurred, but had enjoyed record breaking growth in the

Case copyright © 1989 by James Brian Quinn. Research associate—Penny C. Paquette. Research assistant—Barbara Dixon.

The generous cooperation of the Zayre Corporation is gratefully acknowledged.

early 1980s, and was positioning itself for the rigorous challenges of the late 1980s. What were the key events in Zayre's recent history? And what should its future strategy be?

ENTREPRENEURIAL TIMES

Mr. Stanley Feldberg, Zayre's first CEO, oversaw his company's growth from its 1950s birth to sales of $1.4 billion in 1978. By then there were 251 Zayre discount stores in major metropolitan areas, mainly east of the Mississippi. Like the discount field itself, Zayre had developed rapidly under the entrepreneurial styles of its founders, mostly Feldberg family members. (See organization chart.) The company had been privately held until it went public in 1962, and was still dominated by the founding group and their scions in the late 1970s. Together they held approximately 30% of Zayre's stock. The organization structure was both a cause and effect of Zayre's growth and management style. In the words of Mr. Stanley Feldberg,

> The original founders had always governed themselves as equal partners, and their successors had been groomed to think the same way. People were careful not to let a single person or position dominate the scene. It was often difficult to get a decision implemented in one area, if the head of that area disagreed. There tended to be management by committee and indeed management by consensus. One of the offshoots of this style was that there was not as much emphasis on profitability or "bottom line" as you might have found elsewhere. Profitability was important but could be sacrificed in the short run while you were seeking expansion opportunities.

Expansion Plans and Complications

Around 1969, Zayre went through a McKinsey & Co. organizational study in concert with a 5 year plan to double its stores (from 125 to 250) and its total volume (from $500 million to $1 billion). McKinsey suggested a much expanded executive force and a restructuring to increase Zayre's managerial depth and diversity. Zayre built up its organization rapidly in anticipation of its planned growth, causing a corresponding short-term buildup in overheads. While staying in its traditional market niches, Zayre attempted to decentralize the organization more extensively on a regional basis. Instead of reporting directly to headquarters, district managers began to report to six regional managers, who had their own staffs. These were very large businesses, with some 40–50 stores reporting to each re-

gional manager. While Store Operations decentralized, Merchandising and Real Estate activities stayed centralized. (See organization chart.) And problems soon developed. Said Mr. Stanley Feldberg,

> Frankly, the Merchandising Department had not kept up with our changing customers of the 1960s. We had attempted to keep *absolute* price levels from increasing despite a mild inflation. It finally became impossible to do this and not lose quality in our merchandise lines at the very time our customers' capacity to buy higher quality was steadily growing. We kept advertising prices almost exclusively. In a practice that set my teeth on edge, we sometimes advertised specials with no more than a few days supply on hand to service customers. This brought customers in the door, and kept the store from losing too much on the margins of sale merchandise. But it alienated people who had expected a good buy and couldn't find it.

The merchandising problem was compounded by the fact that Zayre had started to build bigger 80,000 square foot stores (versus 65,000) and to move into suburban areas. Zayre's product lines had to be spread over a larger physical area, creating the impression of thinner inventory coverage. Merchandising techniques of piling goods in aisle bins for quick sale—which had worked so well in lower income areas—failed in the more exclusive suburbs. Ads targeted solely at price didn't bring customers into these stores so readily. And new stores which had been budgeted for $3\frac{1}{2}$ to $4 million volumes, only brought in $1.5–$2 million. Meanwhile Kmart was opening stores budgeted for $9 million sales volumes and had Kresge's massive capital resources to help stock the stores and support them with advertising.

As one executive said, "All this killed our store productivity. As productivity declined, there wasn't enough income to keep the stores current. So we lost more sales. And so on. We wanted the stores to look a bit spartan, but soon our parking lots had potholes, maintenance had to be delayed, roofs began to leak, merchandise coverage dropped even more. Top management was deeply aware of the problem, but it was awfully hard to break out. Then along came the oil crisis and the 1974–1975 inflation-recession—fiscal 1975 (calendar 1974) earnings dropped to only $835,000."

Mr. Stanley Feldberg amplified, "As we disappointed customers at a merchandise level, store sales began to dry up, but overhead percentages began to escalate—not uncontrollably, but enough to hurt badly. Our first response was to cut back expenses at the stores, cleaning services, maintenance, even capital and investment payrolls. We cut back support services at home office too. But profits still dropped and we got

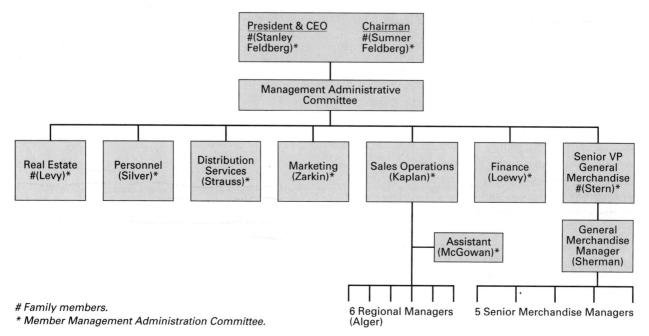

Family members.
* Member Management Administration Committee.

Zayre Corporation Organization Chart Mid-1976
Source: Company records.

Race Tracks and Experiments

into a vicious circle where it got even harder to correct things."

From this low point began one of the greatest turn-arounds in retailing history. Zayre's top managers took a long view and began some experiments designed to reposition its stores for the future. They called in a consultant, Alton Doody, who said that while the Zayre Stores' format had been adequate for the 1960s, it was not well tuned to the future. In 1975 Stanley and Sumner Feldberg authorized a series of experimental layouts, presentations, display changes (etc.) that became known as the "Zayre '75" program. Mr. Doody brought in the concept of a "race track aisle" that carried the customers rapidly around the store to various departments. Each department was arranged around this aisle with "windows" on the aisle and "vistas" to invite the customer into the department. And new display techniques were developed to let each department put the "best foot forward" for its merchandise. Some experiments worked; others did not. "Zayre '75" was followed by another series of experiments in "Zayre '76" and again later in "Zayre '77." Sumner and Stanley Feldberg personally supported all these experiments, but they still had to be carried out with limited capital because of tight operating margins.

1976 brought several other major events. First, Zayre returned to stronger profitability, as the oil crisis receded. Second, Mr. Malcolm Sherman, later president of Zayre Stores, combined several features of the 1975–1976 experiments in some Indianapolis stores, along with a more complete inventory showing adapted to the local clientele. He later said, "I put together everything in this experiment I could without making capital demands." And store sales shot upward in this "Indy 1976" experiment. Another experiment in 1977 called the "loop design" led customers around its test stores—rather than through the central aisles—with good effect. And so on. But third, and perhaps most importantly, in 1975 Stanley and Sumner Feldberg had begun the search for a CEO to carry Zayre into the 1990s. And for the first time Zayre was looking seriously outside the family's ranks.

A TIME OF CHANGE

After an intensive three-year search Mr. Maurice Segall joined Zayre Corp. as its first nonfamily CEO in February 1978. Mr. Segall was a trained economist who had started his career as chief economist and director of planning and organization at Steinbergs, a large food supermarket operation headquartered in Montreal.

He later became director of operations for the Treasure Island Stores chain of J. C. Penney, and finally (1974–1978) president of American Express' Credit and Card Division, where he is widely credited with tripling that organization's volume in a series of highly entrepreneurial and insightful moves. Mr. Segall said, "Many people thought I was crazy to go into a family-dominated situation in a difficult industry like retail discounting. But I had gotten to know Stanley and Sumner Feldberg very well over the last couple years. I knew they were people of quality and high integrity who would follow through on all commitments made to me—and they would not second-guess me. And frankly, while Zayre was a real challenge, I thought it had very high potentials for the future."

Mr. Segall's five-year contract called for a base salary of $300,000 a year plus substantial bonuses if he increased net income per share from continuing operations at rates of 10–20% a year in the first three years and 7.5–15% a year in the last two years. It also provided for a signing bonus of $200,000 in the first year, plus deferred compensation of $500,000. In an interview with *Chain Store Age Executive* Mr. Segall said, "The most successful retail executives are people with a real desire for continuing challenge. There are few companies where they can receive such stimulation year in and year out. . . . The people who have what it takes, the people who thrive on that challenge, are real risk takers. There are few industries other than retailing which offer these people such opportunities."[1]

First Steps

The Board had placed no constraints or set any specific goals for its new CEO. Mr. Segall immediately began a three-month series of travels around to all the stores. Knowing he would be gone constantly, he had kept his family home in Long Island, so his wife would have a familiar environment and close friends nearby while he traveled. In May 1978, Mr. Segall came back to Sumner and Stanley Feldberg and said, "Now I know what I have to do. I like all the experiments. But I want to stop the experiments, put them together, and do the chain."

There were many things that most agreed were crucial to getting Zayre stores back onto their growth curve again. Various executives and outside sources contributed the following composite view:

1. Because of the economic constraints and the corresponding morale problems of the cutback years, many of the stores had become unattractive and some were not well managed at the local level. Frequently, merchandise was not kept neatly arranged. In some cases store cleanliness was even a problem. Many stores did not have complete stock positions, and there was a lot of bickering between the field operations people and the home-office merchants. "When anything was wrong, some other party always seemed at fault."

2. Physically, many stores were in difficult shape. There were numerous stores with leaky roofs and peeling wallboard and plaster. Some of the store fronts were run down and display fixtures were broken or in ill repair. Even stores which had been refurbished were often not properly maintained because of capital constraints. And it would cost millions to bring the chain up to a desired standard.

3. While Zayre had an outstanding financial control system, merchandising control had been a major problem. Merchandising had been centrally managed in detail. Stocking plans for each store were close to identical, even though store sizes and locations varied significantly. Zayre's merchandising group used mainly a "push" system of trying to get good buys on desired merchandise and then pushing goods out through the stores with a standardized plan. This approach had worked well enough when the chain was small, but it began to break down when the company had a complex group of some 250 stores.

4. Many of the stores' presentation techniques in terms of merchandise displays, lighting intensity, wall colors and floor coverings, were not up to date. Long checkout lines and service people not being available to assist on the floors were serious problems. Said one long time Zayre executive, "boxes often littered the floor, and you could look at shelves and see gaps in the merchandise lines. A facelift was necessary both in physical terms and in terms of the morale of employees who had been discouraged during the tight financial period by these surroundings."

Everything at Once

While these were widely recognized issues, action had been difficult to take because of both capital and organizational constraints. Mr. Segall said,

First, it was evident we had to fix up our physical plant and keep it in shape. We needed enormous amounts of money to do the job. But it's not sufficient just to fix up a store. There are a lot of nice stores that go out of business. You have to update your marketing and advertising for that store, and you have to make sure you get the right merchandise in that store and maintain its stocks. None of this works without good people. The problem is you can't do it one step at a time. This chain had 250 stores, and it would take a lifetime to do it that way.

But we had to do it right. And we didn't have the luxury of time. A key point in all this was to zero in on what our mission was and what our customer definition was. We agreed we should not change the definition of our target customer (the working class customer looking for good value), but would try to get to that customer more effectively. We were not going to suddenly become an upper middle class discount store.

Between May and September 1978, Mr. Segall—and a few people (notably Malcolm Sherman and Bob Alger) he had identified for their future executive potentials—developed a strategy called the Marketing Development Program (MDP) to present to the Board in September of that year. Before that meeting Mr. Segall decided to reorganize the entire field structure of Zayre Stores. He later said,

> You have to send some messages, and I decided the then executive vice president of Zayre Stores was not the right person to carry this out. There were any number of good people I could have hired from outside. But I decided to look around carefully inside the company and identified Bob Alger (age 39) as the right person for the job.
>
> We had long discussions about what needed to be done, but I wanted Alger to find the players. Deciding that the whole thing should be done over one weekend, I asked Bob Alger, the V.P. of Personnel, and two promising young executive protégés of Mr. Alger to lock themselves in their hotel rooms at the Logan Hilton for three days and come out with names of all the new district and zone managers for the Zayre chain. It was done in three days without anyone knowing it. Then I asked Mr. Sherman and Mr. Zarkin to develop the kinds of merchandising and advertising strategies we had discussed. All this went into the fall Board presentation.

The proposal asked for $30 million (later $40 million) for a remodeling and updating program and another $25 million for an electronic point-of-sale (EPOS) program to convert all the cash registers and point of sale controls to a computer basis. Mr. Segall later said, "It was a bet-your-company strategy. It was either going to work and be successful, or it would drive us into bankruptcy." Exhibits 1 through 4 set forth some of the key background data for this 1978 strategy meeting.

Zayre Stores did not want to change its basic concept. Zayre was to remain a neighborhood, convenience, self-selection, general merchandise, discount department store chain. Its target customer was the lower part of the middle income class and the upper part of the lower income class—the great working class of America.

Other Zayre Operations

In 1976, Sumner Feldberg had been very impressed by the concept of off-price retailing which he saw at the then young ($120 million volume) Marshall's chain. Off-price stores sold quality brand-name merchandise at 20–60% below regular list prices. Zayre tried to buy Marshall's but was outbid by Melville's. Consequently

Mr. Feldberg rapidly developed a similar concept for Zayre which became the T. J. Maxx chain, with ten stores in calendar 1977. T. J. Maxx's target was the middle-income customer who wanted a good value at a good price. It appealed to the female homemaker buying for a whole family. As *Forbes* said, "The chain catered to people who were snobby enough to want brand names, but didn't want to pay the full price for them."[2] T. J. Maxx carried brands like Calvin Klein, Gloria Vanderbilt, and Liz Claiborne for women; Arrow, Van Heusen, and Ralph Lauren for men; Carter's, Healthtex, and Izod for kids; and a wide selection of branded linens, towels, and housewares. T. J. Maxx stores operated in smaller (25,000 square foot) units in urban and suburban shopping malls. And like most start ups it had lost money in the first few years of operations.

Zayre's other off-price chain was Hit or Miss (H or M), originally acquired as a 10-store Boston chain in 1970, which grew to 17 units by year end. After a promising start, Hit or Miss had begun to top out in the mid-1970s. *Chain Store Age,* said, "In its first eight years, Hit or Miss had become a less than successful teenagers' and low-end girls' apparel chain which emphasized teeny bopper fads, accessories, and fringes."[3] In this very competitive market, H or M had operated 4,000 ft^2 shops in less expensive suburban strip malls where overheads were lower. Its format had been spartan, with bright exposed fluorescent lamps, lots of merchandise "up front" on racks, and heavy use of self-service promotional signage. Although by 1978, H or M was targeted more towards the price-conscious young woman buying for herself, in the words of *Chain Store Age* "Hit or Miss was missing more than hitting" and was a net money loser for the Zayre Corporation." Although its profitability figures were not broken out in Zayre's published statements, observers said H or M's problems were getting worse in the late 1970s.

The 1978 Competition

The major competitors of Zayre were positioned and moving roughly in the following directions in 1977–1978. Traditional department stores had moved to "top-of-the-line" positions in suburban areas or refurbished central cities—or by and large they had failed.

SEARS, ROEBUCK. With sales of $17.2 billion and a 6.23% market share of U.S. general merchandise sales in 1977, Sears was the largest of the major chains. Its *Annual Report* in 1977 stated that its mission was "to provide quality merchandise at competitive prices across the nation." Its current sales distribution was 71% through store outlets, 20% catalogue sales, and 9% other. In the late 1960s Sears moved upscale to the middle- to upper-middle-income market vacated by the big full-line department stores. Sears anchored its big (up to 200,000 ft^2) full-line stores in the more expensive malls and backed its presentations with a greater number of service personnel than most of its chain competitors.[4] Part of the upscale move was toward fashion goods which some thought did not fit too well with Sears' strong (65% of sales) competitive hard goods image.[5] Sears had a strong private-label position especially in white goods, and with its high volume Sears could have quality merchandise made inexpensively with the special features it desired.

By 1978 Sears had 366 full-line (200,000 ft^2) stores, 371 semi-full-line (78,500 ft^2) stores, and 135 hard line (24,000 ft^2) outlets. Sears also held significant equity in some of its suppliers, and owned 49.9% of a Canadian chain, which had sales of $2 billion. And Allstate insurance contributed some $400 million to profits. Its catalogue sales were 55% from in-store centers; only 45% were handled by telephone or through free-standing catalogue stores.

KMART. The second largest chain was Kmart with $9.9 billion in sales, 55% from hard goods and 45% soft lines. Kmart had outlets in 257 of the 275 SMAs of the U.S. Of its 1,395 stores, 795 had been built in the last five years and located mainly in high-growth suburban areas and smaller industrial or agriculturally based cities. Kmart used a one-story format in four basic store types (84,000, 68,000, 55,000, and 45,000 ft^2 formats). These could be "freestanding" stores—not necessarily tied into a shopping center—which could locate in any convenient, available space even in less populated rural or older, high-density city markets as well as in the suburbs. Kmart had grown at 20% per year mainly by opening new stores. Kmart had been S. S. Kresge's vehicle for diversifying out of the maturing variety store business in the 1960s. By 1977 Kmart accounted for 95% of Kresge's sales, and the parent had changed its own name.

J. C. PENNEY. Nearby was J. C. Penney with its $9.4 billion in sales, 59% from full-line stores, and 23% from soft line stores. In 1977 it had 460 full line stores (averaging 88,000 ft^2) mainly in shopping centers of major metropolitan markets. Its 1,226 soft line stores (average 12,000 ft^2) tended to be in the downtown areas of medium sized cities or the "main streets" of smaller communities, where J. C. Penney had built its reputation for reliable quality at a good price. In 1977 its expansion plans were focused around its full-line stores, with modernization and some relocation of its soft line outlets. Penney had recently begun a push toward higher profitability by adding more fashionware to its apparel lines and emphasizing home furnishings to combat the competition it faced from department stores in its shopping center locations.[6] Its other operations included 37 freestanding discount stores (the Treasury Stores) which averaged 97,000 ft^2 and were not very successful in 1977. Penney also had 229 drug store outlets (8,000 ft^2) which were performing adequately, a profitable $1 billion catalogue business, and a small insurance business which it was just beginning to integrate into its retail outlets.

WAL-MART. A small but fast-growing regional chain was Wal-Mart with $900 million in sales, 68% in hard goods. Wal-Mart had 195 stores in a ten-state area (Texas to North Central states) located within 400 miles of its headquarters and distribution center. Its average store size was 43,000 ft^2, ranging from 30,000 to 60,000 ft^2. Wal-Mart was building 30 to 40 new stores a year in standardized formats built around 36 departments. Wal-Mart stressed rock-bottom priced staple goods and emphasized (68% of sales) its hard goods line.[7] Wal-Mart used a "big frog in little pond" philosophy, preferring to be the largest non-food retailer in the smaller 25,000–30,000-person communities. It targeted county seats where it often edged out older J. C. Penney stores by offering a wider selection with more hard goods.[8] Among discounters, department stores, and variety stores, *Forbes* ranked Wal-Mart first over the past five years in average ROE, return on invested capital, sales growth, and earnings growth. In its 1978 *Annual Report* CEO Sam Walton said the secret of success was "nothing more than bringing together men and women who are completely dedicated to their jobs, their company and their communities."

A New Strategy

Mr. Segall was deeply aware of these repositionings as well as the new modes of retailing that were beginning to emerge—especially those associated with direct-mail, "off-price" merchandising, the new wholesale clubs being formed, and the breakdown of traditional retailing structures (i.e., drugs, food supermarkets, merchandise chains) toward "mixed-line" merchandising. He was particularly concerned about the potential impact of the new electronics and communications technologies on retailing. But he had to deal with these from the limited resource base Zayre then had.

1. What should the early 1980s strategy of Zayre Corporation be? What are the critical action sequences?

2. How can Zayre acquire the capital needed for these moves?

3. How should Zayre be reorganized?

4. What other implementing actions must go along with these strategic changes?

EXHIBIT 1 **Zayre Corporation: Expense Comparisons with Cornell Sample of Similar Stores, Fiscal 1976–1977**

Expense Analysis—Percent of Sales (excluding lease or franchised departments)

	Fiscal 1976		Fiscal 1977	
	CORNELL EXCL. ZAYRE	**ZAYRE**	**CORNELL EXCL. ZAYRE**	**ZAYRE**
Total payroll	12.40%	12.76%	12.79%	12.72%
Supplies	0.75	0.87	0.66	0.91
Communications	0.23	0.78	0.25	0.40
Travel	0.21	0.38	0.20	0.39
Services purchased	0.74	0.50	0.67	0.52
Advertising	2.43	2.93	2.66	3.18
Taxes and licenses	1.17	1.33	1.12	1.35
Utilities	1.13	1.39	1.13	1.35
Insurance	0.57	0.70	0.66	0.71
Property rentals	3.21	3.36	3.09	3.56
Equipment rentals	0.35	0.31	0.33	0.30
Depreciation and amortization	0.85	1.13	0.76	1.00
Repair and maintenance	0.48	0.99	0.53	1.05
Donations	0.01	0.02	0.02	0.02
Professional services	0.24	0.17	0.22	0.18
Unclassified	1.05	1.08	1.09	1.11
Credits and allowances	(0.40)	(0.01)	(0.22)	—
Total expense	25.44%	28.39%	25.96%	28.75%

Source: Company records and analyses provided during interview.

Gross Margin, Expense, and Earnings Percent of Sales
(excluding leased or franchised departments)

	Fiscal 1976		Fiscal 1977	
	CORNELL EXCL. ZAYRE	**CORNELL EXCL. ZAYRE**	**ZAYRE**	**ZAYRE**
Gross margin	28.52%	30.15%	28.86%	30.61%
Leased department income	0.80	0.59	0.92	0.65
Gross income	29.32	30.74	29.78	31.26
Total expense	25.44	28.39	25.96	28.75
Net operating profit	3.88	2.35	3.83	2.51
Other income or deductions	(0.23)	(0.80)	(0.06)	(0.69)
Earnings before income taxes	3.65	1.55	3.77	1.82
Federal and state income taxes	1.84	0.78	1.84	0.92
Net earnings after taxes	1.81%	0.77%	1.93%	0.90%

Source: Company records and analysis provided during interviews.

EXHIBIT 2
Zayre Corporation: Location of Operations, January 1978

Source: Zayre Corporation, Annual Report, 1978.

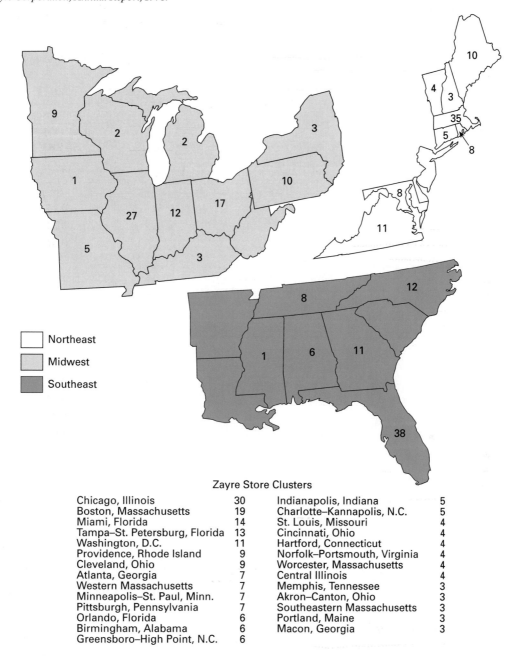

Northeast

Midwest

Southeast

Zayre Store Clusters

Chicago, Illinois	30	Indianapolis, Indiana	5
Boston, Massachusetts	19	Charlotte–Kannapolis, N.C.	5
Miami, Florida	14	St. Louis, Missouri	4
Tampa–St. Petersburg, Florida	13	Cincinnati, Ohio	4
Washington, D.C.	11	Hartford, Connecticut	4
Providence, Rhode Island	9	Norfolk–Portsmouth, Virginia	4
Cleveland, Ohio	9	Worcester, Massachusetts	4
Atlanta, Georgia	7	Central Illinois	4
Western Massachusetts	7	Memphis, Tennessee	3
Minneapolis–St. Paul, Minn.	7	Akron–Canton, Ohio	3
Pittsburgh, Pennsylvania	7	Southeastern Massachusetts	3
Orlando, Florida	6	Portland, Maine	3
Birmingham, Alabama	6	Macon, Georgia	3
Greensboro–High Point, N.C.	6		

EXHIBIT 3 **Zayre Corporation Financials,* 1974–1979**

Statement of Consolidated Earnings

($ millions)

	1979	1978	1977	1976	1975	1974
Net sales	$1,394.1	$1,261.3	$1,160.6	$1,084.0	$1,045.5	$996.4
Cost of sales	1,076.7	987.3	907.9	850.7	827.2	777.7
Gross profit	317.5	274.0	252.7	233.3	218.4	218.7
Operating expense	271.5	234.5	212.8	208.1	201.4	190.8
Interest expense	20.0	17.7	18.3	11.1	16.1	12.1
Income before tax	26.9	21.8	21.5	14.1	0.9	15.8
Federal income tax	12.9	10.8	11.3	7.2	0.2	7.2
Net income	$ 14.0	$ 11.0	$ 10.2	$ 4.9	$ 0.8	$ 9.1

Consolidated Balance Sheet

($ millions)

	1979	1978	1977	1976	1975	1974
ASSETS						
Cash	$ 23.0	$ 23.5	$ 25.9	$ 26.1	$ 38.7	$ 36.6
Accounts receivable	5.5	4.7	4.5	2.8	3.6	5.6
Inventories	254.0	242.3	211.0	187.8	177.6	191.5
Other current assets	19.9	17.9	16.8	15.0	13.6	3.9
Total current assets	302.4	288.5	258.2	231.6	233.5	237.6
Net fixed assets	173.8	168.2	96.0	102.5	112.0	118.5
Total assets	$476.2	$456.8	$354.2	$334.1	$345.4	$356.1
LIABILITIES						
Current installment, long-term debt	$ 9.2	$ 10.0	$ 11.4	$ 9.8	$ 13.7	$ 9.3
Accounts payable	73.3	76.1	57.6	52.0	60.4	70.6
Accrued expenses, taxes, etc.	62.5	53.7	44.2	35.8	30.5	31.0
Total current liabilities	145.1	139.8	113.1	97.6	104.6	110.9
Long-term debt	188.6	190.0	115.5	122.0	131.3	136.6
Stockholders' equity	142.5	128.0	125.5	114.5	109.5	108.7
Total liabilities and equity	$476.2	$456.8	$354.2	$334.1	$345.4	$356.1

*Fiscal year ends January of year designated, refers to operations of preceding calendar year.

Source: Company records.

EXHIBIT 3 (continued)

Operating Results of the Zayre Company by Its Major Segments, 1978–1979
(amounts in thousands)

	January 27, 1979[a]			January 28, 1978[a]		
	CONSOLIDATED	DISCOUNT DEPT. STORES	SPECIALTY STORES	CONSOLIDATED	DISCOUNT DEPT. STORES	SPECIALTY STORES
Sales and operating revenues	$1,394,109	$1,222,900	$171,209	$1,261,301	$1,141,422	$119,879
Operating income	$ 46,778	$ 38,630	$ 8,148	$ 38,190	$ 33,542	$ 4,648
General corporate expense	7,941			6,695		
Interest expense	11,913			9,653		
Total income before income taxes	$ 26,924			$ 21,842		
Identifiable assets	$ 476,243	$ 401,376[b]	$38,214[b]	$ 456,754	$ 395,561[b]	$ 25,656[b]
Depreciation and amortization	$ 18,941	$ 17,738	$ 1,203	$ 17,561	$ 16,678	$ 883
Capital expenditures	$ 21,174	$ 17,108	$ 4,066	$ 10,536	$ 5,793	$ 4,743

[a]Includes the effect of SFAS 13. "Accounting for Leases." The prior year amounts have been restated accordingly. For further information see notes in company's annual report.

[b]Identifiable assets are those assets of the Company associated with an industry segment and do not include cash and marketable securities.

Source: Zayre Corporation, *Annual Report*, 1978.

EXHIBIT 4 Zayre Corporation: Number of Retail Establishments in Operation, Various Years from 1965–1978

	Reported in January of Year Indicated					
	1965	**1970**	**1975**	**1976**	**1977**	**1978**
Zayre (discount dept. store)	72	153	258	254	255	252
Hit or Miss (apparel)			62	87	118	173
T. J. Maxx (off price)						10
On Stage/Nugent's/Bell (apparel)	43	48	36	34	36	31
Beaconway (fabrics)		7	46	44	42	34
Gasoline stations	2	37	95	95	95	7
Shoppers City (food and nonfood supermarkets)		8	10	10	10	9
Spree! (discount toy stores)			6	5		

editorial assistant, Diane Palumbo

APPENDIX A: SOME ORGANIZATIONAL TERMS IN RETAILING

Merchandising involves the entire group of decisions and tasks involved in determining what merchandise is offered, acquiring it, and having it available in the right assortments at the right places to maximize the store's marketing objectives. In many retail operations merchandising includes the functions of buying, receiving, marketing, and handling all merchandise as well as controlling inventory levels and mixes in the stores. In some large or complex chains, some of these activities may be split off as specialized functions or be decentralized regionally.

Buying is a major line activity in retailing. Buying decisions include what merchandise should be purchased, in what quantities, at what prices, under what terms, and when it should be purchased and received. In some stores the buyer also determines prices, markups, markdowns, and closeouts and plans and coordinates a department's special sales. Buying can be organized according to the class of merchandise purchased, store type, or location served. In most department stores buyers are in charge of all merchandising for their particular departments as well as directing the sales force in these departments. In some decentralized operations, buying and local sales force management may be separated.

Operations include all those activities necessary to maintain the quality and appearance of the physical facilities of the enterprise. In some highly decentralized retail concerns, these activities as well as supervision and control of local salespeople and inventory handling functions are the responsibility of Operations. Service and support activities locally may report either to Operations or directly to other centralized line or administrative functions.

Sales is the face-to-face presentation of the product to the customer and the first recording of that transaction on the store's books through the cash register, sales slip, or electronic charge system. In some cases salespeople report to the buying or merchandise heads; in others they are separated from these functions and report either through Operations or a centralized sales unit.

Promotion generally includes advertising, publicity, displaying of merchandise, and any tactics (other than merchandise selection and pricing) which will induce profitable sales volume. Special attraction techniques like store signs, catalogues, premiums, trading stamps, and nonrecurring interest breaks are considered promotions. Store layout, design, traffic flow planning, rack displays, wall and floor coloring, lighting presentations, and so on are important aspects of in-store promotion which clearly impact the effectiveness of all other line activities.

CASE NOTES

3 GENERAL MILLS, INC.

1. "A Dollop of 'Good, Gutsy Maine Business Sense.'" *Fortune,* July 1976, p. 27.
2. "How to Manage Entrepreneurs." *Business Week,* September 7, 1981, pp. 66–69.
3. "The Second Time Around." *Forbes,* March 2, 1981, p. 70.
4. "The General Mills Brand of Managers." *Fortune,* January 12, 1981.
5. "General Mills: An All-American Marketer." *Dun's Business Month,* December 1981, p. 72.
6. "General Mills Continues to Weed Knits." *Advertising Age,* October 3, 1983, p. 12.
7. Bear Stearns Research Report, September 30, 1982.
8. "When Business Got So Good It Got Dangerous." *Fortune,* April 2, 1983, p. 64.
9. "Farmer to President: Joe Lee of General Mills." *The Cornell Hotel and Restaurant Administration Quarterly,* November 1982.
10. "The Impact of Consumer Trends on Corporate Strategy." Sandra D. Kresch, *Journal of Business Strategy,* Winter 1983.
11. "General Mills' Izod Woes Are Said to Reflect Broader Problems of Company Management." *The Wall Street Journal,* December 4, 1984.

5 SONY CORPORATION

1. Morita, Akio, "International Marketing of Sony Corporation." Monograph, Tokyo, July 14, 1969.

2. ———, "Decision Making in Japanese Business." Monograph, Manila, September 30, 1975.
3. ———, "What Is the Difference Between the Japanese Management and the American?" Chicago, February 17, 1972.
4. ———, "Creativity in Modern Industry." Frank Nelson Doubleday Series, Smithsonian Institution, 1974.

GENERAL SOURCES (for Sony Corporation)

"Akio Morita: Chairman and CEO." *Director,* May 1982.
"The Americanization of Sony." *The New York Times,* March 18, 1973.
"Another Revolution." *Economist,* June 4, 1983.
"A Diversification Plan Tuned to the People Factor." *Business Week,* February 9, 1981.
Drucker, P., *Management.* New York: Harper & Row, 1974.
Enderlin, P. J., Smith Barney, Harris Upham & Co., Inc., *Electronic Imaging—Impact on Consumer Photography.* December 20, 1984.
"Even Sony Sometimes Stumbles." *Forbes,* April 25, 1983.
"The Giants in Japanese Electronics." *Economist,* February 20, 1982.
"Here Comes Projection Television." *Economist,* October 8, 1977.
"Horatio Alger Story with a Japanese Twist." *The New York Times Magazine,* September 10, 1967.
"How to Get Bigger with Smaller Products." *Business Week,* May 25, 1968.
Ibuka, Masaru, "How Sony Developed Electronics for the

World Market." *IEEE Transactions on Engineering Management* Vol. EM-22, No. 1 (February 1975).

"An Incongruous Search for Greener Pastures." *Business Week,* February 11, 1980.

Kobayashi, Shigeru, *Creative Management.* American Management Association, 1971.

Lyons, Nick, *The Sony Vision.* New York: Crown Publishers, Inc., 1976.

Pearlstine, N., "Blurred Image." *Forbes,* September 4, 1978.

6 W. L. GORE & ASSOCIATES, INC.

1. In this case the word "Associate" is used and capitalized because in W. L. Gore & Associates literature the word is always used instead of "employees" and is capitalized. In fact, the case writers were told that Gore "never had 'employees'—always 'Associates.'"

2. GORE-TEX is a registered trademark of W. L. Gore & Associates.

3. Fluroshield is a registered trademark of W. L. Gore & Associates.

4. Gore's ASOP is similar legally to an ESOP (Employee Stock Ownership Plan). Gore simply does not use the word "employee" in any of its documentation.

5. In comparison, only 11 of the 200 largest companies in the Fortune 500 have had positive ROE each year from 1970–1988 and only two other companies missed only one year. The revenue growth rate for these thirteen companies was 5.4% compared to 2.5% for the entire Fortune 500.

7 NATIONAL WESTMINSTER BANK USA

1. Due to an increase in loan reserves of $295 million in 1987 (against loans to developing countries who are experiencing debt servicing problems) NatWest suffered a loss in 1987 of $212 million. Without the extra-ordinary item, the 1987 ROA would have been approximately .70. See financial Statements in Exhibit 2.

2. Exhibit 4 provides a summary of recent market research at NatWest, and gives an indication of the degree to which NatWest has been successful in differentiating itself with regards to customer service.

12 ZAYRE CORPORATION (A)

1. "Turnover at the Top: Cause and Effect." *Chain Store Age Executive,* May 1984.

2. "Making Money at the Low End of the Market." *Forbes,* December 17, 1984.

3. "Hit or Miss on Target with New Look." *Chain Store Age Executive,* February 1983.

4. "Too Big for Miracles." *Forbes,* June 15, 1977, p. 26.

5. "Sears' Strategic About-Face." *Business Week,* January 8, 1979.

6. "J. C. Penney's Fashion Gamble." *Business Week,* January 16, 1978, p. 66.

7. "Wal-Mart: A Discounter Sinks Deep Roots in Small Town, U.S.A." *Business Week,* November 5, 1979, p. 145.

8. "A Day in the Life of Sam Walton." *Forbes,* January 1, 1977, p. 45.

BIBLIOGRAPHY

ABELL, D. F., *Defining the Business: The Starting Point of Strategic Planning.* Englewood Cliffs, N.J.: Prentice Hall, 1980.

ACKERMAN, R. W., *The Social Challenge to Business.* Cambridge, Mass: Harvard University Press, 1975.

ADVISORY COMMITTEE ON INDUSTRIAL INNOVATION: FINAL REPORT. Washington, D.C.: U.S. Government Printing Office, 1979.

AGUILAR, F. J., *Scanning the Business Environment.* New York: Macmillan, 1967.

ALLISON, G. T., *Essence of Decision: Explaining the Cuban Missile Crisis.* Boston: Little, Brown, 1971.

ANSOFF, H. I., *Corporate Strategy: An Analytic Approach to Business Policy for Growth and Expansion.* New York: McGraw-Hill, 1965.

ARGYRIS, C., "Double Loop Learning in Organizations," *Harvard Business Review,* September–October 1977, pp. 115–25.

ASTLEY, W. G., & C. J. FOMBRUN, "Collective Strategy: Social Ecology of Organizational Environments," *Academy of Management Review,* 1983, pp. 576–87.

BACON, J., *Corporate Directorship Practices: Membership and Committees of the Board.* Conference Board and American Society of Corporate Secretaries, Inc., 1973.

———, & J. K. BROWN, *Corporate Directorship Practices: Role, Selection and Legal Status of the Board.* New York: The Conference Board, 1975.

BADEN FULLER, C., et al., "National or Global? The Study of Company Strategies and the European Market for Major Appliances." London Business School Centre for Business Strategy, Working Paper series no. 28 (June 1987).

BAKER, EDWIN L., "Managing Organizational Culture," *Management Review,* July 1980, pp. 8–13.

BARREYRE, P. Y., "The Concept of 'Impartition' Policy in High Speed Strategic Management." Working Paper, Institut d'Administration des Entreprises, Grenoble, 1984.

———, & M. CARLE, "Impartition Policies: Growing Importance in Corporate Strategies and Applications to Production Sharing in Some World-Wide Industries." Paper Presented at Strategic Management Society Conference, Paris, 1983.

BARTLETT, C. A., & S. GHOSHAL, "Managing Across Borders: New Strategic Requirements," *Sloan Management Review,* Summer 1987, pp. 7–17.

BATE, PAUL, "The Impact of Organizational Culture on Approaches to Organizational Problem Solving," *Organizational Studies* 5, 1 (1984), 43–66.

BATY, G. B., W. M. EVAN, & T. W. ROTHERMEL, "Personnel Flows as Interorganizational Relations," *Administrative Science Quarterly,* 1971, pp. 430–43.

BAUER, R. A., I. POOL, & L. A. DEXTER, *American Business and Public Policy.* New York: Atherton Press, 1968.

BAUMBACK, C., & J. MANCUSO, *Entrepreneurship and Venture Management.* Englewood Cliffs, N.J.: Prentice Hall, 1975.

BECKER, G., *Human Capital.* New York: National Bureau of Economic Research, 1964.

BEER, S., *Designing Freedom.* Toronto: CBC Publications, 1974.

BENNIS, W. G., & P. L. SLATER, *The Temporary Society.* New York: Harper & Row, 1964.

BERLEW, D. E., & D. T. HALL, "The Management of Tension in Organization: Some Preliminary Findings," *Industrial Management Review,* Fall 1964, pp. 31–40.

575

BERNSTEIN, L., "Joint Ventures in the Light of Recent Antitrust Developments," *The Antitrust Bulletin,* 1965, pp. 25–29.

BOSTON CONSULTING GROUP, *Strategy Alternatives for the British Motorcycle Industry.* London: Her Majesty's Stationery Office, 1975.

BOWER, J. L., "Planning within the Firm," *The American Economic Review,* 1970, pp. 186–94.

BOWER, M., *The Will to Manage.* New York: McGraw-Hill, 1966.

BOWMAN, E. H., "Epistemology, Corporate Strategy, and Academe," *Sloan Management Review,* Winter 1974, pp. 35–50.

BRAYBROOKE, D., "Skepticism of Wants, and Certain Subversive Effects of Corporations on American Values," in *Human Values and Economic Policy,* S. Hook, ed. New York: New York University Press, 1967.

—— & C. E. LINDBLOM, *A Strategy of Decision: Policy Evaluation as a Social Process.* New York: Free Press, 1963.

BRENNER, S. N., & E. A. MOLANDER, "Is the Ethic of Business Changing?" *Harvard Business Review,* January–February 1977, pp. 57–71.

BROOK, P., *The Empty Space.* Harmondsworth, Middlesex: Penguin Books, 1968.

BROOM, H. N., J. G. LONGENECKER, & C. W. MOORE, *Small Business Management.* Cincinnati, Ohio: Southwest, 1983.

BRUNSSON, N., "The Irrationality of Action and Action Rationality: Decisions, Ideologies, and Organizational Actions," *Journal of Management Studies,* 1982(1), 29–44.

BUCHELE, R. B., *Business Policy in Growing Firms.* San Francisco, Calif.: Chandler, 1967.

BURNS, T., "The Directions of Activity and Communication in a Departmental Executive Group." *Human Relations* 1954, pp. 73–97.

——, & G. M. STALKER, *The Management of Innovation,* 2d ed. London: Tavistock, 1966.

BUSINESS WEEK. "Japan's Strategy for the 80's," December 14, 1981, pp. 39–120.

CARLZON, J., *Moments of Truth.* New York: Ballinger Press, 1987.

CHANDLER, A. D., *Strategy and Structure: Chapters in the History of the Industrial Enterprise.* Cambridge, Mass.: M.I.T. Press, 1962.

CHANNON, D. F., "The Strategy, Structure and Financial Performance of the Service Industries," Working Paper, Manchester Business School, 1975.

CHEIT, E. F., "The New Place of Business: Why Managers Cultivate Social Responsibility," in *The Business Establishment,* ed. E. F. Cheit. New York: John Wiley, 1964.

CHRISTENSON, C. R., K. R. ANDREWS, & J. L. BOWER, *Business Policy: Text and Cases.* Homewood, Ill.: Richard D. Irwin, 1978.

CLARK, B. R., *The Distinctive College: Antioch, Reed and Swarthmore.* Chicago: Aldine, 1970.

——, "The Organizational Saga in Higher Education," *Administrative Science Quarterly,* 1972, pp. 178–84.

CLARK, R. C., *The Japanese Company.* New Haven: Yale University Press, 1979.

COHEN, K. J., & R. M. CYERT, "Strategy: Formulation, Implementation and Monitoring," *The Journal of Business,* 1973, pp. 349–67.

—— & J. P. OLSEN, "A Garbage Can Model of Organizational Choice," *Administrative Science Quarterly,* 1972, pp. 1–25.

COHN, T., & R. A. LINDBERG, *How Management Is Different in Small Companies.* New York: American Management Association, 1972.

COLE, A. H., *Business Enterprise in Its Social Setting.* Cambridge, Mass.: Harvard University Press, 1959.

COLE, R. E., *Japanese Blue Collar: The Changing Tradition.* Berkeley: University of California Press, 1971.

——, *Work, Mobility and Participation.* Berkeley: University of California Press, 1979.

COPEMAN, G. H., *The Role of the Managing Director.* London: Business Publications, 1963.

COYNE, K. P., "Sustainable Competitive Advantage," *Business Horizons,* January–February 1986, pp. 54–61.

CROZIER, M., *The Bureaucratic Phenomenon.* Chicago: University of Chicago Press, 1964.

CVAR, M. R., "Case Studies in Global Competition," in *Competition in Global Industries,* ed. M. E. Porter. Boston: Harvard Business School Press, 1986.

CYERT, R. M., W. R. DILL, & J. G. MARCH, "The Role of Expectations in Business Decision Making," *Administrative Science Quarterly,* 1958, pp. 307–40.

CYERT, R. M., & J. G. MARCH, *A Behavioral Theory of the Firm.* Englewood Cliffs, N.J.: Prentice Hall, 1963.

DAFT, R. L., "The Evolution of Organizational Analysis in ASQ, 1959–1979." *Administrative Science Quarterly* 25 (1980), 632–36.

DAVIS, R. T., *Performance and Development of Field Sales Managers.* Boston: Harvard Business School, 1957.

DEAL, T. E., & A. A. KENNEDY, *Corporate Culture.* Reading, Mass.: Addison-Wesley, 1982.

DEAN, R. C. "The Temporal Mismatch: Innovation's Pace vs. Management's Time Horizon." *Research Management,* May 1974: 12–15.

DELBECQ, A., & A. C. FILLEY, *Program and Project Management in a Matrix Organization: A Case Study.* Madison, Wis.: University of Wisconsin, 1974.

DOERINGER, P., & M. PIORE, *Internal Labor Market and Manpower Analysis.* Lexington, Mass.: Lexington Books, 1971.

DOUGLAS, S. P., & Y. WIND, "The Myth of Globalization," *Columbia Journal of World Business,* Winter 1987, pp. 19–29.

DRUCKER, P. F., *The Practice of Management.* New York: Harper & Row, 1954.

————, *Managing for Results.* New York: Harper & Row, 1964.

————, *Management: Tasks, Responsibilities, Practices.* New York: Harper & Row, 1974.

————, "Clouds Forming Across the Japanese Sun," *The Wall Street Journal,* July 13, 1982.

EDWARDS, J. P., "Strategy Formulation as a Stylistic Process," *International Studies of Management and Organization,* Summer 1977, pp. 13–27.

ELECTRONIC BUSINESS, "Services Get the Job Done," September 15, 1988, pp. 87–90.

EPSTEIN, E. M., *The Corporation in American Politics.* Englewood Cliffs, N.J.: Prentice Hall, 1969.

————, "The Social Role of Business Enterprise in Britain: An American Perspective; Part II," *The Journal of Management Studies,* 1977, pp. 281–316.

ESSAME, H., *Patton: A Study in Command.* New York: Charles Scribner's Sons, 1974.

EVERED, R., *So What Is Strategy?* Working Paper, Naval Postgraduate School, Monterey, 1980.

FARAGO, L., *Patton: Ordeal and Triumph.* New York: I. Obolensky, 1964.

FIRSIROTU, M., "Strategic Turnaround as Cultural Revolution: The Case of Canadian National Express," doctoral dissertation, Faculty of Management, 1985.

FLEISHMANN, E. A., E. F. HARRIS, & H. E. BURT, *Leadership and Supervision in Industry: An Evaluation of Supervisory Training Program.* Columbus, Ohio: The Ohio State University, 1955.

FOCH, F., *Principles of War,* trans. by J. DeMorinni. New York: AMS Press, 1970. First published London: Chapman & Hall, 1918.

FORRESTER, J. W., "Counterintuitive Behavior of Social Systems," *Technology Review,* January 1971, pp. 52–68.

FRANKLIN, B., *Poor Richard's Almanac.* New York: Ballantine Books, 1977. First Published, Century Company, 1898.

FRIEDMAN, M., *Capitalism and Freedom.* Chicago: University of Chicago Press, 1962.

————, "A Friedman Doctrine: The Social Responsibility of Business is to Increase Its Profits," *The New York Times Magazine,* September 13, 1970.

GALBRAITH, J. K., *American Capitalism: The Concept of Countervailing Power.* Boston: Houghton Mifflin, 1952.

————, *The New Industrial State.* Boston: Houghton Mifflin, 1967.

GAILBRAITH, J. R., "Strategy and Organization Planning," *Human Resource Management,* 1983, pp. 63–77.

GARDNER, J. W., "The Anti-Leadership Vaccine," in *Carnegie Corporation of New York Annual Report,* 1965.

GARDNER, M., "Creating a Corporate Culture for the Eighties," *Business Horizons,* January–February 1985, pp. 59–63.

GARSON, G. D., "The Codetermination Model of Worker's Participation: Where Is It Leading?" *Sloan Management Review,* Spring 1977, pp. 63–78.

GERTH, H. H., & C. WRIGHT MILLS, EDS., *From Max Weber: Essays in Sociology.* New York: Oxford University Press, 1958.

GHISELLI, E. E., "Managerial Talent," in *The Discovery of Talent,* ed. D. Wolfe. Cambridge, Mass.: Harvard University Press, 1969.

GILDER, G., *Wealth and Poverty.* New York: Basic Books, 1981.

GILMORE, F.F., "Overcoming the Perils of Advocacy in Corporate Planning," *California Management Review,* Spring 1973, pp. 127–37.

GLUECK, W. F., *Business Policy and Strategic Management.* New York: McGraw-Hill, 1980.

GOSSELIN, R., *A Study of the Interdependence of Medical Specialists in Quebec Teaching Hospitals.* Ph.D. thesis, McGill University, 1978.

GREEN, P., *Alexander the Great.* New York: Frederick A. Praeger, 1970.

GREGORY, K. L., "Native-View Paradigms: Multiple Cultures and Culture Conflict in Organizations," *Administrative Science Quarterly,* 28 (1983), 359–76.

GREINER, L. E., "Evolution and Revolution as Organizations Grow," *Harvard Business Review,* July–August 1972, pp. 37–46.

————, "Senior Executives as Strategic Actors," *New Management,* Vol. 1, no. 2, Summer 1983.

GRINYER, P. H., & J. C. SPENDER, *Turnaround—Management Recipes for Strategic Success.* New York: Associated Business Press, 1979.

GROSS, W., "Coping with Radical Competition," in *Business Policy: Selected Readings and Editorial Commentaries,* ed. A. Gross & W. Gross, pp. 550–60. New York: Ronald Press, 1967.

GUEST, R. H.,"Of Time and the Foreman," *Personnel,* May 1956, pp. 478–86.

HAITANI, K., "Changing Characteristics of the Japanese Employment System," *Asian Survey,* 1978, pp. 1029–45.

HAMERMESH, R. G., M. J. ANDERSON, JR., & J. E. HARRIS, "Strategies for Low Market Share Business," *Harvard Business Review,* May–June 1978, pp. 95–102.

HARRIS, S. G., AND R. I. SUTTON, "Functions of Parting Ceremonies in Dying Organizations," *Academy of Management Journal,* Vol. 29 (1986), 5–30.

HART, B. H. L., *Strategy.* New York: Frederick A. Praeger, 1954.

HATTORI, I., "A Proposition on Efficient Decision-Making in Japanese Corporations," *Management Japan,* Autumn 1977, pp. 14–20.

HAYES, R. H., & W. J. ABERNATHY, "Managing Our Way to Economic Decline," *Harvard Business Review,* July–August 1980, pp. 67–77.

————, & D. A. Garvin, "Managing as if Tomorrow Mattered," *Harvard Business Review,* May–June 1982, pp. 70–79.

HAZAMA, H., "Characteristics of Japanese-Style Management," *Japanese Economic Studies,* Spring–Summer 1978, pp. 110–73.

HEDBERG, B. L. T., "How Organizations Learn and Unlearn," in *Handbook of Organizational Design,* ed. P. C. Nystrom and W. H. Starbuck, Vol. 1. New York: Oxford University Press, 1981.

———, & S. A. JÖNSSON, "Designing Semi-confusing Information Systems for Organizations in Changing Environments," *Accounting Organizations and Society,* 1978, pp. 47–64.

———, P. C. NYSTROM, & W. H. STARBUCK, "Camping on Seesaws: Prescriptions for a Self-designing Organization," *Administrative Science Quarterly,* 1976, pp. 41–65.

HIRSCH, P. M., "Organizational Effectiveness and the Institutional Environment," *Administrative Science Quarterly,* 1975, pp. 327–44.

HOFER, C. W., & D. SCHENDEL, *Strategy Formulation: Analytical Concepts.* St. Paul, Minn.: West Publishing, 1978.

HOSMER, A., "Small Manufacturing Enterprises," *Harvard Business Review,* November–December 1957, pp. 111–22.

HOUSE OF REPRESENTATIVES, Staff Report to the Antitrust Subcommittee of the Committee on the Judiciary, *Interlocks in Corporate Management.* Washington, D.C.: U.S. Government Printing Office, 1965.

HOUT, T., M. E. PORTER, & E. RUDDEN, "How Global Companies Win Out," *Harvard Business Review,* September–October 1982, pp. 98–108.

HUGHES, T., "The Inventive Continuum," *Science 84,* November 1984.

HUNT, R. G., "Technology and Organization," *Academy of Management Journal,* 1970, pp. 235–52.

IACOCCA, L., with W. NOVAK, *Iacocca: An Autobiography.* New York: Bantam Books, 1984.

IRVING, D., *The Trail of the Fox.* New York: E. P. Dutton, 1977.

JACOBS, D., "Dependency and Vulnerability: An Exchange Approach to the Control of Organizations," *Administrative Science Quarterly,* 1974, pp. 45–59.

JACQUES, ELIOTT, *The Changing Culture of a Factory.* London: Tavistock Institute, 1951, p. 251.

JAMES, D. C., *The Years of MacArthur, 1941–1945.* Boston: Houghton Mifflin, 1970.

JAY, A., *Management and Machiavelli.* New York: Penguin Books, 1970.

JENKINS, C., *Power at the Top.* Westport, Conn.: Greenwood Press, 1976.

JENNINGS, E. E., *The Mobile Manager.* Ann Arbor: University of Michigan, 1967.

JOHNSON, S. C., & C. JONES, "How to Organize for New Products," *Harvard Business Review,* May–June 1957, pp. 49–62.

JOMINI, A. H., *Art of War,* trans. by G. H. Mendell and W. P. Craighill. Westport, Conn.: Greenwood Press, 1971. Original Philadelphia: J. B. Lippincott, 1862.

JÖNSSON, S. A., & R. A. LUNDIN, "Myths and Wishful Thinking as Management Tools," in *Prescriptive Models of Organizations,* ed. P. C. Nystrom and W. H. Starbuck. Amsterdam: North-Holland, 1977.

JORDAN, W. A., "Producer Protection Prior Market Structure and the Effects of Government Regulation," *Journal of Law and Economics,* 1972.

KAHN, R. L., D. M. WOLFE, R. P. QUINN, J. D. SNOEK, & R. A. ROSENTHAL, *Organizational Stress.* New York: John Wiley, 1964.

KAMI, M. J., & J. E. ROSS, *Corporate Management in Crisis: Why the Mighty Fall.* Englewood Cliffs, N.J.: Prentice Hall, 1973.

KANO, T., "Comparative Study of Strategy, Structure and Long-Range Planning in Japan and in the United States," *Management Japan,* 1980(1), 20–34.

KATZ, D., & R. L. KAHN, *The Social Psychology of Organizations.* New York: John Wiley, 1966.

KATZ, R. L., *Cases and Concepts in Corporate Strategy.* Englewood Cliffs, N.J.: Prentice Hall, 1970.

———, "Time and Work: Towards an Integrative Perspective," in *Research in Organizational Behavior,* ed. B. M. Staw and L. L. Cummings, Vol. 1. Greenwich, Conn.: JAI Press, 1980.

KIDDER, T., *The Soul of a New Machine.* Boston: Little, Brown, 1981.

KIECHEL, W., III, "Sniping at Strategic Planning (interview with himself)," *Planning Review,* May 1984, pp. 8–11.

KONO, T., "Comparative Study of Strategy, Structure and Long-Range Planning in Japan and in the United States," *Management Japan,* Spring 1980, pp. 20–34.

KOTLER, P., & R. SINGH, "Marketing Warfare in the 1980s," *Journal of Business Strategy,* Winter 1981, pp. 30–41.

KOTTER, J. P., & L. A. SCHLESINGER, "Choosing Strategies for Change," *Harvard Business Review,* March–April 1979, pp. 106–14.

KUHN, T., *The Structure of Scientific Revolutions.* Chicago: University of Chicago Press, 1970.

LAND, E., "People Should Want More from Life. . . ," *Forbes,* June 1, 1975.

LAPIERRE, L., "Le changement stratégique: Un rêve en quête de réel." Ph.D. Management Policy course paper, McGill University, Canada, 1980.

LEARNED, E. P., C. R. CHRISTIANSEN, K. R. ANDREWS & W. D. GUTH, *Business Policy: Text and Cases.* Homewood, Ill. Richard D. Irwin, 1965.

LENIN, V. I., *Collected Works of V. I. Lenin,* edited and annotated. New York: International Publishers, 1927.

LEVINSON, H., "On Becoming a Middle-Aged Manager," *Harvard Business Review,* July–August 1969, pp. 51–60.

———, *Executive Stress.* New York: Harper & Row, 1970.

LEVITT, T., "Marketing Myopia," *Harvard Business Review,* July–August 1960, pp. 45–56.

————, "Why Business Always Loses," *Harvard Business Review,* March–April 1968, pp. 81–89.

————, "Marketing Success Through Differentiation—of Anything," *Harvard Business Review,* January–February 1980, pp. 83–91.

————, "The Globalization of Markets," *Harvard Business Review,* May–June 1983, pp. 92–102.

————, *The Marketing Imagination.* New York: Free Press, 1983.

LEWIN, K., *Field Theory in Social Science.* New York: Harper & Row, 1951.

LIKERT, R., *New Patterns of Management.* New York: McGraw-Hill, 1969.

LINDBLOM, C. E., "The Science of 'Muddling Through,' " *Public Administration Review,* 1959, pp. 79–88.

————, *The Policy-Making Process.* Englewood Cliffs, N.J.: Prentice Hall, 1968.

LODGE, G. C., *The New American Ideology.* New York: Alfred A. Knopf, 1975.

LOHR, S., "Japan Struggling with Itself," *The New York Times,* June 13, 1982.

MACAVOY, P. W., *The Economic Effects of Regulation.* Cambridge, Mass: M.I.T. Press, 1965.

MACMILLAN, I. C., "Seizing Competitive Initiative," *Journal of Business Strategy,* Spring 1982, pp. 43–57.

————, "Preemptive Strategies," *Journal of Business Strategy,* Fall 1983, pp. 16–26.

————, & P. E. JONES, "Designing Organizations to Compete," *Journal of Business Strategy,* Spring 1984, pp. 11–26.

————, M. MCCAFFERY, & G. VAN WIJK, "Competitors' Responses to Easily Imitated New Products—Exploring Commercial Banking Product Introductions," *Strategic Management Journal,* 1985, pp. 75–86.

MACE, M. L., & G. G. MONTGOMERY, *Management Problems of Corporate Acquisitions.* Boston: Harvard Business School, 1962.

MACHIAVELLI, N., *The Prince, and the Discourses.* New York: Modern Library, 1950.

MACKWORTH, N. H., "Originality," in *The Discovery of Talent,* ed. D. Wolfe. Cambridge, Mass.: Harvard University Press, 1969.

MAJONE, G., "The Use of Policy Analysis," in *The Future and the Past: Essays on Programs.* Russell Sage Foundation Annual Report, 1976–1977.

MAO TSE-TUNG, *Selected Military Writings, 1928–1949.* San Francisco: China Books, 1967.

MARCH, J. G., & J. P. OLSEN, *Ambiguity and Choice in Organizations.* Bergen, Norway: Universitetsforlaget, 1976.

————, & H. A. SIMON, *Organizations.* New York: John Wiley, 1958.

MARSHALL, G. L., *Predicting Executive Achievement.* Ph.D. thesis, Harvard Business School, 1964.

MARTIN, JOANNE, & CAREN SIEHL, "Organizational Culture and Counter Cultures: An Uneasy Symbiosis," *Organizational Dynamics,* Autumn 1983, pp. 52–64.

MARTIN, L. C. "How Beatrice Foods Sneaked Up On $5 Billion," *Fortune,* April 1976, pp. 119–29.

MATLOFF, M., & E. M. SNELL, *Strategic Planning for Coalition Warfare (1941–42).* Washington, D.C.: Office of Chief of Military History, Department of the Army, 1953.

MAYO, E., *The Social Problems of an Industrial Civilization.* Boston: Harvard Business School, 1945.

MCDONALD, J., *Strategy in Poker, Business and War.* New York: W. W. Norton, 1950.

MCINTYRE, S. H., "Obstacles to Corporate Innovation," *Business Horizons,* January–February 1982, pp. 23–28.

MILLER, D., & P. H. FRIESEN, "Archetypes of Strategy Formulation," *Management Science,* May 1978, pp. 921–33.

————, *Organizations: A Quantum View.* Englewood Cliffs, N.J.: Prentice Hall, 1984.

————, & M. KETS DE VRIES, *The Neurotic Organization.* San Francisco: Jossey-Bass, 1984.

————, *Unstable at the Top.* New York: New American Library, 1987.

————, & H. MINTZBERG, *Strategy Formulation in Context: Some Tentative Models.* Working Paper, McGill University, 1974.

MINTZBERG, H., "Research on Strategy-Making," *Academy of Management Proceedings,* 1972, pp. 90–94.

————, *The Nature of Managerial Work.* New York: Harper & Row, 1973.

————, "Strategy Making in Three Modes," *California Management Review,* Winter 1973b, pp. 44–53.

————, "The Manager's Job: Folklore and Fact," *Harvard Business Review,* July–August 1975, pp. 49–61.

————, "Generic Strategies: Toward a Comprehensive Framework," *Advances in Strategic Management,* Vol. 5, pp. 1–67. Greenwich, Conn: JAI Press, 1988.

————, D. RAÌSINGNANÌ, & A. THÉORÊT, "The Structure of 'Unstructured' Decision Processes," *Administrative Science Quarterly,* 1976, pp. 246–75.

————, & J. A. Waters, "Tracking Strategy in an Entrepreneurial Firm," *Academy of Management Journal,* 1982, pp. 465–99.

————, "Of Strategies, Deliberate and Emergent," *Strategic Management Journal,* 1985, pp. 257–72.

MONTGOMERY, B. L., *The Memoirs of Field-Marshal The Viscount Montgomery of Alamein.* Cleveland: World Publishing, 1958.

MORITANI, M., *Japanese Technology: Getting the Best for the Least.* Tokyo: Simul Press, 1981.

MOYER, R. C., "Berle and Means Revisited: The Conglomerate Merger," *Business and Society,* Spring 1970, pp. 20–29.

NADLER, D. A., & E. E. LAWLER, III, "Motivation—A Diagnostic Approach," in *Perspective on Behavior in Organizations,* ed. J. R. Hackman, E. E. Lawler, III, and L. W. Porter. New York: McGraw-Hill, 1977.

NADLER, D., & M. L. TUSHMAN, *Strategic Organization Design.* Homewood, Ill. Scott Foresman, 1986.

NAISBITT, J., *Megatrends.* New York: Warner Books, 1982.

NAPOLEON, I., "Maximes de Guerre," in *Roots of Strategy,* ed. T. R. Phillips. Harrisburg, Pa.: Military Service Publishing, 1940.

NATHANSON, D., & J. CASSANO, "Organization Diversity and Performance," *The Wharton Magazine,* Summer 1982, pp. 18–26.

NEUSTADT, R. E., *Presidential Power: The Politics of Leadership.* New York: John Wiley, 1960.

NORMANN, R., *Management for Growth,* trans. by N. Adler. New York: John Wiley, 1977.

NYSTROM, P. C., B. L. T. HEDBERG, & W. H. STARBUCK, "Interacting Processes as Organization Designs," in *The Management of Organization Design,* Vol. 1, ed. R. H. Kilmann, L. R. Pondy, & D. P. Slevin. New York: Elsevier North-Holland, 1976.

OGILVY, D., *Ogilvy on Advertising.* New York: Crown, 1983.

OHMAE, K., *The Mind of the Strategist.* New York: McGraw-Hill, 1982.

ONO, H., "Nihonteki Keiei Shisutemu to Jinji Kettei Shisutemu" ("Japanese Management System and Personnel Decisions"), *Soshiki Kagaku,* 1976, pp. 22–32.

OUCHI, W. G., "Market, Bureaucracies and Clans," *Administrative Science Quarterly,* 1980, pp. 129–40.

———, *Theory Z.* Reading, Mass.: Addison-Wesley, 1981.

———, & A. M. Jaeger, "Type Z Organization: Stability in the Midst of Mobility," *Academy of Management Review,* 1978, pp. 305–14.

———, W. G., & B. Johnson, "Types of Organizational Control and Their Relationship to Emotional Well Being," *Administrative Science Quarterly,* 1978, pp. 293–317.

PARSONS, T., *Structure and Process in Modern Societies.* Glencoe, Ill.: Free Press, 1960.

PASCALE, R. T., "Perspectives on Strategy: The Real Story Behind Honda's Success," *California Management Review,* Spring 1984, pp. 47–72.

PAUL, N. L., "The Use of Empathy in the Resolution of Grief," in *Perspective in Biology and Medicine.* Chicago: University of Chicago Press, 1967.

PENCE, C. C., *How Venture Capitalists Make Venture Decisions.* Ann Arbor, Mich.: UMI Research Press, 1982.

PERROW, C. "The Analysis of Goals in Complex Organizations," *American Sociological Review,* 1961, pp. 854–66.

———, *Organizational Analysis: A Sociological Review.* Belmont, Calif.: Wadsworth, 1970.

———, *Complex Organizations: A Critical Essay.* New York: Scott, Foresman, 1972.

PETERS, T. J., "A Style for All Seasons," *Executive,* Summer 1980, pp. 12–16.

———, & R. H. WATERMAN, *In Search of Excellence: Lessons from America's Best Run Companies.* New York: Harper & Row, 1982.

PFEFFER, J., "Size and Composition of Corporate Boards of Directors: The Organization and Its Environment," *Administrative Science Quarterly,* 1972a, pp. 218–28.

———, "Merger as a Response to Organizational Interdependence," *Administrative Science Quarterly,* 1972b, pp. 382–94.

———, "Size, Composition and Function of Hospital Boards of Directors: A Study of Organization-Environment Linkage," *Administrative Science Quarterly,* 1973, pp. 349–64.

———, "Administrative Regulation and Licensing: Social Problem or Solution?" *Social Problems,* 1974, pp. 468–79.

———, *Management as Symbolic Action: The Creation and Maintenance of Organizational Paradigms.* Working Paper, Stanford University, 1979.

———, & H. LEBLEBICI, "Executive Recruitment and the Development of Interfirm Organizations," *Administrative Science Quarterly,* 1973, pp. 449–61.

———, & P. NOWAK, "Patterns of Joint Venture Activity: Implications for Antitrust Policy," *The Antitrust Bulletin,* 1976, pp. 315–39.

———, "Joint Ventures and Interorganizational Interdependence," *Administrative Science Quarterly,* 1976b, pp. 398–418.

———, *Organizational Context and Interorganizational Linkages Among Corporations.* Working Paper, University of California at Berkeley, no date.

———, & H. LEBLEBICI, "The Effect of Uncertainty on the Use of Social Influence in Organizational Decision-Making," *Administrative Science Quarterly,* 1976, pp. 227–45.

PFIFFNER, J. M., "Administrative Rationality," *Public Administration Review,* 1960, pp. 125–32.

PHILLIPS, T. R. ED., *Roots of Strategy.* Harrisburg, Pa.: Military Service Publishing, 1940.

PORTER, M. E., *Competitive Strategy: Techniques for Analysing Industries and Competitors.* New York: Free Press, 1980.

———, *Competitive Advantage: Creating and Sustaining Superior Performance.* New York: Free Press, 1985.

———, "Generic Competitive Strategies," in M. E. Porter, *Competitive Advantage,* pp. 34–46. New York: Free Press, 1985.

———, "From Competitive Advantage to Corporate Strategy," *Harvard Business Review,* May–June 1987, pp. 43–59.

———, "Competition in Global Industries: A Conceptual Framework," in *Competition in Global Industries,* ed. M. E. Porter. Boston: Harvard Business School Press, 1986.

POSNER, B., & B. BURLINGHAM, "The Hottest Entrepreneur in America," *Inc.,* January 1988, pp. 44–58.

POSNER, R. A., "Theories of Economic Regulation," *Bell Journal of Economics and Management Science,* 1974, pp. 335–58.

580

PRICE, J. L., "The Impact of Governing Boards on Organizational Effectiveness and Morale," *Administrative Science Quarterly,* 1963, pp. 361–78.

PUCIK, V., "Getting Ahead in Japan," *The Japanese Economic Journal,* 1981, pp. 970–71.

———, "Promotions and Intra-organizational Status Differentiation Among Japanese Managers," *The Academy of Management Proceedings,* 1981, pp. 59–63.

PURKAYASTHA, D., *"Note on the Motorcycle Industry—1975."* Copyrighted Case, Harvard Business School, 1981.

QUINN, J. B., "Strategic Goals: Process and Politics," *Sloan Management Review,* Fall 1977, pp. 21–37.

———, *Strategies for Change: Logical Incrementalism.* Homewood, Ill.: Richard D. Irwin, 1980.

RAPHAEL, R., *Edges.* New York: Alfred A. Knopf, 1976.

REESER, C., "Some Potential Human Problems in the Project Form of Organization," *Academy of Management Journal,* 1969, pp. 459–67.

REID, S. R., *Mergers, Managers, and the Economy.* New York: McGraw-Hill, 1968.

RHENMAN, E., *Organization Theory for Long-Range Planning.* New York: John Wiley, 1973.

ROHLEN, T. P., *For Harmony and Strength: Japanese White-collar Organization in Anthropological Perspective.* Berkeley: University of California Press, 1974.

ROSNER, M., *Principle Types and Problems of Direct Democracy in the Kibbutz.* Working Paper, Social Research Center on the Kibbutz, Givat Haviva, Israel, 1969.

ROSS, I., "How Lawless are the Big Companies?" *Fortune,* December 1, 1980, pp. 56–64.

RUMELT, R. P., *Strategy, Structure and Economic Performance.* Boston: Harvard Business School, 1974.

———, "Evaluation of Strategy: Theory and Models", in *Strategy Management: A New View of Business Policy and Planning,* ed. D. E. Schendel & G. W. Hofer. Boston: Little, Brown, 1979.

———, "A Teaching Plan for Strategy Alternatives for the British Motocycle Industry," in *Japanese Business: Business Policy.* New York: The Japan Society, 1980.

SAHLMAN, W. A., & H. H. STEVENSON, "Capital Market Myopia," *Journal of Business Venturing,* Winter 1985, pp. 7–30.

SAKIYA, T., "The Story of Honda's Founders," *Asahi Evening News,* June–August 1979.

———, *Honda Motor: The Men, the Management, the Machines.* Tokyo, Japan: Kadonsha International, 1982.

SALTER, M. S., & W. A. WEINHOLD, *Diversification Through Acquisition.* New York: Free Press, 1979.

SAYLES, L. R., *Managerial Behavior: Administration in Complex Organizations.* New York: McGraw-Hill, 1964.

SCHEIN, E. H., "How Graduates Scare Bosses," *Careers Today,* January 1969.

SCHELLING, T. C., *The Strategy of Conflict,* 2nd. ed. Cambridge, Mass.: Harvard University Press, 1980.

SCHENDEL, D. G., R. PATTON, & J. RIGGS, "Corporate Turnaround Strategies: A Study of Profit Decline and Recovery," *Journal of General Management,* Spring 1976, pp. 3–11.

SCOTT, W. E., "Activation Theory and Task Design," *Organizational Behavior and Human Performance,* September 1966, pp. 3–30.

SELZNICK, P., *TVA and the Grass Roots.* Berkeley: University of California Press, 1949.

———, *Leadership in Administration: A Sociological Interpretation.* New York: Harper & Row, 1957.

SHUBIK, M., *Games for Society, Business, and War: Towards a Theory of Gaming.* New York: Elsevier, 1975.

SIMON, M. A., "On the Concept of Organizational Goals," *Administrative Science Quarterly,* 1964–1965, pp. 1–22.

SMITH, L., "The Boardroom Is Becoming a Different Scene," *Fortune,* May 8, 1978, pp. 150–88.

SMITH, W. R., "Product Differentiation and Market Segmentation as Alternative Marketing Strategies," *Journal of Marketing,* July 1956, pp. 3–8.

SOLZHENITSYN, A., "Why the West Has Succumbed to Cowardice," *The Montreal Star: News and Review,* June 10, 1978.

SPEER, A., *Inside the Third Reich.* New York: Macmillan, 1970.

SPENCER, F. C., "Deductive Reasoning in the Lifelong Continuing Education of a Cardiovascular Surgeon," *Archives of Surgery,* 1976, pp. 1177–83.

SPENDER, J.-C., *Industry Recipes: The Nature and Sources of Managerial Judgement.* London: Basil Blackwell, 1989.

STARBUCK, W. H., "Organizations and Their Environments," in *Handbook of Industrial and Organizational Psychology,* ed. M. D. Dunnette. Chicago: Rand McNally, 1976.

STARBUCK, W. H., & B. L. T. HEDBERG, "Saving an Organization from a Stagnating Environment," in *Strategy + Structure = Performance,* ed. H. B. Thorelli. Bloomington: Indiana University Press, 1977.

THE STATE OF SMALL BUSINESS, A REPORT TO THE PRESIDENT. Washington, D.C.: U.S. Government Printing Office, 1984.

STERN, L. W., B. STERNTHAL, & C. S. CRAIG, "Managing Conflict in Distribution Channels: A Laboratory Study," *Journal of Marketing Research,* 1973, pp. 169–79.

STEVENSON, H. H., "Defining Corporate Strengths and Weaknesses," *Sloan Management Review,* Spring 1976: 51–68.

STEVENSON, W., *A Man Called Intrepid: The Secret War.* New York: Harcourt Brace Jovanovich, 1976.

STEWART, R., *Managers and Their Jobs.* London: Macmillan, 1967.

STIGLER, G. J., "The Theory of Economic Regulation," *Bell Journal of Economics and Management Science,* 1971, pp. 3–21.

SUN TZU, *The Art of War,* trans. by S. B. Griffith. New York: Oxford University Press, 1963. Original 500 B.C.

TAYLOR, W. H., "The Nature of Policy Making in Universities," *The Canadian Journal of Higher Education,* 1983, pp. 17–32.

TECHNOLOGICAL INNOVATION: ITS ENVIRONMENT AND MANAGEMENT. Washington, D.C.: U.S. Government Printing Office, 1967.

TERKEL, S., *Working*. New York: Pantheon, 1972.

THOMPSON, J. D., *Organizations in Action*. New York: McGraw-Hill, 1967.

THOMPSON, V. A., *Modern Organizations*. New York: Alfred A. Knopf, 1961.

TILLES, S., "How to Evaluate Corporate Strategy," *Harvard Business Review,* July–August 1963, pp. 111–21.

TIME. "The Most Basic Form of Creativity," June 26, 1972.

TOFFLER, A., *Future Shock*. New York: Bantam Books, 1970.

TREGOE, B., & I. ZIMMERMAN, *Top Management Strategy*. New York: Simon & Schuster, 1980.

TSUJI, K., "Decision-Making in the Japanese Government: A Study of Ringisei," in *Political Development in Modern Japan,* ed. R. E. Wards. Princeton: Princeton University Press, 1968.

TSURUMI, Y., *Multinational Management: Business Strategy and Government Policy*. Cambridge, Mass.: Ballinger, 1977.

TUCHMAN, B. W., *The Guns of August*. New York: Macmillan, 1962.

VANCIL, R. F., "Strategy Formulation in Complex Organizations," *Sloan Management Review,* Winter 1976, pp. 1–18.

———, & P. LORANGE, "Strategic Planning in Diversified Companies," *Harvard Business Review,* January–February 1975, pp. 81–90.

VAN DOREN, M., *Liberal Education*. Boston: Beacon Press, 1967.

VARNER, V. J., & J. I. ALGER, EDS., *History of the Military Art: Notes for the Course*. West Point, N.Y.: U.S. Military Academy, 1978.

VICKERS, G., "Is Adaptability Enough?" *Behavioral Science,* 1959, pp. 219–34.

VOGEL, E., *Japan as Number One*. Cambridge, Mass.: Harvard University Press, 1979.

VON BÜLOW, D. F., *The Spirit of the Modern System of War,* trans. C. M. deMartemont. London: C. Mercier, 1806.

VON CLAUSEWITZ, C., *On War,* trans. M. Howard and P. Paret. Princeton, N.J.: Princeton University Press, 1976.

VON HIPPEL, E., "Get New Products From Customers," *Harvard Business Review,* March–April 1982, pp. 117–22.

VON NEUMANN, J. & O. MORGENSTERN, *Theory of Games and Economic Behavior.* Princeton, N.J.: Princeton University Press, 1944.

WARD, L. B., *Analysis of 1969 Alumni Questionnaire Returns.* Unpublished Report, Harvard Business School, 1970.

WEBER, M., "The Three Types of Legitimate Rule," in *A Sociological Reader on Complex Organizations,* ed. A. Etzioni, trans. H. Gerth. New York: Holt, Rinehart and Winston, 1969.

WEICK, K. E., "Educational Organizations as Loosely Coupled Systems," *Administrative Science Quarterly,* 1976, pp. 1–19.

WESTLEY, F., & H. MINTZBERG, "Visionary Leadership and Strategic Management," *Strategic Management Journal,* 1989, pp. 17–32.

WHEELWRIGHT, S. C., "Japan—Where Operations Really Are Strategic," *Harvard Business Review,* July–August 1981, pp. 67–74.

WHITE, T. H., *In Search of History: A Personal Adventure*. New York: Warner Books, 1978.

WHITEHEAD, A. N., *Aims of Education and Other Essays*. New York: Macmillan, 1929.

WHYTE, W. F., *Street Corner Society*. Chicago: University of Chicago Press, 1955.

WILLIAMSON, O. E., *Markets and Hierarchies: Analysis and Antitrust Implications*. New York: Free Press, 1975.

———, *The Economic Institutions of Capitalism*. New York: Free Press, 1985.

WISE, D., "Apple's New Crusade," *Business Week,* November 26, 1984.

WITTE, E., "Field Research on Complex Decision-Making Processes—The Phase Theorem," *International Studies of Management and Organization,* Summer 1972, pp. 156–82.

WODARSKI, J. S., R. L. HAMBLIN, D. R. BUCKHOLDT, & D. E. FERRITOR, "Individual Consequences versus Different Shared Consequences Contingent on the Performance of Low-Achieving Group Members," *Journal of Applied Social Psychology,* 1973, pp. 276–90.

WOO, C., & A. COOPER, "Strategies of Effective Low Share Businesses," *Strategic Management Journal,* 1981, pp. 301–18.

WORTHY, J. C., "Organizational Structure and Employee Morale," *American Sociological Review,* 1950, pp. 169–79.

———, *Big Business and Free Men*. New York: Harper & Row, 1959.

WRAPP, H. E., "Good Managers Don't Make Policy Decisions," *Harvard Business Review,* September–October 1967, pp. 91–99.

WRIGLEY, L., "Diversification and Divisional Autonomy," DBA dissertation, Graduate School of Business Administration, Harvard University, 1970.

YOSHINO, M., *Japan's Managerial System*. Cambridge, Mass.: M.I.T. Press, 1968.

YOSHINO, M. Y., "Global Competition in a Salient Industry: The Case of Civil Aircraft," in *Competition in Global Industries,* ed. M. E. Porter. Boston: Harvard Business School Press, 1986.

YOUNG, D., *Rommel: The Desert Fox*. New York: Harper & Row, 1974.

ZALD, M. N., "Urban Differentiation, Characteristics of Boards of Directors and Organizational Effectiveness," *American Journal of Sociology,* 1967, pp. 261–72.

ZALEZNIK, A., "Power and Politics in Organizational Life," *Harvard Business Review,* May–June 1970, pp. 47–60.

NAME INDEX

SUBJECT INDEX